Rod Machado's How to Fly an Airplane Handbook

Written and illustrated by
Rod Machado

Published by The Aviation Speakers Bureau

Copyright Information

First Edition
Update 3/30/2020

Please visit (and *bookmark*) our web site for any additional book updates: *www.rodmachado.com*

Published by: The Aviation Speakers Bureau,
P.O. Box 6030, San Clemente, CA 92674-6030

All rights reserved. The contents of this manual are protected by copyright throughout the world under the Berne Union and the Universal Copyright Convention.

No part of this publication may be reproduced in any manner whatsoever—electronic, photographic, photocopying, facsimile—or stored in a retrieval system without the prior written permission of the author: Rod Machado, care of: The Aviation Speakers Bureau.

Nothing in this text supersedes any operational documents or procedures issued by the Federal Aviation Administration (FAA), the aircraft and avionics manufacturers, any aircraft's Pilot Operating Handbook (POH) or approved flight manual (AFM). Don't for one second think that the generic recommendations found in this book override the common sense recommendations of your flight school or flight instructor for a specific airplane or situation or a given set of circumstances.

The author has made every effort in the preparation of this book to ensure the accuracy of the information. However, the information is sold without warranty either expressed or implied. Neither the author nor the publisher will be liable for any damages caused or alleged to be caused directly, indirectly, incidentally or consequentially by the information in this book.

The opinions in this book are solely those of the author and not the publisher.

Don't even think about using any performance chart in this book for performance computations in your airplane. Find a performance chart appropriate for your airplane and use that one. All of the charts, graphs and tables in this book are for training purposes only.

Cover layout by Diane Titterington
Front cover photograph from Fotolia.com by Mark Rasmussen
All material created, written and produced by Rod Machado
All illustrations in this book designed and drawn by Rod Machado (QuarkXPress, Corel, Photoshop, Poser 2010, Vue 9, iClone 5, CrazyTalk Animator, Blender)
Photographs (unless marked otherwise or in the public domain) by Rod Machado

Copyright 2020 by Rod Machado

Table of Contents

Acknowledgments..iv
Dedication..v
About the Author..vi
Introduction...vii
Message to Instructors.......................................viii
Updating Your Book..xi
Book Prerequisites..x

1 Chapter One
Pages 1-1 through 1-38
Let's Go Flying
Basic Piloting Skills

2 Chapter Two -
Pages 2-1 through 2-38
Flying Straight And Level And Turning

3 Chapter Three
Pages 3-1 through 3-28
Climbs and Descents
Understanding the Basics Of Flight

4 Chapter Four
Pages 4-1 through 4-28
Slow Flight Delight
How and Why We Fly Slow

5 Chapter Five
Pages 5-1 through 5-60
Stalls and Spins
The Ups, Downs and Arounds

6 Chapter Six
Pages 6-1 through 6-40
Takeoffs and Climbs

7 Chapter Seven
Pages 7-1 through 7-38
Ground Reference Maneuvers

8 Chapter Eight
Pages 8-1 through 8-26
The Airport Traffic Pattern
The Lowdown On Gettin' Down

9 Chapter Nine
Pages 9-1 through 9-30
Approaching to Land
Gettln' Low, Gettin' Down

10 Chapter Ten
Pages 10-1 through 10-36
The Roundout and Flare
You Have the Nod To Hit the Sod

11 Chapter Eleven
Pages 11-1 through 11-22
Crosswinds and Slips
Flying Sideways Is Fun

12 Chapter Twelve
Pages 12-1 through 12-28
Advanced Landing Skills
Not All Runways Are Created Equal

13 Chapter Thirteen
Pages 13-1 through 13-34
Advanced Maneuvers
Tools to Help You Become Proficient

14 Chapter Fourteen
Pages 14-1 through 14-28
Night Flying
Taming the Dark Side

Appendix-1..15-1 through 15-12
Editors...15-13 through 15-14
Aviation Speakers Bureau..15-14
Product Information.......................15-15 through 15-20
Index..15-21 through 15-28

Acknowledgments and Credits

All the folks at ASRS, Moffett Field, CA
Andrew Shacker
Barry Jones
Brian Weiss of Wordsworth
Bridgette Doremiere
Bruce Williams
Cammie Patch
Captain Ralph Butcher
Carenado (for their use of the Carenado C152 II sim model)
Chris Connor
Chris Felton
Danny Mortensen
Diane Titterington
Federal Aviation Administration
Fernando Herrera
Flightsim.com
Fotolia Photo Contributors (each named in photo)
Fotolia Photo source
Fotolia.com
Gabhan Berry
Gary Sequeira
General Aviation News
Helen Woods
Jim Szajkovics
John Bliss
Just Flight (www.justflight.com)
Larry Diamond
Larry Nelson
Marty Blaker
Matt Abrams
Meg Godlewski
Orange County Flight Center
Orion Lyau
Pam Hengsteler
Paul Svenkeson
Peter Muehlegg
Prof. H. Paul Shuch
Ralph Alcock
Remos Aircraft Company
Richard Sanchez
Rick Crose
Scott Philips
Sheri Coin Marshall
Sporty's Pilot Shop
Steve DiLullo
The Aviation Speakers Bureau
Tim Olson
William Stevick

Microsoft Inc. and their Microsoft Flight Simulator software (for many of the flight sim screen shots used in this book)

The New Piper Aircraft Corporation. Charts and graphs provided by Piper are to be used for information purposes only. The Pilot's Operating Handbook is the only true source of information.

The Cessna Aircraft Company. Cessna authorized the use of their materials with the understanding that they are to be used for training purposes only, not the actual operation of an aircraft.

Clipart from the following companies:
3G Graphics, Archive Arts, BBL Typographic, Cartesia Software, Image Club Graphics Inc., Management Graphics Ltd., One Mile Up Inc., Studio Piazza Xilo Inc., Techpool Studios Inc., Totem Graphics Inc., TNT Designs, SmartPics.

Note: If I missed crediting or acknowledging any contributor to this book, please forgive me. I promise to give you credit and apologize again (big time!) as soon as you let me know.

Dedication

DEDICATION

If you're lucky enough to have someone in your life that can give you an honest appraisal of your work, then you're really lucky.

I'm lucky.

For the past 25 years I've been fortunate enough to have one editor for all my book projects. He's a master wordsmith and one of the wisest men I know. He's also the one responsible for keeping my grammatical sails trimmed and my educational course true.

Mr. Brian Weiss of *WORD'SWORTH* has always told me the truth about what works and what doesn't work in print. Were it not for his wise counsel I'm not sure that the products I've produced would have been so well received by the aviation community.

I consider this book to be one of the most important I've written and there is no one I would prefer to dedicate this book to more than my editor and dear friend, Brian Weiss.

About the Author

Rod Machado traded his motorcycle for flying lessons at the age of 16. His parents were delighted he gave up riding with the vegetarian motorcycle gang known as the *Sprouts*. Captured by the romance and adventure of flight in a Taylorcraft L-2 at Amelia Reid Aviation in San Jose, California, Rod has remained hooked ever since. In fact, he is one of the few airline-transport-rated pilots who still gets excited by a Cessna 150 fly-by.

Rod is a professional speaker who travels across the United States and Europe delighting his listeners with upbeat and lively presentations. Machado truly loves mixing it up with the audience. His unusual talent for simplifying the difficult and adding humor to make the lessons stick has made him a popular lecturer both in and out of aviation. Rod speaks on both aviation and non-aviation topics, including risk assessment, IFR charts, aviation weather, in-flight emergencies, and safety awareness. He is also known for his rapid fire, humorous banquet presentations.

A pilot since 1970 and an active flight instructor since 1973, Rod is also a National Aviation Safety Counselor. You might recognize Rod as the instructor on Microsoft Flight Simulator or as the author of seven aviation books. He has over 10,000 hours of flight experience earned the hard way—one CFI hour at a time. Since 1978, Rod has taught hundreds and hundreds of flight instructor revalidation clinics and safety seminars across the United States and Europe. He was named the 1991 Western Region Flight Instructor of the Year. You can read his monthly column, "License to Learn," in *AOPA Pilot* magazine as well as his monthly columns in *Flight Training Magazine*.

Rod Machado

Rod's eclectic interests are reflected by his equally varied academic credentials. He holds degrees in aviation science and psychology.

Rod believes you must take time to exercise or you'll have to take time to be sick. Holding black belts in the Korean disciplines of Tae Kwon Do and Hapkido and ranking in Gracie Jujitsu, he gets his exercise from practicing and teaching martial arts. He also runs 20 miles a week and claims it's uphill both ways.

Visit Rod's web site at
www.rodmachado.com.

Introduction

Are you thinking about learning to fly an airplane? Or are you a pilot who wants a better understanding of basic flying skills? Are you a flight instructor who'd like to teach your students the basic principles of stick and rudder flying? Then this is the book for you.

No matter what your level of flight experience, from zero flight time to thousands of hours of cockpit experience, I can assure you that this book will be a wonderful guide in helping you learn to fly or learn to fly better. If you're an instructor, this book will help you teach others to fly. That's my promise to you.

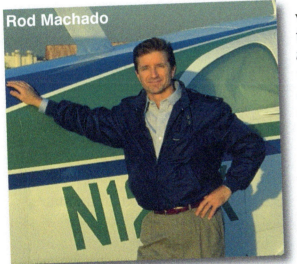

How can I make such a promise? A long time ago I was fortunate enough to learn at a flight school where the flight training emphasized the principles of *basic attitude control*. Many of our school's flight instructors taught others to fly during WW II or were the educational disciples of these same instructors. Airplanes of that era weren't equipped with autopilots or auto-throttles. Nothing was *automatic* about them. You had to manually fly them and you did so by feel, by the seat of your pants using all your senses to make the airplane do what you wanted it to do. This was done mainly by looking outside the cockpit, not at your flight instruments. That's how these war-era pilots kept from being vaporized by the enemy and by their airplanes.

While I never learned how to engage enemy airplanes, my early lessons emphasized the basics of attitude controls (pitch, bank, roll and yaw) while using all my senses—visual, tactile, auditory, kinematic—to maneuver the airplane. Back then, this was known as *stick and rudder* flying. It was the best education a student pilot could have.

The payoff for that type of early training was a deep confidence in knowing that the airplane will do exactly what I wanted it to do, all the time, every time. Many pilots flying today were not taught the basics of stick and rudder flying. Consequently, they are often unable to predict how their airplanes will behave. How disconcerting is that? They might, for instance, stall during uncoordinated flight (not a good idea) and end up in spin. They might even attempt a landing during a moderate crosswind, fail to apply adequate drift correction and end up being blown off the runway rather than landing on it. When these same pilots are questioned about these types of events, they often reply, "I don't have any idea what happened," or, "The airplane just developed a mind of its own and did its own thing." Unpredictability, right?

Therein lies the main reason I've written this book.

If you want to fly your airplane safely, with poise and confidence, you have to make your flying machine do precisely what you want it to do. Nothing more, but certainly nothing less. You must learn the basics of *stick and rudder flying* to do this. That's what this book teaches and what I want you to learn.

Rod Machado

A Message to Flight Instructors About This Book

In *A Connecticut Yankee in King Arthur's Court*, Mark Twain wrote, "...she was wise, subtle and knew more than one way to skin a cat." Disregarding the cat, we're completely justified in applying the same principle to an airplane. There's more than one way to fly one.

More than a few instructors today emphasize the use of flight instruments and cockpit automation as the primary means of aircraft control. Even airplane manufacturers producing airplanes with sophisticated glass cockpit technology now sanction this idea. For them, it's automation that keeps a pilot safe, not basic flying instincts.

Granted, if a pilot has poor flying instincts, he or she has no choice but to rely on automation to help fly the airplane. However, there are occasions when a pilot finds him- or herself pushed to the edge of the normal operating envelope. If and when this happens, pilots must tap into a deeper layer of airmanship where their basic flying skills reside. At this point pilots are only as safe as the strength of the foundation upon which their basic flying skills are built.

The situations where a pilot must rely on basic skills are numerous. For instance, a pilot might need to land for fuel, but willingly overfly a perfectly suitable airport because a report of moderate crosswinds gives him pause. He'd rather dip into his reserved fuel than attempt a landing that any capable stick and rudder pilot could handle. Or, while making a hurried descent to visit the loo, he might not have the instincts to keep his controls coordinated during the turn from base to final. A skidding turn at insufficient speed might easily turn an airplane into a lawn dart. This is just a small sample of the many situations where a pilot must rely on basic flying skills instead of automation to keep him or her safe. That's why this book is about basic flying skills, not automation.

Many of these tips and techniques might seem unfamiliar to many instructors. For instance, it's common to introduce rudder and aileron coordination skills by emphasizing the inclinometer. While I include that information in this book, I also show two additional techniques used by good stick and rudder pilots to keep their flight controls coordinated. One involves looking through the windscreen to hold the nose (the longitudinal axis) relatively stationary as the airplane *rolls* into and out of a turn. The last thing we want to do is give our students another reason to keep their heads inside the cockpit by staring at the inclinometer when entering or exiting a turn.

Another technique that's used by good stick and rudder pilots is the means by which they assess their angle of attack. These pilots seldom rely *solely* on their airspeed indicator to fly an airplane. Instead, they evaluate their angle of attack by looking at the horizon and the wing's imagined chord line while paying attention to what their other senses (sight, sound and feel) tell them about the airplane's speed and performance. For these pilots, flying is a sensory experience, not a digital one. These are just a few of the many good instincts you might want your students to learn.

Finally, it's difficult to have a one-size-fits-all technique for different makes and models of small airplanes. Nevertheless, I've tried to be general enough in my descriptions so that one size might indeed fit most of the small airplanes we fly.

When you come across a technique different from the way you teach, try it as an experiment. If it works for you, then you've just added another tool to your teaching kit. As Abraham Maslow once said, "If the only tool you have is a hammer, then everything looks like a nail." Remember, there's more than one way to skin a cat and more than one way ato fly an airplane.

Rod Machado

Updating Your Book

Updating Your Book

Because the world of aviation changes quickly, you should make it a regular practice to update your book by visiting my web site located at:

http://www.rodmachado.com

Visit the book/slide update page for any changes that may affect this text or changes in the FAA knowledge exam.

Author's Note

Any errors found in this book are solely the responsibility of the author, Rod Machado.

Rod Machado's How to Fly an Airplane Handbook

Prerequisite Reading

In writing a "How to Fly" handbook I had to assume that the reader will have a basic knowledge of aviation (i.e., aerodynamics, powerplants, airport operations, etc.) upon which to build the concepts provided in this book. Sure, I could have written a combination *knowledge* and *how to fly* book but the resulting tome would swell to the size of a small planet. This just wasn't practical since there are no backpacks that big. Therefore, I'm assuming that the reader of this book has read, is reading or is at least familiar with the basic aviation concepts covered in *Rod Machado's Private Pilot Handbook*.

Advanced Knowledge in this Book

Sometimes things are important but they just don't fit. That's why this book has the occasional addendum placed at the end of each chapter known as a *Postflight Briefing*. These are add-on items of knowledge that are nice to know, but not necessarily need to know. They might contain more detailed explanations of concepts that simply can't be discussed in greater detail in the body text. Therefore, I've included these Postflight Briefings for your study as a sort of *graduate level* information for the inquiring mind. Read these if and when you can. They contain some very useful and practical information.

Chapter 1
Let's Go Flying
Basic Preflighting Skills

Flying is a multisensory experience. That's part of the fun. And nowhere is it more important to use your senses *and* your common sense than during the preflight. The preflight is your first, last, and only chance to keep from taking a problem into the air with you.

Properly done, you will look, listen, touch, smell and occasionally even taste during the preflight. Learning to do a great preflight is about developing awareness of the data your built-in body sensors are gathering, and overcoming a dangerous tendency that is referred to by psychologists as *confirmation bias*. If you start with the assumption that everything is OK, you tend to interpret all the incoming information as confirming the conclusion you started with.

That's what happened at a Southern California airport in the late 1970s when the co-owner of a Cessna 182 arrived at the airport and parked underneath the airplane's wing. He was starting a short business trip and anxious to get going. He raced through the preflight, entered the cockpit, started the engine, and taxied for the runup. He assumed the entire airplane was there and his cursory inspection confirmed his bias.

Unbeknown to him, his partner had removed the elevator two days prior in order to have it painted. This information was not conveyed to the co-owner, who managed not to notice that a very important part of the airplane had gone missing. He made this not-so-uplifting discovery when rotating for liftoff. Pulling back on the yoke did not make the airplane fly. He probably set a land-speed record in a Cessna 182 before running his machine into a barrier at the far end of the runway.

There are three ways to mess up on a preflight. First, don't do it, or at least don't do it thoroughly (as Mr. No-elevator Man found out). Second, make sure you don't know what you're looking for when you do the preflight. Third, don't do anything about something that your gut tells you needs to be dealt with. Commit one or more of these errors and you'd better make sure that all of your flying is done over a trampoline factory.

A good preflight is absolutely essential to flying safely. While it's only natural for most pilots to speed up the preflight process so they can fly, taking off with a problem that could have been prevented simply speeds up the likelihood of an unhappy ending.

So the question is, how do you preflight properly and minimize the risks of confirmation bias and its twin evil, complacency? How do you fully employ your senses and really understand what they're conveying? Well, that's what this chapter is all about. So let's talk about the *walkaround* (preflight) which isn't the same thing as the aboriginal *walkabout*, but it is your right of passage to a safe flight if done correctly (it also takes only 15 minutes instead of six months...whew!).

What is THAT Thing?

Along with confirmation bias, *complacency* is one of the biggest preflight problems. In fact, complacency and confirmation bias are co-conspirators. They interact in a powerful way to create danger for pilots.

In the span of your flying years, you will conduct hundreds and perhaps thousands of preflights. It is very easy to fall into a routine, and that is doubly true if you fly the same aircraft every time. It's the same old, same old. Nothing is ever wrong, so don't worry, be happy. Old Faithful will fly again.

Or not. If you become complacent about the preflight, it heightens your existing tendency toward confirmation bias. The airplane has always flown before, it will fly again. Nothing is ever really wrong. Before you know it, you're looking without seeing, hearing without listening.

I learned a long time ago as a flight instructor that preflights often become routine quite quickly. That means you're likely to rush or skip over important parts of the airplane, or at least not pay as much attention to them as you should. That's why I recommend that everyone occasionally preflight the airplane in a direction opposite the one normally followed (Figure 1). If you usually preflight in a clockwise direction, go counterclockwise. By breaking your routine, things will look different. You're simply likely to pay more attention to what you're doing by trying something different.

One way of combating these threats to safety is to try and view whatever airplane you are preflighting as something totally unknown and strange. Pretend it's a recent arrival from Area 51. You

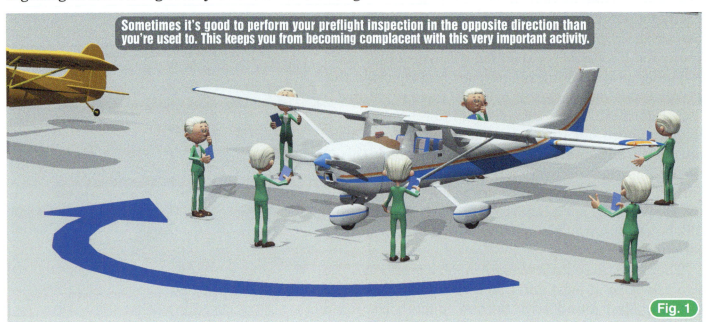

Sometimes it's good to perform your preflight inspection in the opposite direction than you're used to. This keeps you from becoming complacent with this very important activity.

Fig. 1

Chapter 1: Let's Go Flying

have never seen such a thing. Wonder at its strange shape. Gaze upon it as though its contents were completely unknown to you. Deliberately look for things you've never noticed before. And until proven otherwise, assume it wants to hurt you.

Why Is My Airplane Tilting?

So, when does the preflight of this now-alien object begin? Sooner than you might think.

The preflight begins the moment you first spy the alleged airplane on the ramp or in the hangar. Remember, you're not even sure it's an airplane. Good spy that you are, when you see this object from afar, keep it in sight. Sure, from that distance it looks like a tiny model airplane, but the absence of a large cardboard carton should remind you that it's not (unless a giant man is standing next to it).

As you approach the airplane, look for symmetry (things being the same on both sides) as shown in Figure 2. Airplanes, like people, are generally mirror images if split down the middle lengthwise (don't actually *do* the splitting, just imagine it). So, both sides should be the same. Are the wings and tail equidistant from the ground? Is one wing or horizontal stabilizer higher or lower than the other? Is a giant man leaning on the wing? If things don't look right, it's probably because they aren't, and you need to find out why.

Notice an angle to the dangle? It's possible that a main gear tire has gone flat or that the airplane is parked on a sloped surface. Either situation might produce the asymmetry (lack of symmetry) you see. That's a good thing in that it means your airplane isn't broken. It might, however, be a bad thing if the unlevel surface allows fuel to leak out the wing's fuel vent line. Given the expense of fuel these days, you don't want to lose it if you're planning on using it, right? This is one reason pilots try and park airplanes on relatively level surfaces, especially on warm days when air expansion in the fuel tank might push fuel out of a vent line.

He's Bent Out of Shape

Several years ago I looked at a Cessna 150 for possible purchase. As I approached the airplane from a distance, it was clear that one wing was lower than the other—three inches lower at the tip to be exact. It turned out that the left landing gear strut was bent (not an uncommon issue on many airplanes, especially those used for flight training). It just so happens that, on this model airplane, Cessna allows up to four inches difference in wing tip height with regards to a bent landing strut before that strut needs replacing.

No, I didn't purchase the airplane which wasn't what disappointed the owner. He was disappointed because in all the years he had owned the airplane, he never noticed that one wing tip was lower than the other. He had never approached the airplane from the front with the intent of making a macro observation about the airplane's fitness. Since he hardly flew the airplane, he most likely purchased the airplane in this condition. Fortunately, this gentleman has a sense of humor and laughed when I told him that he could now tell his friends that his airplane was specially built for left turns and landing in left crosswinds.

The preflight begins the moment you first spy your airplane on the ramp. Does it look symmetrical? Is one wing higher than the other? Does the horizontal or vertical stabilizer appear tilted?

- Is vertical stabilizer vertical?
- Horizontal stabilizer symmetry
- Tires inflated properly?
- Landing gear strut symmetry?
- Liquid leaks?
- Same height as other wing?

Fig. 2

Rod Machado's How to Fly an Airplane Handbook

Fig. 3 — Some airplanes (such as the Cessna 210 model) require a level surface to accurately assess fuel tank levels. Dipping the fuel tank to check for fuel quantity.

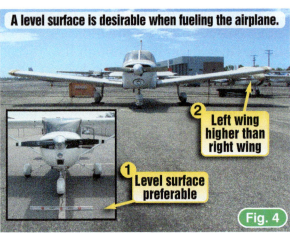

Fig. 4 — A level surface is desirable when fueling the airplane. 1. Level surface preferable. 2. Left wing higher than right wing.

Another reason to park on level surfaces is that some airplanes, such as the Cessna 210, have fuel tanks that can't be accurately dipped (checked with a fuel level dipstick) unless the airplane is on a nearly level surface (Figure 3 and Figure 4, position 1).

If the airplane appears to tilt while parked on a level surface, it's possible that the landing gear's oleo strut (any of the shock absorbing mechanisms that are part of the airplane's landing gear) needs inflation, has sprung a leak (some oleos are filled with hydraulic fluid and some with gas) or is damaged and bent. Sometimes oleo struts simply stick, resulting in the airplane resting with one wing lower than the other. Lubrication usually solves the problem.

Our flight school had a Piper Warrior that was notorious for having its right gear oleo stick in the compressed position, resulting in the left wingtip of this airplane being about five inches higher than the right (Figure 4, position 2). One pilot came into the flight school refusing to fly the airplane. In jest, I tried to tell him that this particular machine was built especially for flying right traffic patterns, and would please him greatly if he would just give the machine a try. He didn't buy it, so I went out, pushed the left wing up by placing my hand on the spar and solved the problem (the mechanic eventually oiled the oleo, which was a better solution).

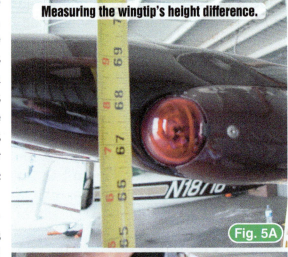

Fig. 5A — Measuring the wingtip's height difference.

On the other hand, if the airplane has solid, flex-type landing gear and the wings appear tilted, it's possible that a tire is low on air (or flat) or one gear strut is bent. At my flight school years ago, a pilot landed a Cessna 150 hard enough to actually bend the left main landing gear. If you looked at the airplane from a distance, it was clear that the landed gear was bent, but from a nearby vantage point the damage was difficult to detect. That explains why the pilot who previously flew this airplane claimed he hadn't noticed the problem after tying down the airplane and leaving for the day (had he shown up for his next lesson wearing a neck brace, I wouldn't have accepted his explanation). If the next pilot on the schedule had walked up to the airplane without first perusing it from a distance, he might not have noticed the damage (Figure 5). On some airplanes, Cessna allows four inches difference in wingtip height before a more thorough inspection is required.

Fig. 5B — Differences in wingtip height can be caused by unequal tire inflation or bent landing gear.

Chapter 1: Let's Go Flying

Fig. 6 — Auxiliary fuel tanks on the wingtips can carry a lot of extra weight which makes it easier to bend a wing during a hard landing. Auxiliary tank on each wing.

The horizontal stabilizer should be horizontal. Elevator. Horizontal stabilizer.

Stabilator

Should be appx. the same height as other side of the stabilizer

Fig. 7

Instead of landing gear problems, it's possible (albeit quite rare) for one wing to be bent. Take for instance airplanes that have auxiliary tip tanks (Figure 6). These tanks can hold 10 to 15 extra gallons of fuel (think 60 to 75 pounds). That's a lot of extra weight on a wingtip as an add-on accessory item. During an extremely hard landing, that extra weight could bend one of the airplane's wings. This is why an aeronautical engineering friend of mine always checks airplanes with wingtip tanks extra carefully. At least that's the tip on tip tanks that he offers.

Another thing best noticed from a distance is when a horizontal stabilizer is bent at an angle (Figure 7). This is something that's not right—or left. The part is called a *horizontal stabilizer* for a very good reason—it's supposed to be horizontal. So how does it get bent? Well, it can be rough out there on the ramp. In one case I'm familiar with, a fuel truck backed into the airplane, then drove off without reporting the problem. Given the mass of a fuel truck, it's not hard to see how it can make a mess of an airplane. Think rhino vs. VW. And given the difference in size, the decibel level to which the fuel boy has his iPod cranked up, and the ambient noise at an airport, it's certainly possible to have hit some part of flying machine and not be aware of it. This is especially true if the gas boy (the *liquid petroleum allocation engineer*, who can most definitely be a girl) doesn't have good hearing or is not good at interpreting sounds such as *thump* and *crunch*. This is just one more reason why all gas dispensing personnel should attend "thump and crunch" sound identification class.

While your preflight actually begins when approaching the airplane, it's when you can actually sniff, look, poke and feel the airplane that the finer details of the machine's airworthiness (or lack of it) are revealed.

Rod Machado's How to Fly an Airplane Handbook

Looking, Sniffing, Poking and Feeling

One of the very first things I *don't* do after opening the airplane door is turn on the airplane's master switch (Figure 8). That's right, I don't do that. Why? Because I don't want to let myself down. If the airplane has retractable gear, someone could have accidentally moved the gear switch to the retract position while exiting the craft, detailing the interior, getting a Hobbs meter reading, etc. It's happened (Figure 9).

Imagine kneeling on the step of a low wing, complex airplane, turning on the master switch and having the gear retract because a *squat* switch has gone bad (the squat switch detects gear compression on the ground, thus preventing gear retraction). Your first thought would probably be, "Holy cow, I need to take off a few pounds!" That's why I always open the airplane door, look at the gear switch, and make sure it's in the down and locked position.

But even before doing that, I sniff. Huh? Sniff? Am I checking to see if there's fine leather or cheap perfume aboard? Nope. I'm on the hunt for anything that smells like fuel or burning insulation (Figure 10). It makes sense to check for scents before doing anything else. When you first open the cabin door, there is a momentary opportunity to smell that something is wrong. Odors that communicate danger are concentrated because the cabin has been closed.

This is the best time to detect fuel leaks in the fuel plumbing mechanism. Airplanes are not deliberately designed to provide *eau du gas* in the cabin, so if you detect any, you should say, "Oh, the gas!" and start looking for a mechanic. There should *never* be a strong smell of avgas inside the airplane. Keep in mind that gas, when combined with spark, goes boom. That's what it's supposed to do, but only when confined to the cylinder of the engine.

Then again, I've been in many older airplanes where I detected a *slight* whiff of avgas and still felt that the airplane was perfectly safe to fly. These are typically fabric covered airplanes (Figure 11) that more easily retain fuel residue when the tanks are filled to the brim and beyond by an overenthusiastic gas boy. As a young gas boy, I was so motivated that I could get 50 gallons of fuel into a 40 gallon tank. That means I'd occasionally overfill a tank, much to the consternation of the owner. My

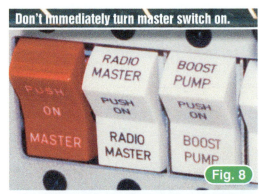
Don't immediately turn master switch on.
Fig. 8

Check gear handle position as "down."
Fig. 9

Sniff for avgas fumes upon entering cockpit.
Fig. 10

Fabric airplanes can retain the scent of avgas.
Fig. 11

NTSB Report on Baron Explosion

"A Beech C55 about to depart Tulsa, OK in April of 1980 on a cargo flight to Dallas, Texas had a wing explode. It was 9:30 a.m. and the wings were warming in the sun when the pilot started his engines. After stabilizing the RPMs at 1,100 on both sides the pilot reached for the radio switch and the right wing exploded. He shut down and vacated the aircraft. Investigators found fuel stains along the interior of the lower wing skid. The aux tank vent and the antisyphon line had become disconnected where it joined the vent line. All the hose clamps on the bent system lines and vapor return line were found loose."

Apparently the spark from the radio switch ignited the fuel fumes. This is a very good reason to sniff the cockpit as you enter before turning on anything electrical.

Chapter 1: Let's Go Flying

Fig. 12 — Fuel Stains. Blue dye is an indication of a fuel leak.

Fig. 13 — Old, rusty, leaky fuel tank vent lines.

Fig. 14 — Dihedral pools leaked fuel/fumes toward belly. Fuel and fumes can pool in this area.

Fig. 15 — Your mechanic can check for leaks to locate source of fumes. © philippe maville

bad, and I did apologize. Fuel that flows off a wing can soak into the fabric, thus allowing the airplane to retain the avgas smell for some time. If the tanks have been overfilled recently, you might be able to see some of the colored fuel dye on the wing behind the fuel cap or even on the bottom side of the wing.

If I were to avoid flying every fabric covered (older) airplane having a very slight smell of fuel in the cockpit, there would be few for me to fly. The deciding factor here is the intensity of the fuel smell. Ultimately, your decision to fly rests on the basic idea of how concentrated that fuel smell is and whether or not it's coming from a leak or from the occasional overfilling of the tanks (Figure 12).

On older airplanes (fabric or metal covered) it's common for the plumbing that connects the tank to the overflow vent lines to crack over time (Figure 13). This means fuel that would ordinarily flow from the tank to the ground via the cracked vent line actually drips into the internal wing structure (which can cause more than just a hint of avgas odor). Since airplane wing tips are often higher than the wing roots (we refer to this as *dihedral*), the fuel tends to sink to the lowest point in the wing structure (near the wing root). You can imagine the danger this poses (Figure 14).

Fuel is volatile—it evaporates easily. The fumes can go anywhere, and they are highly explosive. Years ago, the pilot of a Beechcraft Baron jumped into the cockpit, turned on the master switch, turned on the radio to obtain his clearance and had the right wing literally explode (see NTSB report on Page 1-6). Avgas had leaked from a cracked fuel line down into the belly of the airplane. The pilot apparently didn't notice the avgas odor and he ignited the fuel vapor with his radio switch, which essentially acted like a BBQ striker as a spark jumped between its contact points. Economic booms are good. Wing booms are bad.

This is why the gas company tells those folks who live in homes piped for natural gas to sniff as they enter the house instead of immediately flicking a light switch. A distinctive "rotten egg" odor is added to otherwise-scentless natural gas so you'll know it has escaped its boundaries. The tiniest spark, even inside a light switch, can cause a housing boom.

If you sense a strong fuel smell, it's wise to have a mechanic check the airplane for leaks (Figure 15).

If you detect the smell of burning electrical insulation when you take that opening whiff, find out why before leaving the ground. It might indicate an undetected electrical short somewhere behind the instrument panel. We're inclined to think that all electrical shorts will pop a circuit breaker, but that's not always true. Sometimes circuit breakers are old and have lost their "popness." OK, that's not an official word, but circuit breakers can oxidize, stick, break or just fail over time, losing their ability to open a circuit when excessive current flows through them.

The smell of anything burning in an airplane is worthy of an investigation, though it's better to call an airplane mechanic than the FBI. One fellow started his Cessna 152 and taxied out, only to smell something burning. He immediately returned to the tiedown area and called for a mechanic. The mechanic looked inside the cowling and removed a small, still-smouldering bird's nest from the top of a cylinder. I wasn't there, so I can only hope the mechanic held the nest up in his hand and, in his best British accent, said, "Sir, your eggs are done." I sure hope it wasn't the guy's fledgling flight.

Gust Locks and Gear Handles

Once you've opened the door, sniffed for fuel and electrical issues, and are satisfied that the landing gear handle (if your airplane has retractable landing gear, of course) is in the down and locked position, you want to remove the airplane's internal gust lock (and the external ones if they exist). This frees the flight controls for inspection. It also frees your airplane to fly (Figure 16).

Believe me when I say that you want to remove the gust lock now. A locked-in gust lock is a serious impediment to getting and staying airborne. One pilot in a Cessna 182 managed to preflight, taxi out and take off with his gust lock still installed (I couldn't make this stuff up if I wanted to because it's just too weird). Somehow, with whatever combination of flaps and aircraft loading he had, the airplane came off the ground and climbed. At this point he realized that his gust lock hadn't been removed. The really unfortunate problem here was that his gust lock was an actual lock, whose key was on the ignition key's key ring. Houston, we have a problem.

But never fear, the pilot had a solution, or so he thought. He turned off the ignition, pulled out the key, and tried to unlock the gust lock, hoping he could get the key back in the ignition slot and the engine restarted before hitting the ground. Well, that plan didn't quite work out the way he intended. He managed to vaporize himself and the airplane. OK, a little alcohol was involved in this accident, too—and not because the pilot wanted a sterile cockpit, either.

With all that in order, you are now ready to turn on the battery side of the master switch (assuming your airplane has a split master switch) as shown in Figure 17. Make sure your avionics switch is turned off first (Figure 18), then turn the master (battery) switch on. Ensuring the avionics switch is off means you won't waste valuable and limited battery energy. It also means you won't cause an electrical spike that could harm the airplane's electrical equipment.

Fig. 16 — Remove internal and external gust locks before flight. External gust lock

Fig. 17 — Activate battery side of master switch for power.

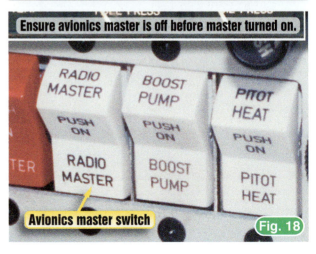

Fig. 18 — Ensure avionics master is off before master turned on. Avionics master switch

Chapter 1: Let's Go Flying

1-9

Overlooked Checklist Item

Completing every item on the checklist is the key to "unlocking" the secret of flight.

"On takeoff roll, when the airspeed reached 60 knots, I started to pull the yoke back, but the nose of the aircraft did not lift. I then pulled back the throttle to abort the takeoff, applied heavy braking, and ran off the side of the runway into a swamp. When I examined the plane afterwards, I found that the control lock had not been removed from the control yoke. A more thorough preflight and better use of the checklist would have prevented this incident."

NASA Report

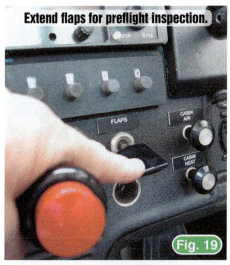
Extend flaps for preflight inspection.
Fig. 19

Once the master switch is on, move the flap handle and fully extend the flaps (Figure 19). The flap handle is the one that is flat and feels like a flap. Don't touch that gear handle. It's the one that's round and feels like a tire. As an aside, before you move the flap or gear handle, you always say, "Flap (or "gear") handle confirmed," as you touch it. This is just another way of ensuring that you know what you're touching, which is always a good idea in life.

As the flaps extend, listen carefully. You're not listening for a flapping sound, but rather for several different types of sounds, the loudest of which is the electric flap motor extending the flaps (if you hear an "ouch," the flaps just hit your flight instructor on the head because you didn't warn her about flap extension). Listen carefully for any signs that metal or cables are binding (or grinding) as the flaps extend.

Electric gyro-based instruments can make noise when master is activated.
Attitude indicator
Turn coordinator
Fig. 20

You may also hear the gyro on your electrically powered turn coordinator or artificial horizon spinning up (Figure 20). In addition, you'll probably hear the rotating beacon on the tail of the airplane spinning (Figure 21). Most pilots leave the airplane's rotating beacon switch in the on position after engine shutdown since it's recommended that this beacon be on when the airplane engine is in operation, regardless of whether it's day or night.

Each airplane sings its own particular flap-lowering sound, so if you fly the same aircraft repeatedly you'll soon know what the music should be. Anything that sounds strange or out of the ordinary is out of the ordinary and deserves your attention (or a spot on American Idol).

As the flaps extend, note the readings on the fuel gauges (Figure 22). Of course you'll make a visual inspection of the fuel before you depart (Figure 23), but this is a good time to check the fuel quantity readings. If the gauges indicate that the tanks are full and you

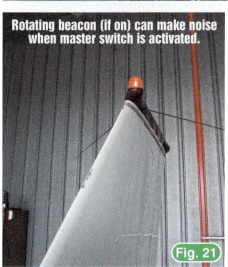
Rotating beacon (if on) can make noise when master switch is activated.
Fig. 21

Check fuel indication when you first enter cockpit and turn master on.
Fig. 22

Always make a visual inspection of the fuel tanks.
Fig. 23

Rod Machado's How to Fly an Airplane Handbook

You'll look very strange if you preflight while wearing the scarf and goggles.

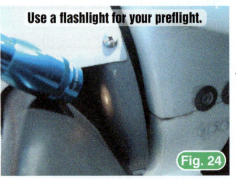

Use a flashlight for your preflight.

Fig. 24

Here is where a flashlight is important.

Fig. 25

A flashlight is also important for looking into small crevices.

Fig. 26

know the tanks aren't full, then you have a gauge problem. If the gauges say empty and you know there's fuel aboard, there's a gauge problem. Yes, rheostat-type fuel gauges are notoriously inaccurate, but this is still something to mention to your mechanic.

Once the flaps are fully extended, turn the master switch off and grab the flashlight out of your flight bag, or from behind the seat or the glove compartment (assuming you wear gloves, that is. Don't wear the goggles. You'll attract way too much attention to yourself at the airport). Now you get to poke and feel your way around the airplane, which will be illuminating since you've got your own light source (Figure 24).

In my opinion, you need a flashlight to do a good preflight, *especially* during the day. That seems a bit ironic, right? During bright daylight hours your pupils have likely slammed shut to the size of a pinhole, which means there's very little light entering your eye. That in turn means you can't see into the dark crevices and metallic folds of your machine without shining some light on the subject. I'm particularly thinking of the areas under the engine cowling as shown in Figure 25 (assuming your engine cowling isn't easily openable) or where the horizontal stabilizer connects to the elevator (Figure 26).

Care for a Stroll? A Walkaround, Perhaps?

So, where do you begin the walkaround portion of the preflight? Most people begin by making a visual inspection of the fuel (Figure 27). This allows them to call for fuel service early if it's needed and avoid delaying the flight. You don't usually need the flashlight to check the fuel level. That's why there are dipsticks (Figure 28). But if you do look into the tanks with your flashlight, be careful not to drop the flashlight into the hole. This is something you couldn't do once in a thousand tries if you were trying, but which it's amazingly easy to do when you're not trying. If the flashlight does go down the gas hole, you'll need to call a mechanic to pull it out. He usually keeps a special pair of tongs in the building for this purpose (tongs aren't Chinese pliers, either).

Unless you recently swallowed an entire bag of Miracle Grow, you'll often need a ladder to make a visual inspection of the fuel

A flashlight helps identify the tank's fuel level.

Fig. 27

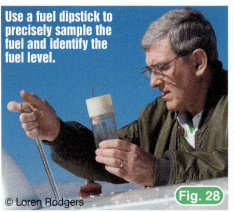

Use a fuel dipstick to precisely sample the fuel and identify the fuel level.

© Loren Rodgers

Fig. 28

A small ladder is often necessary to preflight fuel levels.

Ladder

Fig. 29

Chapter 1: Let's Go Flying

Airplane Flight Manuals (AFM) and POHs

All airplanes weighing more than 6,000 pounds and all airplanes manufactured after March 1, 1979 require an FAA-approved *airplane flight manual* (AFM). This rule covers the vast majority of the airplanes most of us fly.

If you own an airplane weighing 6,000 pounds (gross weight) or less or own one that was manufactured before March 1, 1979, the airplane doesn't require an approved AFM.

AFMs are labeled with a specific part number and are assigned to a specific airplane serial number. The AFM is the official information source for the airplane. It is continuously updated by the airplane owner or mechanic from data provided by the airplane manufacturer. This is where you'll normally find the airplane's weight and balance information, information on the operation of airplane equipment, performance charts, emergency procedures and so on. The AFM is usually in binder form so it can be easily updated.

The AFM is *the* word on any specific airplane. Nothing anyone says, nothing any writer writes, overrules or countermands the official word of the AFM. It is a very good idea to take the time to read the AFM cover-to-cover every so often, perhaps as part of your spring housecleaning or celebration of the winter solstice. You'd be surprised how many pilots have never read the AFM for their airplane. To them, it's just a cabin adornment. The AFM has lots of really interesting charts, and information that you might not have time to look for when you most need it.

You will often hear reference to the *pilot's operating handbook* (POH). This isn't necessarily the AFM, but it might be. To be an official AFM, the POH must contain the airplane's complete AFM as part of its contents. The way you can easily determine this is to look at the POH and see if it contains the airplane's weight and balance information, along with a reference to the airplane's serial number. If the term *pilot's operating handbook* is used in the main title of the book in the airplane you'll fly, there should be a statement included on the title page indicating that sections of the POH are FAA approved as the AFM.

You might on some occasions fly airplanes with only an owner's manual as the official information source. Most airplanes built before 1979 have one of these. The owner's manual along with markings, weight and balance info and placards meets the certification requirement for airplanes manufactured before March 1, 1979.

According to AOPA, the one exception to this is Beechcraft airplanes. The Beech company has provided AFMs with airplane-specific serial numbers for many of their airplanes manufactured since the early 1950s.

level in a high wing airplane (Figure 29). Some airplanes, of course, have hand grips and steps on the side of the fuselage for just this purpose (Figure 30). On occasion, I've called the gas boy over and borrowed his or her ladder for this purpose. It's better, however, to purchase a small, collapsible ladder that can be kept in the airplane to do this job. Either way, there's no excuse for taking off without making a visual inspection of the fuel. This is one of those rules that's just not negotiable. Period.

Now it's time to begin the walkaround. Unless you have your own special way of doing this (and I don't mean whether you should skip or goosestep, either), follow the airplane manufacturer's recommendation in the *airplane flight manual* or *pilot's operating handbook* (Figure 31).

If you're an instructor, you may want to make up your own checklist that includes more than the minimums specified by the manufacturer (Figure 32). I've known flight instructors to make a real-

Fig. 30

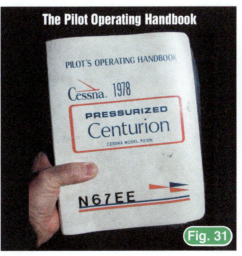
Fig. 31

Fig. 32

time preflight audio recording that their students can listen to and use to guide them as they walk around the airplane (don't get this mixed up with your aerobics tape or you'll be too exhausted to fly after the preflight). This, along with a written checklist, helps beginning students remember important items during the preflight.

If you begin the preflight walk around in the front left of the airplane (as viewed from the pilot's seat), you'll check the left wing's leading edge for dents, the strut (if there is one) and the pitot tube, to ensure it's not plugged. Whatever you do, don't blow into a pitot tube to remove foreign objects, such as insects (Figure 33). Think about it. Where do you think that bug is going if you blow into the tube? There is no "bug" exit port. You'll just blow the detritus farther into the tube while causing the airspeed indicator (which is connected to the pitot tube) to swing to Mach 1. The only thing this will blow is your budget, which will suddenly have to stretch to cover repair or replacement of the airspeed indicator mechanism.

If a pitot cover is in place, now is a good time to remove it (Figure 34) along with any other covers and plugs protecting the airplane and its components (Figure 35). One Air Force pilot told me he departed in a formation of fighter aircraft and noticed that his plastic pitot cover was still attached. He knew his pitot heat was really hot, so he activated it and literally burned through the plastic, which let the airstream pull it free. Let's just say that he got lucky. His plane and pitot heat were bigger than yours. Don't even think about using this technique in a smaller airplane, because it's not likely to work, though it is another way of creating an expensive repair opportunity. If you insist on supporting your mechanic, why not just adopt him?

If you're preflighting a low (or high) wing airplane, you'll want to drop down and make a close inspection of the gear (Figure 36). Here is where the flashlight (and a knee pad, perhaps) comes in handy. Look under the brake disc for leaking brake fluid or hydraulic fluid from the gear's oleo mechanism (Figure 37). Touch the brake line very lightly to ensure that it is connected properly. You should be a big touchy-feely person when it comes to preflighting airplanes. Sometimes looking just isn't enough when you want to know

Chapter 1: Let's Go Flying

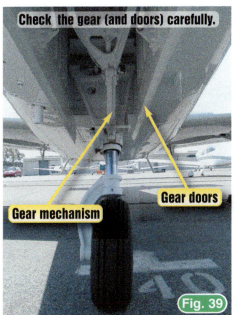
Check the gear (and doors) carefully.
Gear mechanism
Gear doors
Fig. 39

if two items are in the process of separation, disconnection or disintegration. So feel free to touch the brake lines, brake pads and brake discs (Figure 38), but only if you're sure they're not hot from recent use (otherwise you'll scream and do a little shuffle on the tarmac, also known as *brake dancing*).

Why do we preflight the landing gear! To prevent this from happening.
An actual TRUE story.

Make it a point to look at every nut and bolt you can see on the gear's structure as well as the gear doors (if your airplane has them) as shown in (Figure 39). Under the influence of vibration and expansion and contraction from temperature changes, these things can unwind themselves. An unscrewed nut and a screwed-on nut look very similar. That's why you "touch" and go.

Several years ago, a student pilot whom we'll call Ms. Dropsy departed in a Piper Warrior that had just come out of maintenance—specifically, gear maintenance. The mechanic had removed the two main (fixed) gear for repair and reinstalled them without also reinstalling the two pins than hold the gear onto the airplane's structure. Ms. Dropsy took off and both main gear fell off her airplane. Really. I'm not kidding. This is a maneuver that controllers don't get to see every day. Perhaps the controller thought, "Now that's what you call lowering the gear." Ms. Dropsy managed to return and land safely from her solo flight. She even did a short field landing, although she really had no choice in the matter.

Even the best mechanics occasionally have bad days and forget things.
© Andres Rodriguez
Fig. 40

One little lesson I learned many years ago is that if there's ever a time for something to go wrong with an airplane, it's when it has just come out of maintenance. That's not a knock on our mechanic friends, either (believe me, your mechanic is your friend). It's an affirmation of our human nature. Humans occasionally make mistakes. Mechanics are like doctors in that they both usually do great work. But even good doctors and mechanics occasionally have bad days and leave a tool behind, or remove something that should have stayed installed, or forget to tighten something up (Figure 40). *You* are the ultimate quality control inspector, so do your job.

Fuel Sampling

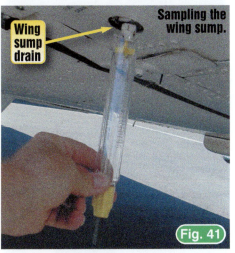
Wing sump drain
Sampling the wing sump.
Fig. 41

While you're under the wing of a low or high wing airplane, it's a good time to sample the fuel in each tank with your fuel sampling cup (Figure 41). No, don't taste it. It's not that kind of sampling. I'm speaking of something known as *sumping* the tank, which means to drain a little for inspection. If you find material in the tank, then sumptin' must be done about it.

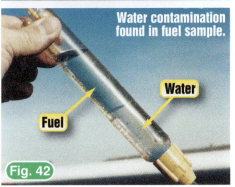
Water contamination found in fuel sample.
Fuel
Water
Fig. 42

What are you looking for when collecting a fuel sample? You're checking for two things—that you have the right stuff in your tank, and that there isn't any type of contamination, be it in solid or liquid form (Figure 42).

The right stuff is the fuel that your engine runs on. Believe it or not, putting jet fuel in your piston plane does not make it fly faster. Aviation gas (avgas) is colored to enable you to more easily distinguish one type from another. Today, the most prevalent fuel for piston aircraft is 100LL (low lead), which is colored a light blue. If you get no color or a different color, it's time to ask questions.

The most common fuel contaminant is water, which is heavier than fuel so it rests in the bottom of the sampling cup and is relatively easy to see (Figure 42). It's easy to see, that is, unless the entire sample cup is filled with water. Then you might just assume that this is all fuel, when it's not. That's one reason why fuel is dyed a specific color. If you've got clear liquid, it's either water or kerosene (jet fuel). If you'd like to know which, then sniff it or, if you're brave enough, taste it (Figure 43). This isn't going to damage the taster unless he/she performs about a thousand tests a day as a result of other instructors all using Ted the Tester.

Many years ago, one of general aviation's famous aviators experienced a double engine failure on takeoff when the gas boy accidentally filled his piston powered Shrike Commander with jet fuel. There was enough fuel in the line for taxi and the initial climbout before both engines failed. An off-field landing followed.

The problem with mixing jet fuel and avgas is that your sample can be dangerously contaminated with kerosene but still look somewhat like 100LL. Fortunately, there is a test you can perform to check for jet fuel contamination in 100LL fuel. Here's what you need to know to perform this test.

Kerosene is oily and when you place a few drops of it on a white piece of paper, it leaves a distinct dark area as the sample dries (Figure 44, position A). Avgas, on the other hand, evaporates clear as shown in Figure 44, position B.

If you suspect jet fuel contamination in your 100LL fuel supply, place a few drops of the suspected fuel on a white piece of paper (Figure 45, position A). If there's an oily spot in the middle of the sample as it dries (Figure 45, position B), then your fuel supply is contaminated.

Chapter 1: Let's Go Flying

1-15

Gas trucks need draining, too. (Fig. 49)

The gas truck's fuel drain location. Drain truck sump here (Fig. 50)

Fuel sample tossed on ground. (Fig. 51)

Water in My Fuel Tank? How So?

Why should you fill up your fuel tanks after flight? One very good reason is to prevent water from accumulating in that tank. Read on.

If you don't have fuel in your tank, then air fills the empty space. As you know, air contains water vapor (water molecules). As that air cools overnight, these water molecules move slower and vibrate less. Eventually, the collisions between water molecules are slow enough to allow them to stick together. In other words, the water molecules can't remain as vapor (gas) any longer, so they return to the liquid state in the form of water condensing and falling to the bottom of your fuel tank (water is heavier than fuel).

You know this process as *The Mystery of the Sweating Glass*. Why does a glass get damp on the outside when you pour cool lemonade in it on a hot summer's day? Hot air, carrying lots of moisture, comes in contact with the cool surface of the glass. The suddenly-chilled air can't hold its water. Droplets form on the glass.

Jet fuel tastes oily, somewhat like bad Mexican food, but with more explosive power. Aviation gasoline tastes similar to the fuel you tasted the time you were forced to siphon gas for your car. Water should be tasteless, unless you live in a really bad area. If there's something in there that shouldn't be there, the tank must be completely drained and cleaned before flight. In other words, you aren't going flying in that airplane that day.

If it's water in the tank, you might be able to fix the problem and fly. Keep sampling the fuel until the water's gone or you feel it's hopeless. You may have to rock the wings slightly to get all the water to collect near the tank's sampling areas for draining (in a moment I'll talk about how to properly rock the wings). There have been times that I've had to sample the fuel 10 or more times to get all the water out of a tank. Now that's a drain. On some older Cessna 182s with bladder tanks (rubber tanks instead of metal ones), it's recommended by the manufacturer that you push down on the tail once or twice similar to the way I'm showing it in Figures 47 and 48 (check manufacturer's recommendation to be sure). This moves water in these older tanks over any ridges in the rubber, toward the aft-located drain spouts.

So much for liquid that lurks. What about solids that sink? What's the deal with that? Contamination can come from a couple of sources. It is possible (though infrequently the case) that something in the fuel system is deteriorating (lines, linings). The more likely scenario is that the bad stuff went in with the gas. How does that happen? Fuel is typically stored in underground tanks that are subject to all sorts of stuff falling, creeping, or crawling into them. In theory, each morning before the gas truck is used, the gas boy is supposed to drain its fuel sumps (Figure 49). He is, after all, refueling the fuel truck's tank every evening or every morning from a main fueling reservoir. If he doesn't drain the truck's tank, the next stop for the gunk is *your* fuel tank (Figure 50).

Most of the time you can drain away contaminants and be satisfied that the source isn't deterioration of the fuel system's plumbing. If "stuff" keeps showing up tank after tank, you'll certainly want to talk to the mechanic. He's going to have to ground the airplane and inspect those tanks, but it will pay for his trip to Europe next summer so he'll accommodate you.

Is that you standing there with a cupful of freshly decanted fuel? Where are you going to put it? Don't worry, I'm not going to make any rude suggestions. Most pilots just throw the sample on the asphalt and let it evaporate (Figure 51). If it's a small sample and no one is sunbathing nearby, that pretty much works, though "evaporate" is another word for "create air pollution." If you do this, don't tell the airport authorities. They are often required to enforce strict environmental regulations. You could be kidnapped and strapped to a slow moving glacier by ecoterrorists. Some airports recommend that you place the displaced fuel in its own container and drop it off at the

Rod Machado's How to Fly an Airplane Handbook

The airport recycling center. Fig. 52

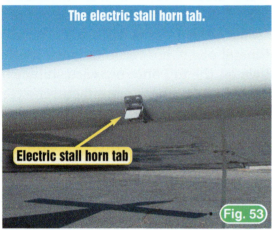
The electric stall horn tab. Electric stall horn tab. Fig. 53

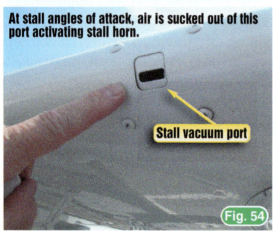
At stall angles of attack, air is sucked out of this port activating stall horn. Stall vacuum port. Fig. 54

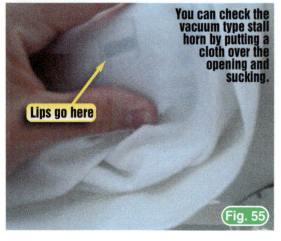
You can check the vacuum type stall horn by putting a cloth over the opening and sucking. Lips go here. Fig. 55

airport's recycling center (Figure 52), though I'm unable to confirm if anyone anywhere has ever done this. As pilots, we do have an obligation to minimize our impact on the planet whenever possible. If the fuel sample is uncontaminated, then it's completely proper to return it to the fuel tank.

Let the Stall Blow Your Horn

As we move on to the left wing's leading edge, you're likely to encounter one of two types of stall warning systems (the left wing is the favored location for these devices since the left wing is the one most likely to stall first because of the airplane's power-induced left turning tendency. You'll learn about this when we discuss stalls and spins later).

The first is the electric stall horn tab (Figure 53). At the higher angles of attack associated with a stall, the air lifts the tab up, closing a circuit and activating an electric horn or light (or both) in the cockpit. You can lift the tab to see if it lifts easily (it should). Don't expect the stall horn to sound unless the master switch is on. Then again, this depends on how your airplane is wired. It may actually sound during the preflight with the master switch off. After all, it's good to have a stall horn if you've shut down the electrical system in flight due to an electrical fire, right? Either way, make sure you check the operation of the electric stall horn every once in a while, just to make sure it is working.

An open port on the left wing usually belongs to the vacuum-type (pneumatic) stall horn (Figure 54). At high angles of attack, air flows over this port creating a vacuum that draws air in through a horn located near the cockpit. The common way to check this port is to place a thin cloth over it and suck on the opening (Figure 55). The stall horn should activate. If you didn't use a cloth and just sucked on the opening, you might unexpectedly swallow a bug, which will activate your gag horn. Then again, a nice fat bug might be a bit more tasty than your typical airport vending machine fare, and will usually have far more protein. If you're a student, don't let your flight instructor make you suck on the stall port, either. If he suggests it, just tell him you've already got a mouthful of vintage jet fuel and that it simply doesn't go well with common bugs.

Tips on Wing Tips

As you reach the right wing you'll want to be sure that the wingtip and position lights aren't damaged (you want to check the position lights for proper operation with the battery-half of the master switch on if you're planning a night flight) as shown in Figure 56. Damage in this area could mean that someone used the wing as a fence detector in-

Chapter 1: Let's Go Flying

Check the left wing position light.

Check the right wing position light.

Check the tail light and rotating beacon.

Fig. 56

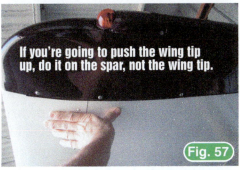
If you're going to push the wing tip up, do it on the spar, not the wing tip.

Fig. 57

stead of the lift producer it was meant to be. Some pilots like to move the wing tip up and down to check for unusual sounds that identify an overstressed wing. This serves more of an emotional need than a practical one, since it would be rather difficult to identify wing damage by this method. If you want to do this, then don't move the wing by the wing tip. Instead, move inward a few inches and press up or down slightly on the area where the spar is located (Figure 57). This keeps the very tip of the wing—often made from fragile plastic—from flying off during flight. Take it from me, that's a good tip, so don't lose it.

As a practical matter, if you're going to detect wing damage (resulting from overstressing the airframe) on an airplane, you should look at the top and bottom of the wing for sheared rivets and metal with waves in it (Figure 58). These are typical signs that the wing has been overstressed. Given how strong wings are, finding this type of damage is *extremely* rare on an airplane.

Ailerons and Flaps

At the trailing outboard edge of the wing you will find (or should find) an aileron (Figure 59). Here's where your flashlight once again comes in handy (Figure 60). Lift the aileron up (your control lock isn't still in, is it?) and touch all the hinges as well as the guide extension lever that extends and retracts the device. One word of caution here. Hold the trailing edge of the aileron up with one hand and use the finger on the other hand to do the touching. If you didn't hold the aileron up, a strong wind might cause the aileron on the other wing to lift, pinching your finger in the process. Not surprisingly, this will cause you to emit a high pitched noise similar to that of a stall horn or a bat going out on the evening hunt. Then again, stall horns and bats don't say, "Ohhh chee mama!"

You will also be checking the control surface's counterweights (Figure 59). These are weights that dampen the aileron's tendency to oscillate with increasing amplitude such that it might eventually lead to control surface flutter. For now, take my word for it—this is not good. Most (but not all) control surfaces have these counterweights. Those that don't use (control) cable tension to dampen or restrict control surface oscillation.

Check the top and bottom of the wing for signs of overstressing.

Fig. 58

You'll inspect the left wing aileron, its hinge, counterweights, etc.

Counterweights

The aileron

Fig. 59

Use your flashlight to help you inspect the aileron hinge.

Fig. 60

Examine the aileron hinge carefully. Fig. 61

Check that flaps move symmetrically. Fig. 62

Check flap hinges and bearings. Flap hinge. Fig. 63

Bent propeller tips. Fig. 64

When you're done touching and inspecting the hinging and control mechanism, hold one end of the aileron up and shine your light on the hinge, bracket and counterweight areas. You're checking for cracks that might indicate that these items are weakened or broken (Figure 61).

The flaps are next up for your thorough inspection (Figure 62). Flaps don't have counterweights, so all you're concerned about here is making sure that both flaps are traveling the same distance downward (upward, too). You also want to ensure that the flap rails and bearings (or hinges if the flaps don't slide rearward) are not binding (Figure 63).

Years ago a flight instructor friend was preflighting a high performance, retractable geared airplane when he noticed that the inside under-edge portion of the flap's trailing edge was scraped and bent slightly upward on both flaps. This made him curious, so he walked to the front of the airplane and looked at the propeller. Sure enough, the tips of the propeller were slightly bent (Figure 64). Apparently the prior pilot had almost landed gear up with full flaps. Upon realizing his mistake, he managed to lift the airplane off with full power and get the gear down for landing. According to this fortunate (unfortunate?) pilot, he thought he had narrowly escaped a bad situation, not realizing that he had in fact damaged the airplane. Is it possible that he didn't hear the scraping of the flaps and the prop? Sure it is. After all, airplanes are noisy places, so I'll take him at his word on that one.

The Fuselage

One of the often overlooked areas during the preflight is the aft part of the fuselage as it merges into the empennage (Figure 65). This is the place to begin checking for the effects of tail strikes. I remember looking at our flight school's Piper Tomahawk that had just suffered a tail strike. The airplane has a T-tail (Figure 66), which makes it easier to over-flare these airplanes. The damage was subtle in that the metal in the mid-point of the fuselage showed an accordion effect as a result of the tail structure being bent upward when striking the ground. Rubbing a hand over the surface revealed the wavy metal and the extensive damage. The tail tiedown ring can also reveal the effects of a tail strike (Figure 67). The Tomahawk's tiedown ring was noticeably bent.

Examining the empennage. Fig. 65

Some "T" tail airplanes are easy to overflare, resulting in a tail strike. Fig. 66

Examine the tail tiedown ring for damage. Scraped, but no damage to tail section. Fig. 67

Chapter 1: Let's Go Flying

Fig. 68 — Looking for excessive oil leakage. Excessive oil.

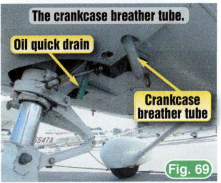
Fig. 69 — The crankcase breather tube. Oil quick drain. Crankcase breather tube.

Fig. 70 — Fuselage/empennage (water) drain holes. Drain holes.

Fig. 71 — A few of the airplane's antennas.

Take a good look under the fuselage while you're in a position to do so. On many airplanes, it might look as though the machine just landed on an oil slick (Figure 68), especially if the airplane's owner doesn't regularly wash his or her airplane (or has a wash crew that thinks "topping it off" means washing only the top of the airplane, not the bottom). Your objective here is to see if there is excessive oil leakage along the bottom of the fuselage (which is one reason to keep the bottom part of your airplane nice and clean).

Since the engine's crankcase breather tube normally runs downward beneath the engine (Figure 69), oil is sometimes blown backward along the belly of the fuselage. Is this common? Well, yes it is. It's a function of the way airplanes are designed. If an engine is filled with too much oil (which still may be less than the maximum allowed by the dipstick), oil can blow out of the breather tube and backward along the belly. If excess oil has to go somewhere, on the belly sure beats having it blow on your windshield, right?

The problem is that this oil and dirt can sometimes plug drain holes on the bottom of the fuselage or empennage (Figure 70). These are holes that allow water entering the fuselage to escape. That means an increase in corrosion or even damage to electrical equipment located in the aft section of the fuselage. If those holes are plugged, then unplug them with something the size of a toothpick (but don't use that same tooth pick to clean your teeth (or tooth), at least not without washing it). While you're down under, take a good look at the antennas (Figure 71), ensuring that none are missing or bent (in a way that they shouldn't be bent).

Static Ports

The static port (or ports) can be located almost anywhere on the side of (or even below) the airplane's fuselage (Figure 72). This is a good time to check that this port isn't plugged by a foreign object (or even objects from this country). The most likely port plugging culprit is the nice person who waxed your airplane (Figure 73). Sure, you told him not to wax that part of the airplane but the wax in his ears may have prevented him from hearing you. So look closely at the static port (there may be more than one on your airplane, too) and make sure it's free of obstructions.

Fig. 72 — Static ports can be found in several different locations on the airplane. Variations in static ports. Two holes for the static port.

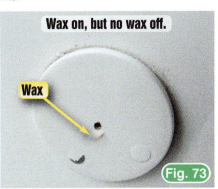
Fig. 73 — Wax on, but no wax off. Wax.

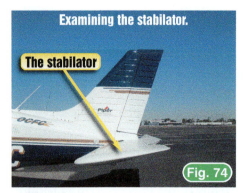
Examining the stabilator.
The stabilator
Fig. 74

Examining the elevator hinge from above.
Fig. 75

Examining the elevator hinge from below.
Fig. 76

Close up inspection of elevator hinge.
Fig. 77

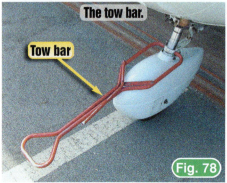
The tow bar.
Tow bar
Fig. 78

Once again, please don't blow into or suck on the static port to clear an obstruction away. If it's not easily cleared away by use of your finger, then have a mechanic remove the obstruction for you.

The Empennage

One thing you can't afford to have problems with in flight is your airplane's tail section. Over the years, several reports surfaced about airplanes having elevator hinges break in flight, and the results were always scary. So begin your empennage preflight by looking carefully at both the horizontal stabilizer and the moveable elevator (some airplanes have a single moveable aft surface known as a *stabilator*) as shown in Figure 74. Your job is to ensure that every hinge, rivet, bracket, bolt and nut is in good working order. The only way you can do this properly, in my opinion, is to use your flashlight (Figure 75). You often have to point the beam into those tiny dark crevices to see if the rivets on the hinge bracket are secure and that there are no cracks in the bracket. That often means kneeling down underneath the elevator, lifting it up, and shining your beam up into the bottom side of these brackets, too (Figures 76 and 77).

I once gently and very lightly applied a little up and down pressure near the tip of a Cessna 172's elevator control. There was an unreasonable amount of vertical movement in the horizontal stabilizer. This was movement beyond what you might expect from the structure's normal elasticity. Despite it not being election day, I elected not to fly the airplane, but I did send it to the maintenance hangar for inspection.

It turned out that the center bracket holding the horizontal stabilizer onto the aft end of the fuselage had broken. The likely reason for this fracture was that pilots would often sit on the horizontal stabilizer to move the airplane backwards into its tiedown spot. Isn't this why airplanes have tow bars? There's no "rear end goes here" sign on any horizontal stabilizer that I've ever seen. A tow bar (Figure 78) is a much better and less damaging method for moving an airplane than using your derriere to sit

Just Pulling Your Nose

I pulled my aircraft out of my hangar using my electric pulley and had it fueled up. After fueling I did my preflight. The attending mechanic said I needed oxygen and decided to fill up the tank. Apparently he had to move the airplane and chose to use the tow bar without my knowledge. When I landed, Ground [control] informed me that the tow bar was still attached. [This] pilot now realizes that walk-arounds should be performed as the last thing prior to flight, especially when an aircraft has been serviced.
ASRS Report

Chapter 1: Let's Go Flying

> **Tow Bar Tantrums**
>
> For two General Aviation pilots, not stowing the tow bar before engine start resulted in a painful experience.
>
> My partner and I pulled our Beechcraft 35H straight out of the hangar in order to see if the engine would start. We believed the battery to be low and I had a planned flight in two days. We did not intend to do anything other than start the engine, shut it down, and return the aircraft to the hangar and so we left the tow bar attached to the nose wheel strut. My partner was in the left seat and started the engine. The engine turned over several times before it started and the propeller cleared the tow bar. As it started, the nose came down and the propeller struck the tow bar, sending it about thirty feet away. The engine was immediately shut down. We got our mechanic to come look at the propeller damage and then returned the aircraft to the hangar.
>
> ASRS Report

Checking the elevator counterweights.
Elevator counterweights
Fig. 79

down on the job. Besides, using a tow bar is a great source of amusement for the playful instructor (see Page 1-31).

On another occasion, I was preflighting an airplane with my tiny flashlight and noticed a nice crack across the entire span of the left elevator hinge. I mentioned this to the mechanic. When he took a look at it, he said, "Oh my gosh, that's nasty." Now, if I'd just been gored by a bull in Pamplona (or bit by a pitbull in Pomona), I'd expect my doctor to say something similar at the first viewing of my wound. But when a mechanic says that about the state of my airplane, it really makes me nervous. The airplane was taken off the flight line for immediate repair. It still makes me nervous to think that other pilots flew the airplane with the bracket cracked.

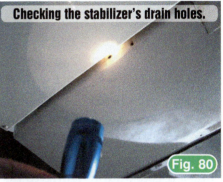

Checking the stabilizer's drain holes.
Fig. 80

While you're snooping around in back, take a look to ensure that the elevator's counterweights are secure (Figure 79). Look carefully at the elevator and the stabilizer to ensure that their drain ports (small holes) aren't plugged (Figure 80). Any water that happens to creep into the elevator needs a place to drain. If it didn't drain, this could cause an imbalance in the elevator control, increasing the potential for control structure flutter. And if you live in a cold environment, un-drained water might freeze in this area, increasing the potential for dangerous control surface flutter.

Ensure that all static wicks are in place.
Fig. 81

If you have static wicks on the airplane, make sure one isn't missing (Figure 81). Static wicks are used to channel static electricity so that it doesn't accumulate on other surfaces such as radio antennas, where it might interrupt communication or navigation. If you get ramp checked while a wick or two short of a full set, the FAA inspector won't be too happy. These items are most likely required by the airplane's *data* or *type certificate* and must be replaced if missing. One wicked corporate pilot I know carries a few extras with him for just this purpose.

Examine the rudder/tail structure.
Fig. 82

Next, take a look at the vertical stabilizer and rudder (Figure 82). How could the vertical stabilizer get damaged? Lots of ways. Pulling the airplane forward in the hangar and striking a bank of lights or an overhead beam will do it (Figure 83). So will the impact of a wing of a taller airplane that is being pushed or towed in the hangar, or is out moving around under its own

Use caution when towing out of the hangar.
Tail can hit overhead lights when towing airplane out of hangar
Fig. 83

power (Figure 84). The rudder, too, is vulnerable. Check its hinges and counterweights (yes, the rudder might have counterweights, too) and its movement about the vertical stabilizer (Figure 85).

Watch out for hangar doors, too.
Fig. 84

I remember one occasion where a flight instructor friend was preparing to do a flight review with a fellow who had arrived in a twin engine airplane. During the preflight inspection, the sharp instructor noticed that the rudder moved a little too freely, and didn't jiggle the cables as it moved. He looked a little closer and noticed that the weld on the rudder bracket had failed. Sure, the bracket moved, but the sheared weld point didn't rotate the rudder surface, meaning that you could move the airplane's rudder pedals but the rudder itself didn't turn. Imagine what would have happened if the pilot of this airplane had been forced to operate on a single-engine. He simply wouldn't have been able to maintain control of his airplane.

Rudders also might have counterweights.
Older type counterweights
New type
Fig. 85

This is one reason why we check the flight controls in the runup area, isn't it? Of course, it's often hard to see if the rudder moves unless you stick your head out an open door in the runup area. That's a reasonable thing to do if you want to check the rudder's operation, but a bad thing to do if you don't want to lose your sunglasses. If this doesn't work for you, then check the rudder's operation before engine start or maneuver in the runup area in such a way that you can see the shadow of your tail feathers from the cockpit (Figure 86). You can tell if the rudder moves from its shadow. And some have said that if you can see that shadow, you can expect at least six more weeks of winter.

Check rudder shadow for movement.
Rudder shadow
Fig. 86

That takes care of the airplane section aft of the leading edge of the wings. Now it's time to move up front and have a look at the engine, propeller and nose gear.

The Propeller

Rodney Dangerfield's famous line was, "I don't get no respect." If propellers had emotions, I suspect they'd feel the same way. There's no way to put a good spin on it. The propeller is probably the one item on an airplane that most pilots most take for granted. Even the airplane's tires seem to have more attention paid to them than the propeller.

Use fingers to check for prop nicks.
Nick
Fig. 87

The propeller moves at very high speeds and experiences tremendous loads. This is why you must ensure that there are no nicks or scrapes on its surface (Figure 87). Even a small nick can eventually lead to a stress fracture and possible separation of all or part of the blade in flight. That's why mechanics will *dress* a propeller if it's damaged (that doesn't mean he'll put pants on it. That's called *dressing up* a propeller). Run your finger along the propeller's leading edge and check for nicks. Then run your hand along the face of the propeller (Figure 88). The face is the side facing you as you sit in the cockpit. It's normally painted a flat, non-reflective black color and it's the side that's also exposed to

Check the face (back side) of the propeller.
Fig. 88

Chapter 1: Let's Go Flying

Fig. 89 — Check prop for excessive movement. Pull up and twist shaft (don't pull on heating element)

Fig. 90 — Check for oil leakage on CS propeller.

Fig. 91 — Check spinner plate for cracks.

Fig. 92 — Prop's swing arc hazard area. No entry

pebbles, stones and other objects that may enter the propeller's swing arc. Because of the dark color, it's often difficult to actually see any nicks, which is why you should run your hands along the surface. Any nick that's noticeable to the touch is one that should be addressed for dressing by your mechanic.

If your airplane has a controllable propeller, you'll want to pull outward gently along the propeller's axis to check for movement (Figure 89). Of course, the propeller shouldn't move in this direction. Each blade shouldn't wiggle or rotate about its axis as you twist it slightly, either. Since the angle of attack of the propeller on most single-engine, complex airplanes is changed by the hydraulic use of oil pressure, you'll also want to check that there's no oil leaking from seals at the propeller hub (Figure 90). If a British Petroleum representative claims to have discovered an oil field under your propeller hub, you've got a bad leak. No flying for you today.

Since you're up front, take a look behind the propeller spinner as well as the plate behind the spinner (Figure 91). There should be no cracks in that plate. If there are, there's a chance that the plate and the spinner could come off in flight. The last thing you want is some guy on the ground finding this assembly and thinking that a pilot's metallic dunce cap fell off in flight or, even worse, that Buzz Lightyear lost his helmet in flight.

One last word of caution here. With the exception of having to touch (but not turn or move) the propeller to preflight it properly, never place any body part within the swing arc of the propeller, especially if these body parts belong to you. I recall an old military picture that had red rectangles painted on the ground at the tiedown where the airplane's propeller swung (Figure 92). If any person entered the area above and within that rectangle, it was mandatory kitchen duty peeling potatoes for a week, which was more than sufficient time to appreciate how useful two hands can be.

Engine Cowling

Some airplanes have cowlings that easily open for inspection, which make it very convenient to take a peek under the hood, so to speak (Figure 93). Then there are airplanes that require the removal of many screws to separate the upper half of cowling for engine inspection (Figure 94). Of course, removing the cowling when preflighting these airplanes isn't practical on every flight. Then

Fig. 93 — Some cowlings open for easy inspection.

Fig. 94 — Some cowlings aren't easily opened.

Smartphones for Smart Preflights

One of the very nice features of most smartphones is the ability to place them in video record mode and have a lighted image appear in the screen. How could this help you better preflight an airplane? By placing the phone into the deeper and darker recesses of your cowling, you can actually see things you might not ordinarily see. The phone not only illuminates dark crevices inside your engine cowling, it also allows you to see around the corners under the cowling. Now that's a smart way to preflight. (Picture of smartphone under cowling with image.)

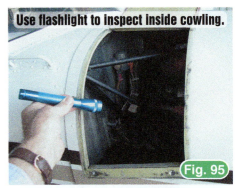

Fig. 95 — Use flashlight to inspect inside cowling.

again, with a flashlight you don't really need to remove the cowling to do a thorough preflight inspection. All you need to do is take that flashlight and poke it into the air inlets on the front side as well as around the small doors surrounding the oil filler and dipstick (if these doors exist on your airplane) as shown in (Figure 95). A good light will illuminate the insides of the cowling sufficiently to let you identify most problems that may exist.

What kind of things are you looking for under the cowling? Well, there should be an engine under there, but that's a given (unless it's been taken). Assuming your engine is still there, it's wise to begin the inspection by sticking your nose near the air inlet and taking a big sniff (Figure 96), which is easy to do if you have a big nose (which means that if you lie down in a sailboat, it will change headings). You're sniffing for that nefarious burning smell that's not supposed to be there. Sure, you might smell the remnants of hot oil, but you shouldn't smell burning insulation, much less anything else. I know of one mechanic who left his handkerchief on the top of the engine, then sealed up the cowling after inspection (he tried to deny that he did this). The pilot who first flew that airplane made an emergency return to the airport when the handkerchief slid onto the hot exhaust manifold and caught fire. So the rules here are, poke and sniff, and never use a monogrammed handkerchief when you work on an airplane (that's how the FBO identified him). The nose knows.

Fig. 96 — Stick your nose in and smell.

As I mentioned earlier, I'm a big touch and feel guy when it comes to metal and plastic. It's always best to reach under the cowling and ever so slightly and very gently feel those fuel injector feed lines to make sure they're not loose (Figure 97). Don't wiggle them hard. Just feel if they're loose. The last thing you want is fuel squirting over a hot engine in flight (which is a terrible way to light up your own runway at night). Do the touch-and-wiggle procedure with everything you can touch. Over the years I've found loose exhaust stacks (that means the potential for carbon monoxide in the cockpit), loose fuel lines (that means the potential for fuel leaks), and many other loose or broken little things that needed fixing. Let your fingers do the work for you here. But don't stick your hand under the cowling containing a hot engine unless you want a full sleeve of cylinder-fin arm tattoos.

Fig. 97 — Lightly touch fuel lines for integrity. Fuel lines

Fig. 98 — Drain all fuel sumps.

Chapter 1: Let's Go Flying

Fuel sample tossed on ground.

Water in sample first seen.

Water more easily seen now.

Water clearly visible in sample.
Fig. 99

Draining the fuel sump located just prior to the fuel pump should be done next if you haven't already done so (Figure 98). This is the lever that's usually located inside the panel that you open to access the oil dipstick. It's also the "shoeshine removing lever" if you're not careful. If possible, it's best to drain the fuel into your sampling cup instead of onto the tarmac. This may, however, require you to have the flexibility of a yoga master, since pulling the lever and holding the cup under the cowling is like milking a cow and scratching its ear at the same time (and what cow gets that lucky?). If fuel does drain on the ground, you can still see any water that's present as the fuel evaporates (Figure 99).

When you check the engine oil, keep one thing in mind. Always wipe the dipstick off then place it back in position before you remove it to take the reading (Figure 100). Why? Because it's easy to slide the dipstick against the surrounding surfaces and obtain a false oil level reading. So remove it, wipe it off, put in back in position, followed by removing it for a proper oil reading.

How much oil is enough? Only your engine manufacturer knows for sure, so see what your POH recommends. On the other hand, it's a good bet that filling your crankcase up with oil to its maximum limit will cause some of that oil to be lost through the crankcase breather tube. The majority of smaller airplanes perform quite well with one quart less than the maximum recommended oil level (but only your POH knows for sure). Remember, airplanes are often like a James Bond's cocktail—shaken but not stirred. As a result, oil is likely to find its way out of the crankcase and onto the bottom of your airplane. So know the maximum limit as well as the minimum oil limit for the airplane you're flying.

The Nose Gear

The nose gear should be checked next, since it's directly underneath you at this point in your preflight (Figure 101). On those airplanes having fixed gear with castering nose wheels (Figure 102), you'll want to ensure that the nose wheel casters easily (and if it doesn't, you don't want to feed it caster oil. Call a mechanic, instead). This is best done when you check the airplane's tires by pulling the airplane forward with the tow bar (we'll discuss tires in a bit).

Clean dipstick first before taking reading.
Fig. 100

Check nose gear mechanism carefully.
Fig. 101

Check castering nose gear carefully, too.
Fig. 102

On fixed gear airplanes having nose gear struts, you're interested in seeing that the strut is sufficiently inflated (Figure 103). Too little inflation and the airplane may be difficult to turn on the ground during taxi. An insufficiently inflated strut also means that the prop arc is closer to the ground, creating a greater chance of a propeller strike as well as having foreign objects drawn up into the prop's swing arc (Figure 104). When the propeller spins, a tiny vertical vortex sometimes forms directly underneath the lowest portion of the prop arc. You can occasionally see this vortex on airplanes during runups on wet pavement, since it looks like a miniature tornado being drawn into the prop arc. The problem is that it's possible to draw pebbles into the arc and damage the propeller, a problem exacerbated when the oleo strut is insufficiently inflated.

On some airplanes, an overinflated strut can prevent you from turning during taxi (Figure 105). Some nose gear struts lock in place when they're fully extended. This should make sense, since you don't want the nose gear to turn in the air. A fully extended nose gear strut while on the ground allows rudder application but no nose wheel steering, which isn't good for you (especially if you like to avoid hitting solid objects while taxiing). Of course, you're looking closely at the gear's swivel arms, making sure that the gear remains connected during liftoff. Remember Ms. Dropsy?

Finally, if this is a retractable gear airplane, you'll want to check the gear doors (if installed) to ensure that the often-delicate door control mechanism isn't bent or detached (Figure 106). You'll also want to have a look at the nose wheel swivel stop points that limit the nose wheel's turning arc (Figure 107). Overzealous line personnel sometimes use powerful tow trucks that attach to the nose wheel and can easily damage the nose gear and its turning mechanism. This doesn't bode well for you if you don't notice the damage during the preflight. It's entirely possible that you could depart, retract the gear and have the nose wheel jam during the process. So look carefully at the mechanism during the preflight.

Tires Galore

One of the most frequently overlooked things on a preflight is the tires. They're at the bottom in more ways than one. Pull the airplane forward with the tow bar. You're looking to see that there is adequate tread all the way around on all the tires, which there should be unless you're buying your rubber from the Bald Eagle Tire Company. You're also looking for flat spots on the tire where tread is missing, perhaps even revealing the internal layers of the tire. Yikes. Proper tire inflation is also a must (Figure 108).

Windscreen

As a personal recommendation, avoid flying any airplane with dirty windows (Figure 109). Dirty windows make it hard to see and avoid other airplanes and they strain your eyes when flying in bright sunlight. I've seen pilots taxi by with windows so dirty that I could

Check nose strut for proper inflation. Fig. 103

An insufficiently inflated strut. Fig. 104

An overinflated strut. Fig. 105

Check gear doors if appropriate. Gear door Fig. 106

Check nose wheel swivel stops. Nose gear swivel stop limits Fig. 107

Chapter 1: Let's Go Flying

Check tires for inflation and wear. Fig. 108

Don't fly airplanes with dirty windows. Fig. 109

Use water to remove dirt before cleaning. Fig. 110

Then use plastic cleaner and soft cloth. Fig. 111

barely see who was inside. The only excuse for this is if you're in the government's witness protection program. Then again, I doubt the feds would let you do much flying in that program.

The essential point in cleaning airplane windows is to remove as much of the dirt as possible using water before the cleaning and/or polishing begins (Figure 110). You may not float your boat, but you do want to float your dirt. This minimizes the potential for having dirt and grit scratch the window's plastic surface. Pour or spray enough water on the window to remove any non-adherent dirt particles. You can pour a bottle of water on the window, which also does the deed, but it's a lot messier. Of course, this recommendation only applies to the outside windows, not the inside side.

Once the heavy particles are removed from the windscreen, use your plastic cleaner and a soft cotton cloth for a more thorough cleaning (Figure 111). It's best to move the cloth up and down in a straight motion rather than in a circular motion (Figure 112). This minimizes the circular ring formations often seen on unpolished plastic windows (Figure 113). These rings are caused by small particles that remain stuck to the window or that were on the cloth to begin with. Of course, this means you're likely to get a few vertical scratches, instead. But vertical scratches tend not to scatter the light as much as a similar number of circular scratches. You'll want to use plastic polish every so often to remove these scratches and reduce the glare they cause. A good window specialist can actually remove all the scratches from your windscreen.

Of course, you can't keep polishing away scratches without eventually degrading the integrity of the windscreen. This is why some smaller pressurized airplanes such as the Cessna P-210 limit the amount of "scratch repair" that can be done on a window before the window must be replaced. While window cleaning can be done before every flight, polishing should be done only when necessary (and according to the limitations of your POH, too).

If you're flying around with dirty windows and decide to clean them, you may be in for a big surprise. Your sudden increase in vision could allow you to discover unusual and interesting things about your airport, such as the fact that it has two runways instead of one or that it has an air traffic control tower that you never knew was there. Of course I'm just kidding, but do clean those windows.

Wipe windows using up and down strokes, not a circular pattern. Fig. 112

Scratches from circular cleaning motion. Fig. 113

One Last Thing

You're not quite done with the preflight yet. This is the point where you stand back and take a look at the overall airplane (Figure 114). What are you looking for? How about anything you left lying on or hooked to your flying machine? Years ago I placed my pager (I said years ago, right?) on the horizontal stabilizer during preflight and taxied out without noticing it was there. Several days later I received a call from airport operations wanting to know if I was missing a pager with my name on it. They described it as a "once nice looking pager that was slightly flattened with tire tracks on it." I'm guessing that my fellow flight instructors saw it and conducted a spot landing contest, with my pager as the spot. It's not unusual for pilots to leave tools, window cleaner, and an assortment of other items somewhere on the airplane during the preflight.

And that's the little stuff. Other left-behinds include wheel chocks that are still in place, the tiedown ropes still untied, or that nasty tow bar that's still attached (Figure 115).

I remember sitting with a student when we saw a small airplane taxi by with a tow bar connected to the nose wheel. I ran over and stopped the pilot in his tracks. He opened the window and I yelled, "You can't take off. You left the tow bar attached!"

He looked at the flight instructor in the right seat and said, "Ah, we just landed!" Ouch! He apparently took off with the tow bar attached and landed with it still attached, which is not impossible in a Cessna 150 as long as the nose strut is properly inflated. Had he compressed the nose strut too much during landing by excessive brake usage, the prop would have knocked the tow bar completely off.

Finally, stand back and take a look at the overall airplane.

Fig. 114

Cockpit Management

There's a great story about an airline pilot having dinner at home with his wife. He looks around for the salt and can't find it in its normal location on the table. She points to the salt on a nearby tray. Then she asks, "Why is it that you can find Detroit in a snow storm but can't find the salt?"

He responds by saying, "Because they don't move Detroit."

It's hard to find things when they're moved, which is one reason you want to organize your cockpit to find a place for the things needed to fly the airplane. I'm speaking of charts, pens, paper, flashlights and so on. That's why I believe that you should always have

Look for anything unusual left on the airplane. Towbar?

Courtesy: Jim Szajkovics

Fig. 115

some sort of lapboard or kneeboard when you fly (Figure 116). Lapboards are the most convenient, but kneeboards give you that gladiator feeling, like you're ready for battle.

Before you start the engine, organize your charts in the order of use. Sounds simple, right? But I've seen pilots twirling and twisting charts right after takeoff in a way that threatens anyone nearby with lethal paper cuts. Sure, you may want to get your gallon and a half (blood donation) pin from the Red Cross, but you certainly don't want to earn it in one sitting.

I've always found it wise to obtain any clearances and airport information before engine start if possible. You can do this using the airplane's battery power, but some pilots carry portable VHF

Chapter 1: Let's Go Flying

Fig. 116 — Lapboard or kneeboard is essential.

Fig. 117 — Always use the engine start checklist.

Fig. 118 — Open window and yell clear before start.

Fig. 119 — Follow POH priming recommendation.

Fig. 120 — Prime may not go to all cylinders.

radios for just this purpose. This allows you to set your radios before engine start as well as plot your taxi route using your airport diagram chart.

Once you have your clearance (if needed) in hand and your charts organized, it's time to ensure that your seat is properly adjusted for taxi and eventual takeoff. Your seat should be moved forward enough so that during taxi your heels or the instep of your foot can push the bottom of each rudder pedal to its full forward position. This means that the balls of your feet should be able to move the top of the rudder pedals (the brakes) to their full forward position for maximum braking.

Engine Start

So far, we've kicked the tires, and now it's time to light the fire (but don't kick the fire and light the tires, unless you like to land hot). In other words, you've completed the preflight and are ready to start the engine. Before you do, consider this. If you're a good, cautious pilot, you'll always use at least the manufacturer's recommended checklist for engine start (Figure 117). Yes, I know that it doesn't take a rocket scientist to start the engine of a small airplane, but I do know an actual rocket scientist who tried to take off with his fuel selector on a nearly empty tank. Had he used a checklist, he would have been instructed to set the fuel selector to the fullest tank before takeoff. Apparently he was used to starting a rocket, which is pretty easy to do since this only requires a Zippo lighter and ear muffs (and perhaps an asbestos leisure suit).

Before you engage that starter, I hope you'll open your window, place your hand over your headset mic, and yell the word "clear" in the loudest voice you can (Figure 118). Yelling "clear" or "clear the prop" seems to have become a lost behavior on the part of some pilots and that's a terrible shame. You at least want to give any person who's near your propeller a fighting chance to get away. Yelling "clear" also causes other pilots to look in your direction and that means someone might immediately point out something that is dangerously close to your airplane or still attached to it, such as a tow bar or a small child.

As a general rule, pilots tend to overprime their engines on cold days and underprime them on hot days. To begin with, always follow your POH's recommendation for priming (Figure 119). That said, consider that on many carbureted engines, fuel from the priming line(s) might only go to one side of the induction system, instead of both sides (Figure 120). Why? Because it's a less expensive system that still works. It just doesn't work quite as well as priming all the cylinders.

That's why some pilots elect to pump the throttle during engine start as a means of priming. If you're one of these people, some caution is in order. When pumping the throttle on carbureted engines, you're activating the carburetor's *accelerator pump* (Figure 121). The accelerator pump is a tiny pump within the body of the carburetor that squirts a small amount of fuel into the carburetor's throat to accommodate the sudden increase in airflow following a rapid increase in throttle.

On airplanes with updraft carburetors (think Cessna 150 whose carburetor moves air and fuel upward toward the cylinders), unless the starter is engaged and the engine cranking (thus, drawing air and fuel into the cylinders), this fuel can accumulate at the bottom of the carburetor structure and increase the potential for an engine fire (a possibility if the engine backfires).

If you insist on priming this way (and assuming this behavior isn't prohibited by your POH), do so only when cranking the engine. Use no more than two or three pumps of the throttle, then return the throttle to the recommended start position. Engines don't start well when the carburetor's butterfly valve is in motion, since this results in an uneven fuel-air mixture entering the induction system, making combustion difficult. Engines always start much better when you prime them, then move the throttle to its recommended start position and leave it be. While this does vary between airplanes, most engines start nicely when the throttle is moved forward about a quarter to a half of an inch and left alone until the engine starts (Figure 122).

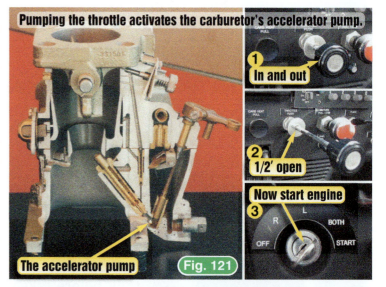

What would you do if you smelled smoke while attempting to start the engine? Run for your life? Put on that asbestos leisure suit? Take up smoking? Engine fires during start are often the result of overpriming, something that's more likely on cold days. That means fuel is most likely being expelled through the induction system, which is more likely to happen on airplanes with updraft carburetors.

This is a good time to get cranky. Many POHs on airplanes with carbureted engines recommend that you continue cranking in an attempt to draw the flames and fumes back into the induction system and cylinders (which are excellent fire containing devices). If the en-

gine doesn't start, you should pull the mixture to idle cutoff (full out), fully open the throttle, and crank for a bit longer, perhaps for as much as 30 seconds, in hopes of removing the fire's fuel source. This procedure normally handles the problem quite well. But after such an event, you aren't going flying until you have a mechanic check for damage to the air filter and engine accessories.

If you have an engine fire when starting a fuel injected engine, it often results from fuel being expelled through the exhaust system. That's because on some fuel injected engines, the fuel used for priming is injected directly into the cylinders, not the induction system. Overpriming can cause that fuel to pool in the exhaust system. If the fuel ignites (because some of it is burning as it leaves the cylinder), a fire can start.

Several airplane manufacturers recommend following the same ground-fire procedure used for carbureted engines. Other manufacturers recommend that you pull the mixture to idle cutoff, turn the fuel selector to its off position and leave the airplane immediately. On airplanes with fuel injected

Chapter 1: Let's Go Flying

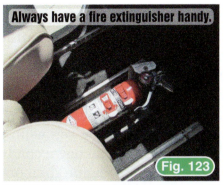
Always have a fire extinguisher handy. Fig. 123

The fuel recirculation line. Recirculation line. Fig. 124

Keeping the high boost pump ready. Split boost pump switch. Fig. 125

How Flight Instructors Are Towed From Place to Place
Courtesy: Barry Jones Chief Pilot OCFC

engines, I'm inclined to do the latter, since the fire is probably an external one that won't be diminished by continued cranking. Of course, you should take your fire extinguisher with you and use it to put out the fire and minimize engine damage. What? You don't have a fire extinguisher? Well, now is a good time to put one in your airplane (Figure 123).

What about starting airplanes with fuel injected engines? Under normal conditions, these are relatively easy to start. With fuel being injected into or near each cylinder, it's more likely that the engine will start quickly and easily. Easily, that is, if it's not too hot to trot.

If a hot engine has been shut down for 15 minutes or so, it's likely to have become *heat soaked*. That means there's a possibility of vapor in the fuel distribution lines, resulting in vapor lock. If you prime the engine, it's possible that little or no fuel will move through those lines and into the cylinders. As a result, the engine is actually underprimed and difficult to start. The inevitable result is that the pilot pushes and pulls throttle levers and fuel pump buttons, ultimately flooding the engine. Here are a few things to consider in such instances.

First, if your airplane has a fuel recirculation line (a line that takes fuel not used by the fuel control unit and returns it to the fuel tank and found mainly on bigger bore Continental engines), that means it's possible to circulate cold fuel through the fuel distribution mechanism and back into the fuel tank (Figure 124). That of course assumes such a procedure is recommended by your POH. If so, it's possible to pull the mixture back to flight idle, move the throttle full forward and engage the auxiliary (electric) fuel pump for 30 or more seconds to provide cooling in the fuel distribution system. This can help dissipate the vapor that's preventing engine start. With the mixture pulled to flight idle and the throttle full open, the fuel circulates but none gets into the cylinders. Once cooled, try your normal start procedure.

This procedure obviously doesn't work on airplane engines not having fuel recirculation lines. There are other procedures to use in those instances. Given that fuel vapor may impede fuel flow into any or all cylinders, consider using your auxiliary fuel pump during the actual engine start, instead of just for priming. For instance, after the engine is primed and a start attempted, there may be sufficient fuel in the far (cylinder) end of those distribution lines to start the engine, only to have the engine falter and stop as the vapor in those lines enters the cylinders. Keep your finger in the ready position on the high boost pump switch (assuming that you have a split high-low boost pump switch) as shown in Figure 125. The moment the engine starts to falter, press the high boost pump switch to move that vapor through those lines quickly, thus keeping the engine running. Of course, you want to ensure that this procedure is in compliance with what's recommended in your POH for hot engine starts.

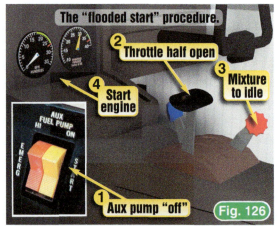

The "flooded start" procedure. (Fig. 126)

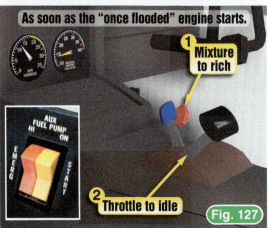

As soon as the "once flooded" engine starts. (Fig. 127)

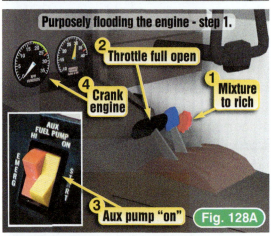

Purposely flooding the engine - step 1. (Fig. 128A)

Apply "flooded start" procedure again - step 2. (Fig. 128B)

Your engine should start using these procedures. If it doesn't, then it's probably flooded. How do you know the engine is flooded? Do you receive a flood warning? In many instances, you actually do receive the airplane version of a flood warning. It's in the form of a distinct smell of fuel. Those on the outside of the airplane might see fuel dripping from the exhaust manifold (thus, the reason you're smelling fuel). Don't fret. At least a flooded engine is a known condition and it's often easier to start a flooded engine than one that's vapor locked.

How do you handle a flooded engine? Move to higher ground? Life vests? The general procedure is to reduce the fuel input while increasing the air input. That should make sense, since there's already enough fuel in the cylinders. Begin by ensuring that the auxiliary fuel pump is off, then open the throttle halfway, pull the mixture to flight idle and start cranking (Figure 126). You're letting a great deal of air into the engine in hopes of burning the fuel that has already accumulated in the cylinders.

Now you have to be quick on the draw. As soon as the engine starts, move the mixture to its full rich position to continue combustion and reduce the throttle to flight idle to avoid blasting anyone nearby with your propwash (Figure 127). This procedure usually works quite well with flooded engines. Just remember that airplanes and their engines are not all the same. So follow the recommendation in your POH as the first course of action in solving these problems.

As a final note on engine starts, what do you do if the engine is not quite flooded and just won't start? The answer is to flood it, then apply the flooded start procedure (Figure 128A). Now I say this with caution, because you don't want to overflood the engine, which might increase the potential for an engine fire on the ground. But if you think you're in this situation (and your POH approves), move the mixture full forward, move the throttle full forward, and crank the engine for five to 10 seconds with the boost pump on. It's unlikely that your engine will start under these conditions, but it sure is likely that a lot of fuel will enter those cylinders. Now pull the mixture to flight idle, open the throttle halfway, turn off the boost pump and start using your flooded start procedure (Figure 128B. As soon as the engine starts, move the mixture to its start position and the throttle to flight idle position.

After Engine Start

Once your engine starts (after not having run for a while), you want to make sure you don't over-rev the

Chapter 1: Let's Go Flying

engine. There's a great deal of engine wear that occurs right after engine start. That's because the thin sheen of lubricating engine oil has drained from the engine's moving parts and flowed into the crankcase. With a properly lubricated piston and cylinder, the engine's moving metal parts ride up, down or sideways while separated from each other by a thin layer of oil. There's very little metal-to-metal contact in these instances. Right after engine start, that protective layer of oil is greatly diminished, especially in the cylinders where raw fuel has helped remove oil from the cylinder walls. So always be kind to your engine. How kind? The "reduce the RPM immediately after engine start" kind.

Right after engine start, you'll want to look at your oil pressure gauge to confirm that you have sufficient oil pressure (Figure 129). If the oil pressure doesn't increase to normal levels within 30 seconds, shut the engine down and figure out why. I've been in cold areas where it seems to take a non-preheated engine nearly all of those 30 seconds to register an acceptable oil pressure reading. Preheating for the engine (and the pilot, too) is certainly recommended in these circumstances.

What else could cause a lack of oil pressure after engine start? Well, how about the fellow who drained his engine oil, reset his quick release oil drain, then became distracted when a friend dropped by the airplane for a chat. Later in the day he starts his engine and taxis to the runup area, where his engines seizes, much like his heart almost did when he realized what he had done. The only thing missing was oil. So always check that oil pressure immediately after engine start.

There's one other thing you should do on startup. Look at your ammeter to check for any abnormal indication (Figure 130). It's quite normal to see a slight "+" indication on a *charge/discharge ammeter* or a reading slightly above your expected current drain on your *loadmeter*. This makes sense, since your battery needs a bit of recharging after using all that energy to crank the engine. What you shouldn't see is an abnormally large reading on either type of ammeter. If you do, shut the engine down immediately.

Why? Because it's possible that your starter didn't disengage from the starter gear and is now being spun by the engine. In these instances, it's possible for your starter to become its own electrical generating source, thereby damaging your electrical system or its delicate components. While this situation is rare, you should still check the ammeter immediately after engine start. Engines make a lot of noise, so you're not likely to hear the still-engaged starter. Your ammeter might provide the only telltale clue to this problem.

Taxiing

As you apply power to move the airplane, make a quick check of the brakes. If for some reason the brakes aren't working properly, this is your chance to reduce power and avoid hitting something. If worse comes to worse, you can shut down the engine and "attempt" to physically stop the airplane by hand, using what can only be described as the Fred Flintstone braking system. Then again, I don't recommend putting your foot under a tire unless you want to become an honorary member of the Big Foot Society. Remember, the airplane you're flying probably weighs a ton or more. So it's like trying to push a small imported automobile or stop one by hand.

I have only one rule that you should always consider following during taxi, and that is to taxi the airplane and do nothing else (Figure 131). That means no fiddling with switches, or if you don't play the fiddle, performing other activities such as copying a clearance, reading your clearance, folding charts, texting or anything else that takes your eyes off the road.

If you must do something other than taxi, inform Ground Control that you'll be coming to a complete stop on the taxiway (assuming you're at a controlled airport). Why inform the controller? Because pilots aren't used to having airplanes stop on the taxiway other than near the runway threshold. Announcing your intentions buys you a little protection, though it would be far better to postpone the non-taxi activity until reaching the runup area (Figure 132).

A big source of confusion and contention for pilots is taxi speed. There are really no hard and fast rules that apply here. Taxi as fast or as slow as is reasonable for the conditions and that leaves you in full control of the airplane. That means taking into account other traffic, visibility, the number of obstacles, and many other factors. Pilots are often told that you shouldn't taxi faster than you can walk, which can only decrease your airport popularity. Do you know how long it takes to walk a mile? Well, try taxiing at that speed on a taxiway that parallels a 5,000 foot runway (Figure 133).

There's absolutely nothing wrong with taxiing at a faster speed as long as wind conditions, other airplanes and your airplane itself don't make such behavior hazardous. Then again, when taxiing some taildraggers, it's often necessary to taxi at a slow enough speed that you can use a serpentine motion to see airplanes ahead of you. A serpentine motion isn't used to avoid snakes on the taxiway nor is it used to intimidate other pilots. It's the right and left directional change while taxiing (similar to that made by a snake in motion) that allows taildragger pilots to see what's ahead of them (Figure 134).

During taxi, you want to maximize your use of the rudder pedals for turning (these are usually the bottom part of the

Chapter 1: Let's Go Flying

Don't ride the brakes during taxi.
Fig. 135

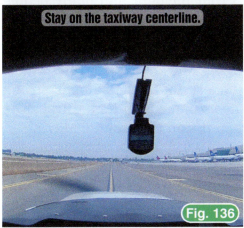
Stay on the taxiway centerline.
Fig. 136

The runway hold lines mean HOLD unless you're cleared beyond them.
Runway hold lines
Fig. 137

Turn slightly while holding to observe any traffic that might be on final approach.
Fig. 138

swivel pedal), while minimizing your use of the brakes (usually the upper part of your swivel pedal). Give your plane a break and don't taxi with constant pressure on the brake pedals, also known as riding the brakes (Figure 135). This puts extra wear on the brake assembly and the brake pads, to say nothing of it being bad form.

You can learn a lot about a pilot by how he or she taxis. For instance, a good pilot begins the taxi by applying power to overcome the airplane's inertia, then reduces power to the minimum necessary to maintain the desired taxi speed. He or she initially uses the rudder pedals for ground steering. If a tighter turn is necessary and full deflection of the rudder pedal doesn't turn the airplane sharply enough, then he'll apply right or left brake pressure as appropriate.

If the pilot is taxiing too fast, perhaps because there's a tailwind when taxiing parallel and opposite the direction of the landing runway (as there often is), then she'll apply equal brake pressure sufficient to slow the airplane to the proper taxi speed, then release the brakes. She'll do this as often as necessary to return to the proper speed rather than riding the brakes during taxi.

If you really want to impress someone with your polished taxiing skills, then make all your stops by applying brake pressure smoothly, and just before you come to a complete stop, release that pressure slightly then reapply the pressure to stop the airplane. That's how you make a good stop without being a jerk, and without jerking your passengers around. Done properly, no one will notice that you've stopped. Of course, that means nobody will compliment you, either. Just know you did a great job.

There's a yellow taxiway centerline on the taxiway for a very good reason (Figure 136). That's where the center of your airplane should always be if you want to have the best chance of avoiding objects around the airport. Now, I said the *best chance*, not the *guaranteed way* to avoid objects. Sometimes you may have to move to the side of the taxiway to avoid another airplane that's traveling the opposite direction. If so, your wing may be in no-man's land. Use a little eyesight and foresight by slowing down and looking for obstructions that your wing might clip.

When approaching the runway for the purpose of holding short of the solid double yellow hold lines, it's a good idea to turn your airplane slightly toward the final approach path (but don't let any part of your airplane cross those double yellow lines until you have a clearance to do so) as shown in Figure 137. This is especially important in a high wing airplane, where one wing can easily block your view of traffic on final (Figure 138). Looking is important if you don't want to have another airplane do a touch-and-go on you. Even at tower controlled airports, it's best to look out for your own (airplane) skin by checking for inbound planes before you taxi onto the runway.

Rod Machado's How to Fly an Airplane Handbook

Control placement for left quartering headwind.
Fig. 139

Control placement for right quartering headwind.
Fig. 140

Control placement for right quartering tailwind.
Fig. 141

Control placement for left quartering tailwind.
Fig. 142

I've had several experiences where an airplane was on a long final approach and the tower controller told me to line up and wait (cleared me onto the runway). I don't have a problem with this as long as there is no delay in receiving my takeoff clearance. On the other hand, it's entirely possible to have the airplane on final approach land on the holding airplane if someone messes up. This happened at Los Angeles International airport many years ago, when a larger airliner landed on a commuter airliner holding in position on the landing runway. The airliner was landing toward the west, into a setting sun, making it difficult to see the airplane on the runway. Several mistakes were made in that incident and many people lost their lives in an accident that was entirely preventable.

Control Placement During Taxi

Every pilot should know about how to taxi in strong winds, despite the fact that it's often best not to be taxiing in strong wings. Keep in mind that the airplane is in its natural state only when it's flying, not when it's on the ground. Moving an airplane on the ground when it's windy is like carrying an umbrella in the same conditions. Move that umbrella the wrong way and you can lose control of it (or have it flip inside out, which the airplane can't do, fortunately). That's why knowing how to move the flight controls when the airplane is on the ground is important, especially if you want to keep the airplane attached to the ground.

We'll discuss ailerons first, and the procedure applies to both tricycle geared airplanes and taildraggers. The general rule for aileron placement is to *turn into a headwind* and *turn with a tailwind*. For instance, if you're taxiing into a left quartering headwind, there's a chance that a strong enough wind could raise the upwind wing unless you manipulate the ailerons in a way that helps force it downward (Figure 139). That's why you should turn your yoke or joystick into the wind (which should bring you much joy because you won't be flipping over). In a right quartering headwind, you would turn the yoke to the right (Figure 140). The aileron on the upwind wing now moves up, causing the air to force the upwind wing downward.

What about a quartering tailwind? Here is where it's possible that a strong enough wind can lift the upwind wing. Turning your yoke or joystick with the wind helps force the upwind wing in a downward direction. With a quartering tailwind from the right you should move your yoke to the left as if you're turning with the wind (Figure 141). A quartering tailwind from the left means you should move the yoke to the right (Figure 142). Now the aileron on the upwind wing is deflected downward, thus exposing aileron surface area in a way

Chapter 1: Let's Go Flying

that allows the wind to push downward on that wing. You aren't concerned about what the aileron on the downwind wing is doing, since this aileron has less influence on the airplane's behavior, mainly because the fuselage diminishes the effect of the wind flowing over it.

Keep in mind that quartering tailwinds can be a real challenge. In a tricycle geared airplane, they can tip an airplane over, because tricycles are unstable in the forward quartering direction. When children fall while riding their tricycles, it's usually a fall toward the front right or front left direction (Figure 143). Combine a sharp turn in a tricycle geared airplane with a quartering tailwind and you have all the ingredients necessary to tip over—a tip you should avoid, of course.

In a taildragger, a quartering tailwind can make the airplane very difficult to control since the wind wants to swing the tail around the main gear (the pivot point) in the same way that it swings a weathervane. It often takes substantial differential braking action (using one brake or the other) to keep a taildragger in control in strong quartering tailwinds.

So much for the ailerons. What about the elevator control when taxiing in a strong wind? While use of the aileron is the same in either type of airplane, there is an instance where elevator use is different between a taildragger and a tricycle geared airplane. In a tricycle geared airplane, you want to keep the elevator control neutral in a headwind and move the yoke or joystick forward in a tailwind (Figure 144). If you applied forward elevator pressure in a headwind, the airplane's nose gear might compress sufficiently to make ground steering difficult. If you applied back elevator pressure in a headwind, you could literally lift the nose gear off the ground (otherwise known as *popping a wheelie*), making ground control difficult.

When taxiing with a tailwind in a tricycle geared airplane, moving the yoke or joystick forward causes the aft wind to push the tail surface downward. This is much better than having it blow upward on this surface, possibly causing the tail end of the airplane to lift upward (otherwise known as *wheelbarrowing*).

Use of the elevator on the ground in taildraggers requires a different technique when taxiing into a headwind. In a headwind, you always want to hold the yoke or joystick full aft. This helps keep the tail firmly on the ground. With a tailwind, however, you want to move the yoke or joystick forward to keep that tail forced to the ground, just as you would in a tricycle geared airplane (Figure 145).

Many years ago I was with a student in an Ercoupe, taxiing behind a twin-engine Cessna 310 on the taxiway. The Cessna made a sudden stop on the taxiway and commenced doing his runup instead of waiting until reaching the runup area like everyone else. It was all I could do to keep the Ercoupe from nearly flipping over since it was being buffeted by the Cessna's turbulence. That's why you want to treat airplane engines, especially jet engines, with a great deal of respect. Stay as far behind these airplanes as necessary to avoid their high velocity thrust. How powerful can that thrust be? On one occasion I witnessed a Piper Cherokee 140 (a four-place, single-engine airplane) get blown over on its wing when the pilot of a Boeing 737 got a little too aggressive with his thrust levers. That's thrust you can't trust.

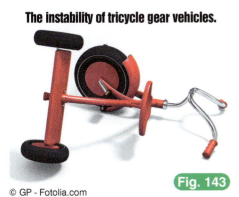
The instability of tricycle gear vehicles.
Fig. 143

Elevator control placement in a tailwind for tricycle gear and taildragger airplanes.
Fig. 144

Elevator control placement in a headwind for taildragger airplanes.
Fig. 145

Leaning the Mixture While Taxiing

Despite using low lead fuel, it's still possible for modern airplane engines to experience sparkplug fouling when idling or using low power settings for longer periods of time. It's true that a properly adjusted idle mixture setting will certainly minimize the chance of plug fouling. Of course, the carburetor or the injection system's idle mixture jet has to be adjusted by a qualified mechanic. But this adjustment is typically useful for a specific density altitude only. So it's reasonable for pilots to manually adjust their mixture on the ground once the engine starts, in order to minimize the chance of plug fouling.

The easiest way to do this in most airplanes is to idle the engine and pull the mixture back slowly. Since most idle mixtures are on the slightly rich side, you'll see a slight increase in RPM as the idle mixture becomes leaner and the engine idles more efficiently. You can stop leaning when the RPM peaks (see sequence A to B to C to D, below). That is, you can if you want to but I don't want you to. Here's why.

If you're going to lean to prevent plug fouling, you want to lean aggressively. So lean as much as you can until the engine begins to sputter, then enrichen the mixture slightly. Why? You want the idle mixture lean enough so that adding full throttle for takeoff causes your engine to really sputter and almost stop running. This is the one foolproof way to prevent you from taking off with the mixture leaned, which can cause engine overheating—a very serious problem. By aggressively leaning, you can still apply taxi power without any issue, but applying takeoff power just isn't in the stars for you until you richen the mixture. There's also no chance of causing any engine problems with such a lean mixture during taxi operations since very little engine power (thus heat) is developed in this condition.

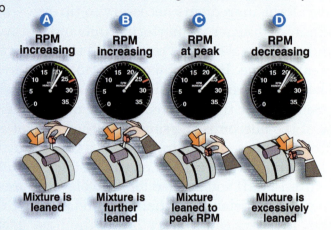

Idle Thoughts

When someone spends a lot of time flying airplanes, they eventually come to the conclusion that the most difficult problems that might be encountered in flight can often be preempted by a good preflight.

The question is, how does one compel him or herself to take the time to preflight the airplane properly? After all, pilots were meant to fly, not touch, poke, feel and check liquids, right? Well, not really. All of these actions are important.

Perhaps James Bond can help us understand our dilemma.

In Ian Fleming's book *Casino Royale*, James Bond, a newly anointed *double-0* agent is having trouble with the moral dilemma of deciding who the bad or evil people actually are. Fortunately, a French agent named Mathis tells James that he should understand evil in terms of something personal, rather than letting it be the abstract principle that has confused him. Bond begins to consider what it would be like to eliminate the bad guys in terms of gaining revenge for the hurt the bad guys have caused others, rather than for some high moral reason.

In this way, he becomes a more effective agent. In the psychological sense, this is how you can find the conviction to thoroughly check your airplane before every flight. And I don't mean by eliminating your enemies, either (unless you want to, of course). Instead, I'm saying that you have to make it *personal*.

That's right. The preflight has to be something that becomes important to you because you've made it important, which is entirely within your power to do. So make it important. Make it personal, because it is.

Now it's time to talk stick and rudder or elevator and pedal. Here's where it really gets fun.

Chapter 2
Flying Straight and Level And Turning

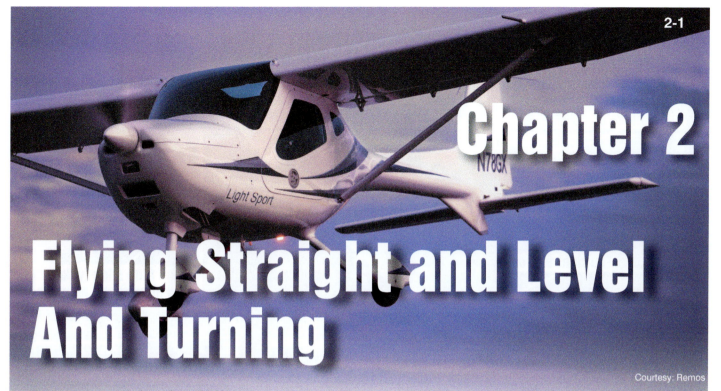

Courtesy: Remos

For some people, the skills necessary to fly an airplane are mega-order mysteries no less compelling than Amelia Earhart's final destination, the number of UFO's in Hangar 18 or whether the Iron Age was actually a time when people wore neatly pressed clothing.

Let me assure you that the knowledge you need to fly an airplane can be acquired in a relatively short time. No mystery here, because like any other sophisticated behavior you've already mastered (such as walking upright), flying an airplane is nothing more than acquiring a set of basic skills, then putting those building blocks together in various ways to accomplish any specific task. Learn the basics and you can assemble any more complex maneuver from them. That's the truth. Believe it.

The basic skills are all things you can learn and learn to do well. My job is to help you acquire those skills, so I'll present the first two of them to you (straight and level flight and turns) in this chapter and the next two (climbs and descents) in the next chapter. I'll do this in the exact same way I've presented them to all the students I've taught since the early 1970s.

No-Mystery History

Let's start with a bit of history. Over the past 100 years, nothing much has changed about how airplanes fly. Airplanes themselves have changed. They now come in all sizes and shapes (much like flight instructors). They also come with cockpit instrumentation ranging from analog devices looking like miniature antique clocks (Figure 1) to advanced and complex electronics that make it look as though you're on the deck of the Starship Enterprise (Figure 2).

What remains unchanged is that the cockpit flight controls of an airplane—the yoke or stick and the rudder pedals—perform essentially the same function they did more than a century ago when Orville first pulled back on the wheel at Kill Devil Hill and turned a short flight into a long stretch of history. So what's the deal with Orville's wheel?

Rod Machado's How to Fly an Airplane Handbook

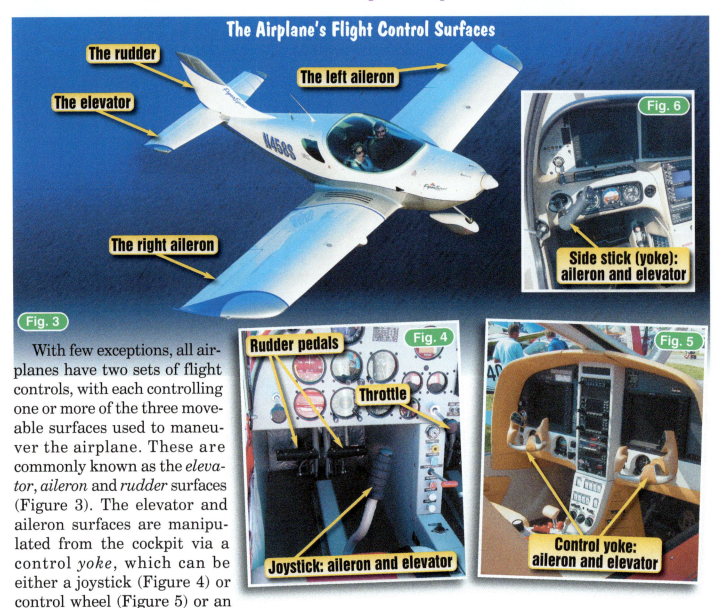

The Airplane's Flight Control Surfaces

Fig. 3 — The rudder, The elevator, The left aileron, The right aileron

Fig. 4 — Rudder pedals, Throttle, Joystick: aileron and elevator

Fig. 5 — Control yoke: aileron and elevator

Fig. 6 — Side stick (yoke): aileron and elevator

With few exceptions, all airplanes have two sets of flight controls, with each controlling one or more of the three moveable surfaces used to maneuver the airplane. These are commonly known as the *elevator*, *aileron* and *rudder* surfaces (Figure 3). The elevator and aileron surfaces are manipulated from the cockpit via a control *yoke*, which can be either a joystick (Figure 4) or control wheel (Figure 5) or an alternate version of the control wheel known as the *side stick* control (Figure 6). The rudder surface is manipulated by a set of rudder pedals found on the airplane's floorboard as shown in Figure 4.

That there are three types of moveable surfaces is no coincidence, because the airplane has three axes about which it can rotate. Think of it in terms of a metal rod (not a Rod Machado) being the axis; the plane, if it were small enough or you were big enough, could then be made to rotate around that axis.

The elevator control rotates (pitches) the airplane about its lateral axis (Figure 7), which runs sideways parallel to the wings (just like a *lateral* or sideways pass in football). The rod runs wing tip to wing tip; the plane rotates tail-over-nose.

The aileron control rotates (rolls) the airplane about the long axis running from the nose to the tail, also known as the *longitudinal* axis (Figure 7). The rod runs like a spine, and the plane rotates like a chicken on a rotisserie.

The rudder controls (yaws) the airplane about its vertical axis (Figure 7), much as you stand and rotate right or left about the length of your body in the morning when you yawn (think *yaw*-n). Fortunately, the airplane doesn't make the same sounds you do when you yawn, otherwise no one would fly it. (While the engine throttle isn't technically called a flight control, I have pointed it out in Figure 4.

Chapter 2: Flying Straight and Level and Turning

The Airplane's Axes

Fig. 7

Having an Attitude

In aviation, words sometimes mean something a little different. And so it is with *attitude*.

While it is not necessarily good for your teenager to have an attitude, it is something your airplane always has, and that's not bad. It has more to do with pitch than petulance.

In the aviation, world *attitude* means the orientation of one of the airplane's three axes relative to the horizon or another reference line. So, when we speak of the plane's *pitch attitude* having increased, it means that the angle between the horizon line and the place the nose is pointing is greater (vertically) than it was previously.

We'll discuss its use in detail later in this chapter.) The rod runs top to bottom (cockpit ceiling to wheels) and the plane rotates around it in a circle.

All three flight controls allow you to rotate the airplane about one or more of its axes. Combining these rotations in the right way, at the right time, yields one or more of the following four basic flight maneuvers: *straight and level flight*, *turns*, *climbs* and *descents*. There are your building blocks. Everything you'll do (or undo) in an airplane is a combination of one or more of these basic flight maneuvers, and all are done by manipulating the flight controls.

Let's put you in control by looking closely at how each flight control operates.

Yoke and Pedal

You manipulate the airplane's elevator surface from the cockpit by forward and aft movement of the *yoke*. Moving the yoke forward or aft rotates the nose up or down around the lateral axis, changing the airplane's pitch attitude relative to the horizon. Rotating the yoke right or left (causing rotation along the longitudinal axis) banks the airplane relative to the horizon.

Pulling the yoke toward you (pulling back) deflects the elevator surface (located at the rear of the airplane) upward, causing the moving air to deflect the tail downward (Figure 8). This results in the airplane's nose pitching upward about the lateral axis. Moving the yoke forward deflects the elevator surface downward causing the tail to move upward (Figure 9). This results in the nose pitching downward about the lateral axis.

Rod Machado's How to Fly an Airplane Handbook

Deflecting the Yoke to the Left Deflects Both Ailerons as Shown and Starts a Left Turn

Fig. 10 — The left aileron moves up — The right aileron moves down

Deflecting the Yoke to the Right Deflects Both Ailerons as Shown and Starts a Right Turn

Fig. 11 — The left aileron moves down — The right aileron moves up

Of course, when you hear the term *elevator,* your first thought is that of a lovely box with glowing buttons and soft music moving up and down. Instead, the only thing you can count on moving up and down relative to the horizon is the airplane's nose. Whether or not the airplane actually goes up (climbs) depends on the amount of extra engine power available as *thrust* to pull the airplane uphill (to allow it to climb).

Besides moving forward and aft, the joystick or yoke also swings or rotates left (Figure 10) and right (Figure 11). This deflects the moveable surfaces on the outboard trailing edge of each wing known as *ailerons*, causing the airplane to bank left or right. The term *aileron* comes from the French word *aileron* meaning *little wing*. Now you can tell your friends you speak French, though if they say, "Wee-wee" I'd consider landing sooner rather than later.

Rotating the yoke right or left deflects one aileron surface up and the other down, thus moving them in opposite directions (no, the airplane isn't broken despite the fact that it looks that way). This decreases the lift on one wing while increasing it on the other, causing the airplane to roll about its longitudinal axis. This rolling motion is called *banking*, though you will not receive a deposit slip for your changes.

Entering a Left Turn

The airplane banks because of a reduction of lift on one wing (left) and an increase in lift on the other (right).

Move stick left to bank left

Fig. 12

Chapter 2: Flying Straight and Level and Turning

At this point, it should be clear that you have to deflect one or more of the airplane's control surfaces to change the airplane's attitude or direction of flight. For instance, a bank or a turn to the left is initiated by turning the yoke to the left, which moves the left wing's aileron upward (deflecting the left wing down) and the right wing's aileron downward (deflecting the right wing upward) as shown in Figure 12. If you want to make the airplane turn, you must bank it in the direction you want to turn. This deflects the wing's vertical lifting force sideways (horizontally), pulling the airplane in the direction of bank.

The Effects of Adverse Yaw

Fig. 13

The airplane banks to the left but adverse yaw caused by an increase in drag from the lowered aileron on the right wing yaws the airplane to the right.

It's natural for most people to think that an airplane will always turn once it's banked, but you can't always bank on the bank. Here's why. Banking an airplane always generates a small penalty, much like the interest you pay when borrowing money from a real bank. While the upward deflected aileron reduces the wing's lift and lowers one wing, the downward deflected aileron increases the other wing's lift and raises that wing. The penalty paid for producing this extra lift on the wing is known as *drag*.

The drag produced by the lowered aileron on the rising wing adversely yaws the airplane's nose opposite the direction you want to turn (Figure 13). That's why this penalty is called *adverse yaw*. You attempt to turn in one direction and the airplane acts as if it's got a mind of its own by yawing in the opposite direction. It's like walking your dog on a leash when it spies a fire hydrant. You pull in one direction, while Fido heads off to sniff around and check his latest messages. Fortunately, the airplane is equipped with rudder to compensate for adverse yaw. It's the use of the rudder pedals that keep the nose (OK, the *longitudinal axis*) pointed in the direction of the turn.

The rudder surface (Figure 14) is controlled by two rudder pedals located just above the cockpit floorboard (Figure 15). The swivel top of some rudder pedals control the brakes on each main landing gear wheel (Figure 16). The floorboard is where you put the heels of your feet during flight. It's also where you find things that fall out of your instructor's pockets, such as his book of relaxation mantras and the rubber stress ball he squeezes when giving flight lessons.

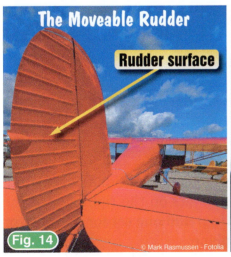
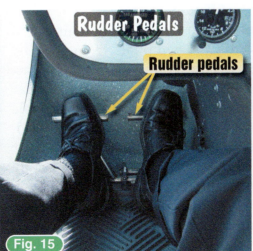
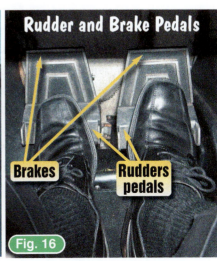

When entering a turn (left turn in this example) you apply enrough left rudder pressure to keep the nose pointed in the direction of turn during the roll-in.

The airplane's rudder does one very important thing: *It keeps the airplane's nose pointed in the direction of turn*. It does this by moving the airplane around its vertical (cockpit ceiling to wheels) axis. Push the left rudder pedal and the airplane's nose yaws to the left. Push the right rudder pedal and the nose yaws to the right. When *entering* a turn, you'll push on the appropriate rudder pedal to compensate for adverse yaw and keep the nose pointed in the direction of turn as shown in Figure 17.

How much rudder should you use when entering a turn? We'll discuss this in greater detail soon. I know, you can't wait. It gives me utter rudder shudder, too.

Why Two Sets of Flight Controls?

Do airplane manufacturers place two sets of flight controls in an airplane (Figures 18, 19 and 20) to keep pilots from fighting over who flies? Haven't you wondered why automobile manufacturers don't do the same? You don't have to be a Rhodes scholar (or a highway scholar, either) to understand that when two people try driving at the same time, it's hard to remain on the road. Sometimes, however, it's necessary to have two people with their hands on or near the flight controls at the same time, especially when one of them (the student) has no idea how to fly. That's why airplanes traditionally have two sets of flight controls. One set is for the flight instructor who typically sits on the right side of the airplane (or in back if the airplane has *tandem* or front and aft seating) and one set for the pilot or *pilot in command* (PIC) who typically sits on the left side of the airplane.

Aileron Deflection is Not Equal

Did you know that your ailerons were not being treated fairly? Well, they aren't. It's just not fair that when you turn the yoke and deflect the ailerons, one aileron is deflected downward to a lesser degree than the aileron that moves upward. There's no equality among ailerons. In this instance, inequality is a really good thing.

The aileron that moves upward diminishes the lift on the wing, resulting in that wing moving downward. Fortunately, reducing lift on a wing doesn't increase the drag on that wing. In fact, it reduces the drag produced by that wing. The aileron that moves downward creates lift and causes that wing to rise. Anything that creates more lift, however, also creates more drag. This is the drag that pulls the rising wing aft slightly and adversely yaws the airplane opposite the direction you want to turn.

Engineers decided to reduce the adverse yaw on the rising wing by limiting the downward movement of one aileron (the one on the rising wing) compared to the upward movement of the other aileron (the one on the descending wing). The result is that there's less adverse yaw during the roll, despite the fact that some adverse yaw is always present when the ailerons are deflected.

Chapter 2: Flying Straight and Level and Turning

Two Sets of Flight Controls

Fig. 18 — Rudder pedals, Joysticks

Fig. 19 — Rudder pedals, Control wheel or the "yoke"

Fig. 20 — Rudder pedals, Front, aft joysticks

While it's hard to pinpoint the historical reasons for this seating arrangement, it most likely results from the tradition of making left turns at the airport in preparation for landing. Color me a skeptic here, but I think it's good to know where the airport is when you're trying to land there. Sitting in the left seat means the pilot is better able to keep the runway and other airport traffic in sight when turning left. With that in mind, the pilot in command (PIC) in a side-by-side, two-place airplane, typically places his or her left hand on the yoke, the right hand on the throttle and feet on the rudder pedals. Now the question is, How should you hold those flight controls? To find out we need to discuss arms control.

Get a Grip or Not: How to Hold the Flight Controls

In calm air, the yoke is typically grasped lightly so that you can properly sense the pressure you're applying to it and it applies to you (Figure 21). Grab the yoke tightly and it's difficult to sense how much elevator or aileron pressure you're actually applying, much less feel the response of the flight controls. In other words, you'd be deprived of feeling the smallest pressure your hand is capable of sensing, otherwise known as the *pressure discrimination threshold* (See *Webers Law* sidebar on Page 2-8). This is important since elevator, aileron and rudder control application is frequently based on *pressure*, not necessarily the degree or amount of control *movement*.

Think about it this way. It you were given a rare and expensive Fabergé egg, you certainly wouldn't squeeze it too hard, right? You'd probably hold it lightly in your hand, allowing you to sense the pressure you're applying so that you avoid damaging the egg (much as you would do if you were holding the rare and delicate Fabergé chicken that laid that egg).

Sure, there are times when you need a tighter grip on the control yoke, particularly when doing steep turns, accelerated stalls or landing in gusty winds. Good pilots, however, never use more force

How to Grip the Control Yoke

The proper way to grip the control yoke.

Too tight a grip on the control yoke.

Not an effective way to grip a control yoke.

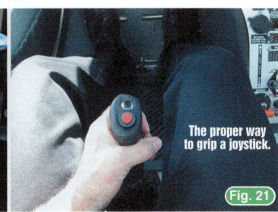

The proper way to grip a joystick.

Fig. 21

Weber's Law

Try the Liquid Experiment

If you closed your eyes, held out a cup, and asked someone to gently pour water in it, how much liquid would need to be added before you noticed a change in weight? One drop? Probably not. One ounce? Maybe. The answer is called the discrimination threshold for detecting weight differences. Interestingly enough, it depends on how heavy the cup is. By the way, don't try this experiment in a public place or the change you notice will be the coins at the bottom of your cup and you could get arrested for panhandling.

Ernst Weber (an 18th century German physician considered one of the founders of experimental psychology) discovered that there is a relationship between the degree of stimulation you're receiving and the amount it must change before you can recognize the difference. For instance, the discrimination threshold for sensing a change in pressure on the skin is approximately 16% (discrimination thresholds vary for different senses). Vary the pressure by 10% and people will not reliably notice the change. This finding has some interesting cockpit applications.

Let's assume that you've just entered a climb from straight and level flight. After establishing the nose-up pitch attitude, you find yourself holding so much elevator back pressure that you look over at your passenger and say, "Hey, spot me!" Being an astute student, you immediately spin the trim wheel with the enthusiasm of a Wheel of Fortune contestant, hopefully not while yelling, "Come on a thousand!" Suddenly, a great deal of hand-yoke pressure disappears, which is easily recognized because the change exceeded the discrimination threshold of 16%. (If 10 pounds of force is being applied to the elevator, this means there must be a change of at least 1.6 pounds for the change to be noticed.)

The Pressure Discrimination Threshold

10 Pounds of Pressure

16% or 1.6 Lbs

Discrimination Threshold

But what happens if you trim away less than 16% of the yoke pressure you're holding? You might not notice the pressure change. This is precisely what happens to timid trimmers. They trim a little bit, but not enough to notice any real difference in yoke-hand pressure. They then release the controls, only to notice a deviation in airplane attitude. Unfortunately, they repeat this process several times, wasting a lot of valuable time in the process.

When you watch experienced pilots trim their airplanes, you'll often see them make several large twists of the trim wheel (come on ten-thousand!) so they can easily feel the sudden decrease in control yoke pressure. With the airplane near its trimmed condition, they'll maintain very light hand contact with the yoke (that's right, they don't let go), then they'll apply additional trim as necessary to keep the nose attitude stabilized. The final trim adjustment is done visually by comparing the nose attitude with the horizon. Attempting to make the final trim adjustment using only the sense of touch can be difficult since the pressure change needed often does not exceed the minimum threshold for pressure detection.

Discrimination thresholds apply to other areas of flight. For instance, the discrimination threshold for sound is about 10%. Our ability to detect a change in pitch, however, is about 33 times more sensitive, with a discrimination threshold of .3%. Holy bat talk! That's sensitive. Now you know why singing off key drives people away, unless it's karaoke night, which brings them together.

This is one reason a pilot might not notice the sound of decreasing engine power, which could result from an accumulation of induction system icing or from an aft sliding throttle. However, he might more easily notice a pitch change resulting from an increase in propeller speed (perhaps due to a loss of oil pressure in an airplane having a constant speed propeller).

The discrimination threshold for determining differences in the perceived length of a line is approximately 1%, meaning that we're quite sensitive to detecting such visual changes. This is one reason we can effectively use our perception of length difference between the near and far end of the runway as a means of detecting a deviation from a previously stabilized glidepath. As you climb above or descend below a previously stabilized glidepath, the distance between the near and far end of the runway increases or decreases, respectively.

There are many variables that alter or affect Weber's law. One of them is time. If a stimulus changes slowly, you might not notice the change. This helps explain how a pilot can get into an accelerated stall when turning from base to final with an excessive bank, yet not notice the increase in pressure on his derriere (i.e., increasing g-force).

Here are discrimination thresholds for a few sensory stimuli in order of our decreasing sensitivity to them: pitch .3%; length 1%; brightness of lights 1.6%; odor 5%; loudness 10%; pressure on skin 16%; and saltiness of food 20%.

Of course, we don't usually use our sense of taste to fly. This is fortunate for two reasons. One, we aren't very sensitive to a change in it. Two, no one can ever tell you that your landings taste a bit "pancake like."

Excessive pressure applied to the yoke

Grip the control yoke too tightly and you will not be able to feel the subtle changes in pressure that the yoke exerts on you.

Chapter 2: Flying Straight and Level and Turning

on the yoke or pedals than is absolutely necessary. They also don't use any less force on the yoke or pedals than is necessary, either. In this instance, the Force should not be with you (Yoda, forgive me).

This is why nearly all airplanes have an elevator *trim wheel* (Figure 22) that moves an elevator *trim tab* (Figure 23). Turning the trim wheel (or rotating the trim handle in some airplanes) moves the trim tab, which is a small flap-like appendage located on the trailing edge of the elevator surface (Figure 23). Movement of the trim tab aerodynamically deflects the elevator surface up or down, which keeps you from having to apply pressure on the yoke to physically maintain your target attitude.

You move the trim wheel to trim away unwanted control pressures. The most common flight control with a trim tab is the elevator surface, although the aileron and rudder surfaces on many airplanes also have trim tabs and corresponding trim wheels or handles. Once unwanted control pressure is reduced by use of the trim wheel, your airplane will tend to maintain the attitude where you placed it. Imagine that! The airplane does what it's told to do. That's because your airplane already knows how to fly.

A Parting Thought on Body Parts

What about the other parts of your body? Where do you place your elbow when you're using a control yoke? You typically rest it on the armrest (assuming your airplane has one, and assuming you have an arm, of course)

The Airplane's Elevator Trim Wheel

Fig. 22

The Airplane's Elevator Trim Tab

Fig. 23

Sitting High to Fly

Proper seating height is important if you plan on seeing the runway during landing, as well as seeing outside the airplane during flight. Most airplane seats have vertical adjustment levers or handles. If yours doesn't, then you'll want to purchase a nice cushion or two to elevate yourself. It's unfortunate that there aren't aviation jumpsuits with a built-in seat cushion on which your derriere could plop. Then again, I suppose you would have a lot of explaining to do if you wore this jumpsuit anywhere other than the airport.

So, how high do you want to sit? As high as possible, as long as you can still see just below the top frame of the left and right front-seat windows.

A very big, "but" that is often an unrealized problem with many student pilots is that they seldom sit high enough in the seat.

Imagine what it's like when that student approaches to land and he or she can't even see the distant runway over the top of the engine cowling or instrument panel (the engine cowling is the metal or composite hood surrounding the engine, just behind the propeller). This would be about as unnerving as a bullfighter not being able to see over the curtain (cape) he's holding in front of him (which would certainly mean curtains for him).

Of course, you'll learn that you don't need to look directly over the nose of the airplane during the landing flare, but it is desirable to see the center of the runway for as long as possible while you're approaching to land.

The only issue with increasing your sitting height is that pilots with short legs often find themselves falling out of touch with the rudder pedals. It's sometimes necessary to accompany any derriere cushion with a back cushion, too.

I had one short male student who adapted to the short legs problem by wearing really hip clog-type shoes. Clogs are usually confined to women, but they worked just fine for extending his leg range.

For those pilots who don't find height-extending shoes comfortable (or are afraid of being cited by the fashion police) there are rudder pedal extenders available for some airplanes.

Clogs

Rudder Pedal Extensions

Courtesy: Sportys

Rod Machado's How to Fly an Airplane Handbook

How a Stationary Elbow Resting on the Armrest Can Cause a Pitch Change in a Turn

In a left turn, a stationary elbow on the armrest might cause a nose down pitch change. Fig. 24

In a right turn, a stationary elbow on the armrest might cause a nose up pitch change. Fig. 25

Rudder and Brake Pedals

Balls of feet rest here. Fig. 26

Apply rudder pressure here. Fig. 27

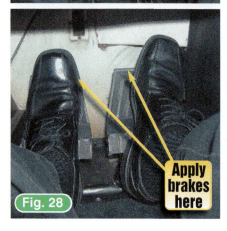

Apply brakes here. Fig. 28

located on the structure of the left door. The secret here is to allow the elbow to slide back and forth easily when making turns (no elbow grease is necessary because you don't need it to grease a landing).

If you keep your elbow stationary when making a turn, the yoke will likely move away from you in a left turn (Figure 24) and toward you in a right turn (Figure 25), based on the mechanics of your arm. Try it. Put your elbow on the desk in front of you, keep it planted there and rotate the imaginary yoke to the right, as if you're entering a right turn. Your forearm, wrist and hand move toward you, causing the nose of your imaginary airplane to pitch up slightly in a right turn. Keeping your elbow stationary when making a left turn results in a nose-down pitch. So let your elbow slide freely when making turns and minimize the chance that you'll apply unnecessary forward or aft pressure on the yoke.

Your feet are another matter that does matter and another place you'll have to toe the line. The heel of each foot should rest comfortably on the floorboard below each rudder pedal (Figure 26). Most airplanes have rudder pedals that

The Electric Trim

One of the benefits of living in a modern society is that manual labor is often replaced by electric devices. Electric shavers, electric nail clippers and even an electric dog polisher make life easier for us (but not necessarily for the dog).

Trim wheel

Electric trim switch

That's why many training airplanes come equipped with a trim motor to move the elevator trim tab with a simple flick of your thumb. That's right. On these airplanes, the electric trim is activated by pressing your thumb against a small switch on the control yoke. Of course, if you're feeling exhausted after every flight because you have to rotate the trim wheel manually, then I'd suggest that you change your diet and stop living entirely off the plant life in the air.

As a general rule, I don't let student pilots use the electric trim in the early stages of training. I want them to have a lot of experience moving the trim wheel manually. Why? Manual movement of the trim wheel allows you to feel the trim inputs you're making. As a rule of thumb, movement of your thumb on the electric trim switch physically disconnects you from the trim that's being applied. It simply takes most students longer to properly trim airplanes using electric trim compared to movement of the trim wheel directly.

Chapter 2: Flying Straight and Level and Turning

Rudder and Brake Pedals

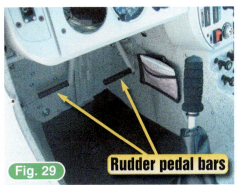
Fig. 29 — Rudder pedal bars

Fig. 30 — Brake hand lever

Fig. 31 — Heel brakes

provide both rudder and brake functions. Rudder pressure is applied with the ball of your foot by pivoting on the heel and pushing forward on the bottom part of the rudder pedal (Figure 27). Brakes are typically applied by lifting the heel off the floorboard, placing your feet flat on one or both pedals and applying pressure to the top of the pedal with the ball of your foot as shown in Figure 28 (you apply brakes on the ground, not in the air because they don't work in the air—mainly because you're not in a Roadrunner cartoon).

On many light sport airplanes, you'll find that the rudder pedals consists of horizontal bars (Figure 29). With a bar-type rudder pedal, pressure is still applied by pushing the pedal with the ball of your foot. Similar to fancy dancing, it's the balls of your feet that do the footwork on the rudder pedals (no, this is not why it's called *ballroom dancing*). The brakes are operated separately by a brake handle which stops both main wheels at the same time (Figure 30). On other airplanes, such as the J3 Piper Cub, you'll have brake pedals and separate heel brakes to control braking on each wheel (Figure 31).

Flying is really a matter of how you feel—that is, how you feel or sense the airplane. If you purposely had all your nerve endings severed so that you had very little feeling in your appendages (perhaps in preparation for a lengthy career as a jack hammer operator), you could probably still fly an airplane. It's doubtful, however, that you'd be considered smooth or delicate with the flight controls, much less able to perform precision flight maneuvers. Precision flying is about feeling your airplane. It's about using most of your senses—sight, sound, tactile, kinesthetic—to understand what the airplane is doing and then making it do your bidding.

You can certainly see the airplane's behavior, and you can hear it, too. You can sense the pressure on the flight controls as well as feel the acceleration and lateral displacement from the uncoordinated use of rudder and aileron (known as slipping or skidding). We call this *flying by the seat of your pants*, even if you don't wear your pants when you fly (but I recommend that you do, especially for your FAA checkride). Ultimately, the strategy to use on every flight is to engage your rear end to help you fly smoothly and precisely. More on seat of the pants flying shortly.

Attitude Plus Power Equals Performance (A+P=P)

Now that you have a basic idea about how the flight controls work, I need to download one very important item into your noggin before placing you in the airplane for your very first flying lesson. I'm going to let you in on a little secret that's really not little at all. It's big. Really big. Once you understand this principle, nothing the airplane does or doesn't do should surprise you (except for birthday parties involving ice cream cake, pilots hate surprises). Think of this as the inside "double" scoop that helps you understand the genetic code of airplane performance. What's the principle? Wait for it.

OK, here it is.

For a given attitude and power condition, the airplane produces a specific level of performance. Symbolically stated, *Attitude+Power=Performance (A+P=P)*. This is an important formula in the air, so think of it as *higher* math for pilots (Figure 32). Attitude is a combination of pitch and/or bank. Power is the thrust produced by the engine/propeller combination. Select a specific nose-up or nose-down pitch attitude and a given amount of engine power and you can expect the airplane to move forward at a specific speed and climb or descend at a specific rate. And that's pretty much your job as the pilot—selecting attitude and power to produce performance.

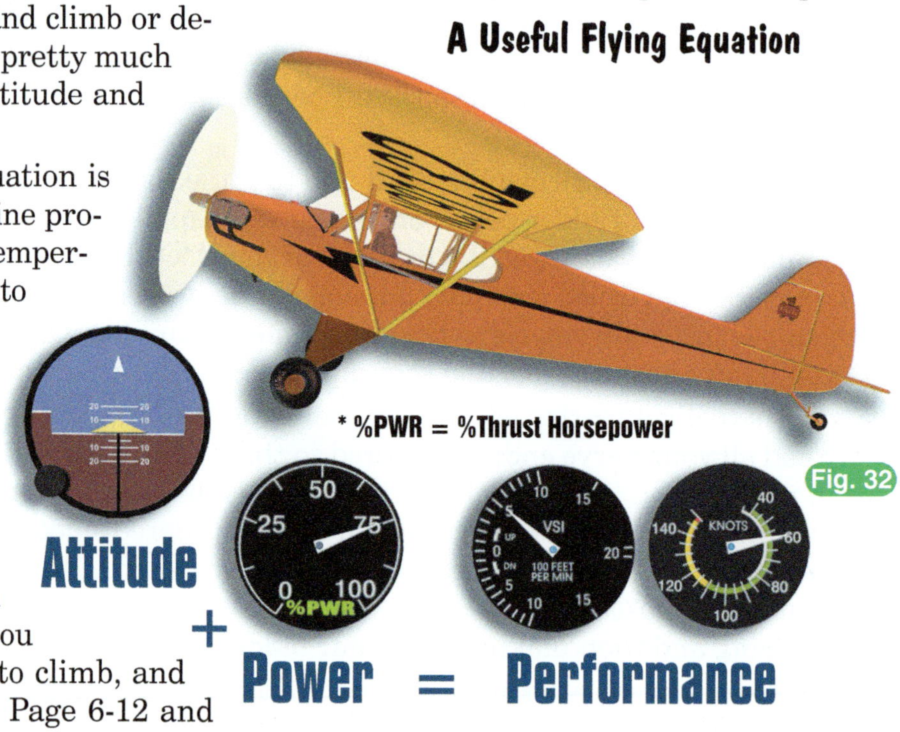

Of course, the performance equation is dependent on the power your engine produces, which is influenced by air temperature, atmospheric pressure and, to a lesser extent, humidity. At higher altitudes, where your non-turbocharged engine produces less power, you can't point the nose upward as high and climb at the same attitude as you would at lower altitudes. That makes sense, right? After all, if you had a powerful enough engine, you could point the nose straight up to climb, and you would climb straight up (see Page 6-12 and read *Climb Attitudes for Airports Having Different Density Altitudes*).

A Useful Flying Equation

* %PWR = %Thrust Horsepower

Attitude + Power = Performance

Fig. 32

The less engine power that is available to you, the less steep the nose-up attitude at which you can climb. Eventually, if the air were thin enough, you'd only have enough power to sustain level flight. And if the air became even thinner, your power production would decrease and your airplane would descend, just as it would if you pulled the throttle all the way back to idle power. If you keep this in mind, the A+P=P equation predicts your airplane's performance quite well.

Just to be clear here, *attitude* isn't *angle of attack*. We'll cover angle of attack in great detail in Chapter's Four and Five. In those chapters you'll learn that we fly attitude but always think in terms of angle of attack. For the rest of this chapter, we'll talk about how to choose a specific attitude and power setting for any flight maneuver. This takes the guesswork out of flying and makes an airplane's performance more predictable in the air.

Straight and Level Flight

We're going to begin your first lesson in the air in straight and level flight (Figure 33). Those aren't two separate maneuvers, either. *Straight flight* means that the airplane's heading is constant

Chapter 2: Flying Straight and Level and Turning

How to Identify Straight and Level Flight

Fig. 33

Fig. 34 — The Instrument Method

because its nose points in some direction and stays pointed in that direction. Flying *level* means that the airplane maintains a constant altitude. In other words, the hands on the altimeter don't move (Figure 34, position A). Sometimes, however, an instructor will use the term *level* with reference to the wings. If an instructor says, "Level out," while turning in level flight, hopefully you'll know he or she wants you to fly straight. Of course, if your instructor doesn't want to confuse you, he or she will simply say, "Level the wings," or "Roll out of the turn," or "Let's roll out now," or even, "I could use a cinnamon roll" (instructors are always hungry).

You can also confirm that you're flying straight by looking at the airplane's artificial horizon to ensure that the miniature wings are on the horizon line and that the skypointer shows a zero degree bank angle (Figure 34, position B). I don't, however, want you to rely too much on your flight instruments. Determining the airplane's attitude can and should be done by looking at the distant horizon through the windscreen ahead of you or through the side window at the wingtip (see next page).

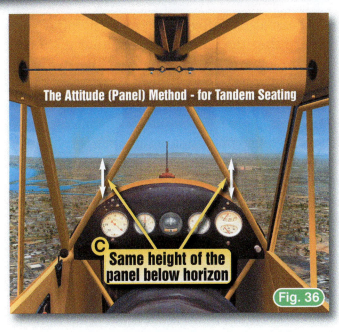

Fig. 35 — The Attitude (Panel) Method For Side-by-Side Seating — Same height of the panel below horizon

Fig. 36 — The Attitude (Panel) Method - for Tandem Seating — Same height of the panel below horizon

In straight and level flight, either side of the engine cowling or instrument panel should be equidistant relative to the horizon line (Figures 35 and 36, position C). If the wings are not banked, then the nose of your airplane remains pointed in one direction, meaning that the number on the index of your heading indicator remains fixed (Figure 34, position D).

How Straight Flight Appears Through the Left and Right Windows

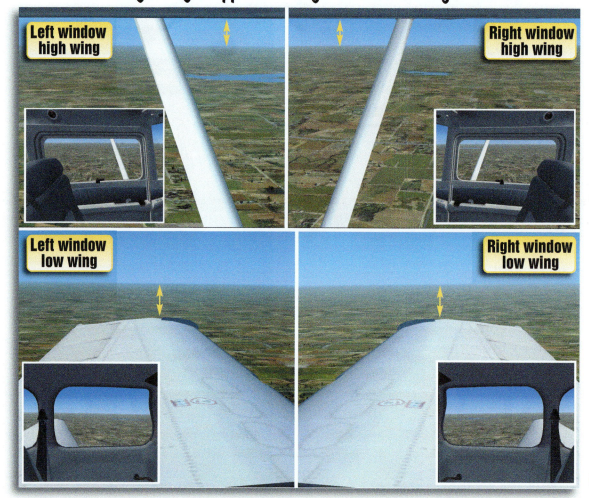

Fig. 37

You can also confirm that you're flying straight by looking out the right and left window and making sure that the wings are at similar distances above or below the horizon, which works for both high and low wing airplanes, too (Figure 37).

When the visibility is good and the horizon is easily identified (meaning that you don't live in Los Angeles), it's relatively easy to keep the wings level. Even when haze is present and the horizon isn't easily seen, there is often sufficient contrast between the area above and below the airplane to help you define, imagine or estimate the horizontal line separating up from down. That's why non-instrument rated pilots (those who aren't licensed to fly in the clouds) can fly in hazy conditions or fly at night without losing control of their airplane (with the legal minimum visibility and cloud clearance, of course).

Something on the Horizon?

Sometimes there is no distinct horizon visible because of the presence of haze or pesky mountains. There's nothing like ancient tectonic plate movement that wrinkles the earth to mess up your flying lesson, right?

How do you deal with this? Fly in Kansas where the authorities have successfully completed their mountain removal project? No. You simply imagine where the horizon line is by letting your brain do what it does best, and that is to make estimates. By using your peripheral vision to sense the location of the ground below you and sky above you, you can actually do a pretty good job of estimating where the horizon line would be as if you had Superman's X-ray vision to look through the haze and hills.

Of course, sometimes there is no choice but to use the artificial horizon to assist in imagining where the horizon line is, especially if you're not Superman. Then again, Superman doesn't need an airplane, does he?

Chapter 2: Flying Straight and Level and Turning

Flying on the Level

On the other hand, how do you perform the *level* part of straight and level flight, also known as *holding your altitude*? To answer that question you need to know what straight and level flight looks like from the cockpit. Not surprisingly, it looks similar to what you see when driving your car on a level stretch of road (Figure 38). Unless your parachute failed to fully open sometime in the past, you typically sit high enough in the car seat so that your dashboard appears below the horizon line. Sit low-rider style in the car seat and the horizon line and dashboard appear to converge.

If you borrowed your dad's car as a two-year old youngster to make a diaper run, then you probably sat so low that your eyeballs, dashboard and horizon all lined up. In an airplane, however, you most likely sit tall enough in the saddle so that the top of the engine cowling or instrument panel appears a little below the horizon line (from now on I'll just refer to the top of the engine cowling or instrument panel as the *cowling*). This observation allows you to keep the airplane in level flight.

Flying level means using the elevator control to place the top of the cowling a few inches below the distant horizon (Figure 39) sufficient to maintain your altitude (i.e., keep the altimeter reading constant).

When the altimeter hands are steady in the instrument, look *directly* ahead of you (*not* slightly to the right toward the center of the cowling) and note the distance the cowling is below the horizon line. Remember this distance. Better yet, use an erasable grease pen to make a small dot on the inside of the windscreen that rests directly over the distant horizon line (get your instructor's permission to do this, otherwise he'll think you are a graffiti artist). A sticky, triangle-shaped corner of a Post-it will also work. So will mascara, chewing gum, and lots of other things though not all may be acceptable to your instructor or the flight school from which you rent the airplane.

The dot on the horizon line helps you calibrate how far below the horizon to place the cowling to maintain level flight. Of course, the dot's location relative to the distant horizon line will vary as you change the airplane's airspeed, power setting or your seating height. That's fine, because the dot is only a rough approximation of the attitude needed for straight and level flight. After one or two flight lessons, you won't even need a dot to fly straight and level, and dot's the truth. Nevertheless, I'll reference the dot throughout these chapters as a means of helping you identify the correct flight attitude.

So there you are in straight and level flight and we have not even talked about what to do with the airplane's throttle. So let's do a little throttle talk.

As you've probably guessed by now, an airplane's throttle is operated by your hand and not your feet (Figure 40). Your feet are busy working the rudder pedals, but your right hand is free for other things like working the radios, holding charts, scratching your ear, and moving the throttle forward and aft. Similar to a car's throttle, you push the airplane's throttle in for more power and pull it back (toward you) for less power.

Maximum allowable climb power (we'll just call this *full power* from now on) is typically used for climbs, approximately two-thirds to three-quarter power is used for cruise flight, and idle (minimum) power is used for power-off descents. The control of engine power is determined by looking at the airplane's engine power instruments such as the engine RPM gauge (Figure 41) or, on complex airplanes, the RPM and manifold pressure gauges (more on complex airplanes later).

OK, time for a pop quiz. What happens to your airplane's airspeed when you increase or decrease the power in straight and level flight? Think about what your car does on a level road when you push the throttle to the floorboard or take your foot completely off the pedal. That's right, you speed up or slow down, respectively. That's why in straight and level flight, your throttle position primarily determines your airspeed.

When the airplane is in level flight, you'll often choose a power setting to obtain a specific airplane performance value such as a specific fuel consumption or specific airspeed. During flight training, however, you'll typically move the throttle to some nominal cruise value such as 2,300 RPM (that's

approximately two-thirds forward throttle travel on many airplanes) and be happy to cruise around at a moderate cruise airspeed. As with all training matters, it's your instructor's wishes that matter. So use the power setting he or she suggests.

Trimming for Level Flight

Earlier, I introduced you to the airplane's trim wheel. Now we're going to learn how to use it correctly.

Suppose you were holding two 25-pound dumbbells (not human). A friend comes by and asks if you want some help, and you give her one of the dumbbells to hold. Lightened your load, didn't it? That's what the trim wheel does. It's a friend who lightens your load.

Chapter 2: Flying Straight and Level and Turning

Elevator Trim Tab and Cockpit Trim Wheel

![Elevator trim tab and moveable trim wheel](Fig. 42)

Controlling the Trim Tab

Fig. 43

In straight and level flight, it might be necessary for you to physically apply forward or aft pressure on the yoke to maintain a specific attitude. Why? When you select a new attitude during flight, you typically alter the aerodynamic forces acting on the airplane. That means you have to readjust the pressure being applied to the elevator control to maintain the correct attitude. This of course becomes tiring after a while. If you wanted that kind of workout, you'd join a gym (or find a guy named Jim to hold the yoke for you). That's why most airplanes have an elevator *trim tab* that's controlled by the elevator trim wheel in the cockpit (Figure 42). Moving the trim wheel changes the aerodynamic forces acting on the elevator trim tab, resulting in the elevator control surface moving up or down, which helps maintain the desired flight attitude.

If you have to apply aft pressure on the yoke to keep the airplane in a level flight attitude, then you should apply *nose-up* trim by rotating the trim wheel downward (or toward your feet), as shown in Figure 43, position A. This moves the trim tab on the trailing edge of the elevator surface downward, thus deflecting the elevator upward (Figure 43, position B). Now the trim tab does your work for you (unfortunately, this doesn't work if you put one on your lawnmower).

The same principle applies in reverse when you must apply forward pressure on the yoke to keep the airplane in a level flight attitude. Give the airplane some *nose-down* trim by rotating the trim wheel upward (away from your feet), as shown in Figure 43, position C. Now the trim tab on the trailing edge of the elevator surface moves upward, which aerodynamically deflects elevator surface downward (Figure 43, position D).

If you're having difficulty identifying the correct way to rotate the trim wheel, mentally enlarge the wheel to a radius of the airplane's length and imagine the airplane in the center of the middle of the wheel. Rotating the wheel aft results in the nose going up (Figure 44, position A) while rotating it forward makes the nose go down (Figure 44, position B).

You never want to use the trim wheel in place of the flight control to which it's attached. In other words, don't use elevator

Trim Tab Visualization

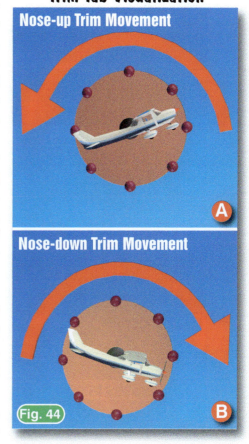

Fig. 44

trim to change your *attitude*. If you want to pitch up, then move the elevator control to change your attitude followed by trimming away the excess elevator control pressure. Trim is *only* used to maintain the desired flight attitude once it's already established.

Now that you know why trimming is important, how do you trim for level flight? The first step involves *pressure*, or more specifically, the lack of it on the elevator control. With the airplane placed in level flight, use the trim wheel to reduce any forward or aft pressure you're applying to the yoke to keep the airplane in that attitude. Your challenge is to feel when the bulk of the forward or aft pressure you're applying to the yoke disappears. When it has, ease up on your grip but please don't let go of the yoke. Now, look at the airplane's attitude over the cowling (Figure 45). The attitude should stay constant without your having to apply any pressure to keep it constant. Of course, if you're in level flight the altimeter hands and the VSI (vertical speed indicator) needle should remain stationary (Figure 45). Any movement of these needles means that the airplane most likely isn't trimmed properly.

If you ease up on the yoke and the airplane's nose pitches upward or downward, apply forward or aft pressure on the yoke to return the airplane to level flight attitude and add a little more nose-down or nose-up trim, as appropriate.

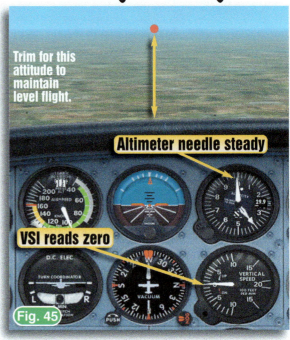

Trimming for Level Flight

Trim for this attitude to maintain level flight.
Altimeter needle steady
VSI reads zero
Fig. 45

Elevator, Aileron and Rudder Trim Wheels

Aileron trim knob
Electric elevator trim switch
Elevator trim wheel
Rudder trim wheel
Fig. 46

Repeat the same process until the airplane remains in level flight without any forward or aft pressure applied to the yoke. The final trim adjustment is made visually (by looking over the cowling) instead of attempting to sense the small pressures the yoke applies to your hand. After all, these small pressures may lie below the threshold of discrimination (remember Weber's Law from Page 2-8?). That's why it's perfectly acceptable for new pilots to use the VSI needle to help trim for level flight. This needle is very sensitive and makes deviations from level flight easy to detect (Figure 45).

As I mentioned earlier, you don't want to let go of the yoke to determine if the airplane is properly trimmed. This is very poor technique. Letting go of the yoke even for a second or two means an untrimmed airplane will pitch up or down, resulting in an altitude

Chapter 2: Flying Straight and Level and Turning

Abuse and Misuse of Your Trim Wheel

One of the big mistakes pilots make with the trim wheel is using it as a substitute for the elevator control. Instead of using the yoke to change the airplane's pitch attitude, they use the trim wheel. It's as if they're spinning the big prize wheel on a game show, except that this is a game where the prizes are really lousy (you could win a chance to have your flight instructor give you the evil eye).

Trying to *raise* the nose by use of trim during a landing is particularly poor technique. It's risky, too. It's entirely possible that you might raise the nose with nose-up trim, then have to suddenly abort the landing. You'll apply full power to go-around, only to find that the airplane *unexpectedly* pitches up because of the combination of nose-up trim and full power.

You are then often forced to apply an enormous amount of forward elevator pressure until a bell goes off in your head reminding you that you've got a lot of nose-up trim already applied. This is just bad form and dangerous, especially for those who don't hear their bell—which earns them the no-bell prize.

change. That means you have to return the airplane to the correct attitude and re-trim, which makes for a lot of unnecessary work (which isn't good unless your flight pay is based on workload). It also tends to be upsetting for passengers, who haven't signed on to take part in a rodeo.

Some airplanes have a trim wheel for the ailerons as well as the rudder (Figure 46). Clearly this is unfair, mainly because your closest relative isn't an octopus and you only have two hands. There is no need to worry, since you only manipulate one trim wheel at a time. In what order do you use the trim wheels if you have more than one? Start by trimming the elevator control first, followed by rudder trim next and aileron trim last. Why in that order? Using elevator trim first stabilizes the one attitude that you can't afford to let wander—the pitch attitude. An airplane that wanders vertically often presents a greater risk to you than one that wanders right or left (especially if air traffic control has instructed you to maintain a specific altitude).

Additionally, elevator trim is hardly affected by use of the aileron or rudder trim. While holding the wings level with aileron pressure, the rudder should be trimmed next. This allows you to compensate any adverse yaw caused by aileron displacement as well any power-induced left turning tendency. It also takes a lot of pressure off your leg if you happen to be in a climb and are holding a lot of right rudder pressure. This is especially true if you have a peg leg because you're a pirate, or heaven forbid, a soon-to-be private pirate.

Finally, you trim the aileron. This is a good trim sequence to use in most airplanes.

Remember, your trim control *doesn't take the place of the actual flight control*. If your airplane's attitude isn't providing the performance you want, then change the attitude with elevator control, not the trim wheel. The trim wheel is only used to remove the pressure you must apply on the flight controls to keep the airplane at the desired attitude.

Trim Truth

There is an important misconceptions about your airplane's trim that you should know. For instance, you can't expect a perfectly trimmed airplane to remain in the flight condition for which it is trimmed. In other words, your airplane may be trimmed for level flight, but if you take your hands off the yoke, the airplane might begin to make slight vertical oscillations. Airplanes are designed to have positive longitudinal dynamic stability. That means when the airplane is disturbed from level flight (perhaps by a gust or by bumping the yoke), the airplane's vertical deviations from level flight should diminish, returning the airplane to its previously trimmed condition as shown below.

These altitude deviations are often typically small, perhaps resulting in a few hundred feet in amplitude, diminishing with time.

Most airplanes seldom demonstrate this ideal behavior. Why? Airplane loading, rigging, age and other factors all affect how the airplane responds when disturbed in level flight. For instance, you're most likely to experience an airplane that demonstrates something closer to *neutral* or *negative dynamic stability* (pictured below) when the airplane is disturbed in its level trimmed condition as shown here.

What does this mean to you? It means that the airplane might oscillate a few hundred feet up and down over relatively long periods of time, with time between peaks measured in tens of seconds or even minutes, depending on the airplane. These types long-term oscillations aren't dangerous at all. They can easily be stopped by an application of elevator pressure.

The takeaway point here is that a perfectly trimmed airplane isn't likely to stay in the condition for which it's perfectly trimmed. That means you'll have to monitor your airplane's flight condition and, when the altitude deviation exceeds your tolerance, you'll have to manually return the airplane to the desired altitude.

Level Turns

So far you're in the top 1% of the class in understanding how airplanes fly straight (sure, you're the only one in the class, but you're still at the top, right?) Now it's time to bring your airplane back home. That means knowing how to make an airplane turn in level flight.

In a second we're going to discuss a lot of "whys" and "hows" for making an airplane turn. But let me preface it with a simple and practical rule. Place the airplane in the desired degree of bank with the ailerons, then manipulate the ailerons to maintain the bank angle. Period. I don't care which way you have to deflect the ailerons as long as the airplane remains at the targeted bank angle. Simultaneously use the rudder to keep the nose pointed in the direction of turn. It's just that simple. If you've got that, then you're on your way to mastering turns.

It is, however, important that you understand *why* and *how* this works, so let's turn our attention to turns.

Making a turn in an airplane is a matter of moving the yoke right or left (Figures 47 and 48) to deflect the ailerons and bank the airplane. Banking the airplane deflects the wing's vertical lifting force in the direction you want to turn. This results in a small horizontal component of that lifting force pulling the airplane in the direction of bank (Figure 49). That's how airplanes actually turn.

As we've previously discussed, airplanes don't turn by yawing the nose right or left with the rudder pedals. Think about it this way. When driving a car, you'll use the steering wheel to make a turn. Turning the wheel allows the friction between the tires and the road to deflect the car's energy in a horizontal direction. Since your airplane's tires aren't touching the ground in flight (at least they shouldn't be, unless they're incredibly overinflated), applying rudder pressure to turn the airplane results in a yaw, not a turn (unless, of course, the yaw actually induces a slight bank which would result in a poorly coordinated turn).

That's right. You heard me correctly. If you don't let the wings bank, then the airplane only yaws with application of rudder pressure. It doesn't turn. There must be some horizontal component of lift involved for a turn to occur. This is why your airplane has ailerons. As you've already learned (and you won't hear this in anatomy class), the nose has a mind of its own and wants to yaw in the opposite direction of aileron application. This is why the airplane is equipped with a rudder. The

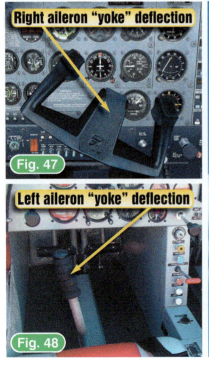

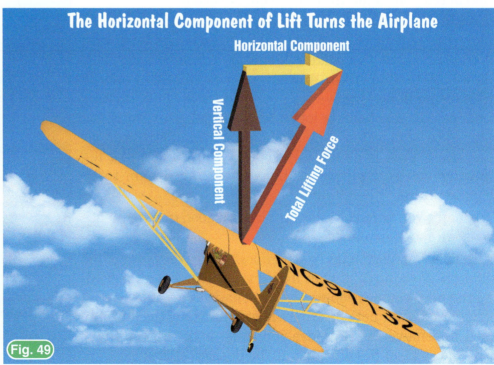

Chapter 2: Flying Straight and Level and Turning

Looking Good...for Traffic Before Turning

One of the clues you can use to determine if you're flying with a traffic-conscious pilot is the way he or she clears the area before turning an airplane. While many pilots will look in the direction of turn to ensure that the area is clear, good pilots *also* look in the opposite direction. They do so because while they're turning in one direction, traffic may be converging on them from the opposite side of the airplane. This is a big concern if the airplane is a low wing. Think about it. If you're making a right turn in a low wing airplane and clear the area to the right, the moment you bank, the left wing rises and blocks the view on the left side of the airplane. An aircraft converging from the left might go unseen.

It's a good habit to ask out loud, "Clear left?" or "Clear right?" before turning. This gives your passengers a chance to look for traffic too, perhaps allowing them to spot an aircraft that you didn't notice. It may also cause your passengers to think that you're defibrillating one side of your heart, but that's a risk worth taking.

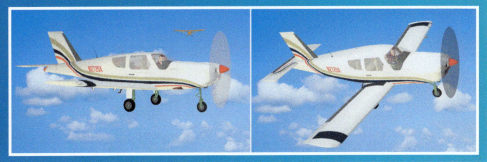

rudder keeps the nose (the longitudinal axis, but remember that we're using the term *nose* to represent this axis from now on) pointed in the direction of turn. Let me explain this in detail by helping you through your first turn.

To begin a turn, you first clear the area. This doesn't mean chasing other airplanes out of your practice area. It means looking ahead, right, left, behind, above and below you to make sure you won't bump into nearby aircraft (See sidebar: *Looking Good...for Traffic Before Turning*). Since there are no "minor fender benders" at 2,500 feet, it is important to always do this.

As you deflect the yoke to the right for a right turn, the right wing aileron deflects upward and the left wing aileron deflects downward (Figures 50 and 51). This causes the airplane to bank to the right. The upward deflected aileron on the wing inside the turn (the right wing is on the inside of the right turn) reduces that wing's lift and its drag.

As we've already discussed, the downward deflected aileron on the outside wing (the left wing in this instance), generates more lift on that wing, causing it to rise, but it also generates more drag, too. This drag pulls aft on the left wing, yawing the airplane's nose opposite to the direction you want to turn. To compensate for adverse yaw during turn entry, you must *simultaneously* press on the appropriate rudder pedal to point the nose in the direction the airplane is banked

How Adverse Yaw Affects the Direction the Airplane's Nose Points

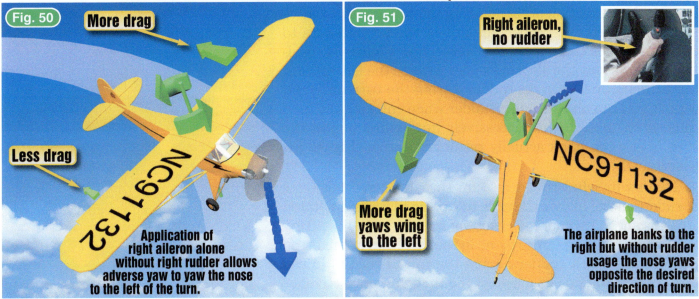

Application of Rudder Compensates for Adverse Yaw - Rolling Into a Turn

Fig. 52 Fig. 53

(Figure 52 and 53). Deflect the yoke to the right and you should *simultaneously* press on the right rudder pedal. Deflect the yoke to the left and you should simultaneously press on the left rudder pedal. As a general rule, the harder and faster that you deflect those ailerons, the harder and faster you apply simultaneous rudder pressure.

How Much Rudder Do You Use to Enter a Turn?

How do you know if you're applying the proper amount of rudder when *rolling* into a turn?

You look directly over the nose of the airplane as shown in Figure 54, position A, then roll into the bank while simultaneously applying sufficient rudder pressure to keep the nose from moving *opposite* the direction of turn (Figure 54, position B). That's the secret to *entering* a coordinated turn (used in this context, the term *coordinated* means that aileron and rudder are being used in such a way that the nose always points in the direction of turn).

Another way of saying this is, if the nose doesn't move opposite the direction of turn during the roll in, then you've at least applied the proper amount of rudder pressure to compensate for the effects of adverse yaw. Figure 54, position C shows how the airplane's nose yaws to the left without the sufficient use of right rudder during the turn entry. Of course, you can use too much rudder when entering the turn causing the nose to yaw excessively in the direction of the turn before the bank actually results in a turn (Figure 54, position D).

That's why, when rolling into any turn, the correct amount of rudder usage allows the nose to *appear* to remain pointed straight ahead (primarily because of inertia) until the lifting force begins pulling the airplane in the direction of turn. Too little or too much rudder during the roll in results in the nose yawing outside or inside of the turn arc, respectively.

Fig. 54

Chapter 2: Flying Straight and Level and Turning

Application of Rudder Compensates for Adverse Yaw - Rolling Out of a Turn

Fig. 55 — Rolling out to the left results in an increase in adverse yaw on the right wing.

Fig. 56 — Applying left rudder during rollout prevents the nose from yawing right or left.

A — Rolling Out of a Right Turn. Before rolling out of the turn. Mountain Reference.

B — Correct usage of left rudder. No yaw.

C — Insufficient left rudder usage. Nose yaws to the right.

D — Excessive left rudder usage. Nose yaws to the left. Fig. 57

The same principle applies when rolling out of a turn. To begin any rollout, you'll apply aileron to reduce the bank angle and simultaneously use rudder in the same direction to compensate for the adverse yaw of the lowered aileron on the rising wing.

For instance, when rolling out of a right turn into straight and level flight, the aileron on the right wing moves downward, which increases the lift as well as the drag on that wing (the aileron on the left wing moves upward decreasing the lift and the drag on that wing). The nose wants to yaw to the right because of the adverse yaw produced by the lowered right aileron (Figure 55). To keep the nose from yawing, you must use left rudder in coordination with left aileron application.

Done correctly, the nose *appears* to stop moving during the rollout with the airplane pivoting about its longitudinal axis as it returns to a zero banked condition (Figure 56). Yes, of course the nose moves a very tiny bit during the rollout, but if you roll out at a moderate rate, you'll hardly notice this horizontal movement. Too much or too little rudder causes the nose to yaw left or right during the rollout. This is how you determine the precise amount of rudder to use when rolling out of a turn.

Figure 57 shows how a rollout from a right turn looks from the airplane cockpit. As you begin the rollout from a right turn (Figure 57, position A) you apply left aileron and left rudder simultaneously. You're using just enough left rudder application to keep the nose from yawing to the right (or the left). Done correctly, you should see the nose appear to pivot about the distant point where the rollout began (Figure 57, position B). Let me emphasize this point one more time. During the coordinated rollout, the nose (the point on the cowling directly ahead of your seated position) actually *appears* to stop its horizontal motion and the airplane pivots or rolls about its longitudinal axis as it returns to a zero banked condition.

This is a very important concept that you must understand if you want to be a good stick and rudder pilot (you do, don't you? Ahh, I knew you did).

Insufficient left rudder (or failure to release any right rudder pressure) when rolling out of a right turn results in the nose yawing to the right (Figure 57, position C). Too much left rudder results in the nose yawing to the left (Figure 57, position D).

Once the wings are level, the aileron and rudder should be neutralized (returned to their non-deflected position). The important thing to remember here is that you make the same inputs (rudder and aileron) when rolling out of a turn to the left or right that you make when rolling into a turn to the right or left, respectively.

Aileron Use When Established in the Turn

After the turn is established, the ailerons are returned to their neutral position. (Fig. 58)

Rolling out of a turn essentially means that you're turning in the opposite direction and stopping the turn when the wings are level with the horizon. Once you know how to use the controls for rolling *into* a turn, you automatically know how to use them for rolling *out of* a turn.

There are several subtleties about turns you should know. First, most airplanes want to turn (yaw) to the left more easily than they do to the right when engine power is being used. The airplane's power-induced left turning tendency means that you won't need much left rudder to enter a left turn or maintain that turn. (See: *The Airplane's Left Turning Tendencies* sidebar and Postflight Briefing #2-2.) Right turns, however, usually require more—and sometimes a lot more—right rudder pressure during turn entry. In many instances, right turns require that you maintain a certain amount of right rudder pressure to keep the turn coordinated once the turn is established. This difference in rudder application diminishes when power is reduced, such as during power-off descents.

Where Do You Place the Flight Controls Once You're Established in the Turn?

Once you've established the desired bank angle for the turn, what do you do with the deflected aileron control? In an ideal world with an ideal airplane, you should return the ailerons to their neutral position, otherwise your bank will increase (Figure 58). If the bank is neither too shallow nor too steep, the bank angle should remain constant. We don't, however, fly in an ideal world or in ideal airplanes. As a practical matter, once you've established the correct bank angle, you should deflect the ailerons in *any way necessary* to sustain the desired bank. Period! That's the rule. It turns out that at shallow bank angles, the bank wants to decrease, requiring aileron deflection in the direction of turn. At steeper bank angles, the bank wants to increase, requiring aileron deflection opposite the turn to sustain the desired bank angle (see *Wing Speed Differential* sidebar on Page 2-29).

Let's assume that you returned your ailerons to their neutral position. So what about the rudder pressure you applied when entering the turn? With the ailerons neutralized, adverse yaw is no longer being created and the airplane's nose *tends to* automatically remain pointed in the direction of turn,

Chapter 2: Flying Straight and Level and Turning

mainly because the fuselage and the vertical stabilizer (the non-moving vertical "fin" structure to which the moveable rudder is attached) keep the airplane aligned with the relative airflow.

Said another way, you don't need to apply pressure on the rudder pedals once the airplane is established in the turn unless adverse yaw or the propeller's left turning tendency displaces the airplane from that position. That's why you should neutralize the rudder pressure simultaneously with returning the yoke to its centered position. Now the airplane turns and the nose points in the direction of turn—most of the time.

I say *most of the time* because, once again, that's how airplanes fly in the ideal world, but things are rarely ideal.

It turns out that the forces of P-factor, propeller slipstream, and torque conspire to deflect the airplane's nose to the left in varying degrees when engine power is used. At higher power settings the propeller slipstream noticeably yaws the nose to the left because rotating airflow from the propeller moves aft and pushes on the left side of the tail surface. At larger angles of attack, P-factor also yaws the nose to the left (see sidebar to the right). If you didn't know better, you might even think that the pilot sits on the left of the cockpit because the engine somehow forced him there against his will (OK, it didn't, but it's not so crazy to think it did).

In many airplanes, you'll find that a right turn (when considerable engine power is used such as in a high speed cruise or a climb) will require some amount of continuous right rudder pressure to prevent the nose from yawing to the left of the turn (i.e., to remain in coordinated flight). How do you know how much rudder to apply *once you're established in the turn*? There are three distinct ways to tell, with the most basic being the use of the *inclinometer*.

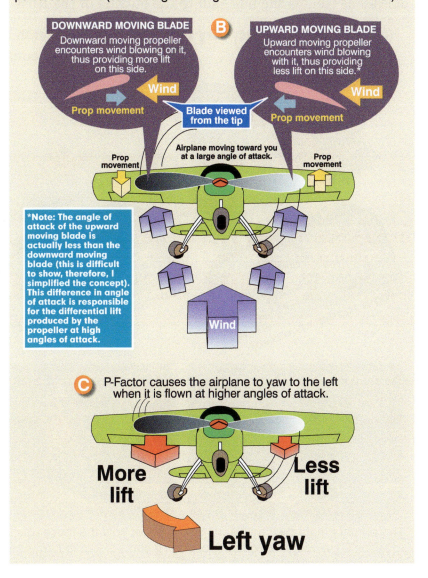

The Airplane's Left Turning Tendencies
Propeller Slipstream

A clockwise rotating propeller imparts a curve or spiral motion to air flowing past the fuselage (position A). Under high power conditions (such as during takeoff or climb), a curved spiral of air swirls around the airplane striking the vertical stabilizer and the rudder, yawing the airplane's nose to the left. At high angles of attack, however, another force known as *P-factor* acts to yaw the airplane to the left.

P-Factor

At a positive angle of attack, the downward moving propeller blade develops more lift than the upward moving blade (position B). This effect is most noticeable at high power settings (i.e., takeoffs and climbs). The net result is that the airplane wants to yaw to the left in both conditions (position C). This is known as *P-factor* or "power (induced) factor." The airplane's propeller *slipstream* (above) plays a major roll in yawing the airplane to the left under high power conditions (see Postflight Briefing #2-2 for technical info on P-Factor).

DOWNWARD MOVING BLADE: Downward moving propeller encounters wind blowing on it, thus providing more lift on this side.

UPWARD MOVING BLADE: Upward moving propeller encounters wind blowing with it, thus providing less lift on this side.*

*Note: The angle of attack of the upward moving blade is actually less than the downward moving blade (this is difficult to show, therefore, I simplified the concept). This difference in angle of attack is responsible for the differential lift produced by the propeller at high angles of attack.

C. P-Factor causes the airplane to yaw to the left when it is flown at higher angles of attack.

Rod Machado's How to Fly an Airplane Handbook

Technique #1–Using the Inclinometer to Fly Coordinated in a Turn

If you've ever made a turn in your car and had your sunglasses fly across the dashboard, you know how it feels to have centrifugal forces act sideways on your machine. Of course, if you properly enter or exit a freeway ramp your Lady Gaga mega-bling sunglasses typically stay put because those ramps are both banked and curved. Banking the ramp and curving it at just the right rate keeps the resultant forces associated with a turn acting straight down through your car seat. Something very similar happens when you bank an airplane with your ailerons, but only if you use your rudder to keep the nose pointed in the direction of the *turn arc* (the airplane's banked flight path through the air).

If the airplane's nose points in the direction of the turn arc, then the turn is coordinated and the force associated with the turn acts straight down through your seat, perpendicular to the airplane's lateral axis. The sunglasses on your instrument panel stay put. Similarly, the moveable ball in the inclinometer (or the slip-skid trapezoidal figure in your primary flight display) should also stay put in its center position (Figure 59, positions B, E and H). You can take that to the bank.

Let the nose point to the outside of the turn arc and the airplane *slips* to the inside of the banked flight path (Figure 59, positions A, D and G). That means those sunglasses and the ball in the inclinometer also slip to the inside of the turn. Let the nose point to the inside of the turn arc and the airplane skids to the outside of the banked flight path (Figure 59, positions C, F and I). Those sunglasses as well as the ball skid to the outside of the turn.

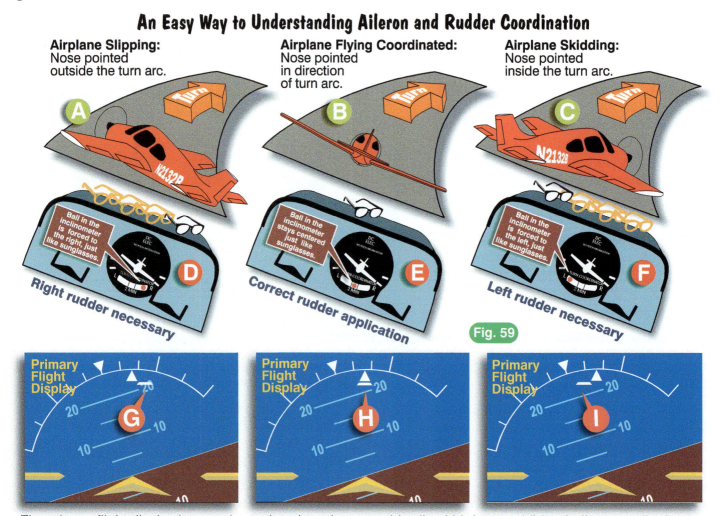

The primary flight display inserts above show how the moveable slip-skid (trapezoid) bar indicates a slipping turn (position G), a coordinated turn (position H) and a skidding turn (position I). These three indications correspond with the indications in inclinometers (D, E and F) above.

Chapter 2: Flying Straight and Level and Turning

Flying coordinated once the turn is established means keeping the ball in the inclinometer centered. If the ball is deflected to the right or left you should add right or left rudder respectively to bring the ball (or the slip-skid trapezoidal graphic in a glass cockpit display) back to the center position. Another way of thinking about this is to simply *step on the ball* to center it in the inclinometer. No, don't raise your foot to the panel and attempt to place it on the little ball. Unless you're a yoga master, this will put you in an awkward position in more ways than one. It might also cause your instructor to hastily scratch a note reminding him to ask his doctor for a stronger valium patch.

Using the inclinometer provides an accurate method of determining how coordinated your flight controls are when *established in a turn*. It's a technique that new pilots are likely to use first, since it's easy to interpret what the ball is telling you. On the other hand, use of the inclinometer isn't my preferred method of determining whether or not the airplane is flying coordinated once the turn is established or when rolling into or out of a turn. The primary reason for this is that you shouldn't be spending more than 10% of your time looking inside the cockpit during flight in VMC (visual meteorological conditions). And when there's even the slightest amount of turbulence, the inclinometer's ball tends to swing back and forth like a yo-yo doing the *rock the cradle* trick. This makes it difficult to use this instrument as a means of flying coordinated.

I prefer two other methods to determine the coordination of your flight controls. The first relies on looking outside the airplane while the second emphasizes how your derriere (your rear end) feels as you manipulate the flight controls. Both methods allow you to keep your eyes looking outside the cockpit instead of staring at the instrument panel. Anything that makes this happen is good.

Technique #2—The Visual Method of Flying Coordinated in a Turn

Under most conditions, when you're established in a turn you can tell if you're flying coordinated by looking over the nose to see if the airplane actually points in the same direction of its curved flight path over the ground. By looking directly ahead of you, it's possible to tell if the terrain you see moving under the airplane's nose is moving directly behind you or at some angle to your longitudinal axis.

If the terrain appears to move at a noticeable angle to the airplane's longitudinal axis, the nose isn't pointed precisely in the direction of turn (with one exception noted in the next paragraph). That means you must apply sufficient rudder to point the nose in the direction you're turning. For example, in Figure 60, position A, the airplane points in the direction it's turning. In Figure 60, positions B and C, the nose points to the outside and inside of the turn, respectively. A simple application of rudder to point the airplane in the direction it's turning will quickly coordinate your rudder and aileron flight controls.

Keeping Coordinated by Looking Over the Airplane's Nose in a Turn

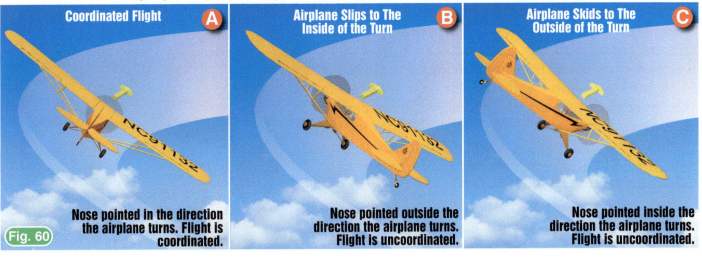

Fig. 60

This method, however, is less effective close to the ground when strong winds blow at an angle to the airplane's flight path. Strong crosswinds, after all, can noticeably alter the airplane's ground track. But at 1,000 feet or higher above the ground, this drift effect becomes less of a factor in visually evaluating your coordination.

Then again, if you're flying 1,000 feet AGL in 100 knot winds, good luck using this technique to help evaluate your coordination. At such a moment, you are probably less worried about flying coordinated and more worried about informing your flight school of their rental airplane's new location 300 miles downwind from the departure airport. And it goes without saying that this method is difficult to use at night. Then again, that's why you'll want to hold onto your pants for the ultimate method of determining your coordination while established in a turn. This method is my favorite and it's known as *flying by the seat of your pants*.

Technique #3—The Seat of the Pantaloons Method of Flying Coordinated

I call this third technique the ultimate method of sensing coordination because it can be used when established in a turn as well as when rolling into or out of a turn. This method allows you to sense whether or not the airplane needs more or less rudder deflection by sensing the pressure distribution on your rear end. We call this *seat of the pants flying* (yes, nudist pilots can use it, too) and you can actually develop sufficient sensitivity to the pressures on your derriere to tell whether or not you need to add or release rudder pressure. So let's talk about your pants (though this also works if you're wearing a dress).

When established in a turn (or even when rolling into or out of a turn), your flight controls are coordinated when the pressure on your derriere is evenly distributed between cheeks. Said another way, you won't feel more pressure on one cheek compared to the other. In Figure 61, position A, the airplane's nose points in the direction of turn and the horizontal component of lift and centrifugal force remain balanced, allowing the resultant force to push you directly downward in your seat. (See *Rod Machado's Private Pilot Handbook* for more information on flight forces.)

Let's assume you rolled into and/or are established in a right turn and haven't use any right rudder at all. Adverse yaw, p-factor, and slipstream all help yaw the

Coordination Rolls to Increase Proficiency

One of the most effective ways of improving your rudder and aileron coordination is with a maneuver known as *coordination rolls*. This maneuver is often erroneously referred to as a *Dutch roll,* which is actually an instability problem experienced in swept wing jets. The coordination roll is something pilots practice to become better pilots.

Here's how it works. You begin by finding an easily seen landmark near the horizon and placing your nose on it. Then you roll into a right turn using rudder and aileron in coordination. While *rolling*, the longitudinal axis will remain steady on the distant reference. Before the airplane can overcome its inertia and begin turning, however, you immediately roll into a bank to the left. Once again, before the airplane begins turning left, you roll back to the right. All the while the airplane's heading stays the same as long as the rudder and aileron are used in coordination.

You can perform this maneuver slowly by rolling into a shallow bank (perhaps 20 degrees or less). Or, you can use a larger bank (perhaps 45 degrees), but this requires a faster roll rate. During the roll, the inclinometer's ball *might* stay centered. This, might not happen in some airplanes, depending on the placement of its inclinometer. The objective is not to keep the ball centered. Instead, it's to keep the nose steady while rolling right and left.

As a graduate of the Torquemada school of flight training, this instructor has devised some very clever ways of conditioning you to fly coordinated.

Chapter 2: Flying Straight and Level and Turning

Flying Coordinated by Sensing the Pressure on Your Derriere

Fig. 61

nose slightly to the outside of the turn, to the left. The nose isn't turning quickly enough for the given angle of bank. The airplane is slipping to the inside of the turn and you feel pressure on the right side of your derriere (Figure 61, position B). The ball in the inclinometer also deflects to the right.

To return to coordinated flight, you need to point the nose slightly to the right, in the same direction of the curved path made by the airplane. By adding a little right rudder (or releasing any excessive left rudder pressure you're applying), the nose now points parallel to the curved path created by the specific bank angle chosen. You'll know the airplane is flying coordinated when you no longer feel the uneven pressure distribution on your derriere (and the ball in the inclinometer is centered).

What do you feel if you bank the airplane to the right and use too much right rudder when rolling into and/or when established in the turn? Now you're attempting to make the nose turn too fast for a given bank angle (Figure 61, position C). The airplane's nose points toward the inside of the turn, causing the entire airplane to skid to the left (outside the turn). As a result, you feel pressure on the left side of your derriere as the ball in the inclinometer deflects to the left.

To return to coordinated flight, you need to point the nose slightly to the left, in the same direction of the curved path made by the airplane. By adding a little left rudder or releasing the excessive right rudder pressure you might be applying, the nose now aligns itself parallel to the airplane's curved path created by the specific bank angle chosen. You'll know the airplane is flying coordinated when you no longer feel uneven pressure distribution on your derriere (and the ball in the inclinometer centers).

Here is where the ball in the inclinometer can teach your rear end a few new tricks—even if you have an old rear end. If you have difficulty telling when you're experiencing uneven pressure on your derriere, purposely deflect the ball in a turn with rudder pressure then consult your rear end. I mean, identify where you feel the uneven pressure. In this way you train yourself to detect and recognize uncoordinated flight. Your fanny is never too old to teach you a few important things about flying, and you can always tell the inclinometer to butt out. So make fanny friendly turns.

Rod Machado's How to Fly an Airplane Handbook

Three Different Types of Turns

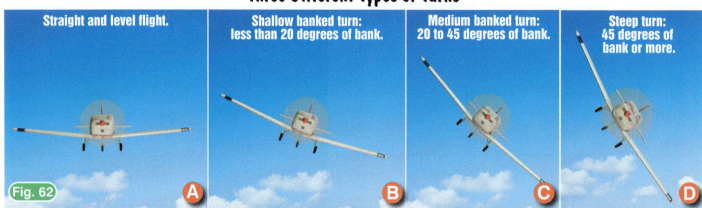

Fig. 62
A — Straight and level flight.
B — Shallow banked turn: less than 20 degrees of bank.
C — Medium banked turn: 20 to 45 degrees of bank.
D — Steep turn: 45 degrees of bank or more.

Three Types of Turns

Choosing the correct bank angle is another aspect of turning an airplane that's important to understand. Turns are traditionally divided into three categories of bank: a *shallow bank* (less than 20 degrees), a *medium bank* (20 degrees up to but not including 45 degrees) and a *steep bank* (45 degrees or more) as shown in Figure 62. The conventional wisdom suggests that, in a coordinated turn, the airplane's lateral stability tends to return the airplane to level flight when the bank is shallow, sustain the bank angle during a medium banked turn and steepen the bank angle during a steep turn. Unfortunately, this is more fiction that fact. The truth is that the airplane's built in lateral stability (the airplane's *dihedral*) only affects the airplane's bank angle when the airplane is *side slipping* and not when the turn is coordinated. Read more about this in Postflight Briefing #2-1 titled, *The Airplane's Lateral Stability* on Page 2-37.

What actually happens in many airplanes is that the bank angle tends to increase on its own as long as the turn is coordinated. This is often true even in a shallow banked turn for many airplanes. It does this because of the differential speed of the wings once the bank is established (see *Wing Speed Differential* sidebar next page).

For instance, in a shallow banked turn the outside wing has a slightly greater turn radius than the inside wing. This gives the outside wing a slightly higher speed relative to the inside wing, thus causing the outside wing to produce slightly more lift. This tends to increase the bank angle unless you counter the effect by holding a slight amount of aileron opposite the turn. Because the turn radius of a shallow banked turn is so large, this overbanking tendency is not very noticeable on most general aviation airplanes. It's a bit more noticeable, however, on aircraft with very long and thin wings, such as a glider.

As you increase the bank angle in a coordinated turn, the airplane's turning radius decreases resulting in a slight increase in speed differential between the inside and outside wing. You can visualize this by imagining a slow flying airplane with a turn radius so

Crossed by Crossed Controls?

Why does it seem like you're flying with your controls *crossed* (left yoke deflection and right rudder application as shown below) in some turns despite the controls being perfectly coordinated? In other words, the inclinometer's ball is centered, the nose points in the direction the airplane turns and you don't feel uneven pressures on your cheeks, yet you're applying left aileron and right rudder.

Generally speaking (even if you don't hold that rank) a turn (often a steeper turn) to the right in most small airplanes requires a left yoke deflection to prevent overbanking and considerable right rudder pressure to keep the flight coordinated. In a right turn, the airplane's power-induced left turning tendency acts like a push on the left rudder and pulls the airplane's nose toward the outside (to the left) of the turn. Sometimes the left yawing tendency in a right turn is so strong (i.e., at full power and slow speeds) that you actually have to add considerable right rudder to keep the airplane coordinated while moving the yoke to the left to maintain the desired bank angle. Despite the controls being crossed, you'll know you're flying coordinated because the nose points in the direction the airplane turns, the ball in the inclinometer is centered and a cheek check indicates that there are no uneven forces on your derriere.

Crossed controls

Chapter 2: Flying Straight and Level and Turning

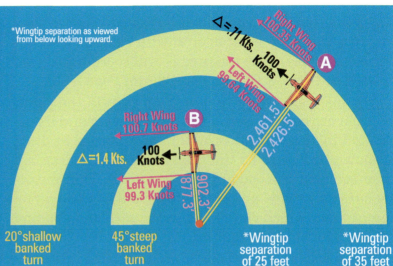

Wing Speed Differential

In a 20° shallow banked turn (airplane A) with a ground speed of 100 knots, the difference in wingtip speeds is: 100.35 knots – 99.64 knots = .71 knots.

At a 45° (steep) bank turn (airplane B) with a ground speed of 100 knots, the difference in wingtip speeds is: 100.7 knots - 99.3 knots = 1.4 knots.

It's clear that in a shallow banked turn (airplane A), the outside wing certainly does move faster than the inside wing, thus explaining the slight over-banking tendency even in shallow banked turns. However, at a steeper bank of 45° (airplane B), the difference in speeds between the inside wing and outside wing is relatively larger despite the distance between those wings decreasing with an increase in bank angle. This explains the slightly larger overbanking tendency in turns at 45° of bank.

small that the wing inside the turn literally pivots on its wingtip while the outside wing moves at a much faster speed (an exaggeration, of course). Therefore, the airplane's overbanking tendency becomes a bit more noticeable as the bank increases (but only up to a point that I'll discuss shortly). As a result, you might find yourself having to hold a larger amount opposite aileron to keep the bank angle from increasing at steeper bank angles.

Yes, it's true that as the bank angle steepens, the wingtips move closer together in the vertical plane, thus diminishing their speed differential (you can visualize this by thinking how 90 degrees of bank results in zero difference in wing speeds relative to the ground). That said, you're not likely to notice any *decrease* in the airplane's overbanking tendency as the bank angle becomes even steeper.

Now, all this is nice to know information but what really happens to your bank angle in an airplane is a bit more complicated. Some high-wing airplanes such as the Cessna 210 produce a *pendulum effect* (big heavy fuselage under the wings) that tend to roll the airplane to level flight in a shallow banked turn. This is the reason these airplanes have a good reputation as being stable aerodynamic platforms. This means you might need to hold aileron *into* the turn to sustain a shallow bank angle. Some low-wing aerobatic airplanes, however, experience very little pendulum effect in a turn. Once a coordinated turn is established in these airplanes the bank angle tends to noticeably increase. This requires you to hold aileron *against* the turn regardless of the angle of bank.

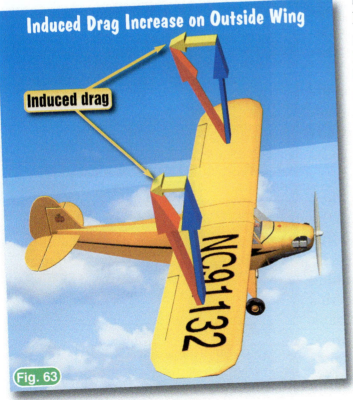

Fig. 63

Ultimately, it doesn't matter what the banking tendency of your airplane is when you're established in a coordinated turn. As a pilot, your job is to establish the turn then use your rudder and ailerons as appropriate to produce a coordinated turn.

This is one reason that you might find yourself established in a steeper turn while holding aileron opposite the direction of turn and simultaneously using rudder in the direction of turn just to keep the controls coordinated. Yes, it appears that your controls are crossed because they are crossed (left or right aileron with right or left rudder, respectively). But the turn is still coordinated (see *Crossed by Crossed Controls* sidebar on Page 2-30).

For instance, if you're in a steep turn to the right, then the increased speed of the outside wing and its associated increase in lift results in an increase in drag, as shown in Figure 63 (induced and parasite drag are discussed near the end of Chapter Three). That means the outside wing is pulling the nose outside the direction of turn, which can result in the airplane slipping unless right rudder is applied.

This is one reason you might need to hold a little rudder pressure in the direction of turn to remain in coordinated flight when turning steeply. Then again, given the higher power conditions and increase in angle of attack associated with a steeper turn, the airplane's left turning tendency might amplify this effect when turning steeply to the right. Steeper turns to the left, however, typically result in the airplane's left turning tendencies being countered by the increase in induced drag on the outside wing. Less rudder pressure is often needed when entering and when established in a steeper turn to the left. These observations, however, do vary from airplane to airplane.

So, we've turned full circle and we're back where we started, which is at *Rod's Turning Pragmatism Rule #1* regarding turns. Place the airplane in the desired degree of bank with the ailerons, and keep it at that bank with the ailerons. I don't care which way you have to deflect the ailerons as long as the airplane remains at the targeted bank angle. Simultaneously use the rudder to keep the nose pointed in the direction of turn. It really *is* that simple.

Identifying Your Bank Angle

One of the challenges of banking an airplane is identifying the bank angle made between the wings and the horizon. There are a few methods that help make this assessment much easier for you.

If your airplane has a high wing and struts, banking the airplane until the strut appears level with the earth's surface gives you approximately 30 to 35 degrees of bank (Figure 64, position A). Of course, this varies between airplanes, so during your next preflight, grab your protractor and then take a picture of the strut with your smartphone. Measure the angle the strut makes with the

Four Ways to Identify Your Bank Angle

Use your strut as a protractor to estimate bank angle.

Use your panel to help estimate bank angle.

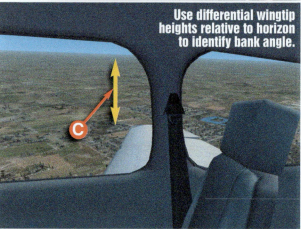
Use differential wingtip heights relative to horizon to identify bank angle.

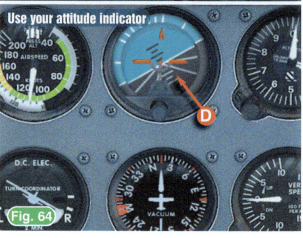
Use your attitude indicator.

Fig. 64

Chapter 2: Flying Straight and Level and Turning

ground. That's your bank angle. Aren't you happy you paid attention during geometry class and that you bought a phone with a camera? You've now strutted your stuff.

In the air, you can estimate your bank angle by the angle formed between the top of the instrument panel and the horizon (Figure 64, position B). It's also possible to determine your bank with a bit of experience by the amount each wingtip is displaced above or below the horizon (Figure 64, position C). For new pilots, it's best to sneak a peek at the attitude indicator to initially determine the correct bank angle (Figure 64, position D). With experience, you'll learn to use outside visual clues to make this assessment, which is preferable to having your eyes focused inside the cockpit. Remember, there are no airplanes in your cockpit.

Determining Your Pitch Attitude in a Turn

When entering a level turn from straight and level flight, you need to properly assess the airplane's pitch attitude to prevent accidentally climbing or descending. In tandem seated airplanes (one person seated behind the other) and side-by-side seated airplanes, you assess your pitch attitude by looking over the part of the cowling that's *directly ahead of you* during the turn. In side-by-side seated airplanes you also look *directly ahead of you* based on your seating position. This means that you're looking slightly to the left of the center of the cowling, but not down the center of the cowling (see sidebar: *Rotation About the Longitudinal Axis*). Where you look is a very important concept, and you absolutely must understand this point.

Rotation About the Longitudinal Axis

No doubt, you've got to be thinking about how the dot-horizon reference can be the same for a right turn as well as a left turn when you're sitting to the left of the airplane's axis of rotation (the longitudinal axis) in side-by-side seated airplanes. Doesn't it seem that rotating right or left about the longitudinal axis would cause the cowling section directly ahead of you to rise or descend in relation to the horizon, respectively?

Well, a lot of things aren't what they seem, such as in my sixth grade Catholic school class when the sister summoned me to the front of the class and demanded that I renounce Satan. It seemed like she said, "Announce Satan." You can imagine how well that went. Amen.

The movement of the horizon-dot reference about the longitudinal axis is different than it seems because it provides the same accurate pitch attitude reference on side-by-side seated airplanes as it does in tandem seated airplanes as long as the dot is placed directly ahead of you (not over the center of the cowling which is slightly to your right) as you sit in the left seat (Picture #1). The reason for this lies in the small vertical separation (in inches) between your eyes and that dot in relation to a very distant horizon line. Here's a non-airplane experiment you can try to prove this point.

Go outside, stand up straight and move your glasses down the bridge of your nose (hopefully you don't have a drawbridge nose) so that the top rim of your glasses is on the distant horizon line. Let the top rim of your glasses represent the location of the dot placed on the windshield over the distant horizon line. The height between your eyes and the rim (i.e., the dot) will remain constant as long as your glasses don't move or your nose doesn't fall off. Now, keep your back straight and bend your knees to move up and down a bit. You'll notice that the top rim of your eyeglasses (the dot) remains on the horizon line, despite your entire body moving up and down.

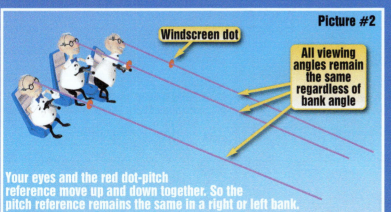

In a similar way, when you make a right and left turn in the airplane, you are rotating about the center of the airplane, thus moving up and down a few inches relative to the longitudinal axis (Picture #2). Since your eyes and the dot move up and down together, you can't detect this vertical movement on a horizon that is so far off in the distance.

This is why a windscreen dot placed on the horizon line directly ahead of your seat provides a good aircraft pitch reference during a right or left turn. Of course, the same thing applies when you're sitting in the right seat as long as you place the dot directly ahead of you in that seat.

In straight and level flight, the top of the engine cowling (or instrument panel) appears displaced slightly below the horizon. That's because your eyes are in your head (a result of your father not being a snail) and your head is above your shoulders and this entire assembly is typically perched high enough in the seat so that you look down at the cowling (I'm assuming you aren't a competitive weight lifter and still have a neck). As we've already discussed, you can place a small dot on the windscreen, or the triangle-shaped tiny corner of a Post-it, to mark the horizon's position based on your seating height. During a shallow banked turn, you only

The Pitch Reference Dot and Bank Angle

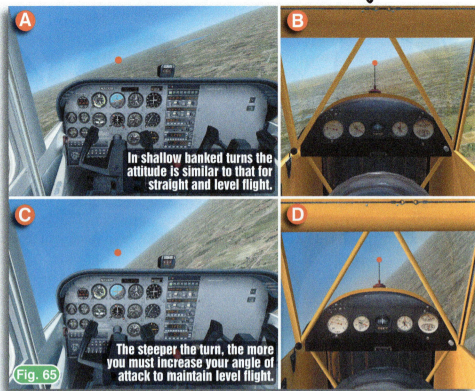

A — In shallow banked turns the attitude is similar to that for straight and level flight.

B

C — The steeper the turn, the more you must increase your angle of attack to maintain level flight. Fig. 65

D

need to keep the dot *approximately* on the horizon to remain in level flight (Figure 45, positions A and B), occasionally cross checking the altimeter to ensure that your altitude is constant.

I said *approximately* because making a turn requires that some of the airplane's lifting force be directed horizontally. Using some of the airplane's total lifting force (the force that's keeping you in the air) to turn sideways, means you'll experience a reduction in the vertical component of lift. This typically results in the nose of your airplane pitching downward slightly unless you compensate by increasing your angle of attack using elevator back pressure. That's right. In a turn you want to increase the angle of attack to generate more lift, so you apply aft pressure on the yoke (see sidebar on Page 2-35: *How to Increase Lift in a Turn*). How much back pressure? The larger the bank angle, the greater the amount of back pressure that must be applied on the yoke to maintain level flight.

For shallow and medium banked turns, as the bank increases the dot will have to be higher above its previous position on the horizon line due to the increasing angle of attack required to maintain altitude in the turn (Figure 65, positions C and D). When performing steep turns, however, the dot's movement is expressed horizontally as well as vertically in the windscreen. You can read about this in Chapter 12 in the sidebar titled, *Dot Is on the Level In Steep Turns*.

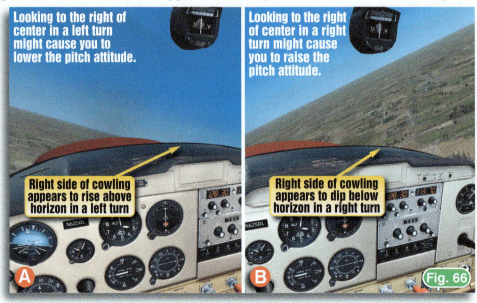

A — Looking to the right of center in a left turn might cause you to lower the pitch attitude. Right side of cowling appears to rise above horizon in a left turn

B — Looking to the right of center in a right turn might cause you to raise the pitch attitude. Right side of cowling appears to dip below horizon in a right turn

Fig. 66

Chapter 2: Flying Straight and Level and Turning

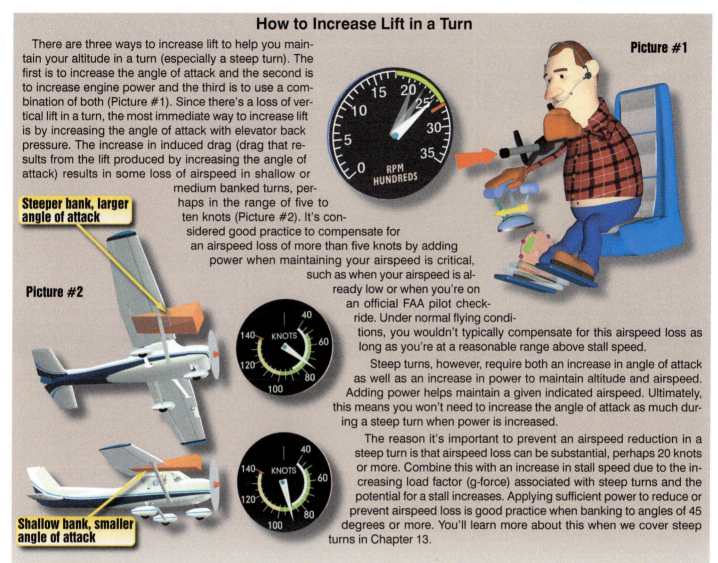

How to Increase Lift in a Turn

There are three ways to increase lift to help you maintain your altitude in a turn (especially a steep turn). The first is to increase the angle of attack and the second is to increase engine power and the third is to use a combination of both (Picture #1). Since there's a loss of vertical lift in a turn, the most immediate way to increase lift is by increasing the angle of attack with elevator back pressure. The increase in induced drag (drag that results from the lift produced by increasing the angle of attack) results in some loss of airspeed in shallow or medium banked turns, perhaps in the range of five to ten knots (Picture #2). It's considered good practice to compensate for an airspeed loss of more than five knots by adding power when maintaining your airspeed is critical, such as when your airspeed is already low or when you're on an official FAA pilot checkride. Under normal flying conditions, you wouldn't typically compensate for this airspeed loss as long as you're at a reasonable range above stall speed.

Steep turns, however, require both an increase in angle of attack as well as an increase in power to maintain altitude and airspeed. Adding power helps maintain a given indicated airspeed. Ultimately, this means you won't need to increase the angle of attack as much during a steep turn when power is increased.

The reason it's important to prevent an airspeed reduction in a steep turn is that airspeed loss can be substantial, perhaps 20 knots or more. Combine this with an increase in stall speed due to the increasing load factor (g-force) associated with steep turns and the potential for a stall increases. Applying sufficient power to reduce or prevent airspeed loss is good practice when banking to angles of 45 degrees or more. You'll learn more about this when we cover steep turns in Chapter 13.

On side-by-side seated airplanes, if you make the mistake of choosing your attitude by looking over the *center* of the cowling (instead of directly *ahead of you*) or even worse, the right side of the cowling, then you'll suffer from something known as a *parallax error*. For instance, looking to the right of the very center of the cowling in a left turn (you're in the left seat) leads you to believe that the nose is pitched above the horizon (Figure 66, position A). You'll probably compensate by lowering the nose, resulting in a loss of altitude. Looking at the right side of the cowling in a right turn (Figure 66, position B) leads you to believe that the nose is pitched below the horizon. You'll probably compensate by raising the nose, resulting in a gain of altitude. This is why some students (who don't use a dot reference directly ahead of their seated position) tend to climb in a right turn and descend in a left turn.

Of course, if you must raise the dot slightly above the horizon to remain in level flight in a turn, then the dot is no longer on the horizon. So how are you supposed to calibrate your pitch attitude properly in this instance? No problem. You just remember the distance the dot is above the horizon and keep it that distance above the horizon in the turn. The dot is simply an initial tool to provide a reference to measure the airplane's attitude as well as to remind you to evaluate your attitude by looking directly ahead of you, not to the middle or right side of the airplane. After a few hours of flight, you won't need a window dot because you'll easily be able to select any attitude or evaluate the airplane's pitch attitude by referencing the cowling's position relative to the horizon, doing so even if the airplane is descending or climbing.

Avoiding a Bad Case of the "Leans"

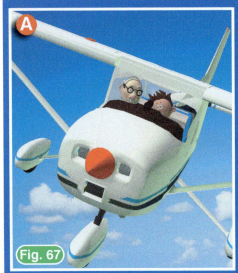

Fig. 67

The student in position A leans to the right in a left turn while the student in position B leans to the left in a right turn. Leaning while turning impedes your ability to evaluate your pitch and bank attitude. The student in position C gets it right. Sometimes instructors will place their hand behind your neck to keep you from leaning in a turn. These instructors often go by the name, "Geppetto."

There is one other very big issue that can nullify everything I've taught you about making turns. I'm speaking of leaning while the airplane banks right or left. This is a very big issue for most people on their first few flights. It's a natural human reaction to attempt to remain upright the moment you feel or see yourself beginning to tilt.

For instance, when first introduced to a left turn, it's common for the flight instructor to feel his student's right shoulder rubbing his left shoulder, which might rub him the wrong way (Figure 67, position A). The student is honoring his biological instinct to remain vertical as the airplane banks to the left. Whenever I sense this happening with my student, I'll use my shoulder to nudge him or her back into the vertical position and mention that now is not a good time for a nap. Of course, in a right turn (Figure 67, position B) the student occasionally attempts to lean to the left. This is often difficult to do since there's a door or a section of the fuselage over there. Although I did have one student lean sufficiently to pop the door open. I suggested to him that it might be best if he waited until we landed to exit the airplane.

The problem with leaning in the seat is that you are no longer looking directly ahead of you where your reference dot is located. This makes it difficult to properly evaluate your pitch attitude much less your bank angle. So keep the idea of remaining upright in your seat in mind (Figure 67, position C). It won't take long before you'll overcome this natural tendency to lean while turning.

I can assure you that if the cockpit door of a big airliner pops open while the airplane is in a turn, you won't see the pilots leaning in their seats. If you do, then don't eat the fish because you might have to help those pilots land. There's a good chance they might not have as much experience as they've indicated on their resumes.

Speaking of flying resumes, let's add more to yours by qualifying you to perform climbs and descents. So it's onto our next chapter dealing with the ups and downs of flight.

Chapter 2: Flying Straight and Level and Turning

Postflight Briefing #2-1 The Airplane's Lateral Stability

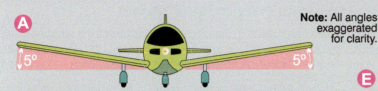

Note: All angles exaggerated for clarity.

Most airplanes have a structural feature known as *dihedral*. Dihedral is the positive angle between the lateral axis of the airplane and a line through the center of each wing (airplane A). The purpose of this feature is to increase the airplane's static lateral stability by returning the airplane to wings-level flight when it's forced into an intentional or accidental sideslip. Here's how this process works.

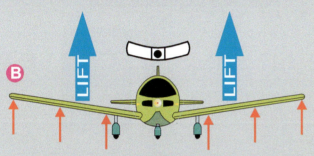

In wings-level flight, the relative wind rises from ahead of and below the wing's leading edge and strikes the wing at something close to a perpendicular angle to its lateral axis (airplane B). The lift produced by each wing is the same in wings-level flight.

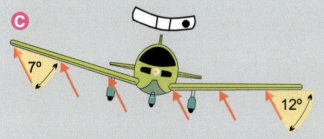

The moment the airplane is forced into a sideslip either intentionally or unintentionally, the relative wind strikes each wing at a slightly different angle (airplane C). The left wing has the relative wind striking its surface at a slightly larger angle than that striking the right wing.

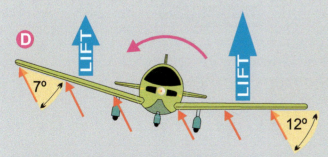

The net result of the sideslip (airplane D) is that the left wing temporarily produces more lift than the right wing, resulting in the airplane returning to wings-level flight.

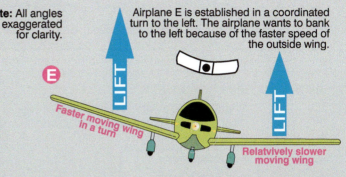

Airplane E is established in a coordinated turn to the left. The airplane wants to bank to the left because of the faster speed of the outside wing.

It's a common misconception among pilots that dihedral affects an airplane in a coordinated turn (in lieu of a sideslipping turn). In reality, dihedral has no effect on an airplane in a coordinated turn. Why? Because the relative wind strikes each wing at approximately the same head-on angle experienced in wings-level flight. So there's no difference in lift produced between each wing by dihedral in a coordinated turn.

On the other hand, we've already seen that the moment a turn begins, the outside wing turns at a slightly faster speed than the inside wing (airplane E). This causes the outside wing to produce slightly more lift and tends to increase the bank angle (as long as the turn is kept coordinated and no sideslip occurs). Therefore, when most airplanes are placed in a coordinated turn (yes, irrespective of bank angle), the tendency is for the bank to increase, not decrease. This bank-increasing tendency, however, does vary between airplanes.

For instance, some high wing airplanes are *less affected* by this *bank increasing* tendency in a coordinated turn because the lateral stability of these airplanes is aided by something known as the *pendulum effect*. As you've probably noticed, high wing airplanes have much less dihedral than low wing airplanes (airplane F).

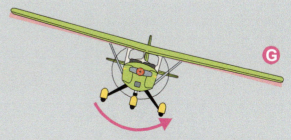

It turns out that the pull by gravity on the fuselage and its contents tends to return the airplane to wings-level flight when the airplane is banked, regardless of whether the bank results in a slip or a coordinated turn (airplane G).

Postflight Briefing #2-2 P-Factor

A. P-Factor (Power Factor) - A Technical Explanation for the Technically Inclined

The motion of the propeller and the airplane combine to produce a *vector* representing the prop's motion through the air (green and blue dashed arrows). At low angles of attack, the prop movement vectors are nearly the same size and make nearly the same angle with the airplane-generated relative wind. Therefore, the upward and downward moving blades have similar angles of attack and produce similar amounts of thrust. Therefore, there is very little P-factor produced thus, no appreciable left tuning tendency is present.

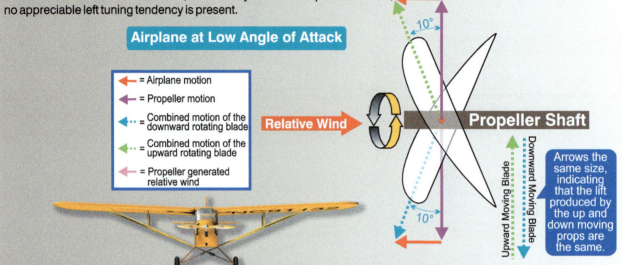

B.

At higher angles of attack, the downward moving blade moves forward slightly in the same direction of airplane motion. Therefore, the net relative wind striking this propeller is a *combination* of propeller motion (pink arrow) and airplane motion (red arrow). The upward moving blade moves opposite the motion of the airplane. Therefore, the net relative wind striking the upward moving blade is found by subtracting the propeller motion from the airplane's motion (brown arrow, as shown by insert). The net result is that the angle of attack and the airspeed of the upward moving blade is less than the angle of attack and the airspeed of the downward moving blade. Therefore, the downward moving blade produces more lift when the airplane is at a positive angle of attack. This results in the airplane yawing to the left as a result of P-factor. This is most noticeable at higher power settings.

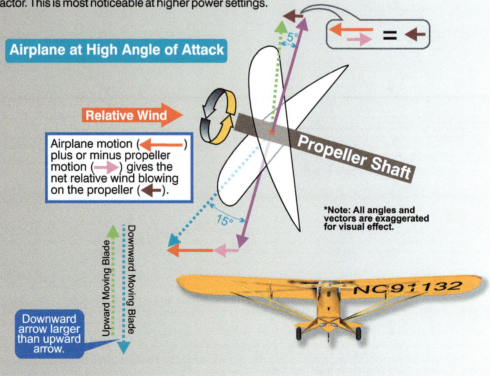

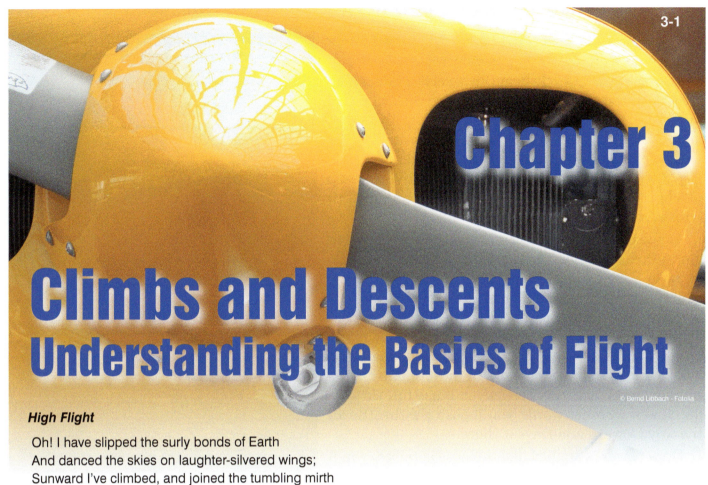

Chapter 3
Climbs and Descents
Understanding the Basics of Flight

High Flight

Oh! I have slipped the surly bonds of Earth
And danced the skies on laughter-silvered wings;
Sunward I've climbed, and joined the tumbling mirth
of sun-split clouds, — and done a hundred things
You have not dreamed of — wheeled and soared and swung
High in the sunlit silence. Hov'ring there,
I've chased the shouting wind along, and flung
My eager craft through footless halls of air....
                              John Gillespie Magee, Jr.

Up? Yeah, yeah, that's the ticket.

Does anything about the first half of John Gillespie Magee's famous poem strike your fancy? Do you have a pulse? Of course you do and of course it does. The poem *High Flight* is epic in several ways not the least of which is that it celebrates what pilots do, can do or think they can do aloft. And the word *aloft* is key here.

You're not doing anything aloft unless you can get there. That's what this chapters is about. It's about the lofty goals of getting your airplane up in the air then finding a way to get yourself back down once you're done high flighting. We call this *climbing* and *descending* and it's the last two of the four basic fundamentals of flight.

So things are starting to look up for you. Or at least they should because that's typically where you focus your attention when you climb. Let's see how to make this happen.

Climbs

To enter a climb, you'll use our previous performance equation: A+P=P. Begin by selecting a nose-up attitude based on your prior experience with climbing in your particular airplane (Figure 1) while always remembering that we fly attitude but think angle of attack. Even if you don't have prior experience in any airplane, climbs always involve some positive nose-up pitch attitude, perhaps in the range of three to 10 degrees or more.

As the pitch attitude increases and the airspeed begins decreasing, apply full power (it's also permissible to raise the nose and apply power simultaneously). Your objective here it to select the climb attitude that gives you the desired climb airspeed. Remember that *full power* is typically the maximum allowable climb power you can use for taking off or climbing, based on what your POH recommends. In most smaller, non-complex airplanes, this means you'll use full throttle for climbs. In other words, you'll push the throttle all the way forward and leave it there.

Once power is applied and the nose is raised, you'll add nose-up trim to reduce any elevator back pressure you're holding to maintain climb attitude (if you're climbing through less than 500 feet, you might want to forgo use of any trim because of the climb's short

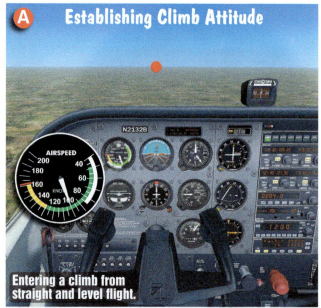

A Establishing Climb Attitude

Entering a climb from straight and level flight.

B Full power added and pitch attitude increased.

C Another useful attitude reference

Climb attitude is established when the desired airspeed is obtained. Then the airplane is trimmed for this attitude.

Fig. 2

Raising the Nose to Climb Attitude

Desired climb attitude and climb speed

Full Power Applied

Fig. 1

Chapter 3: Climbs and Descents

duration). Finally, you'll adjust the pitch attitude slightly to give you the target airspeed for the climb (in the absence of any other recommendation or choice, it's always best to climb at Vy, your airplane's *best rate of climb* speed).

The dot directly ahead of your seated position that was previously placed on the horizon line (Figure 2, position A) is now located a little above the horizon (Figure 2 positions B and C). You can still use the dot as an attitude reference by taking a mental snapshot of its height above the horizon line (you did load your mental camera, didn't you?). You can also use a section of the cowling or instrument panel directly in front of you that intersects the horizon, as shown by the arrow in Figure 2, position C.

Sometimes it's difficult to see the horizon line over the cowling during a climb. So it's perfectly reasonable to match up some portion of your instrument panel with the horizon line to establish your pitch attitude. Since the airplane isn't turning, it really doesn't matter if that panel-horizon calibration point is to the right or left of normal seated-view position (Figure 2, position C). Either choice becomes your new horizon-pitch reference for climbing in straight flight.

How do you make adjustments in pitch attitude to achieve the desired climb airspeed? Take a look at Figure 3, position A, which shows the attitude for straight and level flight, and the attitude for a climb at an airspeed of 80 knots (Figure 3, position B). If your present airspeed is lower than what's targeted (Figure 3, position C), you'll decrease the pitch attitude *slightly* and wait to see how the airspeed changes. Think about it. If the power is fixed (meaning that you're not changing power settings because you're using full power), then lowering the nose results in your climbing a less steep hill. That means you'll speed up a bit.

If your airspeed is too high (Figure 3, position D), then raising the nose results in climbing a steeper hill. That means you'll slow down a little. In both instances, you should lower or raise the nose a small amount and observe the airspeed change. The key here is *not* to chase the airspeed needle, which means you are raising or lowering your nose in an attempt to *immediately* stop the motion of the airspeed needle. This is a very common problem with inexperienced pilots. Because the airplane has inertia, it takes a few seconds for a change in pitch to produce a stabilized airspeed indication.

If you adjust your attitude and expect to see an immediate airspeed change, then you'll end up chasing the airspeed needle over the entire planet, or at least a large section of

Fig. 3

Why Do Airplanes Climb With Full Power?

Because they can't use their arms?

There are several reasons you climb with maximum allowable power in an airplane. First, there's no practical benefit to minimizing climb performance unless there's something above you that's scary, such as the UFO mother ship. Climbing quickly produces several benefits. First, it allows you get to the higher mid-altitudes (i.e., 8,000 to 10,000 feet MSL) as soon as possible. This is a good thing since airplanes typically perform better at these altitudes. It also means that you spend less time in climb attitude where it's always a bit more challenging to see other aircraft ahead of you.

Finally, when the throttle (on most airplanes) is moved to the full power position (that's typically full forward or nearly so), the fuel system's power enrichment valve opens, allowing more fuel to enter the cylinders. This extra fuel helps cool the engine and reduce the high cylinder head temperatures associated with full power climbs. If you tried climbing with the throttle set to less that recommended climb power you might actually generate more engine heat than you would by pushing the throttle forward to the recommended setting.

it. So make a small adjustment then be patient. Wait to see what airspeed you get. If this value doesn't make you happy, then make another small adjustment. Attitude adjustments are the key to in-flight happiness.

Once you've adjusted the pitch attitude to give you the correct climb airspeed, apply the final trim adjustment. Trim to keep the airplane in its present attitude. Look directly over your panel at your grease dot and trim away the pressure on your hand that's holding that dot the desired distance above the horizon line. When the airplane's properly trimmed, you can release nearly all the pressure of your grip and the attitude remains constant. If, however, the attitude begins to change, repeat this procedure.

During your climb entry, you'll notice that I recommended raising the nose first, then adding full power. This is done to prevent an engine over-speed, which is possible in some airplanes in level flight since there is relatively less aerodynamic load on the propeller and because of the high (cruise) power already being used (Figure 4). On the other hand, it's perfectly acceptable to raise the nose and apply power at the same time as long as your engine RPM doesn't exceed its redline value (or other established limits for RPM). This procedure still follows the equation: A+P=P.

One of the big surprises you'll discover when climbing straight ahead is just how much right rudder is required to correct for the airplane's power-induced left turning tendency. Propeller slipstream has a strong influence on the airplane's left turning tendency, and P-factor becomes a big player at the slow airspeeds and higher angles of attack associated with the climb.

As you are increasing your pitch attitude and adding power for the climb, you'll simultaneously but gently apply more right rudder

Prevent Propeller Overspeed

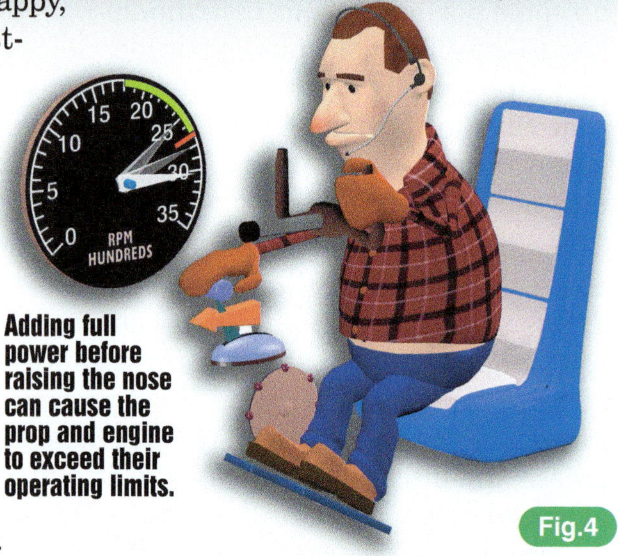

Adding full power before raising the nose can cause the prop and engine to exceed their operating limits.

Fig.4

Entering the Climb

Steps to enter a climb:
1. Increase pitch attitude
2. Add power and simultaneously
3. Add sufficient right rudder
4. Trim the airplane nose up

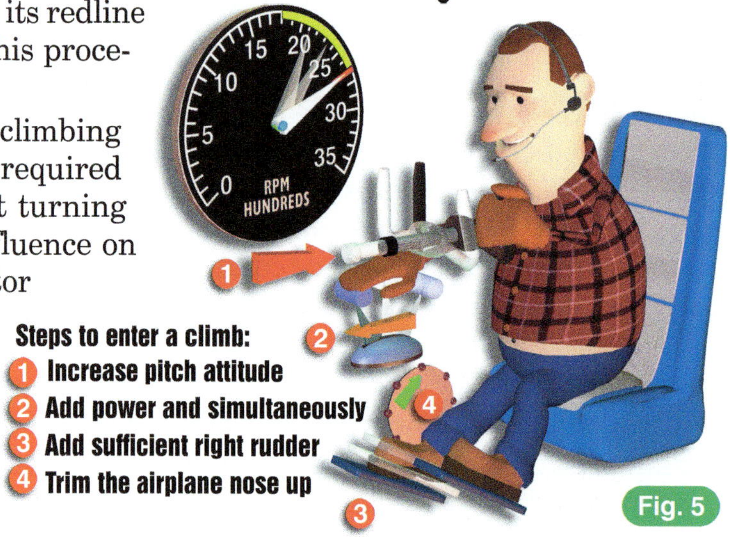

Fig. 5

Chapter 3: Climbs and Descents

pressure to keep the airplane moving straight ahead (keep its heading constant), as shown in Figure 5. Do this by looking directly over the cowling for heading and pitch control. If your airplane has elevator, aileron and rudder trim, then you'll trim the elevator first, rudder next, followed by aileron trim last.

Leveling Off From a Climb

No doubt there's a country western song with an aviation theme titled, *I'm High Over You Because I've Been Climbing Forever*. In the real world, you can't climb forever. Eventually, you climb to a specific altitude and then level off.

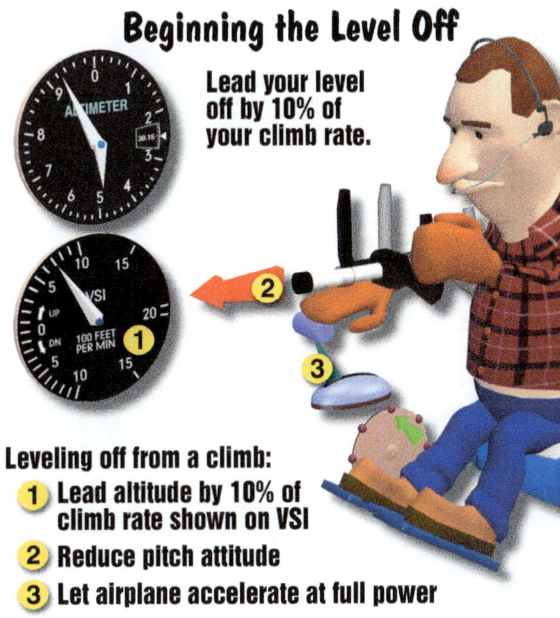

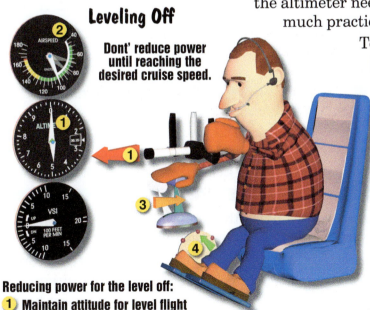

Beginning the Level Off
Lead your level off by 10% of your climb rate.

Leveling off from a climb:
1. Lead altitude by 10% of climb rate shown on VSI
2. Reduce pitch attitude
3. Let airplane accelerate at full power

Fig. 6

Leveling Off
Dont' reduce power until reaching the desired cruise speed.

Reducing power for the level off:
1. Maintain attitude for level flight
2. Accelerate to desired airspeed
3. Reduce power to desired RPM
4. Trim for level flight

Fig. 7

To do so, you use the same principle of A+P=P. Keeping in mind that the airplane is a large piece of machinery with considerable inertia that doesn't change status instantly, and also keeping in mind that the goal is a graceful transition for you and your passengers, you need to start leveling off *before* you reach the final altitude. This is called *leading* the level-off.

The general rule for leveling off is to take 10% of the climb rate (shown on the VSI) and use this as your altitude lead. If you're climbing at 700 feet per minute and want to level off at 5,000 feet, then you'll lead the level-off by 70 feet, meaning that you'll begin the level off when the altimeter reads 4,930 feet (Figure 6). Yes, I know that "five out of four people" have trouble with math, but finding 10% of something is pretty easy, right? Then again, in most of the small airplanes that you'll typically fly, using a 50-foot lead for leveling off works just fine. That's what I do in small airplanes. I wait until I'm within 50 feet of the correct altitude, then apply slight forward pressure, timing this properly to stop the altimeter needle at the target altitude. It really doesn't take much practice to get good at this.

To complete the level-off from a climb, you'll lower the nose to the attitude for straight and level flight (remember your dot?) by applying forward pressure on the yoke. Since your climb speed is slower than your typical cruise speed, you should leave the throttle set at full power until the airplane accelerates to the desired cruise speed. As the airplane accelerates in level flight, apply an initial twist of nose-down trim to help relieve the forward pressure you're using on the yoke.

When the airplane reaches the correct cruise speed, reduce power to the value recommended by your POH. If you don't have a recommended power setting, then just set the power for the approximate value needed to maintain the selected cruise speed (Figure 7). Take your best guess at what this setting

Climbing in a Complex Airplane

If you're entering a climb in a complex airplane (airplanes having a controllable pitch propeller, retractable gear and flaps), you'll want to raise the nose, then slowly move the propeller control forward to achieve the correct climb RPM, followed by movement of the throttle to achieve the desired climb manifold pressure. Of course, if the RPM is already at the value required for climb, then you'll just move the throttle forward to the desired climb manifold pressure.

The general idea here is to think about keeping the propeller lever physically forward of the throttle lever to prevent excessive cylinder pressures resulting from a high power, low RPM condition (Picture #1). In other words, when increasing power, move the prop lever forward first, followed by the throttle. When decreasing power, move the throttle rearward first, followed by the prop lever. (Here I'm talking about the "sequence" of movement between the propeller control and the throttle.)

Keep in mind that when you're climbing in a non-turbocharged airplane having a constant speed propeller, you might need to continually increase the manifold pressure about one inch for every thousand feet of altitude gain. That's because atmospheric pressure decreases about one inch per thousand feet and it's the outside atmospheric pressure that determines how much pressure is available to force air into your induction manifold (Picture #2).

For instance, if you depart a sea level airport and your recommended climb power is 25 inches of manifold pressure and 2,500 RPM, as you climb through 1,000 feet your manifold pressure has reduced to approximately 24 inches (the RPM remains constant because this airplane has a constant speed propeller). At 1,000 feet (and for every successive thousand foot interval) you should move the throttle forward slightly to increase the manifold pressure one inch to maintain 25 inches of climb power.

Of course, when you reach approximately 5,000 of altitude, the outside pressure will be about 25 inches of mercury. In a non-turbocharged airplane this means that your throttle will, most likely, be full forward and your manifold pressure gauge (which now essentially behaves like an altimeter) reads 25 inches. As you continue to climb, your manifold pressure will decrease one inch for every thousand feet of altitude gain, but now there's nothing you can do about it…except buy an airplane with a turbocharger.

This same process applies in reverse when descending. If you're descending with a constant manifold pressure, you can expect the manifold pressure to increase one inch per thousand feet as the atmospheric pressure increases during the descent. That means you'll have to pull the throttle back at every thousand-foot interval to reduce the manifold pressure to the correct power value.

Why do we use 1,000-foot intervals to make these power adjustments? It's simply a matter of convention. Yes, you could do this at 100 foot intervals but it would be hard, if not impossible, to detect 1/10th of an inch of manifold pressure change unless you're wearing Hubble-type telescopic glasses (which require repairs by an astronaut about every five years).

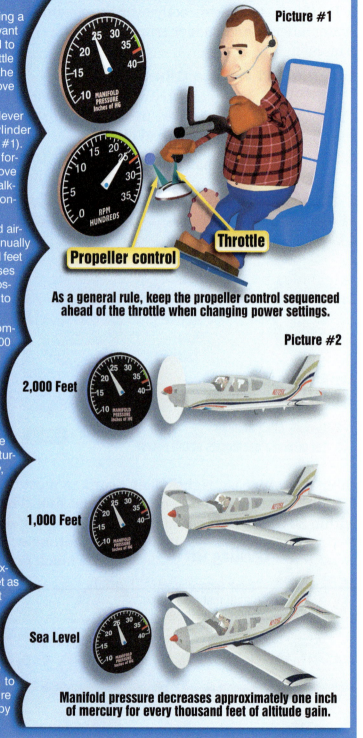

Picture #1

As a general rule, keep the propeller control sequenced ahead of the throttle when changing power settings.

Picture #2

Manifold pressure decreases approximately one inch of mercury for every thousand feet of altitude gain.

is, then modify it as necessary. Once the speed is appropriate, apply the final elevator trim, followed by rudder and aileron trim as necessary (assuming your airplane has these installed).

Keep in mind Sigmund Freud's comment that a cigar is sometimes just a cigar. In other words, sometimes a level-off is just a level-off. You don't always have to level off at some specific airspeed if there's no need to, or if it doesn't please you (you know your happiness is my only concern here). Sometimes you can level off and set your RPM to some moderate power setting or to a known value recommended by your instructor and be happy with the airspeed you get. After all, if you're practicing your basic flight maneuvers in the practice area, there's no need to fly around at the highest

Chapter 3: Climbs and Descents

attainable cruise speed, because you're trying to remain within the boundaries defining that practice area. This is especially true if you go up to sightsee or just to fly without any particular purpose in mind (but still with your mind active, of course).

If you recall, when entering the climb you actually had to apply right rudder to keep the airplane headed straight due to its power-induced left turning tendency. As you reduce power after leveling off from a climb, you'll find that you'll have to release that right rudder pressure to keep the airplane in coordinated flight. And if you used right rudder trim in the climb, you'll need to re-trim the rudder once the airplane is established at cruise speed.

Climbing Turns

Certain things always seem to go together. I'm thinking of things like birthdays and cakes (known as the *birthday cake*), wieners and buns (known as the *hot dog*) and rock stars and parties (known as the *restraining order*). Climbs and turns also naturally go together, and we call this a *climbing turn*. Since you already know how to turn an airplane as well as make one climb, you also know how to make a climbing turn (even if you don't know that you know it).

Normally, climbing turns are entered by simultaneously establishing a nose-up pitch attitude and the desired bank. There's nothing wrong, of course, with establishing the bank angle first, then raising the nose to climb attitude. My preference for student pilots is to pitch first, then bank. As you gain experience, you'll eventually make both attitude changes simultaneously.

The climbing turn is entered the same way you enter a straight climb. Pitch up, apply full power and bank the airplane, followed by adding nose-up trim (remember, A+P=P). The steeper the bank angle used while climbing, the less climb rate you can expect for a given climb airspeed (See: *Why Climb Rate Decreases With Bank Angle in a Climbing Turn* on Page 3-8). This is why it's best to make climbing turns at shallow bank angles for better climb performance. You'll find that the climbing attitude for shallow bank angles is nearly the same as that for a straight climb (Figure 8, position A).

As you increase the bank angle during the climb, you'll find that you can't climb at the same nose-up attitude that you used at shallower bank angles and hope to maintain the same climb airspeed. Why? Steeper bank angles require an increase in angle of attack to compensate for some loss in the vertical component of lift. Since an increase in angle of attack increases the induced drag, you must climb at a slightly less nose-up attitude if you want to maintain the same climb airspeed. The result is that you'll find yourself lowering the nose in a climb to maintain your climb speed as the bank angle increases.

Bank Angle and Climbs

A — Climbing at a shallow bank angle. Pitch - 12 degrees. The intersection of the top of the panel and the horizon (position X) provide an additional attitude reference.

B — Climbing at a steeper bank angle. Pitch - 10 degrees. The intersection of the top of the panel and the horizon (position Y) provide an additional attitude reference.

Fig. 8

Leveling Off in a Complex Airplane

When leveling off an airplane with a constant speed propeller, you should allow the airplane to accelerate to the selected cruise speed before reducing power. As you approach the target cruise airspeed, pull the throttle back (position A) and reduce the manifold pressure (position B) to some known or estimated value that sustains the desired airspeed. Then you'll pull the propeller control back (position C) to reduce the RPM (position D) to the correct value for cruise flight.

Reducing power followed by reducing RPM is another example of how we try to keep the propeller lever physically sequenced ahead of the throttle. The secret to minimizing the number of times you have to tinker with the throttle and propeller control is to reduce the power to a value approximately ½ to one inch of manifold pressure less than the value you want for cruise. You do this because a reduction in RPM typically raises the manifold pressure by approximately ½ to one inch (position E), depending on several engine variables.

Why does the manifold pressure rise with a reduction in RPM? Think about it this way. When the engine is stopped, your manifold pressure equals atmospheric pressure, which is approximately 30 inches of Hg. It takes the pistons moving downward (their intake stroke) to create suction (vacuum) on the engine side of the throttle butterfly valve. This is why the manifold pressure is so low during engine idle (perhaps 14 inches of Hg) with the throttle closed. Those idling pistons want to draw more air into the cylinders but they can't because the throttle butterfly value is closed and the manifold pressure sensor is located on the engine side of this butterfly valve. Very little air gets through unless you open the throttle.

At any given manifold pressure setting, reducing the RPM means the pistons don't move up and down as fast, so there's less piston action providing suction during the intake stoke. That means the manifold pressure must rise a little. In fact, if we were to (theoretically) set the manifold pressure in a twin-engine airplane at 20 inches and then feather the propeller (i.e., stop piston movement entirely), the manifold pressure on the feathered engine would rise to the level of the outside atmospheric pressure.

When entering a right climbing turn, the increase in power and your slower speed make the airplane's power-induced left turning tendency quite noticeable. So be prepared to use a *lot* of right rudder when entering a right climbing turn. In some airplanes, once you're established in the turn, you'll actually need a great deal of right rudder pressure and whatever aileron deflection is necessary just to remain in coordinated flight (Figure 9). Keep in mind that the effects of P-factor and slipstream vary from airplane to airplane, so your mileage will vary depending on the machine you're flying.

In a left climbing turn you probably won't need much left rudder (if any) to enter the turn since P-factor and slipstream are both acting to yaw the airplane to the left (in the same direction you'd use rudder to enter a left turn). Depending on the airplane and the

Why Climb Rate Decreases With Bank Angle in a Climbing Turn

When your daddy told you that you don't get something for nothing, he was talking about life but he might as well have been talking about airplanes, too. The steeper the bank used when climbing, the less the rate of climb you can expect from your airplane. After all, in a turn, you direct the airplane's total lifting force sideways to help pull the airplane in the direction you desire to turn. This reduces your vertical component of lift. To prevent a loss of altitude as you bank the airplane, you must increase the total lifting force so as to maintain the same vertical component of lift. You do this by increasing your airspeed with power and/or increasing your angle of attack (by increasing elevator back pressure).

In a climb, however, you have no power to spare. So, as you bank the airplane in a climb you must increase the angle of attack slightly, which increases the induced drag, resulting in a decrease in airspeed. The only way to maintain your climb airspeed is to lower the nose slightly and climb a "less steep" hill. The obvious result is that your climb rate decreases as you bank the airplane.

It's possible to continue increasing your bank angle during the climb to the point where the climb rate decreases to zero. Now the airplane is maintaining level flight in a very steep turn, but this doesn't do you much good if you wanted to climb, does it? Therefore, the bank limit for a climb is reached when the airplane ends up doing a steep turn in level flight.

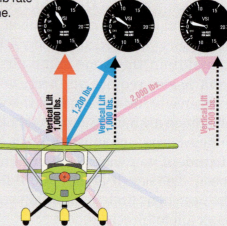

Chapter 3: Climbs and Descents

bank angle, you might even find that once you are established in a climbing left turn, you'll need to hold a little right rudder pressure as well as a little right aileron to keep the airplane in coordinated flight and prevent overbanking (Figure 10).

The same cowling pitch reference used during a straight climb also applies in climbing turns. Refer to your windscreen dot and keep it properly placed above the horizon to maintain the correct climb attitude. Then again, you might find it easier to use a point located at the intersection of the horizon line and the engine cowling or top of the instrument panel directly ahead of you as your pitch reference, since this is vertically closer to the horizon line.

In Figure 8, positions A and B, the intersection of the horizon line with the top of the instrument panel (locations X and Y, respectively) can be used as *additional* attitude clues along with the red dot's displacement above the horizon to aid you in maintaining the desired climb attitude.

Always keep in mind that you need to be ready to make whatever adjustments in pitch attitude are necessary to maintain the desired climb airspeed when changing the bank angle.

Straight Descents

You should be happy that you're not learning to fly during the disco era, in the 1970s. Why? When a flight instructor of that era said, "Let's get down," it usually meant dancing and partying, but no training. Of course, in today's aviation language that's not what the term means (sorry, I hope I didn't disappoint you).

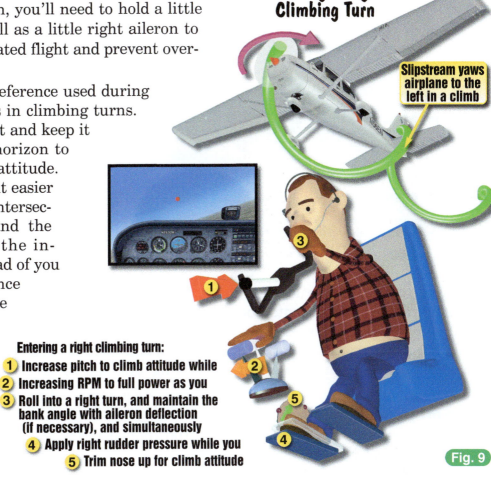

Entering a Right Climbing Turn

Slipstream yaws airplane to the left in a climb

Entering a right climbing turn:
1. Increase pitch to climb attitude while
2. Increasing RPM to full power as you
3. Roll into a right turn, and maintain the bank angle with aileron deflection (if necessary), and simultaneously
4. Apply right rudder pressure while you
5. Trim nose up for climb attitude

Fig. 9

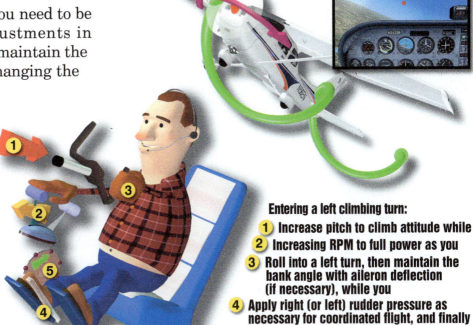

Entering a Left Climbing Turn

Entering a left climbing turn:
1. Increase pitch to climb attitude while
2. Increasing RPM to full power as you
3. Roll into a left turn, then maintain the bank angle with aileron deflection (if necessary), while you
4. Apply right (or left) rudder pressure as necessary for coordinated flight, and finally
5. Trim nose up for climb attitude

Fig. 10

Rod Machado's How to Fly an Airplane Handbook

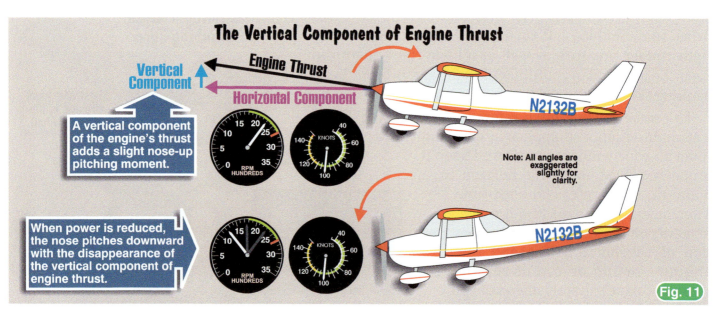

Fig. 11

When your instructor instructs you to get down, he or she wants you to descend. There are good reasons to know about descents, too. It's a downer, but you have to come down sometime, especially if you have a bladder. Airplanes don't remain stuck up in the air, do they? Descents are extremely important because they're pretty much an essential step in landing an airplane. So let's talk about the two common ways of descending, also known as the *power-off* and the *power-on descent*.

Power-off Descents

Let's say your airplane is in level flight at 100 knots using an engine RPM of 2,300 to sustain that airspeed. To enter a power-off descent at 100 knots (or whatever reasonable speed you want), apply carburetor heat (from now on I'll suggest you apply this and you and your POH will decide if it is necessary), then gradually reduce the power to flight idle (pull the throttle all the way back but don't yank it back or attempt to pull the handle completely out of the panel).

As you reduce power, the nose wants to pitch nose-down. It does so mainly because some of the thrust produced by the propeller acts vertically, which helps the airplane sustain a nose-up attitude (Figure 11). As the power is reduced, the airplane pitches forward in an attempt—an approximate

Fig. 12

Chapter 3: Climbs and Descents

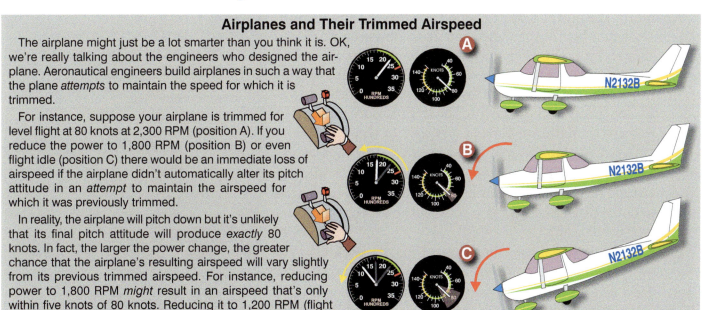

Airplanes and Their Trimmed Airspeed

The airplane might just be a lot smarter than you think it is. OK, we're really talking about the engineers who designed the airplane. Aeronautical engineers build airplanes in such a way that the plane *attempts* to maintain the speed for which it is trimmed.

For instance, suppose your airplane is trimmed for level flight at 80 knots at 2,300 RPM (position A). If you reduce the power to 1,800 RPM (position B) or even flight idle (position C) there would be an immediate loss of airspeed if the airplane didn't automatically alter its pitch attitude in an *attempt* to maintain the airspeed for which it was previously trimmed.

In reality, the airplane will pitch down but it's unlikely that its final pitch attitude will produce *exactly* 80 knots. In fact, the larger the power change, the greater chance that the airplane's resulting airspeed will vary slightly from its previous trimmed airspeed. For instance, reducing power to 1,800 RPM *might* result in an airspeed that's only within five knots of 80 knots. Reducing it to 1,200 RPM (flight idle) might result in an airspeed that's within 10 knots of 80 knots.

Of course these values are only for one particular airplane. There are way too many variables at play here to count on the airplane always maintaining the precise airspeed for which it was previously trimmed when power is reduced or added. This is why you, the pilot, will have to make small adjustments in attitude to produce the targeted airspeed in the descent. It's reasonable, however, to say that the airplane will *try* to maintain something close to the airspeed for which it was previously trimmed.

---

attempt, that is—to maintain the airspeed for which it was previously trimmed (see sidebar: *Airplanes and Their Trimmed Airspeed*).

As power is reduced to flight idle, you should select the nose-down attitude that produces the selected descent airspeed of 100 knots (Figure 12). In other words, using your elevator control, choose the appropriate nose-down attitude for the descent. Use that single dot directly ahead of you on the windscreen to calibrate the correct nose-down attitude. Take a mental picture of that dot's distance below the horizon and remember the picture. This will help you select the correct nose-down attitude for that specific airspeed during later flights.

When power is reduced, allow the elevator control to move forward slightly to establish the proper descent attitude. You'll find that you often have to apply slight back pressure on the yoke to keep the nose from pitching beyond the nose-down attitude necessary to maintain 100 knots. Yes, you heard that right. Most likely you will need to apply a little rearward pressure on the elevator control when you pull the throttle back for the descent. You just lost the small amount of thrust that was acting vertically, so something has to give. After selecting the proper nose-down attitude, apply nose-up trim to reduce any back pressure you're applying to the yoke (Figure 13).

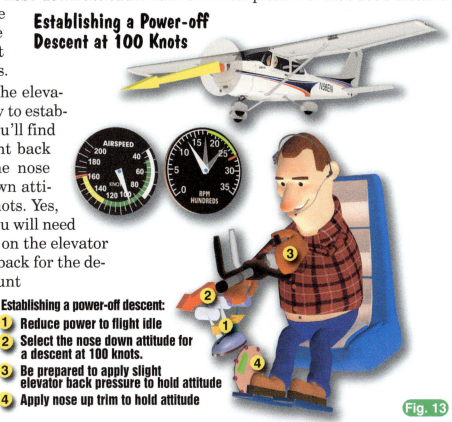

Establishing a Power-off Descent at 100 Knots

Establishing a power-off descent:
1. Reduce power to flight idle
2. Select the nose down attitude for a descent at 100 knots.
3. Be prepared to apply slight elevator back pressure to hold attitude
4. Apply nose up trim to hold attitude

Fig. 13

Normally, the power and pitch attitude are changed simultaneously when beginning a descent. It is, however, perfectly acceptable to reduce power and lower the nose at the same time. Then again, if you watch a pro do this, you'll see that he or she simply reduces power and lets the nose pitch downward automatically while applying the appropriate amount of back pressure to maintain correct airspeed in the descent.

As you've probably already guessed, a steeper nose-down attitude results in a higher descent speed while a shallower descent angle results in a slower one (Figure 14). By adjusting the nose-down pitch attitude, you control the descent airspeed in a power-off descent.

Once again, don't chase the airspeed needle with the elevator control. The airplane has inertia and can take more than a few seconds to change its indicated airspeed. Just change the attitude slightly and see if the result pleases you. If not, make additional small attitude changes until the indicated airspeed pleases you. Figures 15 and 16 show how much time can elapse between an attitude change in a power-off descent to obtain a 20 knot change in airspeed. This "time change" varies from airplane to airplane based on its drag profile. It also varies based on the rate at which you change your attitude, too. I hope this convinces you that chasing the needle is a race you won't win.

Precise pitch control in the descent is achieved by calibrating the cowling's position or your dot's placement below the horizon (hopefully the night janitor didn't remove your dot from the windscreen). Now you'll use the trim once again to keep the airplane's attitude constant and remove any pressure you're applying to the yoke.

An important point to remember about trimming an airplane is that anytime an airspeed change is made either in level flight or in a descent (or if a power change is made when making power-on descent), you must re-trim the airplane. The amount of trim required is based on the change in airspeed or power used. Change either of these and re-trimming is necessary.

One of the things you'll notice when carrying passengers is that suddenly reducing power for a power-off descent can make them a bit nervous. Very nervous, in fact. You might even have one of them actually think you've turned off the engine. You'll know this because he or she will yell, "Hey pal, you turn that thing back on now! Don't make me come up there!" It's good technique to tell first-time passengers what you're about to do and what to expect it to look and sound like *before* making any major configuration changes. This will help minimize scared passengers and unscheduled exits from the aircraft.

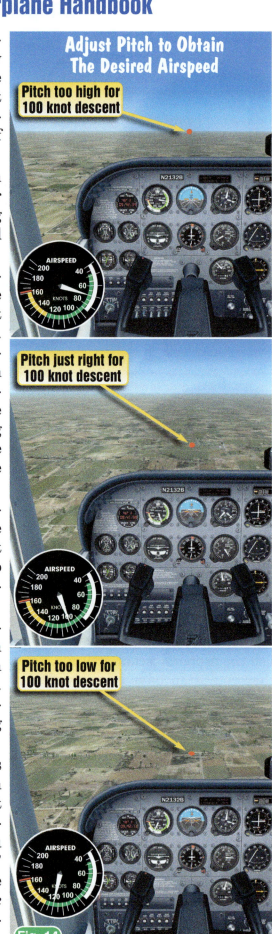

Fig. 14

Chapter 3: Climbs and Descents

3-13

Whatever you do, don't say, "A reduction in sound doesn't mean the engine is no longer working," because I can pretty much guarantee you that all they will hear out of that sentence is "...the engine is no longer working." That's when the unscheduled exits occur.

On the other hand, changes in sound can be helpful to you as a pilot if you listen carefully and know what they are saying. This is your chance to become a plane whisperer. As the airplane speeds up in a power-off descent, the sound of the air rushing past the cabin increases in pitch (but nothing like what you hear in the movies). Slowing down generally results in a decreasing pitch sound. And despite the newest and most efficient active-noise-cancellation headsets that pilots wear nowadays, you can still detect differences in cockpit sounds. You just have to pay attention to how the sounds change under different flight conditions. With practice, you'll easily detect subtle changes in cockpit sounds. You might even be able to discover what your flight instructor is mumbling under his breath during your lessons, too. OK, I'll tell you. He's almost always saying, "Food, I love food. I would sell this airplane for a cheeseburger."

Indicated Airspeed Lag During Attitude Change

The attitude shown below sustains a power-off descent at 80 knots. Time: 39 minutes, 00 seconds on timer.

A 15 degree nose down attitude is chosen and, at 06 seconds past 39 minutes, the airspeed is 90 knots.

It takes approximately 12 seconds for the airspeed to indicate 100 knots at this new attitude.

Fig. 15

The attitude shown below sustains a power-off descent at 100 knots. Time: 42 minutes, 00 seconds on timer.

Note: The airspeed lag can vary noticeably between airplanes depending on their drag profile and the rate at which the attitude is changed.

A five degree nose up attitude is chosen and at 06 seconds past 42 minutes, the airspeed is 90 knots.

It takes approximately nine seconds for the airspeed to indicate 80 knots at this new attitude.

Fig. 16

Leveling Off From a Descent

As a general rule, smaller airplanes descend faster than they climb. That's because gravity is a more powerful engine than the engine you have in your airplane. This is why the altitude lead for leveling off from a descent is usually larger than that used when leveling off from a climb.

In Figure 17, if we assume a descent rate of 500 feet per minute then you should start your level-off at 100 feet above the target level-off altitude. Higher descent rates require larger level-off leads to avoid overshooting the targeted altitude. You'll find that using 20% of your descent rate as a lead when leveling off usually works well. For instance, if you're descending at 1,000 feet per minute, you should lead your level-off by 200 feet, which allows you to make a nice smooth transition to level flight.

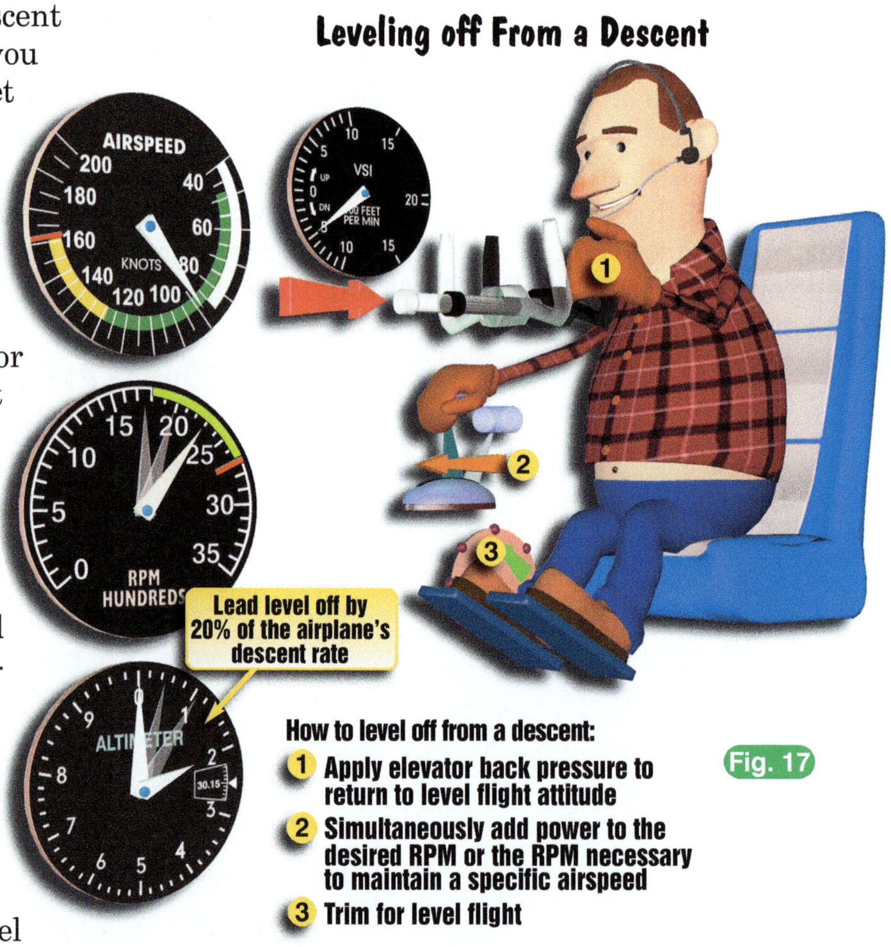

As you approach your target altitude, you'll raise the nose and simultaneously add power to maintain altitude and airspeed. During the initial level-off, it's often wise to trim away the nose-up trim used in the descent. This means that you'll need nose-down trim to maintain a level pitch attitude. As you apply power during the level off, you'll also have to apply forward pressure on the yoke until you apply sufficient nose-down trim. Once the airplane stabilizes at its final airspeed, apply a final adjustment of trim as necessary.

Leveling off From a Descent

Lead level off by 20% of the airplane's descent rate

How to level off from a descent:
1. Apply elevator back pressure to return to level flight attitude
2. Simultaneously add power to the desired RPM or the RPM necessary to maintain a specific airspeed
3. Trim for level flight

Fig. 17

Descending Turns

Descending turns are sort of climbing turns in reverse. The pitch attitude for the descent is maintained by looking over the cowling at your red dot directly ahead of you (once again, not in the center or to the right side of the cockpit). Since the attitude for a descent is lower than that for straight and level flight, the dot-cowling reference will be slightly below the horizon line compared to its position in straight and level flight (Figure 18). Keeping the dot the appropriate distance below the horizon during shallow turns keeps your attitude—and thus your airspeed—constant. As the bank angle of the descending turn increases, the airplane's nose initially wants to pitch downward because of the loss of some vertical component of lift. This requires a slight increase in elevator back pressure to keep the attitude from decreasing beyond that required to maintain the desired airspeed.

If your descent airspeed is below what you want for your power-off descent, lower the pitch attitude slightly and wait for the airspeed to increase and stabilize at a higher speed. If your descent speed is higher than desired, increase the pitch attitude slightly and wait for the airspeed to decrease then stabilize.

Once again, don't expect an immediate change in airspeed with a change in pitch attitude. Small airplanes can weigh several thousand pounds, meaning that they have a lot of inertia. It takes a

Chapter 3: Climbs and Descents   3-15

The Attitude for a Descending Turn

This is the attitude for straight and level flight.

This is the attitude for a power-off descending left hand turn at a shallow bank angle.

This is the attitude for a power-off descending left hand turn at a moderate bank angle.

Fig. 18

short amount of time for airspeed to change with a change in pitch attitude. Patience, Grasshopper. Expecting an immediate deflection of the airspeed needle with a change in pitch means that you'll end up chasing the airspeed needle instead of properly managing your airplane's attitude. In fact, expecting an immediate "anything" when you reconfigure the airplane is always a prescription for frustration. Act, then wait and observe.

Descending in the Absence Of The Slipstream and P-factor

One of the things you'll immediately notice about power-off descending turns is that the airplane's *power induced* left turning tendency has disappeared. Good riddance. I thought it would never leave. With the power at flight idle, there's no P-factor or propeller slipstream to yaw the airplane to the left. The degree to which the power is reduced for the descent represents the degree that the left turning forces are less relevant to you while descending.

During a power-off descending turn, you'll notice that the rudder pedal response will feel a bit mushier, as if you're pushing on a sponge (hopefully it's not the sandwich your hungry flight instructor brought for lunch). With less propeller- induced high velocity air flowing over the rudder surface, the rudder itself might require a greater displacement, thus more push on the pedal to yaw the airplane. This is no time to have timid tootsies.

This need for a big push is even more noticeable when the airplane is slow, such as when you're on final approach to land. So be prepared to apply a bit more pressure on the pedal during power-off turns, especially when compensating for the aileron's adverse yaw when entering or exiting a turn. The essential point here is that the slower the airspeed during power-off descents, the more rudder pedal pressure (and displacement) you'll need to keep the nose pointed where you want it to point. This is one

Attitude Change in Descending Turns - Explained
Anytime you increase the bank angle, you also increase the load factor and experience some diminishment of the vertical lift component. Therefore, you must increase lift by increasing the angle of attack (apply back elevator pressure). On the other hand, an increase in angle of attack means an increase in induced drag. Therefore, in a power off descent, you must lower the nose slightly to allow gravity to accelerate the airplane and overcome the induced drag increase. Doesn't that seem like you're having to move the elevator control in two different directions at the same time? It turns out that when the airplane is banked, any pitch change translates into both vertical and horizontal movement. This allows you to change the airplane's pitch attitude relative to the horizon(a vertical movement) while simultaneously changing the angle of attack (a vertical and horizontal movement in a banked attitude). Ultimately, you are able to find the desired nose-down turning attitude for any given bank angle to maintain the desired airspeed.

of the big reasons student pilots initially have difficulty keeping the airplane properly aligned during landing, when the airplane is typically flying at a much slower speed (more on this in Chapter 10 that deals with landings).

None of this ultimately matters in regard to keeping the airplane in coordinated flight, since you'll use the same visual reference over the nose for coordinating your turns as we previously discussed. You'll press on each rudder pedal as much as needed to keep the nose pointing in the direction of turn or keep it properly aligned with the runway (or at some angle to the runway) during landing. So be prepared to meet the "press" when landing.

Be aware that airplanes are generally rigged for coordinated flight when flying in straight and level cruise. "Rigging" in this case refers to how the plane's aerodynamics are adjusted, not to a game that's been jiggered by an unscrupulous flight instructor to make you think you can't fly so you'll spend more money on lessons. Most planes have flexible rudder trim tabs that are manually bent on the ground to compensate for any left turning tendency in the cruise condition (manually bent by a certified mechanic, that is), as shown in Figure 19.

The Bendable Rudder Tab

The manually bent rudder trim tab

Fig. 19

This makes the plane fly straight in straight and level flight, but it means that during a power-off descent some airplanes tend to turn/yaw to the right a little because there's no power-induced left turning tendency for which to compensate. Here is where you might need to add a little left rudder to remain in coordinated flight (Figure 20). Your feet just can't seem to catch a break, can they? Step on the top part of the pedal and consider it brake dancing.

Making Power-off Descents

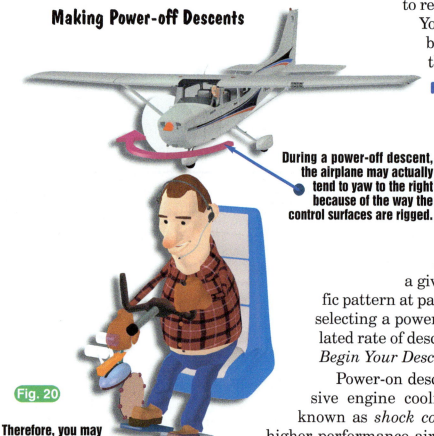

During a power-off descent, the airplane may actually tend to yaw to the right because of the way the control surfaces are rigged.

Fig. 20

Therefore, you may need to use a little left rudder to keep the airplane coordinated in the descent.

Power-on Descents

Of course, descents need not be made with power completely reduced to flight idle. Power-on descents are made for a number of reasons. For instance, power-on descents allow you to control the rate of descent for any given airspeed. That means that you can descend from cruise flight and arrive at a given location (perhaps the airport traffic pattern at pattern altitude) and a given altitude by selecting a power setting that provides for a precalculated rate of descent (see sidebar: *Calculating When to Begin Your Descent From Cruise Altitude*).

Power-on descents are also made to prevent excessive engine cooling. Excessive engine cooling (also known as *shock cooling*) is a concern when operating higher performance airplane engines. Shock cooling can be minimized by maintaining some power during the descent and progressively reducing power at an appropriate rate as necessary.

Chapter 3: Climbs and Descents

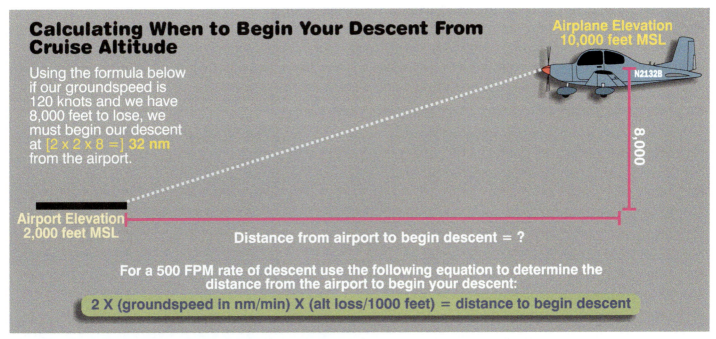

Calculating When to Begin Your Descent From Cruise Altitude

Using the formula below if our groundspeed is 120 knots and we have 8,000 feet to lose, we must begin our descent at [2 x 2 x 8 =] **32 nm** from the airport.

Airplane Elevation 10,000 feet MSL

Airport Elevation 2,000 feet MSL

Distance from airport to begin descent = ?

For a 500 FPM rate of descent use the following equation to determine the distance from the airport to begin your descent:

2 X (groundspeed in nm/min) X (alt loss/1000 feet) = distance to begin descent

Power-on descents are also made to minimize the inner ear discomfort some people feel when changing altitudes in airplanes. No doubt you've experienced this before, either in a car or in the pressurized cabin of an airliner or even when your bigger brother connected one end of the vacuum to your nose. While these escapades are endlessly entertaining for older members of your family, they certainly were discomforting for you, right? A power-on descent means that you can minimize the discomfort by regulating the airplane's descent rate. This prevents your passengers' ears from popping, and keeps them from sounding like you've got bongo players in back of the aircraft.

Making a Power-on Approach

500 feet per minute at 100 knots and 2,000 RPM

Most descents are done at a reduced power setting to obtain a reasonable descent rate. This approach is done with power at a rate of 500 fpm.

Fig. 21

If you're in cruise flight while approaching an airport, you might elect to descend at somewhere around 500 feet per minute (Figure 21). Of course, you may descend at any rate that pleases you within the limits and capabilities of the airplane, but most people's ears can accommodate gracefully to a descent at this rate, assuming they don't have a cold or physiological abnormality. The amount of power you choose for the descent ultimately determines how fast the airplane descends for a given airspeed.

Ultimately, the biggest reason for being proficient at making a power-on descent occurs when you're approaching to land and find that your present glidepath takes you to a place short of the runway (yes, we still refer to this as a *glidepath* even though power is being used, although the term *flightpath* is perfectly acceptable, too). Here's where you add power, reduce your descent rate and extend your glidepath to the correct landing spot rather than into a tree that's short of that spot. You want your landing to be a treat, not a trauma.

There's More Than One Way to Descend, You Know

So far we've covered power-off and power-on descents. At first think, you'd think that pretty much exhausts the possibilities.

Think again. There are three common variations on the types of descents you can make. So let's get chatty about descents at *cruise speed*, descents for a *short-field approach* and descents at the airplane's *best glide speed*.

One of the most common types of descents is known as the *cruise descent*. If you want to begin a shallow descent at cruise airspeeds (say 300 feet per minute at 120 knots), then you'll simultaneously lower the airplane's nose and reduce power sufficiently to maintain 300 fpm and 120 knots (Figure 22). Of course, when you're at cruise airspeed, if you lower the nose to begin a descent and don't want your airspeed to increase, you'll need to simultaneously reduce the power. Reduce it by how much? That depends on many things, such as your current airspeed, the type of airplane you're flying, the airplane configuration, drag profile and so on. But none of that really matters. All that matters is that you take a guess at the power reduction then lower the nose to maintain the desired airspeed, followed by small power corrections to obtain the targeted descent rate. Once you're at the correct descent rate, trim the airplane to maintain your present attitude, which should give you the desired rate and airspeed.

There is another good reason for making power-on cruise descents. No doubt, you're flying an airplane for several reasons, not the least of which is that it's a wonderful vehicle for getting somewhere in a short time. Suppose you're cruising at 120 knots at 10,500 feet MSL (mean "average" sea level) enroute to your favorite vacation spot at Boar's Head airport (where the airport manager wears an actual boar's head to confirm your location). It doesn't make sense to slow down to and descend at 60 knots, does it? You've got a fast airplane, so fly it as fast as it is safe to do based on the atmospheric conditions, the airplane's limitations and your personal limitations. After all, you want to get down and get a picture of that airport manager before he pulls that noggin off his noggin.

Short-field approaches often involve making power-on descents at a steep angle and slow airspeeds.

Chapter 3: Climbs and Descents

On the other hand, there are times when you'll want to make a descent at a steep angle while flying at a relatively slow airspeed. This is known as a descent for a *short-field approach*. You'll most likely use this type of descent when making a landing on a short runway when there's an obstacle in the approach path (Figure 23). Sure, you can fly over the obstacle at a relatively high altitude, but you might not be able to get the airplane down quickly enough to land on, much less stop on, the runway.

Descending at a slower speed and controlling the descent rate with a combination of pitch and power allows you to better project the airplane's trajectory over the obstacle, as well as land immediately after clearing the obstacle and stopping before reaching the end of the runway, all of which are highly desirable. Descents in these conditions are often made with flaps extended and at speeds generally 30% above the airplane's present stall speed or 1.3 Vso (that's 1.3 times the stall speed with flaps extended and landing gear extended). Under normal conditions you won't descend for landing using short-field landing techniques. Instead, you'll most likely make a normal power-off descent with partial flaps (we'll talk more about short-field landings in Chapter 12).

One of the skills you'll acquire as a pilot is the ability to handle a complete engine failure. That means you'll learn how to descend and land safely at an off-airport (off-field) landing site without engine power, much as gliders do. An essential component of this skill is knowing how to obtain the maximum glide performance from your airplane so that you have the best chance of gliding to the emergency landing field of your choice. Doing so requires that you understand something about descending at the *best glide speed*.

Descending at the Best Glide Speed

Airplanes actually glide quite well, often with glide ratios anywhere from 8:1 to 17:1. A glide ratio of 17:1 (read as *seventeen to one*) means that for every foot of altitude loss, the airplane moves forward 17 feet. Open class, high performance gliders (as opposed to an airplane with an engine out) have glide ratios in the range of 60:1. That's why they call them *gliders* (some aircraft, like the space shuttle, should be called *droppers* for obvious reasons).

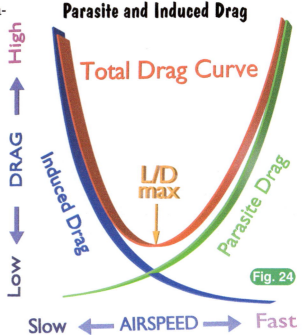

The actual distance over the ground that the airplane glides is dependent on several factors such as the current wind conditions, whether or not the propeller is windmilling (i.e., being forced to spin by the oncoming wind), and the glide speed, to name a few. The actual glide speed used in the glide is the item we're concerned about here.

Almost all airplanes have a recommended glide speed that's found in the POH. This is the speed that the engineers discovered allows the airplane to obtain its maximum glide ratio (8:1, for instance). To best understand the best glide speed, you need to know something about drag, which isn't a drag at all.

As an airplane speeds up, induced drag decreases while parasite drag increases. This is shown by the airplane's total drag curve (Figure 24). As the airplane slows down, parasite drag decreases but induced drag increases (see Chapter Two of *Rod Machado's Private Pilot Handbook* for a detailed discussion of induced and parasite drag). When the induced and parasite drag curves are combined, they produce the *total drag curve,* which always has a low point or minimum drag position.

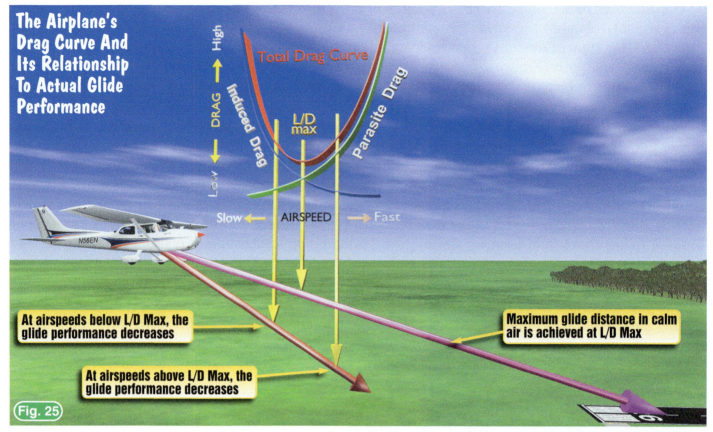

The Airplane's Drag Curve And Its Relationship To Actual Glide Performance

At airspeeds below L/D Max, the glide performance decreases

At airspeeds above L/D Max, the glide performance decreases

Maximum glide distance in calm air is achieved at L/D Max

Fig. 25

The lowest spot on the total drag curve results in a specific airspeed known as the *best L/D speed*. This is pronounced *best L over D speed*, which gives you the best *lift over drag ratio*). It is also often referred to as *L/D max*. This speed yields the airplane's maximum power-off glide range, which is why it's often referred to as the *best glide speed* (Figure 25). Should your engine stop working (most often because the pilot forgot to put fuel in the tanks), you are now the pilot of a glider and should be looking for a landing spot. Here is where you'll immediately establish the proper gliding attitude to obtain the best glide airspeed.

For example, the Remos GX (Figure 26A) has a lift-to-drag ratio of approximately 10 to 1 (or 10:1) at its best L/D speed of 56 knots indicated airspeed. At this speed the airplane experiences minimum total drag (it's now flying at the bottom of its total drag curve) and moves ten feet forward for every foot it descends (in calm winds, of course). On the other hand, high performance gliders (Figure 26B) can have glide ratios in the range of 60 to 1.

The Remos GX Has A Glide Ratio of 10 to 1

Fig. 26A — At the best L/D speed, the Remos will glide 10 feet forward for every foot of altitude lost.

High Performance Gliders Can Have Glide Ratios Of 60 to 1

Fig. 26B — At the best L/D speed, some gliders will glide 60 feet forward for every foot of altitude lost.

Chapter 3: Climbs and Descents

That's impressive when you consider that the space shuttle (a glider when it heads home) has a glide ratio of 1 to 1 at hypersonic speeds which is similar to the glide ratio of a manhole cover. No matter what you do to the airplane (glider, space shuttle or manhole cover), this is the best glide ratio it's capable of attaining. You can rock back-and-forth in your seat and yell, "Come on big fellow, come on, yee-hawww!" and the airplane still isn't going to glide better than ten feet forward for every foot it drops.

Descents are never scary, but are always fun. So, whatever you do, don't dress like this to do them.

Gliding slower or faster than the best L/D speed results in a glide path that falls short of what you could have achieved had you flown at the best L/D. The problem here, however, is that as a pilot sees the ground approaching the airplane, it's natural for a him or her to try stretching the glide by pulling back on the yoke. This simply creates more drag and results in an even shorter glide, but worse than that, it sometimes ends up in a stall or spin (to be discussed in Chapter Five). Burn into your brain the fact that you simply can't do better than the best glide speed.

Of course, you'll want to remember that a change in weight doesn't affect the glide ratio as long as you make a corresponding change in glide speed. To obtain the best L/D for your airplane, a decrease in weight requires a decrease in airspeed. But how do you know what the best glide speed is if it varies with weight? You should refer to the POH or to the owner's manual to find this value.

Some POHs show variable L/Ds for different weight configurations. As a general rule, you should decrease the glide speed 5% for every 10% decrease in gross weight (that can also be read as a 1% decrease in speed for every 2% decrease in gross weight if this is easier for you). Remember, in the event of a power failure, immediately establish the proper attitude to obtain the best glide speed.

To ensure that your airplane does glide as far as possible, you'll want to make sure the flaps and gear are retracted (from now on we'll assume that any mention of retractable landing gear applies only to airplane with retractable landing gear). Gliding with the wind (a tailwind) rather than into it (a headwind) is always better in terms of extending your glide range, too.

Once you have a landing location selected and find yourself above it or nearly so, then there's no practical need to glide at the best glide speed (although you can if it pleases you. I want you to be happy). Instead, you might consider gliding at the *minimum sink speed* (Figure 27). The minimum sink speed is normally found somewhere between stall speed and the best glide speed. It's not, however, a speed that you'll find posted in most POHs. If you know what this speed is, then it makes sense to use it when descending over the desired landing spot since it gives you more time to troubleshoot the engine problem or let someone know you're making an emergency landing. Your final approach and landing, however, should be made at approximately 30% above stall speed.

Pitch and Power Techniques for Flying Your Airplane

Up to this point I've primarily discussed using the elevator control (pitch) and throttle (power) *simultaneously* when making changes in your glidepath and/or airspeed. This is just one of three different ways you can use the yoke and throttle to change either of these two conditions. Before we discuss the other two methods, let's be clear about what we're going to discuss here.

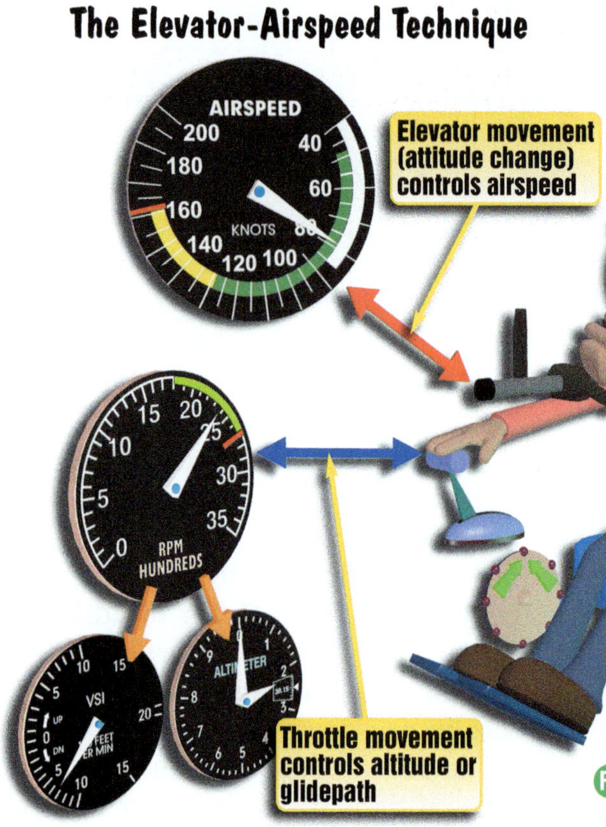

The Elevator-Airspeed Technique

Elevator movement (attitude change) controls airspeed

Throttle movement controls altitude or glidepath

Fig. 28

When we say that you *control* your airspeed, we're saying that you manipulate either the throttle or elevator control to produce a specific airspeed or keep the airspeed at a specific value. When we say that you *control* your glidepath, we're saying that you manipulate your throttle or yoke to produce a specific change in your airplane's vertical speed (which can be a descent rate or a climb rate). This follows from our previous airplane performance equation: *Attitude* (controlled by the yoke)+*Power* (controlled by the throttle)=*Performance* (the resulting airspeed and glidepath).

There are two conditions under which the formula A+P=P applies during flight. There's a *fixed* power condition and a *variable* power condition. Let's take the first condition first.

If you're in an airplane that's either climbing with full power or descending with the throttle set at some value and left alone, then your power (throttle) is considered to be *fixed*. In a fixed power condition, you manipulate the elevator to change your airspeed, which also produces a change in your flight path (either your descent rate or your climb rate if you're climbing with full power).

For instance, during a climb (power fixed) you adjust the elevator to provide a specific climb airspeed and accept the resulting climb rate. During a power-off descent (power fixed at idle), you typically adjust the elevator to yield a specific descent airspeed and accept whatever descent rate results.

What happens when you make the power *variable* instead of leaving it fixed at either full power or flight idle? Now things really get interesting because variable power allows you to have *three*

The story goes like this. Two military C130 pilots decided to play a joke on a General riding jump seat on a flight. When the airplane is aligned with the runway, the copilot says, "Would you mind if I make the takeoff?" The captain says, "Please do." Once airborne the captain says, "That's a mighty fine takeoff for a Landing Pilot. The copilot says, "Oh, I'm not a Landing Pilot. I'm a Takeoff Pilot." At which point the captain replies, "You can't be a Takeoff Pilot because I'm the Takeoff Pilot. Surely they wouldn't have put two Takeoff Pilots on the same airplane, would they?" The look on the General's face was priceless.

Chapter 3: Climbs and Descents

separate techniques for controlling the airplane's airspeed and glidepath. Let's examine all three techniques for dealing with variable power conditions.

Technique #1 involves using the elevator to control the airspeed and the throttle to control the airplane's glidepath. During a descent, you'll make small changes in pitch to maintain the desired airspeed while adjusting the throttle to maintain the required glidepath (Figure 28). The glidepath is determined by referring to the vertical speed indicator or by referring to a reference point on the surface, such as the runway or the VASI or *visual approach slope indicator* (the VASI is a set of colored lights that let you know whether you're above, below or on a normal glidepath to a spot on the runway).

Let's suppose that you're flying a power-on final approach to landing at an airspeed of 80 knots and a descent rate of 500 FPM. Looking at the runway, you see that your airplane is descending to a point short of the intended landing spot (it's getting too low on approach), as shown in Figure 29, position A.

You decide to reduce the descent rate by adding power. With the nose already pointed in a slight nose-down attitude, the addition of power would increase your airspeed unless a slight pitch-up correction is made. So you raise the nose slightly to maintain the desired approach speed and add power to decrease the descent rate (Figure 29, position B). In this way, you've made your glidepath shallower, extending it to a point farther along the approach path by adding power, while maintaining your approach speed of 80 knots by adjusting your attitude with the elevator control.

If you see that you're descending to a point beyond the intended landing spot, then you know you're too high on the approach (Figure 29, position C). You'll want to reduce your power so as to increase the descent rate. Reducing power increases the descent rate, but unless a pitch change is made, it can also reduce your airspeed. You'll need to lower the nose slightly to maintain your desired approach speed (Figure 29 position D). Now you've steepened your glidepath but kept your airspeed constant, which allows you to land at a point shorter than that offered by the previous trajectory.

Let's label pilots who use the elevator to control their airspeed and throttle to control their glidepath as *elevator-airspeed pilots*.

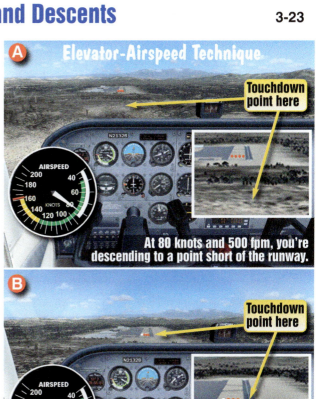

Fig. 29

The Elevator-Glidepath Technique

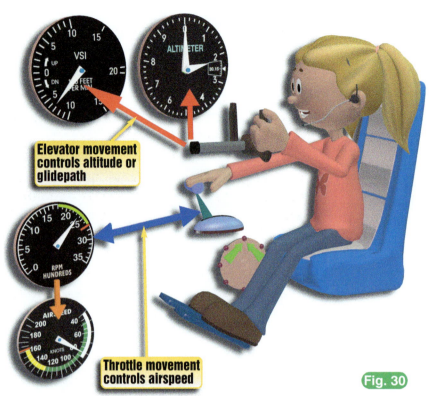

Fig. 30

Technique #2 involves using the elevator to control the airplane's glidepath *and the throttle to control the airspeed.* This is the reverse of Technique #1. During a descent, you'll make small changes in pitch to adjust your glidepath while using throttle to maintain the desired airspeed (Figure 30). Your glidepath is determined by referring to either the vertical speed indicator (VSI) or by referring to a reference point on the ground, which can be a spot on the runway or the VASI.

Let's suppose that you're flying a power-on final approach to landing at an airspeed of 80 knots and a descent rate of 500 FPM. Looking at the runway, you see that your airplane is descending to a point short of the intended landing spot (it's getting too low on approach) as shown in Figure 31, position A. You decide to decrease the descent rate by raising the nose slightly. With the nose pointed in a slightly higher attitude, the airplane begins to slow down, so you increase the power sufficiently to maintain 80 knots. Now you've extended your glidepath to a point farther along the approach path (i.e., you reduced your descent rate), while maintaining your approach speed (Figure 31, position B).

If you were too high on approach and saw that the airplane was descending to a point beyond the intended landing spot (Figure 31, position C), you'd want to lower the nose and increase the descent rate. This naturally increases your airspeed, which requires that you reduce power to maintain 80 knots.

Chapter 3: Climbs and Descents

Now you've steepened your glide path, allowing a landing at a closer spot than that provided by the airplane's previous trajectory, while maintaining your previous approach airspeed (Figure 31, position D).

We'll label pilots who use the throttle to control their airspeed and the yoke to control their altitude as *elevator-glidepath pilots*.

Which Technique Should You Use?

At this point you are probably asking, Which technique should I use? You might even be asking what it's called when someone uses both controls simultaneously without distinguishing what each control controls—ambivalent? Both are good questions, so let's take the last one first.

As you gain experience, you'll tend to move both the yoke and the throttle simultaneously, without giving much thought to what the yoke or the throttle actually controls. This would be the third technique, or **Technique #3**, *meaning that you don't distinguish what the yoke and the throttle actually control*. Instead, you simply move both of them simultaneously as appropriate to produce the right results (say, a 500 foot per minute descent at an approach speed of 70 knots). That's fine. This technique, however, is more reflexive than consciously driven, which is why it's something that most experienced pilots typically do. Regardless of your experience, it's perfectly fine for you to use technique #1, #2 or #3, as you see fit. On the other hand, if you're a pilot in training, you should use the technique selected by your instructor and be happy with that choice. When you gain more experience, you can experiment and try a different technique. We'll call this the *elevator-throttle technique*.

A Rationale for Using the Elevator-Airspeed Technique

If you're already a rated pilot and you want a good reason to choose a specific technique, then consider the following points.

One of the most important concepts for new pilots to absorb is the idea that you never try stretching a glide by pulling back on the yoke. This becomes especially important when attempting to glide to a field and land with an inoperative engine. Keep in mind that the airplane glides best at its best glide speed (L/D max), as shown in Figure 32. Any attempt to stretch the glide by pulling aft on the elevator and slowing the airplane down results in a much steeper descent path (Figure 33).

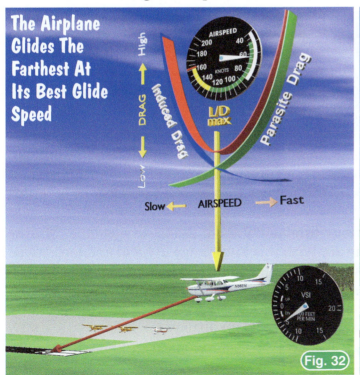
Fig. 32

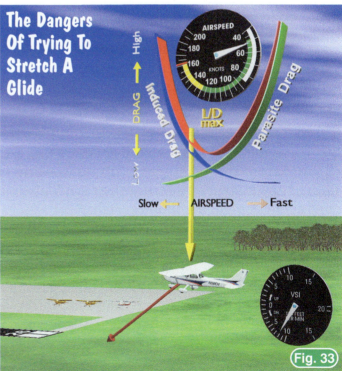
Fig. 33

During an emergency landing, it's much better to fly an airplane into a fence or a small, frangible tree and touch down short of the intended landing spot in a *non-stalled* condition. It's much worse to try stretching the glide, getting too slow and stalling or spinning into the ground (the ground doesn't flex when you hit it). If you accept the importance of this idea, you'll probably want to use Technique #1 favored by *elevator-airspeed pilots*. Why? This technique reinforces the idea of controlling your airspeed by use of the elevator control. This means that you'll be less likely to try pulling back on the yoke to stretch a glide when you're too low, because maintaining airspeed with the yoke is your primary habit. That's why many highly experienced instructors and aviation authors recommend this technique for student pilots.

It's interesting to note that the elevator-airspeed technique is used primarily by the U.S. Navy. The reason is that Navy pilots fly on and off aircraft carriers, and this requires operations at very slow airspeeds. I'm talking about speeds deep in the region of reversed command (which you'll learn about in the next chapter). Any attempt to change a jet's glidepath by raising the nose immediately results in an increased descent rate. Therefore, Navy pilots are taught to control the airplane's glidepath by making power changes while airspeed is controlled with pitch changes.

When you're making an approach in your smaller general aviation airplane at 30% above stall speed, you're usually not in the region of reversed command. Navy pilots typically approach at speeds less than 30% above stall speed, thus their operational techniques are essential for safe carrier operations lest they overshoot the runway and get run over by the airport. Ouch! That has to hurt.

A Rationale for Using the Elevator-Glidepath Technique

On the other hand, there are many instructors who are less worried about a pilot attempting to stretch a glide in an emergency than the chances of those same pilots running off the runway or landing short of it during non-emergency conditions. These instructors feel that using the yoke to control the airplane's glidepath minimizes the chance the airplane will land at other than on the chosen landing spot (non-engine failure conditions assumed here).

Of course, these instructors also assume that if the engine did fail, the pilot would be sufficiently cognizant of not attempting to stretch a glide using the elevator. The FAA's original version of its *Flight Training Handbook* emphasized that all general aviation pilots favor the elevator-glidepath technique. That's because the content for that handbook was originally derived from U.S. Air Force training materials and the U.S. Air Force specifically teaches this technique. That's because Air Force pilots don't land on aircraft carriers, so their approaches and landings aren't done in the region of reversed command. So, there's no specific reason or urgency for them to use the elevator-airspeed technique. Air Force pilots can also use the elevator-glidepath technique as a one-size-fits-all strategy for approaches, landings, bombing runs, in-flight refueling and so on.

Which Technique Do Instructors Typically Use?

It turns out that the many instructors use Technique #1 for beginning students and Technique #2 for their advanced students (those working on their instrument and commercial rating). Then again, if any instructor teaches their students to use Technique #3, there can't possibly be an argument about control dominance, right?

Now you know the essential details about the four fundamentals of flying an airplane. Master these details and there's nothing you can't do in the air. With this knowledge in hand and foot, we're ready to explore the more advanced concepts of slow flight, stalls and spins. Why are we going to study these things? Because all of your training is leading up to one specific skill—*landing an airplane*. Yep, that's right. Everything that you're learning with these basics as well as the upcoming section on slow flight and stalls is really teaching you how to land an airplane.

Can't wait to land? Well, I can't wait to teach you how. But first, we need to know how to fly slowly and recognize and recover from a stall or a spin.

Chapter 3: Climbs and Descents

Postflight Briefing #3-1 Gliding Into the Wind

Best L/D and Wind

Imagine this scenario. Your airplane's best glide speed is 60 knots and you have a headwind of 60 knots. Suddenly, your engine quits and you must glide to an open field just a short distance in front of your airplane. What airspeed should you use for the glide?

If you choose a glide airspeed of 60 knots, then you won't glide any farther than your present position over the ground. Fly at an airspeed slower than 60 knots and you'll move backwards relative to your present position. In this example, it's only logical to glide at a speed a little faster than the airplane's best glide speed if you want to move forward from your present position relative to the ground.

The fact is that when gliding into a headwind, you're better off gliding faster than the airplane's best glide speed. How much faster? The general rule of thumb is to add 50% of the wind speed onto the best glide speed. At least this would allow you to move forward (hopefully this would be toward a desired landing site) instead of making no forward progress at all.

In our "extreme" example above, we would add 30 knots onto 60 knots for a glide airspeed of 90 knots. Sure, at a speed above best glide, you'll come down at a higher descent rate but at least you'll move forward toward the chosen field. Of course, turning downwind might increase your selection of landing sites, assuming there are no acceptable sites directly ahead of you.

Now ask yourself what happens when if you're gliding

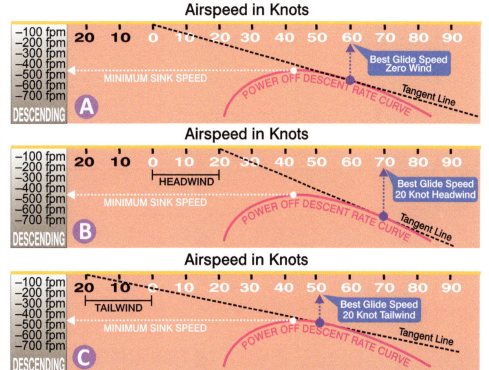

From the engineer's perspective, the best glide speed is found where a tangent line, beginning at the "0" airspeed index, touches the power off descent rate curve. In Block A, best glide speed is found at 60 knots. With a headwind (Block B) or a tailwind (Block C), the best glide speed is found by shifting the beginning of the tangent line an amount equal to the headwind or tailwind, respectively. While adding 50% of the wind's speed applies to headwinds, there is no consistent rule of thumb to use for tailwinds. Let it be said, however, that you should never decrease your speed to less than the minimum sink speed (which would defeat the objective or remaining aloft for a longer period). The minimum sink speed is found at the very top of the power off glide curve. You'll learn more about power curves in Chapters 4 and 5.

into a tailwind. Clearly, gliding with a tailwind extends the glide range of the airplane. However, does it extend the time you'll spend aloft in the glide? No, it doesn't. You'll come down just as fast when using the best glide airspeed regardless of whether you're gliding into a tailwind or headwind. The only thing that changes will be the glide range of the airplane. This is why you might want to operate at a slightly slower speed than best glide speed during an engine failure when you have a tailwind.

The fact is that as the airplane slows below the best glide speed, its glide distance decreases but its descent rate also decreases, at least up to a point called the minimum sink speed. In the following chapters you'll learn about something known as the *minimum sink speed*. This speed is found below the best glide speed and is approximately 10-15% above stall speed.

Therefore, as a practical matter, if you experience engine failure and are gliding with a tailwind, it's not unreasonable to slow the airplane down slightly to decrease the rate of descent (but never slower than the minimum sink speed, of course). Yes, you'll shorten the maximum downwind glide range because you're not flying at the best glide speed. You will, however, remain aloft a little bit longer.

If you're only a few thousand feet above the ground, the extra time aloft won't make much difference to you. If you are many thousands of feet above the ground, then you can possibly add a few minutes onto the time you're aloft, perhaps allowing you to make that emergency call, better plan for the off-field landing or try to find where you put your parachute (just kidding on the last one). That said, make sure you return to best glide speed when you're preparing to make the landing. This places the airplane closer to 30% above stall speed, which is a speed that pilots are used to when preparing for the landing roundout and flare. Finally, make sure you land into the wind, too.

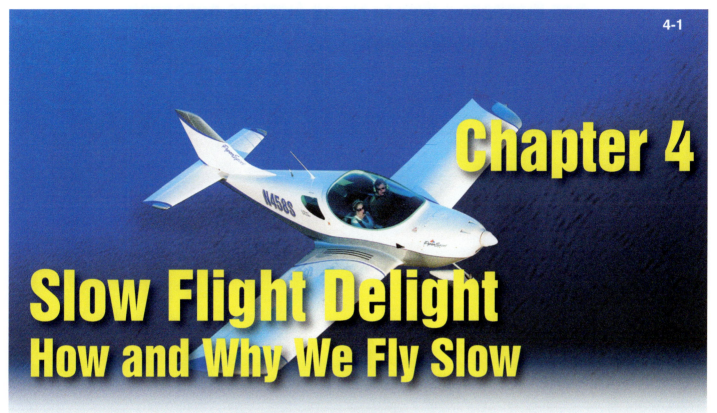

Chapter 4

Slow Flight Delight
How and Why We Fly Slow

Let me introduce you to one of aviation's great ironies—flying low and slow.

How can flying low and slow be the way to go? Isn't the whole point of flying to be fast and elevated? Don't speed and distance from the ground represent safety? Isn't low and slow as risky as being a javelin catcher at the Olympics?

Not really. When you come right down to it, if you want to come right down to it, you are at some point going to be flying low and slow. It's called *landing*.

We practice slow flight because a landing approach is done at a relatively slow speed, typically around 30% above the airplane's stall speed. We have to get close to the ground in order to land, right? If you weren't skilled at slow flight and happened to stall at 5,000 feet above the ground it wouldn't be much of a concern. You could stall, recover from the stall, and have plenty of altitude cushion (about 5,000 feet worth of altitude to spare). It becomes a much bigger concern if you're flying slow and manage to stall a few hundred feet above the ground, where there's less air to spare.

Things happen fast when the plane is slow, and that's what you need to know. The purpose of slow flight is for you to understand the dynamics and aerodynamics of low speed maneuvering and how they differ—sometimes significantly—from what you encounter at cruise speeds.

When the flying is slow the action is fast, so fasten your seatbelt, limber up your legs, actuate your arms, and prepare to step into another flight dimension.

A Very Important Reason to Learn to Fly Slow

Rod Machado's How to Fly an Airplane Handbook

Slow Flight Delight

Learning how to fly your airplane slowly offers several benefits.

The first and most important benefit is understanding how differently your airplane behaves when you fly slowly. The controls are much less responsive, the pitch attitude is often higher, and the airplane is closer to its stall speed (stalls are discussed in the next chapter). That means anything you do to increase the stall speed, such as abrupt maneuvering or making steep turns that increase the load factor, increase the likelihood of a stall. Understanding the behavioral qualities of an airplane in slow flight makes landing a much easier and safer proposition and minimizes the chances you will stall the airplane if distracted or disoriented.

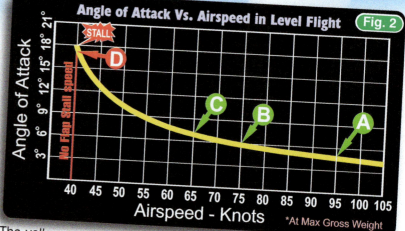

The yellow graph line above shows the angle of attack required for the airplane to remain in level flight at any given airspeed. Decrease airspeed and the angle of attack must increase.

The second benefit is that if you're planning on landing an airplane (I recommend it, especially if you drink a lot of coffee), you'll need to operate in the rectangular circuit flown around an airport's runway, known as the *airport traffic pattern*. That means you'll need to play nicely with others in the pattern, some of whom may even fly slower than you. If you're following a slow flying airplane, you might have the option of passing, but this isn't expected behavior so it has risks and usually won't be approved at a tower-controlled airport where the idea is that everyone flying airplanes with similar capabilities should be able to hit about the same speed and stay in line. No pushing, no hitting allowed.

We're going to build your slow-flight skills a building block at a time, from straight-and-level slow flight to slow flight with a turn, to slow flight in a climb and descent. We'll finish up with ultra slow mo, also known as flight at *minimum controllable airspeed*. This is slower-than-slow flight!

Chapter 4: Slow Flight Delight

Incidentally, Here's Something About Your Wing

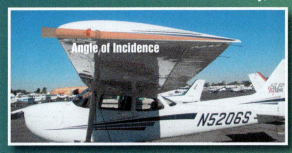

Airplane wings have something known as an *angle of incidence* (AOI) which is typically about 4 degrees on many fixed-wing airplanes. The AOI is the angle the wings' chord line makes with the longitudinal axis of the airplane. In other words, it's the angle with which the wings are attached to the airplane. Airplanes have a built-in angle of incidence mainly so that the airplane doesn't ride nose high during cruise flight. After all, this is where airplanes typically spend most of their time and no pilot, much less his or her passengers wants to spend hours riding in a recliner. With a four degree AOI, the longitudinal axis (or the fuselage) is approximately level with the horizon while the airplane is at the typical cruise airspeed.

Let's begin by placing you in the cockpit of an airplane in level cruise flight at 95 knots (Figure 1, position A). We'll assume your airplane has a power-off stall speed of 40 knots in its clean configuration. "Clean" doesn't mean your airplane has been bathed, dried, and buffed. It means the plane's gear is retracted (if it has retractable landing gear) and that the flaps are retracted. In the cruise condition, your nose attitude is relatively close to the horizon, with the wing's angle of attack at approximately four degrees, and you're typically using somewhere between 65% and 75% of the engine's maximum available power.

Now let's slow you down from 95 knots to 65 knots and maneuver in the clean configuration (Figure 1, position C). Hitting the brakes isn't going to do it, so let's see how you can go about going slow.

Slow (Flying) Pilots at Work

To perform slow flight, you must understand the relationship between angle of attack, airspeed, and lift, as shown in Figure 2 (this graph assumes our airplane is at its maximum gross weight). While cruising at a speed of 95 knots, the wings require an angle of attack of approximately four degrees to generate sufficient lift to allow the airplane to remain in straight and level flight (Figure 2, position A). That *angle of incidence* comes built-in on most planes (see the sidebar *Incidentally, Here's Something About Your Wing*), which means that at cruise speed the airplane is flying in a nearly level flight attitude.

Since you'll be reducing power to slow the airplane to 65 knots, you're going to need a lift in order to maintain level flight. To sustain the same amount of lift you had before slowing down, let's assume that you'll need to increase the wings' angle of attack to approximately seven degrees for this particular airplane model (Figure 2, position C). The airplane's designers gave you a four degree head start, and you have to add three degrees to stay on the up-and-up and maintain level flight.

The aerodynamic relationship that's extremely important to understand is the one between angle of attack (AOA) and speed. It's clearly shown in the *AOA vs. Airspeed* graph in Figure 2. Slow the airplane down in level flight and the angle of attack must increase (the nose must be raised in this level-flight example) to maintain your altitude.

"Increasing the Angle of Attack As I Fly Slower" is an interesting game, but the game definitely has its limits. There comes a point where the airplane moves so slowly that no matter how much you want them to, the wings can no longer curve the air enough to produce sufficient lift for level flight. When you reach that point, you're at the airplane's stall speed in its current configuration. The airplane stalls, as shown in Figure 2, position D (more on stalls in the next chapter).

Fig. 3

Entering Slow Flight

The proper way to enter slow flight is to add carburetor heat, reduce power and simultaneously increase your angle of attack (raise the nose relative to the horizon in level flight in this demonstration) at a rate sufficient to maintain level flight but not so abruptly or slowly so as to allow the airplane to climb or descend (see Figure 3). You'll definitely need to look directly over of the airplane's nose (or slightly to the left if the cowling blocks your view of the horizon) during the transition to slow flight. You'll also need to cross check your altimeter and vertical speed indicator during the transition to ensure that you're maintaining altitude. (See sidebar: *Cross Checking a Flight Instrument* on page 4-7 to better understand how to scan any flight instrument.) You're dividing your attention between outside and inside references during this transition.

The secret is to apply back pressure on the elevator control at a smooth continuous rate that suffices to hold the altimeter and VSI needles steady (Figure 3, position C). That means the nose is slowly but continuously pitching up to hold altitude. You'll find the vertical speed indicator very useful in making this transition, since it's a much more sensitive instrument (because it's sensitive, don't make fun of how it looks or it won't talk to you for a week). Pull back too slowly, and your altitude decreases; too fast, and it increases. With just one or two practice efforts you will be able to hold altitude while transitioning to the targeted speed. During this nose-up transition, feel free to add a few twists of nose-up trim to help sustain the right attitude (Figure 4). The final trim adjustment will come when the correct airspeed and altitude are established.

When you're within five knots of the final slow flight speed (65 knots in our example), begin applying power to hold altitude and adjust the elevator control to maintain airspeed. The key here is to maintain that nose-high attitude as power is applied. Slow flight at speeds close

Chapter 4: Slow Flight Delight

to the airplane's stalling speed typically requires a large nose-up pitch attitude, so don't let that nose drop as you apply power. In fact, you'll find that adding power helps keep the nose up, since engine thrust is now directed in a more vertical direction with the increasing pitch attitude.

Keep that back pressure applied to the yoke and adjust your attitude to get exactly 65 knots. Now add power. How much power should you add? Typically, more power than you think, especially if you're flying close to stall speed and on the back side of the power curve where the induced drag increases dramatically with decreasing speed. (Read the sidebar: *Power Required Curve and the Total Drag Curve* on page 4-11.)

You'll find out how much power is needed during the first few trial runs of slow flight. What you don't want to be is a Slow Mo Sam when it comes to moving that throttle forward to maintain altitude. So get to it. Move that throttle in—move it!—to keep the altitude and vertical speed indicator needles stationary.

This is the start of your education about how different things are in the world of slow flight. A little bit (whether of throttle or rudder) does *not* go a long way in slow flight. Don't be timid. You aren't going to hurt the engine's pistons (or feelings) if you add power pronto, but you will begin to lose altitude if you delay throttle movement. And remember to add the appropriate amount of right rudder pressure (Figure 5) to keep the airplane from yawing to the left, since the power-induced left turning tendency caused by P-factor and propeller slipstream is very strong at slow speeds, high power settings, and high angles of attack—and you've now got all three on your hands (and feet).

Because you might be operating within the region of reversed command during slow flight, my preference is to use Technique #1, the *elevator-airspeed method*, discussed in Chapter Three for controlling your altitude and airspeed. This technique makes slow

How to Reduce Power When Entering Slow Flight

How quickly and to what extent should you reduce power when entering slow flight? The correct answer is, "As quick and as much as you need to." If you've just entered the downwind and are instructed to follow an airplane directly ahead of you that's flying 20 knots slower, then you better

Picture #1

apply that carburetor heat and bring the throttle all the way back quickly as you begin raising that nose (Picture #1). In this instance, you need to slow down quickly, especially since airplanes don't have collision damage waivers (or bumpers).

Now, I'm not advocating that you yank the throttle around, either. Super quick reductions of power can add to the detuning of a crankshaft. Pulling that power back in one smooth consistent motion, however, is not at all harmful. Could this sudden reduction of power "shock cool" an engine? Yes, it will cool the engine, but it's not likely to "shock" cool it since you've already made a power reduction (thus, previously cooling the engine) to enter the traffic pattern. So, shock cooling isn't really an issue here.

On the other hand, under normal conditions or if you're practicing slow flight for proficiency, there's nothing wrong with reducing power slowly to some moderate value and allow the airplane to decelerate at slower rate (Picture #2). You might do this on your private pilot checkride, for instance. The slower rate of deceleration allows you to identify the necessary corrections that you'll need to make if you want to keep the airplane's altitude, heading and airspeed within the required performance limits.

Picture #2

Nose-Up Trim
Fig. 4
During slow flight transition, add nose-up trim to help maintain your attitude.

Adding Right Rudder
As power is applied, right rudder added
Fig. 5
As power is added in slow flight, you'll need a lot of right rudder to fly straight.

flight much easier on first introduction. It's also quite useful when you begin making turns in slow flight (to be discussed soon). Of course, once you gain experience using the elevator and throttle to control airspeed and altitude in slow flight, you'll find that you begin moving the two controls simultaneously, without making a distinction over what controls what (also known as Technique #3 from Chapter Three).

Exiting Slow Flight

Whew. After all that hard work to get into slow flight, we're now going to undo everything we did and exit slow flight. You can't go around with your nose in the air forever.

When the time comes and you want to return to cruise flight (Figure 6, position A), begin by applying maximum allowable power (remember, we're calling this *full power* now) and removing any carburetor heat you applied (Figure 6, position B). Why full power? The airplane is in a high-drag position and full power allows the airplane to accelerate as quickly as possible to cruise speed. There's just no good reason to apply cruise power and wait for the airplane to eventually accelerate to cruise speed at a snail's pace. Just remember, there are no airplanes named after snails (such as the *Escargot-slo*) for good reason.

When applying full power, it's important to lower the nose at just the right rate to maintain your altitude and accelerate to cruise speed. How do you know what that rate is? You cross check the vertical speed indicator and altimeter to keep their needles stationary during the transition (Figure 6, position C). Given the amount of nose-up elevator trim you applied to hold the slow flight condition, you'll need a great deal of forward elevator pressure to initially maintain your altitude during this transition.

It's helpful to immediately apply some nose-down trim after adding power, to prevent the need for excessive forward pressure on the elevator (Figure 6, position B). This isn't supposed to look

Fig. 6

Chapter 4: Slow Flight Delight

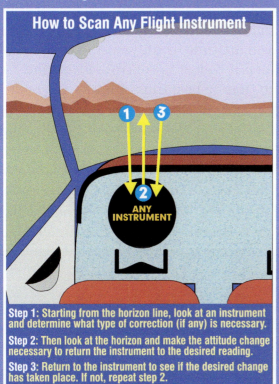

Cross Checking a Flight Instrument

It's often a challenge for new pilots to fly and scan any panel instrument, mainly because they tend to fixate on the instrument while the airplane drifts away from the desired attitude. So here's quick way to crosscheck scan any flight instrument such as the VSI or altimeter when trying to determine if the airplane is holding the desired altitude.

How to Scan Any Flight Instrument

Step 1: Starting from the horizon line, look at an instrument and determine what type of correction (if any) is necessary.
Step 2: Then look at the horizon and make the attitude change necessary to return the instrument to the desired reading.
Step 3: Return to the instrument to see if the desired change has taken place. If not, repeat step 2.

You begin from the horizon line where you've established the appropriate attitude for the maneuver desired. Then you move to a particular flight instrument and determine if it's showing what it's supposed to show (step 1). If you're attempting to hold altitude and the VSI shows a descent, then the VSI is clearly not showing a zero rate indication. Next, you should look back at the horizon (step 2) and make a small pitch or bank correction that makes (or will make) the instrument show the desired value. If you don't know how much of a pitch or bank correction to make, then just take a guess. There's no rule that says you can't crosscheck scan the instrument more than once. Once you make the pitch or bank correction using the visible horizon, return to the instrument (step 3) and see if it's reading properly. If not, just repeat the process until it does.

At no time during this crosscheck scan are you staring at the flight instruments. While I don't care if you stare at the horizon (you're looking outside the cockpit and that's a good thing), I do care if you stare at any panel instrument (because now you aren't looking outside the cockpit and that's a bad thing). As far as the amount of time you spend looking at any flight instrument in step 2, this shouldn't be more than just a fraction of a second (with practice, that is).

like a match between you and the plane, presented by the World Wrestling Federation.

I don't mean to suggest that your muscles are so weak that if someone pinches your bicep it goes flat. I just want you to realize that good pilots don't work any harder than they have to. There's an art to flying smart, and in this case it means using the trim whenever possible to make the airplane easier to handle. By the way, the nose-up pitch response and the subsequent need for forward elevator pressure is very similar to what you'll experience if you're forced to go around (begin a climb) during an approach to landing. That ride can be an un-merry go round. More about go-arounds later.

When applying full power, expect to need more right rudder to keep the airplane flying straight (Figure 6, position B)—a lot more. After all, the airplane is slow and you're applying full power, which initially increases the airplane's left turning tendency. So push on that right rudder pedal enough to hold your heading (keep the nose pointed straight ahead) while keeping the wings level with the ailerons. As the airplane accelerates, you'll find that you need less and less right rudder to keep the airplane flying straight, but you will need more nose-down trim. Use whatever trim is necessary to reduce the forward pressure you're applying through the elevator control.

As you approach the chosen cruise speed, modify the power settings to maintain that speed *or* reduce power to a selected cruise power setting and be satisfied with the resulting speed. It's your choice, but it is a choice. Flying is a series of tradeoffs. In most flight training situations you don't need to cruise at any specific airspeed. Instead, your instructor might have you set power to a previously agreed upon value that produces a speed that keeps you from achieving warp factor seven and exiting the practice area every 15 seconds. You make the call here (and not to Starfleet, either).

Control Response in Slow Flight

One of the critical things to understand about and learn from slow flight is control response—or rather, the *lack* of control response.

Flying slower typically means that the flight controls are less responsive (they feel mushier). This is because the velocity of the air flowing over them decreases. This means that the aileron, elevator and rudder controls must be *deflected* or *displaced* more to maneuver the airplane, compared to the same maneuver at closer to cruise speed. Slow speed is kind of like having a muffler on the controls.

4-8 Rod Machado's How to Fly an Airplane Handbook

We typically think in terms of control *pressures* rather than control *deflection* when operating the flight controls. Flight instructors are constantly harping (or fluting) on the need to be gentle, subtle, and light-of-touch on the controls. And you should be—except when you shouldn't. In slow flight, you must often be a little more aggressive on the flight controls. I want to make sure that you understand (as well as expect) the need for a larger deflection of the ailerons to initiate and sustain the bank angle, and the need for greater rudder pedal displacement to coordinate the flight controls. You should also expect to apply more trim (more rotations of the trim wheel) to sustain a given attitude.

These larger control deflections in slow flight are unfamiliar, and at first students often underestimate how much control pressure it takes to maintain a given attitude or un-yaw a yaw. You need to adjust *your* attitude and realize that "slow needs mo'" when it comes to control movement. I'm not leading you down the primrose path when I say this is no time to be a timid tulip.

In slow flight at a speed close to stall, you'll need a great deal of right rudder pressure to overcome the airplane's power-induced left turning tendency. Keep in mind that the slower you fly, the more power you need to hold altitude. This makes the left-turning tendency quite noticeable. Your right leg is going to get a good workout here, meaning that you can skip the right leg exercises at the gym on the Bowflex machine (which isn't a device for shooting other exercise machines across the gym).

If you have rudder trim I'd be happy to see you using it, but not yet. You can trim to your heart's content after you've done without it a few times. I want you to literally feel just how much right rudder is necessary for most airplanes operating in slow flight. My preference is that you forgo the rudder trim and just tough it out for your first few slow flight practice sessions.

Slow Flight Turns

Now it's your turn to make a turn while in slow flight. Slow flight is where you'll see the airplane's power-induced left turning tendency in its full glory. Let's see how this plays out in a shallow, slow-flight, level turn to the right.

You'll certainly need a little right aileron and rudder to start the right turn. You'll also need to continue to apply a great deal of right rudder pressure to keep the turn coordinated as you compensate for the airplane's natural power-induced left turning tendency.

Remember, you can initially tell if your turn entry is coordinated by looking over the panel and keeping the nose from yawing in a direction opposite the direction of turn. Adverse yaw from the lowered aileron on the left wing is also going to do its best to yaw your nose to the left, but your application of right rudder—and lots of it—

Fig. 7

Chapter 4: Slow Flight Delight

If It Had Claws, It Could Land on a Fencepost

Courtesy - Paul Svenkeson

Do you know that there's a six-place airplane on the market capable of flying at a minimum controllable airspeed of 26 knots? Now that's slow, right? In fact, it's seven knots slower than the stall speed of the Piper J3 Cub. That airplane is the Helio Courier. I've always been fascinated by airplanes that can fly fast (the Helio Courier has a cruise speed of approximately 147 knots) as well as fly slow. The reason this airplane can fly so slow is that it has slotted Fowler flaps and automatic leading edge slats that offer a dramatic increase in wing area when deployed. Big wing, slower flight.

Another unique feature of the Helio Courier is that the airplane won't stall. One owner says that it's possible, with full flaps and slats deployed, to pull the control wheel into your lap and have the airplane descend at 1,200 fpm with full roll authority. This slow speed performance is why the Helio Courier is capable of landing in a distance shorter than that of a J3 Piper Cub, which is 250 feet for the Courier vs. 290 feet for the Cub. That's impressive when you remember that the Courier can carry up to six people while the Cub carries two.

Perhaps one owner expressed it best when he said, "I've seen a local fellow land his Helio Courier on the strip of pavement that connects the taxiway to the runway. The Helio seemed almost to hover onto the taxiway." The pilot did this so he could land into the wind instead of landing in a crosswind that would probably challenge the skills of even the most experienced pilots.

will prevent this. After you establish a shallow banked turn and neutralize the ailerons (assuming that you don't need aileron deflection to maintain the chosen bank angle), you'll most likely find that you have to keep pressure on that right rudder to keep the turn coordinated and the nose pointed in the direction of turn (Figure 7, position A). Once the ailerons are neutralized in a turn there's no adverse yaw pulling the nose away from the direction of turn. So, the right rudder you're applying in the right turn is used only to counteract the effects of propeller slipstream and P-factor.

Sometimes, regardless of whether you're using a shallow or medium banked turn in slow flight, you might have to apply right or even left aileron to maintain the designated bank angle. Like children, flight instructors, and private pilots, not all airplanes behave the same way, for reasons that are way beyond this book to describe (they involve math and stuff). That doesn't matter, because your job is to deflect the controls as needed to make the airplane do what you want it to do. So, do so.

As the lion tamer uses a whip and a chair to control the king of the jungle (thus explaining our current shortage of lion tamers), use your ailerons and rudder in whatever mixture and to whatever extent they are needed to make the airplane do your bidding. That's why you are called the *pilot in command*. Once the right turn is established, apply right or left aileron as needed to maintain the selected bank angle while simultaneously applying whatever rudder pressure is required (right rudder in this instance) to keep the turn coordinated.

Rolling out of a right turn in slow flight and back to straight flight means moving the ailerons to the left, and *releasing* some of the right rudder pressure (or applying left rudder, if necessary). On the other hand, it's unlikely that you'll need much (if any) left rudder pressure to roll out of a right turn in slow flight because of the airplane's power-induced left turning tendency.

Starting a left turn in slow flight often requires just a little left aileron deflection and in many instances very little (if any) left rudder pressure (Figure 7, position B). It's true that using left aileron to roll into the left turn causes the nose to yaw to the right (because of adverse yaw), but the more powerful forces of slipstream and P-factor in the slow flight condition typically overpower this tendency. The result is that the nose tends to yaw to the left, often keeping the turn nearly coordinated during the roll in. It's as if merely thinking about the left turn starts it.

In most instances you can start a left turn in slow flight with a small amount of left aileron deflection and simultaneous release of a little of the right rudder pressure that you were holding to keep the airplane flying straight and the flight controls coordinated. Once you've established a left turn in slow flight, you might need considerable right aileron deflection to maintain the bank as well as a little right rudder to remain coordinated. That's right—*right*. Isn't that interesting? You could be established in a left coordinated turn during slow flight with the flight controls looking for all the world as though they're positioned to roll you into a right turn. You haven't fallen down the rabbit hole or through the looking glass into another world. It's the real world of physics, specifically propeller and slipstream physics. Once again, use whatever combination of aileron and rudder is needed to keep the turn coordinated. Be the pilot in command.

Rolling out of a left slow flight turn typically requires a lot of right rudder pressure along with a reasonable amount right aileron deflection (Figure 8). Why? Because you're essentially making a right turn in slow flight, despite starting that turn from a left banked condition. When rolling out to the right, it's very common for students to apply insufficient right rudder pressure. As a result, the nose of the airplane yaws to the left as the right rollout begins. So if you're asked how much right rudder is needed in rolling out to the right in slow flight, the answer is, "Enough so that the nose appears to stop moving laterally as the airplane rolls into level flight."

At the early stages of your training, keeping the flight controls coordinated should mostly be a *visual* thing. With more practice, it also becomes a *seat of the pants* thing, but you always have the ball in the inclinometer to help with coordination. Good stick and rudder pilots, however, seldom need to look at the inclinometer to evaluate their flight control coordination. So get those legs ready to rumble. Use them, but don't abuse them or the airplane.

Maintaining Altitude During Slow Flight Turns

Maintaining altitude in slow flight turns involves focusing on the airplane's pitch attitude as observed directly ahead of your seated position, just as we discussed in Chapter Three.

Since the slow flight attitude is similar to a climb attitude, the airplane's nose will be several degrees above the horizon. Use the red dot or cowling reference to maintain your attitude during all slow flight maneuvers. The big challenge with slow flight is in learning how to use your elevator and throttle to maintain airspeed and altitude when turning.

Keep in mind that in slow flight near stall speed the airplane might be operating on the back side of the power curve, also known as the *region of reversed command* (see Postflight Briefing #4-1: *The Region of Reversed Command*). In many small airplanes, the

Fig. 8

Chapter 4: Slow Flight Delight

region of reversed command typically begins at approximately 20% (or less) above stall speed (Figure 9). That means if your airplane stalls at 40 knots and you're slow flying at 48 knots (20% above stall speed) then you're probably entering the region of reversed command. In this region, an increase in pitch attitude results in a descent (or a faster descent rate) unless you immediately increase power to hold altitude.

It is very important to understand this concept, because as you start a turn in slow flight you must increase the wing's production of lift for two reasons. First, turning involves some loss of the vertical component of lift. Second, turns increase the load factor, which means the airplane's apparent weight has increased and that results in an increase in stall speed (an increase that's dependent on how steep the bank is, of course).

In other than a slow flight turn, you typically increase lift by applying slight aft pressure on the yoke, which increases the airplane's angle of attack. This results in a slight loss of airspeed, but it's not a problem since you're at cruise speed. Doing this when operating on the back side of the power curve without a commensurate increase in power results in a further decrease in airspeed and a descent (Figure 10). That's why any increase in pitch during slow flight must *immediately* (did I say "immediately" loud enough here?) be accompanied by a *simultaneous* (did I say "simultaneous" loud enough, too?) increase in power to maintain the desired airspeed and altitude. The steeper the bank, the more lift needed, thus the more power needed as you increase the pitch attitude. This is not a time to be dainty with your throttle, either. Said another way, if the throttle snoozes the pilot loses. Of course, you're not moving the throttle like it's a pinball handle, but you are moving it as quickly as necessary to accomplish your objective.

Power Required Curve and the Total Drag Curve

Let me throw you a curve by throwing you two curves. In Chapter Three I talked about the *total drag curve* as it related to the best glide speed and minimum sink speed. In this chapter I introduced you to the *power required curve*. If you look closely, you'll see that both of these curves have shapes that are similar but not the same.

The shapes are similar because the *power required curve's* shape is dependent on the same two types of drag making up the *total drag curve*. The big difference here is that the total drag curve is proportional to the velocity squared while the power required curve is proportional to the velocity cubed.

The important point to understand here is that the minimum power required for level flight (position A) isn't found at the minimum drag speed (position B). In fact, the minimum power required for level flight is found to the left of the minimum drag speed. The main reason for this difference is that the required engine power is more affected by increasing parasite drag than increasing induced drag. Therefore, the minimum power required speed is found to the left of the minimum drag speed, at a point where there is slightly less parasite drag.

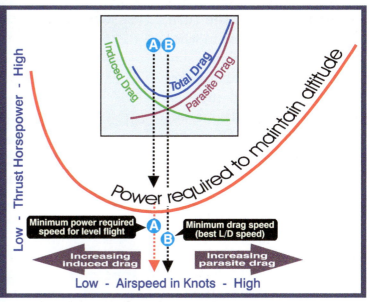

More power also means more left turning tendency, too. So expect to add more right rudder pressure as needed to remain in coordinated flight. When rolling out of the slow flight turn, you'll need to reduce power to maintain the previous straight and level slow flight condition. That means remembering the power setting you had prior to entering the slow flight turn. It just so happens that your short term memory is enhanced by saying out loud the item to be remembered. Say, "Twenty-one hundred RPM" out loud before starting the turn. If anyone questions you or your sanity, just tell them it's your favorite RPM of them all, or the name of a hot new rock group. They'll back away slowly.

As a final note on power application, keep in mind that in slow flight the airplane experiences a great deal of induced drag. That, along with the airplane's inertia, means that it doesn't accelerate quickly when applying power. In other words, the typical small, underpowered airplane is a hog when it's flying slow. This is why the lessons you learn during slow flight are so practical when it comes to landing an airplane. If you're forced to go around just a few feet above the runway, the airplane is low and slow and needs to be flown carefully because you are relatively close to stall territory. (A *go-around* means that you elect to climb rather than land when close to the runway, perhaps because of a traffic conflict, a safety concern, a hog, dog or log on the runway, etc.).

Since slow flight turns are relatively temporary conditions, it's not practical to use additional trim in the turn, only to remove the trim when returning to straight slow flight. Using trim during slow flight turns would increase your workload without any additional benefit. Of course, if you subsist on a vegetarian diet of pigeon milk and wood chips, you might feel weak enough that using trim in the turn actually seems like a good idea. If so, then help yourself to the trim wheel (but not to a cheeseburger).

Fig. 10

Chapter 4: Slow Flight Delight

Slow Flight at Minimum Controllable Airspeed

The term *slow flight* is a relative one. It can mean flying the airplane at any speed slower than your typical cruise speed to a point just above the airplane's stall speed, which is called its *minimum controllable airspeed* (MCA). Flight at MCA is what you call *really slow flight,* because you can't get any slower than that without stalling the airplane.

At MCA, the airplane is hanging by a thread of lift. In this condition, any further increase in angle of attack or load factor, or any reduction of power results in an immediate stall. Since most stall horns or stall warning lights activate at three to four knots above stall, you can expect the stall warning device to be activated at all times when flying at MCA. If you don't have a stall horn or a stall light, you can tell you're at MCA by recognizing the very beginning of the stall buffet on the wings. (Note: during your private pilot checkride, you'll demonstrate slow flight at some speed above the stall horn (or stall light) activation speed. For *checkride purposes* only, the FAA doesn't want to hear, see or feel any stall warning during the maneuver. Increase your speed immediately if the stall horn or stall light activates to deactivate it.)

Before I tell you how to fly at MCA, you're probably wondering why you would ever want to do such thing. Listening to the stall horn isn't exactly a trip to the concert hall. The short answer is, so you'll know an *incipient* stall when you feel it. As a practical matter, if you know how to fly at MCA you are much less likely to unknowingly get so slow or so close to the airplane's *critical angle of attack* that you accidentally stall the airplane. That's the real value in flying at MCA. It's all about the stall, or stall recognition and avoidance. You're learning how to know where you don't want to go.

Flying at MCA is performed just like slow flight at 65 knots except that you're using either the stall warning horn/light and/or the sense of an *imminent stall* to help identify the target pitch attitude (an imminent stall is one where any further increase in the angle of attack results in a stall. More on this in the next chapter). I promise.

Entry to slow flight at MCA is the same as for any slow flight. Apply carburetor heat, reduce power and apply back pressure on the yoke at such a rate that you maintain altitude as your speed decreases (Figure 11, positions A and B). The difference is that you will continue increasing the angle of attack until the stall horn sounds or you feel that a stall is imminent. At that point, apply sufficient power to maintain your altitude (Figure 11, position C). At three to four knots above stall you're at or at least very close to the airplane's MCA.

Fig. 11

Stall Warning Light

Some airplanes have what appear to be two distinct stall horn sounds with the first (a lower pitched sound) activating a few knots above the latter (a higher pitched sound, somewhat similar to your flight instructor's voice when he or she gets nervous). The secret here is to get reasonably close to stall speed without letting the airplane stall. Remember, it's called the "Grand" Canyon because it's grand and it's called "minimum" controllable airspeed because you fly at the minimum controllable airspeed. Keep in mind that flying at MCA instead of some faster speed means that you'll probably need to apply a lot more right rudder pressure than usual to keep the airplane flying straight due to the airplane's power-induced left turning tendency (Figure 11, position D).

What about flight at MCA when the airplane doesn't use a stall horn but uses a stall warning light instead (Figure 12)? Here you have to rely on sight and how the airplane feels to identify the MCA condition. The stall light, which is typically red, will light up when you're three to four knots above stall. Increasing the angle of attack further won't make the light any redder. So when you see red (the red light, that is), consider yourself flying at MCA. If your instructor is a purist, he or she might have you forget the light and fly at MCA using the feel of an imminent stall as your reference. If he or she does, then tell him that he's my new best friend and that I'm calling Neil Armstrong to tell him he's now number two.

What about making a turn in slow flight at MCA? How can you increase the angle of attack even slightly to generate the extra lift needed during the turn without stalling the airplane? After all, any further increase in angle of attack will put you at or beyond the critical angle of attack, and that means you're in a stall. The answer is that you don't increase the angle of attack further because if you do the airplane will stall. Period! You simply can't increase the angle of attack beyond the wing's *critical angle of attack* without stalling.

Instead, when making a turn at MCA, you add more power as you enter the turn and maintain the angle of attack necessary to fly at MCA. The increase in power adds to the vertical component of lift needed to maintain level flight (Figure 13), and keeps you above stall speed (which increases as your bank angle increases).

Adding power in a turn at MCA keeps you above the increasing stall speed that's associated with a slight increase in bank-induced load factor. As a side benefit, the vertical component of engine thrust (yellow arrow) also adds to the total lifting force (dark blue arrow on top) which helps reduce stall speed slightly (it acts against the increase due to load factor).

Chapter 4: Slow Flight Delight

This is a very important point to understand. The addition of power doesn't change the critical angle of attack at which the wing stalls. It can't, because the critical angle of attack is a function of wing design, not power. Adding power helps you remain above stall speed which increases as bank angle (load factor) increases. So, add power immediately when entering a turn at MCA.

Because the typical general aviation airplane doesn't have a very powerful engine, you're better off keeping your slow flight turns in the shallow bank category. While operating at MCA on the back side of the power curve, it's unlikely that you'll have enough power to perform anything more than moderately banked turns.

Of course, as you roll into or out of a bank during a slow flight turn at MCA

you can just imagine how much rudder you'll need to keep the turn coordinated. A left turn in this condition is sure to require a little right rudder pressure to fly coordinated and right aileron pressure to hold the bank angle because of the airplane's prominent power-induced left turning tendency at this slow speed (Figure 14). Isn't that something? It's as though you have to make the controls look like you're entering a turn to the right, while their position simply keeps the bank from increasing to the left during slow flight at MCA. This is generally true for most small airplanes.

Make sure you have that leg cocked and ready when making turns at MCA, and when rolling out of the turn be sure to reduce power to the setting used prior to entering the turn. Yes, that means you should have memorized that setting prior to starting the turn. So say that power value out loud to enhance your short term memory recall.

Slow flight at MCA is best practiced after you're familiar with basic stall recognition and recovery techniques. At least that way you'll know what a stall is and be more capable of avoiding one as well as being more comfortable operating at these slow speeds.

At the slow speeds associated with MCA, it's possible to experience something known as *speed instability*. For instance, when you're at MCA and encounter a little turbulence, your speed might be sufficiently unstable that it could decay quickly (the speed, not your tooth) because your airplane is operating on the back side of the power curve. The induced drag experienced by the airplane will slow it down quickly if the angle of attack increases even slightly without a commensurate increase in power. So be careful about abrupt pitch changes in these conditions, especially if turbulence is present. Be ready to adjust your attitude and immediately apply power as necessary to maintain your airspeed and altitude to prevent further slowing and a possible stall.

Climbing or Descending in Slow Flight Conditions

Taking off or landing are both conditions where the airplane climbs and descends while operating in slow flight conditions. It's true that these climbs and descents are not done at the slowest speeds possible, but they are done at relatively slower speeds. As a training maneuver, it is possible to climb (if you have enough engine power) and descend at slower speeds and even at minimum controllable airspeeds. Let's see how this is done.

If you're in slow flight at any speed down to MCA, you can begin a descent by adding carburetor heat and reducing power. When you do, you must also be prepared to simultaneously lower the pitch attitude to maintain the desired airspeed (or MCA condition). Keep in mind that with power reduced to some *fixed* position and a lower RPM setting, adjusting your pitch attitude with the elevator control is the only means you have of controlling your airspeed. Delaying the reduction in pitch as you reduce power means the airplane will move closer to a stall, which you want to avoid. So, when beginning a descent in slow flight be sure to simultaneously lower the nose as you reduce power.

How much of a power reduction should you make when descending at slow flight? Well, you can certainly do a power-off descent in slow flight, but this would produce a relatively large descent rate, given the low speed and the airplane's position on the back side of the power curve as shown in Figure 15, position A. (See the sidebar *Power Applied vs. Climb/Descent Rates* on Page 4-17.) Since this is a training exercise and not necessarily a practical exercise, reducing power a few hundred RPM is sufficient to demonstrate your skill at the maneuver (although it is challenging to do it with a full power reduction, too). As a final thought on descents, the moment you reduce power for the descent, you'll most likely need to back off on the right leg pressure you're applying to keep the flight controls coordinated. A reduction in power means a decrease in the airplane's power-induced left turning tendency.

Leveling off from a descent at MCA is accomplished by simultaneously adding power, removing carb heat, and raising the nose to the attitude that previously provided the designated slow flight speed. Your success during this transition is all a matter of proper elevator and throttle coordination.

Climbing in slow flight is also possible if your airplane has sufficient power (Figure 15, position B). To do so, you'd apply full power while in slow flight and adjust the pitch to maintain the desired slow flight climb airspeed. I know you know what I'm going to say next. You're right. Be prepared to add a lot of right rudder when adding power in a slow flight condition (Figure 16).

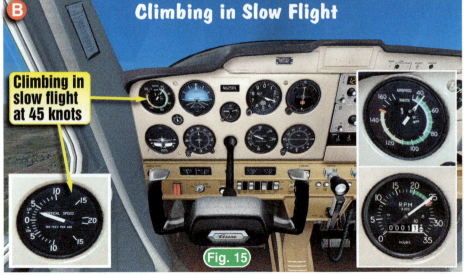

Chapter 4: Slow Flight Delight

Power Applied vs. Climb/Descent Rates

Looking at the accompanying figure, you'll see a different (non traditional) way of expressing the airplane's *power curve* in terms of *vertical speed curves*. The three vertical speed curves shown in different colors below compare airspeed to climb/descent rate for three different power settings. Each vertical speed curve represents the airplane's climb or descent rate (feet per minute on the vertical section of the graph) for a given airspeed (on the horizontal axis) based on three different power settings. Each curve also identifies the region where vertical performance is reversed (region of reversed command) or positive (region of positive command).

At maximum power (magenta vertical speed curve), the airplane's maximum speed in level flight (position A) is approximately 98 knots and its minimum speed in level flight is approximately 45 knots (position C). Starting at position A, if you raise your nose, your rate of climb would increase, eventually reaching a maximum at 69 knots (position B), also known as your *best rate of climb* speed or V_y. Continuing to raise the nose moves you into the *region of reversed command*, the orange shaded area. This results in a decrease in climb rate until you're at 45 knots with zero rate of climb (position C).

When you reduce engine power, you shift the vertical speed curve downward and to the left slightly. For instance, if you reduce your engine power to 2,100 RPM, the minimum speed required to maintain altitude is 62 knots (position D). This is the top of the blue colored vertical speed curve line. To the right of 62 knots is the *region of positive command*, the green shaded area. Lowering the nose and accelerating to 85 knots (position E) results in a 400 fpm rate of descent and pulling aft on the controls and slowing from 85 knots to 62 knots results in a decrease in descent rate leading to level flight. This is a normal (positive) response of the controls and it's what you'd expect when operating in the region of positive command.

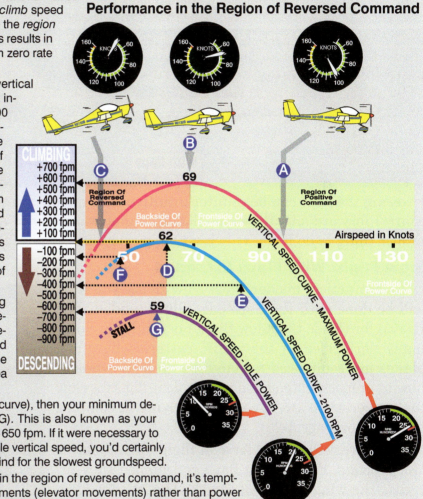

Performance in the Region of Reversed Command

However, pulling aft on the controls and slowing from 62 knots (position D) to 48 knots (position F) results in a descent rate of 150 fpm. This occurs because you're now operating in the region of reversed command. This is the reverse of how you expect the flight controls to work. That's is why we call this area the region of reversed command.

If you reduce power to idle (purple vertical speed curve), then your minimum descent rate occurs at a speed of 59 knots (position G). This is also known as your minimum sink speed and results in a descent rate of 650 fpm. If it were necessary to make contact with the surface at the slowest possible vertical speed, you'd certainly want to use a speed of 59 knots and land into the wind for the slowest groundspeed.

The takeaway point here is that during slow flight in the region of reversed command, it's tempting for you to control your altitude with pitch adjustments (elevator movements) rather than power adjustments. For instance, if you attempted to correct for a descent at minimum controllable airspeed (MCA) by applying elevator back pressure, you'll simply descend faster. If you attempted to correct for a slight climb at MCA by moving the elevator control forward, you'll climb faster. Therefore, in the region of reversed command, it's always best to correct for airspeed changes with pitch (elevator) adjustments and altitude deviations with power (throttle) adjustments.

After adding power, you simply accept whatever climb rate results. And when I say "accept," I don't mean you have to say out loud, "I accept the climb rate and claim it for Spain!" unless, of course, you want to. And please don't expect a substantial climb rate when attempting to climb at MCA. If you do, you're likely to be as disappointed as you were at your 10th birthday party where you hoped for a BB gun and got a record by BB King, instead.

Smaller, underpowered airplanes just don't perform well at slow speeds, and this is something that you should know and understand. The lesson here is that you aren't going to do much climbing, if you climb at all, at speeds near MCA. In most instances, the only way to make an airplane climb at these very slow speeds is to lower the nose and speed up a little. Why? Since you're operating on the back side of the power curve, speeding up decreases induced drag as you move toward the best L/D speed. If you attempt to go around while close to the ground and behind the power curve,

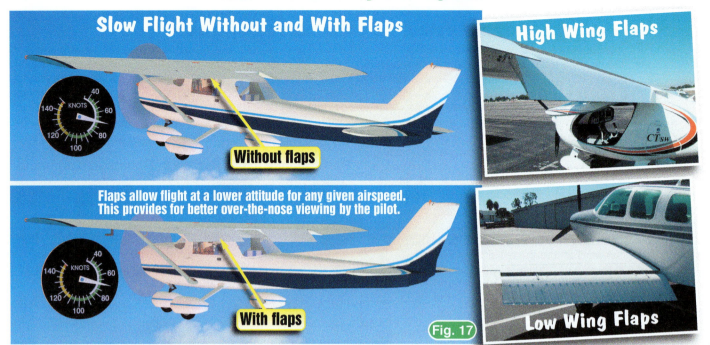

Fig. 17

lowering the nose can be counter intuitive (scary, too). You want to climb, and moving the elevator control forward slightly seems like an unnatural thing to do. It is, however, the aerodynamically proper thing to do if you're behind the power curve, right? Right!

Slow Flight With Flaps Extended

As a practical matter, most slow flying you'll do will be done with the flaps partially extended. The reason for this is that slow flight operations are normally performed in the traffic pattern where airplanes are sequenced for landing. So let's examine how to properly extend and retract your flaps for slow flight operations (we'll cover slow flying in complex airplanes on Page 4-23).

Flaps are very helpful for slow flight operations for two reasons. First, when flaps are applied they increase the wing's angle of attack. That means for a given airspeed, you can fly at a lower pitch attitude and maintain the required angle of attack to generate the necessary lift for flight (Figure 17). The result is that you can see more of what's ahead of and below you when using flaps (Figure 18). How good is that? It's pretty darn good when you consider that this makes it easier for you to see traffic ahead of you in the pattern as well as see the runway below you during your landing approach. The second reason for using flaps in slow flight is that they reduce the airplane's stall speed, which allows you to fly slower and still maintain a reasonable speed margin above stall.

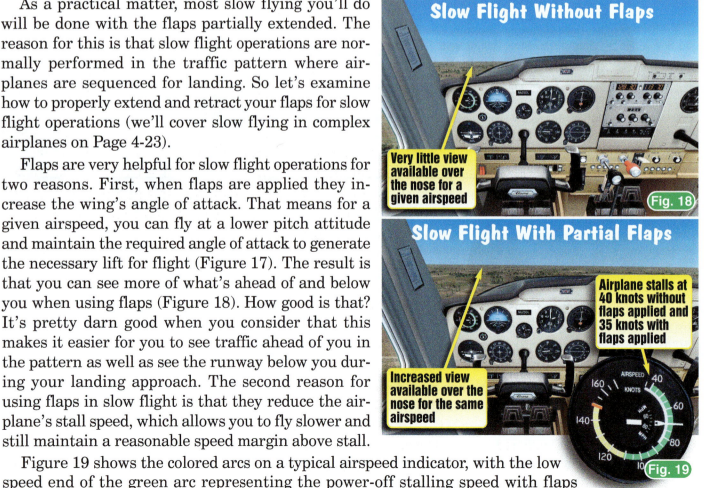

Figure 19 shows the colored arcs on a typical airspeed indicator, with the low speed end of the green arc representing the power-off stalling speed with flaps

Chapter 4: Slow Flight Delight   4-19

Fig. 20 — Manual Flap Extension Handle (Pull handle up to extend flaps)
Fig. 21 — Airplane With Manual Flap Extension

retracted. The low speed end of the white arc represents the power-off stalling speed with flaps fully extended. In our airplane, there is a five-knot difference in stalling speed between the full flap and no flap stalling speeds.

Of course, this being aviation there is neither a free lunch nor free lift. Flaps create lift but they also create drag, meaning that when flying slowly with flaps extended, the airplane accelerates much more slowly when power is applied. Speed instability can also be a bigger issue in the presence of turbulence or abrupt control inputs when flaps are in use. To you, this means a small increase in pitch attitude might result in a relatively large reduction in airspeed. After all, extension of the flaps gives the airplane a higher drag profile as a result of the drag they produce. If you let the nose rise a bit and the speed drops quickly, you must make a quick pitch and/or power adjustment to return to the correct airspeed.

Let's prepare to slow fly with half our flaps extended (or the closest notch of flaps to half-flap extension). Keep in mind that in small airplanes you can apply flaps in increments up to approximately 40 degrees (or more in some STOL or *short takeoff and landing* airplanes). These are typically airplanes with electric flap motors activated by a flap extension switch.

Other airplanes have manual flap extension handles (Figure 20) that allow you to apply flaps in notches or increments with typical extension values of 10, 25 and 40 degrees for the three notches. For instance, the Gobosh, Piper Warrior or Archer have manual flap extension handles (Figure 20).

We'll begin by assuming that you're in level flight at a slow cruise speed and have just entered the downwind leg of the traffic pattern. The intent here is to fly at least as slow as the slowest airplane ahead of you, but only if this is safe to do, of course.

How to Enter Slow Flight With Half-flaps Extended

In this demonstration we'll slow fly at 60 knots with 20 degrees (approximately half flaps) applied. The proper sequence for entering slow flight is to add carburetor heat, reduce power, apply elevator back pressure to hold altitude, and when the airplane is at or below Vfe (the top of the airspeed indicator's white arc or *maximum flap extension speed*), extend the flaps in 10-degree increments. In airplanes with manual flaps handles, you'll extend the flaps one notch at a time by pulling that handle (two notches of pull or 25 degrees will get you closest to half flaps in many airplanes).

So, apply carburetor heat, then reduce power to some value below the present power setting and above flight idle (Figure 22, positions A and B). As you do, maintain altitude by applying elevator back pressure at just the right rate. Remember to cross check the VSI here.

When the airplane reaches Vfe, apply your first 10 degrees (or one notch) of flaps. Keep in mind that the application of flaps on many airplanes causes the nose to pitch upward, so you'll want to be ready to apply a little forward elevator pressure to correct for this pitching movement. On some airplanes, however, the nose pitches *down* with flap application, while on others, it pitches up with the first two notches of flaps and down with the last notch applied (this all depends on the airplane's aerodynamics).

None of this should cause a flap, because it doesn't matter which way the nose goes. Your job is to know and anticipate what your airplane will do, and correct for it. It's simply good airmanship to prevent any sudden pitch change whenever possible (it prevents the "What the heck was that?" verbal query from your passengers not to mention a bad grade on the secret "passenger" post-flight evaluation survey).

After applying the first 10 degrees (or one notch) of flaps and simultaneously correcting for the pitch change, apply the next 10 degrees or second notch of flaps, once again correcting for any pitch changes. Since you're applying flaps while in level flight, you have to keep adjusting the nose to maintain your altitude, but with each successive notch or increment of flap application you'll typically be able to progressively lower the nose and fly at a lower nose-down attitude. This is, after all, one of the benefits of flying slow with half flaps applied. You get a slightly better view over the nose of the airplane.

At about five knots above the slow flight speed of 60 knots (Figure 22, position C), begin adding power at a rate that allows you to maintain altitude while using your elevator to control airspeed. Be prepared to move the throttle forward quickly. A lethargic, sloth-like, near-narcoleptic delay in moving the throttle won't gain you membership in the famed Slow Flight Fan Club (which consists of me and your instructor). While moving the throttle forward, use nose-up trim and apply a little right rudder, as we discussed previously. Congratulations, you now know slow, and in this instance that's good.

Fig. 22

Chapter 4: Slow Flight Delight

One very important thing to keep in mind when engaged in slow flight is that flaps create a lot of drag. What makes this a drag is that the airplane decelerates more quickly with flaps extended. You, connecting the dots, know that this means it's easier to accidentally overshoot the targeted slow flight speed, perhaps by enough to enter a stall, which isn't a ball and could lead to a fall. Once again, you need to be firmly in command. Don't dawdle on the throttle. And be ready to apply that right rudder as you apply power.

I'm sure you're seeing by now that while the airplane can be slow in slow flight, you have to be both quick and firm. Don't be lulled by the airplane's leisurely pace. Slow flight is sort of like being an actor on stage; your gestures have to be somewhat exaggerated in order to look correct.

Generally speaking, you'll operate on the downwind leg of the traffic pattern with 10-15 degrees (one notch) of flap extension. Full flaps are reserved for the landing portion of the traffic pattern (i.e., final approach). You can certainly apply more flaps on the downwind leg if you're following something ahead of you that's really slow, such as a pigeon (a pigeon destined for Squab City if he keeps mixing it up with airplanes). Half flaps will certainly allow you to fly slower, but there is seldom any need to go this slow on the downwind leg given the possibility that there's faster traffic operating behind you. Don't become Bob the Squab.

During training in the practice area, if you want to slow fly with full flaps, continue to apply the remaining flaps in 10-degree (or single-notch) increments as in the previous example. Just remember that with each successive extension of flaps, you'll need to quickly reconfigure the airplane's attitude so as to maintain your desired airspeed.

Slow Flight Maneuvering With Flaps Extended

If you thought that maneuvering in slow flight without flaps required a lot of right rudder, you will be truly astonished at the amount of right rudder pressure that's required to keep the flight controls coordinated when maneuvering with flaps in slow flight. After all, the airplane is now flying slower, allowing its power-induced left turning tendency to have more effect on the airplane. The slower speed also means that your flight controls are much less responsive. So, it's now major pedal-to-the-metal time. You will almost certainly need additional pressure and deflection of the rudder pedals to keep the flight controls coordinated. It's very important for you to understand how the airplane behaves under these conditions. Why? Because this is the behavior you're likely to experience if you have to make a sudden go-around close to the runway during a full flap landing approach.

Returning to Level Flight and Retracting the Flaps

While slow flight with full flaps may be exciting, it's not *so* exciting that you'd want to remain there all day. This implies that at some point you will need to return to straight and level flight with the flaps retracted. Let's do it.

Begin by applying full power, eliminating carburetor heat and lowering the nose at such a rate that you accelerate while simultaneously maintaining altitude (Figure 23, position A). You want to go forward faster, but not up or down. Expect that increasing the power will require significant forward pressure on the elevator control in order to prevent pitching upward. You have nose-up trim applied, so the sudden nose-up pitch isn't (or shouldn't be) a surprise. If you find that your tiny biceps are making violin noises because the muscle strands are humming with strain and exhaustion, please use all the nose-down trim needed to reduce the strain. That's what trim is for, which should be music to your ears (instead of music from your biceps).

Next, reduce the flap setting to the value offering more lift than drag (Figure 23, position B). That often means removing the major drag-causing portion of your flaps, which you'll do by retracting the flaps to their 50% extension level (unless you're already at half-flap extension), or the second notch position if you're using a three-notch, manual flap system. As the flaps are retracted, the airplane's nose typically pitches downward, so you'll need to correct this tendency with rearward elevator pressure.

Right around in here is where the student-in-command usually asks, "If flaps are such a drag, why don't we just retract them all at once and move on?" Good question. You are essentially making your wing area smaller with flap retraction. You need to give the airplane time to get used to this incrementally, so you don't accidentally stall your machine as you reduce the size of its lifting surface. The sequence is: retract a bit, wait for acceleration while anticipating and correcting for pitch change, then repeat (Figure 23, position C).

If for some reason the airplane isn't accelerating properly during flap retraction (perhaps because you're way behind the power curve, literally not figuratively), a complete and immediate retraction of flaps might result in a sudden descent or a stall. How do you know the airplane is accelerating during flap retraction? The first and most obvious clue is that you can see the airspeed increasing and you can feel the acceleration. An equally important clue is that you're sensing no deceleration (i.e., airspeed loss, kinesthetic feel of speed loss, change in sound, etc). It's true. If you can feel subtle acceleration changes when a building's elevator starts and stops, then you can certainly feel these acceleration changes in an airplane, which is essentially an elevator-box with wings.

Fig. 23

Chapter 4: Slow Flight Delight

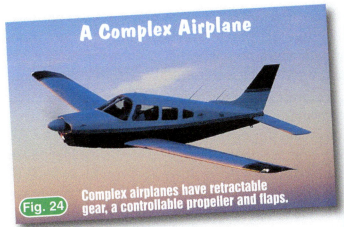

Fig. 24. Complex airplanes have retractable gear, a controllable propeller and flaps.

Slow Flight With Gear And Flaps Extended

If you're operating a complex airplane (one having retractable gear, flaps and a controllable propeller, as shown in Figure 24) you'll normally do most of your slow flying with the gear and flaps extended. So let's examine how to properly extend and retract your gear and flaps for slow flight operations.

Let's slow fly at 80 knots with the gear extended fully and the flaps extended halfway. Let's also assume that we're entering the downwind leg of the traffic pattern at a low cruise airspeed. This is where you'll typically want to have your landing gear extended, followed by partial flap extension.

Start by reducing power sufficiently to allow for a reasonably quick deceleration, but not so much that shock cooling becomes an issue (carburetor heat is not typically found on complex airplanes). Next, lower the gear and apply the initial extension of flaps, in that order (Figure 25, positions A and B). Why this sequence? Extending your landing gear first helps to decelerate the airplane. Since the *maximum gear operating speed* or Vlo is often higher than the *maximum flaps extended speed* or Vfe, it makes sense to put the gear down before the flaps. Begin by reducing power and maintaining altitude with elevator back pressure. When reaching Vlo, extend the gear and make sure it's actually extended (check for the proper gear extension indication). Be careful not to let the gear cause a sudden pitch change as it is extended. Depending on the airplane's gear type

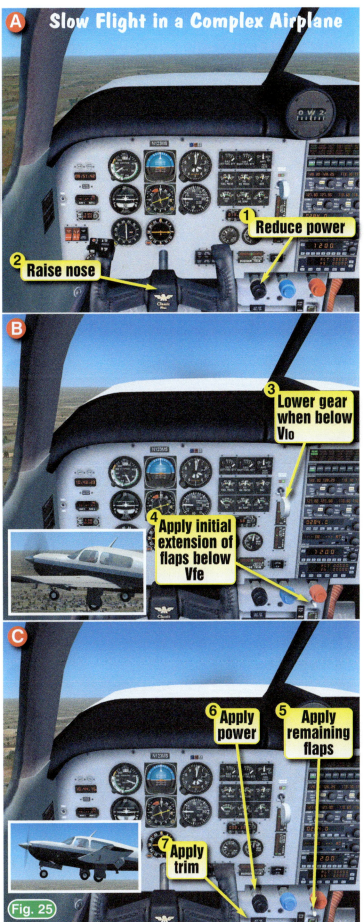

A — Slow Flight in a Complex Airplane
1. Reduce power
2. Raise nose

B
3. Lower gear when below Vlo
4. Apply initial extension of flaps below Vfe

C
5. Apply remaining flaps
6. Apply power
7. Apply trim

Fig. 25

Fig. 26

and configuration, the nose may pitch up or down; you'll quickly learn which is true for your plane and will thus be prepared to compensate for the change with elevator control.

When the airplane reaches Vfe, apply 10 degrees or one notch of flaps. Some airplane manufacturers permit the application of 10 or 15 degrees of flap extension at speeds above top of the airspeed indicators white arc (Vfe). If so, feel free to extend 10-15 degrees of flaps at a higher speed, but not before lowering the gear (remember, the first 10 degrees of flap extension doesn't give you as much drag as it does lift, so getting that gear down early to slow down is important).

Once again, be prepared to correct for any pitch changes when applying flaps. As the airplane continues to decelerate at a *fixed* power setting you're raising the nose to maintain altitude. When you're five knots above the slow flight speed, begin adding power at a rate that allows you to maintain the targeted speed while holding altitude. Of course, you're also using trim and applying appropriate rudder as previously discussed. And as before, keep in mind that flaps and gear create drag, which means the airplane slows down more quickly and your responses must thus be quick and firm.

Exiting Slow Flight in a Complex Aircraft

Now let's clean up the airplane and return to straight and level flight from our slow flight condition. Begin by applying full power, eliminating carburetor heat (if applied) and lowering the nose at a rate that allows you to accelerate while maintaining altitude, as shown in Figure 26 (see the sidebar, *Slow Flight in Complex Airplanes* on Page 4-25 to understand how to coordinate the propeller control when entering and exiting slow flight).

Should the next move be to retract the gear? No. You want to reduce your flap setting to the value offering more lift than drag. That might mean reducing the flaps to their half extended position in 10 degree (or single-notch) increments, depending on the recommendation in your POH. Your intent here is to retract the flaps to their "least drag, best lift" condition while simultaneously using the elevator to prevent a sudden pitch change. Of course, you're also using nose-down trim as necessary during acceleration.

Slow Flight in Complex Airplanes

There are two additional items to consider when operating complex airplanes in slow flight. The first is the operation of cowl flaps (Picture-A). Since the airplane is flying slower at higher power settings, you should be prepared to open or close the cowl flaps to maintain the recommended engine temperatures. Normally, this means opening the cowl flaps fully until you've returned to cruise airspeed.

The second consideration involves the use of the propeller control when entering and exiting slow flight (Picture-B). If you want to use full power when leaving slow flight to return to cruise flight, then it's best to adjust the RPM value to a setting appropriate for the higher manifold pressure you're likely to use. The best way to handle this during the transition to slow flight is to reduce power then, while the RPM is still high, slowly move the propeller lever forward to the setting associated with full power (as stipulated in your POH). Doing it this way means that, as you leave slow flight and apply full power, you don't have to worry about high manifold pressures with inappropriately low RPM values (which could overstress the engine, perhaps even causing detonation).

On the other hand, if you elect to enter slower flight on the downwind leg of the traffic pattern, you don't normally move the propeller control to its full power position. Why? Because you're not normally flying slow enough on the downwind leg that full power will be necessary. You do, however, move the propeller control to its full forward position when you're on short final because it might be necessary to use full power during a go around. (See *Rod Machado's Private Pilot Handbook* for more information on propeller and throttle operations in complex airplanes.)

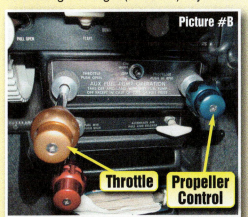

It's vitally important to make sure the airplane is accelerating before making a further retraction of the flaps and before raising the gear. It's entirely possible that with your enthusiasm to return to level flight, you might apply power, reduce flaps to half extension, then raise the gear followed by an immediate but premature retraction of the remaining flaps. This could cause the airplane to start descending or to move into the back side of the power curve or even approach a stall, if not actually stall.

Once again, how do you know the airplane is accelerating? You can see the airspeed increasing and you can feel the acceleration. The most important clue, however, is that you're sensing no deceleration, which would be quite obvious. When the major drag causing portion of the flaps are retracted, retract the gear, then retract the last half of the flaps in 10-degree (or one-notch) increments.

Why didn't I have you retract the gear first instead of removing the major drag causing portion of the flaps? After all, the gear causes a lot of drag, right? You bet it does. The main reason for this sequence is that it simulates the best way to handle a go around when making an approach to a runway.

Suppose you're on final approach at 50 feet above the ground when an airplane accidentally turns onto the runway (the pilot clearly wasn't watching for traffic on final approach and clearly doesn't know how important you are). If you retracted the gear first and were for some reason unable to climb for the go around, you might end up making a gear-up landing to one side or another of the runway (and no, you don't want to land on the guy on the runway, even if you feel as though he deserves it. You'll make an impression but you won't make a friend, nor will you make a biplane, either).

Leaving the gear extended until the airplane proves it can accelerate and climb is generally the wisest move in these instances. At least you can land on the runway, to the side of the runway or even on an unused taxiway if you have to, and that's better than landing gear-up, which won't cheer you up.

OK, I promised you stalls and now we'll discuss stalls without stalling.

Rod Machado's How to Fly an Airplane Handbook

Postflight Briefing #4-1 More Region of Reversed Command

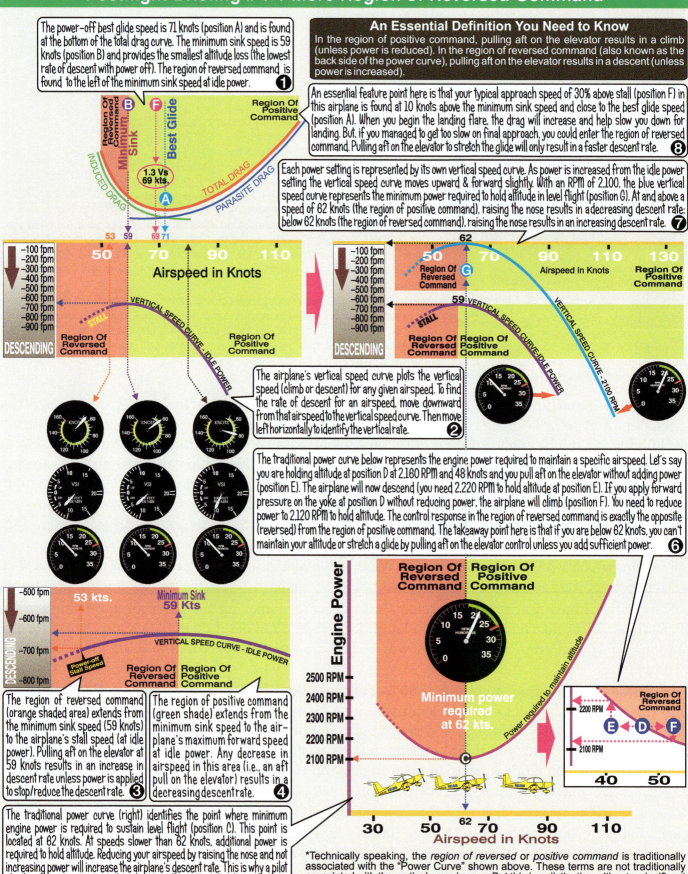

Chapter 4: Slow Flight Delight

Postflight Briefing #4-2 The FAA's New "Not-So-Slow" Slow Flying Strategy

In its 1965 *Flight Training Handbook*, the FAA dedicated over two pages of text to explain the concept of flight at *minimum controllable airspeed* (MCA). Today, the most recent (2018) edition of the FAA's *How to Fly an Airplane Handbook* offers no discussion whatsoever on MCA. If you have the impression that the FAA doesn't want pilots to practice flight at MCA, then you are correct.

It turns out that the FAA now considers practicing slow flight at MCA to be less beneficial (if not harmful) to a pilot's development. The FAA's reasoning is that flight at MCA is typically accompanied by the presence of an activated stall horn or light. As the FAA sees it, any extended exposure to a stall warning that's not accompanied by the immediate application of stall recovery procedures makes a pilot more vulnerable to a stall/spin accident. Whether that makes any sense at all is irrelevant. It is what it is, and obtaining a private pilot certificate today requires you to behave accordingly on your pilot checkride.

For this reason, the *Airman Certification Standards* (ACS) now requires that an applicant demonstrate slow flight in the following manner: *Establish and maintain an airspeed at which any further increase in angle of attack, increase in load factor, or reduction in power, would result in a stall warning (e.g., airplane buffet, stall horn, etc.).*

The FAA is quite clear that slow flight is to be performed without any stall warning present. Therefore, you can fly as slow as desired on your checkride as long as it doesn't involve the activation of a stall horn or light, much less an experience of stall buffet (in case your airplane isn't equipped with a stall horn or light).

To be helpful, the FAA suggests that one way to determine the target airspeed at which to demonstrate slow flight is to "...slow the airplane to the stall warning when in the desired slow flight configuration, pitch the nose down slightly to eliminate the stall warning, add power to maintain altitude and note the airspeed." This will place the airplane a few knots above the speed at which the stall warning activates, or upwards of nine to 10 knots above the airplane's actual stall speed. Given that the ACS allows a pilot to fly up to +10 knots in excess of the selected speed chosen for a slow flight demonstration, it's possible that a pilot could be demonstrating slow flight at a speed above the recommendation many airplane manufacturers suggest for a normal approach.

Before this change took place, pilots regularly demonstrated slow flight at MCA with the stall horn/light activated or with the stall buffet present. This meant that these pilots were just a few knots above actual stall speed—an activity that requires a much deeper understanding of what's happening in the pre-stall regime. Pilots practicing flight at MCA learned about how the airplane handles as it approached a stall. These pilots also learned about the five major clues that typically preceed a stall, thereby helping them identify when they are approaching stall territory. For this reason I would hope all flight instructors would still teach flight at MCA while simultaneously prepping their students to fly at higher speeds during checkride demonstrations of slow flight.

This Page Intentionally Left Blank

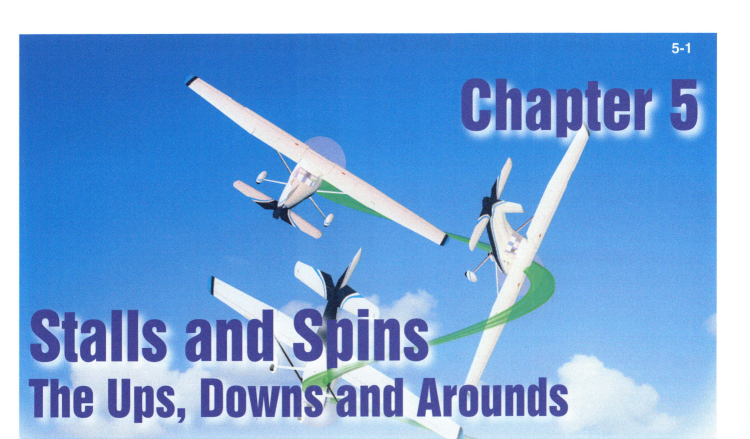

Chapter 5

Stalls and Spins
The Ups, Downs and Arounds

One of the peculiar things about aviation is that you'll often intentionally practice doing what you don't want to do, in order to not do it unintentionally.

Isn't that why you practiced slow flight? You needed to know how slow you could go and what was just below "too slow." Once upon a time, maps showing unknown parts of the world would say, "Here there be dragons." That told you that you didn't want to go there, though somewhere *near* there might prove kind of interesting.

So, dragon slayer that you are, you practiced slow flight and became confident about controlling your airspeed with sufficient skill that you could avoid stalling an airplane, especially while attempting to land.

You're probably not surprised to learn that you now need to go where the dragons are and practice stalls in order to avoid accidentally doing one at an inopportune time. An inopportune time? Is there an opportune time, a tune time, or perhaps an iTunes time, when you might want to do a stall on purpose? You bet. There are certain types of specialty landings, or landings in certain types of airplanes, that require you to essentially stall during landing. These include soft-field landings in tricycle-geared airplanes, and three-point landings in a taildragger. But in general, you'll want to avoid stalls, spins, *and* dragons.

So buckle up, strap in and let's get ready to burble—otherwise known as *experiencing the separation of smooth airflow over the top of the wing*. You are about to learn to go with the airflow.

You don't need a weatherman to know which way the air flows.

What Is a Stall?

What's a stall? It depends on who's doing it.

One reason *stall* creates terror among student pilots is that in day-to-day speech a stall to most people means having the engine in your car stop, which means having the car itself stop. And most people intuitively know that having their airplane stop in midair would somehow not be good.

But *stall* has a different meaning in aviation. What does it mean to stall the wings of an airplane? As you learned in Chapter 3, the production of lift requires air flowing over the airplane's wings. The faster the wings move through the air, the less angle of attack that's needed to generate the lift required to sustain flight. The wings' engineered shape (Figure 1) adds a small curve to accelerate the airflow and generate the needed lift.

The wing is designed to accelerate the air moving over the upper cambered surface as well as deflect the air downward.

As the airplane slows down and the speed of the wing through the air decreases, lift production also decreases. But remember, you're the pilot-in-command, not a passive passenger, so there are things you can (and definitely should!) do to increase airflow and lift. You don't have to just go with the (factory) flow.

One thing you can do is add an additional curve to the air by increasing the *angle of attack* (Figure 2). Increasing the angle of attack bends or curves the air more than the built-in amount allowed by the wings' engineered shape. Now the speed of the airflow over the wings increases,

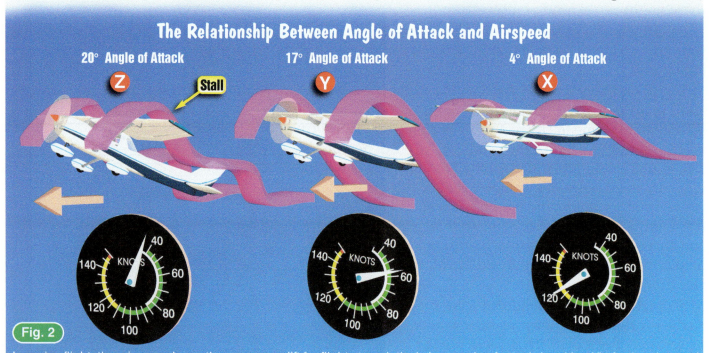

In cruise flight, the wing produces the necessary lift for flight at a relatively low angle of attack (position X). As the airspeed decreases, you must increase the angle of attack to sustain the necessary lift for flight (position Y). At higher angles of attack, this induces the wing to curve or bend the airflow beyond that which the wings' engineered shape alone is capable of doing. When the critical angle of attack is reached (position Z), the wing can no longer add a sufficient curve or bend to the airflow. At this point the wing stalls and the airflow over the top of the wing begins to burble and separate. Now the airplane begins accelerating downward until the angle of attack is reduced and lift regained.

Chapter 5: Stalls and Spins

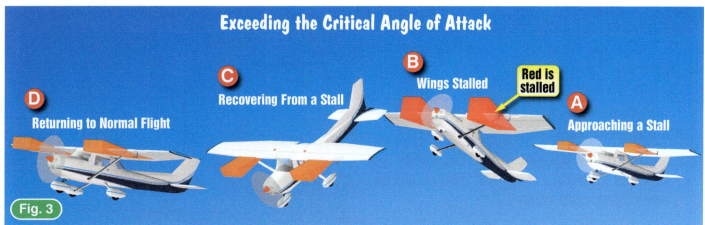

When the airplane's wings exceed their critical angle of attack (position B), the airplane no longer develops the necessary lift for flight and they stall. The required lift for flight is regained when the angle of attack is reduced to less than its critical value (position C). Now the airplane can return to normal flight (position D).

more air is deflected downward behind the wing, and the needed lift is generated. This works great—up to a point. There *is* a very specific point at which more produces less. That point is called the *critical angle of attack*.

The critical angle of attack is the angle beyond which the wings cannot bend or curve the air without disrupting the smooth flow over their upper surfaces. We now say that the wings have *stalled* (Figure 3, position B). At that point, lift dramatically decreases. Dragons be there. The engine is running; the airflow isn't.

The only way to regain the diminished lift and recover from the stall is to decrease the angle of attack to less than its critical value (Figure 3, position C). You can pray, pout, ponder or purse your lips and make funny sounds, but you'll still be in a stall until that angle of attack is reduced to less than its critical value.

For most small aircraft, the airflow breaking point is at approximately an 18-degree angle of attack. You can take this number at face value, or to better understand how we get it, we'll need to take a closer look at the lift equation. If you can wrap your brain lobes around this mighty powerful aerodynamic equation, then you're a spinner's distance ahead of most other folks flying airplanes.

How Not to Slake Your Thirst

I experienced a ditching incident involving an airplane after attempting to take off in my Cessna 150 on a lake creek strip that's associated with a popular Alaska fishing destination.

The airplane was in good mechanical condition and was modified with oversize tires and heavy duty landing gear. The weather in that part of Alaska had been warm that week which explains why I found my arrival landing to be a bit tighter than expected.

Prior to taking off, I paced-off the strip and found it to be about 800 feet long. Consulting with the POH, I determined that the required takeoff distance for the conditions at max gross weight was 748 feet. Since the airplane was well under maximum gross weight, and since the strip ended at the water's edge with no tall obstructions ahead, I determined that a takeoff was possible. I planned to accelerate in ground effect over the water if needed.

Upon takeoff, however, the airplane was unable to establish a climb and, in fact, began to settle over the water. The tires touched down into the water, costing needed airspeed several times. With the conditions of deteriorating airspeed and lack of climb, it became apparent that the airplane would not attain a flyable condition and I elected to do a controlled descent into the water.

Many who have attempted to force an airplane to fly at too low an airspeed have suffered a low altitude, stall-spin accident, dramatically increasing the impact forces upon ground contact. To avoid this, I cut the throttle and entered the water in an upright attitude. The windshield blew inward from the pressure of the water, and I exited the airplane as it sank. The airplane was carried downstream about one mile and washed up on a sandbar, intact and still upright. There were no injuries, or damage to property other than the aircraft and no oil or fuel leakage or oil slick was noted in the water.

Safety Report

Commentary.
This is an excellent example of how a pilot might stumble into a stall-spin accident. The pilot in this report did the right thing in not attempting to pull the airplane into the air when it wasn't ready to fly. The takeaway point here is that when pilots accidentally stall and spin an airplane, they often do so while innocently attempting to perform some other innocent maneuver. You'll read more about how this occurs later in this chapter.

The Lift Equation

Much like a cake recipe, the lift produced by the wings results from several ingredients (although you shouldn't put "icing" on your wing). Lift is a product of the wings':

- coefficient of lift;
- surface area, and
- the dynamic air pressure on the wing (otherwise known as the product of one-half of the air density times the velocity squared).

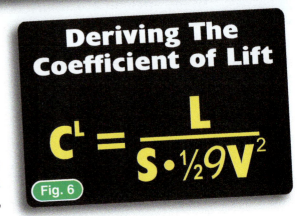

These values should be somewhat familiar to you by now (Figure 4), with the possible exception of the coefficient of lift, otherwise referred to as C^L. To understand the coefficient of lift, we need to see how it's derived.

The coefficient of lift is an experimentally derived value, which means that an *experiment* must be done to derive it. So get that lab coat on and let's break some beakers.

We'll begin with a wing or wing section having a known surface area and place it in a wind tunnel, as shown in Figure 5 (all pilots have a wind tunnel in their garage, right?). Air at a specific density and velocity blows over the wing while its angle of attack is increased in increments. A device similar to a scale measures the lift produced by that wing segment at each incremental increase in angle of attack. The resulting lift produced by that wing or wing segment along with the other values of wing area, air density and air speed are placed back into the lift equation. The only value of the lift equation that is not yet known is the coefficient of lift.

You now use your high school math skills (which doesn't mean paying a smart guy to give you the answer) to isolate the coefficient of lift variable to one side of the lift equation (Figure 6). Insert the previously measured values from the wind tunnel into the variables on the right side of the equation, and quicker than you can say, "Einstein," out pops a coefficient of lift for each angle of attack value.

When you move all the values (except for the coefficient of lift) to the one side of the equal sign, the units of those values (pounds, feet per second, etc.) cancel each other out. It's like getting your

Chapter 5: Stalls and Spins

car washed and waxed—all that's left is the shine, or in this case, a numerical value that has no units. The coefficient of lift is unit-less number, but one that has great usefulness.

Looking at the coefficient of lift on a graph (Figure 7), you can see that there appears to be a linear (straight line) relationship between the angle of attack and the coefficient of lift. Double the C^L and you double the lift, reduce the C^L by one-half and you reduce the lift by one half. The most important thing to observe on the C^L vs. angle of attack graph is that the C^L increases as the angle of attack increases, but only up to a point called C^{Lmax} and by now you have undoubtedly leaped or flown to the conclusion—correctly—that this is the *critical angle of attack*. A further increase in angle of attack decreases the production of lift, and the only way to get that lift back is to decrease the angle of attack to less than C^{Lmax}. That's the takeaway point about that point.

The typical angle of attack associated with C^{Lmax} is about 18 degrees for most small airplanes. This can and does vary a bit based on the size and shapes of the wings. One thing is certain. Wings stall when they exceed their critical angle of attack, and the only way to recover from a stall is to reduce the angle of attack.

The lift equation. It's very uplifting.

How, When and Where a Wing Can Stall

Perhaps one of the most difficult concepts for pilots to wrap their mighty brain lobes around is the idea that a wing, which always stalls when it exceeds its critical angle of attack, can also stall at any airspeed and any attitude.

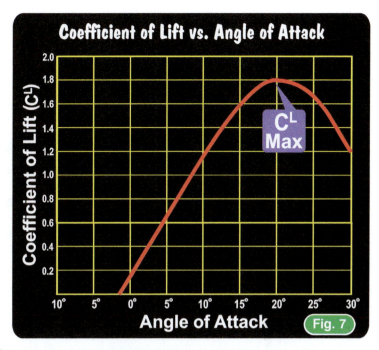

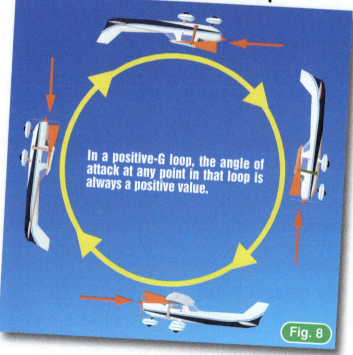

Think about this for a second or two. Too many pilots believe that the only time they can stall a wing is when the airplane is pointed uphill and going slowly. That's bad faith. You can stall an airplane going downhill and fast.

To better understand this concept, let's get a little loopy and examine how an airplane behaves in a loop.

Figure 8 shows an airplane performing a nice 360-degree loop. Here's the statement that often surprises everyone. *At any point during a typical positive-G loop, the angle of attack is always positive*. Do you believe that? Say yes, because it's true. Figure 8 shows how the angle of attack in a loop looks.

The angle of attack is the angle between the wings' chord line and the relative wind (Figure 9). Relative wind is wind that blows at a speed *equal to* and *opposite of* the airplane's motion. If you were to freeze the airplane's motion at any place along the 360 degree loop—yes, I said *any place* and I mean *any place*—the airplane (and its hood ornament if it had one) would feel wind blowing at a slight upward angle to its nose, whether the airplane was pointed up, down or was inverted.

That means the angle between the chord line and the relative wind remains at a positive value throughout the loop (this angle varies based on the number of G's you're pulling during the loop, of course). The point worth noting here is that as long as the angle of attack is less than the critical value, the wings won't stall. It doesn't matter which end is up. What happens if you aggressively pull aft on the elevator at *any place* around that loop? The answer is that the airplane will stall.

That's right. If you pull aft on the elevator control of airplane A in Figure 10, it's possible for the angle of attack to increase beyond the critical angle of attack, resulting in stalled wings. That means the airplane can stall in a nose-up attitude, a level flight attitude or a nose-down attitude (as shown by airplane B in Figure 10).

And (free bonus) the airplane stalls no matter what its airspeed. The key point is that you have to exceed the wings' critical angle of attack to stall, but the stall can occur at any airspeed and any attitude. This is an absolutely essential point for you to understand if you're planning on flying an airplane safely, which seems like the best choice.

As a practical matter, most of your flight hours won't be acquired doing loops. Instead, you'll spend the majority of your flight time in straight and level flight, climbs, and descents (although low performance airplanes make it seem as though you spend all of your time in a climb).

So what is it like to stall an airplane? Let's find out.

A Few Ground Rules

We're about to launch into a discussion of a number of maneuvers involving various versions of stalls and spins.

Some Rod Rules apply each time, so rather than repeat them over and over, I'll say it once and be done with it.

The POH Rules Rule—Most small planes are pretty similar in their fundamentals. The instructions I provide are generic and applicable to most of the aircraft that will be flown by most people. However, under all circumstances *consult and follow* the instructions and limitations set out in the *pilot's operating handbook* (POH) and/or the *approved flight manual* (AFM) for the specific aircraft you're flying. If I say A and the POH says B, then B is almost always the correct answer for your specific airplane (there area few arcane exceptions when this isn't true but they're really rare).

Clearing the Area—There is one very important maneuver you *must* learn before doing anything else, and that's clearing the area above, below and all around you before any practice maneuver.

Chapter 5: Stalls and Spins

Stalling in Any Attitude and at Any Airspeed

An airplane can stall at any attitude and at any airspeed. Airplane B, for example, is stalled in a nose-down attitude. This is a very important concept for every pilot to understand.

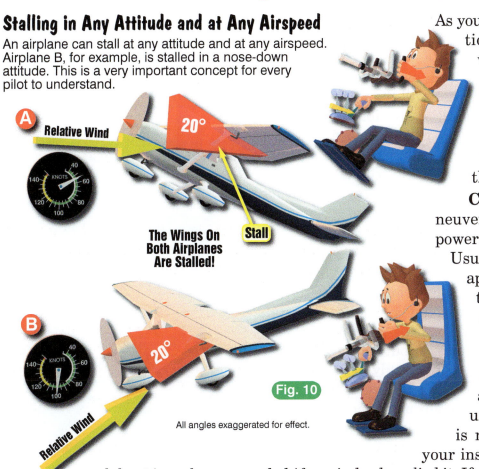

The Wings On Both Airplanes Are Stalled!

Fig. 10

All angles exaggerated for effect.

As you read each of the following sections, consider it to be prefaced with, "After clearing the area..." This is important for your safety and the safety of others. Do not get so focused on doing a stall or spin or anything else that you begin without clearing the area. Ever. Please.

Carb Heat—Many of the maneuvers call for reducing engine power when entering the maneuver. Usually it is a good practice to apply carb heat in such a situation, and I advise doing so *unless* your POH or your instructor says something to the contrary. I'll tell you when in the sequence you should apply carb heat *if* it's normally used and if the use of carb heat is not overruled by the POH or your instructor. And I'll tell you when carb heat is no longer needed *if* you indeed applied it. If you didn't apply it to start with, there's not much need to un-apply it and you can ignore that instruction. If you did apply it, you eventually want to remember to get rid of it, because an engine produces more power with carb heat off, and in smaller GA planes we rarely have a great excess of power.

Recovery Altitude—In most cases, I will say to recover to the altitude at which you began the maneuver. In every case, priority goes to any altitude specified by your flight instructor or FAA examiner. Be sure and practice stalls at an altitude that allows recovery *no lower* than 1,500 feet AGL.

Recovery Attitude—Unless you have a obstacle of some sort looming in your recovery path, you should use your best rate of climb speed (Vy) during stall recovery. If an obstacle is present, then climb at the best angle of climb speed (Vx) followed by Vy once you've cleared the obstacle.

So, assume I've said all the above at the beginning of every maneuver description. Enough said.

How Does Pulling Aft on the Yoke Lead to a Stall in a Nose-Down Attitude?

Got inertia! A moving airplane does because of its mass. That's why any moving object wants to remain moving in its same direction of travel and at its same speed, at least until it's acted on by outside forces. You can change the direction an airplane moves by pulling aft on the yoke. As you do, you increase the angle attack and temporarily increase the lift produced by the wings, which redirects the airplane's motion. Unfortunately, there is a limit to the amount of temporarily lift increase generated by an aft pull on the yoke. That limit is defined by the wings' *critical angle of attack*. Pull aft too hard or aggressively and the angle between the airplane's motion and the wings' chord line increases excessively. Why? While the elevator control can easily rotate the airplane about its lateral (sideways axis) and increase the wings' angle of attack, the airplane's inertia prevents it from responding immediately to the wings' increase in lift. Therefore, if you pull aft on the elevator to move vertically (to pitch upward) or move horizontally (to turn steeply), the airplane wants to keep moving in its previous direction because of its inertia. That means your angle of attack has increased during the aft yoke pull. Therefore, when pulling aft on the yoke, you must make sure that the difference between the airplane's motion and the wings' chord line doesn't exceed 18 degrees (the critical angle of attack for most wings). Pull aft too hard or aggressively and the wings can stall at any attitude and at any airspeed.

The Stall—It's a Ball!

No more stalling on stalling. Let's begin in straight and level flight at an altitude greater than 1,500 feet AGL in a typical fixed gear, non-complex airplane. Begin by applying full carburetor heat (Figure 11, position A), then pull the throttle back to the flight idle position (Figure 11, position B). Hold altitude with elevator back pressure while your airspeed decreases. Use the aileron control to keep the wings level, and use the rudder pedals to keep the nose pointed straight ahead. No trim is needed for this demonstration because you're not going to stay this way for long. You're just visiting. You are going to increase the angle of attack beyond the critical angle and stall the airplane.

Keep the elevator control coming back (Figure 11, positions B and C). Are you noticing the nose-high attitude? What about the airspeed needle pointing just below the beginning of the green arc? Can you hear the stall warning horn (or see the stall warning light)? (If you can't, see a hearing specialist or your airplane's mechanic. Unless, of course, your airplane doesn't *have* a stall warning horn.) You're about ready to stall the airplane (it's technically the wings that stall, but we'll just say "the airplane" from now on since they are normally found together).

As the wings approach their critical angle of attack, you'll feel vibration caused by airflow burbling over the wings' upper surfaces. This tells you that the air is no longer flowing smoothly above the wings, mainly because the bend or curve induced by the wing is too large. The airflow has started to burble, and lift has significantly decreased. Said another way, you've exceeded C_{Lmax} and lift is diminishing dramatically. It hasn't completely disappeared, but it has decreased below the minimum required to sustain level flight (effective lift is now less than the airplane's weight). You should be getting sort of a sinking feeling.

With the elevator held back, and as the airflow burble occurs, the nose pitches downward on its own and the airplane begins to descend (Figure 11, position D). Congratulations! You've just stalled the airplane. No matter how hard you pull back on that elevator, the airplane isn't going to remain in level flight, nor is it going to climb (don't pull the yoke off trying to prove this to yourself, either). The important point to understand here is that the airplane didn't fall out of the sky. That's right. You shouldn't feel what you typically feel when going over the hump in a rollercoaster. That's because there's still some lift left in those wings, despite their stalled conditions. That's why you are descending as the airplane's nose automatically pitches below the horizon.

Why does the nose pitch downward? You have the airplane's built-in longitudinal stability (and its designers) to thank for that. Assuming the airplane's weight and center of gravity are

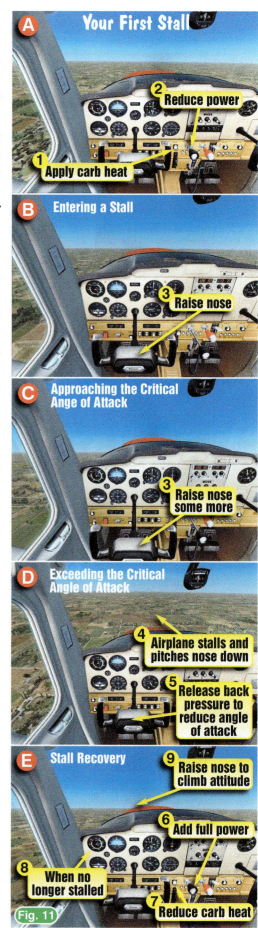
Fig. 11

Chapter 5: Stalls and Spins

within recommended limits, a sudden loss of lift results in the airplane's nose pitching downward. This decreases the angle of attack. The wings regain their full lift potential. It's all built in. Thank you, aeronautical engineers. Show your gratitude by reading about this in the sidebar titled, *The Center of Lift* on Page 5-10.

How can you help the process along? Mostly by getting out of the way. This does *not* involve jumping out of the airplane! All you need to do is allow the nose to pitch downward a bit by not holding the elevator control back. It's a flight, not a fight.

No high drama here, no matter what your elevation. To recover from the stall, you don't need to shove the elevator control rapidly forward, yell a magic incantation, or slay any dragons. You don't need to create what is known as *zero* or *negative g-forces* during stall recovery (also known as the *seeing stuff float around your cockpit* recovery). Just ease the elevator control forward by releasing any elevator back pressure you're holding.

That's it. This simple move allows the angle of attack to decrease below the critical angle. Don't worry, you won't have to do any math on the fly to figure out the coefficient of lift or the angle of attack or the balance in your flight school account. Just lower the nose a little bit below the horizon, look nonchalant, and you'll wind up with a normal stall recovery (Figure 11, position D). Pretend you're British and keep a stiff upper control surface. Go ahead, try it.

As the nose is lowered, the airspeed begins to increase and the burbling of air over the wings stops. Congratulations! You've just recovered from your first full stall, and the airplane did most of the work. Of course, if this was a real stall and you were close to the ground, you wouldn't want to keep the nose pointed below the horizon for very long. Once the wings are no longer stalled, you'll want to move away from the ground by climbing (or, if appropriate, leveling off if you're not at too low an altitude). The correct recovery sequence is to apply full power while *simultaneously* reducing the angle of attack, then remove carburetor heat. When you're assured the wings are no longer stalled, raise the nose to an attitude that gives you the best rate (Vy) of climb speed, as shown in Figure 11, position E (or you can climb at the best angle (Vx) of climb speed if an obstacle looms directly ahead of you).

In terms of training, your objective is to climb back to your starting altitude but no lower than 1,500 feet AGL unless you're over a very large trampoline factory. Figure 12 shows the stall sequence from Figure 11 as observed from outside the airplane.

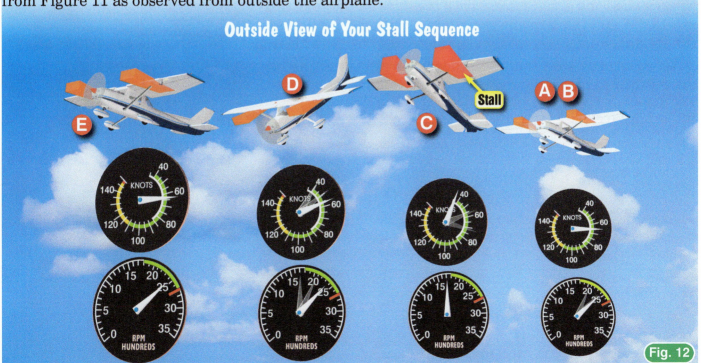

Outside View of Your Stall Sequence

Fig. 12

The Center of Lift

The center of lift is the point where the wings' total lifting force is concentrated. Think of it as the sum or the average of all the lifting forces spread across both wings (simulated by all the little blue arrows). At low angles of attack the center of lift is found farther back along the wing as shown by wing A. As the angle of attack increases, all the little lifting forces move slightly. They tend to become more concentrated toward the front of the wing as shown by wing B. Therefore, as the angle of attack increases, the center of lift moves forward along the wing.

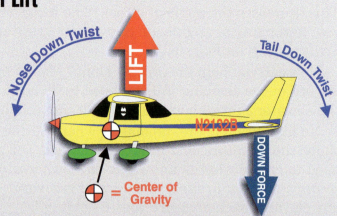

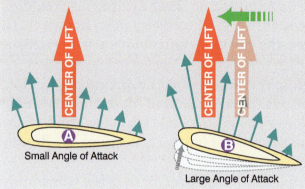

Airplanes are designed so that the center of lift always remains behind the center of gravity (assuming that your airplane is loaded properly). Since all objects rotate about their center of gravity, this causes the airplane to have a nose-down pitching tendency. That's why the tail of an airplane must create a slight downward acting force. This keeps the airplane from nosing end over end. On the other hand, because the center of lift is located behind the CG, the residual lift on the wings of a stalled or stalling airplane will pitch the nose forward, naturally aiding in stall recovery.

As a practical matter, you don't have to climb after recovering from a stall if the stall occurs at a high enough altitude and you are in complete control of the airplane. You can recover to level flight or recover into your previously-established descent, if appropriate. Then again, if you're close to the ground and stall, it's clear that avoiding contact with the surface is your immediate priority. That's why stall practice typically involves climbing after stall recovery. This simulates the worst-case risk of being dangerously close to terra firma and making you super flata.

The *Airman Certification Standards* require that you return to the altitude, heading and airspeed specified by the examiner if you are taking your private pilot checkride.

Let's review a few essential features of the stall you just experienced. Suppose you held the elevator control fully aft as the wings stalled and didn't release back pressure on the yoke (Figure 13). Would the airplane remain in a stalled condition and simply sink quietly (except for your shrieking) to earth? Hardly.

We've already seen that the sudden decrease in lift as you exceed the critical angle of attack causes the nose to *initially*

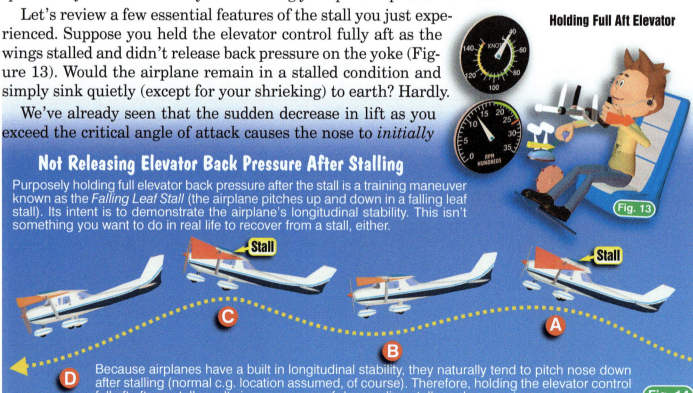

Chapter 5: Stalls and Spins

Mr. Quickdraw, How Fast Do You Apply Power in a Stall Recovery?

One common question asked by pilots during stall training is, "How fast do you apply power during the stall recovery?" Should you shove the throttle forward as if you're a kung-fu master breaking a board with his hand at a martial arts tournament? No, not unless you want to break your panel in half (Picture-1).

During stall training, apply power during the recovery just a bit faster than you'd apply it on takeoff (Picture-2). If you're flying a turbocharged airplane, applying power too quickly during stall training can overboost the engine or overspeed the propeller, and that's not a good thing for your pocketbook or your engine. On the other hand, if you're flying a typical low-powered trainer, you aren't going to hurt the engine with a relatively quick application of power.

Ultimately, the only way to know how fast to apply power during flight training is to ask your instructor for a demonstration. Then again, if you actually stalled an airplane close to the ground, it really wouldn't matter how fast you applied power that one time, would it? In that instance there are far more pressing issues, such as the risk of your airplane becoming a dirt bike.

Another common question pilots ask is, "How much power should you apply during training to recover from a stall?" For small, low powered trainers, apply full power. Since you don't have a lot of spare power to begin with, use every bit that's available to you.

For complex airplanes (Picture-3) with big bore engines (they don't do well at parties, despite having more than 200 HP), the answer is a bit more complex. The short answer is that you should apply full power. Power is good here too, and it helps during stall recovery. You do, however, want to be cautious about not overspeeding the constant speed propeller when applying power during stall recovery practice. When reducing power for stall practice, move the propeller control to its full forward position as shown in (Picture-4). This allows you to develop maximum allowable RPM when your throttle is moved forward during the stall recovery.

When recovering from a stall in a complex airplane, apply power only fast enough to avoid the initial overspeed that could result from the propeller blades having flattened (the blade angle of attack decreased) to the high-RPM position. Applying power too fast could cause the propeller RPM to exceed its redline limit. It's important to be practical when practicing stall recovery. After all, you don't want to place excessive wear and tear on an airplane. Otherwise, it won't be around long to use for more practice. On the other hand, if this were a real stall recovery, your main concern wouldn't be propeller overspeed, right? Right!

pitch downward, based on the airplane's built in stability (Figure 14, positions A and B). But there's more to the story, as the nose knows. When the nose pitches downward, the angle of attack decreases and the airspeed increases. This causes the nose to pitch upward as speed and lift are regained (Figure 14, position C).

Haven't we been here before? If you continued holding the elevator full aft, you would enter into another (secondary) stall (Figure 14, position D). That's why it is essential that you reduce the angle of attack (Figure 15) by releasing elevator back pressure (Figure 16) until the wings are no longer stalled.

You absolutely do not want to hold the elevator control full aft after stalling, despite the temptation to do so (see sidebar: *Stall, Spins and the Conditioned Reflex* on Page 5-38). And believe me, there's a good chance you will be tempted. Why? Because the airplane is going down, and you want to make it go up. At an early stage in your training, up-airplane gets connected in your flying neurons to up-elevator. You later learn that it's a

bit more complicated than that. The only thing capable of making the airplane go up is *excess engine power*, or power beyond that needed to keep you in level flight.

Is lowering the nose and reducing the angle of attack the only thing you have to do to recover from a stall? Technically speaking, yes. As you pitch the nose down in a power-off stall and decrease the angle of attack, you can continue in a descent at the desired airspeed. This is how you'd recover from a stall if you were flying a glider, since gliders don't have engines (unless the pilot keeps one hidden in his pocket). But airplanes do have engines, right? Don't deny it. Fortunately, your engine is very useful in helping you minimize altitude loss during stall recovery.

Minimizing altitude loss during stall recovery means applying full power immediately, while reducing the angle of attack (you should try and do these two things simultaneously, if possible). This accomplishes two things. First, power helps further reduce the angle of attack by accelerating the airplane in a forward direction. This causes the relative wind to come from a more horizontal direction, which naturally reduces the angle of attack (Figure 17, positions A and B). Second, the addition of power increases your airspeed, allowing you to generate the required lift for flight much more quickly. (See sidebar: *A Single Force Can Be a Combination of Smaller Forces* below.)

The most efficient stall recovery procedure is to recognize the stall ("Good morning, haven't we met before?"), reduce the angle of attack to less than its critical value, simultaneously add power, remove the carburetor heat, and once the airplane is no longer stalled, climb back to your original or assigned altitude (or just climb to move away from the ground, which is where the risk is).

The question I know you are asking is, *How do I know when the airplane is no longer stalled so I can begin my climb?* Is it the smile or frown on your instructor's face that provides the necessary

A Single Force Can Be a Combination of Smaller Forces

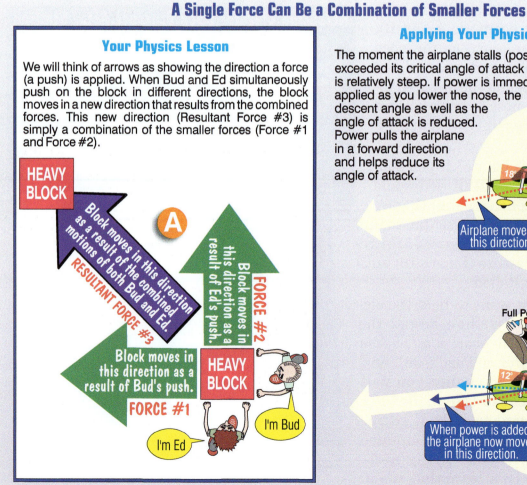

Chapter 5: Stalls and Spins

clue? Sometimes it can be hard to tell if your instructor is smiling, especially if he or she is on a weekly Botox maintenance plan. There's a better way.

Just before you stalled the airplane, what were the sensations you experienced? No, not *those* sensations. I don't mean sensations such as an urge to scream, or throw your hands or lunch up. Stalls aren't scary unless someone makes them scary. I'm thinking of three physical sensations that provide clues a stall is about to happen (Figure 18). This is about knowing before you go messing with the airflow.

Recognizing the Stall

The first of the three sensations that are telling you that you're about to "stall" is *sound*, and I don't mean the sound of your instructor yelling, "Lower the nose!" I mean the voice of the stall warning horn (if your airplane has one) and/or the sound of the airflow striking the airplane at a larger than normal angle, which produces a distinctly different sound than what you otherwise hear. You might also hear the air burbling as it vibrates over the upper section of the wings' structure. This sometimes produces an *oil canning* sound as it vibrates the wings' skin covering.

The second sensation is *sight*, or the visual clues from either a stall warning light and/or a nose-high attitude in relation to the direction the airplane is actually moving. Recall, though, that the nose does *not* have to be pointed above the horizon to stall. On the other hand, if you glance at the wing, you're likely to see a large angle between the horizon (or moving terrain if you're in a turn) and the chord line. If this angle is approaching 18 degrees or more, then you're about to exceed the wings' critical angle of attack and stall, Einstein (Figures 19 and 20).

The third sensation is *feel*, or the change in pressure on the flight controls as well as your body's sense that it is moving

How Power Affects Angle of Attack

Immediately after the stall (critical angle of attack exceeded) with power reduced to idle, the airplane begins a relatively steep descent and the nose pitches downward.

By adding power as the angle of attack is reduced, the airplane begins to move forward at a faster speed. This changes the direction of the relative wind, which results in an increase in speed and a decrease in angle of attack.

Fig. 17

Sensations You Experience Prior to Stalling

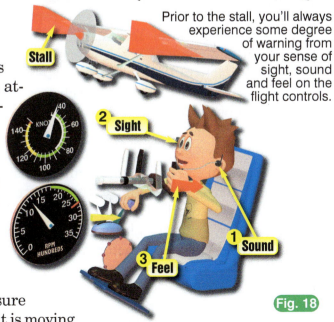

Prior to the stall, you'll always experience some degree of warning from your sense of sight, sound and feel on the flight controls.

Fig. 18

Rod Machado's How to Fly an Airplane Handbook

Estimating Your Angle of Attack in Straight and Level Flight

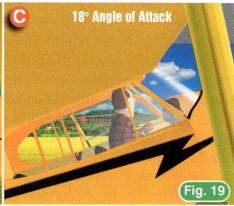

Estimating Your Angle of Attack in a Turn

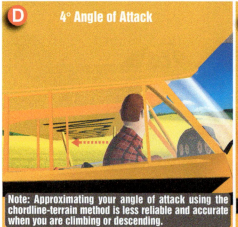
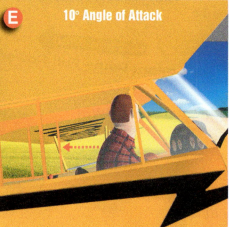
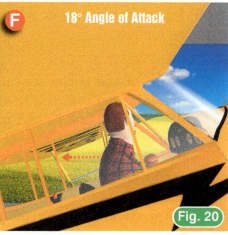

With two good eyeballs, you can easily approximate your angle of attack in most attitudes. In sequence A through C above, the airplane's angle of attack is easily estimated by examining the angle between the wings' chord line and the distant horizon. In a turn, the angle made between wings' chord line and the moving terrain represents your angle of attack as observed in sequence D through F above. When the angle between the chord line and the horizon or moving terrain approaches 18 degrees, then the wings are approaching their critical angle of attack.

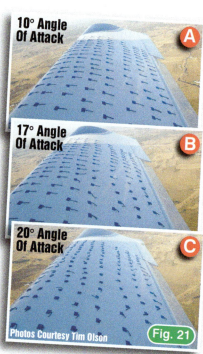

or accelerating, also known as *kinesthesia*. As the airplane's speed decreases, the flight controls become less responsive. This is an excellent clue to an impending stall. You can also feel the vibration on the flight controls as the airflow over the wings burbles and separates. This can be seen clearly in the stall-strip pattern in Figure 21. When the wing reaches its critical angle of attack (position C), the airflow over the wings' upper cambered surface has become chaotic. This wind chaos can be felt on the flight controls and by the seat of your pants.

You might also feel as though you've slowed down a little, in much the same way you can detect the slight accelerations or decelerations in an office building's elevator (though, there should be no music involved when you experience this in an airplane). If the stall occurred during a turn, you might also experience an increase in apparent weight (an increase in load factor) that can be felt in the seat of your pants. We'll talk more about load factor in just a bit. For now, just know that the sense of getting heavier is telling you that the airplane's stall speed is getting higher. This is another way of saying that you don't have to slow down to stall.

Chapter 5: Stalls and Spins

Altitude Loss During Stall Recovery

Did you know that it's possible for the average private pilot to fully stall an airplane and recover with an altitude loss of as little as 25 feet? It's true. You do, however, have to be "Johnny on the spot" during your recovery (which is still possible, even if your name is Fred whose reflexes are dead).

The secret is to reduce the angle of attack to just a little less than its critical value while simultaneously applying full power.

As the airplane stalls (position A), release some elevator back pressure to lower the nose slightly, while simultaneously applying full power (position B). The key here is to reduce the angle of attack to *just less than its critical value,* but not more than that. Lowering the nose excessively (position C) is unnecessary and results in an excessive loss of altitude during the recovery.

Left to its own devices, the airplane will pitch forward and recover. But the price of this built-in service is loss of more-than-minimum altitude. To keep it to a minimum, you apply slight rearward pressure on the yoke after the stall, interrupting the natural and sometimes "excessive" forward-pitching inclination the nose has. Hit the sweet spot just below the critical angle of attack and you get minimum altitude loss as your reward.

I offer this insight to let you know what's possible with stall recovery, rather than what's required. There's absolutely no need to be a fanatic when it comes to uber-minimizing your altitude loss during stall recovery during your practical flight test, either. In fact, the private pilot ACS makes no mention of altitude loss during stall recovery. In my opinion, however, you should be able to recover easily within 100 feet from the altitude at which the stall begins. You can expect the commercial pilot ACS to say that you should have a minimum loss of altitude appropriate for the airplane being flown. (The commmercial pilot ACS is not available as of 5-16-2017.)

It's important to know about these stall clues for several reasons. One is to avoid stalling in the first place (assuming you're not practicing). Another is to avoid a secondary stall during the recovery. Sometimes pilots are overly exuberant in their response to a stall, which creates the conditions needed for another stall. The second one would be a stall recovery with power already applied (called, appropriately, a *departure stall,* which is a power-on stall). If the stall is inadvertent, one is usually more than enough.

Now that you have a clue (three of them, in fact), if you feel the air burbling over the wings during recovery from a stall, you know you need to reduce the angle of attack a bit more to completely recover, while avoiding a secondary stall.

Imminent Stalls

Smart student that you are, I'm sure you're asking why anyone would need to know about stall recoveries. Why not use the stall clues to just avoid a stall altogether? That's a very good question. The answer is, you should.

Many years ago I flew with a student who became so nervous at the sound of the stall horn that he would make a similar sounding noise to match the stall horn. I had to admit that this was quite novel. I had a student with his own, built-in stall horn! Very nice.

Rod Machado's How to Fly an Airplane Handbook

The "Imminent Stall" Recovery Procedure

Fig. 22

Recovering from an imminent stall is much simpler than recovering from an actual stall because the airplane never stalls. You set yourself up for the stall just we discussed earlier (position A). Once you feel that a stall is imminent based on your assessment of the stall clues we just discussed, you release elevator back pressure just enough to keep from exceeding the critical angle of attack (position B) while simultaneously adding power and removing carburetor heat as you return to your previous flight condition.

Up to this point, you've practiced recovering from what is known as a *full stall*. You will also practice recovering from something known as an *imminent stall*. As the name suggests, this is the fun zone right before an actual stall when (if you're listening and paying attention) you hear, feel and see the airplane getting ready to cross the line.

If you're good at recognizing the clues that precede a stall—because you're a good stall detective—there's no reason to actually cross the line. Apply the same recovery techniques—gently lower the nose to remain below the critical angle of attack, while adding power—and you're good to go.

The objective when performing an imminent stall recovery is to take *immediate* stall recovery action the moment you recognize the airplane's about to stall. Since you never let the wings exceed their critical angle of attack, the stall doesn't actually occur. Just release elevator back pressure to decrease the angle of attack while adding full power, removing carburetor heat, and recovering to a point where you feel the airplane is flying safely above stall speed (Figure 22). There will be very little (if any) altitude loss, or excessive nose-down attitude or excessive airspeed associated with the imminent stall recovery, because you didn't stall.

Since you're required to demonstrate stall recovery proficiency on the private pilot checkride, you'll want to return to the flight condition you were in before demonstrating the imminent stall (unless your instructor or the examiner suggests otherwise, and if they do, it's not really a suggestion, it's a command).

Chapter 5: Stalls and Spins

Distractions and Stalls

You'd think that given all the sensory clues regarding stalls available to a pilot, no one would accidentally stall an airplane. Unfortunately, human beings are very good at tuning out extraneous sensory input and focusing on just a few things, and often only one thing. That's why you might not notice an imminent stall, despite all the clues staring you right in the face, yelling in your ears and/or vibrating your fingers.

The most likely place for a stall to happen is in precisely the place it's most dangerous—the traffic pattern, close to the ground. Turning from base to final and on final approach are common places for stalls to occur. Why there? Because it's easy to become distracted by the runway, other airplanes in the traffic pattern, and communications with the tower controller, not to mention thinking about the hamburger you're going to order at the airport grill that goes by the name of "The Nine One One."

Turning Final

As you prepare for landing and turn to align yourself with the runway, you might be too focused on preventing an overshoot of the runway centerline. This is where it's common for pilots to stop paying attention to their airspeed. Sometimes they let it get too slow and stall close to the ground. Sometimes they increase their bank angle too steeply and end up performing an accelerated stall (you'll learn about this later in this chapter) because they're distracted by attempting to align themselves with the runway centerline. This isn't safe, even if your pilot clothing consists of a mattress with holes for head, hands and feet.

You don't need to be in the traffic pattern to have your attention diverted from flying the airplane. Some lovelorn aviators have stalled when they attempted to fly around their girlfriends' houses at dangerously low altitudes. These pilots are so busy trying to impress their lady friends on the ground that they often don't realize how close they are to becoming part of the ground. Activities of this nature, besides being unwise, create distractions that substantially increase the risks associated with flight. I can also assure you that boring a hole in a person's house will blow the roof off the relationship.

An early NASA study found that in 75% of the stall/spin accidents where the pilot survived the event, the pilot reported that he or she didn't hear the stall warning horn or didn't see the stall warning light before the stall. The stall warning horn or light most likely did activate, but the pilot was sufficiently distracted that he or she was oblivious to the event.

This is one very important reason to learn to detect the signs of a stall before it occurs. It's also a very important reason to know how to prevent being distracted when you fly. The best way to do this is to remember the order of your flying priorities: *aviate* (fly the airplane first), *navigate* (point it where it needs to go next) and *communicate* (talk to those you need to talk to, but only after you've honored the first two priorities).

From a practical point of view, you're more likely to depend on stall recognition skills than stall recovery skills. Prevention is always the better course.

There are many circumstances that can lead you to suddenly sense the control response is a bit mushy, and/or the sound of the air flowing over the wings is out of the ordinary. You might even feel an apparent weight increase, as if you're being forced down in your seat (more on load factor soon).

That's why imminent stall practice, and awareness of a stall's look and feel, is extremely important if you want to be considered a good stick and rudder pilot

Use of Ailerons and Rudder In Stall Recovery

During stall entry and recovery, it's very important to keep the flight controls coordinated at all times. You want both wings to stall at the same time, rather than one before the other.

Stalling in uncoordinated flight often leads to one wing stalling before the other. This is how an airplane enters a spin, and that's not an entry you want to make at low altitude. It often winds up being boring—as in, boring a hole in the ground. You do not want to become a young spinster. Later in this chapter we'll discuss how and why one wing might stall before the other and lead to a spin, and we'll discuss spins in more detail.

When practicing stalls, the secret to ensuring that both wings stall and recover at the same time is to use the techniques for coordinated flight that we discussed in Chapter Two. During stall practice, the nose attitude is often artificially high, making it a bit challenging to look over the cowling and evaluate whether or not the nose is pointed in the direction the airplane is moving. If you have this problem, it's perfectly appropriate to glance at the ball in the inclinometer to evaluate your coordination. If the ball is centered, the flight controls are coordinated, meaning that the airplane will stall and pitch downward (away from you) in a direction that's perpendicular to the airplane's lateral axis (its wings), in the direction of the big red arrow as shown in Figure 23, position A. Just so we're clear, there is no big red arrow in the sky when you stall, so don't wait for it.

Stalling in Coordinated Flight

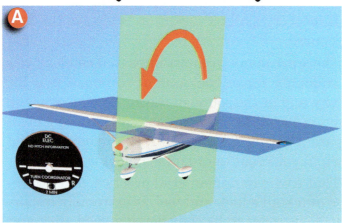

In coordinated flight, the airplane always stalls in a direction that's perpendicular to the airplane's wings (its lateral axis).

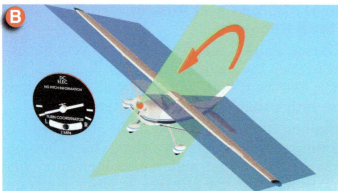

In a left coordinated turn, the airplane will stall and pitch forward (red arrow) in a direction perpendicular to the wings.

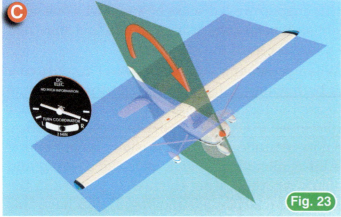

Fig. 23

In a right coordinated turn, the airplane will stall and pitch forward (red arrow) in a direction perpendicular to the wings.

Wing Washout — Wing curves downward at tip. Fig. 24 — Washout results in the wings' tip area being less stalled than the root area

If the controls are not coordinated, then get on the ball and center it by pressing the appropriate rudder pedal. Ball right, right pedal; ball left, left pedal. How easy is that? This means the airplane stalls and pitches from your nose to your toes (directly ahead) and won't *roll* and yaw to the right or left when it stalls. Step on the ball. With only two choices, there's no need to guess.

Even if the airplane is in a coordinated *turn* and stalls (Figure 23, positions B and C), the airplane will pitch forward along a path that's perpendicular to the wings, from your nose to your toes, and won't roll right or left (we'll discuss why the airplane doesn't *roll* and yaw in our spin discussion, coming up).

One of the neat things about the wings on many smaller airplanes is that they twist downward slightly at the tips. This is an aerodynamic condition known as *washout* (which is not something you're going to do in flight school if I can help it), as shown in Figure 24. It means that the outer portion of the wing where the aileron is located has a slightly smaller angle of attack than the middle and inboard sections of the wing. The result is that while the inboard section of the wing might stall, the outboard section near the ailerons isn't stalled or isn't nearly as stalled (Figure 25). That means you often have effective aileron control during the stall. Isn't that amazing? You really need to shake the hand of an aeronautical engineer if you meet one (but don't shake too hard or pens, pencils, protractors, and pocket protectors might go flying).

During stall recovery, once you've reduced the angle of attack on *both wings* and both wings are

Stall Pattern Progression — Washout results in the wings' tip stalling after the wing root. This allows aileron control well into the stall. Photo Courtesy Tim Olson. Fig. 25

Chapter 5: Stalls and Spins

One Wing Might Be Lower Than the Other After the Stall

Fig. 26

After you've recovered from a stall (i.e., your wings are no longer stalled) you might find one wing lower than the other with the airplane in a turn as shown in position A. If so, you should return to straight flight with the coordinated use of your flight controls as show by positions B and C.

developing lift again, one wing might be lower than the other (Figure 26, position A). Why? Well, you could have entered the stall from a turn, which is something we'll discuss in an upcoming section. You might have entered the stall from straight and level flight but gotten a bit sloppy on the controls or a little distracted during the recovery and let one wing get lower than the other (now you know that sometimes "low" happens). If so, your airplane is in a turn but the wings are no longer stalled.

What do you do? Well, since you're expected to recover from a straight ahead stall within +/− 10 degrees of your entry heading, you'll simply return the airplane to straight flight through the coordinated use of the flight controls (Figure 26, position B). Because both wings are *no longer stalled*, it's perfectly reasonable to raise the lowered wing with the coordinated use of the flight controls, just as you would if you were making a coordinated roll out of a turn back to straight flight (Figure 26, position C).

On the other hand, if one wing *drops* during a stall entry (i.e., stalls *before* the other wing—this is a very noticeable and often dramatic wing movement, too) then it does so because the angle of attack on that wing reached its critical value (the critical angle of attack) before the other wing (see sidebar: *Why One Wing Stalls Before the Other* on page 5-20). This is the prelude to a spin. Now the airplane no longer stalls in a direction perpendicular to the wings' lateral axis. Instead, the airplane *yaws* and *rolls* toward the dropping wing. Your first reaction after a wing drops should *not* be to raise that dropping (stalled) wing with aileron, even with the coordinated use of aileron and rudder. Why? Because the use of aileron increases the angle of attack on the dropping wing, potentially deepening the stall, causing the airplane to further yaw and roll, and possibly resulting in a spin.

Stall/Spin Proof Airplanes

There are quite a few airplanes, both new and old, that are either *stall/spin proof* or *stall/spin resistant*. True stall/spin proof airplane are simply unable to stall (and therefore spin since you can't spin unless the airplane stalls first). This is achieved by either of several means, the most common of which is to restrict the degree of aft (or "up") elevator travel, thus limiting the maximum angle of attack attainable by the wings (that limit being a bit less than the wings' critical angle of attack). The early model Ercoupes limited the up elevator movement to 13 degrees, thus preventing the airplane from exceeding its critical angle of attack. Too much "up" elevator restriction, however, might limit the airplane's ability to land slowly. So there is a slight cost to stall protection in an airplane.

Stall/spin resistant airplanes, however, are a bit different in the sense that they are made harder to stall, thus harder to spin. This is accomplished through a combination of flight control restrictions and/or enhanced (wing) leading edge devices that reduce the wings' potential to stall. Cirrus aircraft is a stall/spin resistant airplane. It is not, however, a stall/spin proof airplane since some Cirrus pilots have managed to lure their airplanes into a stall/spin scenario at an altitude where the airplane's BRS or ballistic recovery system (parachute) either didn't work or wasn't deployed.

The Ercoupe
Courtesy: William Stevick

Why One Wing Stalls Before the Other

What causes one wing to stall before the other? The most common way for this to happen is to induce a skid as the wings approach their critical angle of attack. For instance, as the airplane approaches a stall from a left turn (Picture-1, position A), excessive left rudder is applied (or P-factor and slipstream yaw the nose to the left, same effect). This results in the nose yawing to the left, causing the right wing to move forward slightly, giving it a slight increase in speed (and a bit more lift), and the left wing to move aft slightly, giving it slightly less speed (and a little less lift). Now the airplane begins to roll to the left with the nose pointed inside the turn arc.

The rising right wings' angle of attack decreases slightly, while the descending left wings' angle of attack increases slightly, as shown in Picture-1, position B. As the left wing moves down, it generates a relative wind from underneath, which tends to increase its angle of attack. A rising right wing generates a relative wind from above (from a more forward angle), which tends to reduce its angle of attack. Any deflection of the aileron control to the right to maintain the bank angle further increases the angle of attack on the left wing and decreases the angle of attack on the right wing. Ultimately, the left (descending) wing reaches its critical angle of attack before the right (rising) wing and the airplane enters a spin to the left, in the direction of the initial yaw (Picture-1, position C).

This is why a skidding turn at the moment of a stall is likely to result in an airplane entering a spin. That's why you want to prevent the nose from yawing and rolling by applying rudder during the stall if one wing begins to *drop* before the other.

Now you also know why you don't want to raise a *dropping* wing with use of aileron. Attempting to raise a dropping wing means the aileron on the descending wing moves down, which further increases its angle of attack, deepening the stall on that wing.

On the other hand, what happens if insufficient rudder is applied in the turn and the airplane slips at the moment of stall entry? Is this as conducive to spin entry? Let's see.

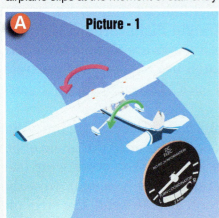

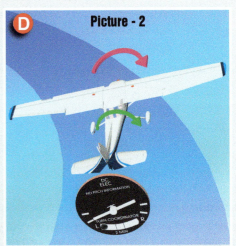

As the wings approach a stall from a left turn (Picture-2, position D), too much right rudder (and/or excessive left aileron control deflection) is applied. This results in a slipping turn to the left with the nose yawing to the right, or outside the turn arc. This causes the left wing to move forward slightly, giving it a slight increase in speed (and a bit more lift) and the right wing to move aft slightly, giving it slightly less speed (and a little less lift).

Now the airplane begins to roll to the right, with the nose pointed outside the turn arc. The rising left wing's angle of attack decreases slightly and the descending right wing's angle of attack increases slightly, as shown in Picture-2, position E. As the right wing moves down, it generates a relative wind from underneath, which tends to increase its angle of attack. A rising left wing experiences a reduction in angle of attack. Any deflection of the aileron control to the left to sustain the left bank further increases (right wing) and decreases (left wing) the angle of attack. Ultimately, the right (descending) wing reaches its critical angle of attack before the left (rising) wing, and the airplane might enter a spin as the left wing goes over the top of the airplane as the airplane yaws and rolls to the right (Picture-2, position F).

Did you notice that I was very careful to say "might" enter a spin there? It's more difficult to enter a spin from a slip than a skid. Why? Looking at the airplane in Picture-2, position E, it should be clear that the slipping airplane is still turning left (it's in a slipping left turn). If a spin does occur in our example, it occurs to the right, which happens to be opposite the direction of the turn. Because the direction of spin (to the right) would be opposite the airplane's momentum (to the left) in the turn, the two tend to work against each other and diminish the potential for the airplane to rotate and enter a spin. The result is that airplanes tend to stall (not spin) more often from a slip.

If they do begin to spin from a slip, the spin *entry* is not as dramatic as one from a skid. That's not to say you can't spin from a slipping turn, because you can. Keep in mind, however, that pilots regularly use slips when landing, and they do so at slower approach speeds. If the potential to spin from a slip were significant, slips certainly wouldn't be such a popular maneuver among pilots, much less a maneuver you're required to demonstrate on a private pilot checkride. Just remember that the aft moving wing always stalls FIRST!

Chapter 5: Stalls and Spins

How does the use of aileron to raise a dropping wing increase the angle of attack on that wing? Figure 27 shows how turning the yoke to the right lowers the aileron on the stalled (left) wing, thus further increasing the angle of attack on that wing beyond its critical value.

Your first reaction whenever a wing drops should be to reduce the angle of attack and simultaneously apply rudder to stop the yawing (or rolling) motion while neutralizing the ailerons. *You can't spin if you don't yaw.* Period! As a general rule during all stalls, if one wing drops (or begins to drop) during a stall, resulting in the airplane yawing and rolling toward the dropping wing, leave the ailerons in their neutral position and release elevator back pressure to reduce the angle of attack on both wings while *simultaneously* applying sufficient rudder pressure to stop the yawing motion.

If a left wing drops, resulting in a yaw and roll to the left, apply right rudder (Figure 28); if the right wing drops, resulting in a yaw and roll to the right, apply left rudder (Figure 29). As you are applying rudder, you are simultaneously reducing the angle of attack.

How much rudder pressure should you apply to stop the yawing motion? Enough to stop the yawing motion!

That's right. Do whatever it takes, and don't be shy about doing it. Push that rudder pedal all the way to the floorboard if necessary. You're usually at a very slow airspeed, which means the

control surfaces aren't nearly as effective as they would be at cruise speed. You often need to fully deflect the rudder surface to stop the yawing motion. You aren't going to hurt the rudder pedal by pushing it to the floorboard. Of course, you're not going to stomp on it while yelling, "Ahh, chupacabra," as if the pedal is the nastiest looking bug you've ever seen in your life. But you will push it all way the way down (if necessary) to stop the yawing motion.

Just to be clear here, I'm talking about using rudder as a wing *drops* during a stall. I'm not talking about using rudder to raise a *low* wing (one that isn't dropping) after the airplane is no longer stalled. In that case, we use both rudder and aileron in coordination to return to level flight (as we discussed previously).

Keep in mind that it's perfectly fine to reduce the angle of attack *and* simultaneously apply rudder pressure to stop the yawing and rolling motion during a *stall*. You're not in a spin. Close, but not yet there. A stall where one wing drops isn't a spin if you prevent the airplane from continuing to yaw and roll.

As you'll soon learn, once you're in a fully developed spin, you want to use rudder *first* to stop rotation. Then (and only then) do you reduce the angle of attack.

Stalling While Turning

As a general rule, you're more likely to stall while turning than while in straight flight. Why? Distractions. While turning, your attention is often directed toward some object outside the airplane, such as the runway when operating in the traffic pattern (discussed in detail in Chapter Eight). This is where pilots most often fail to monitor their airspeed, coordination and bank angle.

As I previously mentioned, as long as the turn is coordinated (the ball is centered in the inclinometer, meaning you're neither slipping or skidding), the airplane will stall in a direction perpendicular to the lateral axis. Despite being in a turn, the airplane stalls and moves in a direction from your nose to your feet (applicable to everyone except a yoga master, of course).

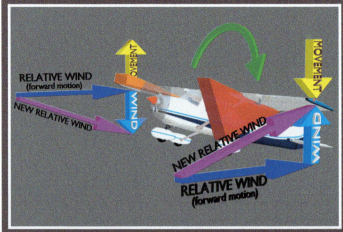

How Angle of Attack Changes With Wing Rotation

What's your vector, Victor?
Let's try wrapping your brain around the idea that rotation about the airplane's longitudinal axis through the use or misuse of rudder can cause a difference between the angles of attack on each wing.

First, let's make sure we understand that applying or not applying rudder to compensate for P-factor and slipstream induces a yaw, which causes the airplane to begin rolling in the direction of that yaw. Let's say that in the figure above, as the airplane approaches a stall (with power on) it yaws and rolls to the left because you failed to use right rudder to compensate for an increase in the airplane's power-induced left turning tendency.

As it rolls left, the left wing moves downward and generates a small component of relative wind blowing upward from underneath, as represented by the upward-pointing light blue arrow. The right wing, however, moves upward and generates a small component of relative wind blowing downward from above, as represented by the downward pointing light blue arrow. Since the airplane is also moving horizontally from right to left, it generates a relative wind opposite to its motion, as represented by a dark blue arrow.

Here comes the best part.
The wind that actually blows on the wing (thus the wind that determines the angle of attack on each wing as represented by the orange and red wedges on each wing (orange wedge on the right wing and red wedge on the left wing) is a combination of both the forward-motion relative wind (dark blue arrows) and the wind generated by wing rotation (light blue arrows). By combining both the dark blue and the light blue arrows, we create a new arrow that represents the actual relative wind that blows on the wing (the magenta arrows) during the left roll.

Although the diagram is an exaggeration of these wind forces, it's clear that the new relative wind on the right wing (orange wedge) strikes the chord line at a smaller angle than the new relative wind on the left wing (red wedge). Therefore, wing rotation induced by a yaw increases the angle of attack on the descending wing while simultaneously decreasing it on the rising wing.

The ultimate effect is that the left wing in our diagram reaches its critical angle of attack first. This allows the lift produced by the right wing to roll the airplane up and to the left (toward the now "stalled" left wing) for a possible spin entry to the left.

When performing a stall while turning, it might appear that one wing has stalled before the other, but this isn't true as long as the turn is coordinated. Both wings stall at the same time and

Chapter 5: Stalls and Spins

the airplane's nose typically pitches forward ahead of you while still in a banked condition (thus the appearance of one wing being lower than the other). The stall recovery, however, is the same as it is for straight and level flight, except that you'll typically recover back into wings-level flight through the coordinated use of aileron and rudder. Let's see this stall in action.

After making clearing turns, apply carburetor heat, reduce power to flight idle, and begin applying sufficient back pressure to hold altitude (Figure 30, position A). Now, place the airplane in a turn that doesn't exceed 20 degrees of bank (Figure 30, position B). Keep the turn coordinated and the airplane turning at a uniform rate as you continue increasing the angle of attack. Be aware of the tendency for the bank to increase with increasing back pressure. Use your ailerons and rudders in coordination to sustain the desired bank (20 degrees in this instance) and prevent overbanking. If the turn is coordinated, the airplane will stall and then pitch forward and downward in a direction perpendicular to the wings.

To recover, reduce the angle of attack by releasing elevator back pressure and simultaneously add full power (Figure 30, position C). When the wings are no longer stalled, use your ailerons and rudder in coordination to level the wings (Figure 30, position D). Now, establish a climb attitude for Vy while maintaining your rollout heading (the heading you rolled out on after you leveled the wings) as you climb to your previous altitude (Figure 30, position E).

Keep in mind that as power is applied during stall recovery, you'll initially need more right rudder pressure to keep the airplane in coordinated flight (Figure 30, position F). Be prepared to push your rudder pedal appropriately. Of course, you don't want to apply power without reducing the angle of attack. Doing so might actually cause one wing to stall before the other, since the addition of power yaws the nose to the left. The combination of a power induced yaw (meaning the need for right rudder) and critical angle of attack is the precise combination of control forces needed to spin the airplane. So be sure to decrease the angle of attack and simultaneously add power, while keeping the flight controls coordinated.

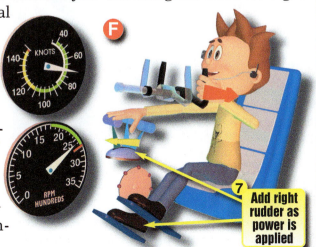

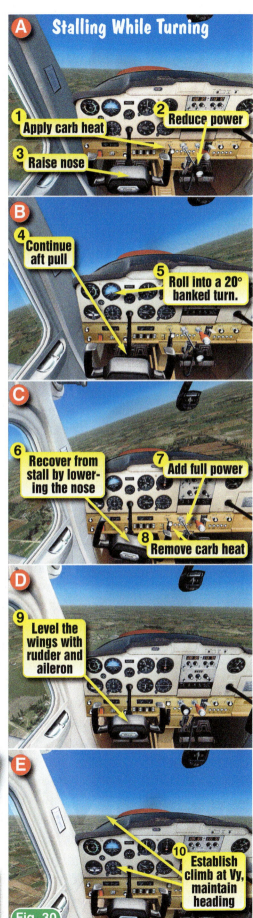

Fig. 30

Stalling With the Nose Pointed Down While Turning

At the beginning of this chapter, I said that an airplane can stall at any attitude and at any airspeed. I wasn't fooling around, either (mainly because I wasn't wearing my propeller hat at the time). This is a very important point for you to understand. Now that you have a foundation for understanding stalls, you're ready to explore a very common stall-spin scenario that can trap the unwary pilot.

Let's assume you're flying at a very slow speed in level flight (meaning that you're using engine power), with the wings near their critical angle of attack (Figure 31). It's clear from this figure that the nose is pointed above the horizon. Let's make a power-off, descending turn from base to final approach at the same angle of attack (Figure 32). This figure shows that the airplane's nose is pointed below the horizon. It's one of those days, you didn't plan your descent perfectly, and suddenly you find yourself at too low an altitude while flying at this large angle of attack. Your natural (although often fatal) instinct might be to pull aft on the elevator in an attempt to shy away from the ground. This might be a subtle, continuous pull and you might not even be aware that you're doing it. Why is that? Read on.

Because the airplane is banked, pulling aft on the elevator control moves the nose at a diagonal to the horizon (Figure 34). In other words, there's a horizontal as well as a vertical component to this motion. This is unlike pulling aft on the elevator in straight flight, which moves the nose only vertically (Figure 33). When applying aft elevator pressure in a descending turn, the nose does rise toward the horizon slightly, but it also moves horizontally (toward the inside of the turn), too (Figure 34).

At 45 degrees of bank the nose moves horizontally as much as it moves vertically with aft elevator pressure. The result is that while you're increasing the angle of attack in a descending turn, you don't see the nose moving vertically as much as you're used to. In previous stall examples, you sensed you were approaching a stall because the nose rose above the horizon to some degree. Here, however, the nose is below the horizon because you're descending and turning. Any increase in elevator back pressure doesn't entirely translate into the vertical movement of the nose because of the banked condition.

When observing the airplane's pitch attitude in relation to the horizon, it might not be apparent to you that the wings are approaching their critical angle of attack when applying elevator back pressure in a descending turn. This is why you want to look at the angle made between the wing's chord line and terrain movement in a turn

Stalling in a Nose-high Attitude

In straight and level flight near stall speed, the airplane's nose is pointed above the horizon and the wings are near their critical angle of attack.

Stalling in a Nose-down Attitude

In a descending turn near stall speed, the airplane's nose is pointed below the horizon with the wings near their critical angle of attack.

Chapter 5: Stalls and Spins

How Elevator Back Pressure Translates Into the Direction the Nose Moves

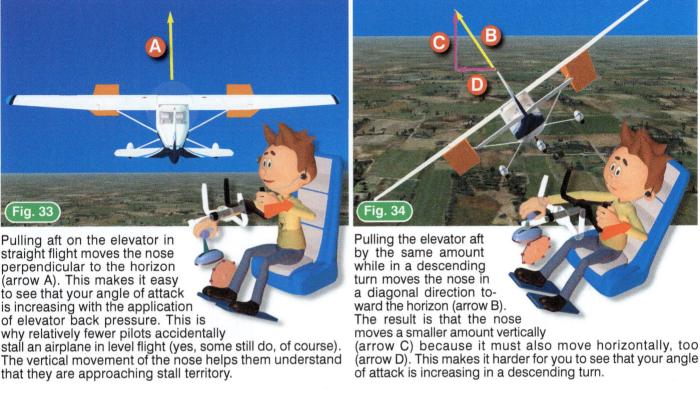

Fig. 33 — Pulling aft on the elevator in straight flight moves the nose perpendicular to the horizon (arrow A). This makes it easy to see that your angle of attack is increasing with the application of elevator back pressure. This is why relatively fewer pilots accidentally stall an airplane in level flight (yes, some still do, of course). The vertical movement of the nose helps them understand that they are approaching stall territory.

Fig. 34 — Pulling the elevator aft by the same amount while in a descending turn moves the nose in a diagonal direction toward the horizon (arrow B). The result is that the nose moves a smaller amount vertically (arrow C) because it must also move horizontally, too (arrow D). This makes it harder for you to see that your angle of attack is increasing in a descending turn.

to get a very *rough approximation* of your angle of attack, as previously discussed in Figures 19 and 20 on page 5-14. Without knowing your angle of attack, it's entirely possible for you to stall with the nose pointed below the horizon. You will undoubtedly be surprised by such an event.

What further complicates this issue is that the airplane's stalling speed increases in a turn because of the increase in load factor (more on load factor when we cover accelerated stalls). If the airplane stalls in this condition, you might initially be confused because the nose is pointed below the horizon in an attitude that you normally select to recover from the stall.

To recover from a stall in a descending turn, you must do what you did before, but now it's a lot more counterintuitive because the nose is already below the horizon and the ground is close. Stay true to your (flight) school. It's just a stall. Release elevator back pressure and lower the nose, reducing the angle of attack to less than its critical value. Yikes! How unnatural is that? It's like wearing swim fins with a tuxedo (and that combination doesn't look good even on a penguin).

The closer you are to the ground, the stronger your tendency is to continue pulling back on the elevator, despite the fact that you may be in a stall. There is a phrase for this in Spanish: *Hasta la vista, baby*. And if you'd like me to complicate this equation even further, just imagine what the stall would be like if the airplane was in a skid at the time of the stall. One wing might stall before the other and the airplane would enter a spin. Believe me, this is *not* what your instructor means when he or she says, "Let's take the plane out for a spin." Spinning close to the ground might easily turn your airplane into a lawn dart. This is why you always want to fly coordinated as well as be hypersensitive to the conditions that precede a stall. Most important, you don't want to fall into the trap of believing that just because the airplane's nose is pointed below the horizon that it can't stall. It can.

Now it's time to look a little more closely at other factors that can affect the stall characteristics of your airplane. Among these are weight, load factor, center of gravity and airplane configuration. Let's examine each.

Stall Characteristics Affecting an Airplane

Weight and balance has an enormous effect on how an airplane stalls and recovers from a stall. In a six-seat twin, there might be a 30-40% difference between day-to-day flying-around weight and maximum gross weight. But you may be surprised at how big a difference a little difference can make.

Let's say you're used to flying your Cessna 172 alone, with limited fuel, at a weight of 1,600 pounds. In that configuration the stall speed is 41 knots. The moment you place your two fishing buddies in the airplane, each weighing 150 pounds (current weight: 1,600+300=1,900 pounds) along with your mother-in-law, the airplane now weighs 2,300 pounds (yes, you're flying your "mom"ster to a Jenny Craig convention but she doesn't know it…yet). At 2,300 pounds, the stall speed increases by nearly 18% to 49 knots (Figure 35). That's a rather large increase in stall speed for the unenlightened (or the unlightened). And in larger aircraft, the difference in weight and stall speed is proportionally larger.

Center of gravity location also affects the airplane's stall characteristics. Move the CG aft and the stall speed decreases slightly. Move it forward and it increases slightly. Why? It's all a matter of the lifting force the wings are required to generate to compensate for the total downward-acting forces on the airplane. (See Sidebar: *How CG Affects Stall Speed*.)

Remember that the tail must produce a downward-acting force to keep the wings from rotating forward (the wings' *center of lift* is located behind the center of gravity, thus imparting a forward twisting moment to the wings). To remain airborne, the wings must produce a lifting force equal to the combined force of the airplane's weight as well as the tail-down force. That means a slightly higher minimum airspeed is necessary to generate the minimum lift for flight.

Said another way, the downward-acting force on the tail increases the airplane's stall speed, in the range of a few knots. Move the CG aft to reduce the tail-down force and now the wings don't have to produce as much lift because there are fewer forces acting downward. That means a slightly slower airspeed will generate the minimum lift for flight. While the angle of attack at which the airplane stalls always remains the same, an aft CG means that the airplane can fly *slower* at (or near) its critical angle of attack to generate the minimum lift for flight. Ultimately, that means the airplane's stall speed has decreased.

How does CG affect stall recovery? As long as the CG is located within its allowable limits, the airplane behaves normally in a stall. That means the nose pitches downward, which aids in stall recovery, and you'll experience normal yoke (stick) forces when maneuvering at high and low speeds.

On the other hand, if you stall an airplane with the CG located aft of the airplane's allowable limits, it will be less stable during the stall. That means that the nose won't automatically pitch downward as easily as it did when operating within the normal CG range. That leads to greater difficulty in stall recovery, and at its extreme can make stall recovery impossible. The accident report will also note that you loaded the plane outside its weight-and-balance specs.

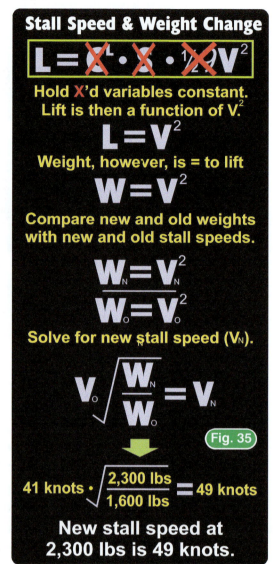

Stall Speed & Weight Change

$$L = \cancel{C_L} \cdot \cancel{S} \cdot \cancel{\tfrac{1}{2}\rho} V^2$$

Hold X'd variables constant. Lift is then a function of V^2.

$$L = V^2$$

Weight, however, is = to lift

$$W = V^2$$

Compare new and old weights with new and old stall speeds.

$$\frac{W_N = V_N^2}{W_O = V_O^2}$$

Solve for new stall speed (V_N).

$$V_O \sqrt{\frac{W_N}{W_O}} = V_N$$

Fig. 35

$$41 \text{ knots} \cdot \sqrt{\frac{2{,}300 \text{ lbs}}{1{,}600 \text{ lbs}}} = 49 \text{ knots}$$

New stall speed at 2,300 lbs is 49 knots.

By holding the variables of the lift coefficient, wing area and density constant, the minimum speed to sustain a specific airplane weight can be determined. This minimum speed is also known as the airplane's *stall speed*.

Chapter 5: Stalls and Spins

How CG Position Affects Stall Speed

A — *Airplane At Stall Speed!*

Note: Only a few forces acting on the airplane are shown here.

LIFT–2000 lbs | WEIGHT–1800 lbs | Force–200 lbs | Nose Down Moment | Tail Down Moment | 18° | ⊕ = Center of Gravity

With the CG at a more forward limit, the center of lift (located behind the CG) results in a nose down pitching moment. This must be countered by a downward acting force generated by the tail of the airplane. Therefore, the amount of lift required to be developed by the wings to sustain level flight is equal to all the downward acting forces. At gross weight and near the critical angle of attack (18 degrees), Airplane A must fly at a minimum speed of 60 knots to generate 2,000 lbs of lift (1,800 + 200) to remain airborne. Therefore, 60 knots is the stall speed for this airplane under the present CG conditions.

B — *Airplane At Stall Speed!*

Note: Only a few forces acting on the airplane are shown here.

LIFT–1800 lbs | WEIGHT–1800 lbs | 18° | ⊕ = Center of Gravity

No tail-down force generated by rear of airplane.

Fig. 36

As the CG moves aft, it make the airplane more "tail" heavy. Therefore, an aft moving CG produces a force that acts in the same direction as the 200 lb tail-down force shown by Airplane A. Move the CG far enough aft so that it eliminates the need for the tail to generate a tail down force, then you've eliminated 200 lbs of downward acting force. That means the wings only need to develop 1,800 lbs of lift to remain airborne. Since the airplane can develop 1,800 lbs of lift at a speed slower than that of Airplane A (at 2,000 lbs), its stall speed has decreased. Airplane B can remain airborne at a minimum speed of 57 knots.

A CG that's forward of the airplane's allowable limits means that your stall speed is higher. The forward CG also means that you'll experience *higher* stick forces on the elevator control, so the control will be less responsive to inputs (Figure 36, position A). After all, with a longer arm between the CG and the tail, you'll need to apply elevator pressure through a longer draw (pull or push) of the yoke to achieve any given amount of pitch change. This means pulling/pushing against a greater aerodynamic load on the elevator control surface (a load caused by air blowing on that deflected surface), thus creating a heavier feel to the elevator control. (See sidebar below: *How CG Position Affects Stick Forces*).

Approaching to land with a CG that's aft of its allowable limits produces *lighter* stick forces on the elevator, making the airplane more sensitive to pitch inputs (Figure 36, position B). With a shorter arm between the tail and the CG, a small movement of the elevator takes less relative force and produces a larger change in pitch. Either extreme in CG location is a no-fly zone.

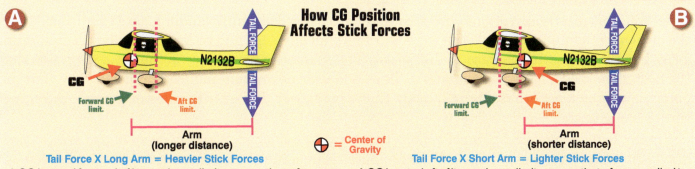

How CG Position Affects Stick Forces

A — Tail Force X Long Arm = Heavier Stick Forces
Arm (longer distance)

A CG located forward of its maximum limits means that a force applied to the tail acts a longer distance away from the CG (the point where the airplane always rotates). This means you'll have to displace the elevator control further forward or aft to produce the desired pitch response (otherwise known as a "heavier" stick force).

B — Tail Force X Short Arm = Lighter Stick Forces
Arm (shorter distance)

A CG located aft of its maximum limits means that a force applied to the tail acts a shorter distance away from the CG (the point where the airplane always rotates). This means you'll have to move the elevator control less distance forward or aft to produce the desired pitch response (otherwise known as "light" stick forces).

Power also affects stall speed (Figure 30). The airplane stalls at a slower speed with power added (the angle of attack at which the airplane stalls, however, *always* remains the same). Why? Because power (thrust, actually) adds a small, upward-acting component of force. As we previously learned, if thrust acts upward, the airplane's wings can fly at a slightly slower airspeed and still generate the minimum lift required for flight. Your stall speed has decreased slightly when using power.

The problem is that if you're close to the stall speed with power applied and you then suddenly reduce power, the airplane might stall sooner than you expect. This is one reason pilots often find the bottom dropping out of their airplane during a slow speed power-on landing when they suddenly reduce power. That, of course, is a figure of speech. The bottom of the airplane doesn't actually detach from the fuselage. The airplane, however, can stall and/or sink toward the ground if power is suddenly reduced while operating close to stall speed.

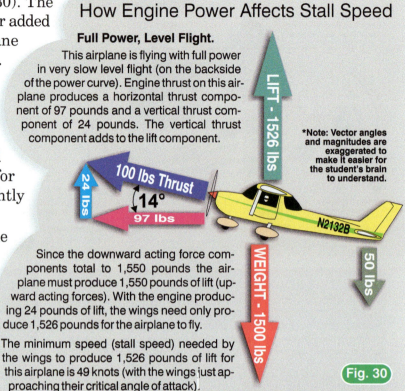

How Engine Power Affects Stall Speed

Full Power, Level Flight.
This airplane is flying with full power in very slow level flight (on the backside of the power curve). Engine thrust on this airplane produces a horizontal thrust component of 97 pounds and a vertical thrust component of 24 pounds. The vertical thrust component adds to the lift component.

*Note: Vector angles and magnitudes are exaggerated to make it easier for the student's brain to understand.

Since the downward acting force components total to 1,550 pounds the airplane must produce 1,550 pounds of lift (upward acting forces). With the engine producing 24 pounds of lift, the wings need only produce 1,526 pounds for the airplane to fly.

The minimum speed (stall speed) needed by the wings to produce 1,526 pounds of lift for this airplane is 49 knots (with the wings just approaching their critical angle of attack).

If we suddenly reduce engine power, we remove 24 pounds of vertically acting engine thrust. Now the wings must produce 1,550 pounds of lift to keep the airplane flying. Since the wings are at their critical angle of attack in this example, the only way to produce 24 more pounds of lift is to increase the airplane's speed by one additional knot. Therefore, reducing engine power increases the stall speed to 50 knots. The takeaway point here is that if you were flying just above a stall at 49 knots with engine power applied and suddenly reduced the power to flight idle, you would stall unless you immediately lowered the nose to accelerate the airplane. This is why the airplane might suddenly stall and smack the runway during landing when it's slow and power is reduced.

Fig. 30

Drag also affects *how* the airplane stalls. While parasite drag and induced drag don't affect the airplane's stall speed, they do affect how quickly the airplane might reach that speed. (A reduction in induced drag in ground effect can reduce stall speed.) A dirty airplane (one with flaps and gear extended, not one that needs a wash job) has a lot of parasite drag. This means that it decelerates much more quickly than one with its gear and flaps retracted. Deceleration means that the airspeed decreases, which is usually accompanied by an increase in angle of attack, which always results in an increase in induced drag.

To you, this means operations with gear and flaps extended (think landings) are conditions where the airplane might quickly approach the edge of its stall envelope and be less quick about accelerating away from it, even with the use of full power. The takeaway point here is that at speeds less than the best glide speed, a dirty airplane (i.e., flaps and gear down) and induced drag can slow your airplane down quickly, perhaps more quickly than you expect. It's as if the slower you go, the slower you're likely to go.

Finally, bank angle also has an effect on stall speed (see sidebar: *Why You Feel Loaded When Banking an Airplane* on the next page). While an increase in actual weight increases your stall speed, it's also true that an increase in *apparent weight* increases your stall speed. An increase in load factor as the airplane's direction of motion changes creates an apparent weight increase. The airplane can't tell the difference between a real weight increase and an apparent weight increase. Since you're in the airplane while it's turning or maneuvering, you'll feel the apparent increase in weight, which is

Chapter 5: Stalls and Spins

Why You Feel Loaded When Banking Your Airplane

During your medical exam, you know when you've put on extra weight because you'll hop on the scale and it will read: Please, one person at a time. Ouch!

There are several ways to gain weight but one of the least recognized is to fly an airplane. In an airplane that's turning or maneuvering, your apparent weight *can* increase. . .a lot. If you could stand on a scale in an airplane that's banking at 60 degrees in level flight, the scale would show that you weigh twice your weight in un-banked, level flight (Picture-1). Isn't that amazing?

How is this possible? An airplane that is turning or maneuvering experiences an increase in its load factor, which is referred to as g-force. The load factor increases when an airplane turns because the airplane's mass tends to resist changing direction.

Mass has inertia, which is the tendency of any object (mass) to resist changes to its motion. As the airplane enters a turn or begins a maneuver, you and the entire airplane want to remain moving in the same direction you were headed before starting the turn. It takes the horizontal component of lift to pull the airplane in a new direction, while the airplane's inertia resists that change. This resistance is known as centrifugal force. Centrifugal force is added to the airplane's actual weight, resulting in an increase in the apparent weight of the airplane and all of its contents (Picture-2).

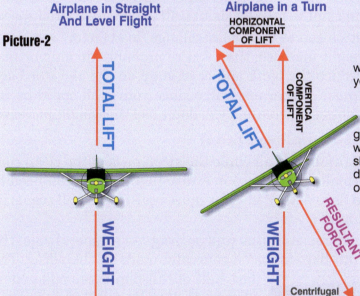

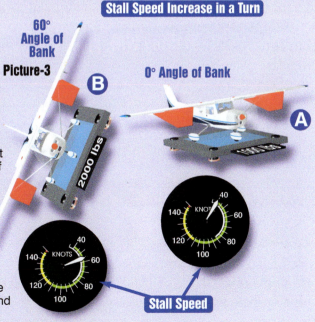

You've experienced this all your life, even if you didn't know what it was. Did you ever ride on a Tilt-a-Whirl at a fair and feel yourself pressed against the frame? Ever ride on a roller coaster and feel yourself getting scrunched into the seat as it rounded a corner? If you're old enough, you might remember being on a merry-go-round as it gained speed and you felt yourself getting heavier in a sideways direction and being pushed outward. You've made a sharp turn in your car, haven't you? The sharper the turn, the more you feel the resistance to a change in direction/motion, making it feel as though you're being forced to one side of your ride. Make an airplane curve or turn more sharply and the resistance to a change in motion increases, which is registered as an increase in *load factor*. You and the airplane apparently feel heavier as a result.

The problem is, if the airplane's apparent weight increases, its stall speed also increases. At a given weight in straight flight, with the wings at their critical angle of attack, the airplane requires a minimum airflow over the wings of 40 knots to develop the required lift for flight (Picture-3, position A). Increasing the apparent weight by banking the airplane requires that you fly at a higher minimum speed to generate the minimum lift that is now needed for flight. This is shown by the airplane banked at 60 degrees (Picture-3, position B), which requires a minimum speed of 56.4 knots to fly at (or just a tiny bit below) its critical angle of attack.

You *cannot* increase the angle of attack to generate additional lift, because the wings in this example are already at the critical angle of attack. Stalls and dragons be there. An increase in apparent weight results in an increase in the minimum speed at which the wings need to move through the air to develop sufficient lift for flight—your stall speed just increased.

The takeaway point here is that your butt is a stall warning device. If you feel as though you're getting heavier during a turn, it means the plane's stall speed is increasing. Be aware. Learn where the limits are and how to handle recovering from a stall in accelerated (turning) flight.

your clue that the stall speed is increasing. This is an extremely important point for you to understand.

During a turn, if you feel as though you've suddenly put on weight (without a doughnut intervention being involved), your airplane will stall at a higher speed. If your airspeed is decreasing as the apparent weight or load factor increases (such as during a steep turn), then it's possible that your stall speed will cross paths with your decreasing aircraft speed. When those two meet, the result is a stall. This is one reason that pilots typically avoid banks in excess of 30 degrees when flying in the traffic pattern. A bank of 30 degrees typically increases the load factory by a relatively small amount (Figure 31, position A). The stall speed also increases by no more than a few knots (Figure 31, position B). Increase the bank to 60 degrees and you're talking about a 40% increase in stall speed.

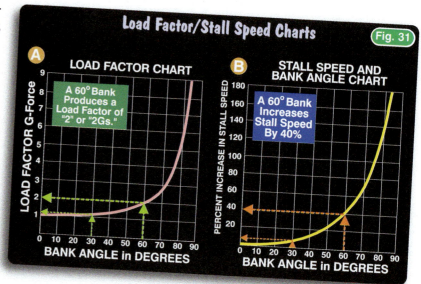

So let your derriere keep you safe by paying attention to the weight change (load factor) you experience while turning. If you feel an apparent weight increase, then you're probably turning or maneuvering too sharply and you might want to reduce the bank and/or ease up on the elevator back pressure (otherwise known as *unloading the wings*). Either one will reduce your stall speed by reducing the load factor. Your stall speed, however, doesn't increase if you don't feel the weight increase.

Stalling with Flaps Extended (Approach to Landing Stalls)

So far we've discussed stalling and recovering from the stall while the airplane is in the clean configuration, which is the configuration you'll normally experience in cruise flight. What you need to learn now is how to recover from a stall with the flaps extended, a far more real-world stall scenario. (We'll cover stalls with gear and flaps extended next.)

As you know, extending the flaps (Figure 32) increases lift as well as drag. As a general rule, the first half of full-flap extension generates more lift than drag. The last half of full-flap extension generates more drag than lift. Now, I don't get all wild and crazy about this point, because the lift and drag effects of flaps vary considerably between airplanes. For example, older Cessnas with their 40 degrees of Fowler flap extension follow this rule. Newer airplanes with plain or split flaps might not follow this rule.

Why is this general rule even important? Stall recovery is about quickly and correctly managing lift and drag. You need to know how to shed as much drag as possible while keeping or getting the maximum amount of lift. Let's

Chapter 5: Stalls and Spins

examine the best way to recover from a stall with flaps extended.

Since you'll typically extend flaps when approaching to land, we'll call stalls in this condition, *approach-to-landing stalls*. In straight and level flight apply carb heat, reduce power to idle and begin by slowing the airplane to the typical approach speed for your plane, as shown in Figure 33 (yes, you can reduce power and lower the nose to begin a descent while slowing down, but this isn't the cleanest or most aesthetically pleasing way to set up an airplane for the stall).

Apply sufficient elevator back pressure to hold altitude as your airspeed decreases. When your speed decreases below the maximum flap extended speed (Vfe) as shown in Figure 34, begin applying flaps in 10 degree or single-notch increments until full flaps are deployed. Ten to 15 degree increments help minimize large up or down pitch changes as you adjust your pitch to maintain the desired full flaps approach speed or 1.3 Vso, for instance. Some airplane manufacturers allow you to apply partial flaps at speeds above Vfe. If you're in such an airplane, then feel free to apply that partial amount of flaps first at a higher speed to help decrease your airspeed. When reaching Vfe, apply the remaining flaps as appropriate.

Once you're established in a power-off descent at the full flap approach speed, you are ready to actually stall the airplane (Figure 35). In this instance, you can trim the airplane as necessary to maintain this condition, especially if your tiny biceps muscles are humming like newly plucked violin strings. Listen to that music and trim away your discomfort. Why trim when this stall demonstration is a temporary condition? Because I want you to know what it's like to feel the actual elevator back pressure associated with deployment of full flaps, trim and full power. As you'll see, you're going to need to initially apply a lot of forward elevator pressure to keep your airplane under control immediately after adding power.

In this example, you'll perform a full stall the same way you did previously, by raising the nose slowly to a nose-up attitude sufficient to exceed the wings' critical angle of attack. Since full flaps are applied, you'll find that you don't have to raise the nose as high to stall as you did when stalling without flaps.

Once the airplane stalls, release elevator back pressure to reduce the angle of attack, while simultaneously applying full power (Figure 36). Because you're simulating flight close to the ground, you don't want to (nor do you need to) use a large nose-down attitude during stall recovery. This creates excessive altitude loss, which you can't afford if you're close to the solid object known as earth. One of the things you'll immediately notice when recovering from a stall with full flaps is how quick and strong the nose-up pitch is with the addition of full power. It's entirely possible that simply releasing back pressure to recover from the stall (as you've done during no-flap stall recovery) won't reduce the angle of attack sufficiently to recover from the stall. With the addition of power, you might have to apply a little forward elevator pressure until the airplane is no longer stalled and is accelerating (Figure 36). Then raise the nose to an attitude near or just a little above the horizon and begin cleaning up the flaps (Figure 37).

At this point, use whatever elevator trim is needed to sustain the desired attitude. So get to it and spin that trim wheel if you have to. Keep in mind that an airplane's pitch-up response with full flaps when power is applied depends on the type of flaps as well as the amount those flaps are extended. The pitch-up response in a Piper Warrior is not as strong as it is in a Cessna 172 with 40 degrees of flaps extension.

Since the flaps are still extended, you don't want to immediately raise the attitude to that used to climb at Vy in the clean configuration. So use a lower pitch attitude, initially. Why? Because your airplane isn't cleaned up yet. It's still in a high drag condition because the flaps (and gear, if retractable) are still extended.

The important thing here is that the initial recovery attitude you select should allow the airplane to accelerate. If the attitude you select at first is too high, lower it a bit. It's

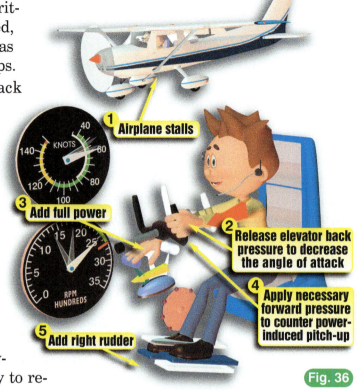

Recovering From the Full Flap Stall

1. Airplane stalls
2. Release elevator back pressure to decrease the angle of attack
3. Add full power
4. Apply necessary forward pressure to counter power-induced pitch-up
5. Add right rudder

Fig. 36

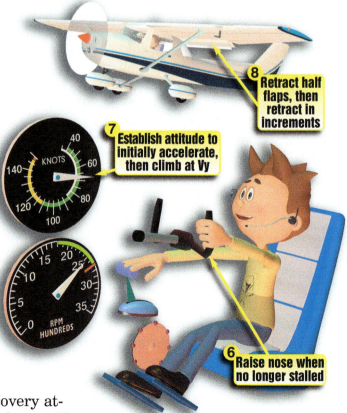

Establishing the Post Stall Attitude

6. Raise nose when no longer stalled
7. Establish attitude to initially accelerate, then climb at Vy
8. Retract half flaps, then retract in increments

Fig. 37

Chapter 5: Stalls and Spins

The Danger of Premature Flap Retraction

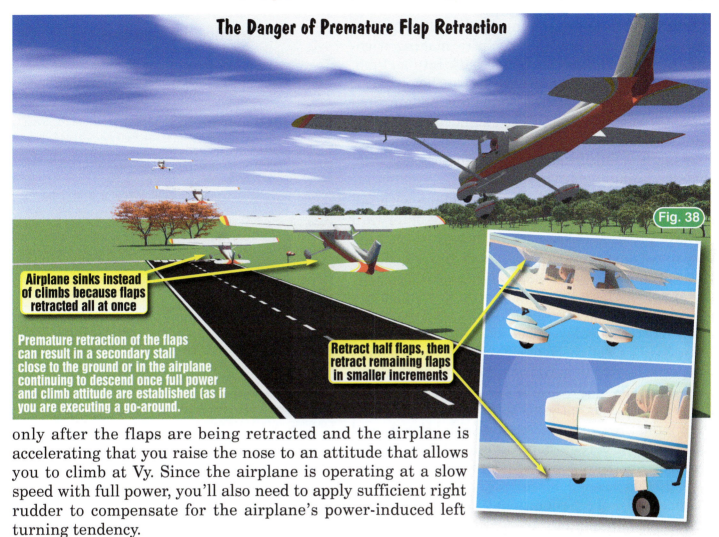

Fig. 38

Airplane sinks instead of climbs because flaps retracted all at once

Premature retraction of the flaps can result in a secondary stall close to the ground or in the airplane continuing to descend once full power and climb attitude are established (as if you are executing a go-around.

Retract half flaps, then retract remaining flaps in smaller increments

only after the flaps are being retracted and the airplane is accelerating that you raise the nose to an attitude that allows you to climb at Vy. Since the airplane is operating at a slow speed with full power, you'll also need to apply sufficient right rudder to compensate for the airplane's power-induced left turning tendency.

Now comes the important question. What do you do about the flaps? If you retract them all at once you'll certainly reduce their drag, but you'll also deprive the airplane of the extra lift they provide. Also, if you removed all the flaps at once, the airplane might begin sinking. As it sinks, you might be psychologically unwilling to keep the nose lowered enough to accelerate the airplane, especially if you are close to the ground and there's a nice big tree ahead of you. You know what that sinking feeling means, right? Or rather, what your reaction to it means. You could enter a secondary stall close to the ground, without much altitude for recovery. It's tradeoff time. You first want to remove the portion of the flaps causing the greatest amount of drag to avoid installing a living treetop air freshener in your cockpit.

Your airplane's POH is the ultimate source of information about correct flap reduction procedures, but in general:

In airplanes having 40 degrees of high-lift/high-drag flaps, you'll typically reduce flaps to 20 degrees of extension (their least drag, max lift condition), followed by reducing the remaining flaps in 10-degree increments as long as the airplane is accelerating to Vy (Figure 38).

In airplanes with manually extended flaps, you'll usually reduce the flaps to the second notch of extension (which is typically the least drag, max lift condition unless specified otherwise by the airplane's POH), followed by each remaining notch as long as the airplane is accelerating to Vy.

In airplanes having 30 degrees of moderate-lift/moderate-drag flaps, remove the last (full-flap) notch of flaps, followed by the remaining flaps in 10-degree (or single notch) increments as long as the airplane is accelerating to Vy.

When the flaps are coming up, it's often best to recover from the stall as if you're making a go-around. That means recovering back into a climb, then leveling out at the altitude at which you began the stall. After all, if you actually did stall on final approach with gear and flaps extended, you might want to go-around and try that approach again, once your heart is fluttering at a speed slightly less than that of a hummingbird's wings.

Please keep in mind that when stalling with full flaps you're likely to need a large amount of forward elevator pressure to keep the airplane from pitching up excessively; apply too little and you could find yourself in a secondary stall. This is especially true if you applied nose-up elevator trim to compensate for your airplane's nose-down pitching behavior when flaps are deployed (see sidebar: *The Elevator Trim Stall*). Over the years, I've observed students who were unable to keep the nose from pitching up as power was applied, and not because they had grape-sized biceps, either (I think one acted as if he were pumping elevator iron and said, "Hey, I need you to spot me here."). Sometimes pilots are just unprepared for the amount of forward elevator pressure that is needed to sustain the proper climb attitude under these conditions.

What about simulating an approach to landing stall while turning? You already know how to recover from a stall in a turn, and you'll apply the same procedures in this case. After establishing a full-flap descent with power at flight idle, begin a coordinated turn at a bank of 20 degrees or less while slowly and continuously increasing the angle of attack and turning at a uniform rate (even if you're not wearing your uniform). Plan on turning at least 90 degrees during the stall entry, to simulate a base-to-final turn. This just adds a bit of realism to the stall and makes the FAA examiner happy (his or her happiness is your goal, right?). As with all turning stall recoveries, you should reduce the angle of attack, add full power, then level the wings with the coordinated use of rudder and ailerons while maintaining your rollout heading throughout the stall recovery. You'll most likely need a lot of right rudder (at least initially), given the slow speed and large amount of engine power.

The one thing you'll need to be careful about is keeping the flight controls coordinated when enter-

The Elevator Trim Stall

The possibility of a secondary stall increases during stall recovery when a great deal of nose-up elevator trim is applied prior to stalling. If you understand the airplane's tendency to pitch nose-up when applying full power during a full-flap stall recovery, then you have a good idea of how the airplane reacts when you apply full power with a relatively large amount of nose-up trim applied. And you can just imagine the nose-up pitching moment you'll experience when both full flaps *and* nose-up trim are in place for the stall. Talk about double trouble.

In a typical landing configuration, you're approaching the runway with full flaps and a relatively large amount of nose-up trim applied. Stall recovery (or, for that matter, a go-around from this condition) requires that you initially apply substantial forward elevator force while adding full power. This is no time to be dainty or delicate. Your goal is to control the nose-up inclination of the plane while adding nose-down trim and getting to an attitude that permits initial acceleration, then acceleration to Vy. Once nose-down trim is added and/or flaps are retracted, elevator forces normalize.

If you don't apply sufficient forward elevator pressure as full power is applied, it's possible for the airplane to stall, or enter a secondary stall. Stalls that result primarily as a result of nose-up trim are known as *elevator-trim stalls*.

Ask your instructor to demonstrate the nose-up pitching moment associated with this trimmed condition. Practice recovering from a stall in this condition, as well. To do this, establish a normal, full flap, power-off descent, and then apply a sufficient amount of nose-up trim to sustain the descent attitude. Now stall the airplane, as before.

After applying full power during the recovery, you may need to immediately add nose-down trim before you can retract the major drag-causing portion of the flaps. This of course depends on the strength in your arms. If you can do it, apply sufficient forward pressure on the yoke, then retract the first increment of flaps, then apply nose-down trim. This simply allows you to accelerate to climb speed sooner, which is always a good thing.

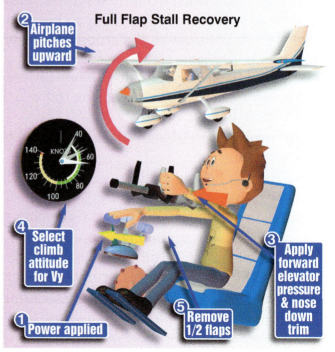

Full Flap Stall Recovery
① Power applied
② Airplane pitches upward
③ Apply forward elevator pressure & nose down trim
④ Select climb attitude for Vy
⑤ Remove 1/2 flaps

Chapter 5: Stalls and Spins

ing a full flap stall as well as when applying full power during the recovery. Some airplanes don't stall peacefully if the flight controls are uncoordinated the moment the critical angle of attack is reached and full flaps are deployed. Cessna 150s are a good example here. If you're skidding at the moment you stall with 40 degrees of flaps deployed, one wing can stall before the other, and by the time you've added rudder to stop the yaw, you've probably turned 180 degrees, or more. These airplanes can fly quite slow with full flaps deployed, and slower flight means less rudder effectiveness. The same full flap stall in a skid, however, isn't as dramatic on other airplanes, such as the Piper Warrior. It's just good pilot practice to keep the airplane's nose pointed in the direction it's moving during the stall (in other words, keep the ball in the inclinometer centered).

When recovering from the full-flap stall, if you allow the airplane to enter a secondary stall and you haven't already applied right rudder pressure to compensate for the power-induced left turning tendencies, then you're headed for Spin City, which is a pity. So the moment you apply power during the stall recovery, apply right rudder to keep the nose pointed in the direction it was originally headed (once again, keep the ball in the inclinometer centered).

Stalling with Gear and Flaps Extended

Given the upward mobility of pilots in terms of the airplanes they fly, it's likely that you'll eventually end up operating a complex airplane. That means flying an airplane having retractable gear as well as flaps and a controllable propeller. Let's examine how to recover from stalls in the approach-to-landing configuration in a complex airplane.

You don't have to be as smart as a fifth grader to know that extending the landing gear increases parasite drag. It's called *parasite drag* because there are no offsetting in-flight bennies—such as lift—that result from extending the landing gear. This is why you'll never hear someone say, "I think we need some more lift, get that landing gear down." On the other hand, retracting the landing gear during a climb helps you to accelerate and climb faster, which is always a good idea in a small airplane. So let's do an approach to landing stall with the gear and flaps extended.

From straight and level flight, slow the airplane to its maximum landing gear operating speed (Vlo) and extend the gear (Figure 39). Let's begin by reducing power (which is typically referred to as your *manifold pressure* in a complex airplane) and applying sufficient back pressure to hold altitude as the airspeed decreases (Figure 39). Bring your power back to a value, say 18 or 20 inches (this value is often on the low end of the manifold pressure gauge's green arc). Given the short duration of the power reduction and the decreasing speed, engine shock cooling isn't an issue here.

When slowing to at or below your gear operating speed, lower the gear. To ensure that the landing gear is fully extended, check that

Fig. 39

gear the annunciator lights indicate the gear is down and locked (that normally means three green lights, one for each landing gear). With the gear fully extended, reduce power to flight idle and continue to slow the airplane in level flight, to the maximum flap extended speed (Vfe).

Once you are below Vfe, apply full flaps and establish the attitude necessary for a power-off descent at your typical full-flap approach speed, as shown in Figure 40 (1.3 Vso is a good speed to use here). Feel free to use sufficient nose-up trim to maintain the established attitude and airspeed. Since airplanes with retractable landing gear are normally complex airplanes with controllable propellers, you should treat the propeller control just as you would if you were on a short final approach to land, meaning that you move the prop control to its full forward position (remember, the power is at idle and the airspeed is slow, so the propeller won't overspeed here as long as you move the propeller control forward in a slow, smooth manner). Keep in mind that you're simulating an approach to landing stall in a high drag condition. That's why you'll need maximum allowable RPM during the recovery. Moving the prop lever forward maximizes the engine's horsepower (thrust) production when power is applied. Now you're ready to stall the airplane.

Begin by raising the nose slightly above the horizon and hold it there until you've exceeded the critical angle of attack. Once the airplane stalls, you'll release elevator back pressure to reduce the angle of attack, while simultaneously applying full power. Sound familiar? There's no need to shove the throttle forward, either. Simply apply power at a reasonable rate, perhaps just a bit faster than you would during a normal takeoff. Why? Given the wind that's already blowing on the propeller, it's quite easy to exceed the maximum engine RPM with rapid throttle application, to say nothing of overboosting your engine if it's turbocharged. Yes, we're trying to create a realistic stall environment here but we must also be good stewards of the machines we're flying. Of course, if this were a real stall recovery you wouldn't worry about overspeeding the prop or overboosting the engine, right? Right!

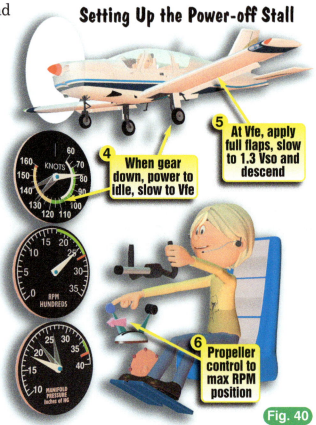

Fig. 40

Fig. 41

It's also good to remember that, because you're simulating being close to the ground, you don't want (or need) to have a large nose-down attitude to recover from this stall. You only need to reduce the angle of attack sufficiently to break the stall (a fancy term meaning to *recover* from the stall). As soon as the stall breaks and the airplane is accelerating, raise the nose to the climb attitude for Vy

Chapter 5: Stalls and Spins

Retracting the Flaps and Gear

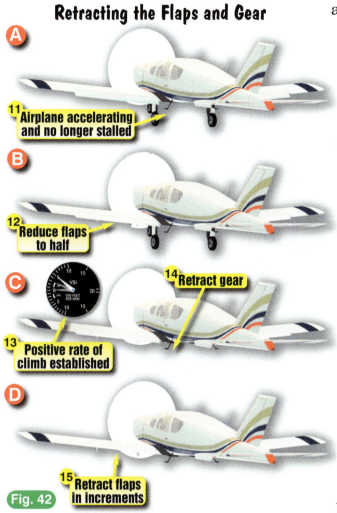

Fig. 42

and clean up your machine (Figure 41). This does not mean shampooing the rugs, vacuuming the floor mats, and dusting the shelving.

Now, how do you do a cleanup when landing gear is involved? Do you raise the gear or the flaps first? (Figure 42, position A). The answer is that you first eliminate the lowest-risk thing causing the most drag. And the winner is, the major drag-causing portion of your flaps. Do that first (Figure 42, position B). Once that's completed and the airplane is showing a positive rate of climb, retract the gear (Figure 42, position C), followed by the remaining flaps in 10-degree increments or single-notches (Figure 42, position D).

If you retracted the flaps all at once, the airplane could move into the region of reversed command, perhaps leading to a descent or a secondary stall, as we discussed previously. Raising all the flaps at one time creates a lot of risk. It can even create a flap. Not worth it.

On the other hand, if you stalled while on a short final approach or while attempting a go-around, raising the landing gear first is risky because you may be unable to establish a positive rate of climb during the stall recovery (go-arounds will be discussed in detail in Chapter Eight). You might continue settling toward the runway, eventually landing gear-up (which is as embarrassing as wearing a propeller hat on your private pilot checkride).

While the landing gear offers no lift, it still produces parasite drag at the slow speeds associated with stalling (and going around). All things considered, raising the landing gear before the flaps might be risky. So the optimal order of precedence is:

1. Raise the major drag causing portion of flaps first,
2. Raise the landing gear when a positive rate of climb is established, and then,
3. Raise the remaining flaps in increments.

(See sidebar: *When POHs Reveal Nothing About the Gear-Flap Retraction Sequence*.)

When POHs Reveal Nothing About the Gear-Flap Retraction Sequence

Please keep in mind that not all airplane POHs recommend the same thing in terms of the flap-gear retraction sequence during stall recovery. On the other hand, using the gear-flap retraction recommendation in the aborted/balked landing checklist often works just fine for stall recovery. For example, the A36 Bonanza doesn't offer a stall gear/flap retraction recommendation, but the balked landing recommendation suggests raising all the flaps first, then retracting the gear.

On the other hand, one Cessna P210 manual recommends only flap retraction on the go-around. It says nothing about retracting the gear. Nevertheless, you might intuit the correct gear-flap retraction procedure in some manuals by examining the retraction sequence offered for short-field takeoffs (which typically require the use of half flaps, not full flap extension). For instance, the short-field takeoff in the same P210 manual suggests raising the gear, followed by retraction of the remaining 20 degrees of flaps in 10 degree increments. Therefore, the correct gear-flap retraction sequence for a go-around should be, raise the flaps to 20 degrees, retract the gear, followed by the remaining flaps in 10 degree increments.

The Piper Turbo Arrow IV also has no gear-flap retraction recommendation during a go-around. Therefore, using the short-field takeoff gear-flaps retraction recommendation, you'd raise the gear first (with flaps extended to 25 degrees or two notches), then retract the remaining two notches of flaps.

There is a method to my madness here, because the flap-gear-flap retraction sequence is the same procedure you will use when making a go-around in a complex airplane. It's nice when a "one size fits all" procedure is available during training.

Departure (Power-on) Stalls

A departure stall is essentially a power-on stall. This is the condition you might find yourself in immediately after takeoff if you over-rotated during liftoff or became distracted and allowed the nose to pitch up sufficiently to stall the airplane.

You might also find yourself in this situation when departing a high-density-altitude airport if you tried using the same climb attitude immediately after liftoff that you use at airports closer to sea level.

You'd think a stall at low altitude is bad enough, but that's not always the end of the story, and how the story ends is often not good. Being distracted enough to let the airplane stall suggests that the pilot is also distracted enough to not to keep the flight controls coordinated as the plane stalls. You already see how this is going down, don't you?

Departure stalls most often occur with the inclinometer's ball deflected to the right, due to the power-induced left-turning tendency. This induces a left yaw and left rolling motion to the airplane, causing the descending and aft-moving left wing to reach its critical angle of attack before the right wing. The left wing stalls first, and because of the high pitch attitude and the lower speed (associated with full power) the airplane enters a spin to the left. This is a spinner that's not a winner.

How can pilots get so distracted on takeoff that they stall or spin the airplane? Turns out there are lots of ways, ranging from unwrapping their pita wrap lunch sandwich to not having reset the elevator trim to the takeoff position after landing.

As with most aviation incidents, it's usually a combination of a few unlikely events that leads to trouble, any one of which wouldn't or shouldn't have caused a problem. The excessive nose-up trim left over from landing is a distraction, though not one that necessarily leads to a power-on departure stall. But what happens if you also left the tugging end of a seatbelt strap outside the door when closing it? The answer my friend, is blowin' in the wind. With all that engine power, the strap is likely to start snapping against the

Stalls, Spins and the Conditioned Reflex

In Chapter Three you learned that many pilots are taught the elevator-airspeed method of control usage. This technique helps reinforce the behavior of using the yoke to control the airspeed and the throttle to control altitude. Many instructors believe that this technique minimizes the chances of a pilot attempting to stretch a glide in order to make a distant landing site in the event of an engine failure.

Does it? Yes it does despite the fact that there's another "brain trainer" with contrary inclinations being applied hundreds of times on every flight.

In straight and level flight, at the slightest change in altitude we make a correction by applying a slight push or pull on the elevator. Every turn requires a slight pull on the elevator to prevent an altitude loss (and we make hundreds of turns, great and small, on every flight). We even pull back on the elevator to meet the ground at an acceptable angle during the landing flare. The list goes on and on and on.

With each rep, your brain is saying, "Hmmm, if the altitude changes, then pull or push on the yoke to return to the targeted altitude." This occurs hundreds of times on every flight.

So, if push comes to shove (or pull), and it's a real emergency landing and you're feeling kind of low, what will *you* do? Unfortunately, too many pilots pull a bad one by pulling a tad on the yoke. Their aft pull on the elevator suddenly becomes a glide stretcher, which of course it really isn't.

What's a pilot to do?

First, combating this type of reinforcement starts with recognizing that it exists and why it exists. Once recognized, you can consciously override an impulse to pull aft on the elevator to stretch a glide. Yes, believe me when I say that you may be a well trained pilot in emergency procedures, but that doesn't mean you won't have the impulse to try stretching a glide when you need to stretch a glide.

Second, you need to develop a powerful countermeasure to combat this habit. Stall recognition and awareness is one answer (perhaps the only significant answer, too). Nevertheless, given that most pilots actually spend relatively little time practicing stall recoveries (compared to practicing landings, for instance), you can see how difficult it is to counteract this conditioned reflex.

So think. Train. Rinse and repeat. Don't change strategies. Be prepared to just say "No" if and when you have the urge to stretch a glide if you're literally powerless to sustain your airspeed. Get as much extra stall proficiency training as your budget allows. Not only will you be a safer pilot, you'll also be a more confident pilot.

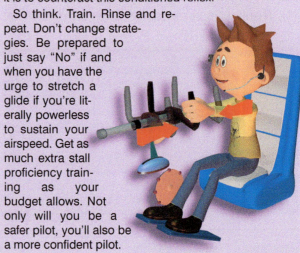

Chapter 5: Stalls and Spins

side of the airplane. Now you're fighting with an airplane that's trying to pretend it can climb straight up like an F-16, the seatbelt sounds as though someone's firing an automatic weapon from or at your bird, the pita wrap is coming undone, your passengers are shrieking in terror, and you are on your way to a departure stall.

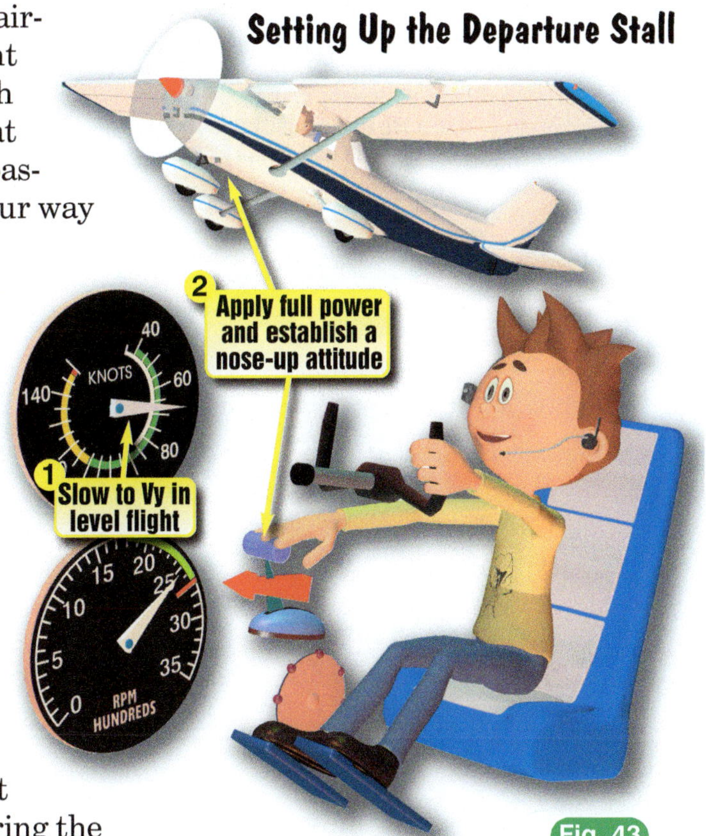

It's time to see how to enter, recognize, and recover from a departure stall. The best way to set the airplane up for the departure stall if you're starting from straight and level flight is to reduce power and slow down to Vy while holding altitude. When reaching Vy, you should apply full power and begin a normal climb at this speed (Figure 43). This best simulates the conditions you'll experience immediately after takeoff. Keep in mind that, during the departure stall, you want to avoid exceeding a 30-degree nose-up pitch attitude unless everyone on board is wearing a parachute (not just you) as stipulated in FAR 91.307 (stand by for a technique that will help you avoid an excessive nose-up pitch during the departure stall).

Setting Up the Departure Stall

1. Slow to Vy in level flight
2. Apply full power and establish a nose-up attitude

Fig. 43

After establishing a climb attitude, gently raise the nose a little higher to an attitude that will decelerate the airplane and increase the angle of attack to its critical value (don't exceed 30 degrees nose-up pitch!). Look at those wingtips to help evaluate your pitch attitude. Wise pilot that you are, you'll coordinate use of aileron and rudder to keep your wings level and maintain your heading as the airspeed decreases.

Performing the Departure Stall

3. Gently raise nose to stall attitude (don't exceed 30° pitch)
4. Add right rudder as airplane decelerates
5. Crosscheck ball to keep it centered

Fig. 44

As the airspeed decreases, increase pressure on the right rudder pedal to keep the inclinometer ball centered and the nose pointed straight ahead (it's OK to cross check the ball here since you can't easily see over the nose in a departure stall). You can also look at the left wing tip and apply rudder to keep it from moving horizontally, fore and aft. This tells you that the nose isn't yawing and that the controls are coordinated (Figure 44).

What you do *not* want to do is stall in an uncoordinated condition. Here there be dragons there. Avoiding that spot is going to take a *lot* of right rudder. I mean really a lot, as in twice as much as you're thinking. Don't wimp out here. Man (or wo-man) up. Push that right rudder pedal forward as needed to

Rod Machado's How to Fly an Airplane Handbook

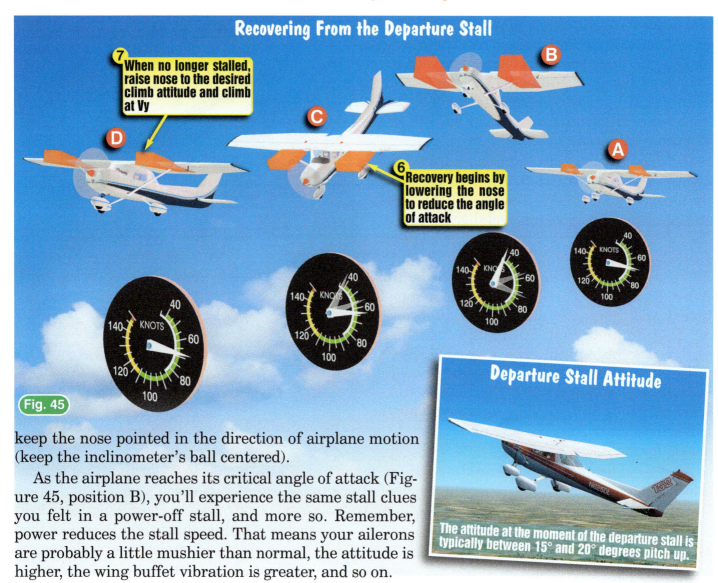

Fig. 45

keep the nose pointed in the direction of airplane motion (keep the inclinometer's ball centered).

As the airplane reaches its critical angle of attack (Figure 45, position B), you'll experience the same stall clues you felt in a power-off stall, and more so. Remember, power reduces the stall speed. That means your ailerons are probably a little mushier than normal, the attitude is higher, the wing buffet vibration is greater, and so on.

When the critical angle of attack is reached and the airplane stalls, the nose will naturally pitch forward and downward (Figure 45, position C). Let it, but control it. Release elevator back pressure and lower the nose to an attitude slightly below the horizon to break the stall (but don't break anything else, because airplane owners hate that). You can't add full power because you're already *at* full power. There isn't a lot to do other than staying out of the airplane's way. Let the airplane accelerate. As soon as it's no longer stalled, raise the nose to climb attitude and reestablish the climb at Vy (Figure 45, position D). Finally, return to your starting altitude, heading and airspeed. Of course, you'll continue the climb in a way that doesn't induce a secondary stall. The last thing you want is to be forced to recover from another departure stall, right? Right.

So there you have it. You've just done your first departure stall.

What I've just described is the pure form of a departure stall. What you need, however, is a bit of impurity in your flying (much like you'll find in the airport coffee pot). So let me tell you about how you'll want to practice these stalls in real life, as well as demonstrate them on your pilot checkride.

The attitudes associated with full power can be very steep. That's why I asked you to set yourself up for the stall by first slowing the airplane in level flight to Vy (Figure 46, positions W, X and Y), then applying full power and establishing a nose-up attitude that allowed the airplane to stall (Figure 46, position Z). This helps prevent the excessive nose-high attitude that's common with airplanes having larger horsepower engines. No matter how you head for the stall, don't exceed 30 degrees of

Chapter 5: Stalls and Spins

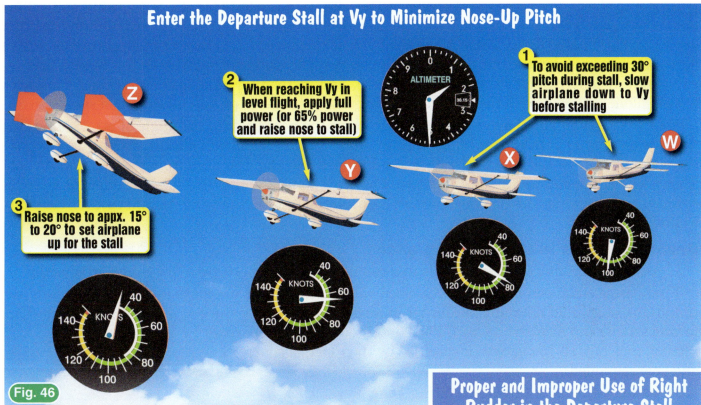

Fig. 46

Fig. 47

nose-up pitch. Finally, don't pull aft on the elevator so quickly during the stall entry that you accelerate the airplane upward and generate a pitch attitude that's unnaturally high for your climb speed. Often the best way to enter the stall is to raise the nose about 15-20 degrees above the horizon and just keep applying elevator back pressure to keep it there. The airplane eventually *will* stall.

In many airplanes (not just high performance ones, either) you might elect to use less than full power during the departure stall, but no less than 65% power for the departure stall (use your POH to determine the throttle setting for this power value). This also helps prevent an excessively steep nose-up pitch attitude that might exceed the 30-degree pitch limit I mentioned. With the triple combination of slowing down in level flight, using 65% power instead of full power and raising the nose slowly to let the speed bleed off, there's no reason why you would exceed (or even come close to) the 30 degree pitch limit.

Unfortunately, some students manage to let the flight controls become uncoordinated at the moment of stall, meaning that they don't keep the wings level with the ailerons and use enough right rudder input to keep the nose pointed straight ahead (Figure 47). If this happens, you can bet that this will induce one wing to stall before the other. And you can also bet that this is not going to be a gentle wing drop as it was in the power-off stall examples.

As noted above, the presence of power in this situation exacerbates the left yawing and rolling tendency, making one wing (the left wing in this example) more likely to stall (drop) than the other during uncoordinated flight. What do you do if it does? You need to get the order of operations correct here. Size may not matter, but order does. If you don't respond correctly with the rudder first (as you simultaneously reduce the angle of attack), and instead try raising the dropping wing with aileron alone, you will push the descending wing into a deeper stall, and ultimately a spin.

Your first action must be to simultaneously lower the nose (reduce the angle of attack) and stop the yawing motion with rudder input. Think "stop=STOMP." You will almost always need to push the rudder pedal all the way to the floorboard in order to stop the nose from yawing right or left. That's why the pedals are there. Use them. They *like* being stepped on. Once the angle of attack is reduced and the wings are no longer stalled, use aileron to level the wings as you recover back into a climb at Vy.

Departure Stalls in Complex Airplanes

If you're performing departure stalls in a complex airplane, here are a few things to consider.

First, these stalls can be done in the clean configuration, but it's more realistic to simulate the conditions you would normally encounter immediately after departure in a complex airplane. That means setting the airplane up with flaps deflected to their departure setting, typically 10-15 degrees (if specified by the POH, of course) and gear extended.

Here's how to set up the stall. Bring your power back to some value (say 20 inches or so) on the low end of the manifold pressure gauge's green arc and slow the airplane down in straight and level flight to "at or below" Vlo, then extend the gear (Figure 48, position A and B). If a change in RPM is

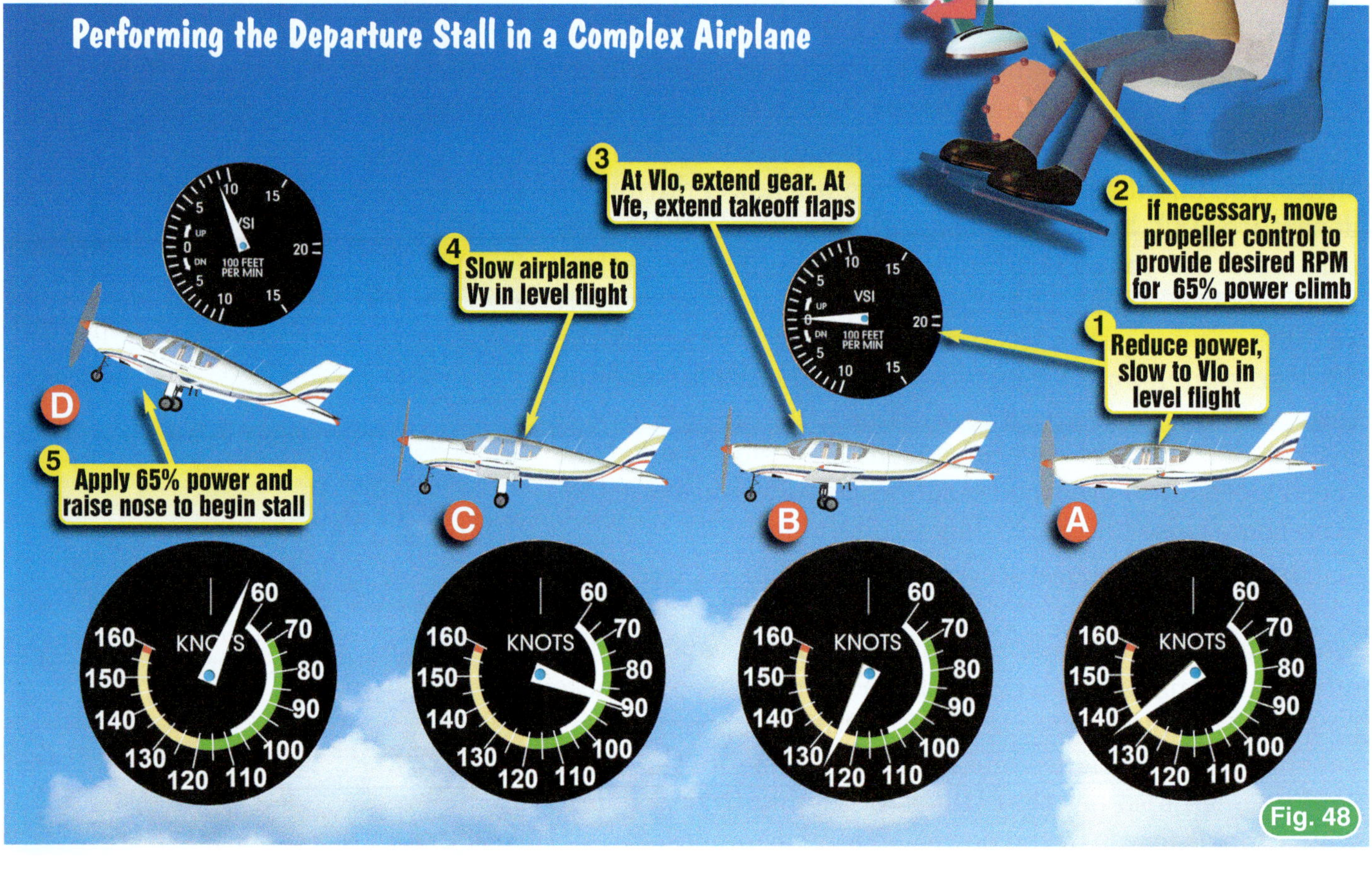

Performing the Departure Stall in a Complex Airplane

1. Reduce power, slow to Vlo in level flight
2. if necessary, move propeller control to provide desired RPM for 65% power climb
3. At Vlo, extend gear. At Vfe, extend takeoff flaps
4. Slow airplane to Vy in level flight
5. Apply 65% power and raise nose to begin stall

Fig. 48

Chapter 5: Stalls and Spins

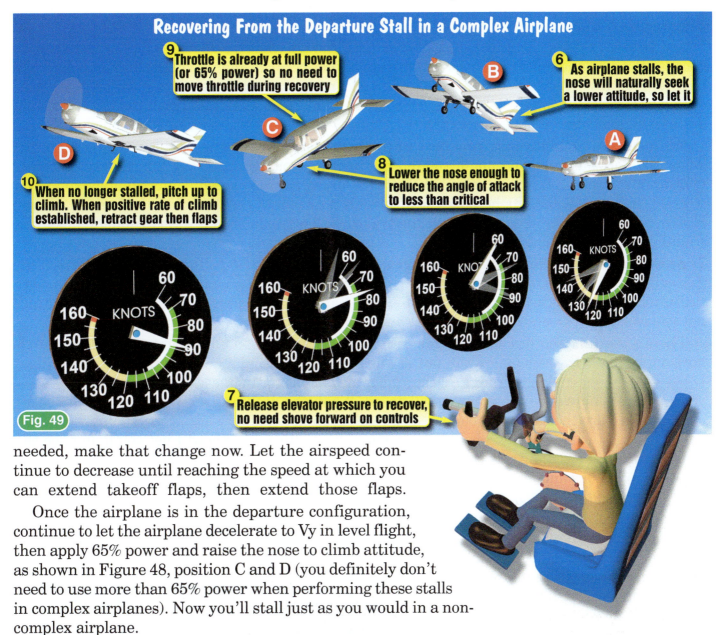

Fig. 49

needed, make that change now. Let the airspeed continue to decrease until reaching the speed at which you can extend takeoff flaps, then extend those flaps.

Once the airplane is in the departure configuration, continue to let the airplane decelerate to Vy in level flight, then apply 65% power and raise the nose to climb attitude, as shown in Figure 48, position C and D (you definitely don't need to use more than 65% power when performing these stalls in complex airplanes). Now you'll stall just as you would in a non-complex airplane.

The initial stall recovery procedure is the same as it is in a non-complex airplane (Figure 49, position C). Release elevator back pressure and decrease the angle of attack, perhaps even lowering the nose below the horizon if necessary to break the stall. Once the airplane is no longer stalled, raise the nose and establish a climb attitude for Vy (since you're typically using 65% power to simulate full power during the stall, there's no need to move the throttle forward during the stall recovery). When you've established a positive rate of climb, retract the gear first, followed by the flaps (Figure 49, position D). Why gear first, then flaps? Because the flaps are already set to their minimum-drag, maximum-lift setting.

Let me explain. In non-complex airplanes, you don't typically use flaps for a normal takeoff. On the other hand, it's common to use 10-15 degree of flaps for a normal takeoff in a complex aircraft. You can feel pretty sure that the engineers have done their homework and that whatever takeoff flap configuration they specify, it's the optimal minimum-drag, maximum-lift condition. During a departure stall recovery with this flap setting, it makes sense to remove the drag caused by the gear extension, not the extra lift provided by the partially deflected flaps.

Accelerated Stalls

Accelerated stalls (sometimes called *whip stalls,* although there's no actual whipping taking place because the airplane hasn't misbehaved) are stalls that occur at higher speeds and increased load factors. They also tend to be abrupt stalls, often occurring at much lower nose-down pitch attitudes than a pilot typically might experience. This is what makes an accelerated stall close to the ground quite risky, and why we are going to practice them to help you avoid accidentally doing one.

For instance, while turning from base to final approach during a descent (your nose is pointed below the horizon here), you might tighten the turn to avoid overshooting the runway centerline (Figure 50). The load factor increases in the turn, hiking the stall speed. Unfortunately, you're not worried (and you should be), because the airplane's nose points slightly below the horizon. To you, it might seem as if you're nowhere near the typical stall attitude (this is a very common misunderstanding about how airplanes stall).

As we discussed earlier (and it's worth repeating), with the nose pointed below the horizon in a descending turn, rearward elevator pressure moves the airplane's nose in both a horizontal and vertical direction, not just in a vertical direction. Pulling aft on the elevator increases the angle of attack, but you won't see the nose rise as much as you would if you were in level flight.

There's the rub. You feel some degree of comfort because the nose is pointed a little below the horizon, which is the same place you put it when recovering from a normal stall in straight flight. Looks good. What could go wrong? All the while, the load factor increases as you pull aft on the elevator control, increasing the plane's stall speed. When the declining airspeed and the increasing stalling speed are the same number, it's a "bingo" you really didn't want. And you don't just stall, you stall with the nose pointed below the horizon, while turning. Whew! I bet you didn't see that coming, right? What a big surprise for the unwary. So let's practice a typical accelerated stall and recovery so it looks and feels like what you might actually experience.

We'll enter this stall from a power-off descent at your normal approach speed of 1.3 Vs1 (the flaps and gear retracted stalling speed). While maintaining a constant heading, apply carburetor heat, reduce power to idle, and slow the airplane in level flight to your normal approach-to-landing speed (Figure 51, position A). Technically speaking, you can do these stalls at any speed less than the airplane's maneuvering speed, but it takes longer to demonstrate the stall at a higher speed and there's no real benefit (unless you have an appointment for a root canal after your flight lesson and aren't in a rush to get there).

When you reach the desired speed, allow the airplane to begin descending. There's no sense trimming for this speed since you won't be using it for long. Now roll the airplane into a 45-degree bank (keep the rudder and aileron coordinated). Once established in the turn, increase the elevator back pressure

Accelerated Stalls

Airplane stalled at high speed

During a descending turn from base to final approach, the airplane's nose is pointed below the horizon. If you tighten the turn to prevent overshooting the runway, it's entirely possible to exceed the critical angle of attack and stall with the nose pointed below the horizon. This is a common way pilots fall victim to accelerated stalls close to the ground.

Fig. 50

Chapter 5: Stalls and Spins

Fig. 51

A Performing the Accelerated Stall
1. Apply carb heat & reduce power
2. Hold altitude, slow to approach speed of 1.3 Vs1

B
3. Roll into a 45° bank with coordinated use of flight controls
4. Pull aft on elevator to increase load factor (don't let bank increase)
5. Hey! I said pull! You've got to pull to experience an increase in g-force

C
6. Release elevator back pressure to decrease angle of attack
7. Add full power
8. Remove carb heat

D
9. When no longer stalled, level wings with coordinated use of rudder and ailerons
10. Raise nose to climb attitude, climb at Vy

so you feel an increase in load factor (Figure 51, position B). You'll have to pull back briskly on the elevator, and at the same time prevent the bank from increasing beyond 45 degrees.

You should definitely feel an increased load factor associated with the steeper bank. If you don't, then you're not pulling aft hard enough on the elevator control. Don't worry, there's no way you're ever going to overstress the airplane when performing these stalls at a speed so far below the airplane's current maneuvering speed. The worst that will happen is that your glasses will slip down over your nose (or your hairpiece droops over your forehead, in which case you'll probably yell, "Squirrel in the cockpit!"). If you have to pull with two hands on the yoke, do so. Eventually, you'll sense that the stall is imminent, but I want you to experience the full stall. So keep that elevator coming back briskly. Wait for it. Wait for it. There it is.

If you stalled in coordinated flight, the airplane will pitch directly away from you in a path perpendicular to the lateral axis of the wings (from your nose to your toes). If you're slipping during the stall (the inclinometer's ball moves to the inside of the turn arc) the airplane will likely roll rapidly to the outside of the turn as the outside wing stalls first. If you're skidding during the stall (the inclinometer's ball moves to the outside of the turn arc), the airplane is likely to roll to the inside of the turn as it would during a spin entry (more on accelerated stalls in uncoordinated flight in the spin section of this chapter). So, don't allow the flight controls to become uncoordinated unless you have a deep interest in rock and roll.

As with all our stall recoveries, release elevator back pressure to reduce the angle of attack while simultaneously adding full power and removing carburetor heat (Figure 51, position C). When you're no longer stalled, level the wings with the coordinated use of aileron and rudder, then raise the nose to the attitude for Vy as shown in Figure 51, position D. Your objective is to lose as little altitude as possible and recover fully before entering a climb attitude.

As a general rule, accelerated stalls tend to involve larger pitching and rolling motions at the moment the stall breaks. Once the stall actually breaks, there's no longer as much of a horizontal component of lift pulling the airplane in its previous direction of turn. As a result, the airplane tends to follow the direction of its momentum, meaning that it wants to move straight again. Think of this as twirling a rock on a string. The moment you let go of the string (which is the analog of the stall breaking), the rock flies off in a straight direction (and, if you're lucky, hits a bully named Goliath and you get your name in print for more than 2,500 years). This is why accelerated stalls generally involve larger pitching motions as the airplane pitches away from its previously banked attitude.

Accelerated stalls are also likely to occur during steep turns (this is one reason we practice turning steeply), aggressive stall/spin recoveries, and aggressive maneuvering (such as a pilot pulling back on the elevator as he buzzes a helpless house). There are two important takeaway points from our accelerated stall lesson. The first is that an airplane can stall in any attitude and any airspeed. If that's not clear to you by now, then you've been skipping school (I'll need a note, thank you). The second point is that any increase in load factor is a memo to you that the airplane's stalling speed is increasing. In this sense, your derriere becomes an ancillary stall warning device, which is proof that you were designed to fly! If you have these two points planted in your mental lobes, you've just risen to the top of the class (not that you ever left the top, of course).

Just to be clear here, you won't perform an accelerated stall (or any other maneuver) if it is prohibited by the POH for your specific airplane. Then again, I know of no small airplane POH that prohibits the practice of accelerated stalls, because they can't possibly hurt the airplane (or you). Why? Because these stalls are done at speeds well below the airplane's maneuvering speed, with flaps retracted (because of flap load limitations) and the bank restricted to no more than 45 degrees. A stall is guaranteed well before there is any danger of structural problems.

Stalls and Cross-Controlled Flight

One of the risks associated with stalling, especially when approaching land, occurs when the flight controls (right aileron and left rudder, for instance) are crossed—applied in different directions—resulting in uncoordinated flight (the "cross" in cross control is not something that happens only when you fly over the Vatican).

From an earlier discussion, you've learned that it's possible to have crossed controls and still be in coordinated flight. Certainly a steeper right turn in slow flight typically requires you to keep right rudder and left aileron applied, resulting in a cross-controlled but completely coordinated condition. Keep in mind that this cross-controlled condition results from the additional forces of slipstream and p-factor (i.e., the reason for rudder use) and the airplane's overbanking tendency (the reason for aileron use).

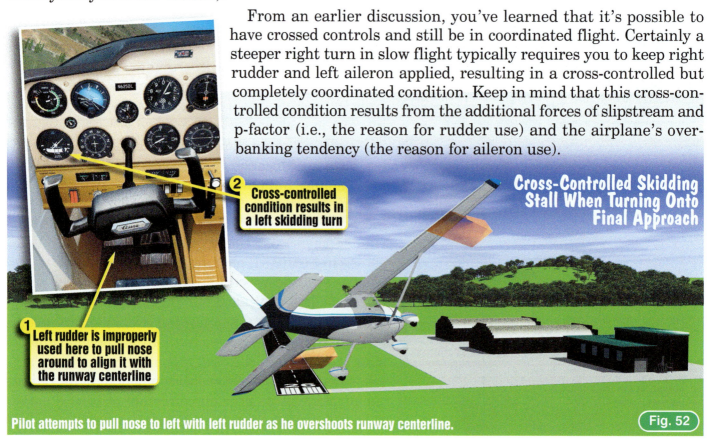

Pilot attempts to pull nose to left with left rudder as he overshoots runway centerline.

Fig. 52

Chapter 5: Stalls and Spins

Cross-Controlled Skidding Stall When Turning Onto Final Approach

4 Pilot adds right aileron and aft elevator pressure to counter the left roll and nose-down pitch

3 Nose pitches down as airplane rolls and yaws left

The left skidding turn results in a yaw and roll to the left, increasing the angle of attack on the left (descending wing). Right aileron application helps the left wing stall sooner.

5 Left wing stalls first

Fig. 53

It's when the controls are crossed and produce an uncoordinated condition that the risks of spinning the airplane increase. There is one very common scenario that often causes unwary pilots to cross their controls and it involves the use of excessive rudder input when turning onto final approach.

Imagine making a left turn onto the final approach path for landing. During the turn you notice you're about to overshoot the runway centerline (Figure 52). In this situation, many pilots tend to (improperly) use left rudder pressure to pull the airplane's nose toward the inside of the turn to align it with the runway centerline.

If a pilot doesn't have good stick and rudder skills, his or her desire to align the airplane with the runway centerline often overrides any inclination to keep the flight controls coordinated. If power is used, the airplane's power-induced left turning tendencies further yaw the airplane to the left (a likely proposition given the relatively slower speeds and higher angles of attack associated with landing). This results in a *skidding* left turn to final approach.

Unfortunately, the left yawing tendency also induces a left roll, which steepens the bank and reduces the vertical component of lift. The nose drops further below the horizon and the bank steepens. The pilot counters the roll and nose-down pitch with opposite aileron and elevator back pressure, which increases the load factor and raises the stall speed (Figure 53). No matter what the orientation is of the runway, this flight is going south. The flight controls are uncoordinated and crossed, with aileron deflected to the right (which further yaws the nose to the left—adverse yaw, remember?) and rudder deflected to the left. This is a classic *skidding turn to final approach*, with the nose deflected toward the inside of the turn on final approach, typically at a very low altitude.

If the pilot in this scenario didn't have a middle name, he's got one now—it's *Trouble*. If the airplane stalls, the left wing will stall first, with the airplane yawing and rolling to the left. This is also known as an *under the bottom* stall (the concept of *under the bottom* or *over the top* is based on what the wing inside the turn does in a stall). In this case the left wing stalls first and goes under the bottom of the airplane as the airplane enters a spin to the left.

It's important to remember that skidding turns on final approach often result from using too much rudder in the direction of turn, but they can also be generated by applying a little rudder in the direction of turn (left rudder in this example) along with aileron applied opposite the direction of turn (right aileron in this example). This is quite common when the pilot realizes his bank is excessively steep and uses aileron to reduce the bank angle. The adverse yaw caused by the lowered aileron on the inside wing (left wing in this example) pulls that wing aft, further yawing the airplane to the left, opposite the direction of turn (Figure 53). The result is a classic cross control condition that exacerbates the skid, possibly leading to the wing inside the turn (left wing in this example) stalling first.

Now let me put a kink in your wheel pants by saying that a skidding turn onto final approach in a right turn is less likely to occur than one in a left turn. How can that be? It's all about engine power. At the slower airspeeds and higher angles of attack associated with power usage, the power-induced left turning tendencies tend to counteract the extra right rudder the pilot might apply to pull the airplane's nose to the right and align it with the runway centerline (I'm assuming the pilot has poor stick and rudder skills and is attempting to correct for a centerline overshoot). Given that most pilots are likely to *underuse* rather than *overuse* their rudder pedals, in a right turn to final it's more likely that they'll accidentally end up in coordinated flight (or something close to it) rather than skidding. Of course, the airplane can still stall, but without the skid it's not as likely to stall and then spin.

On the other hand, the pilot might attempt to correct for the overshoot by increasing the bank angle only (not using excessive rudder in this instance), as shown in Figure 54. He's increasing the bank angle by adding right aileron with insufficient right rudder pressure. Adverse yaw pulls the nose to the left, outside the turn, with the left yawing tendency exacerbated by the power-induced left turning tendency. As the left wing moves aft, its speed decreases, decreasing the lift on that wing, resulting in it moving downward slightly. The downward movement increases the angle of attack on the left wing, which makes the wing outside the turn more likely to stall first (Figure 55).

This type of stall results from a slipping turn onto final approach. If the airplane does stall from a slip, the right wing (the wing inside the

Chapter 5: Stalls and Spins

turn) moves up and over the airplane, resulting in an *over the top stall*. While the airplane can still stall in a slipping condition, it's less likely to spin given that the left rolling momentum is countered slightly by the airplane's original right turning momentum. Don't get me wrong here. The airplane can of course still spin while slipping. But the spin entry is likely to be less violent. This, however, is one reason pilots are allowed (and required) to demonstrate *slips to landing* instead of demonstrating *skids to landing*, which would be extremely dangerous (more on slips later).

As a general rule, an uncoordinated cross-controlled condition is more likely to occur when applying elevator back pressure in a turn to maintain your attitude (or to reduce the descent rate) in a turn and the rudder is misused. It's also likely to occur during base-to-final turns, when attempting to correct for a runway overshoot. Unfortunately, a skidding cross-controlled stall often leads to a spin, which can be a dangerous condition if you're close to the ground. You must avoid falling into the trap of cross controlling when confronted with a runway centerline overshoot. Overshooting the runway isn't the end of the world (or at least it shouldn't be). If it looks like you're going to overshoot, apply the coordinated use of your flight controls to reduce the bank angle, then apply full power and go-around if necessary. Cross-controlled stalls are another reason why it's very important to always fly coordinated as well as to recognize the signs of an imminent stall. Nothing—absolutely nothing—gives you a greater chance at avoiding the low level stall-spin scenario than the ability to keep your aileron and rudder coordinated. Stick and rudder skills are a must here.

You can demonstrate cross-controlled stalls at a safe altitude by configuring the airplane to perform a no-flap power-off stall in the landing configuration as shown in Figure 56, position A (the landing gear is extended if you're in a complex airplane since this type of stall is more likely to occur when approaching to land). Since we don't want to practice spins yet, we'll do this stall in the slipping configuration. With the airplane trimmed for the descent at 1.3 Vs, power reduced and carburetor heat applied, establish a 30-degree banked turn to the right. Now apply left rudder pressure while using aileron to maintain the bank, as shown in Figure 56, position B.

You're now in a slipping turn to the right. Go ahead and increase the angle of attack and let the airplane stall. When it does, you'll notice that the left wing drops a little, but not as much as it would drop if this were a skidding turn, which would most likely result in an entry to a spin

Fig. 56

(Figure 56, position C). Recovery is made by reducing the angle of attack (lowering the nose) and using rudder to stop any yawing or rolling motion, adding full power, and when no longer stalled, leveling the wings and returning to coordinated flight (Figure 56, position D).

It's pretty hard to deny that I've used the word *spin* quite a bit in the last few paragraphs, and for good reason. So we're now ready to move from wash and rinse to the spin cycle. Wait! Come back here Rocket Pants! Not to worry. You don't have to do spins in your private or commercial flight training, but I'm hoping you will. They're perfectly safe to do, and highly educational. So let's discuss them.

No-Spin Talk on Spins

There are few things that worry pilots more than spinning an airplane. A lot of this is fear of the unknown, which we're about to solve by removing the secret coating so you can see what's really there.

If you are aware of how spins occur and what you can do to prevent them, you might find them fun to do. They're safe. After all, the FAA makes them a required maneuver for those working on their flight instructor certificate. This isn't the FAA's way of eliminating flight instructor candidates. Just make sure that any airplane in which you want to practice spins is approved for that maneuver—some aren't and some are but only in certain limited configurations of weight and balance. Check the POH.

The easiest way to describe a spin is to say that it involves an autorotating airplane descending in a corkscrew fashion with one wing completely stalled while the other wing isn't stalled as much, as shown in Figure 57 (if you perked up when I mentioned *corkscrew*, you need to cut back on the vino). As the airplane spins, the rising (outside) wing is the one that's not stalled as much as the descending (inside) wing. This differential in lift between wings creates a rolling, yawing and pitching motion as the airplane descends.

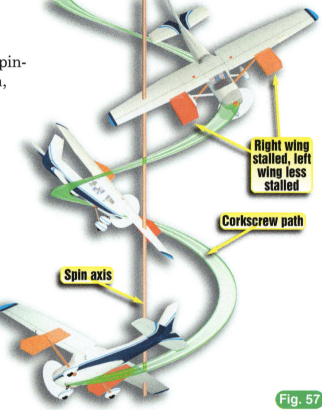

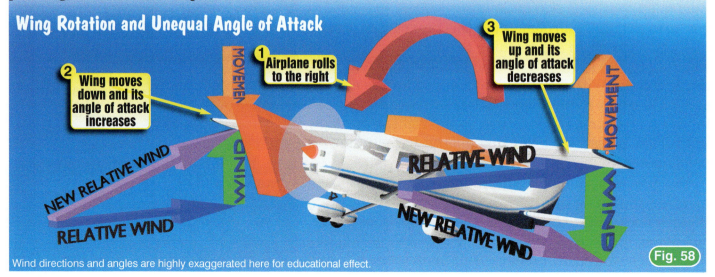

Chapter 5: Stalls and Spins

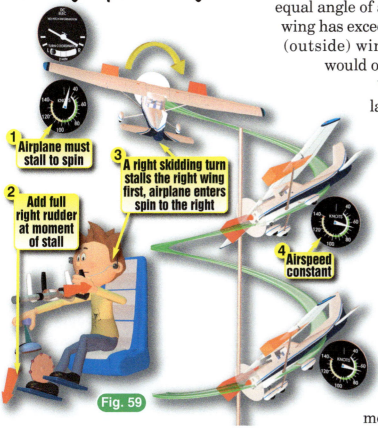

Entering a Spin to the Right

1. Airplane must stall to spin
2. Add full right rudder at moment of stall
3. A right skidding turn stalls the right wing first, airplane enters spin to the right
4. Airspeed constant

Fig. 59

Entering a Spin to the Left

A spin to the left is performed in a similar manner as a spin to the right, except that full left rudder is applied at the moment of stall. If, however, you are using power the airplane's left turning tendency will produce nearly the same effect of adding full left rudder at the moment of stall.

Fig. 60

The airplane's autorotation in a spin results from the unequal angle of attack on each wing. The descending (inside) wing has exceeded its critical angle of attack, but the rising (outside) wing is not quite as stalled (Figure 58). Why would one wing stall ahead of the other?

We've discussed several scenarios in which lack of coordinated flight can cause one wing to stall before the other. To spin, the airplane must first be *stalled* in either a skidding or slipping condition, with the skid being the easiest way to induce the spin. No stall, no spin. So sorry. You can't spin if you don't stall first. Do NOT forget this point! Avoid the stall and you'll avoid the spin. See how important stall recognition is?

For example, if you raise the nose to stall the airplane, hold the wings level with aileron, and then apply right rudder just as the airplane is about to stall (i.e., is near its critical angle of attack), you'll induce a downward and rearward motion on the right wing and an upward and forward motion on the left (Figure 59). The right wing's angle of attack increases beyond its critical value and stalls, while the left wing's angle of attack is near its critical value and isn't stalled as much. The airplane enters a spin to the right, in the same direction you applied the rudder.

On the other hand (or foot), if you raise the nose to stall the airplane while holding the wings level and apply full left rudder at the moment of stall, the airplane enters a spin to the left (Figure 60). Left rudder induces a left yaw and a left roll, which moves the left wing downward and rearward, increasing the left wing's angle of attack beyond its critical value. The right wing, by default, moves upward and forward, which reduces its angle of attack. The net result is that the airplane enters a spin to the left.

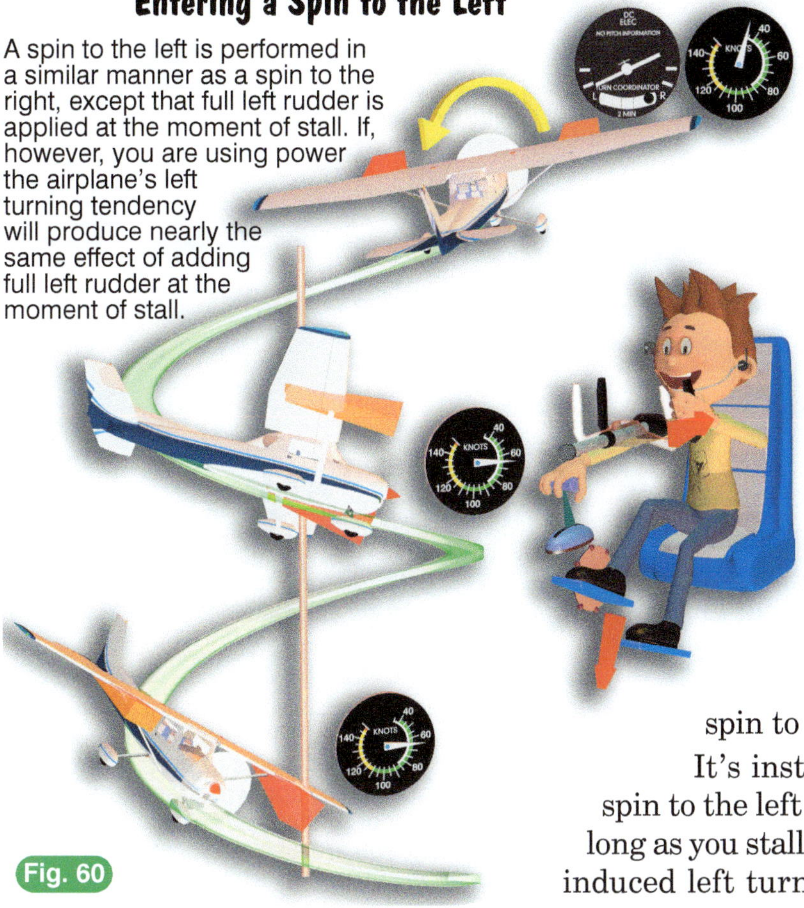

It's instructive to note that you can also enter a spin to the left without purposely applying left rudder, as long as you stall with power applied. The airplane's power-induced left turning tendency substitutes for the rudder application to produce a left-leaning yaw at the moment of stall. This is why uncoordinated departure stalls can result in a spin entry to the left for the unwary.

Do you need any further reason to avoid stalls and uncoordinated flight? I hope not. The big question on your mind here has to be how do you prevent entering a spin?

Preventing Entry Into a Spin

Before you next get into an airplane, take a look at the tail. It could be what saves *your* tail.

The rudder is the one flight control surface that still functions quite well when the airplane is stalled. Why? Recall the stall—in a stall, it's the *wings* that are stalled, not the rudder. The rudder sticks up into the free airstream behind you, always ready to work. That's why you must use it to prevent spin entry and assist in spin recovery. You can forget the Alamo if necessary, but always remember the rudder!

You know that when stalling an airplane in uncoordinated flight, the wing opposite the direction of the skid or slip (think "opposite" the direction of ball deflection) drops at the moment of stall, followed by the airplane yawing and rolling, then pitching downward. Most people's gut reaction is to use the control linked to that thing that's gone wrong to try and make it right. But if you use the ailerons to try and raise the dropping wing, you'll deepen the stall on that wing and accelerate the airplane's rolling motion, further exacerbating the spin condition.

So, remember the rudder! What you need to do, without further ado, is use rudder to prevent the lowered wing from further yawing and rolling (of course, you must simultaneously reduce the angle of attack, too).

As the airplane stalls during a skid and the wing opposite the direction of the skid drops, the nose yaws in the direction of the lowered wing (Figure 61, position A). Your airplane may be about to enter a spin. You're remembering your rudder right now, aren't you?

Because you aren't in an actual spin yet, use the same recovery technique that you've used for all other stall recoveries where a wing drops. Reduce the angle of attack with the elevator and simultaneously stop the yawing motion with the rudder (Figure 61, positions B and C). The main, important, ultimate point here is that the airplane can't spin if the nose doesn't yaw. Repeat after me. *The airplane can't spin if the nose doesn't yaw!* That's why the rudder is your heavy metal friend. Step on it!

Of course, there's a big difference between preventing a spin entry and recovering from a fully developed spin. To understand how to recover from a spin, you should know how to do one.

Preventing entry into a spin is a simple matter of preventing the airplane from yawing. Therefore, as soon as the airplane stalls and one wing begins to drop (right wing in this example), you want to apply rudder in the opposite direction (left rudder in this example) and stop the yaw. Simultaneously, you are also reducing the angle of attack and adding full power.

Chapter 5: Stalls and Spins

Spin Prelim

Spin training is not a real great do-it-yourself project. I do not want you reading out of this book while spinning an airplane for the first time, especially if you're a slow reader. Find a well-maintained airplane and a well-maintained instructor. While the FAA encourages the use of parachutes during spin training, a parachute isn't required when spin training is being provided by either a certified flight instructor or a pilot with an airline transport pilot (ATP) rating.

During spin practice the FAA recommends that you be high enough to completely recover from a spin at no lower than 1,500 feet above the ground. In my book, that means you should begin spin practice at an altitude between 3,500 feet and 4,000 feet AGL. This altitude allows you to spin through several turns without worrying about recovering too close to the ground. Before doing a spin, it's extremely important to clear the area below you. It is apparently upsetting to other pilots to see an airplane spin down right in front of their line of flight, and it can also cause over-stimulation of your adrenal glands. Look before you spin.

Now for the spin itself. The spin can be divided into four distinct stages: *entry*, *incipient*, *developed*, and *recovery*. Let's take the first stage first.

The Entry Stage of the Spin

An intentional spin is typically created by reducing power, raising the nose to an attitude that induces a stall, and just before the airplane stalls applying full rudder in the direction you intend to spin (Figure 62, position A). During the entry, hold the elevator full aft and keep the ailerons neutralized. At this point, the airplane will yaw and roll directly into a spin. Congratulations, you're there. You've just experienced the *entry stage* of the spin.

In the entry stage, it's not uncommon for the inside wing to move completely under the bottom of the airplane (Figure 62, position B). This makes it feel as if the airplane has gone nearly inverted for an instant. In fact, it might have, depending on the airplane and the entry. Despite the dramatic motion, the airplane soon settles into the corkscrew motion that typically defines a spin (Figure 62, position C).

As we previously discussed, it's possible (but not easy) to enter a spin from a slipping rather than a skidding turn. Because the direction of the spin is opposite to the direction of the slip, the forces involved tend to cancel one another. The spin entry here is much less dramatic, with the airplane often simply stalling straight ahead, avoiding the spin entirely.

Here's how a spin from a right slip could occur. As the airplane approaches a stall, the pilot initiates a right turn with right aileron and applies left rudder to initiate the right slip. Left rudder application moves the left wing aft, reduces its speed and generates a roll to the left. This causes the angle of attack on the left wing to increase. If the airplane is close to the stall, the left wing will stall first, resulting in the airplane rolling to the left. This is called an over-the-top stall because the right wing (the one on the inside of the turn) rises up and over the airplane in a left roll.

Keep in mind that it does take relatively aggressive action to induce a spin from a slip in most airplanes. If this were not the case, pilots would be disappearing left and right (no pun intended) by performing slips on final approach, a rather common maneuver. The slip is a perfectly safe maneuver *as long as you keep the airplane from stalling*.

Fig. 62

The Incipient Stage of the Spin

The incipient stage of the spin is defined as being between the time when the airplane stalls and begins to yaw and rotate and the time when the spin fully develops. This takes one or two complete turns for most airplanes. In this stage, the airplane's aerodynamic and inertial forces haven't established equilibrium. Aerodynamic technicalities aside, it's clear from the cockpit that the airplane is in a spin (or you're having flashbacks from eating too many PopRocks in the 1980s). The airspeed is still near or below stall speed, while the turn coordinator's turn needle shows the direction of turn in the spin (Figure 63).

Why would the turn coordinator be important here? Believe it or not, it can be difficult to know which way you're spinning, especially under reduced visibility conditions, at night, or when the spin occurs unexpectedly. You can always look at the turn coordinator needle to determine the direction in which you're spinning (right needle, right spin; left needle, left spin). This allows you to push the rudder opposite the direction of spin to stop the rotation (but only when it's time to do so). The ball in the inclinometer is often quite useless in a spin since the direction it deflects is subject to several variables. We won't solve for those variables, either, mainly because I don't want you using the ball in spin.

Normally, instructors teach spin recovery procedures within the incipient stage, without letting the airplane fully develop into a spin. That means they'll practice spin recoveries prior to the completion of a 360-degree turn. There's nothing wrong with this. Some students don't necessarily want to see the fully developed spin, and that's fine. Just knowing what the entry looks like and how to recover during this phase of the spin help you protect yourself. On the other hand, why not see it all as long as you're here?

The Fully Developed Stage of the Spin

When the spin has fully developed (Figure 64), the vertical speed stabilizes (typically at several thousand feet per minute) in a nearly vertical flight path and the airspeed also stabilizes. Contrary to what some think, the airspeed doesn't continue increasing in a spin. That's because the airplane is not moving forward as it is in a spiral (which isn't a spin). See sidebar: *When a Spin Isn't a Spin, It's a Spiral on Page 5-56*). Instead, it's moving in a circular direction (horizontally), meaning that it can only go as fast around a vertical axis as the laws of physics allow. As a result, the horizontal speed stabilizes at a relatively low airspeed above stall (65 to 75 knots in most smaller airplanes).

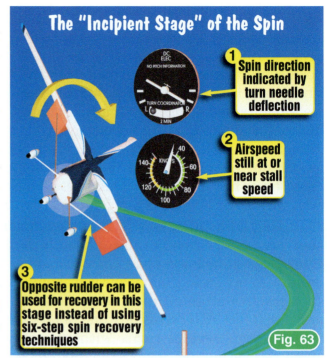

Fig. 63

Fig. 64

Chapter 5: Stalls and Spins

The Recovery Phase of the Spin

To recover from the spin you must stop the autorotation and reduce the angle of attack to below the stalled wings' critical value. While you should always follow the manufacturer's recommendation for recovery, there is a general six-step spin recovery procedure that works for nearly any small airplane.

Step 1: Reduce power to flight idle. You don't want to have power on during the spin recovery for a number of reasons, the most important of which is that it might make it difficult to break the stall and diminish the airplane's rotational movement. Not to mention the very high speed such power would induce when you recover from the spin. So pull that power completely off during spin recovery (Figure 65, position 1).

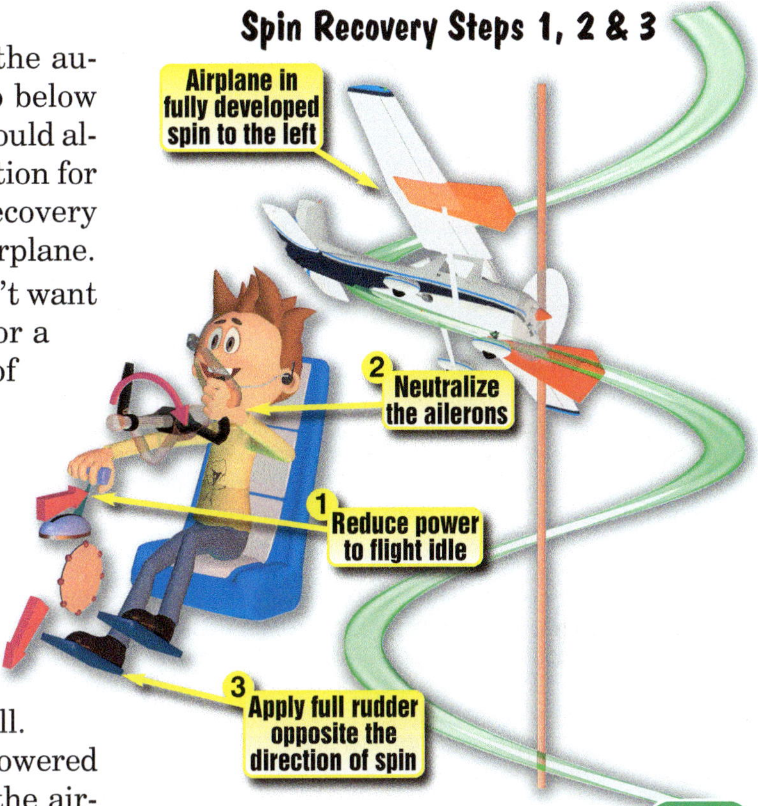

Step 2: Neutralize the ailerons. Any aileron input is sure to aggravate and deepen the stall. In some instances, aileron used to raise the lowered wing (the wing inside the turn) can induce the airplane to flat spin (Figure 65, position 2).

Spin Recovery Steps 1, 2 & 3
- Airplane in fully developed spin to the left
- 1 Reduce power to flight idle
- 2 Neutralize the ailerons
- 3 Apply full rudder opposite the direction of spin

Fig. 65

Step 3: Apply full rudder opposite the direction of spin and hold it there. Here is where your intuition about spin recovery could clash with reality. You may want to use rudder to stop the rotation along with the simultaneous use of brisk forward elevator pressure to break the stall. This isn't a good idea when the airplane is already *established* in the spin. Your primary objective in using the rudder is to reduce the rotational motion of the airplane. Rotational momentum might easily overpower any elevator control application intended to break the stall. So, first apply full rudder opposite the direction of spin (Figure 65, position 3). Then, when approximately one-half of an additional turn is made, apply the brisk forward elevator pressure set out in Step 4.

Step 4: Briskly move the elevator to the full forward position (Figure 66, position 4). When the stall breaks, the rotation stops. Don't shove the elevator forward too fast or your instructor's glasses (or propeller hat) will fly off. And always remember that the use of elevator occurs only after rudder usage.

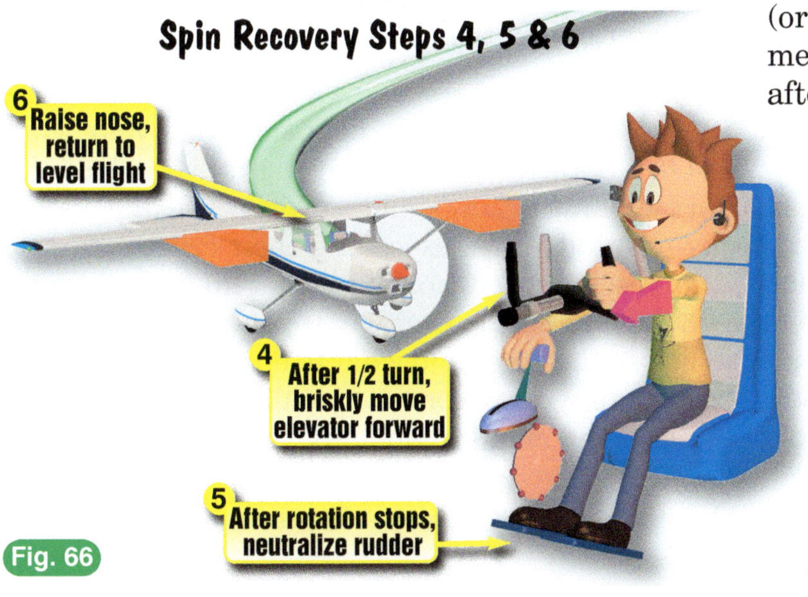

Spin Recovery Steps 4, 5 & 6
- 6 Raise nose, return to level flight
- 4 After 1/2 turn, briskly move elevator forward
- 5 After rotation stops, neutralize rudder

Fig. 66

Step 5: After the rotation stops, neutralize the rudder (Figure 66, position 5).

Step 6: Apply elevator back pressure to raise the nose and return to level flight. Be careful to avoid excessive g-loading and airspeeds during recovery. As it is, the airspeed needle will likely venture into the yellow arc. That's OK, assuming the air is smooth. You want to avoid exceeding Vne, of course.

When a Spin Isn't a Spin, It's a Spiral

Some pilots are confused about the difference between a spin and a spiral. Let's put on our un-confuser hats and sort this out.

In a descending spiral, the wings aren't stalled, meaning that the airplane isn't in a stall nor is it in a spin. The airplane accelerates around a spiraling path during the descent, with the spiral often tightening on its own as the airspeed, bank angle and load factor increase (Picture-1).

Why is a spiral inclined to tighten by itself? As the airplane accelerates, it tends to pitch up, especially if some nose-up trim was already there. Since the airplane is already banked when this happens, the pitch-up acts both upward and in a sideways direction, which tends to further increase the airplane's bank. Increasing the bank results in the airplane's nose dropping, with a loss of vertical lift component.

Now the airplane speeds up, and the entire process repeats itself as one continuous smooth action where the speed, bank angle and load factor continue to increase. Unless a pilot deliberately recovers from the spiral, the airplane can experience flutter, leading to airframe damage. Or, as a bad alternative, the pilot might misuse the flight controls in a spiral with the higher speeds and load factors leading to airframe destruction.

So how do you recover from a spiral? It's quite simple. You pull the power to flight idle, level the wings with the coordinated use of aileron and rudder, and then return the airplane to straight and level flight. Because of the higher airspeed, it might be necessary to apply a great deal of forward (or even aft) elevator pressure to maintain level flight as the wings are leveled. So be prepared to move the elevator control as necessary to keep the airplane in a level flight attitude. On the hand, move the elevator control in such a way that you prevent overstressing the airplane's structure.

How might you accidentally enter a spiral? You might be an instrument rated pilot flying in the clouds while being vectored for an instrument approach with the airplane trimmed to maintain your approach speed. You might even be entering the traffic pattern at an airport with featureless terrain, at night, where you have very few attitude clues.

If you're distracted long enough and you input a bit of aileron deflection, the airplane can enter a bank, resulting in the nose dropping and the airplane accelerating. Instead of reducing power and rolling into level flight, some pilots feel the elevator control moving toward them as a result of the nose-up trim. They instinctually push forward to counter the aft-directed elevator pressure. Unfortunately, all this does is allow the airplane to continue accelerating, eventually leading to excessive airspeed and possible airframe destruction.

So always remember to reduce power, level the wings and return to a level flight attitude if you find yourself in a descending spiral.

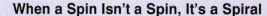

The Descending Spiral

Neither wing stalled in a spiral

Turn tightens in a spiral and load factor increases

Airspeed increases in a spiral

Picture-1

Today's Modern Airplanes and Spins

Some of today's modern airplanes such as the Cirrus, are not certified for spins. The airplane uses modified outboard leading edge (MOLE) technology to help the ailerons remain effective in a stall (the outboard wing sections are drooped and have less of an AOA than the inboard wing sections). The MOLE system, says Cirrus, makes accidental entry into a spin unlikely. On the other hand, Cirrus does have a spin recovery technique in their AFM and it involves activating the Cirrus Airplane Parachute System (CAPS). That's right. If you actually enter a spin, then you pop the parachute. Period.

Whew! What a Whirl That Was

This has been a whole lot of work on your part to understand what happens when your wings stop working (stalls), or one stops working (stalls) before the other. But that was only the half of it. The other half involves getting those wings to start working again (stall recovery). The one undeniable fact no pilot can deny—don't deny it, either—is that wings exceeding their critical angle of attack experience a dramatic reduction in lift. Gone, yes; forgotten, no. To get that lift back the angle of attack must decrease to something less than 18 degrees on the average. If you understand that, along with understanding how one wing can stall before the other and what to do when it does, then you understand more than many pilots who have flown for years. Honest! I wouldn't lie to you. Good for you, too. In much the same way that clothes make the man (or woman), this knowledge make you a much safer pilot.

So now your training is about to takeoff, and I mean takeoff. Our next chapter is on what it takes to get your airplane safely airborne.

Chapter 5: Stalls and Spins

Postflight Briefing #5-1 Mythconceptions About Applying Flaps in a Turn

Everyone believes in a myth at one time or another. This is especially true for those convinced that the world would expire on December 21st, 2012 because the Mayan stone calendar abruptly ends on that date. Well, we're still here, aren't we? More than likely, the massive five by seven foot stone calendar simply fell on the guy doing the carving before he could finish the job. That was the original meaning of getting stoned.

Pilots occasionally believe in myths, too. One such "mythtake" revealed itself at a local FAA safety seminar (held in May of 2012) when an attendee mentioned that he never extends flaps in a turn for fear of stalling. When I asked how this might happen, he simply sat there dumbstruck, never having thought the idea through. I playfully reminded him that he needed to respond before December 21st of this year, while we were still around to hear the answer.

No, extending flaps while turning from base to final approach won't *cause* you to stall—unless you let it cause you to stall. Flaps aren't the culprit here. It's your reaction (or lack of it) to flap extension while turning that causes you to stall, which is often accompanied by a personal introduction to *Ah Uuc Ticab,* the Mayan god of the earth.

Extending flaps allows you to maintain a particular angle of attack at a lower nose-down attitude (Figure 67, positions A, B and C). Flap extension also creates drag, requiring a lower nose-down attitude to sustain the target airspeed during a descent. While it's easy to see how much the nose should be lowered in wings-level flight (lower the nose by eight degrees, for instance) it's much more difficult to determine this value in a descending turn, especially as flaps are deployed.

During a descending turn to final approach, changing your pitch attitude moves the airplane's nose along some diagonal to the horizon as discussed in Figure 34 on page 5-25. The angle of the diagonal depends on the degree of bank you're using at the time. The net result of any pitch change is that the nose moves a little in the horizontal direction and a little in the vertical direction. In a 45 degree bank, the nose moves horizontally as much as it does vertically. If you could sustain a 90-degree

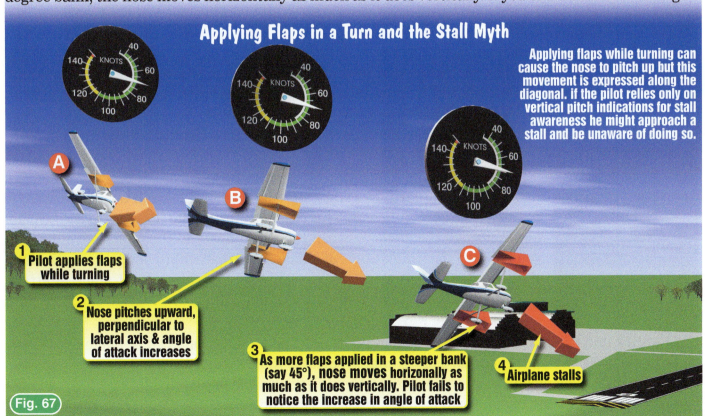

Fig. 67

bank (request a landing clearance from Ah Uuc Ticab tower, first), any pitch change would result in only horizontal movement of the nose—there would be no vertical movement whatsoever.

The takeaway point here is that changing your pitch attitude in a descending turn doesn't provide the same vertical displacement of the nose that you experience in wings-level flight. This is where applying flaps in a turn from base to final approach could bite you in the empennage.

Let's say that you're in a descending turn from base to final approach in an airplane whose flaps generate a nose-up pitching moment when deployed (partially or fully). As you extend the flaps in the turn, the airplane's nose pitches up along a diagonal, from your toes to your nose (as seen from the cockpit). You compensate for this motion by applying forward elevator pressure to sustain the desired nose-down attitude to maintain your approach speed.

The problem is that flap deployment in a turn results in both a horizontal and vertical component of nose movement, instead of pure vertical motion of the nose as experienced in wings-level flight. Therefore, you don't see the nose pitch up vertically toward the horizon by the same amount it does when applying flaps in wings-level flight. Without the obvious vertical pitch movement toward the horizon, some pilots simply fail to apply sufficient forward elevator pressure to sustain their approach airspeed. Ultimately, this can lead to airspeed decay and eventually a stall.

There is an additional factor that increases an unwary pilot's potential for stalling as flaps are applied in a turn. The increase in elevator back pressure necessary to sustain your attitude in a descending turn at steeper banks often masks changes in elevator pressure resulting from flap application. In many airplanes, applying flaps moves the center of lift forward and increases the downwash on the tail. The result is often a change in elevator control forces that helps remind you to adjust your attitude and maintain your approach airspeed. The aft elevator pressure that you're already applying in the descending turn, however, might mask this flap-induced change in elevator force. The net result is that you could miss a valuable clue (a change in elevator pressure) that reminds or prods you to maintain the correct approach speed.

Ultimately, it's a myth to believe that applying flaps in a turn results in a stall. On the other hand, it's absolutely true that a pilot who doesn't understand how flap application in a turn affects an airplane is more likely to stall. So, during a descending turn, glance out your left window and compare the wing chord to ground movement for an approximate assessment of your angle of attack. Look at your airspeed indicator and be especially cognizant of your attitude in a descending turn, making a special effort to adjust it immediately to maintain the right approach airspeed. That's how to fly stall-free when applying flaps in a descending turn.

It's also how to keep your lifespan calendar from getting rocked and ending abruptly.

Postflight Briefing #5-2 Angle of Attack Indicator Anyone?

One very popular new gadget on the market for small airplanes today is the *angle of attack indicator*. This is a mechanism that attaches to the airplane and measures the angle between the chord line and the relative wind, which you know as the wing's *angle of attack*. If you can afford one for your airplane, then have at it. It can certainly teach you something about angle of attack. But if money is an issue (and when is it not?), then don't feel as if you're being left out in some way.

The stick and rudder skills that you're leaning in this book are all you need to make a sufficient and practical assessment of your airplane's angle of attack. Remember, the angle of attack indicator is *most* useful to you when the wings' approach their *critical angle of attack*. But we've already discussed how sight, sound and feel can be used to assess this condition (page 5-13, Figure 18).

Chapter 5: Stalls and Spins

Postflight Briefing #5-3 More Angle of Attack Indicator Insight

Not long ago, researchers at Carnegie Mellon University discovered that using a cell phone while driving is distracting—it results in a 37% reduction in brain activity (and it's often best to use your entire brain while driving). Since distractions often lead to accidents, common sense suggests eliminating this distraction. How? Don't use a cell phone while driving. Check please.

Nearly 40 years ago, NASA researchers discovered that distractions while taking off or landing are also responsible for the majority of stall/spin accidents in airplanes. Unfortunately, it's often difficult to eliminate distractions in an airplane. What we can do is teach pilots the skills necessary to resist being distracted during critical flight times. Curiously, the FAA and NTSB have elected to attack this problem from a different angle by recommending that pilots install *angle-of attack-indicators* (AOAI) in their airplanes.

Other than slow-running Hobbs meters, nothing would give me more pleasure than knowing that AOAIs would eliminate or even substantially reduce stall/spin accidents. No doubt that the AOIA is a wonderful device for helping pilots better understand the concept of angle of attack. It's also a useful device for informing them when the airplane's wings are approaching their critical angle of attack. The problem with the previous sentence, however, is the word "informing."

An early NASA study indicated that in those stall/spin accidents where the pilots survived, three out of four didn't recall hearing the stall horn prior to the accident. Why? They were distracted, and distractions typically redirect a large percentage of our brain power to something other than controlling the airplane. We're now less likely to behave properly in the presence of aural and visual cockpit warnings. The question is this: How useful can an AOAI be as a stall-prevention device when distractions keep pilots from paying attention to it?

To be fair, there are AOAIs that do a better job of getting your attention even when you're distracted. These are models with verbal warnings, such as "Angle! Angle! Push!" Verbal warnings are superior to the continuous tone warnings of your typical stall horn.

According to recent research involving stall/spin accidents, there's an even more superior stall-warning device than the angle of attack indicator. It's called a *stickshaker*. Unfortunately, the only stickshaker found in most general aviation airplanes is the flight instructor, who often accompanies stick shaking with the following two phrases: "Let go of the controls!" and "I mean it this time."

On the other hand, we shouldn't expect AOAIs to be the antidote for preventing stall/spin accidents. Consider that a 1971 NASA study suggested that the use of an AOAI, "...did not show a significant improvement in performance and flight safety." To date, no study has shown the AOAI as being effective in preventing stalls and spins. However, proper training—especially spin training—has been shown to have a positive effect on reducing spin accidents.

Research indicates that the stick shaker is a very effective means of warning a pilot about an impending stall.

That said, if you're going to use an AOAI, then give it the best chance of serving you. Become a distraction denier by learning to recognize and avoid those situations that increase your chances of being distracted. Modern-day distraction training doesn't do the best job of helping pilots avoid distraction. It typically consists of an instructor tossing a pencil on the cockpit floor and asking the student to fetch it. The proper answer to that request is "No" or "No. Pencils are evil!" We might be better served if we elevate our cognitive game by training pilots to "avoid" those situations where we are likely to be distracted.

For instance, we should avoid flying tight traffic patterns or patterns flown at low altitudes on base and final approach. Flying a tight pattern compresses the amount of time in which we have to act, and that increases our chance of being distracted. There's no sense flying as if you're in a Red Bull competition when Red Bull isn't in town.

Flying low in the pattern requires that a pilot pay more attention to spying a harder-to-see runway, much less trying not to notice the rapidly moving ground beneath him. Stabilizing an approach on base and final approach with proper trim control reduces the likelihood that the airplane will deviate from the desired attitude if a pilot is distracted. Additionally, if ATC says, "Can you make an immediate takeoff?" sometimes the best answer is, "No" or "No! Immediate takeoffs are evil!"

These are just a few of the many—MANY!—things you can do to avoid being distracted during takeoffs and landings. The payoff? If and when a stall alert appears in the cockpit, you'll be more likely to notice it.

Postflight Briefing #5-4 Complete Stall Recovery Procedure

The most important thing for you to remember about recovering from a stall is to reduce the angle of attack. Period! Nothing is more important. However, it's entirely possible you might be in an airplane with the autopilot on and experience a stall. How might this happen? You might be operating the autopilot in the *altitude hold* mode and make a significant power reduction for the purpose of maneuvering and fail to deactivate the autopilot (autothrottles not assumed here). If so, the autopilot servos will apply elevator back pressure to maintain altitude as the airspeed decreases. This, of course, will eventually lead to a stall if you fail to recognize the decreasing airspeed.

If the airplane stalls, you should immediately reduce the angle of attack by lowering the nose—perhaps having to apply strong forward pressure initially to overcome the autopilot's servo. Recognizing that the autopilot is on, you should immediately disconnect it. At this point you'll apply full power (if needed), and simultaneously level the wings. If any spoiler or speed brake is deployed, you should immediately retract it and return to the desired flight path as appropriate.

There's a difference between the FAA's recommendation for leveling the wings then adding power, compared to my recommendation (above) of adding power and *simultaneously* leveling the wings. If both are done simultaneously, then there is no significant difference in procedure here.

Stall Recovery Procedure

1. Wing leveler or autopilot	1. Disconnect
2. a) Pitch nose-down	2. a) Apply until impending stall indications eliminated
b) Trim nose-down pitch	b) As needed
3. Bank	3. Wings Level
4. Thrust/Power	4. As needed
5. Speed brakes/spoilers	5. Retract
6. Return to the desired flight path	

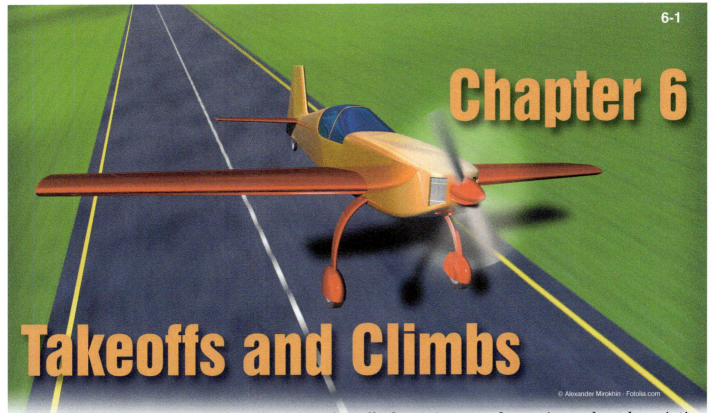

Chapter 6
Takeoffs and Climbs

Takeoffs are something special. They are, after all, the topic most often written about by aviation poets, not the least of whom was Gillespie Magee. You read his famous poem, *High Flight*, at the beginning of Chapter Three. It began with, "Oh! I have slipped the surly bonds of earth…" It's clear that a takeoff must be involved in order to have "slipped the surly bonds of earth" without the ingestion, inhalation, or injection of illegal substances.

Just in case you haven't noticed, there are very few poems that begin with an elevated and moving description of a landing. In fact, I can think of no such poem. Takeoffs are special because that's where the action is. It's where an airplane begins behaving like an airplane, not a clunky ground vehicle. It's where we stop being ground-bound and do something most people will never get to do. It's where the mystery and mystique of flying begin. It's where poems are made.

Since every flight begins with at least one takeoff, just as every journey begins with a single step, let's examine what it takes do a takeoff properly and safely. And while there are taildraggers and tricycle geared airplanes, I'll focus this takeoff discussion on tricycle geared airplanes. These days, there are more of them.

The Big Takeoff Picture

A takeoff involves taxiing to a runway (unless you're flying a vertical takeoff and landing—VTOL—jet, which I doubt), taxiing onto it, applying power, accelerating and lifting off when the airplane attains sufficient airspeed. A takeoff is normally done into the wind as a means of minimizing the runway distance and time required to become airborne. After all, airplanes weren't designed to spend a lot of time on the ground, especially when moving at higher speeds. Lacking proper shock absorbers, they make for shockingly bad ground

Rod Machado's How to Fly an Airplane Handbook

transportation. So the sooner you get airborne, the quicker your airplane does what engineers intended it to do—fly, and inspire poetry (well, OK, the engineers don't have too much to do with the poetry part, but they're not averse to it).

As you're accelerating along the runway to liftoff speed, you're also looking ahead and to the side of the takeoff path to ensure that there's no one else nearby trying to share what should be yours and yours alone at the moment (Figure 1). You're also paying attention to every possible clue that might suggest the flying machine doesn't want to fly today. That includes hints such as poor acceleration, parts or liquids leaving the airplane, or a longer than normal ground run, to name a few. If they all occur at once, it's a really bad sign.

Runway incursions are always a possibility. During takeoff you should keep your eyes open for anyone attempting to use the runway on which you're departing.

A Bit More "Big" for Our Big Picture

Every takeoff begins with a *takeoff roll*, which is not an aerobatic maneuver you perform immediately upon liftoff. It is also not something you can order at the airport sushi bar. The takeoff roll is also known as the *ground roll*, and it's the total distance from where the airplane starts the takeoff to the point where the wheels leave the runway, usually referred to as the *liftoff* point (Figure 2, position A).

Depending on the airplane, the liftoff point typically coincides with the place where the airplane is *rotated* for takeoff. Rotation, in this case, does not involve spinning the airplane around in circles. It means that the airplane is rotated about its lateral (wingtip to wingtip) axis by application of elevator back pressure. This increases the angle of attack, resulting in a nose-up pitch increase and the airplane's wheels leaving the ground as it continues to accelerate. Once the airplane lifts off and has reached the best rate of climb speed (Vy) the *initial climb* begins (Figure 2, position B).

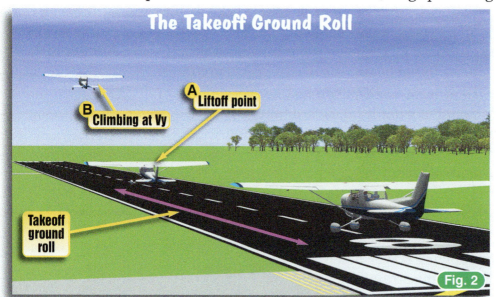

The initial climb is usually considered completed when the airplane reaches a safe maneuvering altitude, typically 500 feet AGL. After the initial climb, the airplane can be established in a cruise climb condition, which is a climb that's generally done at a slightly faster airspeed when you're operating a higher performance airplane. In smaller airplanes, it's not unreasonable to climb at a speed slightly higher than Vy because it keeps the nose a bit lower and makes it easier to scan for traffic.

Now that you have the big picture of the takeoff, let's look at all the details that describe how to perform the maneuver safely and effectively.

Chapter 6 - Takeoffs and Climbs

The Trip to the Runway

The liftoff is somewhat similar to parachuting out of an airplane in the sense that once you begin, you're committed to the act. That's because you're often out of runway and thus out of choices at that point. Here is where the old aviation adage speaks a great truth: *There's nothing more useless than the air above you or the runway behind you.* Keep this idea handy in your frontal lobe cache memory, because once those wheels leave the ground and you're climbing, you're committed to fly (at least for a while). Unlike the flight simulator, there's no reset button on this ride.

This imminent commitment is why pilots typically do a *runup* prior to takeoff. This involves checking the flight controls, instruments, levers, dials, and engine in some designated area near the departure end of the runway while using a good runup checklist (Figure 3). Strange sounds or strange responses from your flight controls (or even your passengers) are good reasons to delay the takeoff, at least until you're assured that it can be done safely. All must be good in the "hood" and under the hood, too.

Pilots, quite reasonably, do not like surprises. Well, maybe for their birthdays, but not for their flights. Surprises lead to distractions. Distractions lead to accidents. Surprises, distractions, *and* accidents are all to be avoided.

I recall taxiing out for takeoff once and hearing a muted banging sound coming from the rear of the airplane. At first I thought it might be a stowaway, or perhaps my pet chinchilla. It turned out that the rear baggage door was flapping in the breeze. On most small airplanes, an open rear baggage door probably wouldn't be a serious problem on takeoff. There have been occasions, however, where the nose-area baggage door on a Seneca (a small twin-engine airplane) came off in flight and damaged the airplane's horizontal stabilizer. Floored by a door. You can imagine what kind of emotional baggage you'd tote around after that experience.

If you hear unusual banging or clanging noises prior to or even during the takeoff roll, they're most likely coming from either an open door, an open window, or the seatbelt strap you left hanging out of the door when you shut it (Figure 4). Make it a point to check those window and door latches during the runup, to make sure they're secure. The most likely time for a door or window to come open is on the takeoff roll. That's when the differential in air pressure between the inside and outside of the cockpit can increase sufficiently to unlatch a weakly (or even daily) latched door or window. The vibration caused by the takeoff roll helps the process along, too.

Tissue's the Issue: Jammed Rudder Pedals During a Takeoff

While taking off...the left rudder jammed and I rejected the takeoff.... We then cleared the runway and returned to the ramp to troubleshoot the problem. After we were clear of the runway, I saw a small tissue box under the rudder pedal. This box apparently was already forward of the rudder pedals out of sight when we took over the aircraft. When takeoff power was applied, the tissue box slid back under my foot and rudder pedals causing the rudder to jam. Directional control was difficult but maintained during the rejected takeoff maneuver.

Tissue boxes, flashlights, water bottles, and manuals have all managed to interfere with rudder travel. Usually a visual preflight and a flight control check will detect these objects prior to takeoff. Flight crews should make sure that items that go missing during flight are located prior to turning the aircraft over to the next crew.

ASRS Report

A window popping open or a back door banging in the breeze won't typically affect the airplane's performance on most general aviation airplanes (cockpit canopies are another story). It might, however, affect your performance. It's the distraction that does the most damage.

If you've already lifted off and are climbing when something pops or bangs, just keep flying the airplane. Nothing matters more than keeping the airplane under control. You got into the air, didn't you? Then you'll be able to stay there. Just because the window is unhinged doesn't mean you should follow suit. First and foremost, fly the airplane. Plan on returning for a normal landing to close the window or door. If you elect to close the window or door in the air, do so when you're at a safe maneuvering altitude and with the airplane under control. Follow the POH's recommendation on shutting things that have come loose or popped open in flight. Passengers who come loose or pop open require special handling and aren't covered by the POH. Use your judgment.

Get Set

The FAA has become very concerned in recent years about runway incursions (i.e., two airplanes trying to use the same runway or same parts of the runway at the same time). It causes bad things to happen, and they don't like it when bad things happen. So, they're watching to make sure all the rules about getting on and off the runway are followed.

Start by making sure you hold short of the runway at the runway hold lines when told to do so (Figure 5). Remember that at a tower-controlled airport you must be explicitly cleared to taxi onto the runway. This is a party to which you cannot invite yourself, though you can and do ask for an invitation.

Acknowledge any runway hold-short clearance given by the tower controller. Holding short of the runway means not letting your spinner cross those double solid-yellow

Takeoff Over an "Airplane" Obstacle

A Cessna had landed and pulled completely off the runway to the north. I pulled onto the runway, announced on UNICOM that I was, "Taking off on Runway 24," and seeing no airplanes on the runway, I applied full power.

After a roll of about 500 feet, I saw the Cessna start across the runway, from north to south. Since I was already at about 80 MPH, I concluded that I could safely climb above the plane crossing the runway rather than try to stop.

I continued the takeoff, passing over the Cessna by more than 250 feet AGL. The Cessna failed to made a call on UNICOM to state his intentions. It was clear to me that he started across the runway after I had started my takeoff roll.

I can't suggest any remedial measures, except to emphasize that all pilots should look before they cross a runway and use UNICOM to announce their intentions. There is nothing that I could have done to avoid this situation.

Operating from a non-towered airport, the pilot of a light aircraft had to takeoff prematurely to avoid an aircraft which had previously landed and exited the runway but then turned back and was recrossing the runway despite the reporter's declaration of his takeoff given on UNICOM.

ASRS Report

At airports where an air traffic control tower is in operation, you are required to hold short of the runway hold lines (solid double-yellow lines) until you've received either a clearance to cross the runway or your have been given permission to *line up and wait* on the runway (meaning you can taxi onto the runway and hold in position for your takeoff clearance).

Chapter 6 - Takeoffs and Climbs

hold-short lines until you're cleared onto the runway (or elect to taxi onto it in the case of a non-towered airport). The FAA considers your spinner to be part of the airplane that shouldn't cross those lines until cleared to do so. There's no way to spin yourself out of such a violation, either. So hold short of the runway when instructed to do so, and don't hold one inch short of it, either. Stop a few feet short of the line for good measure, in case you can't measure.

Before taking the active runway (you can't actually take it, because it's way too heavy and that would constitute a runway excursion), I always like to use the memory aid, *lights, camera, action* to remind me of critical things to do before departure.

Lights reminds you to turn on the landing light as an aid in helping other pilots see you. *Camera* reminds you that your transponder should already be turned on to the ALT selection and that you should be squawking the VFR code of 1200 unless you have been assigned a specific code. This allows ATC and pilots with traffic observing equipment to see you electronically. *Action* reminds you to move things forward, such as the mixture control, prop control and finally the throttle control (Figure 6). If you prefer, there's nothing wrong with using a written/graphic *before takeoff checklist*, either.

When cleared onto the runway, or when taking the runway at a non-towered airport, make sure you look carefully at the arrival path on final approach. Trust no one but yourself on this. Look high and low before you go. You need to be sure that no aircraft is about to use your takeoff spot as its landing spot (Figure 7). It's a wise idea to listen closely and form a mental picture from the tower's conversations about where everyone is in the pattern. If someone is unaccounted for when you're cleared onto the runway, don't hesitate to ask where the bogie might be.

While holding short, it's OK to be a little cocky. Cock the airplane at an angle toward final approach so you can see who, if anyone, is approaching to land. This is particularly important to do in

a high wing airplane, since without X-ray vision (you don't have it) you can't see through the wing or top of the fuselage. When you apply power to move onto the runway, please be careful not to taxi into another airplane that might be holding short next to you.

Do keep in mind that once you're on that runway, you can't see what's behind you. Many years ago a small commuter plane taxied onto a runway at Los Angeles International airport only to have a Boeing 737 land directly on it. It was late afternoon and the 737 was approaching into a setting sun, making it difficult to see. This is why ATC will normally avoid issuing a landing clearance to an arriving airplane when another airplane is holding in position for takeoff.

If you do taxi into position and hold, your ears now become your eyes (my apologies to Mr. Darwin). You must listen carefully for position reports or tower clearances, just in case someone's on final or the tower forgot about you and cleared someone to land on the runway you're presently occupying. You might want to get into a biplane some day, but having someone land on you isn't the preferred way of going about it.

By the way, if you're not comfortable with a clearance onto the runway to take off, decline it! It's an invitation, not a mandate. If you don't want to accept the "line up and wait" or "takeoff" clearance, don't. If you think someone is on short final and the tower has forgotten them, decline the clearance. If you think you just heard the engine hiccup, find out what's going on before going on the runway. You never *have* to go. As PIC, safety of yourself and your passengers is the highest priority and should govern everything you do.

Takeoffs–The Way of the Runway

Pilots take off into the wind for several reasons. First and most important, taking off into the wind reduces the takeoff ground roll distance (Figure 8). After all, it doesn't take much for a takeoff to turn into a land-speed record attempt. Think about it this way. Taking off into a 10 knot headwind means you already have 10 knots of airspeed while sitting on the runway. Free airspeed! How great is that? If you typically rotate (liftoff) at a speed of 50 knots, you're already 20% of the way there and you haven't even moved yet.

On the other hand, taking off with a 10 knot tailwind means you start out with an airspeed deficit of 20%. You have to accelerate 10 knots just to have zero airspeed, and then accelerate 50 knots beyond that to lift off. You'll eat up a lot of runway this way. In fact, if you take off in the wrong direction with a 10 knot tailwind instead of a 10 knot headwind, it's not unusual to consume 50% more runway before becoming airborne.

Once on the runway it's important to align yourself with it. That's because

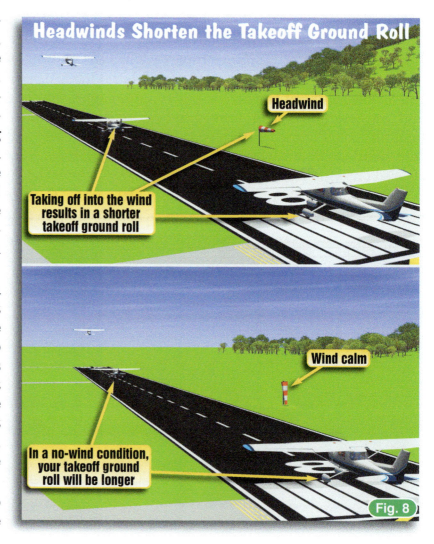

Chapter 6 - Takeoffs and Climbs

when you first apply power, your airplane's propeller slipstream is going to do everything in its power (its engine power, that is) to move you to the left of the centerline. Since the pilot's seat is rarely in the middle of the airplane, it can be a bit of a challenge to know when the airplane is aligned with the runway centerline.

There are several clues that can help you here. If you're sitting in the left seat, the runway centerline shouldn't be directly underneath you (Figure 9). It should clearly be off to your right a bit, perhaps by a foot or more from the center of your derriere. If you just lean over to the right for a second or two, you'll be able to confirm that the center of the engine cowling is indeed aligned with the runway centerline (do let your instructor know what you're doing otherwise he or she might think you want him to pat you on the head for encouragement before takeoff).

Making this alignment assessment by leaning is easy to do on the ground when you're not moving. Once you know the airplane is aligned with the runway centerline, you have the proper sight picture to maintain when sitting upright in the left seat.

Lining Up With the Runway Centerline

During your first few flights it's OK to lean over before takeoff to calibrate your "lined up" sense

When lined up on the centerline for takeoff the centerline is to the right of your right leg

Fig. 9

Toe brakes applied when holding in position for takeoff

Release brakes and place heels on floor for takeoff

Fig. 10A

Fig. 10B

When cleared for takeoff, you'll want to ensure that the heels of your feet are resting on the floorboard with the balls of your feet off the brakes on airplanes with toe brakes (i.e., the top of the rudder pedal).

In small airplanes, you'll make a normal takeoff by releasing brake pressure and applying full power. That doesn't mean you jab the throttle in like you're applying a karate punch to the abdomen of an evil adversary. You want to apply power smoothly but not so fast that it causes the engine to falter, the engine manifold pressure/RPM limits to be exceeded, or your passengers to have whiplash.

Conversely, you don't want to dally (or dilly) with the throttle for fear of hurting your pistons. Your pistons don't have feelings, only cylinders. Move the throttle forward with your hand at about the same speed you initially press your automobile's throttle with your foot when grandma is in the car.

A big problem typically experienced by students during takeoff is that they don't lower their heels to the floorboard and control the steering portion of their rudder pedals (the top part) with the balls of their feet as the airplane accelerates (Figures 10A and 10B). Instead, they keep the balls of their feet elevated and resting on the brake (upper) portion of the rudder pedals. This is very bad form and can certainly cause your tires and brake assembly to overheat, if not smoke (and this is a no-smoking flight, right?). It also really slows down your acceleration.

As soon as you apply takeoff power, get those heels on the floorboard and control the airplane's alignment with the lower portion of the rudder pedals. You'll find that the rudder pedals will easily keep the airplane aligned with the runway once the propeller's slipstream flows over the tail assembly. As you accelerate you'll find that the rudder response increases, and that less and less rudder deflection is needed to keep the airplane properly aligned with the centerline.

If you're operating an airplane with heel brakes (such as the Piper J3 Cub), then you'll want to make sure that you release heel pressure prior to and during the takeoff roll (Figure 10C).

Heel brakes are typically found on tailwheel airplanes. You apply them by sliding your heel forward on the floorboard to activate each main wheel brake individually.

Once power is applied, the airplane's left turning tendency acts to move the airplane toward the left side of the runway (Figure 11). Engine torque rotates the airplane to the left (opposite the propeller's rotation), slightly increasing the pressure and friction on the left main wheel. Propeller slipstream also applies a force to the left side of the vertical stabilizer, resulting in the nose yawing to the left.

These forces combine to yaw the airplane to the left of the runway centerline as you accelerate for takeoff. Once the airplane increases its angle of attack during rotation, p-factor also plays a part in the left-yawing tendency. So as power is applied, it may be necessary to use a great deal of pressure on the right rudder pedal, and on occasion even a little *initial* right brake pressure to keep the airplane aligned with the runway. But with sufficient speed, you'll want to slip those heels to the floorboard and become a pedal pusher to control the airplane's direction of roll.

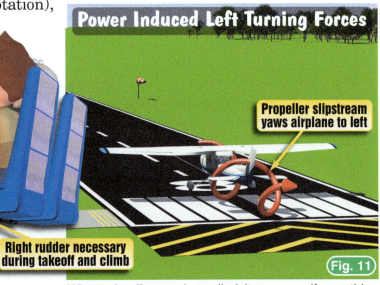

When takeoff power is applied, it seems as if everything in the world forces the airplane to the left side of the runway (i.e., prop slipstream and torque).

Of course, any crosswind experienced during takeoff needs to be dealt with and we'll chat about that in a few paragraphs.

Take It Off—Take It All Off

As the airplane accelerates for takeoff, check to make sure that your engine instrument indications are where they're supposed to be. Needles, bars or symbols should be in the green and not in the red. It's also a good time to quickly look right and left to see if

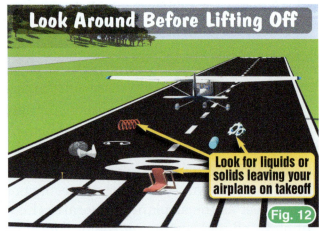

The most important time to catch anything going wrong with your airplane is before you lift off, in which case you'll abort the takeoff.

Chapter 6 - Takeoffs and Climbs

Position for the Elevator Trim Detent Prior to Takeoff

A — Let the elevator assume a neutral position for takeoff

B — Set trim detent to the takeoff position (Trim tab)

C — Airspeed moving into green range

Fig. 13

Assessing when the airplane is ready for liftoff means using several inputs. First, the airplane should feel like it is accelerating properly and feels like it wants to fly. Second the elevator control feels responsive. Third, the airspeed is in the green range.

anything is leaving your airplane, such as fuel, oil, gas caps, loose wingtips, passengers, etc. (Figure 12). I don't want to give you the impression that this happens often. It doesn't. In fact, it will probably never happen to you. But it's a good practice to look for anything that looks bad, wrong, weird, strange or peculiar while you're on the ground and while there's still time to abort the takeoff instead of having to deal with a problem after you're in the air.

During the takeoff roll, let the elevator control assume an aerodynamically neutral position (Figure 13, position A). Pushing forward on the elevator might cause the airplane to wheelbarrow on the nose gear, while pulling aft causes a premature increases in the angle of attack and slows acceleration. The sweet spot is the elevator's natural position that it assumes when power is applied. Of course, I'm assuming that you did check to see that the elevator trim was in its takeoff position (Figure 13, position B), right? OK, good. I knew I could trust you.

The big question is, How do you know when the airplane is ready to fly? There are several ways to determine this. First, you can assume that the airplane is ready to fly when it feels like it wants to leave the ground by itself. Airplanes tend to do this on their own because of their built in *angle of incidence* (see sidebar: *Incidentally, The Wings' Angle of Incidence.*). This, however, sometimes occurs beyond the speed at which the airplane might actually begin flying.

Looking at the airspeed needle and rotating the airplane for takeoff when the needle has moved and continues to move into the green range (the airplane's normal operating range) is another perfectly reasonable way to help assess when an airplane is ready to fly (Figure 13, position C). On the other hand, since you're holding the yoke during takeoff, you can physically sense when the elevator comes alive—that's pilot talk for *it becomes responsive to your control inputs*. The secret in assessing the airplane's readiness to fly lies in using *all* the clues that are available. Clues are to use, Sherlock.

The Wing's Angle of Incidence

0° Pitch Attitude

Chord Line — 4° Angle of incidence — N2132B

In a level flight attitude, the chord line of the wing makes a small angle with respect to the longitudinal axis of the airplane. This angle is known as the *angle of incidence*. The angle of incidence is somewhere around 4 degrees for many airplanes. This allows the fuselage to remain level at cruise speeds (where the airplane typically spends most of its time). The result is that the pilot and passengers sit perpendicular to the earth's surface (a comfortable position) during cruise flight. With the elevator in the neutral position during the takeoff roll, the airplane will naturally want to lift off on its own, but often do so at a higher than normal speed.

Airplane Attitude When Climbing at the Best Rate of Climb Speed (Vy)

Good stick and rudder pilots rely primarily on the attitude that the nose and the wing make with the horizon to initially obtain the desired climb airspeed. Once the initial attitude is established the airspeed indication is used to fine tune that attitude.

Initial attitude selection for climb at Vy

Climb attitude also assessed by angle wing makes with horizon

Fig. 14

At this point, you'll want to rotate the airplane to a nose-up attitude sufficient to produce a climb at the best rate of climb airspeed (Vy). How do you know what that attitude is? Get used to it. You'll have to see it a few times to remember it, so expect your instructor to help you identify the correct attitude during your first few takeoffs. Until then, when the airplane's ready to fly, rotate and point the nose slightly above the horizon, as shown in Figure 14. That's good enough for starters, right? But please don't yell out, "To infinity and beyond," at the moment of liftoff, even if you are excited about it. It will scare your instructor.

As soon as the airplane lifts off the runway, be aware of its tendency to pitch upward a little higher than you might like. Why? Because the landing gear is the pivot point at the initial rotation. Once the airplane is airborne, all rotation then occurs about the airplane's center of gravity (c.g.). Since the c.g. is located forward of the main gear in a tricycle geared airplane, this means that the distance from the elevator surface to the rotation point (the "arm") actually increases slightly with rotation. And that means the force you were applying on the elevator control suddenly has a little more leverage (a longer arm, right?).

The net result is that tricycle geared airplanes tend to pitch up a little bit more than new pilots anticipate. So, rotate the airplane and make sure it pitches up to the attitude you want, not the attitude the airplane wants (this is usually more noticeable on airplanes having four or more seats). Reminder—you are the pilot in command. So, be in command. Don't let the airplane fly you; you fly the airplane.

You also want to be careful not to force the airplane into the air. Believe it or not, airplanes can start flying before they have enough speed to really start flying. How can that be? Let me introduce you to *ground effect,* something we'll discuss at greater length in a while. Because of the reduction of induced drag in ground effect, it is possible to rotate and become airborne at a speed and or

Chapter 6 - Takeoffs and Climbs

Attempting to Climb Prematurely Out of Ground Effect

Fig. 15

A premature climb out of ground effect might require you to lower the nose and accelerate to climb speed in ground effect before resuming the climb.

attitude that won't let you do anything outside of ground effect except sink back to the runway like a non-rolling stone. The problem with ground effect is that you need to be near the ground to enjoy its benefits. Try climbing out at too slow a speed and you'll be more grounded than a teenager coming in after curfew. The only way to begin the initial climb here is to lower the nose, accelerate to the proper speed, then raise the nose to an attitude that allows the airplane to climb (Figure 15).

It's worth noting that in non-turbocharged airplanes when density altitude is high, you don't want to try climbing out at the same nose-up climb attitude that you use for lower density altitude conditions. The reduction in power at higher density altitudes is going to make that a no-go. You must select a slightly lower climb attitude to attain the correct airspeed. (See sidebar: *The Right Attitude for a High Density Altitude Takeoff on Page 6-12*).

An equally bad scenario is to accelerate, force the airplane into the air while still in ground effect, then have it sink toward the runway as you run out of runway altogether (Figure 16). You get to watch your pristine flying record go down the drain that's located in that sink.

Ultimately, you've got to listen to your airplane. If you listen it will speak, in its own way. Pay very close attention to what your airplane does immediately after liftoff and you will know if wants to continue flying. If the controls feel too mushy, if the airplane doesn't want to climb or if it's sinking back to the runway, then you're not ready for *prime climb* time just yet. This would be a perfect moment to abort the takeoff, perhaps while yelling, "To infinity and beyond someday, but not now."

Insufficient Runway Available for Landing When Climb Not Possible

Fig. 16

Attempting to climb out of ground effect when a climb isn't possible might result in a loss of sufficient runway for landing.

Here's a thought experiment. Imagine you are climbing out from an airport located at sea level. During the climb the airplane's nose is pointed upward at some relatively nose-high attitude. Now, what would you have to do to that attitude if I pulled the airplane's throttle back a bit? You'd have to lower the nose to maintain the same climb speed, right? The ability to climb depends on the availability of excess power. So if you suddenly have less power available to you in the climb, you can't climb as steeply, which means your climb angle must be shallower.

This is precisely what can happen when taking off. In high density altitude conditions, your engine doesn't develop as much power. If you raise the nose and attempt to climb at the angle that's familiar to you from your sea-level departures, your airspeed decreases because of the large amount of induced drag associated with higher angles of attack.

When departing a high density altitude airport, rotate and keep a nose-low attitude initially, at least until you see that the airplane is accelerating to climb speed (Vy). Then continue raising the nose attitude to keep the climb speed at Vy. Think of it as the old high-low.

Since you're working with less power because of the density altitude (just as in our thought experiment), you'll find that the climb angle is much less, and the rate of climb is less, too.

Climb Attitudes for Airports Having Different Density Altitudes

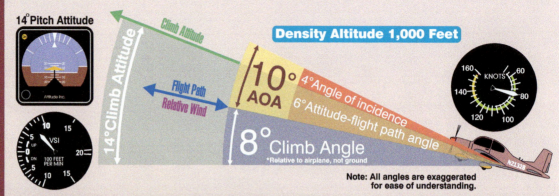

During a climb from a low density altitude airport (i.e., 1,000 feet DA) at the best rate of climb speed (Vy), the airplane climbs at a 14° nose up attitude at a best rate of climb speed of 80 knots. Its *angle of attack* (AOA) is approximately 10° and the climb rate is 700 FPM. The AOI or *angle of incidence*—the angle the wing's chord line makes with the longitudinal axis—is approximately 4°. Therefore, the airplane's nose-up pitch attitude during climb is a combination of the angle of attack (10°) plus the climb angle (8°) minus the wing's AOI (4°), which equals = 10° + 8° − 4° = 14° nose-up pitch attitude. This formula reads as follows:

Pitch Attitude = Angle of Attack + Climb Angle − Angle of Incidence or PA = AOA + CA − AOI.

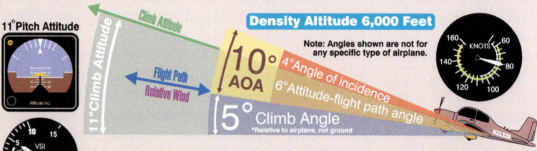

Now let's assume that you're departing an airport at a higher density altitude (6,000 feet in this instance) and want to climb out at Vy (always a good speed to use unless obstacles are present). In a non-turbocharged airplane, you just can't climb at the same angle you did when you departed at a lower density altitude (power ultimately determines how steep your climb angle can be for a given airspeed). In other words, you can't rotate to the same climb attitude used at an airport with a density altitude of 1,000 feet and expect the same climb performance. Instead, you need to rotate to a smaller climb attitude to climb out at Vy. Using your formula (**PA = AOA + CA − AOI**), the airplane's nose-up pitch attitude during climb is a combination of the angle of attack (10°) plus the climb angle (5°) minus the wing's AOI (4°), which equals = 10° + 5° − 4° = 11° nose-up pitch attitude. Eleven degrees nose up pitch gives you the climb angle of attack (10°) necessary to produce the most altitude gain for a given amount of time, otherwise known as Vy. Climb any steeper and your airspeed will be less, perhaps approaching stall speed.

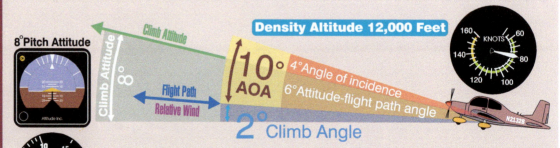

At an airport with a much higher density altitude (i.e., 12,000 feet), you'll need to climb out at a much lower pitch attitude if you want to use Vy as your climb speed. Using your formula (**PA = AOA + CA − AOI**), the airplane's nose-up pitch attitude during climb will be a combination of the angle of attack you want during climb (10°), plus the climb angle (2°) minus the wings' AOI (4°), which equals = 10° + 2° − 4° = 8° pitch attitude. Of course, you won't know the climb angle for your airplane during takeoff, but that doesn't matter. What you do know is that you will achieve the desired climb airspeed at a lower pitch attitude when departing a high density altitude airport. So raise the nose to climb, but don't raise it as much as you would when departing at a lower density altitude.

Chapter 6 - Takeoffs and Climbs

There are two problems students typically experience during the initial takeoff. The first is that they tend to be either ham fisted or ballet-dainty on the elevator control—either pulling aft too hard or not hard enough. The second big takeoff issue occurs when insufficient right rudder is applied just after liftoff. Until liftoff, P-factor (which increases with an increase in angle of attack) has no affect on the airplane. As soon as the angle of attack increases during rotation, the left yawing tendency of the nose increases (Figure 17, position A). You must apply sufficient right rudder to keep the airplane aligned with the extended runway centerline and keep it coordinated, too. Whatever you do, don't be like the pilot whose rudder skills are so poor that the only reason his airplane appears to fly straight on takeoff is because of the coriolis force. Adding right rudder also means applying whatever aileron deflection is needed to keep the wings level (Figure 17, position B).

How do you know if you're aligned with the runway centerline after liftoff? The best reference is to look directly ahead of you at either the end of the runway (if you can still see it over the airplane's nose) or some distant reference you spied just before takeoff. Sometimes that's a bit challenging, given the high nose-up attitude that's normal during climb. You simply can't see through your instrument panel

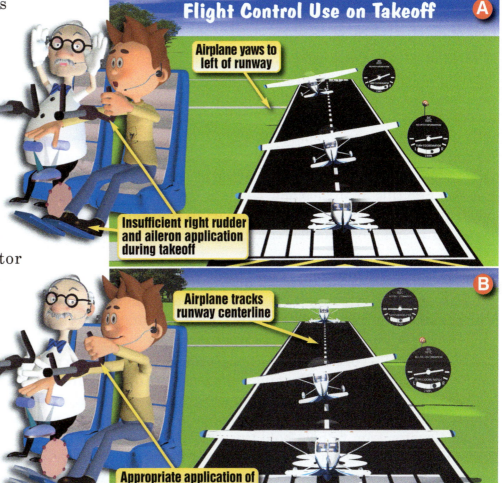

During the takeoff roll and subsequent climb, apply sufficient right rudder pressure to compensate for the airplane's power-induced left turning tendency or the airplane will track left of the centerline.

Squeeze Play
This instructor and student used the POH to calculate the rotation speed but neglected to follow the procedure for leaning the fuel mixture [for takeoff]. They put their C172 into a spot where there was not enough speed to takeoff and not enough runway left to abort.

...With full tanks and increasing density altitude, the engine was unable to produce the needed power to achieve the rotation speed of 48 knots. After passing the intersection of Runway 13/31 we were at 42 knots. At this point we decided to rotate because there was not enough runway left to abort the takeoff.... Unfortunately, after rotation, the stall warning horn sounded at about 10 feet. We did not have enough distance to climb and clear the obstacles at the departure end of the runway. We decided to cut the power and land.... At this point we believed that there was some runway and hard grass surface to stop the plane. Unfortunately, the brakes did not catch the wet grass and we slid into the plowed field 200 feet south of the runway....

In my opinion, if we had tried to keep it in the air the outcome could have been much worse. However, there were some errors in our judgement. The density altitude was significantly higher than it had been in the last several months. Keeping the high density altitude in mind, apparently one thing that we could have done to produce more power [would have been to] lean the mixture for takeoff....

ASRS Report

(if you can see through your panel, you need to buy more instruments to fill up the holes). So you might want to look out the left side of the airplane to see the runway below, or at least the left side of it. Sometimes you can actually take a glance behind you if you have windows back there.

Most of the time you can get a good initial approximation of alignment by simply glancing at the heading indicator and ensuring that it reads the same value it read when you began your takeoff (no crosswind assumed). If you can lift off and establish the correct climb speed and a wind correction angle, then you can fly whatever heading you're on and track the runway centerline.

I personally prefer keeping my eye on some distant reference to help me remain aligned after takeoff. This is *not* a good time to be staring at your flight instruments, even if they're showing the latest hit film or app. If you like staring at the instruments, buy one, take it home, and stare at it. But don't do this in an airplane. Glace at it, but keep moving and look elsewhere, too. Outside is a particularly good place to look. You need to continuously scan for traffic, obstacles, runway alignment, birds and anything else that can present an issue during climb.

Climb Time

Once the airplane has lifted off and is indeed climbing, you'll want to adjust its attitude to keep the airspeed at Vy, the best rate of climb speed. This speed gives you the most of what you need at the moment, which is a lot of altitude for a given amount of time, compared to using Vx, or the best angle of climb speed (Figure 18, position A).

We're assuming, of course, that there's no obstacle looming at the end of the runway, which would initially require the use of Vx immediately after liftoff (Figure 18, position B). Vx gives you the most altitude gain for a given distance over the ground. Ultimately, Vx results in a steeper angle of climb, which is precisely the angle you want when obstacles loom in your departure path. You'll also want to use elevator trim to help hold this attitude, so don't be a stingy twister with that trim wheel. Twist that wheel and get the trim you need to keep the airplane in the proper attitude.

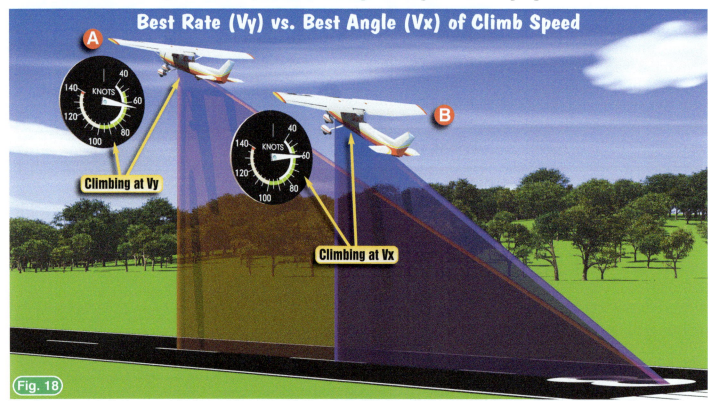

Fig. 18

The best rate of climb speed (Vy) provides you with the most altitude gain for a given amount of time. This is the speed you would typically use for normal climb operations. The best angle of climb speed (Vx) provides you with the most altitude gain for a given distance over the ground. You would use this speed when an obstacle is present in the departure path.

Chapter 6 - Takeoffs and Climbs

In complex airplanes, you typically take off using *takeoff power*. That means throttle to the firewall. After liftoff and when reaching a safe *maneuvering* altitude, which is typically about 500 feet AGL, the normal recommendation is to reduce power to its climb setting.

Why do we wait until reaching a maneuvering altitude to reduce power? The first reason is that we want to get to a safe maneuvering altitude as quickly as possible. With most airplanes it takes less than a minute to get to 500 feet AGL. A little altitude buys you a lot of insurance during departure. Some airplane manuals, however, recommend maintaining takeoff power until reaching 1,000 feet.

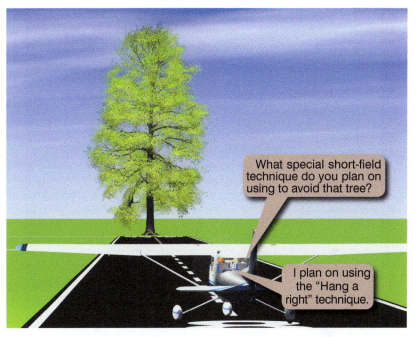

What special short-field technique do you plan on using to avoid that tree?

I plan on using the "Hang a right" technique.

The second reason involves an unwarranted concern about power reduction and engine failure. For years, some pilots have argued that it's best not to change from takeoff power to climb or METO power (see sidebar: *Three Engine Power Conditions*) until reaching at least 1,000 feet AGL. The reason, they argue, is that any big bore engine is more likely to fail during a rapid power reduction. Except for the fact that there has never been any study (or evidence) to support this theory, it's not an unreasonable thought, and some pilots still behave as if the theory were indeed a fact. I don't think you have anything to worry about. Do what your POH recommends and be a happy pilot.

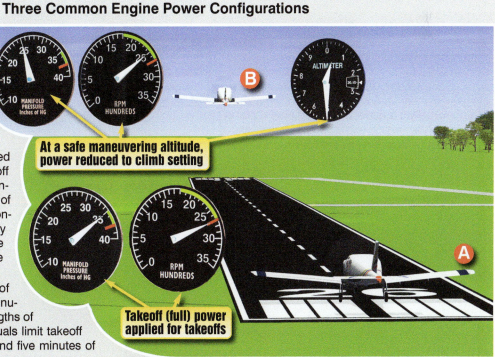

Three Common Engine Power Configurations

Engine power is a continuum, from none to maximum, but there are three common power configurations you'll likely use when operating a complex airplane (one with a controllable propeller, flaps and retractable landing gear).

The first is *takeoff power*. This is where the throttle is typically pushed all the way to the firewall for takeoff (no fire and no wall are actually involved here). The maximum amount of engine power is produced in this condition (position A) and this is precisely what you want to get your airplane airborne and climbing away from the runway.

Takeoff power, however, is a lot of power and most engines can't continually operate at this level for long lengths of time. That's why most engine manuals limit takeoff power to anywhere between one and five minutes of continuous use.

At a safe maneuvering altitude, power reduced to climb setting

Takeoff (full) power applied for takeoffs

The power setting at which the airplane can operate continuously is called METO power or *maximum except takeoff power* (position B). This is the setting that is used for climbing once the airplane has reached a safe maneuvering altitude. We commonly call this *climb power*. Once the airplane reaches its cruising altitude, the power is normally reduced to a *cruise power* setting (not shown). Cruise power is selected by the pilot based on several variables such as fuel economy, speed, range, etc. As in most of life, it's a tradeoff between these variables. You choose which one you want at what level, and the others fall into place.

When to Raise the Landing Gear in a Complex Airplane

When is the best time to retract the landing gear on a retractable geared airplane? The best answer is, when you don't need to use it any more. That means when the airplane is positively established in a climb (Picture #1). The last thing you want is to retract your gear and then somehow settle back onto the runway without benefit of wheels. This means you get to make new friends at the local FAA office and your mechanic gets to take that long-awaited cruise vacation on the income from the repair.

Then again, pilots who fly retractable gear airplanes often hear that they should not retract the landing gear until the aircraft is positively airborne and insufficient runway remains for landing. The caveat regarding insufficient runway is based on the premise that if the engine were to quit, it would still be possible to land with the gear down on the remaining portion of the runway. This is good advice, assuming that you have any runway remaining ahead of you once you've lifted off.

Pilots are often overly optimistic in estimating how much runway is needed to take off, have an engine fail, land, and roll out. This distance is probably a lot longer than you think (Picture #2). In a typical small complex airplane at sea level on a standard day with no wind and at full gross weight, it takes approximately 1,500 feet of runway to clear a 50-foot obstacle on takeoff. To land over a 50-foot obstacle under the same conditions takes approximately 2,000 feet of runway. Thus, to climb to 50 feet, have an engine failure, and land to a complete stop requires at least 3,500 feet. Keep in mind that those numbers are based on a professional pilot operating a new airplane and knowing in advance that he's going to start and stop. As a practical matter, your mileage is going to vary and not in your favor.

The distance I quoted to land over a 50-foot obstacle is based on a full flap approach, which is accomplished at a slower speed than that used for a normal departure. But we don't typically climb this slowly, nor do we use full flaps for takeoff. Furthermore, many pilots don't bother to use the very beginning of the runway for takeoff (the full length of the runway) nor do they maximize their performance on every takeoff.

As a general rule, the actual length of runway you'd use in the event of an engine failure on takeoff will be longer than what you'd expect on a typical short-field landing over a 50-foot obstacle. Given these considerations and the fact that a skilled test pilot determined the takeoff and landing distance shown in the performance chart, it's safe to say that the average pilot is looking at 4,000 feet or more of runway to climb to 50 feet, then land to a full stop in the event of an engine failure in a complex airplane.

Unless you're departing on a long runway (one over 4,000 feet, for instance), it's likely that you'll use up all your available landing distance the moment you lift off. This is why the best course on average-length runways is usually to raise the gear after liftoff once a positive rate of climb is established. Then again, if you're departing JFK or LAX on a 6,000 to 10,000-foot runway, there's nothing wrong with leaving the gear down a bit longer after takeoff.

What do you get in return if you raise the gear as soon as a positive rate of climb is established? The airplane climbs faster—several hundred feet per minute faster in some cases. This extra bit of altitude is your insurance against needing to use your insurance. It gives you more options if the engine quits (or other problems arise that require an immediate return for landing or an emergency landing). If the engine quits and you are only a few hundred feet off the ground, you still have sufficient time to lower the gear for landing in most airplanes.

You might even elect to keep the gear up and belly-in after an engine failure. This becomes a wiser choice if the increased glide performance with the gear up means reaching an acceptable landing site. Personally, I'd rather have additional altitude to glide to a vacant field and land gear up than land gear-down in less hospitable territory (which doesn't mean that are no hospitals nearby, but does mean that there are cars, telephone poles,

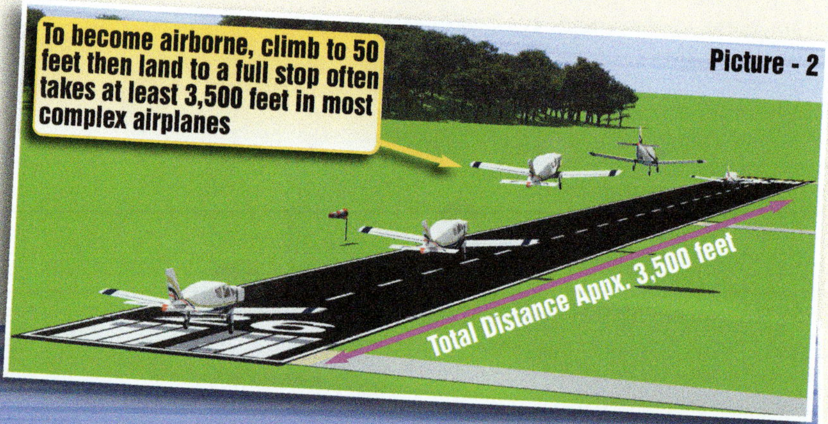

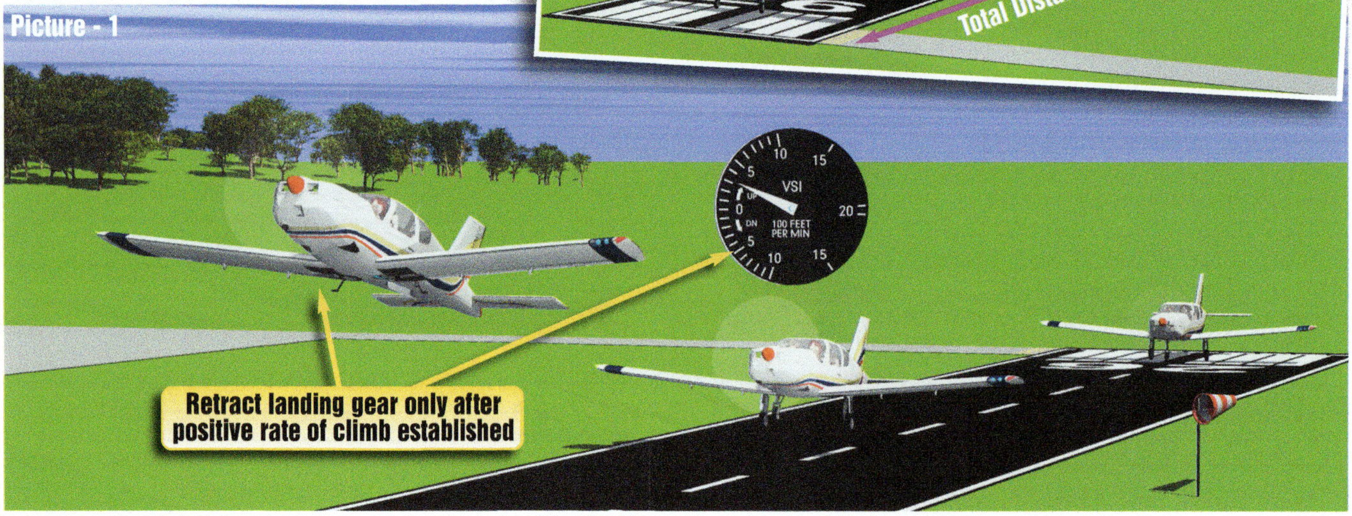

Picture - 2
To become airborne, climb to 50 feet then land to a full stop often takes at least 3,500 feet in most complex airplanes

Total Distance Apxx. 3,500 feet

Picture - 1

Retract landing gear only after positive rate of climb established

Chapter 6 - Takeoffs and Climbs

How to Not Be Crossed Up by Crosswinds

If runways could be placed on a swivel and allowed to rotate into the wind, you'd never need to worry about taking off or landing with a crosswind again. There are only two places where this can actually happen. One is on an aircraft carrier, where the breeze is always down the runway (though the runway is bobbing up and down). The other is in the Fantasy "Landing" section of Disneyland.

As it stands, large crosswind angles for takeoffs and landings aren't all that frequent. That's because runways are usually aligned to the average wind direction for

Without correcting for a crosswind on takeoff (right crosswind in this instance), it's possible for the airplane to have its wing lifted (A), to weathervane into the wind (B) or even begin to yaw and roll immediately after takeoff (C).

that location. Just take a look at any aviation chart where airports are close to each other and you'll see that they pretty much point the same way, with some minor variations and occasional exceptions.

But it's an unpredictable world, and averages are made up of a range of data points. Sometimes, the wind just doesn't behave in an average way. That's the way the wind blows, and that's the way it goes. So, all pilots must learn to take off and land in crosswinds. It really isn't all that difficult as long as you know and use the proper technique.

The technique for taking off in a crosswind is similar to that for taxiing in a crosswind, at least as far as aileron placement is concerned. Your goal is to avoid being blown off the runway or having a wing lifted up before or during the takeoff roll (which might turn the takeoff roll into an actual roll on takeoff). See Figure 19, position A.

In a very strong wind, it's not unusual for the airplane to attempt to weathervane into the wind given the rather prominent tail surface on the rear of the airplane (Figure 19, position B), which come to think of it *does* make an airplane look sort of like a weathervane.

Crosswinds can also cause the upwind wing to lift and the airplane to roll as you accelerate (Figure 19, position C). The wind might not be strong enough to lift the wing while the airplane is sitting still, but once it moves, there is less and less weight on the wheels. That means the airplane might start skipping across the runway and that could lead to directional control problems. "Hop, skip, and a jump" is not a description of the ideal takeoff. Side skipping places a great deal of unnecessary side stress on the landing gear, which you always want to avoid. You want the gear to be supportive when you next make a landing.

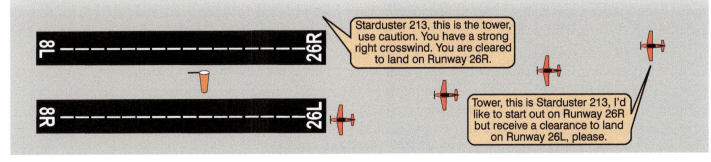

Fig. 20

Fig. 21

Here's how you'll prevent side-stress distress from happening. When you're aligned with the runway, take another look at the windsock or other wind indicator to determine the direction the wind is blowing in the runway environment (don't worry if there's no wind indicator nearby). As a good stick and rudder pilot, you can simply feel what the wind is doing to your airplane as you begin moving and immediately apply the appropriate correction. Now turn your control wheel (or deflect your joystick) *fully* into the side from which the wind is blowing (Figure 20, position A). This raises the aileron on the upwind wing and provides a downward force to that wing as you accelerate.

You might be concerned that a full deflection of the control wheel into the wind will cause the upwind wing to strike the ground as you accelerate. That's not going to happen. As the airplane sits on the runway before takeoff, there's no downward force on the upwind (right) wing. As the airplane accelerates, you'll actually sense the increasing aileron control response because the upwind wing begins to lower just a tiny bit. That's the response you're looking for during a crosswind takeoff. As your speed increases, reduce the aileron deflection just enough to keep that upwind wheel firmly planted on the runway, at least until you lift off (Figure 21, position C). Now you're assured that the airplane won't be skipping sideways due to the crosswind's influence.

As soon as you lift off, the upwind wing will want to drop because of the aileron input (Figure 21, position D). That's to be expected. Since you're lifting off, however, the upwind wing will also be moving away (vertically) from the runway, so it's not going to strike the ground, even in low wing airplanes. The point here is that you don't want to be stingy about deflecting that control wheel into the wind to correct for crosswind drift during the takeoff roll.

Chapter 6 - Takeoffs and Climbs   6-19

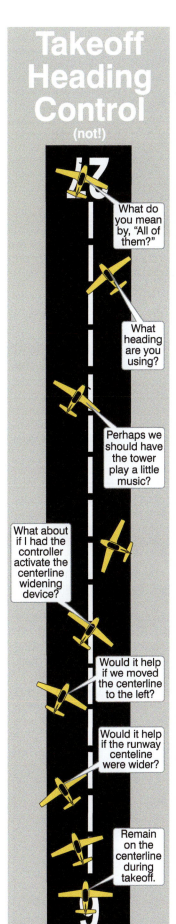

During the takeoff roll, as the airplane accelerates you want to keep its longitudinal axis aligned with the runway centerline. That means you have to be ready to dance on those rudder pedals (not the brakes) to keep the nose pointed straight down the runway (Figure 20, position B). During the takeoff roll and before liftoff, propeller slipstream wants to yaw the airplane to the left. If you happened to have a left crosswind during takeoff, then both the crosswind pushing on the left side of the airplane's tail surface along with the airplane's left turning tendencies combine to yaw and weathervane the airplane to the left, into the wind. Yes, your airplane appears to have a mind of its own, unless you do something about it. Substantial right rudder is often needed to keep the airplane going straight in this condition. Sometimes a crosswind can work for you. In a right crosswind, for instance, wind blowing on the right side or the tail helps counter the airplane's left turning tendency during the takeoff roll.

When do you rotate for takeoff in a crosswind? As long as the crosswind isn't gusty, you'll rotate at the same speed at which you always rotate. With gusty winds, it's better to leave the airplane on the ground for an extra five knots or so to give you a little more control response immediately after liftoff. Higher airspeeds mean more effective control response, which makes it easier to counter the pitch and bank effects of gusty winds immediately after takeoff.

As I stated previously, at the moment of liftoff with aileron applied into the wind, your upwind wing wants to drop. At this point, the airplane may be side slipping slightly into the wind (one wing is low and the nose is aligned with the runway. That's a *sideslip*).

In a strong crosswind, however, there is nothing wrong with the airplane being in a *slight* and *temporary* sideslip after takeoff, since this keeps the airplane closer to the runway centerline. It also helps prevent excessive side loads on the landing gear should the airplane unexpectedly settle back to the runway immediately after lifting off. The obvious benefit to this is that it provides you with a runway on which to touch down, instead of touching down to the downwind side of the runway (or the dirt off the side of the runway, and you don't want to do anything dirty, do you?).

Your objective immediately after liftoff is to establish a slight crab angle to help track the runway centerline (Figure 21, position D). This means lifting off and making a slight, shallow turn into the wind with the coordinated use of aileron and rudder. Do keep in mind that you're already using a great deal of rudder to counteract the airplane's left-turning tendencies. That means a lot of right rudder will be needed to make a slight right turn into a right crosswind.

On the other hand, if you have a left crosswind you might make a left turn into the wind by simply releasing a bit of the right rudder pressure already applied. Whatever you do, please don't ever forget this point: *You do not crab into the wind by using only rudder*. That's a big no-no on takeoff. You always use rudder and aileron in coordination when you make a turn, and crabbing into the wind always involves a turn, followed by a rollout, not a rudder-induced yaw. Period!

Rod Machado's How to Fly an Airplane Handbook
Crabbing Into the Wind After Takeoff

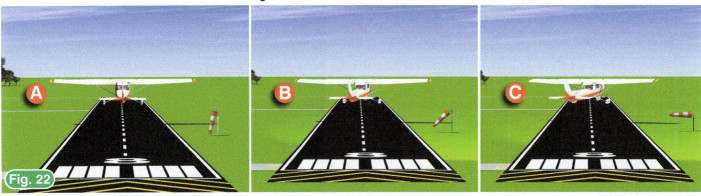

After takeoff, when the wind is calm, no crab angle is necessary to track the runway centerline (A). As the speed of the crosswind increases, a larger crab angle is necessary to track the runway centerline immediately after departure (B and C). Remember, crabbing into the wind requires a coordinated turn into the wind, not just an application of rudder.

The big question is, How much of a turn into the wind should you make after takeoff to correct for wind drift? The answer is, Just enough to track the runway centerline. You really don't know how much of a turn you need until you turn a bit and observe the results of the crab (Figure 22). If you turned into the wind a little and are still drifting, then you need a larger crab (they come in several sizes). Make another small coordinated turn into the wind. You might have to make two or three small turns into the wind during your initial climb, since the crosswind tends to change in direction and/or velocity as altitude is gained. The important thing here is to not take sides—I mean sides of the runway. It's the centerline you want to track immediately after takeoff, so do what you have to do to track it.

Of course, when you gain some experience with crosswind takeoffs you won't have to do much turning after departure to keep the airplane aligned with the runway. When a pro makes a crosswind takeoff, he or she will immediately turn into the wind as soon as the airplane becomes airborne. Given that a wing is likely to drop a bit after a crosswind takeoff (based on your aileron input), the pro simply applies the appropriate amount of rudder to roll into a slight coordinated turn into the wind, then rolls out at the appropriate crab angle. Nice eh? That's why they call him or her a pro. You can fly like a pro, with a bit of practice.

There's a (Crosswind) Limit

There are two limits on how much of a crosswind component you can accept for takeoff and landing. The first is the airplane's limit, based primarily on the aerodynamic potential of the rudder. The second is your personal limit, based on your skill and experience.

Check the POH and you will most likely find a crosswind component limit for takeoffs and landings. For instance, the Cirrus SR20 POH says that its maximum demonstrated crosswind component is 21 knots. Additionally, the FARs require airplanes be satisfactorily controllable with no exceptional degree of skill or alertness on the part of the pilot in 90° crosswinds up to a velocity equal to 0.2 V_{SO}. (For example: .2 X 50 Knots. = 10 Knots.)

It is interesting to note that POHs don't list a maximum crosswind component beyond which the airplane shouldn't be flown. Instead, they offer a maximum "demonstrated" crosswind component.

POHs do this because airplane's aren't required to be tested to determine what the maximum crosswind is that they're capable of handling. That's why the Cirrus POH also says that its 21 knot *demonstrated* crosswind component isn't limiting, meaning that pilots with sufficient skill can handle direct crosswinds of greater velocity. (That's a lot of skill, by the way.)

Then again, just because the POH says 22 knots was "demonstrated" that doesn't mean *you* can accept 22 knots, though. Here we encounter the second limit—yours. It takes a while to get comfortable enough to maintain control of the airplane in a strong crosswind, especially gusty ones. Start low, and work up slowly. Set a limit and stick to it. Of course, you have to be able to calculate the crosswind component. It's rare that the wind is blowing at exactly 90 degrees to the runway. Any time it's at any other angle, not all the breeze is causing unease. The figure to the right is a typical crosswind component chart.

For instance, a 40-knot wind blowing at 90 degrees to the runway has a crosswind component of 40 knots. Crank that wind around to where it's blowing at a 45 degree angle to the runway, and of those 40 knots only about 28 of them are

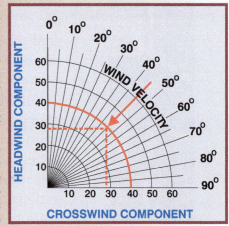

Chapter 6 - Takeoffs and Climbs

The Effects of Ground Effect

Can you get something for nothing? The casino owners in Las Vegas want you to think so, but their large, glittery, and very expensive buildings should convince you otherwise. Then again, you sure come close when you come close the runway and operate in something known as *ground effect*.

Ground effect occurs as a result of the ground's effect on the airflow over an airplane's wings. The total lift produced by the wings acts in a slightly rearward direction when the wings are not influenced by ground effect (Figure 23, position A). The vertical component of the total lifting force (gray arrow) is known as *effective lift* (but we'll just call it *lift* from now on), while the rearward component (yellow arrow) is known as *induced drag* (drag induced by the wing's lifting force). Aerodynamically speaking, the total lifting force (red arrow) is always generated perpendicular to the local or "average" relative wind that's making contact with the wing. Because of the wing's influence on the air around it, the local relative wind contacting the wing is bent downward slightly compared to the general relative wind found many feet ahead of the wing. (See Sidebar: *Downwash and the Average Relative Wind* on page 6-22.)

Here's how this airflow gets bent out of shape. As air approaches the wing, the low-pressure area above the wing induces a slight upward movement of the air. As the air flows over the wing, it's deflected downward, thus inducing a downwash to the wind. This means that the relative wind in the *local* vicinity of the wing (the *local relative wind*) is angled downward slightly as a result of the upwash and downwash created by the wings. Therefore, when the wing is not in ground effect (Figure 23, position A), the total lifting force (red arrow) tilts slightly rearward because it's acting perpendicular to the local relative wind. Any time the total lift is tilted rearward there's less lift acting vertically, right? That can't be good. Rearward acting lift acts just like drag, which is why we call it induced drag (induced by the wing's upwash and downwash).

As soon as the airplane wing enters ground effect, the upwash and downwash angle of the wind diminishes, resulting in slightly straighter airflow over the wing (Figure 23, position B). How can that be? I call it the *solid-object* phenomena. The wind can't come from out of the runway ahead of the airplane nor can the wind be blown into the runway behind it. The solid runway surface straightens out the local relative wind, despite the wing's attempt to bend it, making it more like the relative wind that lies ahead of the airplane. That means the total lifting force must tilt forward slightly to remain perpendicular to the relative wind, thus reducing induced drag.

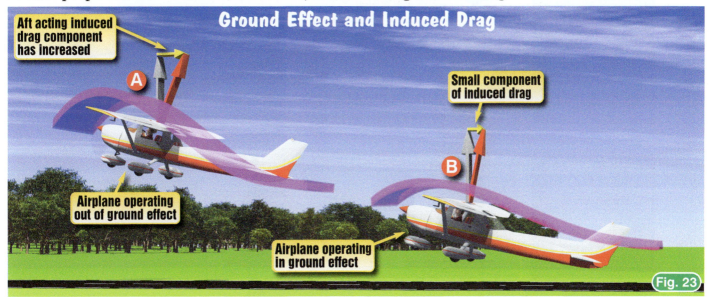

In ground effect (B), the airplane's total lift component (red arrow) points more vertically than aft, thus producing a relatively small aft acting component (yellow arrow) of induced drag. As the airplane moves out of ground effect (A), changes in the wing's *local relative wind* tilt the total lift component rearward, thus increasing the aft-acting component of induced drag.

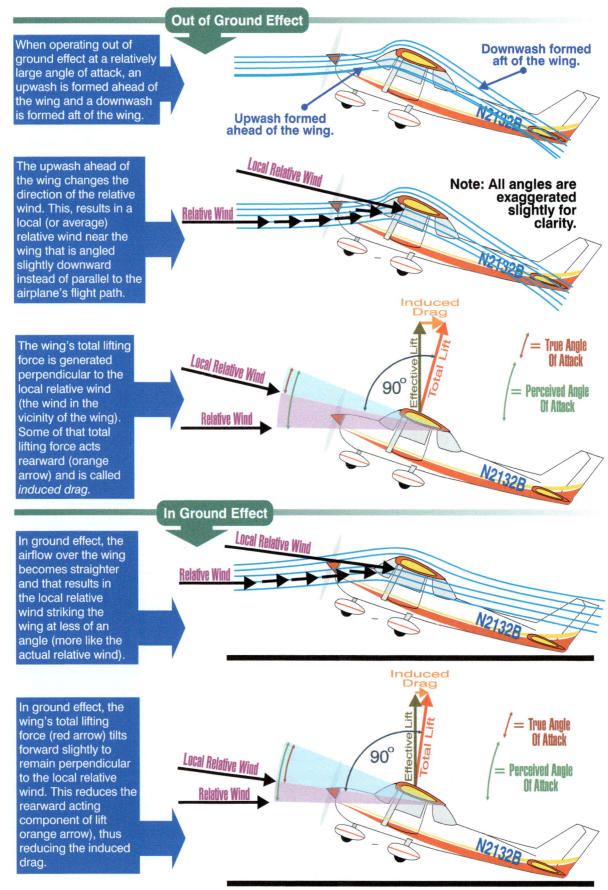

Chapter 6 - Takeoffs and Climbs

Ground effect can begin to affect the airplane when it's within a wingspan's height (30-40 feet for most 2-4 seat GA airplanes) above the runway (Figure 24). The reduction in induced drag, however, becomes most noticeable when the wing is much closer to the runway surface.

For instance, induced drag is reduced by 25% when the airplane's wing is at a height of approximately one-quarter of its wingspan above the ground and by 50% when within one-tenth of its wingspan above the ground. By definition, of course, that means low wing airplanes experience the effects of ground effect a little more than high wing airplanes, unless you like to land inverted (which I don't recommend because you don't have feet on your head).

Ground Effect and Takeoffs

How does ground effect affect you? It's possible for your airplane to become airborne at a slightly lower-than-normal speed in ground effect—a speed at which it can lift off but not climb. If you rush the takeoff and became airborne in ground effect, any attempt at a climb will find you settling back to the runway. And why should you settle for that?

If you became airborne prematurely in ground effect, the best thing to do is keep the airplane close to the runway and accelerate to the proper initial climb speed before attempting to climb. This assumes, of course, that the climb path ahead of you is free of climb-inhibiting obstacles, such as a tree, building or mountain. It also assumes that your departure won't make you an honorary member of DORP—the "Departure Obstructions Removal Program." You don't want the tower paging for a wet cleanup on Runway 32. That's Dorpy.

There's also a slight nose-up pitch change that you'll experience when climbing out of ground effect (Figure 25). Since operating in ground effect reduces the angle of downwash behind the wing, there's less downwash on the horizontal stabilizer. You'll notice this phenomenon when you climb out of ground effect, because the sudden increase in downwash on the tail surface results in the nose pitching upward slightly. This requires you to apply a slight amount of compensating forward pressure on the elevator control to prevent an excessive nose-up attitude.

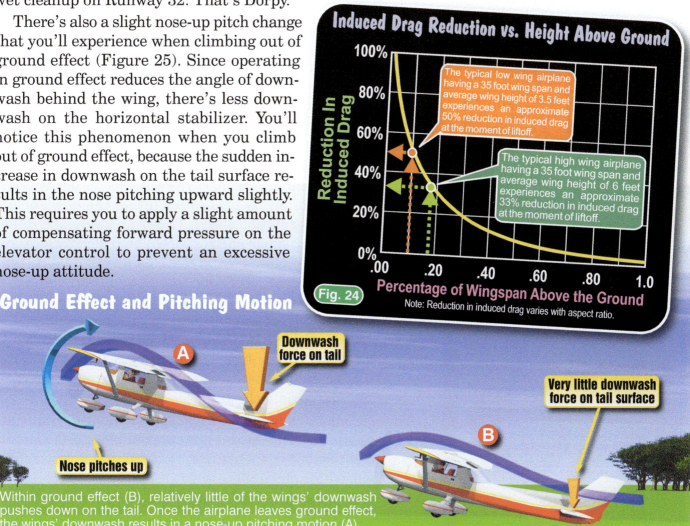

Fig. 24

The typical low wing airplane having a 35 foot wing span and average wing height of 3.5 feet experiences an approximate 50% reduction in induced drag at the moment of liftoff.

The typical high wing airplane having a 35 foot wing span and average wing height of 6 feet experiences an approximate 33% reduction in induced drag at the moment of liftoff.

Note: Reduction in induced drag varies with aspect ratio.

Ground Effect and Pitching Motion

Within ground effect (B), relatively little of the wings' downwash pushes down on the tail. Once the airplane leaves ground effect, the wings' downwash results in a nose-up pitching motion (A).

Fig. 25

Static Pressure Reduction In Ground Effect

Did you know that you're under pressure to understand ground effect? Well, technically speaking, you are. There is a slight increase in local static pressure around your airplane just before and just after leaving the ground. How can that be? It occurs because of the way that air passes between the wing and the ground when the airplane is close to the runway. This results in a slight compression of the local airflow, resulting in an increase in local atmospheric pressure near your static source, which can result in an incorrect static pressure reading.

Why am I giving you static about this? Because it means that your airspeed might read slightly less than normal in this condition. Remember that your airspeed reading is derived from the difference between dynamic air pressure and static air pressure. Make static air pressure greater and your airspeed will read slightly less as a result. Your altimeter will also read a little lower and your vertical speed indicator will indicate a slight descent, too. This shouldn't be a problem for you, since you shouldn't be flying on instruments immediately after takeoff as a VFR pilot. It's just nice to know what's causing your instruments to read strangely when you're not flying in the Bermuda Triangle.

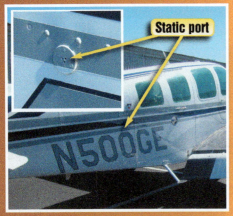

Suppose you allow the airplane to become airborne too soon in ground effect during a high density altitude takeoff (a condition in which airplane performance is often considerably reduced). You might find that you are indeed airborne, but the moment you try climbing out of ground effect, the airplane's nose pitches upward slightly. If you don't correct for this, the increase in angle of attack will generate more induced drag. This can result in your settling back to the runway, much to your chagrin and bent shins if you run into that fence at the end of the airport.

It's also possible to become airborne in ground effect on a high density altitude day and simply be unable to climb out of ground effect. It's like Hotel California—you can check out any time, but you cannot leave. How nice is that? You think you're able to fly because you're actually flying, but you just can't fly higher than permitted by the effect of ground effect. The problem with this is that if you don't recognize that you can't climb, you may go into that fencing at the end of the runway. And that's not the way to get into fencing—the type of fencing that you learn for fun, if you get my point.

The big question is, How do pilots allow themselves to become airborne in ground effect when the airplane can't fly out of it? We discussed this a bit earlier, but it's worthy of additional exploration. It's true that I told you earlier that you should lift off when the airplane feels like it's ready to fly. I also said that this isn't the only clue you should use. You should also use airspeed and control response to help you make this judgment.

Then again, if you have a short runway or have obstacles in the distance, it's often natural to try lifting the airplane off below your normal rotation speed. This is an automatic reflex that you need to recognize and resist. On high density altitude days, you'll want to place a little more emphasis on ensuring that you have sufficient speed for liftoff before attempting to actually lift off. You'll also want to rotate to a lower attitude than you would when departing at an airport under lower density altitude conditions. If you do manage to lift off at a speed below your targeted climb speed, it's perfectly reasonable to lower the nose and accelerate the airplane in ground effect to achieve the appropriate climb speed.

There is one time, however, when you should use ground effect to become airborne at the slowest possible speed. Care to guess when that is? It's when you're departing a very rough or soft field, where any unnecessary ground run could possibly snag or damage the gear. This is called a *soft-field takeoff* and we'll discuss the procedure soon. Wow, I had no idea your kung fu was so strong. You've compelled me to discuss it next.

Chapter 6 - Takeoffs and Climbs

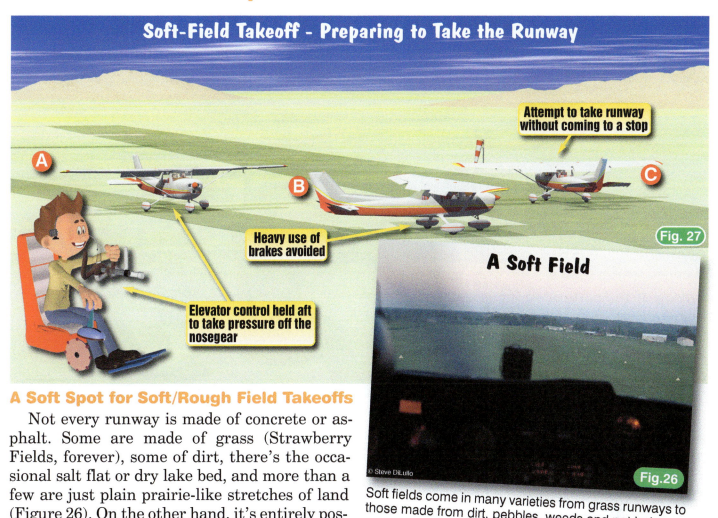

Fig. 27

Fig. 26 Soft fields come in many varieties from grass runways to those made from dirt, pebbles, weeds and pot holes.

A Soft Spot for Soft/Rough Field Takeoffs

Not every runway is made of concrete or asphalt. Some are made of grass (Strawberry Fields, forever), some of dirt, there's the occasional salt flat or dry lake bed, and more than a few are just plain prairie-like stretches of land (Figure 26). On the other hand, it's entirely possible that you may have landed on dry sod (grass) only to have it rain and you must now depart on soft, wet sod, which could be a sod story if you didn't know how to do this properly. That's why you need to know how to make a soft-field takeoff (not to mention where to buy glow-in-the-dark mud flaps).

Your objective in making a soft-field takeoff is to transfer the weight of the airplane from the tires to the wings as soon as possible, while protecting the nose gear from damage during the takeoff roll. Normally, we don't associate an obstacle with a soft-field takeoff, so our main concern is to avoid letting the airplane get bogged down in the soft-field or having the landing gear be damaged by any rough spots in the field (divots, holes, rocks, etc.).

Your first concern when taxiing on a field that's really soft is to avoid coming to a complete stop (Figure 27, position A). If you aren't moving, there's a good chance you're sinking and it's entirely possible you'll need to call a tow truck to get unstuck from the mud. This is a big problem because the American Automobile Association only recognizes requests for auto assists. You'd have to call an aircraft mechanic to assist you with your dud in the mud.

To minimize the chance that this will happen when taxiing a tricycle-geared airplane, hold that elevator control all the way back to reduce the pressure on the airplane's nose gear (Figure 27, positions A and B). If possible, plan on taxiing to the runway, then onto it, and then into the takeoff roll all without stopping (Figure 27, position C).

This means that you will most likely need to complete the runup where the airplane is parked or at a place where the ground doesn't act like a giant strip of no-fly paper with the potential to bog down your forward motion. You certainly don't want to sacrifice safety to do this. Only taxi onto a

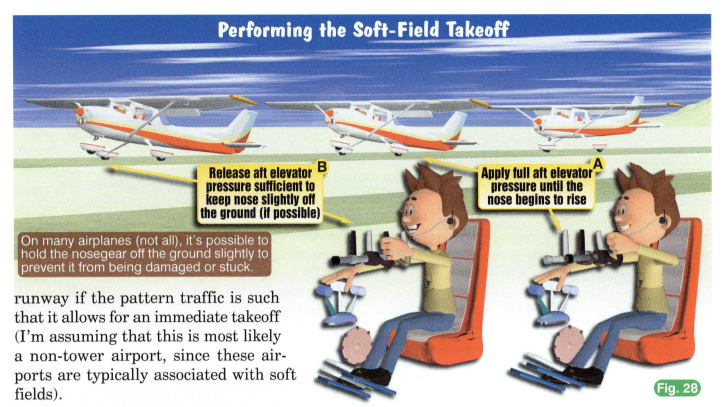

Fig. 28

runway if the pattern traffic is such that it allows for an immediate takeoff (I'm assuming that this is most likely a non-tower airport, since these airports are typically associated with soft fields).

Of course, before takeoff you'll also want to select the appropriate amount of flaps recommended for the soft-field takeoff procedure. Most POHs recommend the use of 10 to 25 degrees of flap deflection for soft-field takeoffs to help make the transition from ground to air a bit quicker. This does vary between airplanes, so be sure to consult your POH.

As you taxi onto the runway and align yourself for takeoff, avoid excessive use of the brakes. Excessive braking might cause your wheels to dig into the soft field and call a sudden halt to the proceedings (and to you being able to proceed). Once aligned with the runway and while you're moving, you'll slowly apply full power for takeoff while holding the elevator fully aft (Figure 28, position A).

In some airplanes with a relatively long fuselage (*long coupled* airplanes) or airplanes with a T-tail, the nose-gear typically rises off the ground while the main wheels remain in contact with the runway. This is a very good thing and you want it to happen. You're popping a wheelie for a reason, and it's not about showing off, either (although it can improve your status if Harley bikers are watching, but only if your tattoo doesn't say, "I Love My Momma").

If your airplane is capable of pitching up during the takeoff roll, then adjust the elevator pressure to keep the nose wheel a few inches off the runway as the airplane accelerates (Figure 28, position B). Don't, however, let the tail strike the runway surface, which is a slightly more common and unplanned occurrence in T-tail airplanes because of the aerodynamic effectiveness of that tail structure. A tail strike can damage the tail and its surrounding structure. You have to know how your airplane responds during a short-field takeoff, which is something an instructor can help you understand.

As you apply full power for takeoff, make sure you move the elevator control forward enough to prevent the nose from coming up too high. It's perfectly acceptable to continue the takeoff roll in this attitude with the nose gear wheel held a few inches off the ground. Remember, your objective is to transfer the airplane's weight from the wheels to the wings as quickly as possible while protecting the nose wheel to the greatest degree possible.

Chapter 6 - Takeoffs and Climbs

Soft-Field Takeoffs in Short Coupled Airplanes

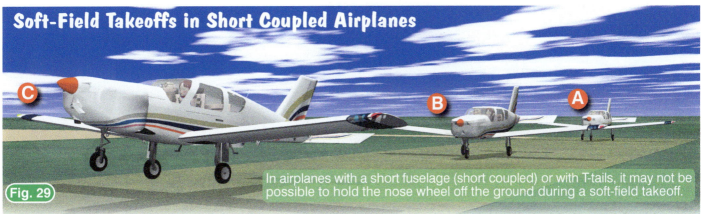

In airplanes with a short fuselage (short coupled) or with T-tails, it may not be possible to hold the nose wheel off the ground during a soft-field takeoff.

Fig. 29

In airplanes having a relatively short fuselage, you might not be able to hold the airplane's nose gear off the ground during the takeoff roll. Trying to do so could cause the nose to pitch up aggressively just before liftoff, with a tail strike being a possible result. The best you can do in these airplanes is to hold the elevator back as far aft as reasonable during the takeoff roll to reduce pressure on the nose gear (Figure 29, positions A and B). When the aft-held yoke feels like it's about ready to lift the nose, quickly move the yoke forward just enough to keep the pressure off the nose gear without causing the airplane to over-rotate and strike the tail.

Once again, the rotation response varies with airplanes and this is why having a good instructor prepares you for the behavioral quirks of individual airplanes.

Regardless of the attitude you have during the takeoff roll, you'll want to immediately lower the nose as soon as the airplane becomes airborne (Figure 30, positions A and B). This is very important. You don't—DON'T—want to try and climb in the steep pitch attitude you're likely to have immediately after rotation during a short-field takeoff. If you tried to climb at this attitude, you probably wouldn't climb and if you did manage to climb for just a bit, it would be a very short bit before it would bite. Your airplane might easily stall in this condition. Thanks, but no thanks. Lower the nose immediately after liftoff to remain a foot or two above the runway in ground effect and accelerate to at least Vx before continuing your climb at Vy, as shown in Figure 30, positions A to B (unless, of course, there's a reason for you to use Vx to avoid an obstacle).

As a practical matter, it doesn't matter how close to the ground you are during the acceleration as long as your wheels don't touch the surface. If you're six inches off the

Soft-Field Takeoff - After Liftoff

After lift off, lower nose and accelerate to best rate of climb speed

Retract flaps in increments

Accelerate to Vx in ground effect

After liftoff in the soft-field condition, you must immediately lower the nose and accelerate to at least Vx in ground effect before continuing the climb.

Fig. 30

After a soft-field takeoff in a retractable geared airplane, let the airplane accelerate, then retract the landing gear first, followed by the remaining flaps in increments.

Fig. 31

ground as you accelerate, then good for you, as long as there is no vegetation or rocks seven inches off the ground. Remember, the airplane has lifted off just above stall speed, which is below the speed at which you normally lift off. So please take advantage of ground effect to help accelerate the airplane before continuing to climb at Vy in this instance.

As the airplane establishes a positive rate of climb after liftoff (meaning that you are moving away from the ground) as shown in Figure 30, position C, you'll want to raise the flaps in increments. Ten degree increments or one notch of flaps at a time is often satisfactory. If you're flying an airplane with retractable landing gear, then you'll want to raise the gear and then the flaps, in that order (Figure 31). Why in that order? Remember that you probably had 50% or less of the flaps deployed for takeoff. So the flaps are already in the "max-lift, low-drag" condition. Therefore, once the airplane is accelerating in ground effect and a positive rate of climb is established, then the landing gear should be retracted. You must, however, be careful not to let the airplane settle back onto the soft field as you're accelerating close to the ground in ground effect.

If there's snow on the runway or the runway is wet, it's best to delay retracting the gear just long enough to let the liquid, snow or mud blow off. You don't want water or mud to collect on the gear mechanism or in the wheel wells and freeze. Frozen liquid or mud certainly won't make the gear work better. If it did, the airplane manufacturer would have put little refrigerators on the wheels, right? Think about it. When was the last time you heard a mechanic say to a pilot, "Bob, if you throw a little frozen mud on those wheels, I bet it will solve those pesky gear problems you've been having." Yeah, I bet you haven't heard that one before.

Most of the time, however, it's not a soft field that poses a problem for a pilot. More often, it's a field that's too short or it's one having an obstacle carefully placed on the departure end of the runway. Let's see how to handle takeoffs in these situations.

Chapter 6 - Takeoffs and Climbs

Short Field Takeoffs

Size *does* matter, at least when it comes to runways. Contrary to what some believe, runway length isn't determined by the amount of asphalt or concrete that was on hand the day the runway was built. It's not the case that when materials ran short, the engineers put big white numbers on the end and simply called it day (and a threshold).

In reality, runway size is often based on the purpose of the airport, property size, obstacles in the peripheral area, desired length, cost and so on. Not all runways are created equal. Some are as short or shorter than 1,300 feet, while others can be over two miles long (Figure 32). Some shorter runways even have obstacles on their departure end. That's why you need to know how to make a short-field takeoff with and without an obstacle off the departure end.

The objective of the short-field takeoff is to get the airplane off the runway in the shortest ground run possible. Since it's also reasonable to assume that a runway might have been built shorter because there was either a natural or manmade obstacle off the departure end, we'll want to know how to combine a short-field takeoff with an obstacle clearance procedure (Figure 33).

Variable Length Runways — Fig. 32

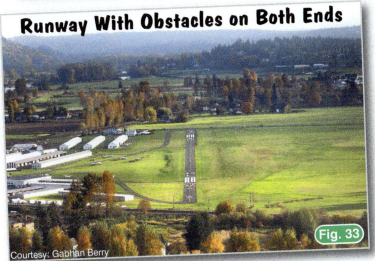
Runway With Obstacles on Both Ends — Fig. 33
Courtesy: Gabhan Berry

Use the procedures recommended in your POH for the short-field takeoff. Not all procedures are the same, as you'll soon see.

Instructor Complacency Doesn't Mean All is Well

A Bonanza A36 pilot receiving recurrent training in short-field takeoff procedures assumed (incorrectly) that if the instructor was not intervening, things must be OK.

Conditions were VMC and Runway XX was in use with ATIS reporting winds calm. I Successfully executed a simulated short-field takeoff with 50-foot obstacle…and simulated short-field landing with 50-foot obstacle…. My next activity after a full-stop and taxi back… was a simulated soft-field takeoff with 50-foot obstacle. I put in approach flaps and confirmed rotation and climb speeds prior to entering runway. I [lined up and waited]… per the controller's instruction.

Once cleared for takeoff, I increased throttle to full while holding yoke back fully and adding right rudder. The aircraft yawed left when the nose wheel lifted so I input additional right rudder. the Aircraft continued to turn left requiring increasing amounts of right rudder to stay on runway and turn aircraft back toward centerline. The main gear lifted off the runway surface so I reduced back pressure on yoke. I observed right wing dropping and attempted to correct this through yoke and rudder inputs. Thereafter, I continued with unsuccessful attempts to stabilize the airplane. My instructor called out, "My plane," and took control…. In the process of recovery, landing, and rollout, the aircraft departed the runway surface for the grass area to the left of the runway and impacted a taxiway sign. He stopped the aircraft on the taxiway and observed damage to left flap. He decided not to retract the flaps. He radioed the tower and confirmed that we did not require assistance and intended to return to the hangar…. We returned to hangar and observed damage to left wing tip, left flap and wing surface at flap attach point, and left horizontal stabilizer….

Here are my initial thoughts as to cause. I believe a misunderstanding of my instructor's instructions and his corresponding control inputs along with my mistaken assumption that he was not intervening, implied that everything was OK. These, unfortunately, were the primary factors in the destabilization of the aircraft and subsequent off-runway landing…. My conclusion? Don't become complacent because you are with an instructor. Fly and make decisions as you would if you were alone. **ASRS Report (Modified)**

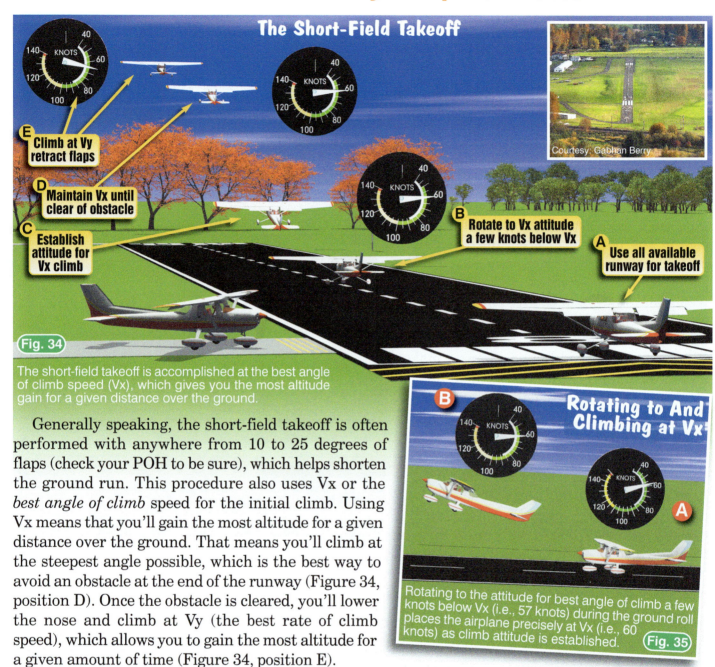

Fig. 34 The short-field takeoff is accomplished at the best angle of climb speed (Vx), which gives you the most altitude gain for a given distance over the ground.

Fig. 35 Rotating to the attitude for best angle of climb a few knots below Vx (i.e., 57 knots) during the ground roll places the airplane precisely at Vx (i.e., 60 knots) as climb attitude is established.

Generally speaking, the short-field takeoff is often performed with anywhere from 10 to 25 degrees of flaps (check your POH to be sure), which helps shorten the ground run. This procedure also uses Vx or the *best angle of climb* speed for the initial climb. Using Vx means that you'll gain the most altitude for a given distance over the ground. That means you'll climb at the steepest angle possible, which is the best way to avoid an obstacle at the end of the runway (Figure 34, position D). Once the obstacle is cleared, you'll lower the nose and climb at Vy (the best rate of climb speed), which allows you to gain the most altitude for a given amount of time (Figure 34, position E).

Keep in mind that Vx is slower than Vy. Sometimes significantly slower. The point here is that when climbing at Vx, you're closer to stall speed than when climbing at Vy. So you have to be careful about maintaining your airspeed (your attitude) during departure to prevent it from becoming too slow.

The other reason to carefully monitor your attitude and maintain the designated airspeed is that even a slight variation from Vx can dramatically reduce the airplane's climb performance. Slow to less than Vx and you might see a several hundred feet per minute reduction in climb rate. That might result in turning a 50-foot obstacle into a 49-foot obstacle and a one-foot cockpit decoration. On the other hand, let your speed increase above Vx and you'll definitely see an increase in your rate of climb. But that's a good thing, right? Wrong. It's not at all good during a short-field takeoff because while the climb rate increases slightly, the angle of climb decreases (see Figure 18 on Page 6-14). It's the angle of climb that you want to maximize during the short-field takeoff.

The first step in making a short-field takeoff is to place the flaps at their recommended departure setting. Then taxi to the very beginning of the runway, or at least the first point where a takeoff is

Chapter 6 - Takeoffs and Climbs

allowed, as shown in Figure 34, position A (you can take off prior to the displaced threshold, but you can't land in this area). Make sure that you use all the runway for takeoff. This doesn't, however, mean holding the airplane on the ground until reaching the end of the runway.

Some instructors recommend that you keep the airplane rolling as you taxi onto the runway (if possible) since this helps minimize the runway required for takeoff. Other pilots recommend that you taxi into position and hold, apply the brakes, apply full throttle, and release the brakes once the engine has achieved full power production.

As a practical matter, you won't find your short-field takeoff performance enhanced by stopping on the runway and powering up before takeoff. In most airplanes, stopping on the runway while applying full power and holding the brakes doesn't allow the engine to develop its maximum takeoff power, mainly because the propeller RPM can't achieve its maximum value unless the airplane begins to move. There's a lot of drag on a spinning propeller when the airplane's not in motion. Since horsepower is a function of RPM, a static power-up doesn't necessarily allow the engine to develop its maximum available power.

On the other hand, if the airplane is already in motion and you have a takeoff clearance, it doesn't make sense to stop on the runway only to accelerate again. Airplanes have inertia, and it takes a lot of energy just to get several thousand pounds of airplane moving. So why stop just to get it moving again? For the minimum takeoff roll, keep the airplane in motion as you taxi onto the runway, then apply full power for takeoff.

Since you'll climb at Vx after liftoff, rotate a few knots below this value, depending on the performance of your airplane. Keep in mind that the airplane is still accelerating during rotation. By choosing to rotate a few knots below Vx (Figure 35, position A), you'll find that you'll be very close to Vx as you establish your initial climb attitude (Figure 35, position B).

Some airplanes want to leave the ground before reaching Vx, and that's just fine. You don't want to hold an airplane like that on the ground against its will. Doing so might cause the airplane to

The Best Angle (Vx) and Best Rate (Vy) of Climb Speed

In the picture below, you'll see the Rate of Climb vs. Airspeed Graph. The magenta curve in the middle represents the rate of climb (ROC) on the vertical speed indicator. At 40 knots (the airplane's clean stall speed), there's zero rate of climb (position A). The top of the magenta curve represents the maximum rate of climb (position B). The maximum speed in level flight (position C) also represents a zero rate of climb. Now for the details.

Vx is the best angle of climb speed (position D). At this speed the airplane gains the most altitude (vertical movement) for a given distance (horizontal movement) over the ground.

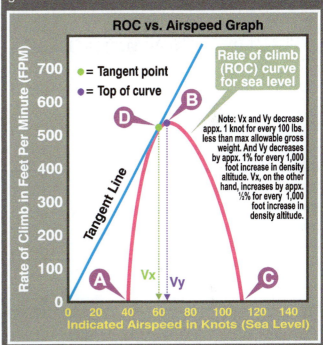

The blue line "Tangent Line" is tangent to the rate of climb curve and the point at which it intersects the ROC curve represents the speed (drop straight down to the IAS scale) for the best angle of climb. Here's why. If I placed you in the far left hand corner of the reference box at the 0-FPM and 0-airspeed corner and asked you to look up from that position and point to the highest part of the ROC curve that you could see, your arm would point directly to the tangent point on the graph (identified by the green dot). Mathematically speaking, the upward angle of this tangent line represents the maximum amount of vertical gain for a given amount of horizontal movement to the right (based on the 0-0 starting position). If you drop straight down from the tangent point (green dot), you'll see that the best angle of climb is achieved at an airspeed of 60 knots at sea level for this airplane. Therefore, Vx is 60 knots (indicated) at sea level.

What about the speed for the best rate of climb (Vy)? Isn't this where you have the greatest amount of altitude gain for a given amount of time. Isn't this just another way of saying that at the best rate of climb speed the VSI needle has the greatest upward deflection? Indeed, it is. Therefore, the greatest rate of climb is show by the very top of the ROC curve (the green dot). If you drop straight down from this point you'll find the speed for the best rate of climb speed (Vy) for this airplane is 65 knots.

wheelbarrow on the nose gear. Wheelbarrowing could compress the nose gear sufficiently to restrict your ability to steer, or it could damage the gear structure. So allow the airplane to lift off if it insists, but make sure to lower the nose sufficiently to accelerate to Vx before beginning your climb.

It's important to maintain the attitude for Vx during the initial climb and not let the airspeed vary. In this transitory condition, you really don't have enough time to apply trim to maintain the optimal attitude, because by the time you do you'll most likely be over the obstacle. I want you concentrating on your attitude and airspeed rather than fumbling with the trim wheel. Once you've cleared the obstacle, lower the nose to the attitude for Vy, retract the gear and flaps, then trim.

Wait a minute. Why do I want you to keep your gear and flaps extended during the climb over the obstacle? Doesn't an airplane climb better with its gear retracted? Yes it does. However, you don't want to be distracted by finagling with your gear and flap handles when there's an obstacle ahead of you. Nor should your attention be diverted from attitude/airspeed control when you're operating at a speed closer to stall. The last thing you want is to stall during a short-field departure, only to end up in some tree off the end of the runway. Good pilots always avoid getting themselves into situations that require using phrases such as, "See me, I'm in the tree?"

It won't take long to climb over a 50-foot obstacle, so gear and flaps won't be much of a concern in these instances (Figure 36, position A). Then again, if the obstacle is farther off the departure end of the runway and a lot higher than 50 feet, you'll want to get your gear up as soon as you've established a positive rate of climb (Figure 36, position B). This is where it's a matter of weighing the risk of a gear distraction with obstacle impaction. Flying is all about risk management and sometimes you have to make the best choices based on the cards you've been dealt (or that you've dealt to yourself). Once you're over the obstacle and have reached a safe maneuvering altitude, reduce power to climb power (if you're in a complex airplane).

So far, we've spoken as if every takeoff roll inevitably results in a takeoff. That's not always true. There may well be takeoff rolls where you suddenly decide that you don't want to continue the takeoff. Perhaps something doesn't sound or feel quite right, you forgot your box lunch, or you spot a tornado

Fig. 36

Chapter 6 - Takeoffs and Climbs

at the departure end of the runway. This stop-after-go procedure is called a *rejected takeoff* and it's something at which you should be proficient.

Rejected Takeoffs

A rejected takeoff doesn't result in a country-and-western song. No feelings are hurt in the making of a rejected takeoff. Pilots normally reject a takeoff when there's a good reason not to fly. For instance, you might hear strange sounds coming from the engine or airframe. The engine might suddenly begin to run rough, or it might not be producing the necessary power required for flight. Sometimes a foreign object or an animal such as a squirrel appears on the runway, necessitating an immediate rejection of the takeoff lest the rubber meet the rodent. If the density altitude is high, you might reject the takeoff if the airplane just isn't meeting your expectation for acceleration (see sidebar: *Takeoff Expectations*). There are an infinite number of reasons to reject a takeoff, and you should be ready, willing, and able to stop rolling if you're not convinced everything is good to go.

There are two times when you can reject the takeoff: either before lifting off or after lifting off (yes, it's still a rejected takeoff even if you've already taken off). Clearly, it's better to reject a takeoff before lifting off. Once the airplane's wheels leave the surface, you will consume a great deal of runway (if there's any runway left to consume) if you abort the landing. A typical small, fixed gear airplane might use a total of 2,400 feet to take off, climb to 50 feet, then

Takeoff Expectations

There are many rules of thumb in aviation, including one for estimating when to abort a takeoff. The rule says you should have achieved 70% of your liftoff speed at the runway's halfway point. If you haven't reached this airspeed value, then pull the power and stop the airplane.

The only problem with rules of thumb is that we often forget the thumb part. For instance, the 70-50 rule certainly works on a long runway, since airplanes can stop much more quickly than they can accelerate. Departing on a 10,000 foot runway, even under higher density altitude conditions, leaves you the luxury of 5,000 feet to stop if you haven't hit the 70% mark halfway down. Try that on a 1,800 foot runway at higher density altitude conditions and you will be surprised at how short 900 feet looks.

If we assume that most small airplanes can be stopped in 500 to 1,000 feet, 900 feet sounds reasonable if somewhat lacking in any margin for error. And therein lies the problem. Remember, it's a rule of thumb, meaning approximations are involved. Exactly where *is* the midpoint of the runway? There's no standard marking for that. Judging where that spot might be is particularly challenging when you're accelerating and the runway is really short. Then you have to factor in a slight amount of time for a delay in deciding to bail out—such decisions are often preceded by hesitation. Mix these and other factors together and you could just end up with an expensive dirt bike instead of an airplane.

While rules of thumb are quite valuable, they shouldn't be the only source upon which to base your takeoff decision. Most of the time the performance charts in your POH are the best source for takeoff information as shown below. Ultimately, you use the performance chart to see if a takeoff is even theoretically possible, then combine this with your rule of thumb and rules of common sense to arrive at a much clearer understanding of whether a takeoff should even be attempted.

In the accompanying figure, the accelerate-stop distance at a pressure altitude of 5,000 feet with an OAT of 41 degrees F is approximately 1,577 feet. So it seems that you'd have no difficulty accelerating to liftoff speed then bringing the airplane to a stop on a runway that's 1,800 feet in length. Having acquired this information, I'd feel much more comfortable applying my 70-50 rule of thumb for departure, knowing that if I didn't reach at least 70% of my takeoff speed by the runway's midpoint I'd probably have sufficient distance to stop the airplane. If, however, my calculated accelerate-stop distance was exactly 1,800 feet, I'd be less inclined to give this takeoff a try despite having a defined point where I'd abort the takeoff. And always make sure to read the notes associated with every performance chart, too.

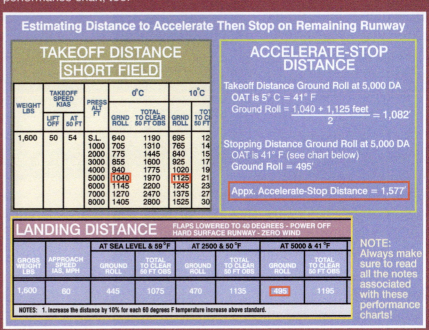

come to a stop on the end of the runway (Figure 37). This distance can be a lot longer if you're operating a complex airplane, as we previously discussed (Figure 38).

The best option, of course, is to reject the takeoff before your wheels leave the ground. The moment you decide to abort, you should pull the power back quickly and apply brakes promptly, without causing the tires to skid. This means that you should expect to apply increasing brake pedal pressure as the airplane decelerates. In fact, the majority of your braking effectiveness takes place in the latter portion of your landing roll. So apply the maximum permissible brake pressure possible without skidding those tires.

While applying the brakes, you must make sure that you also apply elevator back pressure to prevent excessive compression of the nose-strut (Figure 39), which might induce wheelbarrowing or nose-strut oscillation or difficulty in maintaining directional control.

Then again, if the airplane is moving fast enough when you initially reject the takeoff, you'll want to release sufficient

A typical small fixed-gear airplane might use several thousand feet of runway to reject a takeoff that involves a climb to 50 feet above the runway then stopping. (Fig. 37)

Under the same conditions, a complex (higher performance) airplane can use considerably more runway length during an aborted takeoff. (Fig. 38)

Compressing a Nose-Strut Excessive brake application can result in a compressed nose strut leading to wheelbarrowing. Compressed nose strut (Fig. 39)

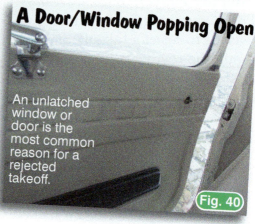

A Door/Window Popping Open An unlatched window or door is the most common reason for a rejected takeoff. (Fig. 40)

back pressure to ensure that the airplane's weight is transferred to the wheels. Braking at a high speed while holding the elevator slightly aft could result in skidding the tires, turning your Goodyears into a *bad year* for your budget.

Of course, if you reject the takeoff because you suspect an engine or electrical fire, you'll pull the power, apply brakes while maintaining directional control, come to a stop, pull the mixture, turn off the mags and get out of the airplane pronto. I probably didn't need to tell you to get out of the airplane quickly, did I? Hot tip.

Chapter 6 - Takeoffs and Climbs

Care to guess what the most likely reason is that pilots reject a takeoff? Good guess. It's when a window or door pops open during takeoff acceleration (Figure 40). As I mentioned earlier, takeoff is the time when doors and windows are most likely to pop open, because of the sudden change in pressure in and around the cockpit.

The big problem with doors and windows opening on takeoff is that there's a sudden increase in noise. That often scares the pilot into doing something he or she later regrets. During the takeoff, if a door or window pops open, it's perfectly reasonable to abort the takeoff, but only if you're sure you have sufficient runway on which to land. If not, then it's often safer to continue the takeoff, fly the airplane around the pattern normally and land normally.

Almost all general aviation single-engine airplanes can fly with a side door or side window open with very little compromise in performance. Your airplane will most likely fly and land just fine as long as you fly it and land it just fine (that means landing the way you normally do). If possible (but only if you have the skill to do so), just before coming to a complete stop, try holding onto the door to keep it from arching forward and bending a hinge.

So, you've now achieved a takeoff, which is among other things a prerequisite for a landing. After all, what good is a takeoff if you can't do anything with it? There are some interesting and useful things to do in between takeoff and landing, and in the next chapter we'll explore one of them—ground maneuvers. You won't need to enlist in the Army to participate. These are activities where you develop your skill at maneuvering around some reference on the ground in order to prepare for the big prize at the flying circus—landings!

Postflight Briefing #6-1 Density Altitude

Density Altitude

Taking off at an airport near sea level usually results in good acceleration and climb performance. The elevation has no effect on performance, temperatures are usually moderate, and the humidity is generally not too high. If we take off from an airport situated at 100 feet MSL, the airplane performs quite well.

Suppose, however, that it's an extraordinarily hot day at our 100 foot MSL airport. Will the airplane perform well? No. Because of the high heat, the air might have a density equivalent to an altitude around 3,000 feet. The term *density altitude* describes how dense the air feels to the airplane, regardless of the airplane's present height above sea level. Density altitude is an extremely important term for you to understand.

In the previous example, even though the airplane was physically at 100 feet MSL, in terms of *airplane performance* the airport has a density altitude of 3,000 feet.

If you've read *Rod Machado's Private Pilot Handbook*, you know that *pressure altitude* was the reference to which airplane engineers calibrate their performance charts. Pressure altitude is what the altimeter indicates when 29.92 inches Hg is set in the altimeter's Kollsman window. In addition to the pressure altitude reference, engineers also calibrate many of their performance charts to a standard temperature of 59 degrees F (15 degrees C) at sea level.

Engineers call the conditions of 29.92 inches Hg and 59 degrees F (15 degrees C) at sea level *standard conditions*. Since you must have a starting point or reference when calibrating the performance of airplanes (and their instruments), standard conditions at sea level is a good starting place. For example, when you ask the teacher how your son Bobby is doing in school, he or she normally compares his performance to that of a previous year. The teacher might say, "Well, compared to last year, Bobby is doing better." If the teacher said, "Well, in reference to all forms of animal and plant life on this planet, little Bobby is holding his own against most species of protozoa," then Bobby is in trouble. Standard temperature and pressure conditions are simply a reference point where a baseline of performance is established.

Of course, if standard conditions existed at sea level all the time, we wouldn't have to worry about changes in air density and its effects on airplane performance. Unfortunately, Mother Nature doesn't like constant, standard conditions (that's why a tornado is similar to a divorce or an earthquake—one of them is going to get your house).

Let's assume you're at an airport at 4,000 foot MSL and standard conditions exist at sea level. Let's also assume that temperatures decrease at 3.5 degrees F (2 degrees C) per 1,000 feet (by now you know that while this is the engineer's standard lapse rate and is used for instrument calibration, it is seldom the actual lapse rate found in the environment). Under these conditions, the temperature at 4,000 feet should be 45 degrees F (4x3.5=14 and 59-14=45 degrees F). Suppose it's really hot, say 100 degrees F (38 degrees C) at 4,000 feet (this is definitely a non-standard temperature). Is the airplane going to perform like it normally would at 4,000 feet? Definitely not. In fact, the airplane is going to perform more like it's at 7,500 feet (I'll show you how I arrived at this value in just a moment).

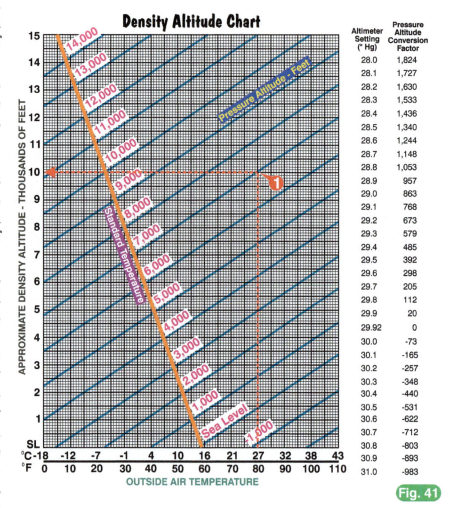

Fig. 41

Because of the higher than normal temperature, the air has a density altitude—a performance altitude, if you want to think of it that way—of approximately 7,500 feet. Think of density altitude as you do personal debt. Whenever debt increases, bad things happen; when debt decreases, good things happen. Increasing density altitude decreases airplane performance; decreasing density altitude increases airplane performance.

Density Altitude Example – Finding the density altitude is easy with the density altitude chart in Figure 41. Along the bottom (horizontal) axis is a temperature scale with Fahrenheit and Celsius markings. Rising diagonally upward from left to right are pressure altitude lines. On the left side of the chart is the density altitude reading along the vertical scale. If you know the pressure altitude and the air temperature for your location, you can easily find the density altitude. Let's see how this works.

Assume your outside air temperature (OAT) is 80 degrees F (27 degrees C) and the pressure altitude is 7,000 feet. Referring to Figure 41, find 80 degrees F (27 degrees C) on the bottom, horizontal scale and move upwards until reaching the 7,000 foot (diagonal) pressure altitude line. Make a mark at this point (position 1) and move horizontally to the left. The number on the left hand vertical scale is the density altitude. In our example the density altitude is 10,000 feet.

Chapter 6 - Takeoffs and Climbs

Postflight Briefing #6-2 Why Vx and Vy Change With Altitude

While you've learned the difference between the best angle of climb speed and the best rate of climb speed, what you might not know is that these speeds change with a change in altitude. So let's take a peek into the mechanics of how this change occurs.

As you know, Vx is the *best angle of climb* speed. At this speed the airplane gains the most altitude (vertical movement) for a given distance (horizontal movement) over the ground. Take a look at Figure 42 which depicts an airplane's rate of climb curve for a given *true airspeed*.

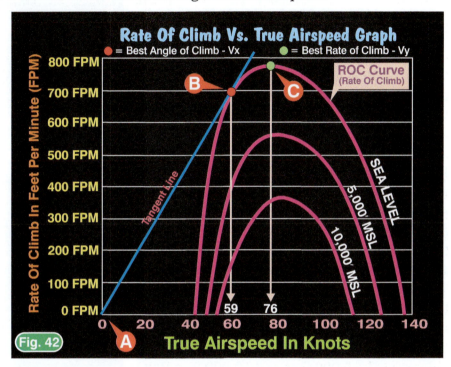

The magenta lines are *rate of climb* curves (rates to the left for a given airspeed on the bottom, horizontal axis). Three curves are shown for performance at sea level, 5,000 feet MSL and 10,000 feet MSL.

Let's say I placed you in the bottom left hand corner of the reference box at the 0-FPM and 0-airspeed corner (position A). If I asked you to look up from that position and point to the highest part of the sea level rate of climb (ROC) curve that you could see, your arm would point up at the same angle of the tangent line shown in the figure at position B. Your arm would point to directly to the tangent point on the graph (identified by the red dot). Mathematically speaking, the upward angle of this tangent line represents the maximum amount of vertical gain for a given amount of horizontal movement (based on your true airspeed shown at the bottom of the graph).

But isn't the maximum amount of vertical gain (or *altitude gain*) for a given distance over the ground also called the *best angle of climb*? Indeed, it is. So if we drop straight down from the tangent point (red dot, position B), we see that the *best angle of climb* is achieved at a true airspeed of 59 knots at sea level. So Vx is 59 knots (TAS) at sea level.

What about the speed for the *best rate of climb*? Isn't this where you achieve the greatest amount of altitude gain in a given amount of time? Isn't this just another way of saying that, at the best rate of climb speed, the VSI needle has the greatest upward deflection? Indeed, it is. Therefore, the greatest rate of climb is identified by the very top of the ROC curve (the green dot, position C). If you drop straight down from this point you'll find the speed for the best rate of climb speed (Vy) for this airplane is 76 knots (true airspeed at sea level).

Keep in mind that I am using *true airspeed* (TAS) in this graph because it allows us to observe the effects of altitude on airplane performance. In other words, true airspeed increases as altitude increases (approximately 2% of your indicated airspeed per 1,000 foot of altitude gain). Using true airspeeds allow you to see how your airspeed varies with a decrease in power as altitude increases (non-turbocharged airplane assumed here). Yes, we actually fly an airplane by looking at the airspeed indicator, which provides *indicated airspeed* (IAS). That's why I plan on showing you how Vx and Vy vary with altitude in terms of TAS first, then I'll show you the same comparison in terms of IAS.

Now, ask yourself what happens to the size and shape of the ROC curve as altitude increases. Since the maximum power (thrust) the engine is capable of producing *decreases* with an increase in altitude, the ROC curve will change shape and grow shorter at higher altitudes (Figure 43). The ROC curve for three different altitudes are shown: *sea level, 5,000 feet MSL, 10,000 feet MSL*. (A non-turbocharged airplane is assumed here.)

It should be clear from Figure 43 that the top of the ROC curve moves down and shifts to the right slightly (positions D, E and F). In addition, a shorter ROC curve causes the "0-0" tangent lines to make less of an upward angle with the horizontal (positions G, H and I). Symbolically speaking, you can think of the lowering tangent line as the path of an airplane climbing at a shallower and shallower angles as a result of an increase in altitude. (The ROC curve shrinks vertically because of a reduction in power, thus ROC decreases. The actual *shape* of the ROC, however, shifts to the right because of changes in drag and in propeller efficiency with altitude.)

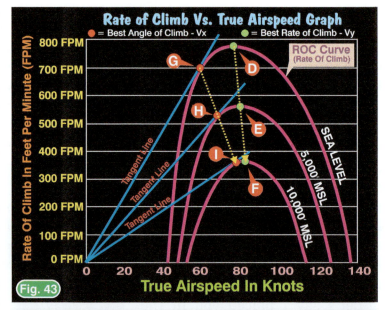

Fig. 43

Dropping straight down from the tangent points for the 5,000 foot and 10,000 foot ROC curves, you'll find that the best angle of climb (Vx) speeds have increased beyond the value found at sea level—59 knots to 69 knots to 77 knots—as shown in Figure 44. Additionally, the best rate of climb speeds (Vy) have increased, too—76 knots to 80 knots to 82 knots.

In terms of true airspeed, both Vx and Vy *increase* with an *increase* in altitude. The reason rests with how the ROC shrinks and shifts to the right as altitude increases.

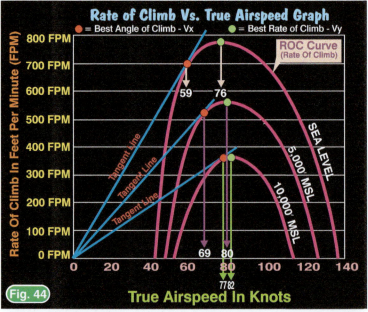

Fig. 44

Let's plot these changing Vx and Vy values as "altitude versus true airspeed" on the graph shown in Figure 45. This figure makes it clear that both Vx and Vy increase with altitude as true airspeeds. But what do they do if we convert true airspeeds into indicated airspeeds? Let's find out.

As a rule of thumb, we know that our true airspeed increases approximately 2% per thousand feet over our indicated airspeed. In

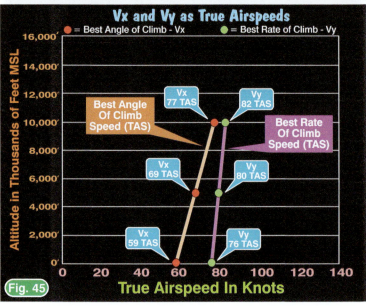

Fig. 45

Chapter 6 - Takeoffs and Climbs

other words, if we're indicating 100 knots at 10,000 feet, then our true airspeed is 20% above this value, or 120 knots. What we need to know now is the indicated airspeed we need to fly in order to produce a certain true airspeed (for sea level, 5,000 feet and 10,000 feet MSL). A simple way to determine these values is with your E6-B flight computer.

Figures 46, 47 and 48 show the E6-B set for standard conditions at sea level, 5,000 feet MSL and 10,000 feet MSL, respectively. You can read the TAS values on the outside scales of each computer in these figures and find their corresponding IAS values on the inside scales (we'll assume that IAS equals *calibrated airspeed* or CAS in these examples).

When you've found these values, they'll look like the plot of indicated airspeeds versus altitude shown in Figure 49. It's clear from this graph that Vx, as an *indicated airspeed*, actually *increases* with altitude while Vy, on the other hand, *decreases* with altitude as an *indicated airspeed* (Figure 49).

Figure 45 makes it clear that the TAS values for Vx increase a little faster than the TAS values for Vy as altitude increases. When you convert these TAS values to IAS values, then it's clear from Figure 49 that both Vx and Vy decrease with altitude, with Vy decreasing a little faster as an IAS than Vx as an IAS.

Thus the two sloped vertical lines will eventually converge and intersect. The point where the intersection occurs is known as the airplane's *absolute ceiling* (Figure 50). This is the point where Vx and Vy are the same (67 knots IAS) and the airplane's rate of climb is now zero. The absolute ceiling for the airplane in this example is 13,000 feet MSL.

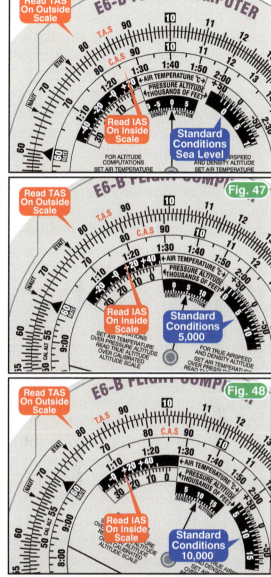

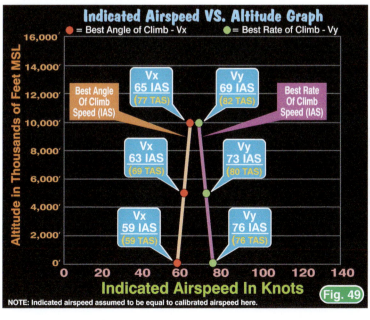

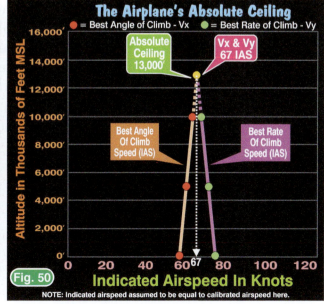

Postflight Briefing #6-3 Preventing Serpentining During the Takeoff Roll

One of the more common issues with student pilots (or even experienced pilots transitioning to different airplanes) is the issue of unintentional *serpentining*. Serpentining is the motion snakes make to move across the ground, mainly because snakes have no legs. In an airplane, unintentional serpentining is the back-and-forth sideways motion made by pilots who are having trouble remaining on the taxiway or runway centerline during taxi, takeoff or landing (Figure 51). Of course, these pilots have legs, but they don't have a leg to stand on when it comes to justifying the behavior. So here's one simple technique that you'll find useful in preventing the airplane from serpentining.

First, the reason pilots typically serpentine is that they overcontrol their rudder pedals. This often occurs because the rudder pedals (and the nose gear mechanism they control) are sometimes stiff and difficult to move. This is a common experience in some light sport airplanes with poorly designed steering mechanisms. It might also occur because the steering mechanism is oversensitive to the touch. So here's how to handle either of these issues.

The easiest way to stop serpentining motion is to apply a quick application of pressure to the rudder, otherwise known as the *pedal pulse*.

If you're attempting to steer the airplane with your feet and find that you're overcontrolling, then try *pulsing* the rudder pedals to stop the serpentining motion. Instead of applying continuous pressure on the rudder pedal, simply apply a pulse to one pedal (quickly push it in and release the pressure) then watch the results. You'll find that this is an effective way to stop the airplane's lateral movement during taxi, takeoff or landing.

Sometimes it might take one, two or even three pulses to return an airplane to the taxi or runway centerline. Then a continuous series of small, spaced pulses might be necessary to keep it there. These pulses are often so small that no one in the cockpit can feel their application.

You will even find the pulse to be effective in flight when transitioning to an airplane that's difficult to control about its longitudinal (roll) axis. Anyone checking out in a twin Cessna 310 knows what I mean. The 310 has its main fuel tanks on the wing tips. Pilots new to the airplane often have a challenging time keeping the wings level the first few hours of flight. A simple pulse on the ailerons stops the serpenting (or rolling oscillations).

You might also find the pulse useful when flying a flight simulator. Sometimes it's very difficult to get the feel for the simulator, which often results in serpentining or rolling motion about one of more of the simulated airplanes axes. So use the pulse, if necessary.

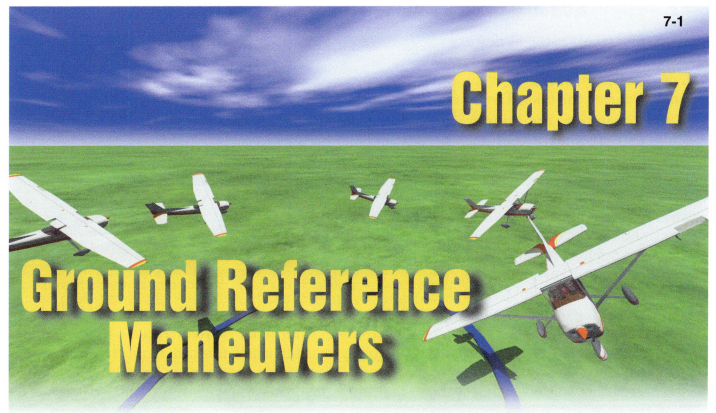

Chapter 7
Ground Reference Maneuvers

You don't need a weatherman
To know which way the wind blows
  Bob Dylan
  Subterranean Homesick Blues

You *don't* need a weatherman, because *you* have ground reference maneuvers and from those you will learn to know which way the wind blows.

Who cares? You do, because you ultimately want to land the airplane and a landing is nothing more than the ultimate ground reference maneuver. It's the primary reason we practice ground reference maneuvers in the first place. And once you get the hang of it, it's a breeze, even with a brisk wind.

This chapter is second in importance only to Chapters Two and Three that cover the fundamentals of flight. Your ability to master the wind, or at least understand how it affects an airplane, is an essential element in being able to land anything that flies and can be piloted (hummingbirds and pterodactyls are excluded). That's why we're going to spend time talking about how the wind affects the airplane during flight.

Let's begin with what happens to the airplane the moment it leaves the ground.

Once Upon a Calm Day

Let's imagine that it's a calm day—a no-wind, you-win situation (and you should run to Vegas and bet big on the wheel because it's your lucky day). Now let's imagine that you are accelerating along the runway and have just rotated to climb attitude. Immediately after liftoff,

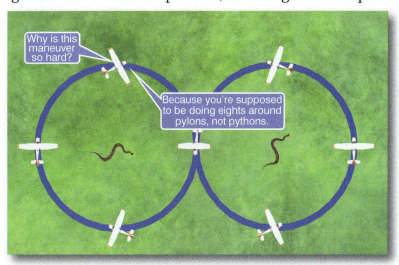

the airplane points straight down the center of the runway, as long as you don't let it get squirrely or hit a squirrel during the takeoff roll.

If you maintain the runway heading, the airplane will continue flying straight down the extended runway centerline. It does so because there is no wind (solar or otherwise) to blow it off that line. This is just another way of saying that the airplane *tracks* the runway centerline (Figure 1). For pilots, the motto is, "Keep on trackin'."

When the wind is perfectly calm, you can point the airplane's nose directly down the runway centerline and the airplane will track directly along that runway centerline.

Think of the term *track* as a reference to the steel rails of a railroad. One thing that's certain about railroad tracks is that they don't move once they're spiked to the ground. They follow an established direction in much the same way an airplane follows a specific path over the ground in a no-wind situation, as long as the heading is constant. Another way of looking at this is that the airplane moves along the ground in the same direction the nose points.

Once there's wind, however, this is no longer true. Game on.

A Wind-Wind Situation

You only have to spend a few hours aloft to begin wondering whether Mother Nature ever intended for an airplane to go where its nose points. She didn't.

Perhaps this explains how pilots who are ignorant of the ways in which wind affects their airplane become lost. They don't so much fly to a specific destination as they unexpectedly arrive at a random one. If it weren't for the airport name on the gas receipt, they wouldn't know what to put in the destination section of their logbook. After awhile, they run out of excuses for their behavior so when they land somewhere they pretend that it's the place they intended to go.

If the wind only blew directly on the nose or tail of every airplane in flight, this chapter would be a lot shorter. In fact, we'd be done by now. Mother Nature, however, is not so accommodating. Most of the time the wind blows at some angle to your intended flight path. Left uncorrected, the effect is to blow the airplane off its intended course. Your job as a pilot is to compensate for this drifting tendency. And just to wind up the wind challenge, the direction from which the wind blows rarely remains constant for very long; it varies both horizontally and vertically as your position changes.

If the wind blows from the north at 20 knots, then the local atmosphere is literally moving across the ground a distance of 20 nautical miles for every hour that passes. If you were in a small hot air balloon and lifted off into this large moving block of wind, you would drift 20 nautical miles in one hour's time, as shown in (Figure 2, position A). Toto, we're not in Kansas any more.

Chapter 7 - Ground Reference Maneuvers

Moving Within a Block of Wind

The balloon is drifting with a block of wind that's moving over the earth at a speed of 20 knots. Without any mechanical form of propulsion, the balloon has a groundspeed of 20 knots.

Moving Within A Moving Block of Wind

The airplane has a true airspeed of 100 knots (we'll let IAS = TAS in these examples). It's flying within a block of air moving at 20 knots that blows directly on the tail of the airplane. Thus, the speed of the airplane over the ground is a combination of the wind speed and true airspeed which gives us a groundspeed of 120 knots.

Moving Within A Moving Block of Wind

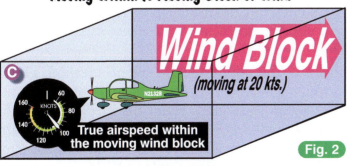

Fig. 2

The airplane has a true airspeed of 100 knots. It's flying within a block of air moving at 20 knots that blows directly on the nose of the airplane. Thus, the speed of the airplane over the ground is the true airspeed minus the wind speed. This gives us a groundspeed of 80 knots.

While drifting, would you feel any wind blowing on you while moving? Not at all (unless it's from localized gusts). That's because you are a stationary object within this moving block of wind (yes, you're an object in this example, deal with it). It's the block of wind that's moving. You, the balloon and the block of wind are all moving the same way, at the same speed. Their speed relative to one another is zero. Stick your arm out over the side of the balloon and you'll find the air to be perfectly still (and other balloonists will think you're signaling to make a turn). In fact, if you didn't look at the ground it's unlikely you'd even know you were moving.

Airplanes also drift with a moving block of wind. In addition to this drift, however, they have forward movement generated by the engine. This movement can be directly with, directly against, or at an angle to the way the block of wind is moving.

The airplane in (Figure 2, position B) has a true airspeed of 100 knots, meaning it is moving at 100 knots through the block of air. The block of air is moving at 20 knots, and as remarkable luck would have it, they are both moving in the identical direction. The airplane's speed over the ground is a combination of the wind and airplane airspeeds. Adding the wind speed to our true airspeed gives us a speed over the ground (groundspeed) of 120 knots. Free speed. Take it while you can, because I'm about to take it back.

The airplane in Figure 2, position C also moves through the block of air at 100 knots. But now the block of air is moving at 20 knots in a direction *opposite* that of the airplane. That's knot as good. We now have a net groundspeed of only 80 knots (100-20=80).

As an aside, it's important to notice that making a 180 degree turn when flying into a 20 knot headwind changes your net groundspeed by 40 knots, not 20 knots (120-80=40). This is why airplanes can have radical changes in their ground tracks and groundspeeds when maneuvering in strong winds. This is one more mighty reason to understand how to maneuver with reference to the ground when wind exists.

Air Bullies

Winds are the bullies of aviation in that they typically push you where you don't want to go. Bad bully! Take a look at what happens to an airplane attempting to follow a road with a wind from the left (Figure 3). While the airplane heads (points) directly down the road in Figure 3, position A, it drifts to the right in Figure 3, positions, B, C and D. Our airplane's *ground track* is a combination of the motion of the airplane and the motion of the air. The angle between the desired course and the actual ground track is called the *drift angle*. It's the amount of air drift by which you're adrift. By determining the drift angle and correcting for it, you can fly a ground track exactly along the chosen course, as shown in Figure 4. This is the aviation equivalent of punching a bully in the nose (or getting one of your homies named Brick Armbar to do it for you).

Let's be clear here. You cannot stop drift (air or continental). What you are going to do is *compensate* so that by flying slightly into the wind, drift acts to put you right where you want to be. You know intuitively how to do this. Think about swimming across a swiftly-moving stream. You know that if you swim straight, the sideways motion of the water will carry you downstream. You have to swim somewhat upstream in order to land directly across from where you started. As a pilot, you have a slipstream rather than a wet stream, but the principle remains the same. You need to swim up the *River Air* a bit.

Flying Without a Wind Correction Angle

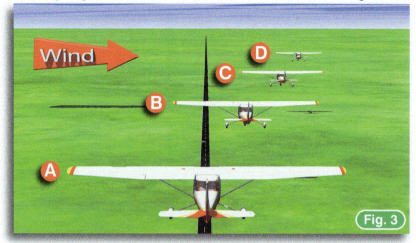

If you don't correct for wind drift, the airplane will drift downwind at a speed equal to the wind speed at your altitude.

Flying With a Wind Correction Angle

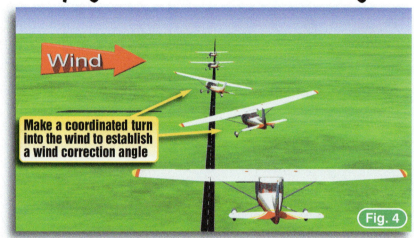

By making a *coordinated* turn into the wind and flying at an angle to the road, a small component of the airplane's speed directly counter's the wind's speed. This is your wind correction angle.

How do you determine the drift angle from the cockpit? You might use the *eyeball* method. That's right. Look out your windscreen at the ground reference you're trying to track and determine the direction of drift. How do you correct for wind drift? Swim upstream. Head the airplane into the wind by making a coordinated turn and rolling out at an angle to the original course that stops the apparent drift and allows you to track the intended ground reference. Get my drift? The amount you turn into the wind to stop the drift is known as the *wind correction angle* or WCA.

Now you're ready to get squared away—well, sort of—because it's time to study your first ground reference maneuver, known as the *rectangular course*. I had a student once who thought I'd said "rectangular Coors" and he kept waiting for a beer can that doesn't roll when you drop it.

But First. . .

There are a few things that apply to *all* the maneuvers we'll discuss in this chapter. It's important to take note of these things, because you will be working at relatively low altitudes and sometimes at

Chapter 7 - Ground Reference Maneuvers

slow speeds and/or steep bank angles. I'll say these things once, with the understanding that you will apply them to every maneuver we're about to discuss.

Mind your FARs. *If* you can meet the requirements of FAR 91.119(c) for being over an uncongested area, then you will perform most of these maneuvers at anywhere from 600 to 1,000 feet AGL and not less than 500 feet above any person, vessel, vehicle or structure (Figures 5A and 5B). If you are over a congested area (Figure 5C and 5D) you must remain at least 1,000 feet above the highest obstacle within a radius of 2,000 feet, in accordance with FAR 91.119(b). A congested area, of course, makes it impossible to perform any maneuver at 1,000 feet AGL unless the houses and buildings are all flattened out to the thickness of a dime. If that's the case, you've entered the alternate dimension of Flatland. So be sure to extend your airplane rental time.

In all the maneuvers that follow, when I propose an altitude of 1,000 feet or less, if you are over a congested area simply adjust that number upward as needed to make you legal. The FARs rule.

Clear. Be doubly certain to always clear the area before each maneuver. You're at an altitude low enough that helicopters, traffic inbound to an airport, crop dusters, and even flying squirrels become traffic factors. You're going to be busy dividing your attention between outside and inside. Make sure you're in the clear before starting.

Fly Coordinated. Always make only a coordinated turn to change direction, even if the change is small. In these maneuvers you will frequently need to make small course changes. Do not—N-O-T—start nudging the nose around using just the rudder. This isn't how you turn an airplane. I *know* it's tempting to just give it a little nudge with the rudder. Don't. Not even a little. In addition to being bad stick-and-rudder technique, this is an invitation to Spin City and you don't want to go there, unexpectedly, at a low altitude.

Limit Your Bank. When performing the maneuvers in this chapter, try keeping bank angles at 45 degrees or less to reduce the risk of stalls. Stall speed does increase a little at 45 degrees of bank, but certainly not as much as it would in a 60 degree bank.

And now we're ready. Even if you're a square, you're about to be rectangular.

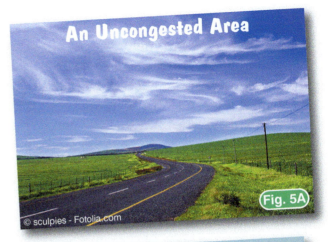
Fig. 5A — An Uncongested Area

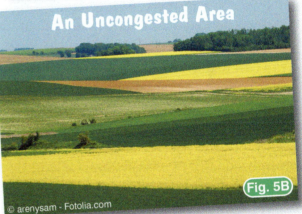
Fig. 5B — An Uncongested Area

Fig. 5C — A Congested Area

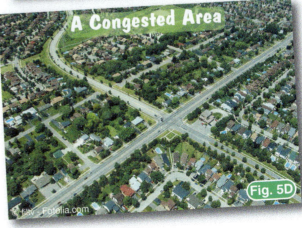
Fig. 5D — A Congested Area

The Rectangular Course

The first ground reference maneuver you're likely to learn in flight training is also the one you're most likely to use, and that's the rectangular course, of course (Figure 6). The *physical objective* of this maneuver is to maintain a ground track that's parallel and offset from a rectangular course while correcting for the effect of wind drift. The *educational objective* is to teach you how to anticipate the effect of wind on your airplane with respect to references on the ground as well as to help you learn to divide your attention between flying the airplane and tracking a ground reference.

The rectangular course uses geometry similar to that used in flying the traffic pattern when approaching to land at an airport. Just to get you in the landing mode and mood, we'll refer to each side of the rectangular course using the same terms we use for the traffic pattern: the *upwind leg*, *crosswind leg*, *downwind leg* and *base leg* as shown in Figure 6 (more on traffic patterns in the next chapter). Master the rectangular course and you're one step closer to being able to land an airplane.

Before you can learn how to track a rectangular course, you need to find one. It's not as if your local flight school uses a bulldozer and an urban renewal permit to dig a rectangular trench through the "hood" that's easily seen from the air and just happens to align most of the time with the wind.

You can usually use a traditional city block or a rectangular field (soccer, football), assuming they have city blocks or rectangular fields where you fly. The ideal is to have each side approximately one mile in length, but you may have to be creative and adaptable. Unless you're a Jedi master with a "road and wind" endorsement on his light saber, it's unlikely you can move roads and alter the wind in search of the perfect rectangle. Sometimes the best you can do is a sub-optimal rectangle where only one side lies at a 90 degree angle to the wind (see *Sometimes You Just Can't Get a Square Deal*).

Let's suppose you've found a rectangular course oriented perpendicular to the wind. Of course, if no wind exists, then tracking those sides is easy. You simply keep the nose pointed parallel with each side as you fly around the perimeter of the course (Figure 6). Easy, huh? Well, hang on a second before you injure yourself patting you on the back.

The Rectangular Course - Without and With Wind

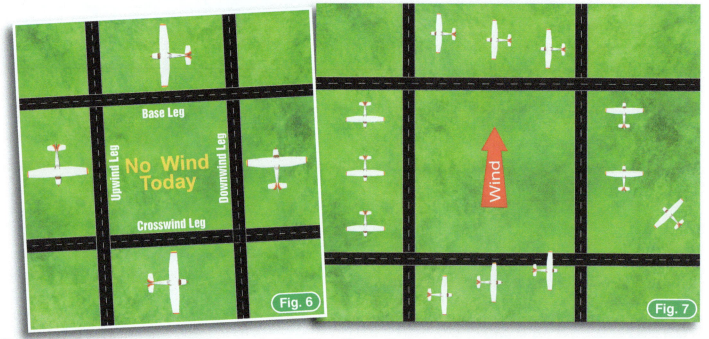

Flying a rectangular course is easy in a no-wind condition (Figure 6). You simply point the airplane's nose parallel to any side of the course and your ground track will remain parallel to the course. Using the same strategy when wind is present (Figure 7), results in the airplane drifting downwind when flown at an angle to the wind's direction.

Sometimes You Just Can't Get a Square Deal

It's unlikely that you know Stribog, the Slavic god of the winds, personally. So it's unlikely that a personal call from you, me or anyone else will convince him to aim his galactic leaf blower in a way that directs the winds precisely perpendicular to the four intersecting roads you selected for your rectangular course. That's why it's doubtful that you'll find a rectangular course having sides precisely aligned with and/or parallel to the prevailing wind.

So be practical. Choose a course with winds blowing as close as possible to 90 degrees (or parallel) to the relevant sides. If you live in a roadless area where it's difficult to find a rectangular course to follow (Picture-1), then improvise. For instance, if you have no official roads because your county still favors the

Picture-1

donkey as its primary means of travel and transport, then find rows of trees or other landmarks you can track from the air. We'll settle for a close approximation of a rectangular course (Picture-2).

Sometimes you can find a rectangular course that lies within the Class D airspace of a tower-controlled airport (Picture-3). If so, and if this course isn't directly in the common path of incoming or outgoing traffic, you've just scored

Picture-2

big time. It's like having a guardian angel with radar. How so? Tower power. The nice controllers in the tower are going to help look out for you. No extra charge. By asking the tower controller if you can practice your rectangular course maneuver within their airspace, you let them know you're there. They in turn are likely to direct traffic away from you whenever possible. If that doesn't happen, you at least have the controller advising other airplanes of your location, altitude and intentions and giving you a heads-up as well. Of course, you'll have to remain in contact with the tower at all times, but that's a small price to pay for the help offered.

Picture-3 — I'd request permission from Lost Alamitos tower to practice maneuvers south of their airport

With wind, you'll need to apply a wind correction angle to track the course. What happens if you try flying a rectangular course without correcting for the wind? You can see the results in Figure 7. By flying a heading parallel to each side of the course without correcting for the wind, your ground track looks more like a wrecked angle than a rectangle. Only an amoeba has fewer parallel edges.

Your airplane will drift with the wind on the upwind and crosswind sides of the course, which is something you wouldn't want happening when you're trying to fly a rectangular traffic pattern at an airport. After all, the traffic pattern helps pilots operate in an orderly sequence for landing. If you get blown away from or toward the runway, that makes it harder for other airplanes to see you, much less follow you (or for you to see and follow other airplanes).

So let's see what it takes to fly this maneuver and make the ground track come out rectangular by applying a wind correction.

Begin by flying in the direction the wind is blowing, which I'll refer to as flying *downwind*. The wind is at your back. You enter the maneuver this way because this is how you typically enter the traffic pattern—downwind.

This means you need to know the wind's direction. How do you find that out? Sticking your hand out the window is *not* going to give you what you need, though it might give you some things you don't need (think "missing watch"). If you are still relatively close to the departure airport, use the wind reported there at takeoff. You most likely departed an airport rather than launching off an aircraft carrier in your Cessna, right?

Rod Machado's How to Fly an Airplane Handbook

Various Ways to Identify Wind Direction

Fig. 8

There are various methods of detecting wind direction from the air. The first is from steam or smoke stacks (position A). Windmills are another good indication since they point into the wind (position B). Cows (and other herbivores) are even known to stand with their tails the wind so as to see downwind and smell predators coming from upwind (position C).

Forgot the wind direction at takeoff? Clues are all around on the ground. Just pick one such as smoke from a smokestack (Figure 8, position A), the direction the local windmills or wind turbines are pointing (Figure 8, position B), the way flags are flying on flagpoles, trash or leaves blowing over the ground, or the direction the treetops and other landscaping are leaning.

Some even say it's possible to estimate the way the wind is moo-ving from the way cows are facing (Figure 8, position C). Lore has it that cows (and other tasty herbivores) stand with their tails facing into the wind so they can keep an eye on predators such as feedlot operators who otherwise might approach undetected from downwind, while using their noses to sniff upwind predators that might be behind them. Any such tail-end predators can be dispatched using the on-board methane gas system.

Once you know the wind's direction, you'll want to enter the maneuver at a 45 degree angle to the downwind leg (Figure 9, position A), then fly parallel to the perimeter and offset by a quarter to a half mile (I prefer a quarter mile, if possible), as shown in Figure 9, position B. We enter at a 45 degree angle because this is also how we enter the traffic pattern. See how useful this maneuver is already?

Since you will normally first practice this maneuver by making all your turns to the left, a quarter mile offset should place you far enough to the side of the course boundary so

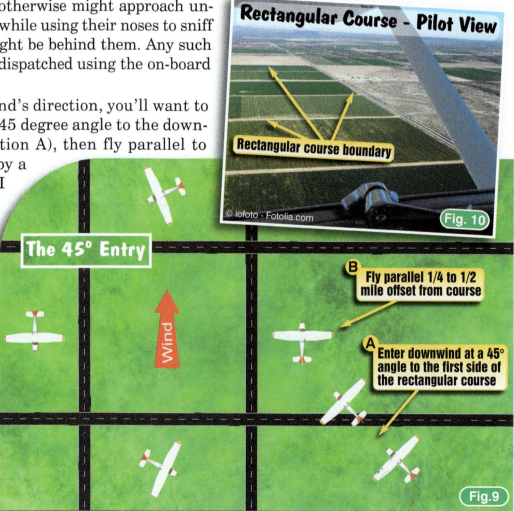

Chapter 7 - Ground Reference Maneuvers

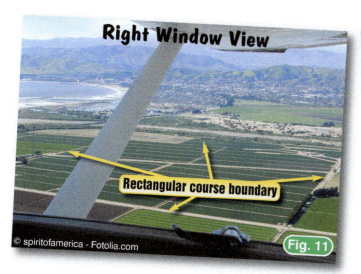

Fig. 11 — Right Window View — Rectangular course boundary

Fig. 12 — The Runway View

you can easily see it out your left window (Figure 10). When doing this maneuver to the right, you might need just a bit more than a quarter mile offset to identify the course boundary over the right window ledge if you're in a side-by-side seated airplane, as shown in Figure 11.

Once again, this is very similar to how you'll fly a traffic pattern at the airport, with the runway (representing one side of the rectangular course) clearly visible out the airplane's side window (Figure 12). What you don't want to do is fly directly over the course perimeter, because you don't (or shouldn't) have a hole in the bottom of your airplane. Flying directly above the boundary makes it difficult to see the course as well as identify any drift.

On the downwind leg, the wind shouldn't cause you to drift right or left when no crosswind exists. Then again, as I mentioned earlier it's sometimes challenging to find the necessary rectangular geometry with boundaries that are exactly parallel and perpendicular to the wind. So it's possible that you may have to apply a slight wind correction on both the downwind and upwind legs. You make the call here.

Correcting for Wind Drift

As you approach the first corner of the course boundary (this will be a turn to the *base leg* of this rectangular course) and when you are abeam it (when it's directly off your left side, as shown in Figure 13, position C), begin your turn.

Keep your bank from exceeding 45 degrees—the bank limit for this maneuver—as you turn (Figure 14). The best way to gauge your bank angle during the turn is to cross-check the attitude indicator

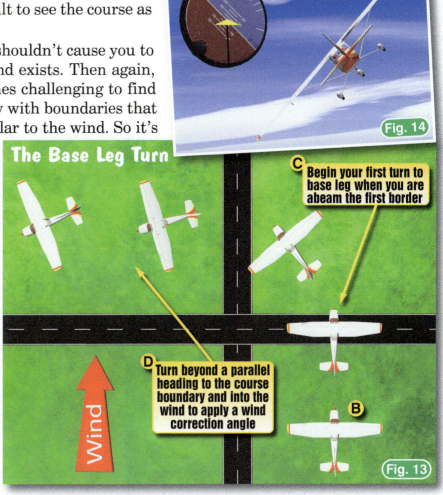

Fig. 14 — 45° Bank Limit

Fig. 13 — The Base Leg Turn
C — Begin your first turn to base leg when you are abeam the first border
D — Turn beyond a parallel heading to the course boundary and into the wind to apply a wind correction angle
B
Wind

and ensure your bank is 45 degrees or less. As your stick and rudder skills develop, you'll find that the top of the instrument panel or engine cowling is useful in making an accurate assessment of 45 degrees of bank without having to look inside the cockpit.

Since you're flying downwind, your groundspeed will be equal to your airspeed plus the wind speed. This higher groundspeed means that you'll need to use a slightly faster rate of roll-in and a steeper bank to keep from exceeding your previously chosen perimeter displacement of a quarter to a half mile. To better understand this concept, please read the *Speed, Rate and Radius* sidebar.

As you turn, you'll want to go at least 10 degrees *past* the heading that parallels the course boundary. This will be your initial estimate for the wind correction angle (WCA), as shown in Figure 15, position B. Sometimes you've just got to make a guess at that WCA and see what happens. That's right. While there's no crying in baseball, there *is* guessing in flying. With experience, your guesses become fairly accurate estimates.

By turning 10 degrees into the wind, you've just made a 100 degree turn to the

Speed, Rate and Radius

Here's a simple mental experiment (the non-mathematical kind) that shows the relationship between your speed and the steepness of turn required to follow a predetermined path on the ground.

Let's say that you're in an unoccupied parking lot and want to circle your car at a radius of 30 feet (the predetermined path) around one of those bright orange reference cones. You begin circling at 10 mph and notice that it requires very little deflection of the wheel to maintain the turning radius. Now you decide to speed things up a little by accelerating to 20 mph. It immediately becomes clear that more speed means that you have to turn the wheel more sharply to maintain the selected radius. At 30 mph it might be impossible to maintain that radius of turn without the car skidding off into some distant corner of the parking lot.

While the physics of cars and airplanes is slightly different, the general principle here remains the same. The faster your speed over the ground in a car, the more sharply you must turn the wheel to maintain a specific distance from some reference point. The faster your speed over the ground (groundspeed) in an airplane, the more steeply you must bank to maintain a specific distance from some ground reference, which is your course boundary in this instance. This is why all ground reference maneuvers require you to use steeper banks when turning from the downwind direction (higher groundspeeds) and shallower banks when turning to the upwind (lower groundspeed).

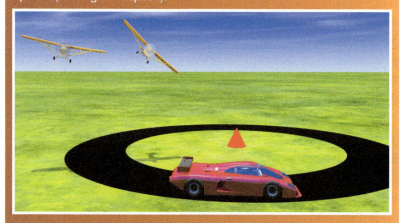

left from the downwind direction (90 degrees plus 10 degrees for drift correction). Now check for airplane drift. If you continue flying parallel to the course boundary, then 10 degrees is a sufficient WCA. Suppose, however, you see that you're drifting downwind, away from the course boundary. What should you do? Call ATC? Use the autopilot? Scratch your head? Scratch your autopilot?

Clearly, you must apply a larger WCA. How do you do that? You simply make a coordinated turn into the wind. Use your rudder and aileron in coordination to turn a little more into the wind, perhaps an additional 10 degrees. Then roll out of the turn just as you would when rolling out of any other turn. If your WCA is sufficient to correct for wind drift, then you'll track along a path that's parallel to the course boundary.

Suppose that the additional 10 degrees causes you to move closer to the course boundary instead of away from it? That means your WCA is a little larger than necessary, right? Apparently a 15 degree WCA would have been the better choice here. So make a coordinated turn to the right of five degrees and roll out. This WCA should allow you to track parallel to the course boundary. If not, then make another small modification to the WCA as appropriate. On the other hand, if you don't apply a sufficient WCA quickly enough, you'll drift beyond the quarter to half mile perimeter before finally finding a WCA that works. If this happens, make an even larger wind correction to return to where you should be, followed by resetting to the appropriate WCA.

Chapter 7 - Ground Reference Maneuvers

When abeam the next course boundary (the *upwind leg* of the rectangular course), you'll only need to turn approximately 75 degrees to fly parallel to it (Figure 15, position E). Why 75 degrees? Because you're already heading 15 degrees into the wind, and 90 degrees minus 15 equals 75 degrees. Remember, when heading directly upwind, there should be no need to correct for wind (Figure 15, position F).

Two-and-a-half down, one-and-a-half to go. When you're abeam the next course boundary (the *crosswind leg* of the rectangular course), make a shallower banked turn using a heading change of less than 90 degrees (Figure 15, position G). Why less than 90 degrees of turn? Because you want to roll out on a heading that applies the *same* WCA used on base leg. You're swimming upstream again.

Unless you're flying a rectangular course precisely over the middle of a mountain range that disrupts wind flow (and I don't recommend this), the WCA for the crosswind and base legs should be exactly the same. That means you'll turn 15 degrees less than 90, or 75 degrees to the left (Figure 15, position H). This leaves you pointing into the wind at a 15 degree WCA, which allows you to fly parallel to the course boundary. Once again, make a coordinated turn to modify your WCA, if necessary.

As you approach the original entry leg of the rectangular course (the *downwind leg*), you'll need to turn 105 degrees to align yourself parallel to the course boundary (Figure 15, position I). Why 105 degrees? Because you're pointed 15 degrees opposite to the direction of turn. In essence, the first 15 degrees just gets you even; you've got 90 degrees to go. Adding 15 to 90 gives you 105 degrees of turn.

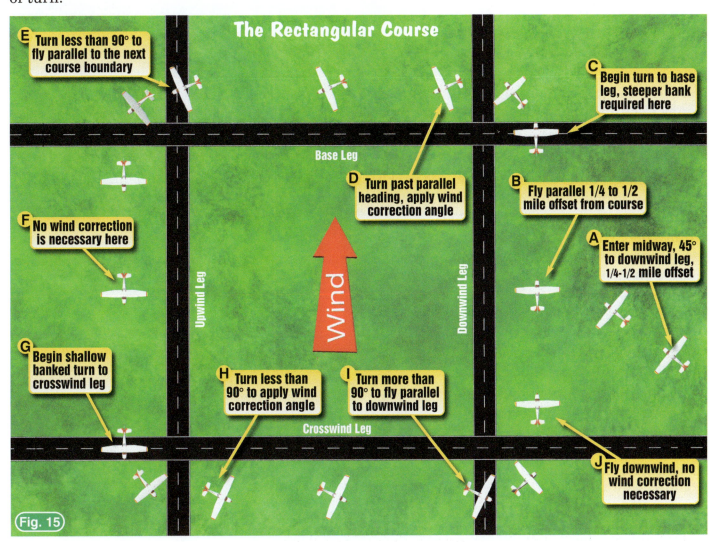

Fig. 15

When abeam the upcoming course boundary (Figure 14, position I), begin your turn and keep in mind that you're now turning downwind. You won't have to roll in quite as quickly as you did when making the turn *from* the downwind to the base leg because you are flying at a slower groundspeed than you were on the downwind leg.

You do, however, have to turn an additional 15 degrees from crosswind to downwind, which requires a bit longer time to execute, so don't be slow to go. In addition, your groundspeed increases in the turn. Both events require you to use a slightly faster roll-in rate to return to maintain the same course boundary displacement you originally had when you entered this maneuver on the downwind leg.

As you cross the downwind entry point (Figure 15, position J), you've passed go and get to collect $200. Ask your instructor for it. Of course, if he just lost his watch, he'll need that money to purchase a new one.

What's Important Here?

The rectangular course is the simplest of the ground reference maneuvers. It is also one of the most practical and important to learn. The skills you acquire here can be put to immediate use, especially if you're planning on landing an airplane. (You have to land, of course. You have to eat and there's no Chinese takeout—or take-up—in the traffic pattern. If the tower says "lo mein, lo mein" they're referring to your tire pressure, not your dinner.)

During this and other ground reference maneuvers, you'll learn to divide your attention between monitoring the ground reference(s) and flying the airplane. That's easier said than done. It's also why you'll initially practice these maneuvers with your flight instructor on board. How do you divide

The Essentials of the Rectangular Course

The *physical objective* of this maneuver is to maintain a ground track that's parallel and offset from a rectangular course while correcting for the effect of wind drift.

Why Do We Do it?—The rectangular course uses geometry similar to that used in flying the traffic pattern when approaching to land at an airport, with the sides referred to as the upwind leg, crosswind leg, downwind leg and base leg. The educational objective is to teach you how to anticipate the effect of wind on your airplane with respect to references on the ground as well as to help you learn to divide your attention between flying the airplane and tracking a ground reference.

Ground Reference Needed—You can usually use a traditional city block or a rectangular field (soccer, football) or any rectangular (trapezoidal) ground reference. The ideal is to have each side approximately one mile in length, with the wind parallel to one of the two long sides, but you may have to be creative and adaptable. Sometimes the best you can do is a sub-optimal rectangle where only one side lies at a 90 degree angle to the wind. The desired altitude for the maneuver is between 600 and 1,000 feet AGL.

You will fly one-quarter to one-half mile outside of the selected rectangle.

The Rectangular Course Maneuver, Step-by-Step—
- Enter the maneuver at a 45 degree angle to the downwind leg, then fly parallel to the perimeter and offset by a quarter to a half mile (I prefer a quarter mile, if possible).
- As you approach the first corner of the course boundary (this will be a turn to the base leg of this rectangular course) and when you are abeam it (when it's directly off your side), begin your turn. As you turn, go at least 10 degrees past the heading that parallels the course boundary. This will be your initial estimate for the wind correction angle (WCA).
- When abeam the upwind leg of the rectangular course, turn to parallel the upwind side of the course, which should take less than 90 degrees of turn given the WCA angle you're already carrying into the wind.
- When you're abeam the crosswind leg of the rectangular course, make a shallower banked turn using a heading change of less than 90 degrees. You want to roll out on a heading that applies the same WCA used on base leg.
- As you approach the original entry leg of the rectangular course (the downwind leg), you'll turn more than 90 degrees to align yourself parallel to the course boundary. You're turning more than 90 degree because you're carrying a WCA into the wind opposite the direction of turn so as to maintain the desired ground track.
- You've now come full circle – or full rectangle, to be precise.

Maneuver Notes—
- Figure (15) makes it clear why you sometimes turn more or less than 90 degrees to "turn the corner" and move from one side to another of the rectangle. Your existing WCA either has to be offset and then a 90 degree turn made or the existing WCA has already made part of the 90 degree turn for you.
- If you have been lucky enough to find a rectangle that has the wind exactly parallel to two of its sides, you will not need a WCA when flying downwind and upwind. Most of the time, you will require at least a small correction.
- Keep your bank from exceeding 45 degrees—the bank limit for this maneuver—as you turn. The best way to gauge your bank angle during the turn is to cross-check the attitude indicator and ensure your bank is 45 degrees or less. As your stick and rudder skills develop, you'll find that the top of the instrument panel or engine cowling in useful in making an accurate assessment of 45 degrees of bank without having to look inside the cockpit.
- The rate at which you roll into your turns is a function of groundspeed. When going downwind, you're moving fast (airplane speed+wind speed) so you need to bank faster and harder when turning crosswind. When turning from crosswind to upwind, your groundspeed is slowing as the turn progresses, so you need to roll into the turn slower and use a shallower bank angle. Remember, it's ultimately about your track over the ground.

Chapter 7 - Ground Reference Maneuvers

your attention? You simply *divide your attention*. You look outside for a bit, check the ground reference, then glance back inside the airplane to ensure that the altitude, airspeed, heading and so on are appropriate. It's the same principle as cross-checking a flight instrument that we discussed in an earlier chapter. The difference being that instead of looking at the horizon, you're looking primarily at the ground *and* the horizon as you occasionally glance at your flight instruments.

The challenge in dividing your attention is that you'll often forget the divide part (especially if you weren't good at math). You might find yourself looking outside and staring almost exclusively at the ground while your airplane and altitude take a nosedive. After just a little practice, most pilots get the idea about dividing their attention. From then on they find it much easier to attend to both the ground reference and the airplane.

As an aside about outside, you should spend most of your time looking outside the airplane. During ground reference maneuvers, you'll probably spend 70% of your time looking at the ground reference and 30% of the time looking inside the cockpit. Pilots with experience typically spend about 17% of their time looking inside the cockpit. Spending a bit larger chunk of time looking inside the cockpit is reasonable for anyone new to ground reference maneuvers, given the need to maintain specific airspeed, bank and altitude requirements. With practice, however, the in-cockpit head time can be steadily reduced.

The Worth of Google Earth

Now here's a perfect way to put your computer to use as a student pilot. Why not install *Google Earth* and use it to find the perfect ground reference for your maneuvers before you practice them? It's free and you can use the features of *Google Earth* to drop a pin over areas that would be suitable for each different type of ground reference maneuver you'll do.

Turns Around a Point

Turns around a point sounds like something a ballerina would do. For you as a pilot, *en pointe* means something a bit different. The *physical objective* of this maneuver is to make the airplane fly a constant radius around a specific point on the ground by correcting for the effects of wind while not exceeding a bank angle of 45 degrees during this maneuver. (Figure 16).

The *educational objective* of this maneuver is to teach you how an airplane's radius of turn is affected by both the airplane's bank angle and the wind's speed and direction. It helps you develop a good sense of your altitude above ground level as well as furthering your development at subconscious control of the airplane while your attention is diverted to references outside the airplane.

This maneuver combines turning and correcting for wind drift while a constant radius of turn is maintained around a prominent and easily identified ground reference. The nice thing about it is that you already know how to do it…well sort of. Think of this as a round rectangle. Let others circle the wagons; you're going to circle the point.

Turning around a point and flying a rectangular course are essentially the same maneuver with the right angles of the rectangular course removed. This is shown by the progressive rounding of the rectangular corners as shown in Figure 17. Now the four legs of the rectangular course (downwind, base, upwind and crosswind legs) are represented by four positions located at 90 degree intervals around the circle.

The only difference between the rectangular course and turns around a point is that the airplane must be kept banked at some angle throughout this maneuver in order to maintain the correct turn radius. You can directly apply to performing turns around a point what you learned in navigating a rectangular course.

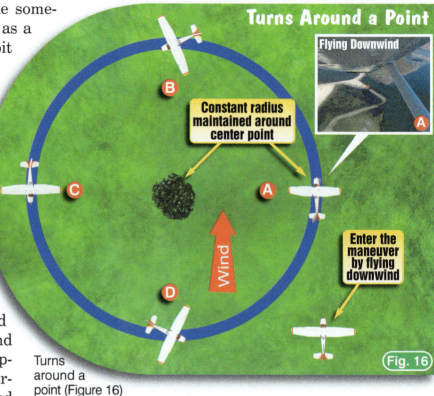

Turns around a point (Figure 16) involves maintaining a constant radius of turn about a ground reference by correcting for wind drift. It is similar to flying a rectangular course (Figure 17) in terms of the wind correction angle applied at points A, B, C and D in both figures. The main difference is that when turning about a point, the airplane is always banked to some degree while the rectangular course involves straight flight on all its sides.

Round off the edges of the rectangular course and you get the same "leg" positions in the newly morphed turns around a point.

Chapter 7 - Ground Reference Maneuvers

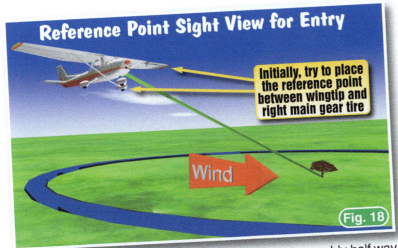

Fig. 18: Enter downwind at a distance from the point that's roughly half way between your wingtip and the main landing gear wheel. You can also apply this same principle to low wing airplanes, too. Remember, this is only an initial approximation of position.

Fig. 19: A high wing airplane can block the ground reference if the turn radius is too large. A low wing airplane can block the ground reference if the turn radius is small.

As was the case with the rectangular course, if there is no wind this is a very easy ground reference maneuver to perform. You'd simply fly a circular path around the point at a constant bank angle and be done with it. But how often is *that* going to happen? When pigs get instrument ratings. Wind affects groundspeed and drift, requiring continuous re-calculation of bank angle and wind correction angle.

For wind of the same direction and velocity, the maximum wind correction angles used when turning around a point are essentially the same as those used for the rectangular course. In other words, if you needed a 15 degree WCA to remain parallel to the base leg in a rectangular course, you'll also need a 15 degree WCA to maintain the correct radius of turn at the 90 degree point when turning around a point. The only significant difference here is that you're constantly banking to some degree in order to fly a constant radius around the chosen point. Let's take a closer look at how to perform this maneuver.

Before we can begin this maneuver, there's an important point to be made. Or rather, found. You need to find a nice point about which to turn. The point can be an intersection, a tree, an outhouse or anything else that's readily visible and relatively pointy. The preferred altitude for this maneuver is between 600 and 1,000 feet AGL, with my personal preference being lower, perhaps at 600 feet AGL. This makes the effects of wind drift more apparent.

Begin this maneuver by flying downwind (Figure 16) at a distance from the point equal to the radius at which you want to fly the maneuver. Keep in mind that the chosen radius should allow you to fly the maneuver and correct for the effects of wind without exceeding 45 degrees of bank at the steepest part of this maneuver. The big question is how far from the reference should you make your initial entry. You can make a good approximation by entering just far enough to the side of the reference point so that it's half-way between the wing tip and the main gear (Figure 18). This will keep you from exceeding 45 degrees of bank but place you in a good position to begin the maneuver.

If you're in a high wing airplane and you choose a radius that's too far from the ground reference during entry to the maneuver your wing will block your view of the reference during the steepest portion of the turn (Figure 19, position 1). This isn't the end of the world (that typically involves a lot of water or a very big flash of some sort), but it's nice to see the reference all the time, if possible. If you're in a low wing airplane and choose a radius of turn that is too small, it's possible that your wing will also block the reference during a portion of the turn (Figure 19, position 2).

As you enter the maneuver downwind, begin your turn (left, in this instance) when you're abeam the chosen ground reference, as shown in Figure 20, position A (it's best to do all ground reference maneuvers to the left the first time you do them. The view is always better out your left window). At this point, you'll be flying at maximum groundspeed. This is also the place where you'll need to apply the maximum bank to maintain the correct radius of turn. Roll crisply into the appropriate bank angle (try some bank angle less than 45 degrees at first). Then be willing to increase or decrease the bank angle as necessary to maintain the selected turn radius. That's right. You gotta know when to hold 'em and know when to roll 'em when it comes to the bank angle, and that means changing the bank as needed to keep the turn radius constant.

As the turn progresses beyond your initial entry and toward 90 degrees of turn (Figure 20, position B), you'll have to gradually reduce the bank angle as groundspeed decreases (the wind is no longer from directly behind you as you continue to turn, so your groundspeed is decreasing).

As you progress toward 90 degrees of turn, you also need to progressively apply a slight WCA to maintain the turn radius. Here is where you'll allow the airplane's nose to *continue turning a little beyond or inside the imagined circular ground path,* to keep from stretching the downwind portion of the turn (Figure 21, position B).

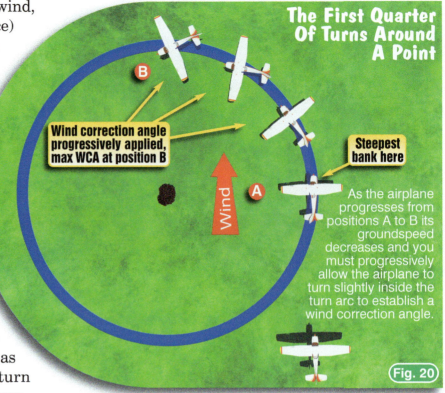

The steepest bank will be at position A (Figures 20 and 21), when you're abeam the ground reference point while flying downwind. Your groundspeed is the highest for this maneuver at this point. From position A to B, the airplane is progressively turned into the wind (a wind correction angle applied) so as to maintain the desired flight radius while the bank angle is progressively decreased.

Turning inside your imagined circular ground path is the equivalent of applying the same WCA used when flying a rectangular course with similar winds. You accomplish this by gradually reducing the bank angle when approaching 90 degrees of turn, but not so fast that the nose turns parallel to or outside the imagined turn arc. This keeps the nose turned slightly inside the desired ground track

Chapter 7 - Ground Reference Maneuvers

arc. This is how you can crab into the wind during the turn while keeping the rudder and aileron perfectly coordinated. Now your radius of turn is constant, which is another way of saying that your ground track is circular.

Continuing the turn past the 90 degree point toward 180 degrees of turn, you're now heading upwind. This means your groundspeed continues to decrease (Figure 22). You must progressively reduce the bank angle to maintain the correct turn radius. At the 180 degree of turn point (Figures 22 and 23, positions C), your groundspeed is the lowest it will be during the entire maneuver and the bank angle is also the smallest. That should make sense, since you're not flying as fast and you don't need to turn as fast to circle the reference point. At 180 degrees of turn you're pointed directly into the wind, so there should be no wind correction angle applied. This is why your left wing is directly in line with the ground reference point.

How to Divide Your Attention Between Airplane and Ground

Dividing your attention between the cockpit and some outside reference is a learnable behavior that involves time-sharing your conscious attention between two things. Here's how you do that.

You typically begin a ground reference maneuver by placing your airplane abeam a ground reference. As you commence maneuvering, you'll initially need to focus your attention outside the cockpit. Once you are established in the initial attitude around or about the ground reference, return your attention to the instrument panel, ensuring that the airplane is in the required pitch and bank attitude needed to sustain that maneuver.

For example, suppose you're downwind and ready to begin the initial turn for the maneuver known as *turns around a point*. You enter the maneuver by looking at the ground reference, then rolling into a steep turn at or below 45 degrees of bank while simultaneously holding altitude. As you glance back at your instrument panel, you need to ensure that the altimeter needle isn't moving and that the attitude indicator shows less than 45 degrees of bank. There's no need to look at the heading indicator or any other instrument that doesn't provide you with immediately actionable information. That's why knowing what instruments you need to look at as you return to the panel is absolutely essential in minimizing the time spent with your head in the cockpit.

While looking back at the panel, any deviation in bank, altitude or airspeed (or whatever performance value is essential here) should be immediately corrected with a slight change in attitude or power, followed by returning your attention to the ground reference. Most of your conscious attention should be focused outside the airplane, not on the instrument panel.

Keep in mind that a change in altitude is often the immediate result of a failure to monitor the airplane's attitude. When you shift your attention back to the panel, the altimeter should be your eyes' first stop. Then it's back to ground.

As you approach the upwind point of the circle (the 270 degree turn point), as shown in Figure 24, position D, your groundspeed begins to increase slightly because the wind is no longer blowing directly on your nose. You'll have to increase the bank slightly to maintain the correct turning radius. However, you'll also need to keep the airplane's nose pointed slightly outside your imagined circular ground track in order to keep your turn radius from decreasing. Apply the same WCA you used at the 90 degree of turn point (the WCA won't change much and if it does change a little, that's due to slight changes in airspeed due to bank angle).

How do you do that? Gradually increase the bank angle to compensate for the increasing groundspeed but not so fast as to pull the nose parallel to or inside the imagined turn arc (Figure 25, position D). In

The Third Quarter Of Turns Around A Point

As the airplane progresses from positions C to D, it experiences less of a headwind but more of a crosswind. Therefore, as its groundspeed increases, you must progressively allow the airplane to turn slightly outside the turn arc to establish the desired wind correction angle.

Fig. 24

Turns Around a Point - Graphically Explained

Sometimes there's nothing like a good graph to help you make sense of a particular maneuver. So let me help you understand how to use the *Turns Around a Point* graph to the right.

On the left side of the graph are three vertical color coded bars representing the wind correction angle, the groundspeed and the bank angle used in this maneuver. The top of these bars represent maximum values (MAX) while the bottom represents minimum values (MIN).

The graph's horizontal axis represents the degrees of turn throughout the maneuver. Position #A represents the beginning and end of the maneuver (0° and 360° of turn) where the groundspeed and the bank angle are the largest (MAX). At positions #B and #D (90° and 270° of turn) the wind correction angle is at a maximum and the groundspeed and bank angle are approximately half of their max value. At 180° of turn all three values are at a minimum.

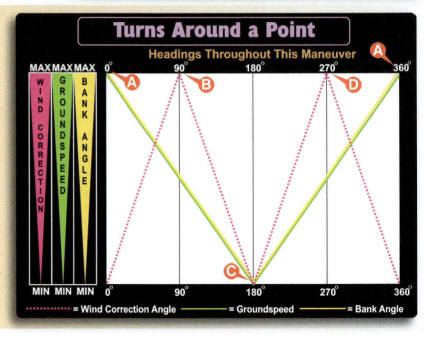

Chapter 7 - Ground Reference Maneuvers

other words, increase the bank angle during the 180-to-270 degree turn, but do so slower than your untrained intuition tells you to. This will keep the nose pointed slightly outside the desired circular ground track.

At and beyond the upwind or 270 degree point (Figure 26, position D) of the turn, your bank should increase as the groundspeed increases. You'll reach the maximum bank at the 360 degree point (Figure 26, position A), which is where this maneuver first began. As you can see from Figures 26 and 27, you're headed directly downwind and your groundspeed is at a maximum and no wind correction angle is needed.

Welcome home. Now keep going! That's right. Don't stop at one turn. Continue this maneuver for at least two full turns as a demonstration of your skill.

Crab Angle Decreased

Wind correction angle progressively reduced

(Fig. 27)

The Fourth Quarter Of Turns Around A Point

Zero wind correction angle and max bank at position A

Groundspeed increasing, wind correction angle decreasing and bank increasing

As the airplane progresses from position D to the starting position A, it experiences increasing tailwinds and less of a crosswind. Its groundspeed increases and you must progressively reduce the wind correction angle.

(Fig. 26)

Why do we practice this maneuver? The first and most important reason is that it furthers your understanding how the wind affects an airplane. Believe me when I say that you can never have too much understanding of what wind does to a flying machine. Comprehending how wind affects the airplane is essential in predicting your airplane's flight track geometry. You absolutely need to have this skill if you hope to land in a crosswind. And I hope you do. Being able to land only when the wind is right down the runway is very limiting.

The additional value in this maneuver is that it helps you learn how to divide your attention between looking outside and inside the cockpit. If you keep gaining or losing altitude while turning, you haven't yet mastered how to divide your attention properly. It shouldn't be much of a surprise to learn that good pilots spend a lot of time looking outside the cockpit. This is a major reason why we fly, isn't it? It's all about the view and avoiding other aircraft in the process. So anything you learn that helps identify when the attitude of the airplane changes is a worthwhile skill to have. Turns around a point help you better understand how altitude can vary with the slightest diversion of attention, which is a dangerous proposition when close to the ground. Take a look at the sidebar *Turn Around a Point - Graphically Explained* the left for a graphic idea about how wind correction, groundspeed and bank angle interrelate during the performance of turns around a point.

The Essentials of Turns Around a Point

The *physical objective* of this maneuver is to make the airplane fly a constant radius around a specific point on the ground by correcting for the effects of wind while not exceeding a bank angle of 45 degrees during this maneuver.

Why Do We Do it?—The *educational objective* of this maneuver is to teach you how an airplane's radius is affected by both the airplane's bank angle and the wind's speed and direction. It helps you develop a good sense of your altitude above ground level as well as furthering your development at subconscious control of the airplane while your attention is diverted to references outside the airplane.

Ground Reference Needed—The point can be an intersection, a tree, an outhouse or anything else that's readily visible and relatively pointy. The preferred altitude for this maneuver is between 600 and 1,000 feet AGL.

Turns Around a Point, Step-by-Step—
- Begin this maneuver by flying downwind at a distance from the point equal to the radius at which you want to fly the maneuver.
- As you enter the maneuver downwind, begin your left turn when you're abeam the chosen ground reference.
- As you progress toward 90 degrees of turn, you also need to progressively apply a slight WCA to maintain the turn radius.
- Continuing the turn past the 90 degree point toward 180 degrees of turn, you're now heading upwind with your groundspeed decreasing (Figure 22). You must progressively reduce the bank angle to maintain the correct turn radius.
- At the 180 degree of turn point, your groundspeed is the lowest it will be during the entire maneuver and the bank angle is also the smallest.
- Approaching the upwind point of the circle (the 270 degree turn point), you'll progressively apply a WCA. As you turn away from a direct headwind, your groundspeed begins to increase and you'll have to increase the bank slightly to maintain the correct turning radius.
- At and beyond the upwind (270 degree) point of the turn, your bank should increase as the groundspeed increases. You'll reach the maximum bank at the 360 degree point, which is where this maneuver first began.

Maneuver Notes—
- Turning around a point and flying a rectangular course are essentially the same maneuver with the right angles of the rectangular course removed (Figure 17).
- If you're in a high wing airplane and you choose a radius that's too close to the ground reference, your wing will block your view of the reference during the steepest portion of the turn.
- If you're in a low wing airplane and choose a radius of turn that is too large, it's possible that your wing will also block the reference during a portion of the turn.
- Turning inside or outside your imagined circular ground path is the equivalent of applying the same WCA used when flying a rectangular course with similar winds.
- A critical part of this maneuver is the initial bank used when entering downwind. You're moving fast in this position and it's easy to be blown downwind of the ground reference if the initial bank isn't steep enough. If you entered the maneuver upwind, then things would happen more slowly and you'd have more time to modify your bank. So be prepared to modify the bank quickly if it doesn't produce the desired turning radius.
- The crab into the wind in Figure 20 is applied by turning just a tiny bit faster (i.e., increasing your bank angle) than you normally would if you were flying this arc in a no-wind condition.
- The crab into the wind in Figure 24 is applied by turning just slow enough to keep the nose pointed outside the imagined turn arc.

S-Turn Across a Road

Now we come to a ground reference maneuver that's essentially a turn around a point on a half shell (or two). In other words, it the same maneuver but sliced in half and set side-by-side (Figure 28).

The *physical objective* of this maneuver is to fly half circles of equal radii along a straight ground reference line (such as a road, fence or field border) at 600 to 1,000 feet AGL. The *educational objective* of this maneuver is to teach you how an airplane's radius is affected by both the airplane's bank angle and the wind's speed and direction. It helps you develop a good sense of your altitude above ground level as well as furthering your development at subconscious control of the airplane while your attention is diverted to references outside the airplane. S-turns across a road is more demanding of the pilot than turns around a point, mainly because of the alternating right and left hand turns experienced throughout the maneuver.

The ground reference line is chosen so that it's perpendicular to the wind's direction, which allows you to apply the same principles learned from performing turns around a point. The only real difference between this maneuver and turns around a point is that each side of the half circle is flown in a different direction instead of using only a right or left bank for the entire maneuver.

I prefer to introduce this maneuver after introducing turns around a point because it's a slightly more challenging maneuver to learn. Why? Because you're correcting for wind drift while turning and following a road at the same time. Complicating matters is the requirement to alternate from right turns to left turns. Additionally, this maneuver requires you to keep in memory the size of your previous half-circle's radius as well as imagin-

Chapter 7 - Ground Reference Maneuvers

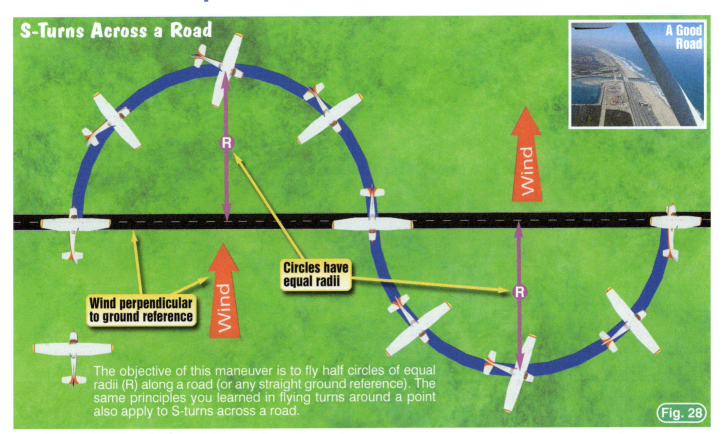

S-Turns Across a Road

The objective of this maneuver is to fly half circles of equal radii (R) along a road (or any straight ground reference). The same principles you learned in flying turns around a point also apply to S-turns across a road.

Fig. 28

ing what a half circle should look like when you have no precise indication of what your flight path is actually like over the ground. Let's remember that most people have a hard enough time drawing a circle, much less trying to visualize and fly half of one. It can be a bit challenging for a student to try making equal half-circles when changing directions from right to left.

To perform this maneuver you must find a straight ground reference (I'll say "road" from now on, but it could be railroad tracks, a row of corn, the edge of a farmer's field, or even a reasonably straight river or stream) that's perpendicular to the wind's direction.

A Slightly Different Explanation as to How the Airplane Crabs Into the Wind When Flying S-turn Half Circles

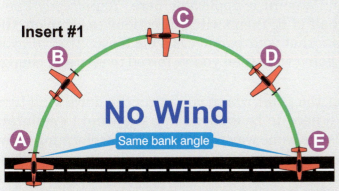

Let's suppose you were instructed to fly your airplane above and along a large green arc painted onto the ground from positions A to E (Insert #1). In a no wind condition, you only need to keep the airplane's nose (OK, its longitudinal axis) pointed in the same direction of the curving arc to remain directly above and over it. If you tried to keep the nose directly over and precisely aligned with the curving arc when wind is present (Insert #2), your airplane would be blown to the outside of the arc (or to the inside with a reversed wind).

For example, when flying from position F to J while attempting to keep the nose aligned with the green arc while flying directly above it, you would be blown to the outside of the arc (position Z). Now you need to turn back toward the arc to intercept it again at position G. Therefore, instead of letting yourself be blown to the outside of the arc to begin with, you should begin your turn at position F and purposely bank the airplane so that the nose initially points just to the inside of the green arc. This is how you crab into the wind to maintain a half-circle ground track. If there were actually a green arc on the ground, then you'd need to turn so as to increase the angle between the arc (into the wind) as you progress to position H (where the maximum crab angle occurs). And, of course, you'd need to decrease this crab angle between positions H and J. The only difference between this example and flying an S-turn across a road you have to imagine the half circle.

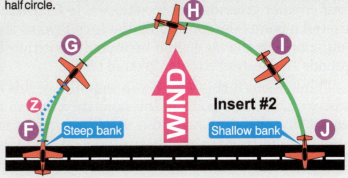

Rod Machado's How to Fly an Airplane Handbook

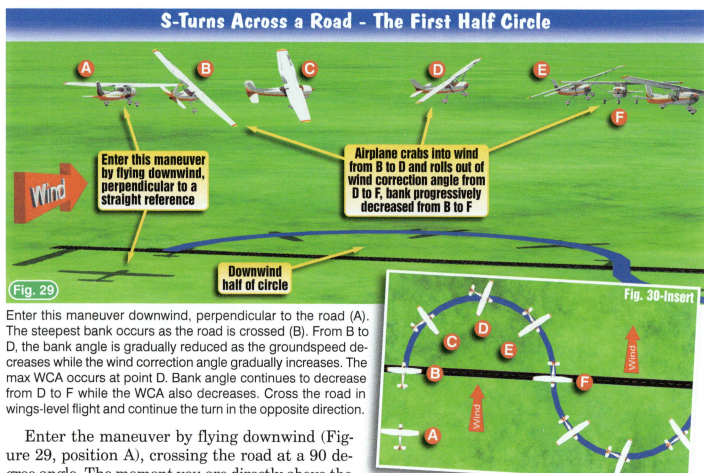

S-Turns Across a Road - The First Half Circle

Enter this maneuver by flying downwind, perpendicular to a straight reference

Airplane crabs into wind from B to D and rolls out of wind correction angle from D to F, bank progressively decreased from B to F

Downwind half of circle

Fig. 29

Fig. 30-Insert

Enter this maneuver downwind, perpendicular to the road (A). The steepest bank occurs as the road is crossed (B). From B to D, the bank angle is gradually reduced as the groundspeed decreases while the wind correction angle gradually increases. The max WCA occurs at point D. Bank angle continues to decrease from D to F while the WCA also decreases. Cross the road in wings-level flight and continue the turn in the opposite direction.

Enter the maneuver by flying downwind (Figure 29, position A), crossing the road at a 90 degree angle. The moment you are directly above the road begin a right or left turn (Figure 29, position B). Your objective is to fly a half circle at a constant radius. How big a radius? Well, that's for you to decide, but it shouldn't be so small that it requires use of more than 45 degrees of bank (even in a strong wind). Ultimately, the radius is determined by the perceived distance from the road. This is where you need to develop an ability to estimate distances and retain this estimate in your short term memory. That's why this maneuver is best practiced after turns around a point (and, perhaps, with a quick shot of *Ginkgo biloba*, too).

Everything you learned performing turns around a point is applicable here. You already know how to do this maneuver, but you only have to do half of it, then switch directions to complete the other half. If this were a date, you could rightly claim that your partner is a big tease. After all, you get halfway through your maneuver and things are going well, then you're forced to stop and change directions.

The rate of roll-in and the steepest bank occur at the point where you begin the downwind turn (position B). Approaching 90 degrees of turn, you'll need to be crabbed into the wind to maintain your circular ground track (positions C to D). Do this the same way you did it when performing turns around a point—by continuing the turn toward the inside of the imaginary circular ground path as you approach the 90 degree turn point (position D). This keeps you from being blown downwind, outside the desired circular ground track.

Think about it this way. If you were flying this maneuver in a no wind condition, your airplane's nose would always point in the same direction as the half-circle ground track. With wind, however, expect that the airplane's nose should always be turned (crabbed) a bit toward the *inside* of the circular ground track on the downwind loop, and toward the *outside* on the upwind loop. This means that you have to turn just a little bit faster than you normally would if you were flying this maneuver

Chapter 7 - Ground Reference Maneuvers

in a no-wind condition. You'll find that you need a moderate bank at position D in Figure 29 along the turn (the 90 degree point), with the bank angle and the wind correction angle continuing to decrease as you approach the 180 degree of turn point (position F).

At 180 degrees of turn (Figure 29, position F), your wings should be temporarily level (0 degrees of bank) as you roll into a turn in the opposite direction. The object is to make the same size half circle that you made on the downwind portion of this maneuver. Be careful here, because you're heading into the wind and your groundspeed is at its slowest at position F. If you roll into a bank too quickly or use too large a bank angle at this point, the turning radius on this upwind circle will be smaller than on the downwind circle.

From positions F to H in Figure 30, you're applying a moderate amount of bank and the airplane's nose is pointed outside of the circling path to establish a WCA into the wind. Once again, the crab into the wind was applied by not turning as fast as you normally would if you were flying this arc in a no wind condition. In other words, your rate of turn up to position H is slow enough to allow the nose to point slightly outside the circular path you're making along the ground.

At position H, the airplane begins to turn with the wind, thus rapidly increasing your groundspeed. The bank angle must also increase if you want to maintain the same circling radius. When reaching position J (180 degrees of turn), groundspeed is once again at its maximum and your bank angle is at a maximum just before you cross the road. As you cross the road, your wings should transition though level flight as you roll from one turn to the next, repeating the maneuver as you travel along the road. Figure 31 shows this maneuver in graphic format. S'good.

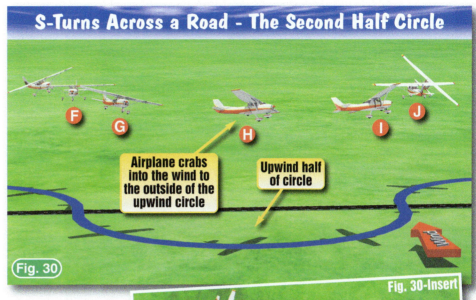

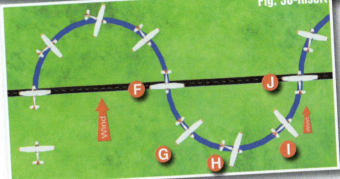

From F to J, the bank angle is gradually increased as the groundspeed increases, while the wind correction angle gradually increases. The max WCA occurs at point H. Bank angle continues to increase from H to J while the WCA decreases. Cross the road in wings-level flight and continue the turn in the opposite direction.

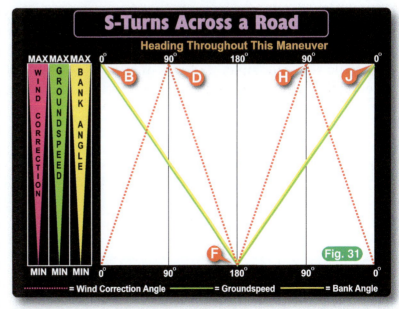

The graphic representation of this maneuver shows that the *max* and *min* values of WCA, groundspeed and bank angle occur at the same place they occur when performing turns around a point.

Rod Machado's How to Fly an Airplane Handbook

The Essentials of S-turns Across a Road

The physical objective of this maneuver is to fly half circles of equal radii in opposite directions along a straight ground reference line (such as a road, fence or field border) at 600 to 1,000 feet AGL.

Why Do We Do it?—

S-turns arcoss a road combine two important elements of flight that you'll often use when operating with reference to the ground: *turning* while *correcting* for wind drift. It develops your ability to follow a desired ground track when the WCA is constantly changing. Your ability to fly while managing the distractions of a ground reference is also developed

Ground Reference Needed—

You'll need a straight ground reference—a road, railroad tracks, a row of corn, the edge of a farmer's field, or even a reasonably straight river or stream that's perpendicular to the wind's direction.

S-turns Across a Road, Step-by-Step—

- Enter the maneuver by flying downwind, crossing the road at a 90 degree angle. The radius is determined by the perceived distance from the road.
- Approaching 90 degrees of turn, you'll need to be crabbed into the wind (toward the inside of the half-circle) to maintain your circular ground track.
- At 180 degrees of turn, your wings should be temporarily level (0 degrees of bank) as you begin an immediate turn in the opposite direction.
- Approaching 90 degrees of turn in the opposite direction, you'll need to be crabbed into the wind (toward the outside of the half-circle) to maintain your circular ground track.
- As you cross the road again, the wings should be level with the airplane rolling into a turn in the opposite direction until told by your instructor or examiner that the maneuver is complete.

Maneuver Notes—

- The half-circle turn radius shouldn't be so small that it requires use of more than 45 degrees of bank when flying downwind (even in a strong wind).
- The rate of roll-in and the steepest bank occur at the point where you begin the downwind turn.
- If you were flying this maneuver in a no wind condition, your airplane's nose would always point in the same direction as the half-circle ground track.
- The object is to make the same size half circle that you made on the downwind portion of this maneuver.
- On the downwind loop, the crab into the wind is applied by turning just a tiny bit faster (i.e., increasing your bank angle) than you normally would if you were flying this arc in a no-wind condition.
- On the upwind loop, the crab into the wind is applied by not turning as fast (i.e., decreasing your bank angle) as you normally would if you were flying this arc in a no-wind condition.
- At 180 degrees of turn the airplane should be passing through wings level flight while rolling smoothly from one bank to another as you cross the ground reference.
- After 90 degrees of turn (while turning into the wind) your closure rate with the road decreases, thus you must reduce your bank accordingly or you'll be perpendicular with the road before crossing it.
- After 270 degrees of turn (while turning with the wind) your closure rate with the road increases, thus you must increase your bank accordingly or you'll cross the road at some angle less than 90 degrees.
- The bank in this maneuver is constantly changing when wind is present.
- There's a general tendency to increase the bank too quickly when turning from 90 to 180 degrees, thus completing the 180 before crossing the road.
- The secret to performing this maneuver correctly is to visualize the circular ground track desired on both the upwind and downwind half-circles.
- Since the evaluation of half-circle ground tracks can be somewhat subjective, an emphasis is placed on a pilot's ability to arrive over the road in wing's level flight as a means of evaluating his performance in this maneuver.

One of the benefits of doing S-turns across a road is that it allows you to practice dividing your attention in both right and left turns. While alternating the direction of turn may not seem like much of a challenge to an experienced pilot, student pilots usually don't get as much practice doing maneuvers to the right as they do to the left.

I still remember making left traffic most of the time as a student pilot. The first time ATC asked me to make right traffic for the parallel runway I thought I was going to lose control of my airplane. I simply wasn't used to making turns in that direction. If you're a student pilot, then you'll want to get used to seeing your ground reference out the left and right side of the cockpit early in your training development.

One of the very common but understandable errors during this maneuver is the inability to visualize the ground track required to make a half circle. This does take practice and that's why I recommend having your instructor demonstrate this maneuver through enough half circles that you get an idea of what a proper half circle looks like from the cockpit.

Positive Exchange of Flight Controls

When one pilot wishes to give the flight controls of the airplane to another pilot, he or she should use the following protocol:

1. "You have the flight controls."

The other pilot should acknowledge this immediately by saying:

2. "I have the flight controls."

The first pilot should say again,

3. "You have the flight controls."

This is a very important procedure to follow every time another pilot wants to use the controls, especially on your pilot checkride. It's an excellent way of always knowing who's flying the airplane.

Chapter 7 - Ground Reference Maneuvers

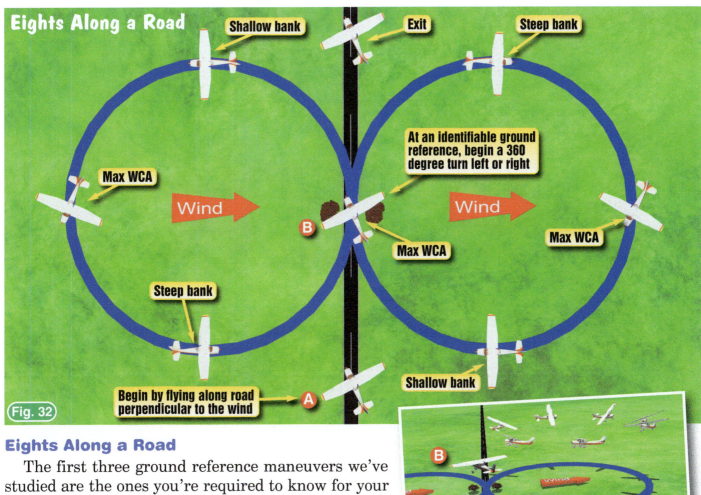

Eights along a road requires you to use the same techniques you used with turns around a point except that you must imagine the circle's center point.

Eights Along a Road

The first three ground reference maneuvers we've studied are the ones you're required to know for your private pilot checkride. The next few maneuvers aren't required for you to become a private pilot, but they're well worth knowing so that you can improve your piloting skills and become an exceptional private pilot. In most cases, they are simply differing combinations and permutations of what you've already done.

The *educational objective* of this maneuver is similar to other ground reference maneuvers in that it helps you develop your skill compensating for wind drift while turning with respect to a ground reference. It also helps you develop a good sense of your altitude above ground level as well as furthering your development at subconscious control of the airplane while your attention is diverted to references outside the airplane. The *physical objective* of this maneuver is to fly a ground track consisting of two complete circles adjacent to each other having equal radii on each side of a road with that road oriented perpendicular to the wind (Figure 32). Looked at from above or below, the maneuver appears to inscribe the figure of an "8" on the ground or in the air, respectively.

Sure, while you're up there doing this maneuver you'll look like a skywriter who's writing with invisible ink. But with a little imagination, observers might see the eight (especially during Octoberfest or an Eighth of July party). This maneuver uses the same skills used in turns around a point and S-turns across a road.

Begin the maneuver by flying directly along a road (or field boundary, or tree line and so on) oriented perpendicular to the wind. This means you'll have a wind correction angle already applied to track the road (Figure 32, position A) prior to beginning the maneuver. Remember the size of this WCA. When you come to an intersection or some definable reference on the surface (obviously not

7-26 Rod Machado's How to Fly an Airplane Handbook

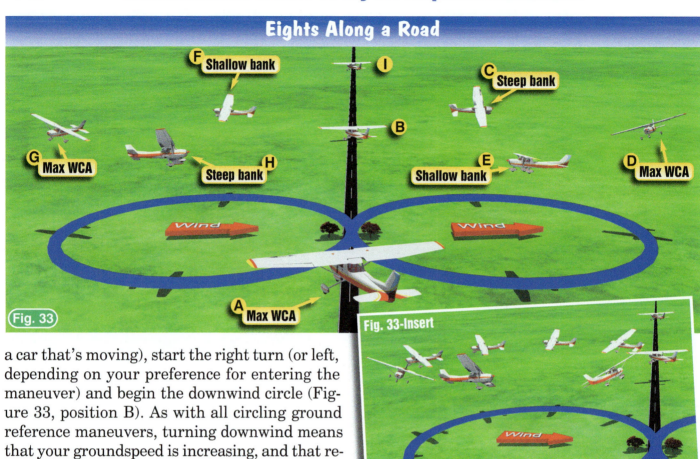

To maintain the imagined circular path for this maneuver, the steepest bank occurs where the groundspeed is the highest (positions C and H) while the shallowest bank occurs where the groundspeed is the slowest (positions E and F). Max WCA occurs at positions D, B and G.

a car that's moving), start the right turn (or left, depending on your preference for entering the maneuver) and begin the downwind circle (Figure 33, position B). As with all circling ground reference maneuvers, turning downwind means that your groundspeed is increasing, and that requires a quick roll-in, reaching the maximum bank angle to be used at position C. Initially, you'll have to do your best to estimate this bank angle but 40 to 45 degrees of bank is a good angle to use in the absence of other information. You can always reduce the bank if it appears to be too steep.

When reaching 90 degrees of turn on the downwind portion of the circle (position C), your groundspeed and bank angle are at a maximum and the wind correction angle is zero. Continuing past this position, begin reducing the bank just slow enough so that your nose turns a little beyond or inside your imaginary circular ground track on the downwind side of the circle. This is how you apply a wind correction angle (and crab into the wind) on the downwind portion of this arc, thus preventing a distortion (stretching) of the circling path. At the 180 degree turn point (position D), you'll have the maximum wind correction angle applied toward the inside of the circular path using a moderate bank, and the groundspeed will be decreasing. As you continue the turn to 270 degrees and head into the wind, the bank continues to decrease commensurate with the decreasing groundspeed. At the 270 degree turn point, the wind correction angle is zero and groundspeed is at its minimum for this maneuver (position E).

Continuing beyond 270 degrees of turn, strive to cross the road at the same starting point used when entering this maneuver. Ideally, you'll also cross it at the same WCA used during your initial track before beginning the first downwind loop. This means making the corrections necessary to cross the road in a wings level attitude at the original WCA then immediately entering a turn in the opposite direction to begin the upwind loop of this maneuver (position B).

Since you're now turning left, into the wind, groundspeed is decreasing so you won't need to use as steep a bank to begin the upwind loop as you did when turning downwind. At the 90 degrees of

Chapter 7 - Ground Reference Maneuvers

turn point (position F), your groundspeed will be at a minimum. To maintain the circular ground track beyond position F, begin increasing the bank just fast enough so that the airplane's nose points to the outside the circling path, thus providing the necessary WCA to maintain a circular ground track. When reaching the 180 degree turn point on the upwind loop (position G), the WCA should be at a maximum.

Turning beyond position G to the 270 degree turning point, groundspeed will now be increasing. This requires an increase in the bank and rate of turn. The maximum bank will be achieved at 270 degrees of turn as you're flying directly downwind (position H).

Beyond the 270 degrees of turn point, maneuver to cross the road at the same point where you began this maneuver. Done correctly, you'll actually turn to cross the road with the nose pointed upwind (into the wind) slightly, which is nothing more than the WCA with which you originally began your eights along a road.

As with all our ground reference maneuvers, this one requires a division of attention between flying the airplane and maintaining a circular flight path along the ground. This maneuver takes the level of difficulty up a notch because you have to visualize the circular ground track being flown. There's no reference point at the middle of the circle by which you can gauge your radius of turn, either. So there is a certain amount of subjectivity as to whether or not your circle is another man's ellipse. That's why arrival over the road at the same starting point and in a wing's level attitude becomes even more important as a means of evaluating your proficiency with this maneuver.

The Essentials of Eights Along a Road

Eights along a road (or a fence or a field border or any straight line reference) consists of two adjacent circles flown on each side of a road that's oriented perpendicular to the prevailing winds (Figure 33). Looked at from above or below, the maneuver appears to inscribe the figure of an "8" on the ground or in the air, respectively.

Why Do We Do it?—The educational objective of this maneuver is similar to other ground reference maneuvers in that it helps you develop your skill at compensating for wind drift while turning with respect to a ground reference. It also helps you develop a good sense of your altitude above ground level as well as furthering your development at subconscious control of the airplane while your attention is diverted to references outside the airplane.

Ground Reference Needed—You'll need a road or reference boundary that's aligned perpendicular to the wind. An altitude between 600 and 1,000 feet AGL is the desired altitude for the maneuver.

Eights Along a Road, Step-by-Step—
- While flying parallel to a road and perpendicular to the wind, begin a right or left turn to start the downwind circle when you come to an intersection or some definable reference on the surface (obviously not a car that's moving).
- Don't exceed 45 degrees of bank at the steepest part of the maneuver (when flying the downwind portion of any circle).
- When reaching 90 degrees of turn on the downwind portion of the circle, your groundspeed is at its maximum, the wind correction angle is zero and your bank is at its maximum.
- Continuing past 90 degrees of, begin reducing the bank just fast enough so that your nose turns a little beyond or inside your imaginary circular ground track on the downwind side of the circle.
- At the 180 degree turn point, you'll have the maximum wind correction angle applied while using a moderate bank, and the groundspeed will be decreasing.
- As you continue the turn to 270 degrees and head into the wind, the bank continues to decrease commensurate with the decreasing groundspeed.
- At the 270 degree turn point, the wind correction angle is zero, the groundspeed is at its minimum and the bank angle is at a minimum for this maneuver.
- Continuing beyond 270 degrees of turn, strive to cross the road at the same starting point used when entering this maneuver.
- When entering this maneuver, ideally you'll also cross it at the same WCA used during your initial track before beginning the first downwind loop.
- Now begin a turn in the opposite direction, into the wind, where the groundspeed is decreasing. You won't need to use as steep a bank to begin the upwind loop as you did when turning downwind.
- The same techniques apply on the upwind loop except that to maintain the circular ground track, you must increase your bank angle just fast enough to allow the airplane's nose to point outside the imagined circling path, thus providing the necessary WCA to maintain a circular ground track.

Maneuver Notes—
- You apply a wind correction angle (and crab into the wind) on the downwind portion of the arc by turning fast enough so that your nose turns a little beyond or inside your imaginary circular ground track on the downwind side of the circle.
- There's no reference point at the middle of the circle by which you can gauge your radius of turn. So you must visualize the circular ground track desired during this maneuver.
- Ultimately, it's your arrival over the road at the same starting point and in a wing's level attitude that offers the best means by which to evaluate your proficiency with this maneuver.
- Since the evaluation of the circular ground track is a bit more subjective in this maneuver than with S-turns across a road, the emphasis is placed on a pilot's ability to arrive over the road in wing's level flight as a means of evaluating his performance in this maneuver.

Eights Around Pylons

If you're interested in improving your ground reference maneuvering skills, you might want to elevate your plane game a bit more by practicing *eights around pylons*. I once taught a ground class to eight students, and when I said that, they all *piled on* (OK, that didn't happen but I could see it in their eyes). Dangerous business, instructing.

The *educational objective* of this maneuver is to use skills learned during the practice of other ground reference maneuvers. Skills such as wind drift assessment and correction, altitude assessment and the ability to fly with your attention diverted to the outside of the airplane.

The *physical objective* of this maneuver is essentially to make circular ground tracks around two different points or pylons in opposite directions while compensating for the effects of wind. From the ground looking up, or the air looking down, this maneuver appears to make the shape of the number eight, as shown in Figure 34 (thank goodness we don't use Roman numerals any more because who could fly something that looks like VIII? Hey, let's do the "V with the three bars" maneuver. What?). This maneuver also requires a lot less subjective evaluation than eights along a road. That's because you're trying to maintain a circular path at a constant radius about two distinct points on the ground. You also don't need to learn anything new here since this maneuver uses only the skills you've learned previously.

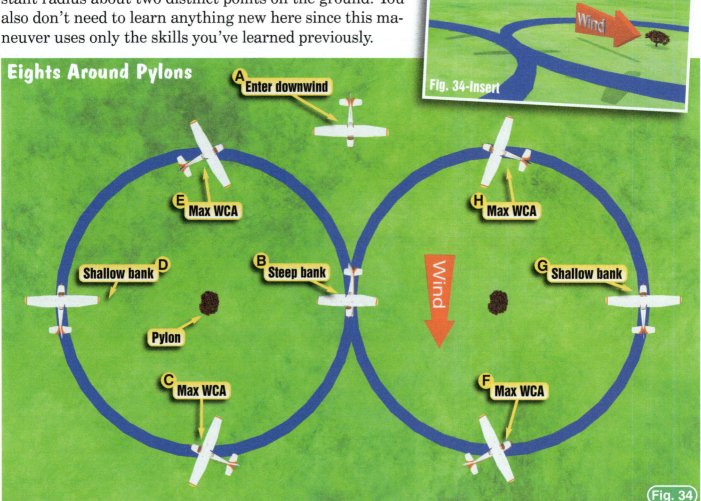

Eights around pylons tests your ability to perform two "turns around a point" in different directions. Your ability to perform them correctly demonstrates your skill at maneuvering right and left while your attention is diverted outside the airplane.

Chapter 7 - Ground Reference Maneuvers

The first thing you want to do is to choose two pylons or ground references oriented perpendicular to the prevailing wind direction. These pylons can be trees, road intersections or any two objects that can be easily seen from at least 600 feet AGL (it's perfectly legal to do this maneuver at 500 feet AGL as long as you meet the minimum altitude requirements in the FARs). Since this maneuver is more advanced than the previously discussed ground reference maneuvers, an altitude of 500 feet AGL increases the skill necessary to pull it off. Why? Because when you're lower, things happen a lot faster, thus requiring more planning and skill on your part (see sidebar below).

You'll begin by flying downwind between the pylons to enter either a right or left turn (we'll enter a right turn in our demonstration), as shown in Figure 34, position A. This maneuver is nothing more than two individual turns around a point that are placed side-by-side. You fly from a turn in one direction to a turn in another direction (Figure 34 Insert, position Z). As Figure 34 shows, to maintain your selected turn radius, the steepest bank is required when flying downwind (position B) and the shallowest bank when flying upwind (positions D and G). Everything you've learned when doing turns around a point applies and should be applied here.

On the upwind and downwind crosswind portions of the loops (positions C, E, F and H), you'll still need to apply the appropriate WCA to make your ground path circular. There's nothing new here except for the change in direction when completing one portion or one half of the eight. At this point, you immediately roll into a bank in the opposite direction to fly a circular track of similar radius.

Why Things Appear to Move Faster When You're Closer to the Ground

It should be no big secret to you that the closer you are to any moving object, the faster it appears to move. Seeing a jet moving overhead at 30,000 feet and 500 mph is a very different thing than seeing the same jet fly overhead at 300 feet. The jet appears to move through your field of vision faster when it's closer to you, which we tend to associate with an increase in speed.

This is one reason why *eights around pylons* is practiced at 500 feet AGL. The intent of this maneuver is to increase your skill level beyond that already gained by performing *rectangular courses, turns around a point* and *S-turn across a road*. This is why you typically practice eights on pylons after (and not before) you've learned the previous three ground reference maneuvers.

30,000' — Happens Slower
300' — Happens Fast

How We Perceive Speed

The Essentials of Eights Around Pylons

The physical objective of this maneuver is essentially to make circular ground tracks around two different points or pylons in opposite directions while compensating for the effects of wind. Done properly, the resulting ground track resembles a figure 8.

Why Do We Do it?—The educational objective of this maneuver is to use skills learned during the practice of other ground reference maneuvers. Skills such as wind drift assessment and correction, altitude assesment and the ability to fly with your attention diverted to the outside of the airplane.

Ground Reference Needed—Choose two pylons or ground references oriented perpendicular to the prevailing wind direction. These pylons can be trees, road intersections or any two objects that can be easily seen from at least 500 feet AGL (the optimal altitude to use for this maneuver as long as it's legal from an FAR perspective of minimum altitudes).

Eights on Pylons, Step-by-Step—
- Establish the desired distance from the pylon in the same way you did during turns about a point.
- Start the eight on a downwind heading while passing between the pylons
- You fly from a turn in one direction to a turn in another direction.
- To maintain your selected turn radius, the steepest bank is required when flying downwind
- To maintain your selected turn radius, the shallowest bank is required when flying upwind.
- The crab into the wind on the downwind loops is applied by turning just a tiny bit faster (i.e., increasing your bank angle) than you normally would if you were flying this arc in a no-wind condition.
- The crab into the wind on the upwind loops is applied by not turning as fast (i.e., decreasing your bank angle) as you normally would if you were flying this arc in a no-wind condition.
- The straight and level portion of this maneuver flown between pylons should be tangent to both patterns.

Maneuver Notes—
- This maneuver is nothing more than two individual turns around a point that are placed side-by-side.
- Unlike the previous ground reference maneuvers, this one can be done as low as 500 feet AGL. The reason for this is that eights around pylons is the most advanced of all the previous ground reference maneuvers. Therefore, performing this maneuver at a lower altitude requires more skill and diligence on your part compared to performing it at a slightly higher altitude. Things appear to happen faster when you're operating closer to the ground.

Rod Machado's How to Fly an Airplane Handbook

Eights-On-Pylons

Also called pylon eights, this is the maneuver you've been waiting for. It's not required for the private pilot test, but it is a required for commercial pilot and flight instructor applicants. If you're a private pilot and want to really sharpen your proficiency, this maneuver is for you. You'll soon be an eights ace. Why? Because *the educational objective* of this maneuver is primarily to teach, develop and test your ability to fly your airplane subconsciously, while your attention is almost entirely focused on ground references.

Unlike eights *around* pylons, this maneuver is about being *on* the pylon, meaning that an imaginary reference parallel to the airplane's lateral axis (as visualized by you from the cockpit) pivots on (about) the pylon. There's a big difference between going *around* something and being *on* something in regard to these two maneuvers. What's common between both maneuvers is that they make a somewhat similar *eight* shape around two ground references (Figure 35). But that's about the only commonality between them.

The maneuver we previously studied, eights *around* a pylon, required you to maintain a constant radius around a ground reference, thus providing a circular ground track. The *physical objective* of Eights *on* pylons, in contrast, requires that you use whatever bank angle and radius from the pylon that are needed to place the imaginary *lateral reference* directly on the pylon and keep it there throughout the turning portion of this maneuver (Figure 36).

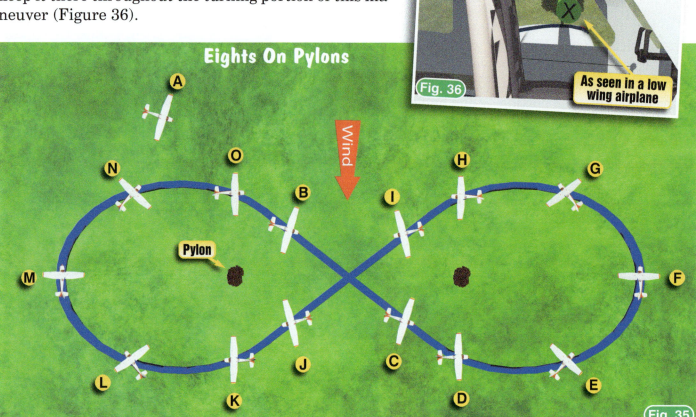

This maneuver is all about *pivoting* on a pylon rather than trying to maintain a constant radius of turn about one. Notice that, except for the straight flight portions of this maneuver (positions between I and J, and B and C) the wing always points toward and pivots about the pylon. This pointing is actually done by a *lateral reference* as seen from the cockpit in Figure 36.

Chapter 7 - Ground Reference Maneuvers

From the cockpit it looks like your lateral axis reference actually pivots about the pylon, thus the reason for the "on" in eights *on* pylons. After flying around the pylon (when wind is present), your ground track isn't circular. Instead, it takes on the shape of an ellipse, with the pylon located at one foci (near one side of the ellipse).

Except for the straight portions of this maneuver, you'll make no attempt to maintain a constant radius of turn or correct for wind using a wind correction angle to manage drift control. If there is any wind present, you'll find that you actually have to *change your altitude* to keep this lateral axis reference on the pylon. Unlike other ground reference maneuvers, this one doesn't require you to maintain altitude or to keep the airspeed constant. In fact, if you're performing this maneuver correctly when wind is present, your altitude *must* vary to keep that imaginary lateral axis reference directly on the pylon as you pivot about the reference.

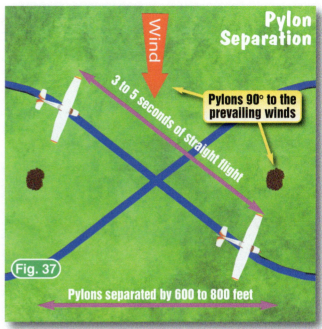

Pick pylons perpendicular to the prevailing winds that are separated by 600 to 800 feet (this allows you to have 3-5 seconds of straight flying between them).

The altitude necessary to make this work is known as the *pivotal altitude* and this value is solely a function of groundspeed. To obtain a good understanding of pivotal altitude, please read the sidebar, *What is This Pivotal Altitude of Which You Speak?* on page 7-32. Let's take a closer look at how to do this maneuver. We'll discuss the intricate details later.

Begin this maneuver by selecting two ground references (the pylons) on an imaginary line lying 90 degrees to the prevailing winds (Figure 37). These pylons should be chosen to allow approximately three to five seconds of level flight crosswise between them. Using a distance of approximately 600 to 800 feet works fine for this maneuver. If you remember what your height above ground looks like at a pattern altitude of 800 feet AGL, then pylons separated at this distance (or a little less) usually work fine when performing this maneuver at a low cruise airspeed of 100 knots in the clean configuration. I find this speed a reasonable value for beginning this maneuver, too.

What about your initial entry altitude for eights on pylons? Having read the sidebar on pivotal altitude, you know that this altitude is based solely on your groundspeed, which depends on your airspeed and the wind speed. If your groundspeed is approximately 100 knots (you're just guessing here and that's OK) as you enter the maneuver, your pivotal altitude is 884 feet. So it's reasonable to enter this maneuver at an altitude of 900 feet, since your initial turn on the pylon occurs at a location where you have a tailwind (where your groundspeed is the highest), thus requiring the maximum pivotal altitude (Figure 38). As you begin your pylon turn into the wind, the pivotal altitude decreases, meaning that you'll have to descend to keep the imaginary lateral reference on the pylon.

Enter eights on pylons by flying downwind between pylons at a "best guess" pilotal altitude of 900 feet AGL (let MSL=AGL here).

What is This Pivotal Altitude of Which You Speak?

It's time to get your bearings, because it's your turn to learn pivotal altitude.

There is an altitude—the pivotal altitude—for any given *groundspeed* at which an imaginary reference line (one that's parallel to the airplane's lateral axis and beginning at the pilot's eye level) appears to pivot on that point as the airplane turns. This altitude is solely a function of the airplane's groundspeed. This means that the pivotal altitude changes if the airplane's groundspeed changes.

Here's why this happens. Airplane A moves at a groundspeed of 100 knots at a 45 degree bank at 884 feet AGL. Because of its speed it flies around a relatively large arc with a large radius of turn. At 884 feet AGL with a 100 knot groundspeed, airplane A pivots about a point on the ground as seen from the line-of-sight view out of the left or right window.

Airplane B moves at a groundspeed of 80 knots at 45 degrees of bank at 566 feet AGL. Because of its slower groundspeed relative to airplane A, it flies around a smaller arc with a smaller radius of turn. At 566 feet AGL with the same 45 degree angle of bank, airplane B also pivots about the same point on the ground as seen from the line-of-sight view out of the left or right window.

Airplane C moves at a groundspeed of 60 knots at a 45 degree bank at 318 feet AGL. Its slower speed means it moves through an even smaller arc with a small turn radius. At 318 feet AGL with 45 degrees of bank, airplane C appears to pivot about the same spot as airplane A and B.

There are two very important points to take away here. First, anything that reduces an airplane's groundspeed reduces the circular arc circumference through which the airplane moves. Therefore, the airplane's pivotal altitude decreases with a reduction in groundspeed, and increases with an increase in groundspeed.

Second, pivotal altitude doesn't vary with the bank angle to any significant degree, as shown in the figure below. It's true that your distance from the pylon affects the bank you use during your pylon turn but this doesn't affect the pivotal altitude. This is seen below with a larger radius of turn needed for a 30 degree bank in place of the 45 degree bank (and shorter radius of turn) used above.

If you're at pivotal altitude and start this maneuver close to the pylon, then you'll need to use a larger bank angle when pivoting about the pylon. If you enter this maneuver farther away from the pylon at the appropriate pivotal altitude for your groundspeed, then your bank will be much less. This is a very important distinction to understand. It's also why, when beginning this maneuver, you'll want to maneuver far enough from the pylon so that the bank at the steepest part of this maneuver doesn't exceed 40 degrees. The recommended bank at the steepest part of this maneuver should be between 30 and 40 degrees, so pick a horizontal distance from the pylon (or modify the distance you're using) that keeps you from exceeding 40 degrees of bank on your initial turn entry.

If you're interested in how pivotal altitude (PA) is derived mathematically, here's the formula. As a general rule, PA= groundspeed^2/11.3 (knots) or 15 (mph). The important thing to understand here is that the formula for PA makes reference to groundspeed and nothing else. Groundspeed is everything in PA.

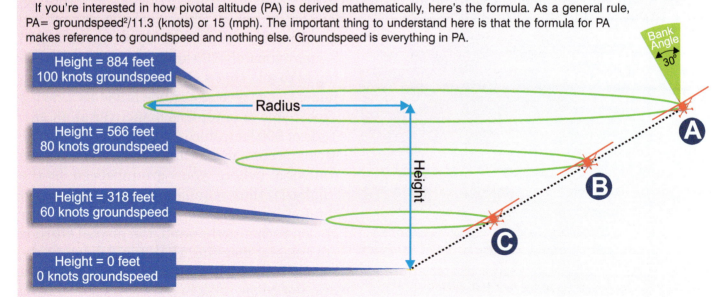

Chapter 7 - Ground Reference Maneuvers

Eights on Pylons - The Details

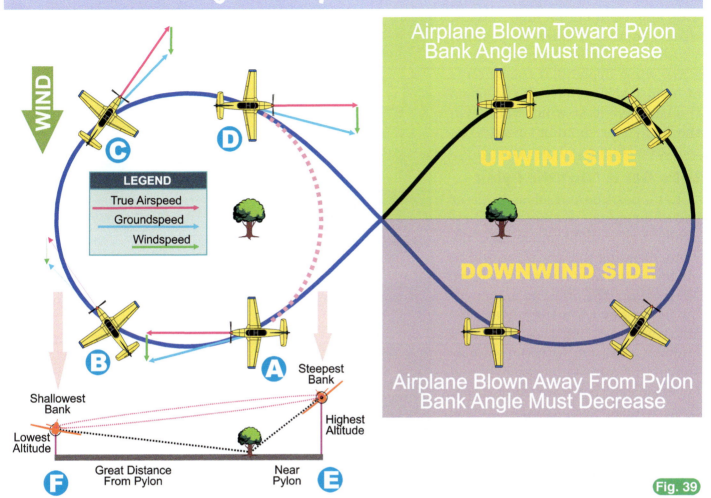

Fig. 39

Here's a point that might not seem intuitive to you. The bank you'll use for this maneuver is entirely dependent on your distance from the pylon. For instance, when you're flying anywhere on the downwind side of the pylon—as defined by a line running through both pylons and perpendicular to the wind—turning about the pylon moves you in a direction that's a combination of the airplane's motion and a wind that blows you away from the pylon (Figure 39, positions A to B). This results in the loop around the pylon stretching outward and forming an ellipse. As you move away from the pylon (from positions A to B) and begin heading into the wind (position B), your ground speed decreases. Therefore, you'll need a shallower bank at a lower altitude to keep your lateral reference on the pylon.

When flying anywhere on the upwind side of the pylon, the wind combined with the airplane's motion moves you inward, closer the pylon (Figure 39, positions C to D). This results in a loop that's closer to the pylon (position D). As you begin to turn downwind (position D) your close proximity to the pylon and the increase in ground speed requires you to steepen the bank to maintain your lateral reference on the pylon.

The bank required when heading directly into the wind (shallow) and when turning downwind (steep) comports with the other ground reference maneuvers we've studied. The only thing that's changing here is the altitude (your pivotal altitude) you must be at to keep your lateral reference on the pylon.

Since you'll want to use banks between 30 and 40 degrees during the maneuver, it's best to start this maneuver with sufficient horizontal distance from the pylon so that the pylon appears a little above the 45 degree diagonal between straight-down and the wing. This applies to both a high and low wing airplanes (Figure 40, position 1). Additionally, as a general rule in a low wing airplane, if the pylon is at or just below your wingtip, then the bank angle at which you begin the maneuver shouldn't need to be too steep (Figure 40, position 2).

Let's Get It "On" the Pylon

Let's position ourselves to enter this maneuver so that our first pylon turn will be made into the wind, meaning that the pylon will be off to our left, as shown in Figure 41, position A. Enter the maneuver by flying downwind (or nearly so since you're flying crosswise in a crabbed condition with the wind as shown in Figure 41, positions B and C.) Once you're positioned properly, fly a wings-level, straight ground track to that pylon by applying the necessary WCA. Of course, entering this maneuver is important but it's not as important as your perform-

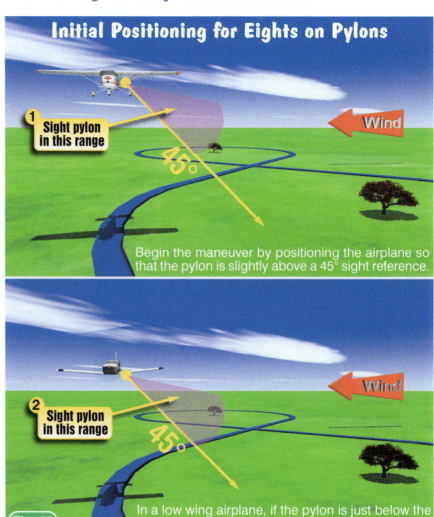

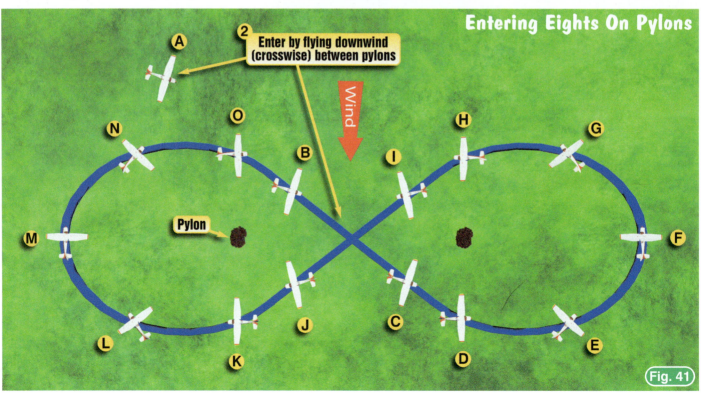

Chapter 7 - Ground Reference Maneuvers

Placement of Your Lateral Reference

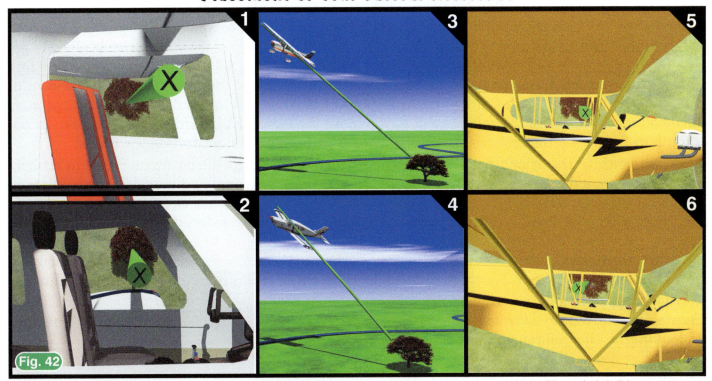

Fig. 42

The lateral reference used to pivot about the pylon isn't the wing's lateral axis. Instead, it's a "line of sight" between your eyes and the pylon that's parallel to the airplane's lateral axis. This occurs below the wing in a high wing airplane (position 1) and above the wing in a low wing airplane (position 2).

ance in the actual maneuver. So don't get your wheel pants wrinkled over getting to the pylon at the precise distance when you first attempt this maneuver. Just do the best you can. With pylon *entries*, there is no do; just try.

Once you're directly abeam the pylon (Figure 41, position D), roll into a turn and place your imaginary lateral reference line (that starts at your eye level and *parallels* the airplane's lateral axis) directly *on* the pylon (Figure 42, positions 1 and 2). Some pilots talk about putting the wing on the pylon, but you're actually placing this imaginary lateral axis reference on it (Figure 42, positions 3 and 4). This imaginary line is parallel to the airplane's lateral axis and often appears at different vertical positions when viewed in high and low wing airplanes (Figure 42, positions 1 or 2). If you're sitting in front or behind in a tandem seated airplane (Figure 42, positions 5 and 6, respectively), then this imaginary reference line will vary based on seating position.

When sitting side-by-side, each seat offers a similar view of where this imaginary reference line is located, assuming both seat occupants have equal seating (eye) heights. The same principle applies in all instances, regardless of where you see this line. Place that lateral reference line directly *on* the pylon. Your objective now is to keep it there. Here's how to make that happen.

As the airplane turns upwind (Figure 43, positions E to F and L to M), its groundspeed decreases. That means pivotal altitude also decreases as shown in the *Pivotal Altitude vs. Groundspeed Graph* in Figure 44. To keep the reference line on the pylon you'll need to apply slight forward elevator pressure to initiate a descent (Figures 45 and 46). If you didn't decrease your altitude slightly beginning at position E and extending through position F in Figures 43, 45 and 46, the reference line will begin to move behind the pylon (or the pylon moves ahead of the reference line) as shown in Figure 47. As a memory aid, think of moving your elevator control in the direction of the pylon. If the pylon moves ahead of the reference line, you move the elevator forward a bit to descend. At position F in Figure 43, the groundspeed is the slowest and the pivotal altitude is the lowest.

As you continue the pylon turn, the groundspeed increases (Figure 43, positions F to G to H). Any turn away from a direct headwind means your groundspeed increases and increasing groundspeed means an increase in pivotal altitude (Figure 44). If you didn't bother to increase your altitude slightly, you'd notice the lateral reference line moving ahead of the pylon (the pylon moves behind the line), as shown in Figure 48. To prevent this, begin a slight climb to keep the reference point on the pylon. Once again, move the elevator in the direction of the pylon. Since the pylon is now moving aft, move the elevator control slightly aft to begin a climb that will return you to the pivotal altitude.

What's happening here is that you're maintaining the required pivotal altitude by looking at the reference point and climbing or descending slightly to keep the lateral reference line on that pylon. Unlike other ground reference maneuvers, you aren't concerned about holding altitude, maintaining a specific radius of turn or maintaining a circular ground track. Nor are you concerned about variations in airspeed, because

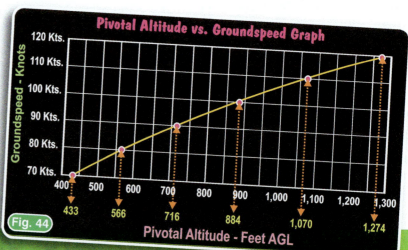

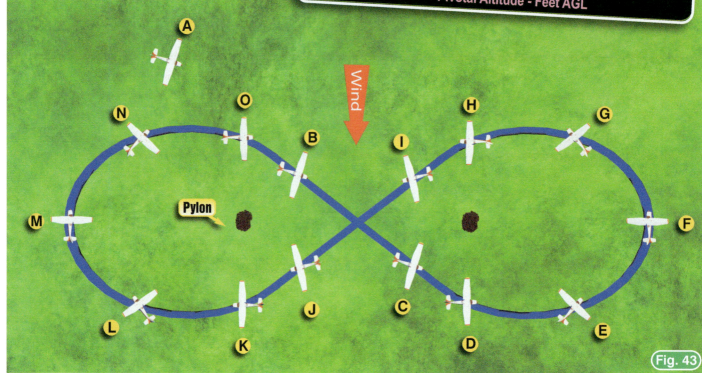

Chapter 7 - Ground Reference Maneuvers

Pivotal Altitude Changes With Changes in Groundspeed

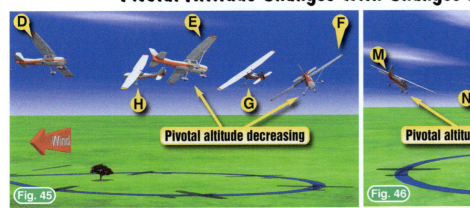

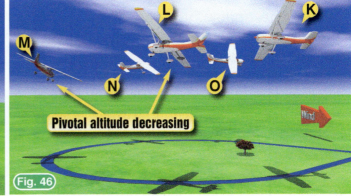

As the airplane heads into the wind (positions D to F and K to M) the groundspeed decreases. Therefore, the pivotal altitude decreases and the airplane must be pointed nose down slightly. As the airplane turns away from a direct headwind (positions F to H and M to O) groundspeed increases and you must apply slight aft elevator pressure to increase your pivotal altitude.

they will occur with this maneuver. That's just fine. This is all about keeping that lateral reference line on the pylon.

As you move from positions F to H in Figure 43, you'll find that you've had to climb a little more to remain at pivotal altitude. When reaching position H, you'll want to roll out, maintain altitude and fly wings-level to position K, where you'll begin a right pivot around the pylon. This means that you must roll out on a heading that allows you to fly for three to five seconds diagonally between pylons and arrive at approximately the same distance from the pylon that you used when beginning your first pylon turn. So you must roll out crabbed into the wind with a wind correction angle applied to correct for drift (Figure 43, positions I and J). Make your best estimate for the WCA and modify it, if necessary, to maintain the selected ground track.

When reaching Figure 43, position K abeam the second pylon, it's time to lower the wing and place the lateral reference line directly on the pylon. Now apply the same techniques used to maintain your pivotal altitude through positions K and O in Figure 43.

Plan on doing two full circuits of eights on pylons to demonstrate that you have sufficient skill and don't hate the eight. With a little practice, you'll become proficient at this maneuver. When you do it says something very positive about your airmanship skills.

Here are a few tips and tricks about eights on pylons.

Sometimes pilots use the term *wingtip* to refer to the lateral reference line, but you're not actually using the wingtip for this maneuver.

You want to choose pylons that are easy to see from the pivotal altitude. Having to hunt for your pylon adds unnecessary difficulty to an already challenging maneuver. Road intersections make ideal pylons. Isolated trees are very good, too. I don't recommend using livestock, since it's best that pylons not move, nor should they yield anything that requires USDA grading. It's also wise to pick pylons both of which are at the same altitude. If one's on a hill and the other in a valley, you add another level of difficulty to this maneuver.

Sometimes turbulence or inattention can cause your heading to change and displace the lateral reference line from the pylon. In other words, one minute your lateral reference is on the pylon and the next minute it's pointed somewhere else entirely. The best way to handle this is to shallow out or increase the bank as appropriate to get that lateral reference line back on the pylon. What you don't want to do here is to use rudder to yaw that reference line into place. This is one of the most common errors among pilots lacking good stick and rudder skills. For them, it's just too easy to slip or skid the airplane to place the lateral reference line on the pylon. Keep in mind that skidding the airplane with rudder is a risky thing to do at such a low altitude. Think spins here.

Now that you're grounded on the essentials of maneuvering with reference to the ground, let's put the airplane on the ground by flying an airport's traffic pattern.

The Essentials of Eights on Pylons

The physical objective is to use whatever bank angle and radius from the pylon are needed to place the imaginary *lateral reference* directly on the pylon and keep it there throughout the turning portion of this maneuver.

Why Do We Do it?—
The educational objective of this maneuver is primarily to teach, develop and test your ability to fly your airplane subconsciously, while your attention is almost entirely focused on ground references.

Ground Reference Needed—
Select two ground references (the pylons) on an imaginary line lying 90 degrees to the prevailing winds and about 600 to 800 feet apart. These pylons should be chosen to allow approximately three to five seconds of level flight crosswise between them.

Eights on Pylons, Step-by-Step—
- Begin this maneuver at a low cruise airspeed of 90 to 100 knots in the clean configuration.
- Enter the maneuver by flying downwind (or nearly so since you're flying crosswise with the wind).
- If your groundspeed is approximately 100 knots (you're just guessing here and that's OK) then use an approximate initial pivotal altitude of 900 feet to begin this maneuver.
- Once you're directly abeam the pylon, roll into a turn and place your imaginary lateral reference line directly on the pylon. Your objective now is to keep it there.
- Since your groundspeed is the highest when entering this maneuver, you'll find that you need a steeper bank to keep your lateral reference on the pylon.
- As the airplane turns upwind its groundspeed decreases and you'll need to apply slight forward elevator pressure to initiate a descent to a lower pivotal altitude.
- As the airplane turns with the wind its groundspeed increases and pivotal altitude increases. You'll have to climb to remain at pivotal altitude.
- You'll roll out and fly wings level between pylons (you must anticipate the WCA to reach the next pylon at the desired offset distance) to a point where you'll begin a pivot in the opposite direction of turn.
- When reaching a position abeam the second pylon, lower the wing, place the lateral reference line directly on the pylon, and apply the same techniques discussed previously to maintain your pivotal altitude.

Maneuver Notes—
- Throughout this maneuver you'll make no attempt to maintain a constant radius of turn or correct for wind using a wind correction angle to manage drift control (except on the straight and level portions between pylons).
- If there is any wind present, you'll find that you actually have to change your altitude to keep this lateral axis reference on the pylon.
- Unlike other ground reference maneuvers, this one doesn't require you to maintain altitude or to keep the airspeed constant.
- If you're performing this maneuver correctly when wind is present, your altitude must vary to keep that imaginary lateral axis reference directly on the pylon as you pivot about the reference.
- Pivotal altitude is solely a function of groundspeed, meaning that pivotal altitude changes if the airplane's groundspeed changes.
- Pivotal altitude doesn't vary with the bank angle to any significant degree.
- You'll want to use banks between 30 and 40 degrees during the maneuver
- It's best to start this maneuver with the pylon a little above the 45 degree diagonal between your seat and the wing on a high wing airplane.
- In a low wing airplane, start with the pylon just below your wingtip.
- If you're sitting in front or behind in a tandem seated airplane, then this imaginary reference line will vary based on seating position.
- The imaginary line is parallel to the airplane's lateral axis.
- Memory aid: move your elevator control in the direction of the pylon.
- You're maintaining the required pivotal altitude by looking at the ground reference point and climbing or descending slightly to keep the lateral reference line on that pylon.

Chapter 8
The Airport Traffic Pattern
The Lowdown on Gettin' Down

What goes up, must come down
Spinnin' wheel, got ta go round

Blood, Sweat and Tears
Spinnin' Wheel

The last chapter had you flying circles and rectangles and angles and I promised you there was a reason for the teasin'; well, there is. Welcome to the *airport traffic pattern,* where you cash in all your hard-earned practice maneuver chips and get something useful for them.

Last chapter, we created building blocks. Now you're at aviation's version of Legoland, and we're going to put the pieces together into something every pilot needs—a way to get down to earth. What goes up must come down, and in order to accomplish that, you've got to go round—round the airport traffic pattern, that is.

The airport traffic pattern is an invisible rectangular box over every runway around which pilots fly at a given altitude and sequence in order to safely transition from air to ground. I want to stress *invisible,* because I've had students who expected to see the lines and labels in the book painted on the ground near the airport. Of course, the same students thought the states would be painted different colors, too (OK, I exaggerate a little...but not much).

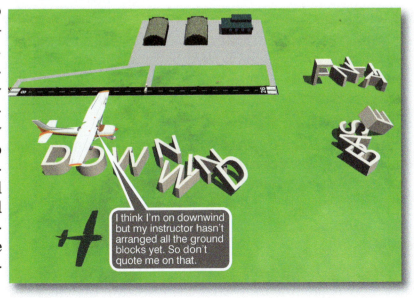

The traffic pattern is like a very large cotillion dance. Every step is carefully choreographed, and improvisation is *not* encouraged or beneficial. Your job in this chapter is to learn the proper dance steps, so that you're never out of step.

The traffic pattern is a place where you are definitely not protected by the "big sky" theory—the notion that it's usually a long way to the next airplane. In the traffic pattern, you often have a large number of airplanes in close proximity to one another. There is nowhere on the aviation landscape where it is more important that pilots be able to have a high degree of confidence they know what all the other pilots are doing and are going to do. Whatever you think of predictability in other contexts, value it in the pattern (Figure 1). Whatever you think of creativity, abandon it in the pattern, where "doing your own thing" can be the undoing of someone else's thing, which is really rude.

The traffic pattern is exactly the opposite of what bees do when circling the hive. While bee flight may not be chaos to the bee, it's certainly not the way we'd want to fly our aircraft when operating in close proximity to each other, is it honey? This is especially important because airplanes don't have bumpers and horns. So our choice is simple: to bee or not to bee. Fortunately the FAA chose "not to bee" by creating recommended procedures for use by all pilots when circling to land—not just small airplane pilots, either.

Each portion of the traffic pattern has a specific name, for easy reference (Figure 2). Good airport citizen that you are, you'll want to know exactly what behavior is expected when operating on each leg of the pattern. In return, you'll benefit by knowing what to expect from other pilots operating in close proximity to you. So let's begin at the beginning.

I See a Pattern Here

> "When I use a word," Humpty Dumpty said, in rather a scornful tone, "it means just what I choose it to mean – neither more nor less."
>
> **Lewis Carroll**
> ***Alice in Wonderland***

And so it is with airport traffic patterns. All airports have them because the FAA says they do, and they mean precisely what the FAA says they mean—neither more nor less.

Fig. 1 — The traffic pattern provides an organized flow of traffic around the landing runway.

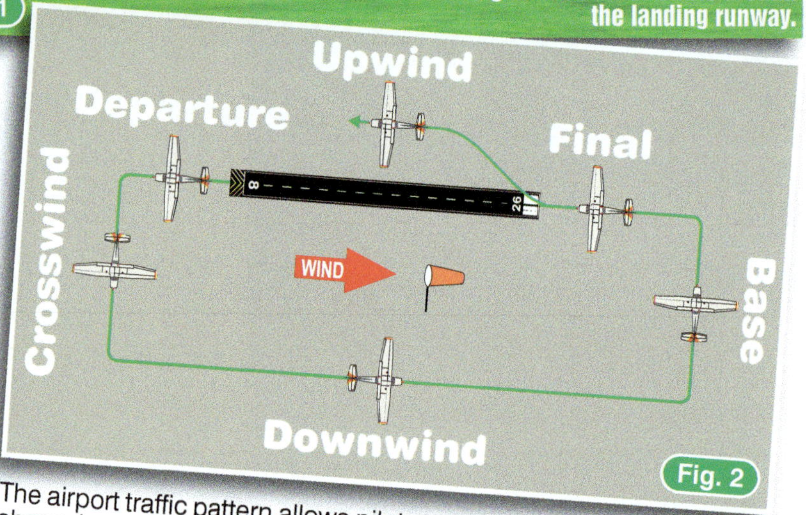

Fig. 2 — The airport traffic pattern allows pilots to fly an organized rectangular shaped pattern around the landing runway. Each segment of the pattern has its own name for easy reference.

Chapter 8 - The Airport Traffic Pattern

Tower Controlled Airports

Tower controlled airports provide airplanes with a takeoff and landing sequence. (Fig. 2A)

Tower controlled airports are shown in blue on a sectional chart. (Fig. 2B)

By and large everyone else agrees that traffic patterns are a good idea. It means you always have some recommendation about how to operate when approaching to land at any airport. This includes airports with operating control towers, called *controlled airports* (Figure 2), and those without operating control towers called *uncontrolled airports,* as shown in Figure 3 (these are sometimes referred to as *non-towered airports* but that's a bit misleading since they might have a control tower that isn't operating at the time. So let's call an airport without an operating control tower an *uncontrolled airport* and be happy with that choice, while acknowledging that "uncontrolled" does not mean "out of control").

At controlled airports, air traffic controllers manage the flow of aircraft. This becomes especially important when the airports are busy. While it's obvious that airports such as Los Angeles, Chicago, and New York need air traffic control towers, there are many general aviation airports that also have a relatively high volume of aircraft traffic. At these airports, pilots fly the established traffic pattern while controllers verbally coax them into an orderly sequence, a job roughly akin to herding ants.

Uncontrolled Airports

Pilots at uncontrolled airports provide their own sequencing and separation between other airplanes. (Fig. 3A)

Uncontrolled airports (airports without an operating control tower) are shown in magenta on a sectional chart. (Fig. 3B)

Old Habit - New Pattern

A Bonanza pilot related how an unfamiliar approach to a familiar field caused some confusion. Proper entry into the traffic pattern is crucial and should be based on situational awareness, not a habit pattern.

I was approaching the airport from the southeast. I contacted the tower and was told to call at three miles for a right base entry to Runway 6. At three miles southeast, I called and was told to watch for traffic on left base for Runway 6. I told tower that the traffic was not in sight. When I finally saw the traffic, it was close off my left wing, about 300 feet below me. I was told by tower that I had flown through the final approach course, very close to landing traffic, and that I was to make a left 180-degree turn to enter final for Runway 6. An uneventful landing was accomplished.

After thinking about the incident, I realized what had happened. I have been to this airport many times, but almost always approaching from the northeast and usually landing on Runway 24. This time I approached from the southeast for a base entry to Runway 6. I was intent on looking for my traffic and mistook Runway 14/32 for Runway 6/24. I was looking at the wrong runway and looking for traffic in the wrong place. When I saw the traffic, I thought he was in the wrong place and I became confused, until the tower told me about flying through the final approach course for Runway 6. I realize that orientation is a full time job, especially when flying in the pattern. When I didn't see the traffic, I should have called the controller and asked for further directions....

ASRS Report

When taking off or landing in the pattern at a controlled airport, be aware that the controller's job is to *sequence you for landing,* not *separate* you for landing. How you separate yourself is your business, at least to a degree. The controller is not typically going to tell you to fly a specific airspeed or maintain so many feet behind another airplane. Besides, air traffic controllers can't physically control your airplane (at least not yet). That's your job, and be happy that it is.

Of course, an air traffic controller isn't going to sit there and let you bump into another airplane in the pattern, either. They hate that, so they may tell you when you are overtaking another aircraft, and suggest a remedy such as S-turns or an altitude change. But how you fly is ultimately your job, so make sure to punch your time clock and get to work when you're in the cockpit.

At airports with less activity, it's difficult to justify establishing an air traffic control tower on the field. At these uncontrolled airports, pilots typically enter, fly and depart the airport's traffic pattern on their own, while announcing their intentions on a *common traffic advisory frequency (CTAF)*. They are left to their own devices in deciding their landing direction and sequence among other aircraft in the pattern.

If the idea of a lot of pilots flying around near an airport without someone telling them what to do raises a few questions, then find solace in the fact that when everyone knows the rules of the aviation road, operation by cooperation usually works quite well.

Think of all the four-way stop signs there are on highways in the U.S. You don't see automobile carcasses piled high at each of these intersections. That's because drivers follow the rules (OK, at least most of the time). Why do they follow the rules? Because bad things, such as increased insurance rates, crumpled fenders (and worse) happen if they don't. Pilots follow the rules for operations at an uncontrolled airport for the same reasons and because they need to be able to predict what other pilots will do in the traffic pattern. *Predictability* is the key to making the system work for everyone.

That's why the concept of the traffic pattern is so important. The traffic pattern represents a very standardized way for pilots to depart from or land at an airport. If everyone does what they're supposed to do in the traffic pattern, then everyone knows what everyone else is going to do. Once you know where you fit in the sequence of traffic, simply take your place in line, sing "Heigh-ho, heigh-ho, it's off to land I go," and happily follow the aircraft ahead of you for landing. All you have to do is not be Dopey.

Let's take a closer look at the airport traffic pattern, and see how to approach and join one.

Chapter 8 - The Airport Traffic Pattern

Traffic Pattern Components

Traffic patterns are rectangular in shape and consist of six segments: *departure leg, crosswind leg, downwind leg, base leg, final approach* and *upwind leg* (Figure 4). Three of these (downwind, base, and final) are part of a normal landing sequence. The departure and crosswind legs are encountered on takeoff and landing circuit practice. And the upwind leg is an exception you'll use occasionally.

Traffic patterns are supposed to be flown in such a way that they produce a rectangular shape. When some pilots fly the pattern, it's clear they didn't do well in high school geometry, let alone kindergarten block time. Their rectangle traces the outlines of a constantly-morphing amoeba. There's a good reason for getting in shape in the pattern—predictability. Being where you're supposed to be gives others confidence that they know what you'll do and where you'll be in the next instant, and it gives you the best shot at seeing them. So there's that word *predict* again. It won't be the last time you see it.

Components of the Traffic Pattern

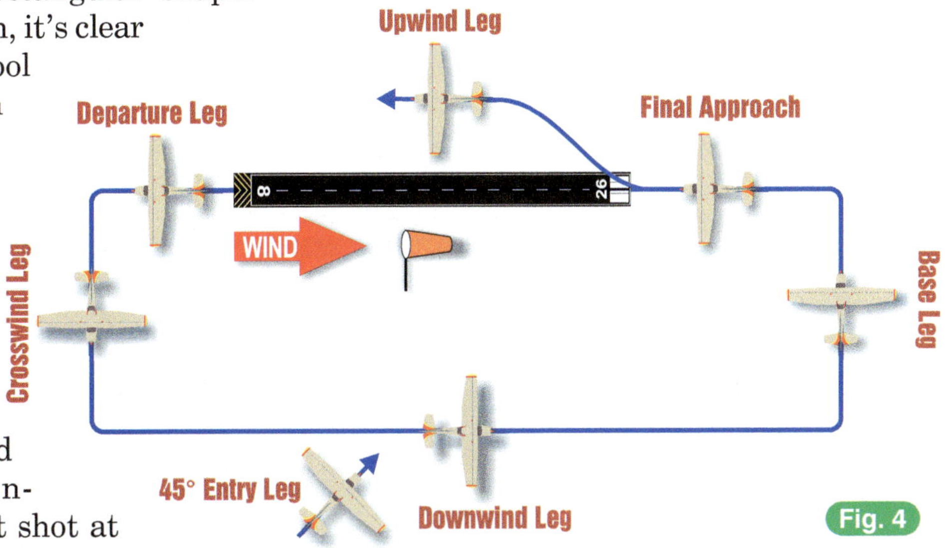

Fig. 4

The Departure Leg

Airplane takeoffs are made into the wind and the takeoff flight path is thus called the *departure leg* (Figure 5). After takeoff, you have two choices—you can either *depart* the traffic pattern (by flying straight ahead and eventually turning), or you can *remain* in the pattern (that's pilot talk for *remain in the airport traffic pattern*), which means you'll fly the full rectangular path and return for landing on the runway from which you just departed. You don't necessarily do this because you enjoy very short flights. You usually do it because you enjoy practicing landings (and who doesn't?). Keep in mind that many airports have local noise abatement requirements that apply heading and/or altitude restrictions on the departure leg. Please honor these restrictions.

The departure leg is made into the wind whenever possible. This shortens your ground run and allows the airplane to become airborne quicker.

Fig. 5

The Crosswind Leg

If you're remaining in the pattern, a turn (a left turn if you're flying *left traffic* or a right turn if you're flying *right traffic*) to the *crosswind leg* (Figure 6) will be made when the airplane is at least a half mile beyond the departure end of the runway and within 300 feet of the TPA or *traffic pattern altitude* (most traffic patterns have a recommended altitude, which can be found in the *Chart Supplement* as shown in Figure 7). This portion of the pattern is called the crosswind leg because the flight path (the airplane's track over the ground) is perpendicular to the runway and generally crosswise to the wind direction.

Most of the time you will arrive at the half-mile position before getting to within 300 feet of traffic pattern altitude. This is particularly true for lower performance airplanes. If you continued flying straight ahead until your altitude was within 300 feet of the TPA, the local pattern traffic might think you're departing the airport. In some instances, you might even fly beyond the normal anticipated rectangular boundaries of the pattern by the time you reach the TPA.

In these instances, it's perfectly reasonable to make your turn to crosswind at a slightly lower altitude. This keeps you closer to the runway and allows other airplanes in the pattern to keep better track of you. Do use a little common sense here. Typically there are no big buildings in the departure path of a runway, because the FAA discourages such things. It's not that they don't *like* big buildings, it's just that they don't like them in the departure path.

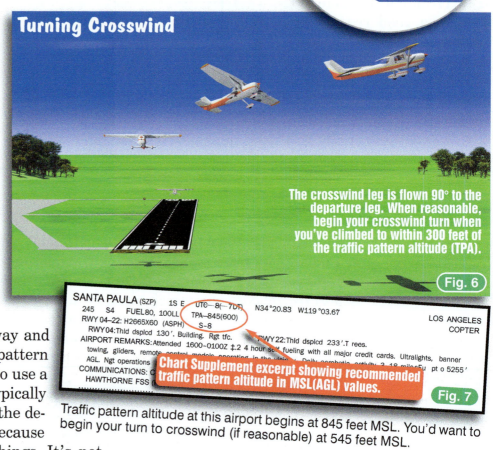

Fig. 6

Fig. 7

Traffic pattern altitude at this airport begins at 845 feet MSL. You'd want to begin your turn to crosswind (if reasonable) at 545 feet MSL.

There can, however, be larger buildings offset from the runway. In these instances, turning an early crosswind might keep you closer to the runway but it could also result in a low and close-in fly-by of an office typist. They tend to get keyed off about such things. Since they know how to type, you don't want one of them sending the FAA a letter of complaint about you, do you? Of course not.

One very common error when turning from the departure leg to the crosswind leg is a loss of attitude control. In a left pattern, when making a left turn to crosswind, it's not at all uncommon for students to let the nose drop toward the horizon, sometimes even below the horizon (Figure 8). That's because they're looking at the *apparently* raised right side of the panel on a side-by-side airplane (Figure 9) instead of looking directly ahead of their seated position for attitude information. They're also attracted to the wonderful view of the ground that has just appeared out their left window.

Chapter 8 - The Airport Traffic Pattern

Fig. 8 — When making a left turn to crosswind, pilots tend to let the nose drop because the right side of the instrument panel appears raised above the horizon. Instead, they should use their normal pitch attitude reference located directly ahead of their seated position.

Fig. 10 — When making a right turn to crosswind, pilots tend to raise the nose because the right side of the instrument panel appears lower than the horizon. Once again, they should use their normal pitch attitude reference located directly ahead of their seated position.

Looking at the ground expands your aesthetic horizons but unfortunately does nothing about giving you horizon (attitude) information. The airplane often descends in these conditions.

Turning to a right crosswind in a right hand traffic pattern, the tendency is to raise the airplane's nose (Figure 10) because students look to the *apparently* lowered right side of the airplane (Figure 11). And the attraction to the view of the ground out the right window is often just too tempting for pilots without the requisite Jedi mind training needed to resist. You can imagine what raising or lowering the nose in either one of these conditions does to the airplane's climb performance, right? We discussed this viewing bias in Chapter Three, but the point is worth repeating here.

Now I want you to make me a promise. First, uncross those fingers. Good. I need you to promise me that during the climb on the crosswind leg that you'll quickly but smoothly lower the nose, look for traffic, then return the nose to climb attitude. That's right. Thumbs up to nose down, for a brief moment. I need you to look for traffic that may be entering the traffic pattern directly ahead of you. In many cases, you just can't see well enough over the nose during a climb to ensure that there's no traffic ahead of you. So lower the nose, look, then return to climb attitude pronto. Promise? OK, I believe you.

The Downwind Leg

As the airplane continues its climb, you will make another turn to the left (90 degrees in a no wind condition). This puts the wind at your tail (roughly), and the airplane tracking parallel to the runway, traveling opposite to the direction of landing (Figure 12). This is called the *downwind leg* because you are now traveling in the general direction as the wind, if any wind is present, of course. Throughout the departure, crosswind and even a part of the downwind legs, the airplane continues to climb until reaching traffic pattern altitude.

Part of your preflight duty is to learn the correct traffic pattern altitude at your intended airport of landing. The information can be found in the *Chart Supplement* (Figure 7), other printed materials, and online in many sources. The TPA varies from one airport to the next because of terrain, obstruction and noise concerns. Expect traffic pattern altitudes to range from 600 to 1,500 feet above the airport elevation, averaging about 1,000 feet AGL.

I want to offer one very big word of caution to those who will be turning from crosswind to downwind in a low wing airplane. It's entirely possible for your raised wing (the wing on the outside of the turn) to keep you from seeing another pilot entering the traffic pattern (from your right side when flying a left hand pattern), as shown in Figure 14. This is why it's extremely important to look both ways before making any turn, especially in a low wing airplane while operating in the pattern.

Turning from crosswind to downwind in a low wing airplane might prevent you from seeing incoming traffic because of the raised outside wing.

Airplanes of different size flying at much different speeds can be found in the traffic pattern. Bigger and faster airplanes typically fly larger, wider and higher traffic patterns.

Chapter 8 - The Airport Traffic Pattern

Bobbing and Weaving for a Better View of Traffic

When the famous bank robber Willie Horton was asked why he robbed banks, he answered by saying that this is where the money is. Well, airports are where the airplanes are, too. That means we need to be especially vigilant for airplanes arriving in the traffic pattern while we're using it. So, just how do you do this?

A good fighter avoids punishing blows from his opponent by bobbing and weaving. This is precisely what I expect you to do in the traffic pattern, too. During your climb on the crosswind leg, it's very difficult to see what's ahead of you. So lower your nose, take a peek at what's ahead, then raise your nose back to climb attitude. This won't cost you more than a few knots in climb airspeed variation, either.

When established on the downwind leg, feel free to make a quick S-turn to see what's above you (if you're in a high wing) or below you (if you're in a low wing airplane).

So you'll look to your left before turning downwind but you'll also look ahead of you and to the right of the airplane's nose to see if anyone is entering the downwind leg, perhaps at some angle that's not considered standard for an entry. We'll talk more about traffic pattern entries shortly.

For smaller airplanes, the downwind leg is flown at an offset of approximately a half mile from the landing runway (Figure 13). I like to keep the downwind leg as close to the runway as reasonable, since this places me within gliding distance of the runway in the event of an engine problem.

Larger multi-engine, turboprop and jet airplanes often fly patterns with the downwind leg offset at higher altitudes and larger horizontal distances—up to one mile—to keep from having to mix it up (or grind it up) with smaller, slower flying machines. They also fly a wider pattern because they have to fly faster to remain in the air (Figure 15). Flying a tighter traffic pattern would result in these larger and faster airplanes having to make much steeper turns to remain within the pattern perimeter, and that results in an increasing stall speed while uncomfortably close to the ground.

If you happen to be operating at an uncontrolled airport with one of these larger airplanes flying a wider and higher pattern, you're still playing follow the leader. The only question is, who is the leader if one airplane is flying faster, higher and wider than the other? This is where you have to use your mighty 1400cc brain to mediate while you aviate. If it's clear that you can land and get off the runway before the larger airplane approaches the threshold, then do so. If you're not sure you can do this, then slow your machine down and find a landing sequence you can live with.

If you are both using the airport's common traffic advisory frequency (Figure 16), then work out a landing sequence between yourselves. Ask the pilot of the larger airplane about his or her intentions and inform him about yours. This is the aviation version of *Let's Make a Deal*. At a tower controlled airport the controller makes the deal for you by providing a landing sequence. When

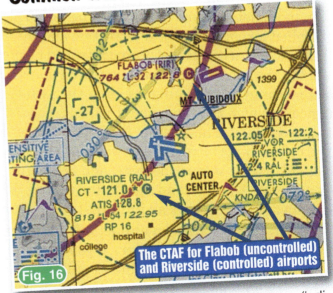

The CTAF or common traffic advisory frequency (indicated by a white "C" on a magenta or blue circle) is used at controlled and uncontrolled airports to communicate with the tower (when it's operating) and with other airplanes, in the case of a non-towered airport.

The Finger-Decoder Method of Pattern Entry

Trying to find the proper runway when entering a traffic pattern can sometimes be a challenge, especially when the airport has more than one runway. So try the finger-decoder method.

Here's how it works. If you were instructed to enter right downwind for Runway 14, then place your pointer finger over the center of the heading indicator and point to that number on the compass rose (position A). Keep the knuckle of your right pointer finger over the center of the heading indicator. Now look through your windscreen and find the runway that most closely parallels your finger. Congratulations! You just found Runway 14. You da man or (wo)man.

If you were instructed to make left traffic for Runway 24, place your pointer finger over the center of the heading indicator as shown in position B and point to the number 24 on the compass rose. That's Runway 24.

The direction your finger points in the direction of the runway on which you'll land. Of course, you'll have to figure out how to maneuver so as to enter right or left traffic for that runway. Nevertheless, this method makes it easier for you to identify runways when approaching an airport.

operating around bigger airplanes, it's always wise to remember the ancient dictum that, *Confucius say pedestrian have right of way but rickshaw have more momentum*. Bigger airplanes have more momentum, too. So don't demand your right of way and be smashed right away.

Now that you know a little something about the downwind leg, what speed should you fly it at in your small airplane? The pattern works best for everyone when everyone is flying more or less the same speed. This minimizes the risk and complications of airplanes overtaking one another.

Keeping in mind that you are setting up for a landing, it's time to slow it down, Big Boy or Girl. The pattern is a transition to the ground. Clearly, you don't want to fly this leg as if it's your shift at Le Mans. Curb your need for speed. You would like to avoid poking your spinner into another airplane's empennage on the downwind leg (Figure 17). How rude.

The flip side of the pattern coin is to never let yourself be rushed. If there is someone behind you who is clearly bigger and faster, don't be shy about making your presence known. Talk and rock those wings. It's his or her job to avoid you, and they'll most likely pass you on the outside of the pattern, away from the downwind leg. Then again, remembering your Confucian lesson, you're not obligated to let someone in a bigger, faster airplane nip at your tailfeathers. If you're operating at a controlled airport, then be a tattle tale and inform the controller of your discomfort. If you're operating at either a controlled or uncontrolled airport, take whatever evasive action is needed to remain safe. On the other hand, you might find yourself rushing to accommodate a controller's request to do something a little different than that which you're used to doing. Pilots develop a definite sequence in which they complete the tasks needed to land, and definite cues for initiating each action in the sequence. This is their *pattern in the pattern*. Interrupt the sequence and you can be headed for trouble. If a controller asks you for a "short approach" (an abbreviated pattern often involving steeper turns, a steeper descent, and less setup time than normal on base leg and final approach), you *can* say, "Unable" and they'll find a place for you farther back in the line. Just don't let yourself be rushed unless there's an immediate need for action.

The first rule of pattern etiquette is to follow the leader (or the airplane you've been instructed to follow by the tower controller), if you can. If you're in a higher performance single-engine airplane and are following a Piper Cub, then pull that throttle back and slow your airplane down. That's one of the reasons you learned how to fly slowly, right? So fly slowly, if you feel it's safe to do so. If you're operating at a controlled airport and can't fly slowly enough to follow the airplane ahead, then let the controller know. He or she might have you make S-turns, pass the other airplane, or have you or the other airplane make a 360 degree turn for spacing. Or, you might request to perform any of these maneuvers, too.

Chapter 8 - The Airport Traffic Pattern

On the other hand, if you're operating at an uncontrolled airport, the best option is often to pass the aircraft to the outside of the pattern (by a wide margin) and not on the runway side of the traffic pattern (Figure 18). For instance, in a left hand traffic pattern, the runway is to the left so don't pass to the left (Figure 19). Doing so would mean placing yourself directly in the turn trajectory of the airplane ahead of you if he or she decides to turn base early. The pilot is eventually going to turn left, so why place yourself on the turn side? If this is a right hand traffic pattern, then pass to the left, toward the outside of the pattern.

Yes, I know that FAR 91.113(f) says you should overtake another airplane and pass on the right, but this is an instance where common sense rules are better than the written rules. Applying the FAR passing rule on the downwind leg when flying *right* traffic is not only terribly unwise, but it is also dangerous. Pilots on downwind are looking for airplanes entering the pattern on a 45-degree angle to the downwind leg (from the outside edge of the pattern). They aren't expecting another airplane to pass between them and the runway.

At an uncontrolled airport, if the pilot ahead of you is flying so slowly that he's acting as though he has an appointment for a root canal, then you often have no choice but to take the lead. So lead. If possible, you'll also want to inform the pilot ahead about your intentions (assuming that both of you can communicate by radio, since he probably doesn't read smoke signals). The thought of making a 360-degree turn on the downwind leg to increase the spacing might enter your mind. In most cases, it's a good idea to let that idea pass on through. While a 360 in the pattern isn't illegal at an uncontrolled airport (it is uncontrolled, right?), doing so can present a real problem if there's someone behind you and you don't realize it (which is certainly a greater possibility at an uncontrolled airport). If

Maintaining Pattern Spacing

If you're flying a higher performance (faster) airplane, you'll want to be slow enough by the time you enter the downwind leg so as to prevent chewing off another airplane's tailfeathers.

Maneuver to the Outside of the Pattern

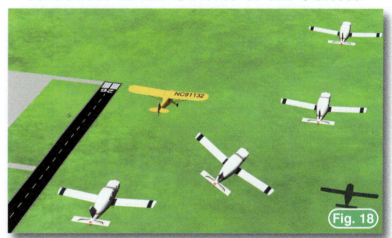

If you're unable to remain behind another airplane, then pass that airplane to the outside of the pattern. This is, after all, where faster and larger airplanes fly their pattern.

How Not to Maneuver Around Pattern Traffic

Maneuvering on the inside of pattern traffic means that the airplane ahead might turn directly into you. This is very dangerous.

you decided that a 360 was necessary at a controlled airport, then ask the controller's permission first.

Please use caution if you decide to make any maneuver in the traffic pattern that's considered unusual or unexpected. All pilots have a responsibility to avoid surprising other pilots in the traffic pattern. Besides, we've already established that pilots don't like surprises (unless they involve shiny gift wrapping or some form of chocolate).

If you are flying a wider pattern to pass a slower airplane and then make your turn to base leg, be aware that your forward progress in the downwind direction has ceased; the other pilot's hasn't, which could make you a spearfish candidate (Figure 20). You *are* going to cross his path; it's just a question of where he is at that instant. If I were you, or even me, I'd make sure there's plenty of "passing room" when you do this.

Turning Toward Another Airplane in the Pattern

When flying a slightly wider downwind leg and turning onto base leg ahead of another slower airplane for landing, use extreme caution. The slower airplane inside of you on the downwind leg might not anticipate your turn base leg turn. Even at pattern speeds, airplanes converge quickly.

Fig. 20

A similar problem exists if you fly a pattern of normal width and a slower airplane departs behind you only to turn downwind inside your flight path (Figure 20). This is a rather common event, too. Apparently these people didn't get the memo about being good pattern citizens. Since you can't revoke their citizenship, you have to pay in adrenaline for these kinds of things. You've got an airplane to your left and behind you (or to your right, inside and behind you in a right hand pattern). So give yourself enough spacing to ensure you maintain a reasonable distance ahead of that airplane.

Can We Talk: Time for a Chat

As a general rule at a controlled airport, when you make your initial contact with the tower for landing, you'll be told to report entering or established on the downwind leg. This is the tower controller asking for his or her own wakeup call, to remind him that you're there. Here is where you'll say something similar to, "Goldenrod Tower, Gasburner 45 Tango, downwind." You will usually be told where you are in line, and whom you should follow. Unless given other instructions, it's up to you when and how to turn base and final and descend to land.

Radio communications are similar, but a little different at uncontrolled airports. Here, it's recommended (and always wise) that you report your position as you enter the traffic pattern, as well as when you're established on the downwind leg, base leg and on final approach.

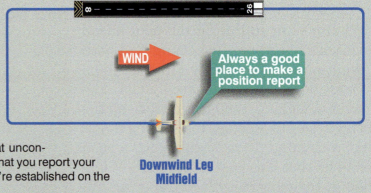

You might, for instance, say, "Big Toad traffic, Cessna 2132 Bravo, entering downwind, Runway 25, full stop, Big Toad." Begin and end your message with the airport name, state what it is you're doing, identify the runway you're using, then tell everyone within ear shot what you plan to do on that runway. For instance, when established on base leg, you might say, "Big Toad traffic, Cessna 2132 Bravo, base leg, full stop, Big Toad." Or, "Big Toad traffic, Cessna 2132 Bravo, final, full stop, Big Toad." You get the point, right? If pilots can't or don't visually detect you, then help them locate you with their ears. Begin your career in broadcasting by making those radio calls. But don't hog the airways, either. Think minimum talk, maximum message.

Traffic Pattern Speed

There are no set rules for how fast to fly in the traffic pattern (except for FAR 91.117 that stipulates a maximum indicated airspeed of 200 knots IAS in Class C and D airspace). So it's good to think of the *basic speed law* that's associated with driving an automobile. In other words, don't fly faster than is safe. It's good to have an idea of what an experienced flight instructor thinks is safe or at least reasonable. As a general rule (and I do mean *general*), there's no sense going anywhere fast in the

As a general procedure when flying smaller training airplanes, fly the downwind leg at 1.5 Vs; base leg at 1.4 Vs and final approach at 1.3 Vs. Fig. 21

pattern. That's why I prefer my student pilots fly the downwind leg at 1.5 Vs (50% above the airplane's present stall speed, but I'm certainly fine with flying downwind at faster speeds). Base leg should be flown at 1.4 Vs and final approach at 1.3 Vs/Vso (Figure 21). These speeds keep your pattern geometry smaller and reduce the larger bank angles associated with higher pattern speeds.

As I previously mentioned, flying fast in the pattern means you must use steeper banks to remain within the desired pattern perimeter. Steeper banks mean a higher stall speed, too. How can that be good when operating closer to the ground? Unfortunately, there are always some pilots who don't like flying slowly, either because they become nervous when they do it because they're frightened of stalls, or they simply aren't proficient at the lower range of speeds. What a shame. In an attempt to remain above stall speed, they actually end up closer to it because of steeper turns made in the pattern. Don't be one of these individuals. Master your airplane, otherwise it will master you.

Configuring for Landing on Downwind

Continue downwind until you're abeam (opposite) the beginning of the runway's landing threshold (Figure 22). This is a good time to begin configuring the airplane for approach and landing.

It's generally a good procedure to begin configuring the airplane for landing when reaching a position abeam the landing threshold (A). At this point, the landing gear should already be extended (if retractable) and 10-15 degrees of flaps extended.

After ensuring that the airplane is below its maximum flap extension speed, applying 10-15 degrees of flaps at this point is usually a good idea. In addition to reducing the airplane's stall speed, the application of flaps also allows your airplane to fly with a slightly lower nose attitude. That means that you can better see what's ahead of you, especially when beginning your descent.

While a few pilots like to begin their descent for

landing when abeam the runway threshold on the downwind leg (or even earlier), I don't recommend that you join their ranks. Descending at this point produces more risk than it's worth. There may be other airplanes entering the pattern, and it's sometimes hard to know whether or not there's someone above or below you. Whether you fly a high or low wing airplane, some portion of the sky is a "blind spot" for you (Figure 23). When all pilots operate at the same altitude on the downwind leg, they're more easily observed and detected by other pilots who look to the right, the left, ahead and behind their airplanes. Descending on the base leg (coming up next) is a far wiser strategy for any pilot.

If you're flying a retractable-geared airplane, you'll want to make sure that your landing gear is down and locked into position while you're on the downwind leg. Besides, you probably extended your landing gear

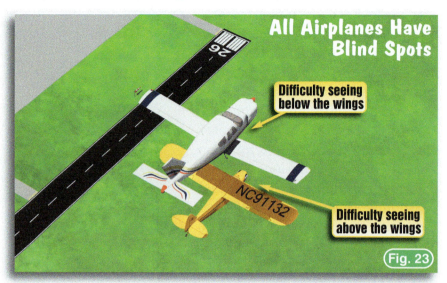

All airplanes have blind spots. Low wing pilots can't see what's below them while high wing pilots can't see what's above them. This is why it's extremely important to maintain pattern altitude on the downwind leg and, if necessary, to make maneuvering turns to see what above or below you.

prior to or while entering the traffic pattern, especially if you were trying to lose altitude to reach pattern altitude. But you can't check for landing legs too often, so there's no downside to seeing what's where in the downwind, and if for some reason you haven't yet lowered the gear, for sure you want to do it now.

That's why it's wise to use a memory aid such as GUMP to prevent yourself from forgetting to properly configure your complex airplane for landing (Figure 24). GUMP stands for *gas* (fuel tank selected that has adequate fuel supply and fuel boost pump on, if appropriate), *undercarriage* (gear is confirmed down and locked into position), *mixture* (full rich or as appropriate for the density altitude conditions during landing) and *prop* (propeller control in the full forward, high RPM position at least by the time you cross the runway threshold). Use this memory aid on downwind, base, final and when crossing the runway threshold (that's four times) to ensure your landing gear is down.

When operating airplanes having retractable landing gear, you should use the memory aid GUMP (gas, undercarriage, mixture, prop) on downwind, base, final and when crossing the threshold. This ritual helps prevent gear-up landings.

And just because a checklist memory aid has an item that doesn't pertain to you doesn't mean the checklist isn't valuable. For instance, you certainly wouldn't switch to another fuel tank (gas) on the downwind leg. That wouldn't be wise at all, unless you're using a tank containing mostly fuel vapors. On

Chapter 8 - The Airport Traffic Pattern

the other hand, the term *gas* also implies use of the fuel pump, which is often required to be turned on for landing in low wing airplanes (or the mixture control properly adjusted for landing). Some airplanes have a constant speed propeller but no retractable landing gear. If you're in that category and using the GUMP memory aid, just don't do anything with your gear, which should be easy since you can't do anything with your gear.

Base Leg

Speaking of *base leg*, let's speak about it, since it's the basis of your landing.

Assuming that traffic isn't a factor, the optimal time to start your turn onto base leg is when the landing threshold appears 45 degrees between the wing and the tail of your airplane (Figure 25). In other words, as you look out the left window, the runway threshold appears to be at a 45 degree angle to the left of the wing (or midway between the wing and the tail). This gives you enough distance from the runway to make a comfortable approach (Figure 26), which is one that doesn't involve steep banks and excessive rates of descent and your passengers holding their hands up over their heads just like they would when riding the world's scariest rollercoaster (Figure 27). Turning base leg before reaching the 45 degree angle position can easily result in your being too high on approach.

Of course, we're assuming that traffic in the pattern permits you to turn base when you want to turn base. As the Rolling Stones taught us, you can't always get what you want (but if you try, sometimes you might find, you get what you need). When other pilots are using the pattern, you must follow the leader. That might mean flying an extended downwind leg as you follow the airplane ahead, whether instructed to do so by a controller, or because you see it's the only alternative. It might

Plan on your turn from downwind to base leg when you can look over your left shoulder (right shoulder for right traffic) and see the runway threshold half way between the tail and the wings (i.e., 45° to your left).

Delaying the Base Leg Turn Because of Traffic

When there's traffic on final approach, you might have to delay your turn onto base leg to maintain the proper spacing for landing. Normally, when the traffic on final passes your wing, you can turn inbound and maintain about a half mile spacing between you and the other airplane. If the traffic you're following is much slower than you (Figure 28), then you might want to delay your turn to base leg a little longer. If you're following faster jet traffic inbound (Figure 29), it still might be wise to delay your turn to base leg a little longer to give the jet's wake turbulence a chance to dissipate before landing.

also mean that you extend your downwind leg to give the person on final approach sufficient time to land and exit the runway. Delaying your turn to base leg until the airplane on final has passed off your wing generally works out correctly in terms of spacing (Figure 28 and 29).

Don't get locked in to *always* turning base at a certain spot at your home runway (or anywhere else). Unfortunately, some pilots get into the bad habit of using a local ground reference at their home airport to decide when to make their turn to base leg. For example, a pilot might use the *Sum Ting Wong* Chinese restaurant to cue him or her when to turn base leg. The problem with this strategy is that you're not likely to find the same restaurant at the same location at every airport, right? That's right. You might look for your "turning" restaurant and it won't be there, which means that either you've got the wrong Wong or it's not your turn.

When to turn base is a separate calculation each time, and it varies with wind, other traffic, airspeed and several other variables. Use a little common sense to figure this out and always err on the side of increasing the distance between you and the other airplane rather than decreasing it. Turning too soon might mean having to execute a go-around if the landing airplane ahead doesn't clear the runway in time. And you don't want to rush someone, any more than you want to be rushed.

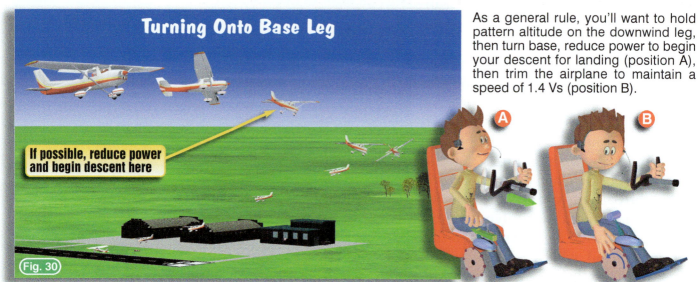

Chapter 8 - The Airport Traffic Pattern

Base leg is a point of transition for landing and that's why it's often wise to begin your descent on this leg and continue that descent throughout final approach and landing (Figure 30). It's the place where important adjustments are made in the airplane's speed and landing configuration.

Final Approach

The *final approach* (for those on a first-name basis with it, it's just *final*) is a critical part of the landing sequence. Sometimes new pilots think *final approach* sounds a bit ominous, like the last roundup or the end of the line. Relax. It's final, not *finito*. It's called final because it's the final leg of the pattern, and anyone who says anything different doesn't have a leg to stand on.

This is the leg on which you align yourself with the runway centerline for landing (Figure 31) and make (we hope minor) adjustments to your glidepath in order to land in the center of the first third of the runway.

A square turn onto final approach is best since it gives you the most time to assess the airplane's glidepath.

Generally, a square turn from base onto final approach is best. This provides you with enough time on the final approach leg to observe your airplane's descent path and alignment with the runway. You can also observe and correct for the effect of crosswinds on the airplane if you give yourself a reasonably long final approach. This is a very important point to consider. The last thing you want to happen when approaching to land is to roll out on final approach without enough time to see how the wind is affecting your airplane.

If your downwind is flown a half mile from the runway and you use the 45 degree wing-threshold-tail reference to cue your turn to base leg, then according to Euclid (who did very well in his high school geometry class) you should now find yourself with at least a half mile final approach (unless you're flying in curved Einsteinian space, which most flight instructors prohibit). A half-mile final approach should be the minimum for any student pilot learning to land.

Learn to See With Your Ears

One of the things you learn when you spend enough time in the traffic pattern is that air traffic controllers can't always monitor the behavior of all the airplanes in the traffic pattern. That's right. Airplanes sometimes enter the pattern at controlled airport without making radio calls. I've even seen airplanes cut directly across the pattern at pattern altitude in Class C airspace without having any radio contact with the tower, much less approach control. Controllers, like pilots, are human and they make mistakes. That means you are ultimately responsible for seeing and avoiding traffic at controlled and uncontrolled airports. Aside from using your eyeballs to do that, you should also learn to see with your ears when operating in the traffic pattern.

For instance, if you're climbing on the crosswind leg and you hear a pilot report inbound on the forty-five (a 45 degree entry onto the downwind leg), then you know there's a chance for this traffic to merge onto the downwind about the time you're downwind midfield. The moment you hear this pilot's report, you should begin searching for that traffic.

Anytime you're operating in the pattern, you should always listen to any airplane making a position report. Keep a mental note of that airplane and its position. Be especially alert if the pilot of the transmitting airplane seems confused about his or her location, too. As a general rule, these are the pilots that are most likely to be somewhere other than they say they are.

When turning from base leg onto final approach, you have an additional opportunity to correct your glidepath if you find that you're either too high or too low. Let's assume that you are making a power-off approach from the base leg and are higher than normal. Of course, you could slip the airplane (we'll talk about slips in Chapter 11, but you will hear nothing about evening gowns), or add flaps to increase your descent rate, but sometimes even full flaps won't help if you're too high. Then again, it's also possible that your flaps have failed or you're in a flapless airplane.

So there you are, with a bit too much altitude. What to do? You'll be happy to know that you do have options. You can deliberately overshoot the turn onto final approach giving you more distance to cover during your descent, as shown in Figure 32. Of course, this assumes that there is nothing that would prohibit you from safely overshooting the centerline, such as the presence of a parallel runway, airplane, or universe.

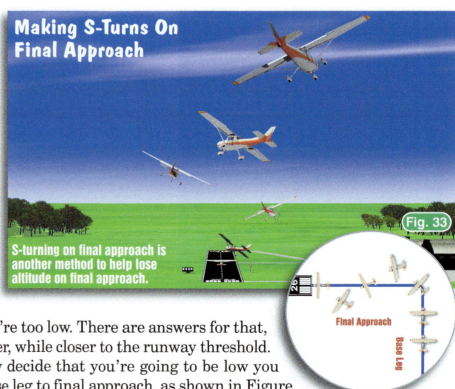

Overshooting Final to Lose Altitude

(Fig. 32)

If you sense that you're going to be high as you turn onto final, then it's perfectly acceptable to overshoot the extended runway centerline which gives you more room to descend (no nearby conflicting traffic assumed here).

Another option is to S-turn on final, as shown in Figure 33. S-turns are simply a series of alternating turns left and right of the runway centerline. Since the shortest distance between any two points is a straight line, anything you do to fly *other* than a straight line lengthens the trip. S-turns should be easy for you, especially if you excelled in penmanship or paid attention in the last chapter. Assuming a constant rate of descent, taking the long way home allows you to lose more altitude.

Making S-Turns On Final Approach

(Fig. 33)

S-turning on final approach is another method to help lose altitude on final approach.

On the other hand, perhaps you're too low. There are answers for that, as well. You can turn base leg sooner, while closer to the runway threshold. While on base leg, if you suddenly decide that you're going to be low you can cut short the turn from the base leg to final approach, as shown in Figure 34. Flying more of a curved path onto final approach means flying less distance during the descent, thus increasing your chances of making the runway.

Chapter 8 - The Airport Traffic Pattern

S-turns, forward slips, change of flight path and use of flaps provide you with several ways of adjusting your glidepath. Adjusting power is another option, assuming you're not in a glider. This knowledge becomes especially important when a precision landing is necessary, such as on a short field or in the event of an engine failure when you have only one opportunity to touch down on the landing spot you've chosen. With a little practice you will be able to put the airplane down precisely where you want.

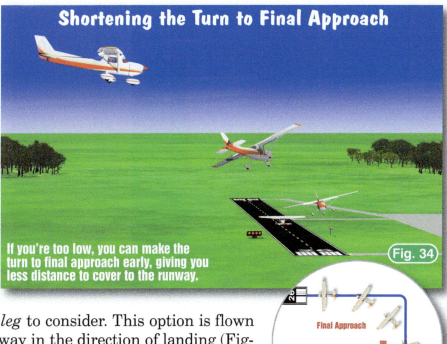

Shortening the Turn to Final Approach

If you're too low, you can make the turn to final approach early, giving you less distance to cover to the runway.

Fig. 34

That leaves us just the *upwind leg* to consider. This option is flown parallel to and offset from the runway in the direction of landing (Figure 35). It's used during go-arounds or overflights to see and avoid departing traffic.

If you're on final approach when a pilot taxis onto the runway, fly to the outside of the runway, offset just enough on the non-pattern side to keep the departing airplane in sight. You don't do this so you can flash your disapproval to the pilot of the offending airplane with one of your aviation gang signs, either. You simply climb, avoid the departing airplane and turn crosswind to fly the pattern for landing again (and hope this guy doesn't have a twin brother who'll do the same thing).

Tips on Flying the Upwind Leg

The upwind leg of the pattern is flown slightly offset from the departure leg. Given the standard left hand traffic pattern, this means you'll be in a position to look down and to your left at departing traffic. I'm speaking of the departing traffic responsible for your having to fly the upwind leg in the first place. You'll typically climb to traffic pattern altitude on the upwind leg and fly it until departing traffic is no longer a factor. Then, when you've past a point abeam the departure end of the runway, you'll commence your left 90 degree turn to the crosswind leg (assuming traffic isn't still a factor, of course).

When flying a right hand traffic pattern, you'll have to fly the upwind leg to the left side of the runway. Because you're sitting in the left seat, you'll want to fly a slightly larger offset so you can see any departing traffic.

The upwind leg, however, is not only used when going around. It might, for instance, be flown at higher altitudes for reconnaissance purposes. I've flown the upwind leg quite a few times over the years while attempting to determine wind direction at the airport.

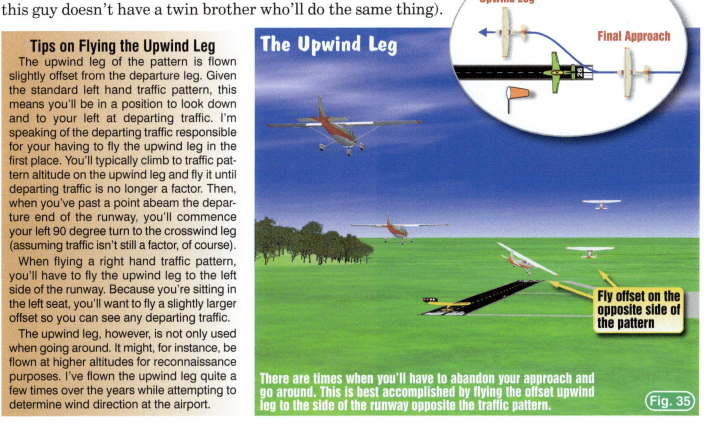

The Upwind Leg

Fly offset on the opposite side of the pattern

There are times when you'll have to abandon your approach and go around. This is best accomplished by flying the offset upwind leg to the side of the runway opposite the traffic pattern.

Fig. 35

Crabbing in the Pattern

The whole story of the pattern is meeting expectations. You have to be predictable, which means being where other pilots expect you to be (and vice versa). Unless you fly where the wind doesn't blow, this almost always involves crabbing, if you get my drift.

Crabbing isn't what happens when your instructor doesn't get enough sleep. Crabbing does, however, describe what the instructor, the tower, and other pilots will be doing if you don't learn how to take account of the wind and adjust for its effects on your airplane in the traffic pattern.

As you know from our prior discussions about ground reference maneuvers, the path your airplane

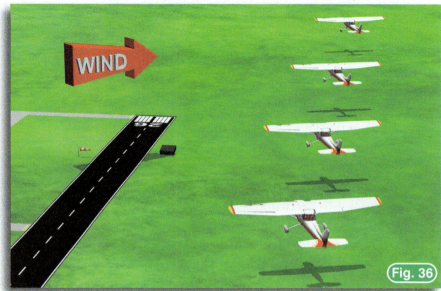

To maintain a downwind flight track parallel to the landing runway, you'll need to crab the airplane into the wind. This is accomplished by making a slight coordinated turn into the wind and not by rudder usage alone (yikes!).

traces over the ground is called its *ground track*. If you sit there fat, dumbfounded, with your brain marinating in a bath of endorphins (i.e., happy) while flying a steady heading of 80 degrees on your highly accurate compass, you will track an 80 degree heading over the ground from any given point only when there is no wind (or the wind blows directly on your nose or tail).

Think of the wind as being a giant and often-friendly hand that occasionally offers a knuckle sandwich if you don't respect it. Because the airplane doesn't have its feet on the ground, it gets pushed around by the wind. Depending on how much wind there is and the angle at which the friendly hand pushes, the effect can be anywhere from slight to considerable.

The only way to create a straight ground track is to compensate for whatever wind there is by pointing the airplane's nose (slightly or more so, depending on conditions) into the wind (Figure 36). For instance, if you're on the downwind leg with a wind blowing from your left, thus pushing you to the right, you'll have to turn into the wind slightly to correct for drift. The nose is now pointed one way while the airplane heads another, which we call crabbing into the wind. The term *crabbing* comes from the fact that crabs walk in a direction other than the one they're facing,

Chapter 8 - The Airport Traffic Pattern

perhaps because they have so many legs that they haven't quite figured out how to coordinate each one (OK, maybe not).

How do you know the precise amount to crab on each leg of the traffic pattern? You apply the same skills you learned when practicing following a rectangular course in the last chapter. This is, after all, why you learned those skills. That means you'll make a slight coordinated turn (say 5 to 10 degrees at first) into the wind, level the wings and watch the results. If the airplane is crabbed properly, it will make a rectangular ground track about the runway. If the airplane begins drifting again, then you'll need to increase your wind correction angle by turning into or away from the wind a little bit more (Figure 37). The moment you find the proper wind correction angle, the airplane will track parallel to the current leg of the traffic pattern.

Applying a Wind Correction Angle

The only practical way to know how much wind correction to apply is to check for potential drift, then either stop it by immediately by applying a wind correction angle, or returning to the desired course after you've drifted slightly then apply a slightly larger wind correction angle.

Of course, the downwind leg is one of the most important places to correct for wind. You're on that leg for a longer period of time and might drift away from or toward the runway without the proper correction. You certainly don't want to find yourself closer to the runway when beginning your base leg turn, given the steeper bank angles required to fly a shortened base leg. You also don't want to be blown away from the downwind leg, since a turn to base leg could place you directly in the path of converging downwind traffic (traffic that did correct for downwind drift and remained a constant distance from the runway on the downwind leg).

Most often the downwind leg has less of a crosswind than either the crosswind or base legs. That's because runways are often built so that they're aligned into the average prevailing winds. Then again, even if the wind blows directly down the runway, that means there will be a direct crosswind on the crosswind leg and base leg. Ultimately, if the wind is not directly aligned with the runway, you can expect to crab on all five segments of the traffic pattern to maintain a rectangular ground track (Figure 38).

One of the more common mistakes made by pilots is the assumption that a lack of wind at the surface means a lack of wind at traffic pattern altitude, or that the wind angle will be constant

Crabbing on All Four Legs of the Pattern

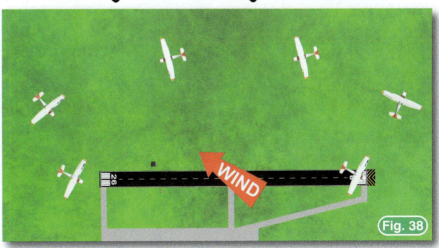

Wind blowing at an angle to the runway often means that you'll need to crab on every leg of the pattern to maintain the desired rectangular ground track.

throughout the landing. As you fly the pattern, you must *continuously* evaluate whether a different WCA is needed. Surface friction as well as natural and man-made obstructions can easily alter the wind's direction and speed. These effects are usually felt more strongly the closer you get to the ground. You might need little or no WCA on downwind, yet suddenly find the need for a substantial WCA on short final (Figure 39). And sometimes it can be the other way around!

Wind Can Vary With Altitude in the Pattern

Winds are often stronger at altitude than they are closer to the ground. Ground frictional effects decrease wind speeds, resulting in directional shift to the left. So don't expect the winds at altitude to be the same on final approach.

When it comes to the local winds at traffic pattern altitude, it's often difficult to make a good guess about its direction and speed. Sometimes you have to take a wait-and-see attitude at altitude. That's why, when operating in the pattern, it's perfectly reasonable to initially apply a wind correction angle based on how the surface wind behaved, while being ready to modify that correction based how the airplane drifts when aloft.

If you let yourself get pushed around by the wind, you won't be where you're supposed to be and that important element of predictability that we're trying for is gone with the wind. It's very difficult for other pilots (and the tower controllers at a controlled field) to predict what you'll do if your traffic pattern doesn't conform to the traditional rectangular shape. It's also hard for you to predict what other pilots will do if they're also drifting with the wind (Figure 40). So be a little crabby when you fly. Apply the appropriate WCA to properly track each leg of the traffic pattern.

Dangers of Failing to Apply Wind Correction

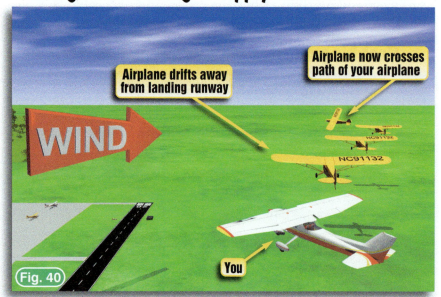

Following an airplane downwind that fails to apply a wind correction can result in a progressively wider pattern. This might result in that airplane turning onto base leg and putting itself in the direct path of your oncoming airplane.

Entering the Traffic Pattern

OK, the dance is in progress, you've been invited to join, but how do you make your grand entry?

It's all about channeling your urge to merge into something—surprise—predictable. Entering the traffic pattern is essentially the art of the merger—merging with the other pilots operating on the downwind leg of the pattern. The essential feature of a good pattern entry is that pilots in the pattern at the time of your merger don't describe your behavior with colorful phrases such as, "What home correspondence course did that guy use to learn how to fly?" Or, "I didn't know you could donate your brain

Chapter 8 - The Airport Traffic Pattern

and still fly." So let's talk about entering the pattern in such a way that no one is surprised by anyone else's behavior. In other words, in a safe and responsible manner.

For some pilots, pattern entries happen to be one of those areas where they feel that self-expression is important and necessary. In other words, they feel like they can enter the traffic pattern in just about any way they want since the FAA only offers a *recommended* traffic pattern entry in the *Aeronautical Information Manual*.

It's true that there is no FAR *requirement* that pilots enter the traffic pattern in a specified manner. The FAA is often quite liberal in the way it approaches pilot regulation and we should all be grateful for that. After all, you probably have enough people bossing you around in your life without having someone else telling you what to do all the time, right? (Answer the question!) Right.

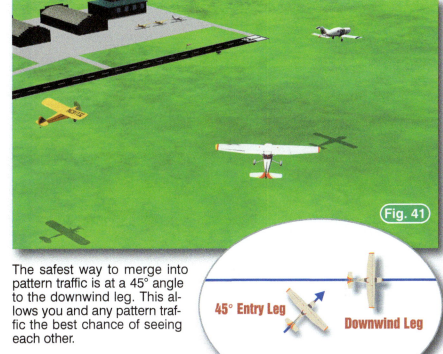

Entering the Traffic Pattern

The safest way to merge into pattern traffic is at a 45° angle to the downwind leg. This allows you and any pattern traffic the best chance of seeing each other.

45° Entry Leg — Downwind Leg

Fig. 41

On the other hand, many accidents have occurred where pilots have elected to express their creativity by entering the pattern in an unorthodox manner, with fatalities the occasional result. In these instances, the entering pilots were held liable for their actions. With these pattern entries falling into the FAA's *recommended* category, NTSB judges adjudicating these cases didn't take a fancy to seeing pilots seek to be unique and creative with their own versions of pattern entries.

So if you need to be unique and creative, I strongly urge you to do it someplace other than the airport traffic pattern entry. Perhaps an art class? Keep the big goal in mind—predictability. You want others to know, with a high degree of certainty, what you are going to do before you do it. This is the aviation version of an ideal community, one where we all look out for one another.

Before actually discussing how to enter the pattern, let's be clear about one more thing. You'll apply the same entry to the traffic pattern regardless of whether you're flying into a controlled or uncontrolled airport. Of course, if a tower controller instructs you to enter the pattern in a way that's different from the FAA's recommendation, then do what the tower controller says (unless you request an amendment to your clearance because you have a good reason to do otherwise). For instance, the controller might ask you to enter the pattern on an extended base leg or fly over the airport and enter the downwind directly. There's nothing at all wrong with doing this as long as the controller is monitoring pattern traffic and providing you with a landing sequence. So let's get into it. The pattern entry that is.

The FAA's recommended pattern entry consists of an approach to the downwind leg at a 45 degree angle (Figure 41). That's a 45 degree angle between the airplane's ground track and the runway as that ground track takes you to the landing runway threshold, too. That's right. It's best not to think about entering the pattern by pointing the airplane (or its ground track) to the middle of the runway. Why? Because this won't take you to the middle of the downwind leg, which is your desired entry point. By pointing the airplane (its ground track) to the runway threshold during the entry, and ensuring the angle of approach is 45 degrees to the runway centerline (this relatively easy to determine), you'll typically enter the downwind leg very close to the midfield point, making the whole entry process easier and more accurate (Figure 42).

Why 45 Degrees?

I was expecting the third degree about the 45 degrees.

If you were one of those individuals who failed trick-o-nometry, then you might not see the relevance of making an entry at a 45 degree angle. Well, there's a good reason for

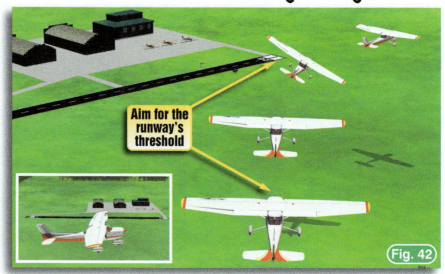

The proper way to ensure a 45° entry to the downwind leg is to point the airplane's nose directly toward the landing threshold, then turn onto the downwind leg at a minimum of one-half mile for the runway centerline.

choosing 45 degrees over 30 or 70 degrees. It allows you to satisfy your urge to merge without scaring the daylights out of pilots on the downwind leg.

At 45 degrees, pilots on the downwind leg can more easily see and track you as you enter the pattern. It also allows you to keep an eye on the airplanes with whom you are merging. Merging at a 45 degree angle allows the merger to happen more slowly relative to merging at a 90 degree angle. And anything less than a 45 degree entry is more an action of overtaking another airplane, rather than merging with one. It's also more difficult to detect another airplane sneaking up on you from behind.

During the 45 degree entry, what happens if the spacing between airplanes on the downwind leg is so tight that there's no room for you to enter the flow of traffic? Do you honk your horn and try to merge, or just barge in? Not unless you're in flying car, right? Cessnas don't have horns. So the best thing to do in these instances is to fly parallel to the traffic outside the downwind leg (Figure 43). From here you're in a better position to find a way to enter the landing sequence (assuming that there's no tower controller giving you a sequence for landing, of course). Either way,

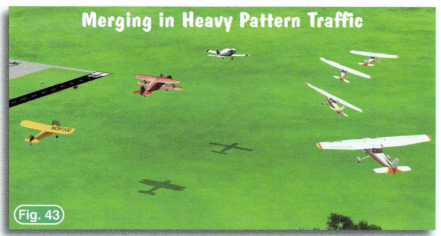

When the pattern is busy, it's often impossible to merge directly between traffic on the downwind leg. In this instance, merge to the outside of traffic and fly a wider pattern as you sequence yourself for landing.

you don't want to try wedging yourself between airplanes where there's no safe space to do so. This type of wedgie isn't just uncomfortable, it can be downright dangerous.

Sometimes there's just no easy way to enter the traffic pattern at the time you elected to do so. Yes, at controlled airports, it's easier for the controller to fit you into a landing sequence because they can slow you down or have you maneuver before you even get to the pattern.

Chapter 8 - The Airport Traffic Pattern

At uncontrolled airports, however, there are times when discretion is the better part of impact (or is that valor?). I've been at uncontrolled airports where a major aviation event was taking place and it gets quite busy. In these instances, it's not unusual to find yourself on the downwind leg with 15 airplanes ahead of you. In such a situation, it might be better to begin a climb, go around and circle somewhere near the airport while waiting for the pattern to thin out before returning to enter the downwind leg. Once again, a little applied common sense and courtesy always helps.

Traffic Pattern Entry Altitude

In terms of making the traffic pattern safe for everyone that's in it, you should always enter the pattern at the recognized traffic pattern altitude (the altitude stated in the *A/FD*). Think about it. If you enter the pattern at a 45 degree angle while descending to pattern altitude, you deprive other pilots of the chance to see and avoid you. Pilots on the downwind leg are typically looking for someone to enter the pattern at their eye level, not from on high (Figure 44) or low. If the pilot on the downwind leg is flying a high wing airplane, it's doubtful that he or she will see you during your entry. It's absolutely essential that you enter the pattern at pattern altitude if you want to make flying safer for yourself and everyone else involved.

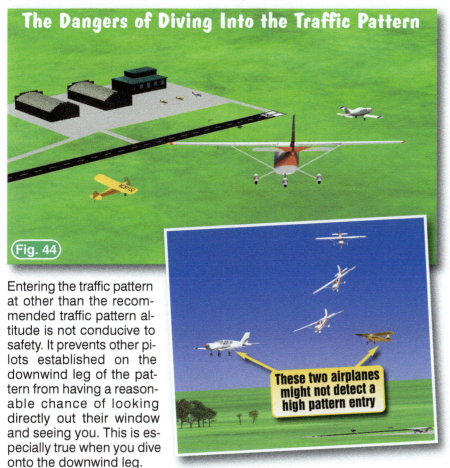

Fig. 44

Entering the traffic pattern at other than the recommended traffic pattern altitude is not conducive to safety. It prevents other pilots established on the downwind leg of the pattern from having a reasonable chance of looking directly out their window and seeing you. This is especially true when you dive onto the downwind leg.

That means you have to plan to get lower way before you enter the airport environment. If you're flying a complex airplane, this is a very good reason to lower your landing gear at least by the time you've begun the 45 degree entry to the downwind leg. Think: Gear down, go down. Yes, you can place the gear down on the downwind leg, but my guess is that by waiting until you're downwind to do so, you're probably also entering the pattern at a very high rate of speed. Proficient pilots plan on entering the pattern at a speed consistent with that of the other traffic in the pattern. This means that if you're in a complex airplane and mixing with smaller trainers making circuits, you should plan on entering at somewhat less than 100 knots indicated airspeed. Your mileage may vary, but this is a good round number for guidance. Always remember that there's a big difference between being a Speedo and wearing one (don't be one in the pattern and don't even think about wearing one if you're over 25).

Finally, when entering the pattern you must keep in mind that there might be someone else entering the pattern on the same 45 degree entry leg. This is an especially big concern at uncontrolled airports, where some pilots might not be communicating their intentions on the CTAF. But it's also an issue at controlled airports. Don't for one second think that tower controllers can watch everyone at the same time. They can't. Many a midair collision has occurred at tower controlled airports because one or more pilots thought the controller was watching out for them at the time.

Believe me when I say that trusting an air traffic controller to keep you safe in the traffic pattern is one way not to keep you safe. Controllers sometimes miss airplanes, or miscommunicate with them, and sometimes pilots just misbehave and don't do what controllers tell them to do. Please remember that the only eyes you can count on 100% of the time are the ones directly wired to your brain.

That's why I want you to fly like a butterfly when entering the traffic pattern and, if necessary, on any leg of the pattern (Figure 45). I don't mean always heading toward a patch of colorful flowers, either. I mean changing headings so that you can see what's below as well as what's above you. Making S-turns to look below and above is absolutely S-ential to pattern safety. If you're descending on the 45 degree entry (or any time you're descending, period!), you need to S-turn to see what's below and above you (Figure 46). So S-turn. How often do you need to do this during the pattern entry? How about just often enough to know what's below you?

If you can S-turn and see that there's no one below and ahead of you all the way to the downwind leg, then there's no more need for S-turning. If and when you suspect that someone has snuck below or above you (perhaps you hear a radio call and position report from this airplane), then make those S-turns. No need to do fancy or aerobatic flight here. Just make a 20 to 30 degree turn right and left a sufficient number of times, then return to your inbound heading.

After all this pitter about pattern, we're now ready to discover why we entered the traffic pattern in the first place. It's time to pull it all together and land the airplane. Land(ing) ho! Let's go!

Checking for Traffic During Pattern Entry

When entering on the 45° entry to the downwind leg, make it a point to perform S-turns to see what's below you. As you're descending on the 45° entry, there may be someone already at TPA below you on the same entry.

Use the Butterfly Technique on the Downwind Leg

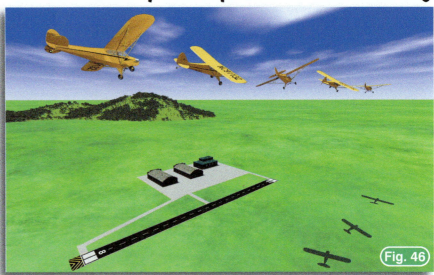

On downwind, it's entirely possible that someone has entered the traffic pattern above or below you. If you suspect that this has happened, then make a short right and left turn to lift you wings and peek above and below you. This is essentially an S-turn maneuver and is best accomplished using your rudder and ailerons in coordination. Fly like a butterfly when you have to.

Chapter 9
Approaching to Land
Gettin' Low, Gettin' Down

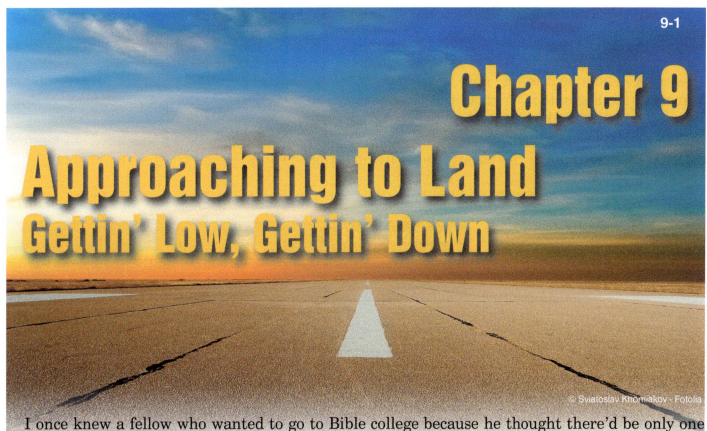

I once knew a fellow who wanted to go to Bible college because he thought there'd be only one book to study. Heaven only knows what he thought after the first day of class. You can make a good case that if an aviation college had only one book, it would be a book on how to land an airplane.

Speaking of Judgment Day, your passengers ultimately base a lot of their opinion about your piloting skills on how well you land the airplane. You can fly with only 10 feet of altitude deviation for three hours while properly correcting the plane's heading to account for a 25 knot wind blowing at 90 degrees to the intended flight path and shifting constantly, but land long, short, or hard and your stock as a pilot sinks faster than the plane did. Being nicknamed "Bounce" is *not* a compliment.

Think of landing as being like writing a symphony. Your goal is to become the Liszt of landings and the Rachmaninoff of the runway. As a student, you learned all the instruments and notes—the four basic flight maneuvers, slow flight, stalls. I'm not Baching up the wrong tree when I tell you that landing is the opportunity to string these things together into a beautiful work that will resonate for you, your flight instructor, and all your passengers.

After years of teaching people how to fly, I can say with confidence that if you have trouble learning to land an airplane, it's because you didn't learn (or learn thoroughly) one or more of the basic fundamentals of flight. There is very little that's new about landing. It's simply the proper sequencing and application of skills you should already have acquired.

For instance, one of the fundamental skills needed to land an airplane is the ability to maintain precise control of the airplane's attitude. Specifically, you need skill at holding heading and airspeed constant. That means you must know how to control the airplane's bank and pitch attitude. If you're on final approach and can't keep your heading constant, how can you expect to put the airplane on the centerline of the runway? If your airspeed needle is swinging faster than a samurai's sword in combat, how can you hope to raise the nose for the landing flare and keep the airplane from floating off the runway or stalling onto it? Without the necessary skill at controlling your attitude, the runway sight picture you see over the airplane's nose is not a pretty sight, because it never stays the same.

Having been an astute student, you now have the nod to hit the sod (even if you're not landing on a grass runway). It's the basics you've learned that have prepared you for the ultimate skill thrill—landings!

What It's All About

Landing is an exercise in energy management. There you are in the pattern, 1,000 feet up, flying along at 100 knots. Somewhere between where you are and the time you get to the runway, you have to dissipate all that energy (altitude is simply energy stored in a different form) so you arrive with barely enough oomph to keep the plane flying. And then, at the moment of landing, you even get rid of the oomph.

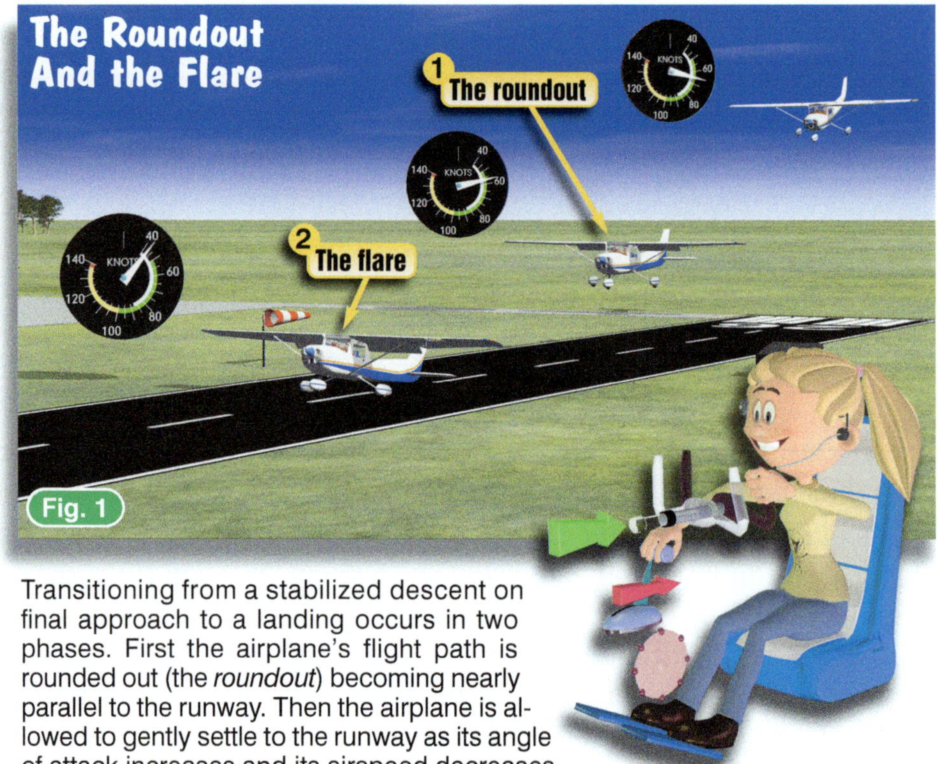

Sound complicated? Well, it may surprise you to learn that you already know how to do almost everything needed to perform this amazing feat, which will astound family and friends. If you look beyond the

The Roundout And the Flare
1. The roundout
2. The flare

Fig. 1

Transitioning from a stabilized descent on final approach to a landing occurs in two phases. First the airplane's flight path is rounded out (the *roundout*) becoming nearly parallel to the runway. Then the airplane is allowed to gently settle to the runway as its angle of attack increases and its airspeed decreases.

basics of flying mentioned above, landing an airplane ultimately involves the acquisition of only one additional skill. That's right, just one. You only need learn how to transition the airplane from descending at a relatively slow airspeed (you already know how to fly slow, right?) to maintaining level flight just a few inches above the runway (called the *roundout*), and then letting the airplane slow down close to its stall speed (the *flare*, Figure 1). That's how you land an airplane. OK, that's how you land if there's no crosswind, which we'll assume for this initial discussion.

You already know how to transition an airplane from a higher speed to a slower speed while maintaining altitude. In a previous lesson on slow flight you used the altimeter's hundred-foot hand to help you maintain altitude during the transition to slow flight. When landing, you'll use the solid surface known as the *runway* to help control your altitude as you make the transition from a higher speed to a slower speed (the roundout and flare). In other words, you'll descend to a point just above the runway, then apply elevator back pressure sufficient to hold the airplane's main wheels about 12 inches or less above the surface until the airplane is near its stall speed. Then you'll allow the airplane to gently settle those last few inches onto the runway. Oomph gone. Landing accomplished.

Let's continue with your training. In the next two chapters I'm going to take you through the approach and landing just as I would if you were my student sitting in the cockpit right next to me (no Hobbs meter, no charge). By the end of this chapter you will be about 10 feet above the runway and

Chapter 9: Approaching to Land

ready for the final steps in making your first landing. Since you'll be left hanging, there will be a strong incentive for reading through to the end of the next chapter!

In this chapter we'll discuss the approach to a landing that involves a minimum number of complications (none, which is pretty much a minimum). In the next few chapters we'll get you from 10 feet AGL to down on the ground, while also dealing with the more complicated elements of landings such as crosswinds and short- and soft-field situations.

Your First Approach and Landing

Your first approach and landing will be what I call a no-brainer (although I can assure you that this will go much easier if you actually use your brain). You're going to make your first landing using only 10 to 15 degrees of flaps, and reducing power on base leg to flight idle at the point where you think you are within gliding distance of the runway (Don't worry, I'll help you decide when to reduce your power on the first few landings.)

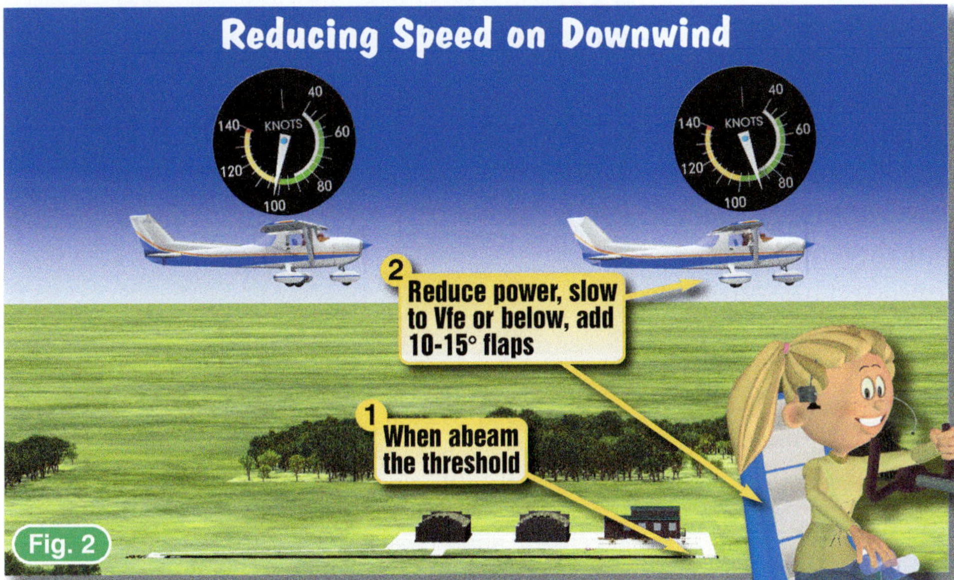

Yes, your first few landings will be made completely power off. There's a very good reason for this. You have to learn how the airplane glides power-off to understand your airplane's glide potential. Of course, you'll add a little power if you're going to end up short of the runway, or add more flaps if it looks like you're going to land long. However, if you judge correctly you'll fly a normal power-off glidepath and land on the centerline somewhere in the first third of the runway.

Fig. 2 — Reducing Speed on Downwind
1. When abeam the threshold
2. Reduce power, slow to Vfe or below, add 10-15° flaps

As you approach a point abeam the landing threshold while on the downwind leg, you'll want to slow the airplane down to at or below its maximum flap extension speed (Vfe) of 90 knots. Do this by reducing power, perhaps by 200 to 300 RPM, depending on your particular airplane. Then you'll apply 10-15° of flaps.

Therefore, for the purposes of your initial training, we'll define a *normal power-off glidepath* as one that allows you to reduce power to flight idle at some point in the pattern and *land the airplane in the center of the first third of the runway*. Please don't forget this definition. It's important because it's the method I'm using to introduce you to landing an airplane. Later in this chapter you'll learn that a *normal power-on glidepath* allows you to fly an approximate three degree glideslope (a shallower glidepath) and land the airplane in the center of the first third of the runway.

Let's assume you're flying at approximately 100 knots while midfield on the downwind leg at a traffic pattern altitude of 1,000 feet AGL and your maximum flaps extension speed is 90 knots (Figure 2). Let's also assume that there's no one else in the pattern, so you're free to turn onto base leg at will. Life is good, flying is better.

As you approach a position abeam the landing runway threshold, reduce power slightly (by about 100 to 200 RPM) and slow the airplane down from 100 knots to Vfe (your maximum flaps extension speed of 90 knots), as shown in Figure 2, position 1. Then, when you're abeam the landing threshold, extend the flaps a small amount (typically 10-15 degrees or one notch of flaps in most airplanes). Why apply flaps in this position on the downwind leg? Flaps not only reduce the stall speed and allow you to descend more quickly, but they also allow you to have a better view directly over the airplane's nose. Flaps make this possible by allowing the airplane to produce the required lift at a slightly nose-low attitude.

As flaps are applied, you will need to apply a little forward or aft pressure on the elevator to keep the nose from pitching upward (some airplanes such as Cessnas typically require forward elevator pressure, while others such as Pipers typically require aft elevator pressure for the initial application of flaps).

Good. Now, adjust the attitude to maintain level flight and trim the airplane for hands-off flying in this condition. Since you were at 90 knots, the airspeed has probably decreased to around 80 knots. That's fine. You're interested in progressively reducing the airplane's speed throughout the landing transition. Remember, you're now in the energy management business. Of course, different airplanes use different speeds, but I'll just assume that you're using a speed of 100 knots on the downwind, and before beginning the base turn you've slowed to 80 knots.

Flaps produce more lift at the cost of producing more drag. That's why your airspeed has decreased to approximately 80 knots (the airspeed reduction you experience will vary between airplanes). And that's OK, because you're going to fly base leg at a speed that's 40% above your present stall speed or 1.4 Vs. Why do you want to use this speed? Mainly because we want to fly the final approach at 30% above stall speed (or the specific speed that the airplane manufacturer recommends, of course). For most airplanes, flying final approach at 30% above the airplane's stall speed for a given configuration means that the airplane will be relatively close to the bottom of the drag curve. That minimizes the likelihood of floating during the landing flare (Figure 3).

Floating is an energy management fail. It occurs when you arrive above the runway with excess energy (see sidebar, *When Lift is a Drag*). Until you get rid of that energy, you cannot put the plane on the ground, so you cruise along just above the runway, humming the theme from Exodus. Very soon, you are not in the first third of the runway any longer. Maybe not even the second third. Depending on how long the runway is, this can go from annoying to dangerous pretty quickly.

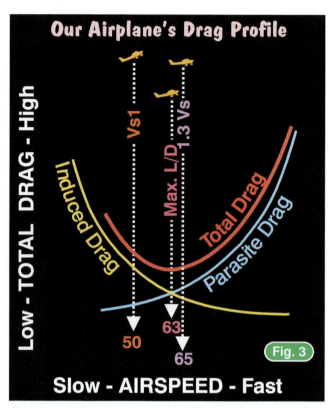

At a speed of 63 knots (this airplane's *best L/D speed*), the airplane experiences its lowest total drag in flight. This speed is relatively close to the recommended approach speed of 1.3 Vs or 30% above stall speed. Therefore, an increase in angle of attack at this speed means drag also increases. That's what you want when beginning the landing flare since it minimizes the chance of floating.

When Lift is a Drag

Recall from our earlier discussion of the lift/drag curve that increasing the airplane's angle of attack reduces total drag—up to a point, otherwise known as the airplane's *best L/D* speed. This is the speed representing the bottom of the total drag curve and occurs at a point somewhere around 30% above the airplane's stall speed. Increasing the angle of attack and further slowing the airplane down beyond the speed for best L/D results in the wings throwing a lot more of their lift backwards (called *induced drag*) rather than directing it upwards (where it's really useful). It's important that you understand this because it helps explain what happens if you attempt to flare at airspeeds higher than 1.3 Vs.

For instance, if you attempt to flare at a speed that's *higher* than 30% above the airplane's present stall speed, then increasing the angle of attack during the landing flare *reduces* the total drag produced by the airplane. This initially results in the airplane floating down the runway. Once you're at or below the lowest portion of the total drag curve, however, any increase in angle of attack still produces the required lift but it also *increases* the airplane's total drag production. The result of this is called an increase in *induced* drag and it's what's responsible for the rapid decrease in speed at higher angles of attack.

If you need a more thorough refresher on the drag curve and L/D Max, see Page 3-19.

Chapter 9: Approaching to Land

For the purposes of this example, the airplane will have a power off stall speed in the clean configuration of 50 knots, so base leg will be flown at 70 knots (we'll also assume that the airplane is at its maximum gross weight—mainly because you brought along 200 pounds of lunch just in case I got hungry). While the stall speed does decrease slightly with 10-15 degrees of flaps added, the change isn't great. So, for the purpose of computing 1.3 Vs, we'll just assume that the airplane still stalls at approximately 50 knots.

When Do I Turn Onto Base Leg?

As we discussed in the previous chapter, you'll know when to turn base (assuming you aren't following anyone ahead of you in the pattern) when you can see the runway threshold behind you, halfway between your left (or right) wing and the airplane's tail. In other words, the threshold has moved 45 degrees behind the wing on the runway side of the pattern (see Chapter Eight, Page 8-15 for details). This is a good reference point to use when there are no other aircraft to follow in the pattern. And if you're ahead of a few other airplanes on the downwind leg, you certainly don't want to unnecessarily extend the downwind leg. That's not how you make friends with other pilots at the airport (think *extend to unfriend* on your Facebook page). The other pilots would like to land in time to make it home for dinner and without needing aerial refueling.

When you're at the 45 degree reference point, begin your turn to base leg. I want to caution you about having a bad attitude at this juncture. It turns out that most students are so focused on looking at either the ground or the runway that they tend to let their nose attitude lower or raise during the base leg turn (Figure 4). Since we're delaying our descent until we're established on base leg, focus on maintaining a level flight pitch attitude using your

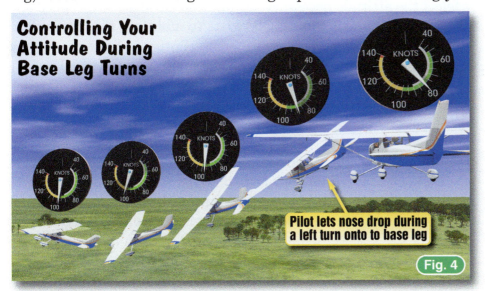

Controlling Your Attitude During Base Leg Turns

Pilot lets nose drop during a left turn onto to base leg

Fig. 4

When turning onto base leg, many students fail to properly control their attitude and let the airplane climb or descend (a descent is common during a left turn). If you're delaying your descent until established on base leg, then make a 90 degree level flight turn followed by a power reduction, attitude selection and trim.

When Do I Begin My Descent for Landing?

Later.

Yes, it's a landing and that implies you want to get down. But there's a right time for everything, and you're not there quite yet. As a general rule, resist the temptation to begin your descent for landing on the downwind leg. As I mentioned in the previous chapter, descending on the downwind leg increases your risk of exchanging paint with another airplane.

On the other hand, some pilots simply can't wait to put their wheels on the runway and therefore insist on beginning their descent when they are downwind and abeam the runway threshold. Yes, even the FAA seems to support this idea. So if you're an early descender, then the earliest point where you should begin your descent is when you're abeam the landing runway threshold. You'd apply your initial application of flaps at this point then reduce power for the descent. I want to make it very clear, however, that I'm not a big fan of beginning your descent when abeam the threshold because it still means descending while on some portion of the downwind leg. You simply increase the risk that you or someone else in the pattern might have fewer descendents if two airplanes happen to vertically merge in his portion of the pattern.

Of course, I'm not a fanatic about this either. If you're sure—and being *sure* is the essential point here—that there are no aircraft below you, then begin your descent for landing when and where it pleases you. On the other hand, if you want to follow a procedure that's conducive to traffic pattern safety, then begin your descent as you're turning onto base leg or begin it on base leg. Under normal circumstances, there will only be one plane on base at a time, so risk is reduced.

When I first introduce a student to landing practice, I take the descent delay a bit farther and have the student delay the descent until established on base leg. This reduces the mental workload and makes the landing experience more meaningful. It's also the way I personally fly an airplane in the pattern, since it minimizes the chance that I'll descend onto downwind traffic or that someone will descend onto me if they're downwind.

Once established on base leg, reduce power to flight idle and begin your descent for landing.

windscreen pitch reference (as discussed in Chapter Two) and hold your altitude during this turn. Using a shallow to medium bank (20 to 30 degrees) is just fine when operating in the traffic pattern. Just don't let your attitude get bad.

What Do I Do Once I'm Established on Base Leg?

As soon as you're established on base leg, reduce power to flight idle, lower the nose to maintain 1.4 Vs (or 70 knots in our example) as shown in Figure 5, and then trim the airplane to maintain this attitude.

Remember, you're trimming to fly a specific attitude and this is initially much easier to detect than trying to trim for a specific airspeed. You should already know how to do this and it should be a snap for you, although you shouldn't hear any snapping noises while doing it (unless it's coming from your instructor's fingers because you're not being Johnny-on-the-spot with that trim wheel). Yes, that's right. One of the qualities you'll see in a good pilot is his or her snappiness with the trim wheel. They don't gently roll it to apply nose up trim. They select the attitude necessary to maintain the desired airspeed and give the trim wheel a few good twists to maintain that attitude.

Fig. 5

To begin your descent for landing on base leg, reduce power to flight idle and establish the pitch attitude that gives you an airspeed of 1.4 Vs. Then give the trim a few quick twists in the nose-up direction to help you maintain this attitude. Fine tuning the trim can be done after you've made the initial trim application.

OK, this time when I say "Land on the numbers," I mean the first set you come to.

After gaining some experience, you'll be able to easily determine when to reduce power for the descent on base leg as well as whether or not the present glidepath will reach the runway as you turn onto final approach. When you begin your initial landing training, however, you won't have the experience to make this assessment. You might end up a bit too high or low on final approach, but that's OK. I'll show you how to correct for that. All you're initially concerned about here is developing the ability to evaluate whether or not you'll make the runway based on your present glidepath.

Ready for your turn to final approach? OK, here's where the real action starts. Let's roll (humor me, I just like saying that).

Chapter 9: Approaching to Land

Finally Turning Final

As you approach the extended runway centerline from base leg, begin your turn to final approach (Figure 6). How do you know when to make this turn? Unless you have some experience making these turns, you simply must guess the first few times. So guess. Take your best shot. This is how you gain experience. Of course, if you begin your turn early and use a shallow bank, then the windscreen picture changes much more slowly than if you wait until the last minute and use a steep bank. If you find yourself overshooting final approach, assuming that there isn't a parallel runway with traffic on the other side, then you can easily turn back to final. Whatever you do, please try to avoid steepening the bank in an attempt to align yourself with the runway since this increases your load factor, resulting in an increase in stall speed. Increased stall speed close to the ground isn't something you're likely to want, even if you're directly over a marshmallow factory.

Fig. 6 — Making a shallow 90° turn onto final allows the windscreen picture to change more slowly, giving you a chance to modify the turn for perfect runway alignment.

Fig. 7 — The "Thigh-land" Method of Runway Alignment. Align your right leg "thigh" with the runway centerline. When turning onto final approach, you can place the airplane very close to the runway centerline by thinking about aligning the extended (imagined) centerline with your right leg thigh.

Turning onto final approach is one thing, but determining whether or not you're lined up with the runway centerline, is another. Sometimes it's just not easy to tell if you're aligned properly. That's why I want you to pretend you're in "thigh" land and initially align the runway centerline with your right thigh, which is relatively close to the center of most side-by-side seating airplanes (Figure 7). This technique actually gives you a good sense of where to point the airplane.

This is another spot where bad attitudes tend to develop. It's quite common to let your pitch attitude decrease when turning onto final approach. Once again, most students tend to fixate on the pretty big black strip ahead of them just after completing their turn, often to the exclusion of almost all else, including attitude control. If you want to look at pretty things, buy a painting; if you want a good landing, divide your attention between controlling your attitude and tracking the runway centerline.

Sometimes the runway centerline is hard to see during the turn from base to final approach. This is a very common problem when flying a high wing airplane, since the wing inside the turn obscures the centerline, preventing you from knowing when to roll out of the turn. You can often solve this problem by leaning forward a little during the turn to find the runway. This is one place where I want you to stick your neck out, literally!

You may even need to have a "peek" experience by leaning forward in your seat and peeking around the window post or the wing in order to spy the runway. Depending on the way the cockpit shell obscures your vision, you might even need to decrease the bank in the turn, take a peek at the runway, then continue the turn for alignment. If so, then fine. Peek and bank, but don't peek and boo. Just do what you need to do in order to get centered.

Once established on final approach at a distance of approximately half a mile from the threshold, slow the airplane down from 1.4 Vs to 1.3 Vs (65 knots in this airplane). This is your final approach speed. Since power is at flight idle for this approach,

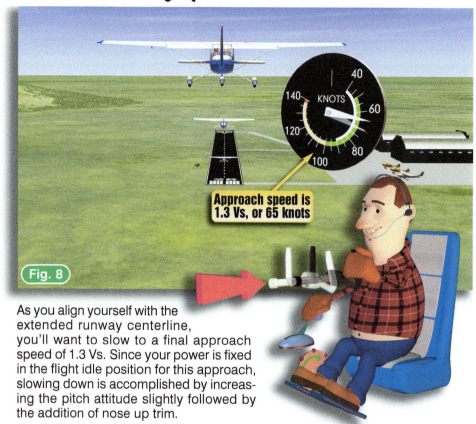

Reducing Speed on Final to 1.3 Vs

Approach speed is 1.3 Vs, or 65 knots

Fig. 8

As you align yourself with the extended runway centerline, you'll want to slow to a final approach speed of 1.3 Vs. Since your power is fixed in the flight idle position for this approach, slowing down is accomplished by increasing the pitch attitude slightly followed by the addition of nose up trim.

the practical way to slow down is to raise the nose ever-so-slightly and add a little nose-up trim. Adjust the pitch to give you a speed of 65 knots (Figure 8), and then make any additional small trim adjustments required to keep the airplane at this pitch attitude. Once again, trim is the secret to helping you keep the airplane under control during your approach to the runway. Whatever you do, please don't forget that your job on final approach is to maintain the attitude that provides the correct airspeed.

As I said earlier, one reason for having you do a power-off approach your first few landings is so you will develop some basic skill at estimating your gliding distance without the use of power. Why? While catastrophic engine failures are extremely rare, engines can and do quit, most often because pilots forget to keep fuel in their tanks. And you will ultimately use your skill at estimating glide distance every time you land an airplane, whether you're using engine power or not during the descent.

A second reason is that I want you to know how to approach a runway and land an airplane without the use of engine power. Airplanes will easily and happily glide to a runway if you start your descent on base leg with sufficient altitude. This even applies to the space shuttle (although, since you haven't soloed yet and because they're no longer flying, you shouldn't be piloting the space shuttle). Of course, if you start your descent too early on base leg, you might need to use engine power in order to make it to the *desired landing spot* on the runway. That's perfectly OK, too. That *is* one of the reasons you have an engine under the hood.

OK, when I say to apply back pressure, I mean to pull back on the yoke, not force your back against the seat.

My other preference for your first landing experience is to have you do it without the use of more than 10-15 degrees of flap extension. The reason is that partial flaps produce less drag than

Chapter 9: Approaching to Land

The Desired Landing Location

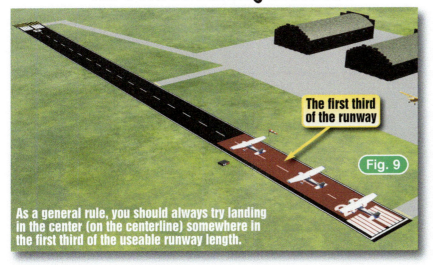

As a general rule, you should always try landing in the center (on the centerline) somewhere in the first third of the useable runway length.

The first third of the runway

Fig. 9

full flaps. As a result, you'll find that your airspeed doesn't decrease as quickly during the landing flare compared to landing with full flaps. Use more flaps and you'll find that everything happens a lot quicker during the landing flare. This reduces the time you have to assess the visual clues needed for landing, especially when figuring out your height above the runway. There are several reasons why it's advisable to use at least partial flap extension on some training airplanes for landing. One is that the sitting position in some airplanes makes it difficult to see the runway over the airplane's nose at slower speeds (higher angles of attack). Using 10 to 15 degrees of flaps allows you to develop the required lift at a lower pitch attitude, and that means better over-the-nose visibility on final approach. More on flaps later.

Once you're on final approach, your goal is to land the airplane as close as possible to the *desired landing spot*, which should be located on the runway centerline somewhere within the first third of the runway (Figure 9). So identify a spot—perhaps a runway marking or a runway light—located in the center of the first third of the runway.

Keep in mind that while the airplane's glidepath intersects the desired landing spot, the airplane will actually touch down a little beyond this spot (this is why I call it a "desired" landing spot). This occurs because the airplane remains airborne as it rounds out and flares for landing. Also note that the airplane's nose (its longitudinal axis) doesn't point to where the glidepath intersects the runway. That's because the airplane always flies at some positive angle of attack during its descent, meaning that the nose typically points above the actual glidepath and beyond the desired landing spot. More on the desired landing spot later. (See Postflight Briefing #9-2 on *Names for Runway Spots*.)

The Truth About Power-Off Landings

One of the unfortunate developments in aviation is the emphasis on flying long, low approach profiles at higher indicated airspeeds. Over the years, as stick and rudder skills became less emphasized than cockpit management skills, pilots began to develop an unnatural fear of flying at slower airspeeds. As a result, it's not unusual to see a pilot in a larger airplane flying a final approach to touchdown 50% or more above the airplane's stall speed. That might work if you have a long enough runway, such as the space shuttle runway at Edwards Air Force Base. Good luck using these speeds on shorter runways.

If power-off approaches to landing were made at these higher airspeeds, then pilots would need to remain higher and delay their descents until they were closer to the runway. This requires a certain amount of skill to accomplish. It's simply easier and requires less skill for fast flying pilots to start their descents early and extend their traffic pattern to fly a long final approach at a lower altitude and higher airspeeds using gads of engine power. Does this landing profile sound familiar to you? It should. It's the landing profile used by airliners. General aviation's cockpit management skills were significantly influenced by the airline community. This influence ultimately affected the way general aviation pilots began flying their smaller machines.

Unfortunately, this isn't a good development because it isn't the best way to fly a smaller airplane. There's no benefit to an extended final approach at too low an altitude while using lots of engine power to reach the runway, and there are several distinct disadvantages. An engine failure here leaves you with very few landing options. Low is where the birds are, to say nothing of antennas, trees and chimneys. And finally, the added noise does not exactly endear pilots to their airport neighbors.

Flying a power-off approach at the lower airspeeds I've recommended in this lesson keeps you closer to the runway (traffic permitting, of course) without the worry of using excessive runway during landing. You can fly power-off approaches in airplanes ranging from a Piper Cub to a Cessna P210 and so on. They're just airplanes, and when power is reduced to flight idle, they're just gliders. OK, not very good gliders, but reasonable gliders, nevertheless.

Some pilots worry about shock cooling when making power-off approaches. But they often forget that the low power settings used in the traffic pattern don't usually allow engine temperatures to reach sufficiently high values to make shock cooling an issue.

I am not by any means saying that you should *always* make power-off approaches in larger single-engine airplanes. But I am saying that you should feel comfortable doing them and comfortable flying approaches at 1.4 and 1.3 Vs/Vso in larger airplanes.

Stabilizing Your Attitude on Final Approach

Fig. 10

One of the essential skills new pilots need to land an airplane is the ability to use rudder and aileron in coordination to keep the nose from yawing right and left and the wings from banking on final approach. This skill, along with the ability to maintain the necessary pitch attitude is *absolutely essential* for anyone learning to land an airplane. Period!

Final Essentials on Final Approach—Things You Must Remember

Since every leg of the traffic pattern has something essential associated with it, let me clue you in to what's essential on final approach. You must—must!—keep those wings level with the ailerons, the nose straight with the rudder and the pitch steady with the elevator, all the way down to landing (Figure 10, position C). I simply can't tell you how important this is, but I will. *Keep those wings level on final approach using rudder and aileron in coordination and maintain a constant airspeed through attitude control.* If your airplane banks to the right, use left aileron and left rudder to level those wings (Figure 10, position A). If the airplane banks to the left, use right aileron and right rudder to level the wings (Figure 10, position B). And don't take your sweet time doing it, or the airplane is going to head off in some direction that involves a landing where there's no runway.

You don't jack the controls around, but you do move them smoothly and quickly to level the wings (we don't use the word "jack" around airplanes, either. For instance, if you see your pilot friend near an airplane, you'd never say, "Hi Jack," unless you want to spend your next birthday at Gitmo).

How Normal Traffic Patterns Aid in Landing

If you've never heard the word *Pythagoras* (which isn't a snake that only strikes at right angles), then you might not know how an understanding of geometry can help you more effectively establish the correct glidepath for landing.

Let's assume you're flying the downwind, half a mile from the runway centerline. If you wait to turn base when the runway threshold is 45 degrees behind your left wing, the perpendicular distance from base leg to the point where you turn final approach will also be half a mile. And the distance from the point where you turn final to the runway threshold will also be half a mile (or approximately so). What's my angle here? If we assume that you will begin your descent as you complete the base leg turn, then you'll need to lose approximately half the pattern altitude on base leg if you want to cross the runway threshold at airport elevation. This, of course, is only a rough approximation and assumes a no-wind condition.

Think about it. The length of your base leg is approximately the same distance you'll fly on final approach to the runway threshold. If your pattern altitude has you at 800 feet AGL, then you should be at 400 feet AGL when turning onto final. If you're at 600 feet AGL when turning final, you are a bit too high. If you're at 300 feet when turning final, you are a bit too low on the approach.

Once again, these are only rough approximations because it's likely that you'll land into a headwind, which will reduce your groundspeed on final approach (meaning you'll have a bit more time to descend on final approach). These calculations reflect the distance to the threshold, but you normally land several hundred feet beyond this point (in the center of the first third of the runway). Nevertheless, this geometric understanding does add one more bit of information with which to better evaluate your glidepath.

Chapter 9: Approaching to Land

Using the IAS and CAS Chart To Determine Approach Speed

On many airplanes "certificated" (not *manufactured*) after 1980, the airspeed indicator's color codes may be presented as *indicated* airspeeds, not *calibrated* airspeeds (check your POH to find out). To you, that means if the POH says fly 75 knots IAS on approach, you fly 75 KIAS on the airspeed indicator. On airplanes "certificated" earlier than this time, the airspeed indicator's color codes are given as *calibrated airspeeds*. And that means the number the airspeed needle points to might not be the actual speed of the wind striking the airplane as a result of pitot/static errors.

That's a problem, because if you're on final approach at 30% above stall speed, you'd better be sure that your indicated airspeed is accurately representing the speed of wind blowing on your wings. This is why you need to calibrate your airspeed indicator by using the *airspeed calibration chart* (shown below) found in your POH. With it, you can determine what *indicated* airspeed you need to fly to produce a specific *calibrated airspeed* (the actual speed of wind striking your airplane).

AIRSPEED CALIBRATION CHART

FLAPS UP						
KIAS	50	60 (B)	70	80	90	100
KCAS	50	63	72	81	89	98
FLAPS 40°						
KIAS	40	50 (A)	60	70	80	85
KCAS	40	54	64	71	80	85

KIAS = Knots Indicated Airspeed
KCAS = Knots Calibrated Airspeed

For instance, we want to fly a final approach at 1.3 Vs. Since the color-coded values on the airspeed indicator are calibrated airspeeds, we can multiply 1.3 x 50 knots (the low speed end of the green arc), which equals 65 knots. So what *indicated* airspeed do we fly to produce a *calibrated* (actual) airspeed of 65 knots? You have to do a little bit of interpolating and guesstimating here. The chart gives us a precise number for 63 knots CAS (position A, with flaps up, or nearly so)—you have to fly an indicated airspeed of 60 knots (position B), or three knots less than what's on the airspeed indicator. We'll take that same three-knot deduction from our target speed of 65 knots CAS and fly 62 knots indicated airspeed.

When using full flaps in this airplane, the CAS-IAS difference is much larger. For instance, 1.3 Vso with full flaps is 52 knots CAS (1.3 x 40=52). To fly a CAS of 52 knots, you fly approximately four knots less on the airspeed indicator or an indicated airspeed of 48 knots.

Keep in mind that color-coded stall speeds are based on the airplane being at maximum gross weight. For the purposes of this chapter, we'll assume that the airplane is operated at this weight and that it has no IAS-CAS errors, either. It's good being the author of this book, because I can create the perfect airplane and configuration for you to fly.

Nothing matters more than flying coordinated if you want to make great landings and do so easily. Nothing! If you can't (or choose not to) fly coordinated, landing is going to be a lot harder (literally and figuratively) until you learn how to do so. Why is this so important? Because you can't begin to properly evaluate your glidepath to the runway, much less your height above the runway, if the runway appears to move up, down, left and right in your windscreen as you approach it.

Imagine for a moment that the Mona Lisa were hanging on your wall, with the picture frame loose but properly framing the painting. That looks good. But what if the frame jumped around every few seconds, so at one instant it framed the top quarter of Mona and a lot of the wall and a few seconds later it framed more Lisa than Mona? Seconds later, it frames the painting in such a way that you can't see the famous smile (rendering it more of a Mona Larry, than Lisa). Wouldn't *that* be a disturbing way to view your expensive treasure?

That's what you're going to get if you don't fly a coordinated final approach. The plane's windscreen is the picture frame, and the runway is your Mona Lisa. The goal is to keep precisely the same picture framed all the way down. The smile is your landing point, and it should start and stay at the center of the picture frame. Do that and *you* will be the one smiling after a great landing.

If you get the picture, you understand why it is crucial to keep the wings level and the airplane aligned with the runway (or at some steady crab angle to correct for a crosswind as I'll discuss in Chapter 11). This is especially important in bumpy weather conditions, where you have to work hard at keeping the runway picture constant in your windscreen. Even in perfectly smooth weather, if you can't fly coordinated, the nose will be yawing to the right and left of the runway, which causes the picture frame to jump around.

Let's assume that you're aligned with the runway on final approach. Now comes the ultimate question of the moment (there will be other questions at other moments). *Will your power-off glidepath allow you to glide to a point located in the center of the first third of the runway?* This is considered a reasonable place to land the airplane on all but the shortest of runways.

How are you supposed to make this assessment? Well, it's not all that difficult. Let's cover a few ancillary details before I reveal my glidepath secrets.

Low Blow

Sometimes flight instructors are reluctant to begin landing lessons on those days when it's windy, preferring calm days for this introduction. There's something to be said for this idea. If the wind creates gusts, that complicates the acquisition of the perceptions needed for the student to gain the proper insights for landing. So smooth conditions, perhaps in the early morning or early evening, are often the best times to introduce students to landings.

There is, however, one condition that lends itself very well to students learning to land and it involves a lot of wind. I'm speaking of a good strong wind right down the runway, with relatively few gusts to continually disrupt the airplane on final approach. Normally this means that there's nothing in the runway environment such as trees or buildings that can create mechanical turbulence.

What's the benefit of learning under this strong but steady wind condition? The landing roundout and flare occur at a slower groundspeed, making it a little easier for the student to see and evaluate his or her closure rate with the runway. If you're a flight instructor, don't be reluctant to introduce landings when you have a good strong, non-gusty wind blowing directly down the runway centerline. The slow groundspeed might just speed up the rate at which your student learns to land.

I'm Setting You Up

In case you haven't noticed, I'm setting you up so that your turn onto final approach places you at an altitude that permits a power-off descent to a spot located in the center of the first third of the runway. Am I doing that just because I'm a nice guy? Well yes, that too. But mostly I'm doing it because for you to know what a normal power-off glidepath to the runway is, you have to know what one looks like.

You only need to watch an episode of the Simpsons to know that your family is emotionally stable and mentally healthy by comparison, right? Similarly, you can't know what an abnormal glidepath is if you don't have a mind's eye view of what a normal one looks like. That's why I told you when to pull power back to flight idle on base leg. I did this when I knew you were in a position from which you could glide to the runway (hopefully, your instructor will do the same).

After two or three power-off approaches, you'll have a basis on which to assess whether your glidepath is just right (you'll land in the center of the first third of the runway), too high (you'll land farther down the runway), or too low (you might land short of the runway threshold if I don't stop you).

Once you make this evaluation, you can either add flaps if you're too high or add power if you're too low, both of which modify the glidepath. For purposes of basic training I'm going to assume that the runway you're approaching doesn't have its own VASI or *visual approach slope indicator* that provides a lighted visual indication of whether your glidepath is correct. That would be too easy. Not every airport has a VASI, and they aren't always working, but you will always have your eyeballs with you. That's why I'm starting you out using the eyeball system of flight path estimation.

The key to the landing treasure is obviously being able to figure out where the glidepath you're on at any moment will take you and whether or not the glidepath angle is too steep, too shallow or just right. This does *not* require a crystal ball, swami attire, or a Ouija board, either. There are two distinct visual clues to help make this assessment. One visual clue involves finding the single spot on the runway that doesn't move (the *stationary spot*) and the other uses changes in the trapezoidal shape of the runway. Let's examine how to use the stationary spot first.

Chapter 9: Approaching to Land

Don't Move! How a Stationary Spot On The Ground Shows Where You're Headed

With the airplane trimmed for approach speed and the descent rate constant, as you look through your windscreen there will always be *one* single spot on the ground directly ahead of you that doesn't appear to move (Figure 11). It's the spot where your airplane is headed (assuming the glidepath doesn't change, of course). If there were a piece of paper there, it would be a stationery spot; otherwise, it's just a stationary spot.

All objects on the surface positioned above the stationary spot (and thus beyond the point where the glidepath intercepts the runway) appear to move *up*, away from that stationary spot as you get closer; those below the stationary spot appear to move down and away from that spot. The points above and below the stationary spot appear to move away because the entire surface picture in your windscreen is getting bigger.

Look at the center of any picture hanging on a wall while moving closer to the center of that picture. The center remains stationary while the upper and lower parts of the picture appear to move up and down away from the center. We'll call this technique for evaluating your glidepath the *stationary spot method*.

The stationary spot *would* be the impact point if you did nothing but let the plane continue on its way in its current configuration. Since this tends to make for unpleasantly abrupt landings, you will round out and flare in order to dissipate the final bit of energy, so the final touchdown point will be a little beyond that unmoving spot.

After turning onto final approach, I *don't* want you to look for the spot on the ground that isn't moving. Instead, I want you to look at the spot where you'd like to land (your *desired landing spot*) as shown by the red dot in Figure 11, and see whether or not it's moving up or down relative to your windscreen. If the spot where you'd like to land remains stationary in your windscreen, then that's where you're headed. Good for you. The universe is once again in perfect harmony. (Remember, you'll touch down a little beyond this spot unless you purposely aim short of it.)

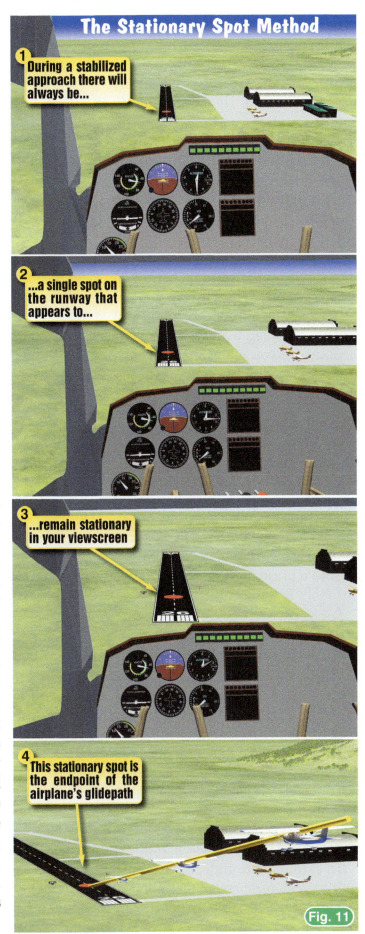

Fig. 11

If the desired landing spot (the red dot in Figure 12) moves up or down, then it's not the spot to which the airplane is presently aimed (which is the green dot in Figure 12). But you *are* the pilot in command, so you are going to issue the "stay" command by modifying your glidepath in order to make the desired landing spot remains motionless in the windscreen.

Let's assume that despite my best efforts to set you up to land on a spot somewhere in the center of the first third of the runway, you are either high or low. What should you do? Let me take over? This is your airplane, so *you* make the appropriate glidepath corrections. It's really pretty easy, so let me show you how.

The Low Down

Let's say that with the airplane trimmed and speed and power constant, the desired landing spot (the red dot) moves upward in your windscreen (Figure 13, position sequence A, B and C). This means that your glidepath is taking you to a place that's short of the desired landing spot, which is shown by a green dot in Figure 13, position D. You need to extend your glidepath to a place farther down the runway, as shown by the red dot in Figure 14. How do you do that? Probably not the way you might at first think.

When the Desired Landing Spot Moves Up or Down

When the desired landing (red) spot moves up in the window (#1,2,3), you're going to land short of it (at the green spot in this example). When the desired landing (red) spot moves down in the window (4,5,6), you are going to land beyond it (at the green spot in this example).

For many first-time pilots, it is unfortunately an intuitive response to raise the nose and point it at the desired landing spot. They're chasing the dot and they are *not* going to catch it. What they discover, sometimes too late, is that this action will cause the landing spot to move upward even faster!

Why does that happen? I don't want to be a drag, but back to the total drag curve for a moment. You are already close to the optimal lift/drag ratio, the low point in the drag curve. Raising the nose moves you toward the back side of the curve, where induced drag increases rapidly and total drag does the same. With more drag and no more power, the plane descends at an ever-increasing rate. You're now flying at a slow speed and with a rapidly increasing descent rate (the power curve is essentially the total drag curve when power isn't used). Pretty soon, you see the ground rushing up, and there is an almost irresistible urge to pull back on the stick, which further increases drag and the rate of descent and. . .is that a stall I see happening? Near the ground? This is why you never ever, ever try and stretch a glide by pulling aft on the elevator. Never! Never! Never! Please read the sidebar titled: *The Elevator Instinct* on Page 9-16.

To extend your glidepath, increase engine power slightly while simultaneously raising the nose to maintain an airspeed of 65 knots (Figure 15). The proper technique is to add just a little bit of power (try an increase of 100 to 300 RPM), then make a pitch adjustment with the elevator control to maintain the correct approach speed. It should be obvious to you by now that adding power without

Chapter 9: Approaching to Land

Fig. 13

raising the pitch attitude will increase your airspeed. The proper technique involves making a *simultaneous* adjustment in power and pitch.

Once you've added a little power and increased the pitch slightly, the runway picture through your windscreen changes for the better. You will now see that the stationary spot has moved up along the surface, into the first third of the runway's length, as shown in Figure 15. Now your glidepath takes you exactly where you want it to. Bravo! The secret to modifying your glidepath is to make a small

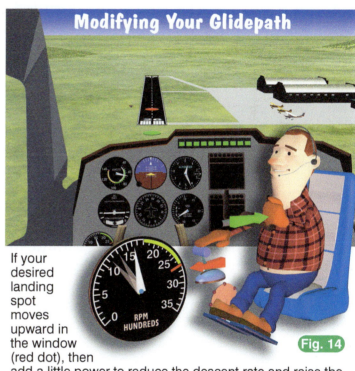

If your desired landing spot moves upward in the window (red dot), then add a little power to reduce the descent rate and raise the nose slightly to maintain the desired approach airspeed.

Fig. 14

Adding a little power and raising the nose slightly allows you to extend your glidepath and maintain your airspeed.

Fig. 15

adjustment in power, and then leave the throttle alone, using pitch adjustment to maintain the correct airspeed. Now wait and see if your desired landing spot remains stationary as viewed through your windscreen. Repeat this procedure as necessary so that the glidepath obeys your demands and your desired landing spot (red dot) becomes stationary. Be sure to always trim the airplane once you've made any change in power.

When you're learning to fly, it's very helpful to think in terms of one thing controlling another. That's why I want you to think in terms of your *throttle* controlling your *descent rate* and the *elevator* controlling your *airspeed*.

As you recall from Chapter Three, I discussed three techniques for controlling your airspeed and descent rate (i.e., glidepath). Some instructors prefer to think of using power to control airspeed and using elevator to control descent rate. There's absolutely nothing wrong with using either technique when you're operating on the front side of the power curve (typically above 1.3 Vs). So, *vive la différence*.

The reason I prefer the throttle-controls-descent-rate method is that you aren't always *on* the front side of the power curve. At 1.3 Vs, you are still above but close to where the back side of the power curve—the region of reversed command—begins. If you do get too slow on final approach and move onto the back side of the power curve, using throttle to control descent rate means you are a lot less likely to pull aft on the elevator control in an attempt to stretch your glide. I like my students—and you—to have this extra margin of safety while they learn.

Bye High

What happens if your landing spot (the red dot) moves *downward* in the windscreen, as shown in Figure 16? The glidepath is taking you beyond where you want to land (you're now headed for the green dot). You're going to land long if you don't make some changes. What to do, what to do? You need to steepen the glidepath without increasing your airspeed (Figure 17).

Let's start with the case where you *are* on approach while using a little power, even though that's not the case in the virtual first landing you're now performing. Your first move should be to reduce any power that's being used (Figure 17). If that alone doesn't get the job done, you might also have to add flaps or additional flaps to increase the descent rate, but don't do this without reducing power first. That would be like driving with the brakes on. Reduce any power applied, in order to steepen the glidepath, and simultaneously lower the nose slightly to maintain the correct airspeed.

The Elevator Instinct

Pilots receive a tremendous amount of reinforcement (reward) for their use of the elevator as a flight path control. If you think about it, this reinforcement occurs hundreds of times on every flight. At the slightest change in altitude, we return to the desired value by a slight push or pull on the elevator. This is the pilot's equivalent of your dog named *Biscuit* getting a treat each time she does something you want her to do again. Every turn requires a slight pull on the elevator to forestall an altitude loss (and we make hundreds of turns on every flight). We even pull back on the elevator to meet the ground at an acceptable angle during the landing flare. The list goes on and on and on. You pull on the elevator, the airplane remains where you want it to, your brain says, "Hmm. Done good. Next time do again." What goes unnoticed by virtually all pilot brains is that each push and pull action has an airspeed reaction, however slight.

Numerically, the reinforcement for elevator as a flight path control (otherwise known as controlling your *altitude* or *glidepath* with the elevator) far exceeds its reinforcement as an airspeed control. Is it any wonder this conditioned reflex causes pilots to stall and spin as they habitually pull on the elevator to raise the nose or stretch the glide? What's a pilot to do?

First, combating this type of reinforcement starts with recognizing that it exists and why it exists. Once recognized, wary pilots avoid putting themselves in situations where they can be victimized by this reflex. In other words, they avoid buzzing and swooping.

Second, pilots need to develop a powerful countermeasure to combat this habit. Stall recognition and awareness is one answer (perhaps the only significant answer, too). Nevertheless, given that pilots actually spend very little time in practicing stall recoveries, you can see how difficult it is to counteract this conditioned reflex.

Behavioral conditioning is a major culprit. In an emergency, pilots may reflexively pull on the elevator to stretch the glidepath, inadvertently stalling the airplane. This hazardous and too-often-fatal tendency must be counteracted. Stall/spin recognition and recovery training is one way to accomplish this.

In the movie "The Untouchables", Sean Connery confronts a lone, knife wielding attacker after the exchange of much gunfire. Confronted with an apparent mismatch of weaponry, Connery says something like, "It's just like a dumb thug to bring a knife to a gunfight." Flying without a deep awareness of stall/spin territory is like showing up unprepared for safe flight. It's a tremendous mismatch. Stall training is the key. Make sure you get your fair share of it.

Chapter 9: Approaching to Land

A Landing Long on the Runway
Desired landing spot

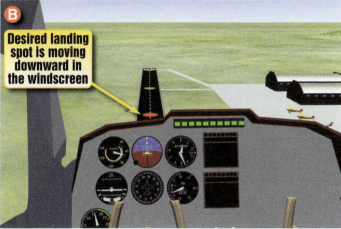

B Desired landing spot is moving downward in the windscreen

C Glidepath taking you to the stationary spot here

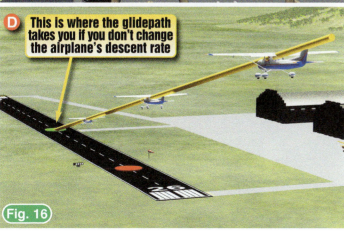

D This is where the glidepath takes you if you don't change the airplane's descent rate

Fig. 16

If you reduce power and don't reduce the pitch attitude slightly, your airspeed will decrease, perhaps to the point where you end up behind the power curve. You don't want to be there. So when reducing power, the nose must move down a bit to maintain the desired approach speed. Now that's a nice place to be.

Observe the spot where you want to land (Figure 18). If it remains stationary (doesn't move up or down in the windscreen), then you're headed directly toward it. Nice job. Keep on keeping on. Is the magic spot still moving downward a bit? Make the same adjustments again (assuming the throttle isn't already at flight idle). Several iterations might be necessary while on final approach

Modifying Your Glidepath

If your desired landing spot moves down in the window (red dot), then reduce power to increase the descent rate and lower the nose slightly to maintain the desired approach airspeed.

Fig. 17

How Your Glidepath Changes

Fig. 18

Reducing power and lowering the nose slightly allows you to steepen your glidepath and maintain your airspeed.

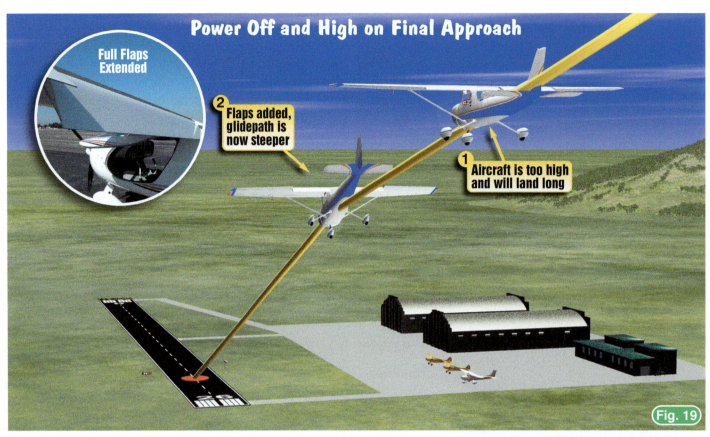

Fig. 19

before you get the landing spot properly dialed in. Even when you nail it, wind conditions can change on the way down, so keep checking. And remember to trim the airplane after you've made any change in power.

The second case is when you are high on final approach with the power already at flight idle. You're powerless to further reduce power, but you're not out of options. You have two choices to help you descend. You can either forward slip the airplane, or you can add flaps or you can even do both, if that rings your chimes and wiggles your wings (assume your POH approves of slipping with flaps extended). We'll talk about slips in the next chapter, so let's add flaps to increase the drag and steepen the descent rate (Figure 19).

When the airplane is high on final approach, there are three options available to you to help increase your rate of descent. You can slip the airplane (to be discussed soon), you can add flaps or you can slip with flaps as long as this is approved by your airplane's POH. When adding flaps, you'll want to lower the nose to maintain the desired airspeed and you'll want to use 1.3 Vso (the new approach speed based on the airplane's reduced stalling speed with full flaps applied.

Fig. 20

Chapter 9: Approaching to Land

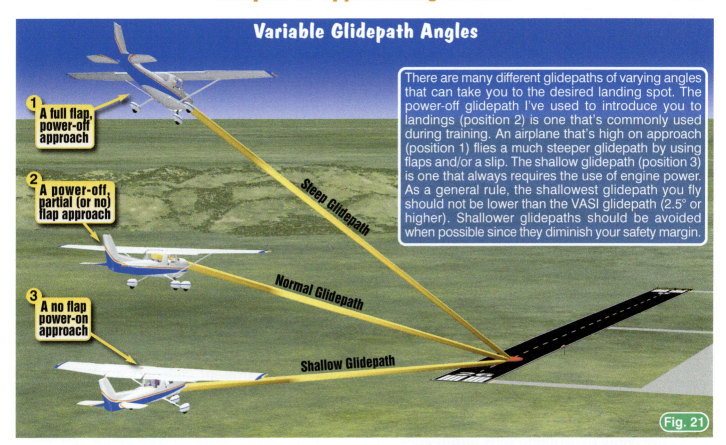

If you add full flaps, keep in mind that your approach speed will change slightly. That's because 1.3 Vso with full flaps is 52 knots. So by adding flaps, you'll need to adjust your attitude to give you this airspeed. This means your attitude will be lower than normal, because flaps allow the airplane to have the correct angle of attack at a much lower nose attitude (Figure 20). That means you can see the runway over the nose more easily. So apply the flaps in 10-15 degree (or one notch) increments and lower the nose smoothly.

So Many Glidepaths From Which to Choose

Now you have some knowledge about establishing a glidepath that takes you to your desired landing spot. But isn't it possible that more than one glidepath—a very shallow one or a really steep one, for example—could also take you to the same landing spot, as shown in Figure 21?

The short answer is, "Yes." After all, if you turn final approach at too high or too low an altitude, you end up flying a glidepath that's either very steep or very shallow, yet both glidepaths will take you to the same landing spot. In fact, there are an almost infinite number of glidepaths that could lead you to the same spot. But isn't there one glidepath that might be preferable to all the others? Of course there is.

How We Define a Normal Glidepath

The POH of our the small training airplane we're using in this chapter lists its power-off glide speed as 63 knots (IAS). This results in a descent rate of approximately 500 feet per minute and gives us a glide angle of about 6° in a no-wind condition. This is how I define the normal power-off glidepath that we've used for your initial introduce to landing.

It's interesting to note that the best L/D speed of our trainer is 63 knots (IAS). This is very close to 65 knots, our approach speed in these examples. Therefore, at 1.3 Vs (even with 10-15° of flaps), we're operating near the bottom of the total drag curve, just above the region of reversed command.

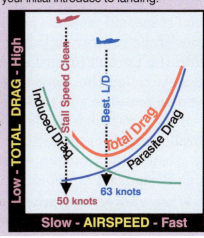

Flying an extremely shallow glidepath (meaning that you're flying a *power-on* approach) means you might get to sample some of the obstacles attached to the ground, to say nothing about knocking a few birds out of their tree nests. Flying a steep a glidepath (obviously this would be a *power-off* approach) means that you're typically landing with full flaps, which isn't always favorable in strong wind conditions. That's why you need to know how to establish a normal glidepath to the runway immediately after turning onto final approach. (For more information on glidepath angles, please read Postflight Briefing #9-1.)

Recall that we've agreed that a *normal power-off glidepath* is one that allows you to make a power-off glide in a typical small training airplane to the center of the first third of the runway. When it comes to making *power-on* approaches, a normal power-on glidepath is one that is typically inclined anywhere between 2.5 and 3.5 degrees (which we'll define as a *normal power-on glidepath*). Of course, if the landing runway is equipped with a VASI, it's easy to identify and fly the correct glidepath angle (see sidebar on Page 9-21). In fact, you are *required* to fly at or above the VASI angle, which is sometimes adjusted to take account of local conditions, including noise abatement and obstacles.

What happens when your landing runway has no VASI? Perhaps it had a VASIectomy. Eye see. Well, it turns out that "eye see" is actually a method you want to use because it uses your eyeballs.

As you turn base-to-final, it's not always clear whether you've set yourself up to fly a steep, normal, or shallow glidepath to the desired landing spot. Here is where the actual shape of the runway as it appears through your windscreen can provide a clue to your present glidepath angle. Let's see how this works.

How Do You Know If You're on a Normal Glidepath Without a VASI?

You are going to estimate your *initial* glidepath angle by examining the runway's apparent *trapezoidal shape*. That's why we call this method (stand by for a big surprise) the *trapezoidal shape method*. This method will tell you three things. First, it will tell you if you'll *begin* your approach too high, too low or somewhere in between (perhaps just right). Second, it will *supplement* the stationary spot method in helping you descend to the desired landing spot. Third, it will help you fly a *stabilized approach* (which I'll define in the next chapter). Can geometry be so useful to us? Absolutely.

Trapezoidal shape? OK, let me be square—or somewhat square—with you about this method. Trust me, this does not involve dressing in tights and maneuvering above a crowd at the circus, though it *does* involve flying through the air.

A trapezoid is a four-sided figure with only two sides that are parallel. As you look at the runway on final approach, it appears to be a trapezoid, an extended rectangle that tapers toward the far end because of the way our eyes perceive three-dimensional objects (Figure 22). Only the near and far ends of the runway trapezoid appear parallel. The sides of the runway appear to taper toward the far end toward a meeting at what is called the *vanishing point*. I want to reassure you that the runway itself *is* a rectangle with *all* its sides parallel, and that no airplane has ever vanished at the vanishing point. There is no Bermuda Trapezoid.

When viewed from where you sit in the cockpit on final approach, it is

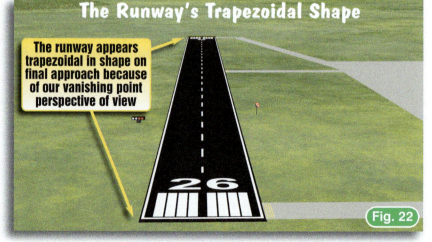

The sides of the runway appear to taper toward the far end, giving the runway its trapezoidal shape as seen on final approach.

Chapter 9: Approaching to Land

The Visual Approach Slope Indicator (VASI)

Without training, it can be difficult to make a determination of the proper landing glidepath with the naked eye. Fortunately there is something known as a *Visual Approach Slope Indicator* (VASI) that provides you with a visual clue as to the proper glidepath to fly.

There are several types of VASIs but the most common one usually consists of two pairs of light-bars along the side of the runway (it's often called a *two bar VASI* for this reason). The two VASI bars are usually 500 to 1,000 feet from the approach threshold. These lights project either a red or white color, depending on your altitude. The colors are constant and don't actually change within the box. What changes is your height, which allows you to look at the VASI from different angles and see different colors. When you are below the proper glidepath, both VASI bars show red. Some pilots remember that this signals trouble by thinking of it as *Red over red, you'll conk your head*. Level off until you see red over white. Red over white means that you're above the glidepath for the bar closest to you and below the glidepath for the bar farther away. This is a complicated way of saying you're on the glidepath that will plunk you down halfway between the two bars. A good way to remember this is *Red over white, you're all right*. Of course, if you're too high, both bars will show white. A good memory aid for this is *White over white, you'll soon be out of sight*. Increase the descent rate until the upwind bar turns red. You can expect the VASI's red and white bars to transition through a pink color as your altitude in relation to the proper glideslope changes.

You shouldn't see a green color on a two-bar VASI unless you're so low that the light is filtering through the grass (OK, that can't happen). But there is such a thing as a tri-color VASI where a green light shows you're established on the desired glidepath.

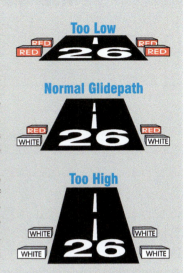

perspective that creates the *illusion* of a trapezoid. Discovering this was a big deal for Renaissance painters. Too bad they didn't have pilots back then; they might have figured it out sooner.

Speaking of painters, let's return to the idea that you are viewing a picture in a frame during final approach. The picture appears to grow in your windscreen (Figure 23) as its outer edges move beyond the frame. If you're on a normal glidepath taking you to the desired landing spot, that spot remains stationary in your windscreen and the ends of the runway (both thresholds) above and below that spot appear to move away from each other. This makes the entire trapezoidal runway shape appear to grow *proportionally* in size, *while the actual shape remains the same* (i.e., the angles of the trapezoid's four corners don't change as long as the glidepath angle doesn't change). As you're about to see, it's this overall *shape* of the runway trapezoid (not its size) that informs you whether you're above, below or on (or ready to begin) a normal glidepath to the desired landing spot. How so? Read on.

Trapezoidal Shape Remains the Same on Stabilized Glidepath

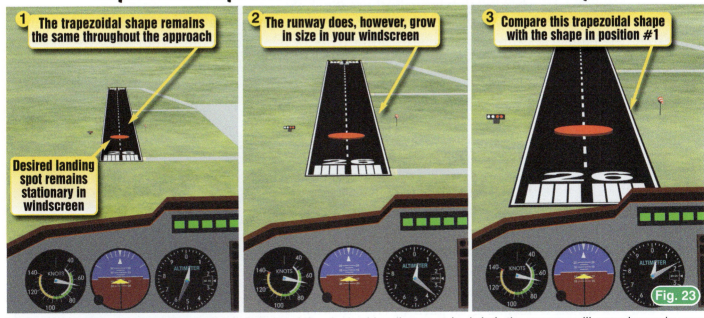

While descending on a *stabilized glidepath* toward the desired landing spot (red dot), the runway will grow larger in your windscreen but its trapezoidal shape will remain the same (but only as long as the glidepath remains the same).

How the Runway Shape Changes Base on Your Glidepath

As your glidepath changes, the trapezoidal appearance of the runway will also change. It's the runway's shape that provides a clue as to the angle of your glidepath. A normal glidepath is shown by the runway in position (A). Clearly the compressed and elongated runway shapes in B and C show you on either too low or too high a glidepath, respectively.

During your first few approaches, as I set you up for a normal glidepath using a power-off descent for landing, you'll want to pay special attention to the shape and length of the trapezoidal runway picture as you turn onto final approach at your home airport. You should see a reasonable distance between both the near and far ends of the runway through your windscreen (Figure 24, position A). If the thresholds are too close together, then you're clearly too low (below a normal glidepath) on this approach (Figure 24, position B). If the thresholds are far apart, then you're clearly too high on approach (Figure 24, position C).

To better understand how runway geometry informs you about your height on final approach, try this experiment. Use a letter size piece of paper to simulate a short, wide runway. Place that paper on the edge of your dinner table, with the runway threshold (the 8.5 inch side of the paper) parallel to that edge. If you want to paint numbers on each end and add a centerline, go for it Picasso. Now stand about four feet away, bend your knees a few inches, and look at the runway's geometry. Consider this the normal glidepath perspective.

Now stand up straight up, while keeping your eye on the paper. As you went higher the runway trapezoid (the paper) appeared to elongate, didn't it? Now bend down until your eyes are just a few inches above the table top. The runway trapezoid appeared to shrink, didn't it? You've just experimented with changing runway perspectives based on height above the runway. You also gave your dinner guests something to talk about for years to come (assuming you didn't explain to them what you're doing). Tell them you're practicing meatball bobbing, which might be a sport in the next Olympics.

Techniques for Returning to a Normal Glidepath

As you turn onto final approach, the trapezoidal shape of the runway provides another means of evaluating whether you're above, below or on a normal glidepath. What you're looking to see as you turn final approach is the *same* trapezoidal shape (not size) that you saw when I first set you up on a normal glidepath to the runway. This will be the baseline shape you want to remember and

Chapter 9: Approaching to Land

keep etched in that steel-trap memory of yours. If the trapezoidal shape isn't similar what you remember (or what common sense suggests that it should be), then you probably need to modify the glidepath angle you use to reach the desired landing spot.

You're Too Low on Final

For instance, if you turn onto final approach and notice that the thresholds appear too close together (as when you were four inches above the dinner table), then you know you're at a lower than normal altitude on final approach (Figure 25, positions A and B). You certainly don't want to continue descending at your previous rate because you might be flying dangerously close to the surface or land short of the runway. The best way to handle this problem is to add additional power to reduce the descent rate (or perhaps decrease it to *zero* temporarily) and simultaneously raise the nose slightly to maintain the correct approach speed (Figure 25, positions C and D).

As both ends of the runway begin to move farther apart from each other, they'll eventually reach the distance you recall as the separation for a normal glidepath (Figure 25, positions E and F). At this point, you would reduce power to flight idle and resume a descent at 1.3 Vs toward the desired landing spot using the stationary spot method discussed previously. This places you in a position to fly a normal glidepath on final approach.

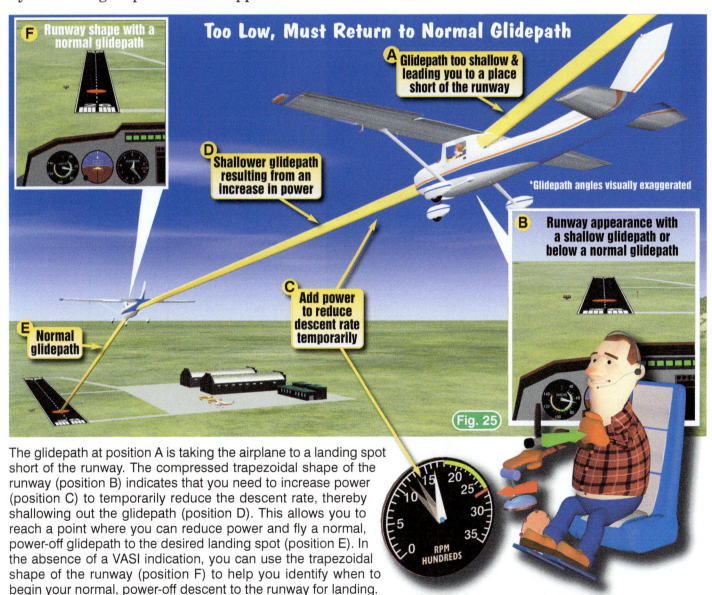

Fig. 25

The glidepath at position A is taking the airplane to a landing spot short of the runway. The compressed trapezoidal shape of the runway (position B) indicates that you need to increase power (position C) to temporarily reduce the descent rate, thereby shallowing out the glidepath (position D). This allows you to reach a point where you can reduce power and fly a normal, power-off glidepath to the desired landing spot (position E). In the absence of a VASI indication, you can use the trapezoidal shape of the runway (position F) to help you identify when to begin your normal, power-off descent to the runway for landing.

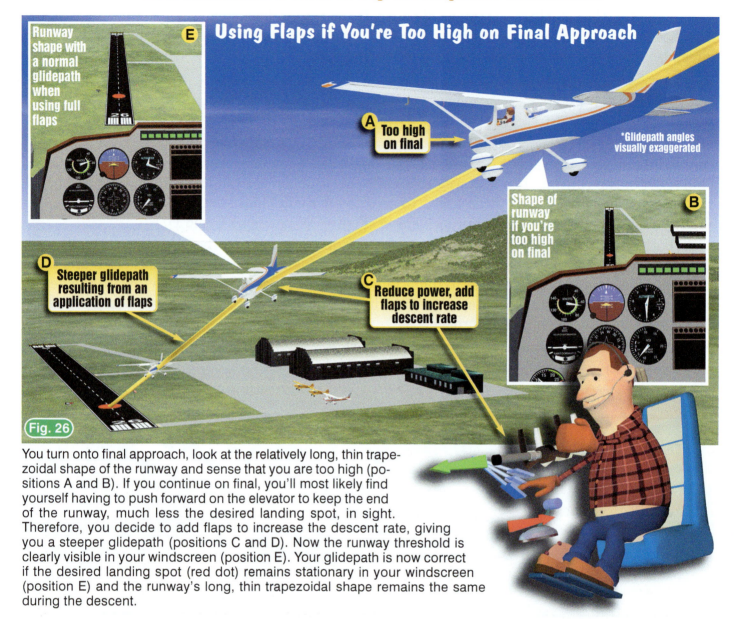

Using Flaps if You're Too High on Final Approach

You turn onto final approach, look at the relatively long, thin trapezoidal shape of the runway and sense that you are too high (positions A and B). If you continue on final, you'll most likely find yourself having to push forward on the elevator to keep the end of the runway, much less the desired landing spot, in sight. Therefore, you decide to add flaps to increase the descent rate, giving you a steeper glidepath (positions C and D). Now the runway threshold is clearly visible in your windscreen (position E). Your glidepath is now correct if the desired landing spot (red dot) remains stationary in your windscreen (position E) and the runway's long, thin trapezoidal shape remains the same during the descent.

You're Too High on Final

If you turn onto final approach and notice that the thresholds are too far apart, then you are higher than normal on final approach (Figure 26, positions A and B). Your *very* natural tendency here is to keep lowering the nose (without adding flaps) to maintain sight of the desired landing spot and/or the landing threshold that's moving beneath the airplane's nose in your windscreen. Lowering the nose is a very bad idea because it results in the airspeed increasing and that means the possibility of not being able to come to a stop on the runway (if you even manage to land on the runway). The fact that your airspeed is increasing because you are pushing the elevator control forward just to keep the runway in sight is a powerful clue that you are high on the approach.

As we discussed earlier, the best way to handle being high is to reduce power (if any is still applied), and add flaps (as necessary) to increase the descent rate while simultaneously lowering the nose slightly to maintain the correct approach speed (Figure 26, position C). This allows you to fly a steeper glidepath to the desired landing spot (Figure 26, positions D and E). Since you're already making a power-off approach with 10-15 degrees of flaps, you should add another 10 to 15 degrees of flaps to increase your descent rate (after you gain a little more experience, you'll know whether to add another 10-15 degrees of flaps to arrive at the desired landing spot or add full flaps if you're excessively high).

Chapter 9: Approaching to Land

It's the flaps' increase in drag that increases your angle of descent. It's also what helps prevent an increase in airspeed at this steeper descent angle. If you choose to add full flaps, your approach speed decreases to 1.3 Vso (52 knots CAS in this airplane).

After adding the appropriate amount of flaps, lowering the nose and trimming for the descent, you'll use the stationary spot method to ensure that you land on the desired landing spot. Yes, your approach is going to be steeper, but that's the price paid for being high in the first place. Of course, you can always climb and return for another landing, otherwise known as a *go-around* (a good option, in many cases) if the approach is too steep for your tastes.

Please keep in mind that the long thin trapezoidal shape of the runway shouldn't change during your steeper descent as long as your glidepath remains stable and takes you to the desired landing spot in the center of the first third of the runway. Why? You were originally high on approach which gave the runway a long thin trapezoidal shape. Since you're still high and coming down at a steeper angle, the runway shape will remain the same despite growing larger in your window as shown by comparing the two cockpit views (Figure 26, positions B and E).

What if your airplane didn't have flaps, or didn't have effective flaps? Fear not and want not. Here is where you can use a forward slip to help steepen the descent angle (Figure 27, position A). I promise to chat with you about slips in Chapter 11 (I know, I'm such a tease) but here it's important to understand that slips allow you to increase your descent rate without adding flaps. For instance, if you evaluate the runway's trapezoidal shape on final approach and determine that you're high (Figure 27, positions B and C), you can place the airplane in a forward slip to increase your descent rate. When the runway's trapezoidal shape appears as it would for a normal, power-off glidepath (Figure 27, position D), you'll roll out of the slip and resume your wings level descent (Figure 27, position F).

The simplest way to increase your descent rate if you're high on final approach is to use a forward slip (position A). You'd slip the airplane until the runway shape indicates that you can fly a normal glidepath to the runway (position D), then you'd roll out of the slip into a wings level attitude (position F).

Now, here is one thing you *don't* want to do. If you're high on final approach, you *don't* want to add flaps, descend to a point where the trapezoidal shape looks normal to you, then retract the flaps and continue with a power-off, no-flap (or partial-flap) descent. This would be very poor piloting technique and could prove highly unsafe in certain instances. Retracting flaps raises your stall speed. If you happen to be a little too slow for some reason and retract the flaps, you could stall your machine. Think of flaps as a one-way decision. If you add flaps to adjust the descent, accept the resulting glidepath.

There's nothing wrong with flying a steeper glidepath using full flaps as long as you maintain control of the airspeed. That *is* one of the purposes of flaps. You get a steeper descent without an increase in airspeed. Then again, there are times when strong surface winds make landing with flaps fully extended inadvisable.

However, this depends a lot on the airplane you're flying. Forty degrees of flaps extension in a Cessna 150 can make the airplane difficult to control in very strong, gusty winds. Given the same winds in a Piper Warrior with full flap extension, this isn't as much of a problem. This is where your instructor's experience and advice will be of great value to you. If you suspect that the winds are too strong to land safely with flaps, you can always go around and return to the pattern for another landing.

Strive to remember the trapezoidal shape of your home airport runway after turning onto final approach when I set you up for your first few normal landings. This is the shape that you'll be looking for during subsequent landings *on this particular runway*. Hmmm, wouldn't it be great if your instructor could take a picture of the runway shape at the point where you turn final on a normal approach, just so that you could memorize it on your own? It's just a shame we don't have portable digital cameras, perhaps combined with a cell phone, or something like that.

Oh wait! My bad. We do have such things. They're everywhere. Let your instructor borrow your phone and take some photos on approach. Perhaps he or she already has pictures of high, low and normal glidepaths, showing how these trapezoidal shapes differ. Perhaps he or she will email them to you so you can imprint these shapes on your learning lobes at home.

Variable Runway Shapes and What They Mean

Now that you have an understanding of how the runway's shape can aid you in evaluating your glidepath, I want to make one thing absolutely clear here. Runway shapes, like pilot shapes, vary from airport to airport. Some runways (and pilots) are long, some short, some wide and some thin. So this technique is a little more challenging to use with the same degree of precision on runways that differ dramatically in length and width from your home runway. In other words, there's a big difference between an 1,800 foot long, 50 foot wide runway and one that's 10,000 feet long and 150 feet wide.

On the other hand, there's not as much difference in trapezoidal runway shapes between a 2,500 foot runway and one that's 4,000 feet in length (variable widths—within reason—don't matter as much in assessing glidepath evaluations. It's the distance between the thresholds that counts most). These are typical runway lengths for the airports at which you're likely to land. That's why there's a strong possibility that the runway shape of your home field (if we assume it's around 2,500 to 3,000 feet long) can be used as a reasonable aid to help you make glidepath evaluations on runways that are a little longer and wider.

Even on a runway that's longer than your home field, if the ends appear really close together, you're definitely low on the approach. If the ends appear separated by a relatively great distance, you're clearly too high on approach. So this method is still useful, especially when it comes to evaluating the extreme high and low ranges of glidepath angles (and this is where it really counts, right?).

Then again, if my home field runway is 2,887 feet in length (position A, shown below), and its trapezoidal shape in imprinted on my lobes, I can use half the length of a 5,701 foot runway to help me make a crude assessment of my glidepath as I turn onto final approach (position B, shown below). Yes, I realize that there's an increase in complexity to this evaluation because a pilot has to imagine the halfway point as the runway's end. The complexity, however, is lessened by the fact that many runways have midfield taxiways, which help pilots divide the runway into sections matching the basic shape of their home field. Of course, once a pilot gains experience landing on different runways, he or she can make accurate glidepath evaluations irrespective of differing runway lengths.

Variable Runway Shapes and Sizes

A — Runway 19L is 2,887 feet long, 75 feet wide

B — Runway 19R is 5,701 feet long, 150 feet wide

Chapter 9: Approaching to Land

What It Means When the Trapezoidal Runway Shape Varies

There's one an additional benefit to being able to assess the trapezoidal shape of the runway, and this occurs when you evaluate how this trapezoidal shape is actually *changing*.

Let's assume you're on final approach to your home airport runway with the ends of the runway separated by the appropriate distance necessary for a normal, power-off glidepath, as shown in Figure 28, position A. If your desired landing spot (the red dot) begins moving upward in the windscreen, you're descending below the desired glidepath and you will notice that the thresholds on each end of the runway are moving closer together (Figure 28, positions B and C). In this way, a *collapsing* runway trapezoid tells you that your glidepath will likely take you to a point short of the desired landing location.

If the desired landing spot begins moving downward in the windscreen, then you're rising above the desired glidepath (Figure 29) and you will notice that the runway thresholds are moving farther apart (Figure 29, positions B and C). An *expanding* runway trapezoid clues you in that your glidepath will likely take you to a point beyond the desired landing location.

When the desired landing spot moves upward in the windscreen and the runway trapezoid collapses, your glidepath will take you short of the desired landing spot.

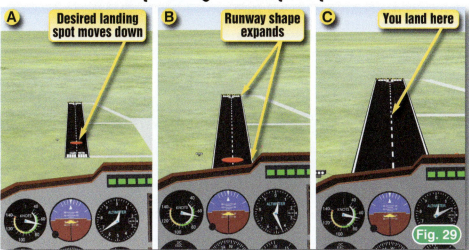

When the desired landing spot moves downward in the windscreen and the runway trapezoid expands, your glidepath will take you beyond the desired landing spot.

By observing the runway's trapezoidal shape as you turn onto final approach, then observing how it changes, you have a very important visual clue to help assess whether or not you're in a position to descend on a normal glidepath for landing.

Combine the trapezoidal shape of the runway with the stationary landing spot method discussed earlier and you have two fantastic methods for determining if you're descending below, moving above or established on a normal glidepath.

As a side note on using the trapezoidal method for evaluating your glidepath, keep in mind that you can begin to evaluate the runway's shape and its changing geometry when you're on base leg. That's right. About midway through base leg, the runway's trapezoidal shape is just as informative as it on final approach.

But wait, there's more. Let me introduce you to something I call, *The Super EZ Glidepath Evaluation Clue*.

The Super EZ Glidepath Evaluation Clue

By now you already know that on final approach, ground references above the stationary spot on the runway move upward toward the horizon while objects below this spot move downward toward your cowling. What you might not yet know is that while the airplane moves toward this spot, it will most likely touch down slightly beyond it, mainly because the roundout and flare extend the landing distance slightly (Figure 30). Here's where you can use this knowledge to your advantage.

Without question, the beginning of the runway is easy to identify. Here's how you can use this to your advantage. When you're lined up on final approach and have established the attitude to maintain 1.3 Vs, trim the airplane, then watch the very beginning of the runway. If it moves upward in your windshield, you're obviously going to land short of the runway because the desired landing spot is on the approach side of the threshold.

If the threshold moves downward in the windscreen, perhaps moving below your engine cowling, then you will definitely land somewhere beyond the landing threshold. How far beyond? Well, here's where you have to look for the area on the runway that appears not to move either up or down (yes, this is one time where you might want to actively look for a spot on the runway that's not moving). To do so, gradually focus your vision up the runway and identify the white runway stripe that appears to remain stationary. That's where the airplane is headed. If it's in the first third of the runway, then bravo for you. But wait, I have more good stuff for you.

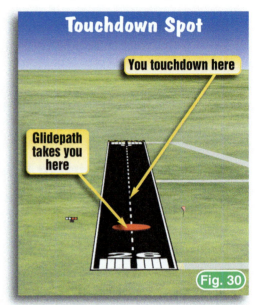

Despite your glidepath taking you to the stationary spot (red dot), you'll actually touch down slightly beyond this spot as the airplane rids itself of its extra airspeed in the roundout and flare.

As long as you're established on a normal glidepath and not dragging the airplane in at a low angle with power, you can choose the runway threshold to be the stationary spot by increasing or decreasing your descent rate (Figure 31). When the landing threshold is the stationary spot in your windscreen, you'll actually touch down slightly beyond the threshold (several variables affect this such as wind speed, true airspeed, density altitude and so on, but 50 to 200 feet is a reasonable estimate of this distance).

This technique produces more of a short-field landing, except that you're not striving for true short-field performance since you're not typically landing with full flaps in your early practice sessions. But I do have to make it clear that you don't want to use the runway threshold as your stationary spot if you're dragging your airplane in at low altitude on final approach. To use this technique, you'll most likely need to use power, so this isn't something you'll do until you've achieved some degree of landing mastery.

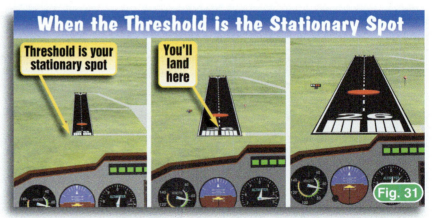

If the threshold is the stationary spot, then your airplane will touch down in the first third of the runway. This is an acceptable short-field technique if there are no relevant obstacles in your approach.

No doubt you'll be able to use all these clues to get you to a point 10 feet above the runway. But what do you do when you get there? To find out, we need to discuss what is known as the landing *roundout* and the landing *flare*. So let's continue our upbeat but downward trend in Chapter 10.

Chapter 9: Approaching to Land

Postflight Briefing #9-1 Glidepath Angles

Glidepath Angles and Power Usage

One concept that all pilots should be familiar with involves how wind affects their glidepath angle. For instance, the glidepath angle in Figure 32, position A is your normal power-off glidepath in a no-wind condition. The desired glidepath is the actual glidepath you fly at your approach airspeed with the throttle at flight idle.

What happens to your glidepath angle if you are flying into a headwind, as you do on most landings? The answer is that your actual glidepath angle is steeper than your normal or desired glidepath angle, despite flying at the same approach speed and same descent rate with power off (Figure 32, position B). Keep in mind that we're talking about the *angle* of the glidepath, not the descent rate, which remains the same in all three conditions shown. The headwind simply reduces the airplane's groundspeed, which means that for every bit it moves downward, it moves forward a little slower than normal. The result is a steeper than normal descent angle despite descending at the same rate as normal. If you're expecting to fly a normal glidepath but the headwind is exceptionally strong, you'll find yourself having to use power to make your desired landing spot.

On the other hand, if you attempt to land with a tailwind, the actual glidepath angle will be shallower than the desired glidepath angle (Figure 32, position C). Here your groundspeed increases, meaning that for every bit the airplane moves downward, it moves forward a little bit faster than normal. This results in a shallower glidepath angle despite the descent rate being normal. If you're expecting to fly a normal glidepath angle while approaching with a tailwind, you're likely to find yourself landing beyond the desired landing spot. It might be possible to add flaps to increase your descent rate, but it's also likely that your touchdown speed and an insufficiently long runway would make a landing unadvisable.

In a no-wind condition in a power-off glide, the airplane glides at an approximate angle of five degrees at approximately 500 feet per minute at approach speed.

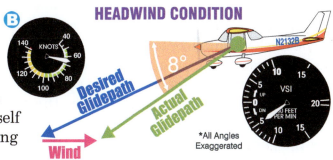

When flying into a headwind at approach speed with no power, the descent rate is the same as it is above, but the descent angle increases. This often requires the use of engine power to reach the desired landing spot.

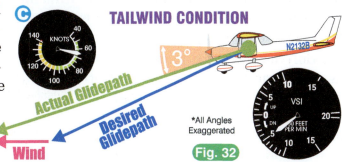

Fig. 32

When flying with a tailwind at approach speed and no-power, the descent rate is the same as it is above, but the descent angle is shallower. This typically results in the airplane being higher on approach, perhaps requiring flap usage for landing.

Postflight Briefing #9-2 Names for Runway Spots

One of the most important ideas a student should learn from this chapter is that the *desired landing spot* should be the *stationary spot* on the runway as viewed through his or her windscreen. That's why I've chosen to use these two terms in this chapter. Other books use several terms to describe the landing: *aiming point, the true aiming point, the touchdown point, the desired touchdown point, the intended landing spot, the desired landing spot* and so on. Over the years I've always found many of these terms to be confusing for student pilots. Let me explain.

Let's suppose a student is on final approach and the spot where he or she wants to land is located on the centerline, exactly one-third of the length of the runway past the threshold. Some students are taught to look through the windscreen and identify the spot on the surface ahead of them that doesn't move. In other words, they have been trained to identify the location where their glidepath intersects the landing surface ahead. Most books call this the *aiming point* because it identifies where the airplane's glidepath is presently aimed. Once the aiming point is identified, these same students are supposed to ask themselves if this is where they'd really like to land. If not, then are instructed to adjust their glidepath so that the aiming point allows them to land on the spot desired. This is an adequate method, but it doesn't involve an extra and unnecessary step. I believe there's an easier and more efficient way for students to evaluate their glidepath.

I find it easier and less confusing to have the student turn final approach and look at the spot where he or she would like to land (which I call the *desired landing spot*) and see if this spot moves in the windscreen. This is, after all, the most important spot on the runway, isn't it? If the desired landing spot remains stationary in the windscreen, then all the student has to do is fly a stabilized approach down to the runway, followed by the roundout and flare at the proper time.

If the desired landing sport moves up or down in the windscreen then all the student has to do is modify the glidepath so that this spot becomes stationary in the proper part of the windscreen. In this way, the student eliminates the need to see where the airplane is presently aimed. There's really no need to know this since the student doesn't want the airplane to go there.

This is why I've only used two terms for landing in this book, the *desired landing spot* and the *stationary spot*. As the student turns onto final approach, his or her objective is to make the desired landing spot the stationary spot in the windscreen. After reading this chapter, he or she will have the skills to make this happen in short order.

The only caveat with respect to the terms is the one I mentioned at the bottom of Page 9-9 where I wrote that the airplane will actually *touch down a little beyond the desired landing spot* because of the roundout and flare (Figure 33). As long as the student understands this, then all is well in the universe. If the student needs to touchdown precisely on a specific landing sport, then he or she should pick a stationary spot that's a little short of this spot. This understanding allows me to use only two terms for landing while avoiding the confusion that often occurs when several additional terms are involved.

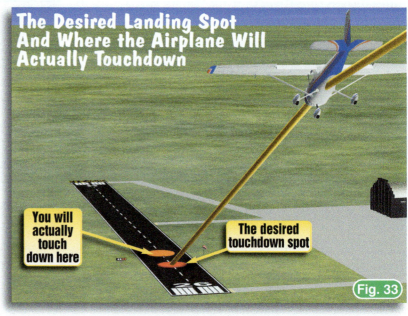
Fig. 33

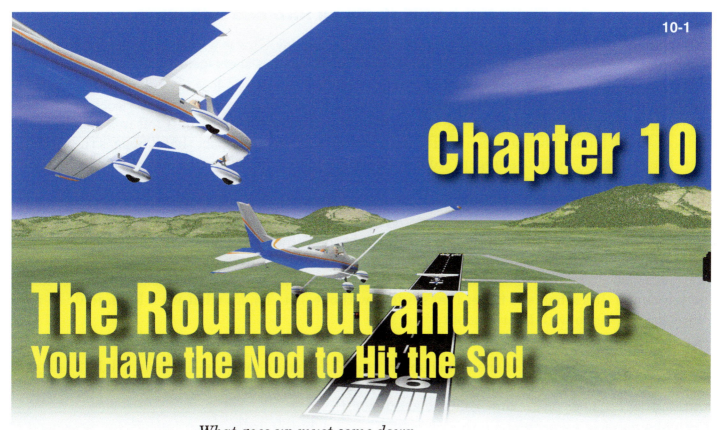

Chapter 10

The Roundout and Flare
You Have the Nod to Hit the Sod

What goes up must come down
Spinnin' wheel got to go 'round
                        "Spinning Wheel"
                        Blood, Sweat and Tears

Are you ready for The Question? Brain engaged? Pampers positioned? As you approach the runway, how and when do you transition from a steeper descent into a shallower one that eventually results in the airplane's main wheels touching down softly on the runway?

This is an important question that every pilot must answer if he or she is to land an airplane. Since we've already agreed that you want to land, let's begin with a thought experiment.

Suppose you maintained the descent rate you had on final approach (approximately 500 to 600 feet per minute) and did nothing else but fly the airplane right onto the runway. Can you see it? Did you land? Hardly. Which is exactly the way you *would* land. Hardly.

You most likely approached at a nose down angle, and got nose hosed when the airplane's nose wheel contacted the runway before the main gear as shown in Figure 1. That can result in a broken

nose gear and even a bent propeller. Bad gear, bad prop, bad day. This is why tricycle-geared airplanes sometimes come back to the FBO as bicycle-geared or sometimes shear-geared.

If you managed (in your mind) to contact the runway at a slightly less nose-down angle (but on the nose gear, nevertheless), you probably performed the aviation version of the ricochet. You hit the runway, then bounce back into the air, performing a maneuver that's best left in a Roadrunner cartoon. These types of bounces can lead to low altitude stalls or an impact that damages the landing gear, the propeller, your passengers' confidence in you, your dignity, and more. Beep! Beep! No thanks.

Avoiding ricochets, beep-beeps from your stall horn and squeak-squeaks from your passengers during landing requires knowing how to *round out* the landing approach (transition from a steep to a shallower descent rate) and *flare* the airplane onto the runway (allow the airplane's main gear to settle onto the runway when the airspeed has decreased to just above stall speed). These are the two steps necessary to land on your main gear, under control, while maintaining a constant state of landing happiness. It's a ballistic ballet that's a feat without feet. That's what we'll learn to do in this chapter. Let's begin with the roundout.

The Roundout

As you recall, at the end of the last chapter, I didn't let you down. Well, I mean I didn't talk you all the way down to the runway, leaving you a bit up in the air. My apologies, but I intend to make it up to you, because we are now going to get down!

Final approach has gotten you this far, which is good, but in order to land nicely you now need a different approach. This is where you'll begin the first part of the landing maneuver known as the *roundout* (Figure 2, position A).

The roundout begins with you, the pilot in command, reducing power (if any is still being applied) to flight idle while simultaneously applying sufficient elevator back pressure to *break the glide* and transition to a shallower descent angle. OK, you're not actually breaking anything, so if you're a Demolition Derby king or queen, don't get all excited and giggly. Your objective is to raise the nose so that the longitudinal axis of the plane is initially parallel with the runway.

A safe and successful landing requires transitioning from the approach descent by raising the nose to a level flight attitude (A-the *roundout*), slowing the airplane down (B-the *flare*), followed by touching down on the main wheels (C-the *touchdown*).

Chapter 10: The Roundout and Flare

The immediate result of this action is that your airspeed begins to decrease. As you continue pulling aft on the elevator control, the airplane should continue to settle toward the runway at a very low descent rate of perhaps 100 to 200 feet per minute. It's the reduced descent rate caused by the roundout that provides you with time to assess your closure rate with the runway. You're seeking a cue for the next act, which is the *flare,* for which you will develop a flare, I'm sure.

Because you're approaching at 30% above stall speed, you have just enough kinetic (airspeed) energy to control your closure rate with the runway during this maneuver. Yes, you're eating into a limited airspeed allotment, but that's OK. The goal is to land slightly above stall speed.

Oh look, there's the runway about a foot away. Now that you're there, it's time to flare.

The Flare

The landing flare follows the roundout, and technically begins the moment the airplane's nose rises above a level flight attitude with the continued application of elevator back pressure. In other words, the nose gear rises above the main gear during the landing flare as the angle of attack increases and the airplane continues to decelerate (Figure 2, position B). The landing flare accomplishes two very important things. First, it allows the airplane's initial contact with the runway to be on the main gear, thus protecting the more fragile nose gear from damage (Figure 2, position C). Second, it allows the airplane's speed to continue decreasing to just above stall speed, meaning that the airplane becomes less and less likely to continue flying once the wheels make contact with the runway (also known as the *touchdown*).

From the position of an observer standing alongside the runway, the landing flare appears to be your attempt to keep the main gear from touching the runway, at least until the airplane finally has insufficient speed to remain airborne. Psychologically speaking, this is how you should conceptualize the landing flare. After the initial approach path is rounded out and made shallower, you'll let the airplane gently settle from a height of 12 inches or less onto the runway surface. This is how the landing flare is accomplished in a tricycle geared airplane.

Now that you know of the two components associated with landing, we'll discuss both in more detail. Our objective is to answer two questions. *When do you begin the roundout? How fast do you flare for landing?*

Why Ground Shy?

One of the very interesting phenomena to observe when introducing students to landings is how they almost instinctively

---

Why Two Terms for Landing Instead of Just One?

In some aviation training literature the process of landing an airplane is described with one term, the *flare,* without any mention of the *roundout.* In other literature (in particularly FAA literature), the roundout and the flare are used synonymously without any distinction made between the two. In this book I use both terms. Why? Read on.

From a psycholinguistics perspective, if you have more terms available to you to define *specific* and *distinct* events in reality, then you're more capable of describing that reality to others. For instance, someone from the equatorial regions might typically have one word to describe snow and that's "snow." Without much (if any) experience with snow, they would have a hard time understanding the many different varieties of it.

On the other hand, a typical American skier has several different words at his disposal to describe snow: powder, drift, flurry, etc. The more experience someone has in a particular discipline the richer that person's vocabulary is in relation to that discipline. It's this richer vocabulary that helps convey the details and subtleties of this discipline.

I use the terms roundout and flare because they represent two distinct actions performed by a pilot as he or she transitions from approach to landing.

The first action the pilot performs (the roundout) is to pull aft on the elevator so as to alter the initial approach glidepath from a downward trajectory to a near level trajectory. This is a necessary and distinct action because at 30% above stall speed, there is still quite a bit of energy to be dissipated before the airplane is at the proper angle of attack to actually touchdown.

The second distinct action (the flare) blends the airplane's now shallower glidepath with the runway. It's this action that allows the pilot to raise the nose sufficiently above the horizon to prevent the nose gear from touching the runways before the main gear.

Without the use of these two terms, it becomes much harder to accurately convey the details about how to land an airplane.

pull aft on the elevator as the runway comes closer. I've even seen this behavior in students while descending toward a solid, flat stratus layer of clouds during an instrument approach. The student automatically reacts by pulling back at the sight of what appears to be a solid surface.

This reflex is nearly as natural to a five-hour student as putting your hands out to break a fall. This shouldn't really be a surprise to anyone, since riding 2,000 pounds of sheet metal on a trajectory toward a solid surface (the runway) or one that appears solid (a flat cloud deck) does stir certain primal survival instincts. As far as your brain knows, nothing good can come of the impending impact.

Unfortunately, this can lead to what might best be called *air flare*. The pulling aft action is often begun at 20-40 feet above the runway, which is about 19-39 feet too high. Worse, students are not even aware that they are doing it. The problem with the aft pull at too high an altitude is that the airplane often doesn't have enough energy (think *airspeed* here) to do a proper roundout and flare, resulting in a rough or dangerous landing.

The antidote to this problem is brain drain. You have to drain your brain of the train of thought that it's on and get on a different track by recognizing that the air flare phenomenon exists, and then train your brain to think differently.

It's your flight instructor's job to point it out when he or she sees you pulling aft prematurely on the elevator. For instance, you might hear your instructor say, "Don't do that," in reference to a premature pull on the elevator. This, and a hand gently placed on the elevator to prevent you from pulling it aft prematurely should help form a new and move favorable behavior pattern. Then again, most students get the idea once it's pointed out them.

When Do You Begin the Roundout?

It is beyond a doubt time to round out. You begin rounding out the airplane for landing when you're 10 feet above the runway (Figure 3). Believe it or not, several million years of evolution have equipped you with a very functional 10 foot height detector. That's right, pilot, you come equipped with the necessary skill built in. (See: *The Runway Expansion Effect* on Page 10-6.)

One of our two basic, instinctual fears is the fear of falling. Even a very young infant will shy away from a perceived edge of a precipice. We're pretty good at estimating the height from which a fall could really hurt; those who couldn't do so were summarily dismissed from the gene pool a long time ago. It's not surprising that most of us who have survived can, just by looking, make a reasonable guess as to what a dangerous height is.

When it comes to landing, however, you can't look straight down at the ground out your left window because the ground will appear blurry and thus offer little or no surface details with which to gauge your height. At a typ-

Fig. 3 The roundout begins when the airplane is 10-15 feet above the runway as shown above.

If the Shoe Fits...

I set out to fly...to brush up on cross-wind taxi/takeoff/landing procedures. On the second landing, while in the flare, my left shoe fell off while applying left rudder. The shoe landed in front of the left rudder pedal and heel brake. The right crosswind started to pivot the aircraft to the right, and I discovered the shoe blocked access to the left rudder pedal and brake. Without left rudder capability, I was unable to prevent the aircraft from turning right into the wind. The aircraft departed the runway to the right onto a level grass area. I finally kicked the shoe free of the pedals and braked to a stop with one shoe off, one shoe on. Taxied back to the ramp and shut down for a thorough inspection. No damage to aircraft or airport property.

Despite nearly 20 years experience, I was unable to overcome the effects on an errant shoe on a crosswind landing. In the future, I will pay more attention to the fit of my shoes before commencing flight.

NASA Report

Chapter 10: The Roundout and Flare

Sensory-Rich Runway Environments

The more sensory-rich the runway environment, the easier it will be to properly gauge the height for roundout. But every place isn't Hollywood or New York, so sometimes the airports you're landing at are just plain plain, which is a pain. No bells, no belles, no whistles, no thistles. The runway has few markings (or they've faded over time) and few surface clues (the rabbits ate all the bushes and the locals ate the rabbits, leaving the pilots to stew). It's possible to compensate for this problem to some degree by having the tower activate the runway edge lighting (or activating it manually to its highest setting if there is pilot controlled lighting). Because we see lighted objects better peripherally, this has helped some students to better gauge when to begin the roundout for landing (lights are not always available during the day, unfortunately). Additionally, make sure you aren't wearing polarized sun glasses during landing practice, which can reduce your visual input, especially in terms of the detail associated with the runway environment.

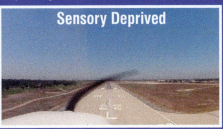
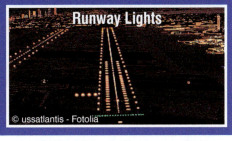

ical approach speed of around 50-60 knots, you *can* look 50 to 80 feet straight ahead during a descent and make a good guess as to when you're 10-15 feet above the ground (Figure 4). Couple your crude (instinctual) height evaluating skill with the fact that you've spent your life gauging your height above the surface by looking forward and slightly downward in the direction you're moving and there's your prepackaged basic skills for getting a righteous roundout reading.

As you begin your roundout by looking at a point on the runway 50 to 80 feet ahead of you, your ability to gauge your height above the landing surface is aided by a (hopefully) rich runway environment. "Rich" in this context doesn't mean you'll see stacks of stocks and bonds. It means a runway foreground that contains shrubbery, runway lights, VASI light boxes, a windsock and runway markings and other runway accessories that are to a pilot what Louboutins are to a fashionista. These visual clues (except the Louboutins) aid you in estimating your height above the ground. What a feat.

A 2006 study conducted by the Australian Transportation Safety Board found that a rich runway foreground improves a student's ability to more accurately time the landing flare (estimate his or her height above the ground). Remove all these visual clues and you create an environment similar to landing a ski plane on a featureless bed of snow or a floatplane on glassy water. Anyone who has tried landing on this type of surface knows that judging height above that surface is extremely difficult. This is why floatplane pilots are taught to establish a *very* shallow descent all the way to touchdown when landing on a mirrored water surface (hopefully they won't be glancing at that mirror and fussing with their hair while saying "Oh yeah, who's your daddy?" just as they're ready to touch down). Flaring isn't necessary during these types of landings because the airplane is at a very slow speed in a slight nose high attitude and is literally flown *onto* the snow or water.

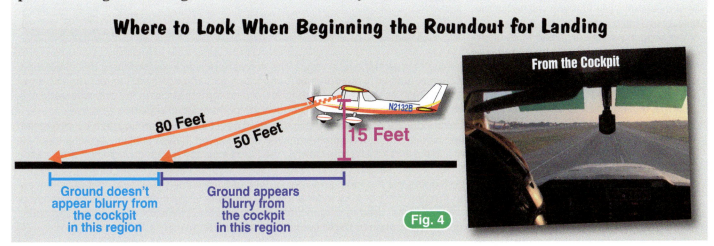

Fig. 4

Rod Machado's How to Fly an Airplane Handbook

The Runway Expansion Effect that Cues You To Begin the Roundout

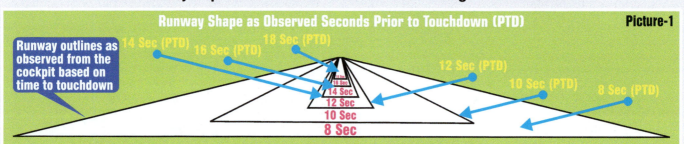

There is one very important but little recognized clue that tells you precisely when to begin the roundout for landing. I call it the *Runway Expansion Effect*. Here's how it works.

As you approach the runway during a stabilized approach at 1.3 Vs, the runway's trapezoidal shape appears to grow in your windscreen. For instance, the outlines of the runway shown on the next page are presented in Picture-1 from a period between 18 seconds prior to touchdown to eight seconds prior to touchdown. It's clear from these outlines that during a stabilized approach to a desired landing spot somewhere in the first third of the runway, the runway's size appears to increase while its trapezoidal shape remains relatively the same. On the other hand the *rate* at which the runway grows (expands) in your windscreen isn't linear.

Looking at the width of the runway threshold as a measure of its size, you can see in Picture-1 that from 12 seconds to 10 seconds prior to touchdown, the runway threshold width appears to expand approximately four times as you observe it from the cockpit. From 12 to eight seconds prior to touchdown, the runway threshold width appears to expand 10 times in your windscreen (this includes what you see with your peripheral vision, too).

This expansion isn't a linear at all. In fact, it's more of a geometric expansion as shown by Picture-2. This figure graphs your perception of the runway's width (as you observe it from the cockpit starting at 18 seconds from touchdown) and compares its growth all the way to touchdown in two-second intervals. During the period from 12 to eight seconds prior to touchdown, the runway appears to increase in size 10 times (Picture-1). The most rapid period of growth in any two second interval occurs from 12 to 10 seconds prior to touchdown (Picture-2). The 10 second cue is the point where the runway expansion can be used to alert you to begin the roundout for landing.

While flying a stabilized approach to the desired landing spot on the runway, the moment you notice a *sudden* increase in runway width, you should raise the nose and place the airplanes longitudinal axis level with the runway. Congratulations, you've just performed the *roundout* and are now approximately 10 feet above the runway. Believe me when I say that you will notice the runway expansion effect. In fact, it's because of the sudden runway expansion that pilots often become spooked at a point approximately 10 seconds prior to touchdown and overflare their airplane as a result. The secret here is in knowing about this effect then looking for it as a cue to begin the roundout. Of course, how fast you roundout is important, too. You don't want to roundout so slow or so quickly so as to either hit the runway or flare too high, respectively. Looking at the landing sequence on the opposite page, it's clear that the roundout takes place in a little less than two seconds, which is about right for most small airplanes.

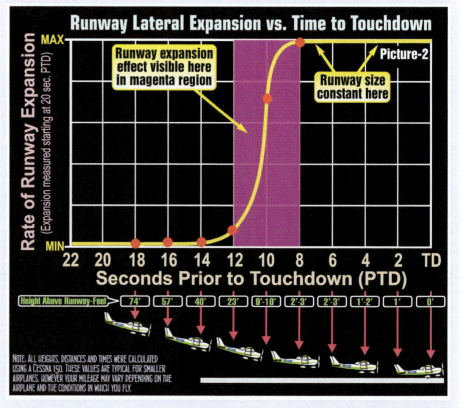

If you don't have excessive airspeed during the roundout, then you can easily transition directly into the landing flare by raising the nose just a bit more and placing the top left-hand side of the cowling on the horizon and keeping it there until the airplane touches down (excess airspeed means you must transition to the flare much more slowly). The flare sequence is shown beginning at four seconds prior to touchdown on the next page. This raises the nose gear high enough to allow the main gear to touch down first.

While this is a rather mechanical method of performing the roundout and flare, it does use the same visual cues that experienced pilots use when landing, especially when landing at night. It is, however, independent of any other visual cues you might have learned to help assess your height above the runway. Nevertheless, used in conjunction with your previously learned visual landing cues, you've got a powerful method to assist you in determining when to begin the roundout for landing.

Chapter 10: The Roundout and Flare

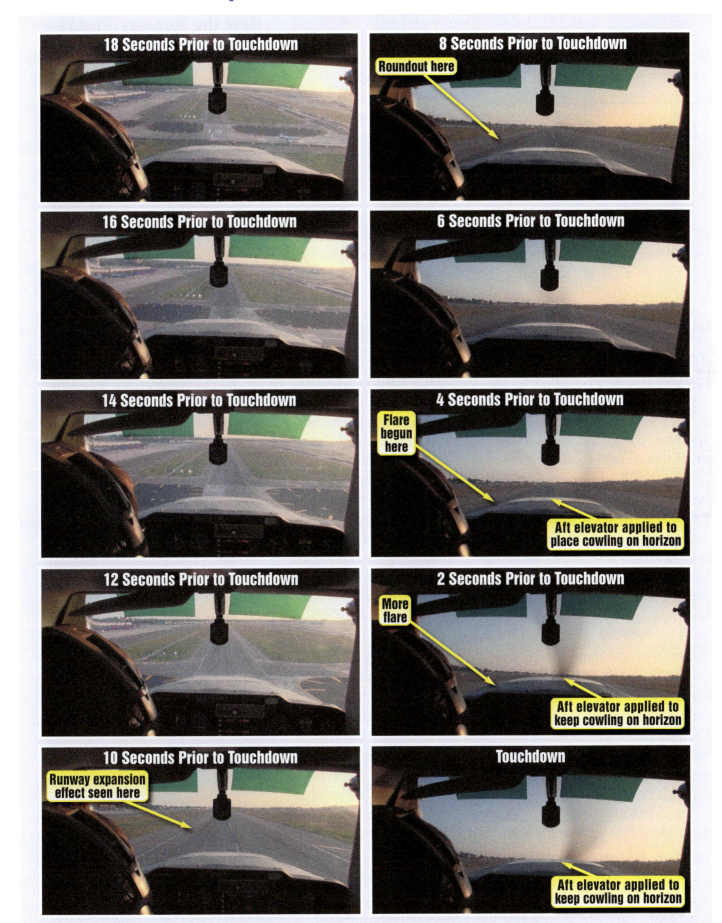

Unfortunately, it's very difficult to fly an airplane onto a runway in a similar manner. Lakes and snowfields tend to be really long, runways much less so. That's why it's necessary to learn how to flare the airplane for landing.

Identifying a height of 10-15 feet above the runway is relatively easy for most student pilots, especially when they have a chance to see what this height looks like from the seated position inside the cockpit.

What most pilots aren't accustomed to is having the runway ahead of them disappear from their sight as they raise the nose during the roundout and subsequent landing flare (Figures 5, 6 and 7). Say again. That's right! The runway can disappear from sight as the nose comes up and blocks the pilot's view of the landing surface, which isn't a pretty sight from the cockpit (mainly because there's no sight to see). Before we can examine the details of the landing flare, we need to solve the case of the missing runway.

The Case of the Missing Runway

Here's how your runway can become a runaway during the roundout and subsequent landing flare.

As you pull aft on the elevator to perform the roundout, the nose comes up and the cowling goes with it (this is, generally speaking, good). Continuing to pull aft on the elevator for the landing flare raises the cowling above the horizon, which is where the vision thing becomes a problem. You can't see through the cowling (well, most of us can't, but most of us aren't affected by Kryptonite, either), so the runway directly ahead of you suddenly disappears from sight. Gone, but not forgotten. How nice is that? The thing you were using to gauge your height above the runway—the runway ahead of you—now disappears from your view. Only a mad scientist or a normal flight instructor could think up a worse way to torment a student in flight training.

You've got to sit high in the saddle, pardner. An important element in keeping the runway in sight involves sitting high enough in the seat so that you have the best chance of seeing the touchdown area for as long as possible during the roundout and subsequent landing flare. Trust me when I say that most students seldom—yes, I said it, "seldom"—sit high enough in the seat to assist them in seeing what's ahead of their flying machine. So, I'll give you the lowdown on sitting high. And I don't want you to take this lying down.

Sitting Height

It turns out that your mother and teachers were right. You need to sit up straight, despite the fact that you graduated from the Quasimodo posture school with honors.

How the Runway Disappears

While on your approach to the runway, it's relatively easy to keep the runway in sight, especially when some flaps are used.

During the roundout, the runway ahead become less easy to see.

During the flare, the runway ahead becomes almost entirely blocked from view.

To have the best chance of seeing the runway over your panel, make sure you sit high enough so that your eyes are located just below the top of the window frame.

Chapter 10: The Roundout and Flare

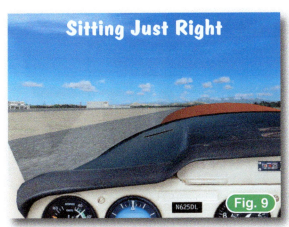

Sitting closer to the panel (as close as is comfortable, of course) provides you with a better view of the runway during the roundout and flare.

Sitting too far away from the panel makes it difficult to see the runway ahead of you.

In high or low wing airplanes, you should be sitting high enough so that your eyes are just below the top of the left window frame (Figure 8). This allows you to see aircraft out your left window without having to bend your head forward like a giraffe that suddenly decided to try grazing grass (or a high school student texting). It also gives you the best shot at seeing over the panel. Sitting as close as feasible to the panel also helps, since this lets you peer down at the runway at a steeper viewing angle (Figure 9).

This isn't a circus act, and I'm not trying to make you into a contortionist. I don't want your legs cramped and the elevator control touching your belly. Sit close enough to the panel so you can apply full rudder travel using the balls of your feet. Of course, sitting too far aft will make it difficult to see the runway over the panel (Figure 10). So find a good horizontal and vertical seating position and remember it.

Do whatever it takes to get into this position. Ironically, women are better at doing this than men. Women know they are shorter (on average) and they aren't afraid to add a cushion here or there. It's men who are too often cushioning their egos instead of their butts. Ultimately, you may need to sit on cushions (Figure 11) *and* have a cushion behind you to move you forward in the seat (Figure 12). I don't care how you do this or whose furniture you have to rob to make it happen. Just get those cushions and move on up. Take my word for the fact that if you can't see the runway, this landing thing is going to be a whole lot more difficult.

No matter how well cushioned your landing, there comes a point where the rising cowling makes seeing the runway over the engine cowling during the roundout and flare impossible in most airplanes. That's why you *don't* want to look straight ahead over the nose during the landing flare when the nose is at flare attitude.

A good seat cushion often makes all the difference in terms of the ease with which you learn to land.

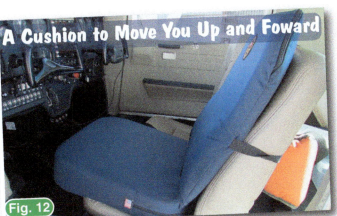

If your legs are a bit shorter than normal, a good backseat cushion helps with visibility and rudder usage.

The Best Place to Focus Your Vision During the Roundout and Flare

Fig. 13

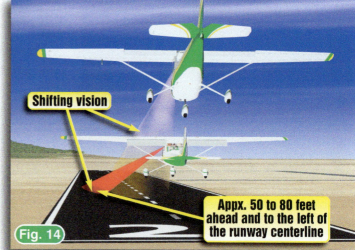

Fig. 14

On final approach, it's easy to see the runway over the panel. When you begin the roundout and subsequent flare, however, you'll want to shift your vision to a spot slightly to the left of the runway centerline approximately 50 to 80 feet ahead of the airplane. This allows you to see the landing surface as well as the distant horizon.

Instead, you want to shift your vision from looking straight ahead to looking slightly left of the engine cowling and focusing on a point to left side of the runway centerline that's still visible to you (Figure 13). This means looking down and to the left slightly, at an angle of about 10 to 15 degrees. This directs your eyes to a spot on the runway 50 to 80 feet ahead of you. Based on your present speed, the runway at that spot appears *neither* blurry nor motionless, which we'll call the *sweet spot* (Figure 14). In other words, you're looking far enough ahead of the airplane to see a portion of the runway surface that's sufficiently detailed that it allows you to continue to estimate your height above the ground. The far end of the runway as well as the distant horizon are also visible to the left side of your cowling, allowing you to use your normal and peripheral vision to help evaluate pitch attitude during the flare.

If you look straight down out your left window during landing, the runway will appear blurry to you. You simply can't see the ground well enough to identify surface details, thus preventing you from estimating your height for the roundout, much less the flare. (See sidebar: *Driving and Landing*.)

If you look too far ahead, such as only looking at the distant horizon, you'll lose your ability to perceive your rate of closure with the runway surface, which also prevents you from properly estimating your height above the ground. This is why you look at that portion of the runway—the sweet spot—ahead and to

Driving and Landing

You bring a lot of experience to the cockpit to help you flare even though you may have never practiced landings. How so? If you've driven on the freeway in a typical automobile, you were sitting at a height and moving at a speed similar to that of a small plane pilot in the landing flare. In a sense, your depth perception is already calibrated (to some degree) for the speed and height you experience in an airplane. That means you already know where to look (to the left of your car's hood) and how far to look forward (perhaps 50 to 80 feet) to identify the spot where the ground ahead is neither blurry nor motionless. The problem is that you don't know that you know this. Well, now you know.

The only big structural difference here is that while sitting in a car you can see most of the road directly ahead of you all the time. In an airplane, you can't see the road (runway) ahead of you when you need to most—during the landing flare! This makes knowing where to look and knowing when to shift your vision an important factor in helping you know when and how to flare the airplane.

Note that this does not work in a 1960s lowrider car, mainly because from the outside looking in, the low bucket seats make it appear that no one is actually in the car. Apparently, low riders thought this would fool the police. It turns out that the police tend to notice driverless cars more so than those that are clearly under the control of an actual human being. Go figure.

Chapter 10: The Roundout and Flare

your left, where the blurry motion stops yet the runway still appears to move. Now you have the depth perception necessary to gauge your height above the landing surface. See how I let you down by not letting you down with these important tips? Now it's time to sweeten things up by taking a closer look at the sweet spot.

The Sweet Spot

The sweet spot for us is typically framed by the left side of the engine cowling, the right side of the window post (on those airplanes with window posts, of course), and the horizon. The frame takes the shape of a pizza slice through which you're viewing a portion of the non-moving runway and the horizon (Figure 15). This is only available as takeout, by the way.

Looking anywhere besides in the pizza slice during the landing flare generally means you're looking in all the wrong places and won't know how high you are above the ground. And how much fun can that be when a large solid slab of solid runway is rising to meet you?

You should also be aware that the sweet spot ahead of you where the blurry motion stops will appear to move toward you (horizontally) as the airplane slows down during the landing flare (Figure 16). In other words, the sweet spot is approximately 50 to 80 feet ahead of you as you begin the roundout and flare, then it moves closer (think 40 feet, then 30 feet, then…you get the idea, right?) as your speed decreases.

Think about it for a second and you will see just how much sense this makes. When the airplane is stopped on the runway, you can look directly down out your left window and see a non-moving section of the runway with perfect clarity. How sweet is that? That's why you have to continually shift your vision just a little closer toward the airplane during the landing flare to maintain visual contact with the sweet spot.

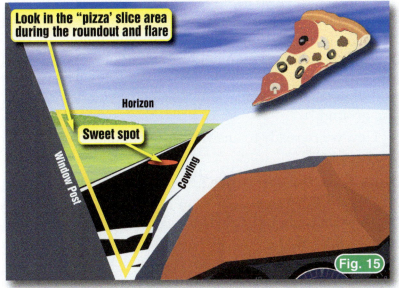

The sweet spot is framed by the "pizza slice" triangular area formed between the horizon, the window post and the engine cowling.

In addition to looking at this non-blurry sweet spot ahead and to the left, you are also using peripheral cues associated with the runway environment to help assess your height above the runway. Sure, there aren't a lot of obvious vertical peripheral cues in this area such as buildings, huts and men holding large rulers vertically. But the white runway stripes, the runway lights, the grass, the rabbits and so on all add dimensional perspective that helps you assess your height above the ground.

Now we're ready to answer the question, "How fast should you flare for landing?"

How Fast Do You Flare?

The answer to this question is rather simple. *With power reduced to flight idle, you pull aft on the elevator to progressively raise the nose and reduce the airspeed while the airplane remains a foot or less above the ground.* Stating this, however, is much easier than doing it. So let's examine this question in more detail.

During the roundout, as the airplane rotates through a level flight attitude you'll transition directly into the landing flare by continuing with the aft pull on the elevator control. At this point, you'll shift your attention from the runway directly ahead of you to the sweet spot located ahead and to the left of the cowling.

During the flare, if you pull the elevator control back too quickly the airplane will pitch up and climb because its airspeed is still above stall speed. That's not good. Power is at flight idle, airspeed is slow and decreasing and right about *now* the stall warning horn is singing your song.

My friend, there is no silver lining in that dark cloud. The chance of stalling or settling hard onto the runway increases dramatically if you don't release elevator back pressure to lower the nose and apply a little power to increase your airspeed (if it's too slow) and decrease your descent rate (if it's too high). If, on the other hand, you don't pull back fast enough, there's a good chance that you will hit the runway on the nose wheel or with all three wheels at the same time (which is not how you land a tricycle geared airplane).

It's clear that the rate at which elevator back pressure is applied is a totally new experience if you've never landed an airplane before. After all, you've never had to calibrate changing the airplane's trajectory with reference to a solid surface just below the airplane, have you?

Probably the only semi-similar experience you've had in the plane was leveling off at a specific altitude by reference to a tiny altimeter needle representing an altitude, which doesn't offer the same resistance a runway would if you tried to fly through it. There is, after all, nothing physically solid about an altitude unless it represents the beginning of something physically solid. Ultimately, it will take you a few landings to get a feel for how much back pressure to apply to the elevator to prevent under- or over-flaring the airplane. But that doesn't mean there aren't a few exercises that might help you develop this skill.

The Fallacy of Looking Only At The Horizon During Landing

It's actually quite common for flight instructors to tell their students to look over the engine cowling at the end of the runway and/or the horizon during landing as a means of gauging flare attitude and flare height. Yes, the distant horizon is useful for helping you gauge the attitude necessary to begin the roundout. During the landing flare, however, the rising cowling above the horizon often obscures the distant horizon line located directly ahead of the airplane. Furthermore, the horizon line tells you very little about your height above the runway.

So why do instructors often tell their students to do this? Because this is the landing clue that they *personally* use. That's right. Most experienced pilots will initially look over the cowling during the flare to gauge their landing flare attitude. As the nose comes up, they'll shift their vision slightly (and often unknowingly) to the side of the airplane, while using their highly developed peripheral vision to precisely gauge their height above the runway. They can do this because they have a great deal of experience landing airplanes. You should do the same, but only when you gain a similar level of experience.

If you're just learning to land an airplane, you need to look at the pizza-sliced frame to the left of the engine cowling during the flare. This is the place that allows you to see a portion of the horizon as well as a non-moving section of the runway. Other than having your instructor make all your landings for you, the pizza-slice view offers you the best chance of making smooth, consistent landings.

Chapter 10: The Roundout and Flare

Fig. 17

The low level pass down the runway at roundout height is a valuable training exercise for student pilots learning to land. It's a maneuver best accomplished with no more than 50% flap extension and no slower that 30% above stall speed.

The Ultimate Training Exercise for Learning the Landing Flare

Here's a wonderful training exercise that you can do with a competent and capable flight instructor on board to help you calibrate your rearward pull on the elevator control during the flare.

Under your instructor's supervision, approach the runway with no more than 10-15 degrees of flaps at a speed of 1.3 Vs. As the airplane reaches a height of 10-15 feet above the runway, simultaneously raise the nose and apply sufficient power to hold 10-15 feet of altitude at 1.3 Vs (Figure 17). Your objective is to track the runway centerline at approach speed while holding altitude. At first this will be quite challenging simply because you'll have no idea what type of pitch response results from the pressure you apply to the elevator.

You may find yourself wandering all over the runway, mainly because you now have a chance to see how easy it is to over- or under-control the airplane when given a distinct reference by which to measure your deviation. What you learn from this example is the relationship between elevator movement and pitch change. It will only take a few trips down a reasonably long runway for you to calibrate your pitch inputs with airplane response. Once you get that idea into your noodle, you're unlikely to over- or under-flare an airplane during landing practice.

This lesson is extremely useful because most pilots spend as much as 10 minutes flying one circuit around the pattern just to make one landing. Yet the part of the landing that pilots need the most exposure to is the part that's a few inches above the ground and that lasts 10 seconds at most, otherwise known as the landing flare. So while you might make 10 landings in one training session, you only experience 100 seconds or less than two minutes in the environment where you learn how to flare.

Frankly, it's amazing that anyone can actually learn to land as quickly as they often do with so little exposure to the landing flare. That's why this training exercise is so valuable. It gives you much more exposure to the landing flare environment.

It's also important to make sure that you begin your departure climb in sufficient time to avoid any obstacles at the end of the runway. You don't want to turn a great training exercise into a hedge clipping debacle. That said, this is one of the most valuable training exercises you can do to further your feel for how to land an airplane. It's also a wonderful exercise to help you learn about crosswind landings, too. We'll chat more about that in the next chapter.

The Aft Elevator Pull and How It's Not What It Seems

One of the peculiar things about moving the elevator aft during the landing flare is that it becomes less effective in raising the nose for a given amount of pull as the airspeed decreases. The slower you go, the more aft you must pull, as shown in Figure 18.

This provides you with the *initially* strange experience of having to pull aft on the elevator at an ever increasing rate as you try and maintain an ever decreasing descent rate during the landing flare descent. Of course, the amount of aft elevator movement applied varies between airplanes and even between the same airplane based on how it's loaded, its trim condition, and so on. Nevertheless, it does take a few attempts at landing to "roughly" gauge the rate at which the elevator should be moved aft in the flare.

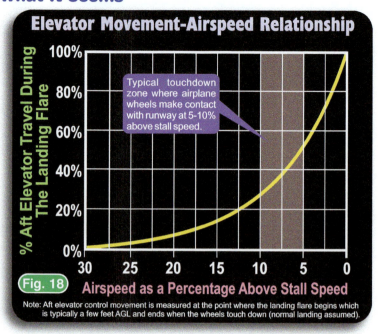

The important thing to identify here is that the aft elevator movement required to flare the airplane isn't linear. Starting the roundout at 30% above stall speed, you'll find that a little aft pull easily raises the nose and levels the airplane's longitudinal axis with the runway. This is why it's easy to overflare during the roundout but relatively less so during the actual landing flare. As the airplane decelerates because of the drag caused by the increased angle of attack, the aft elevator travel necessary to keep the nose coming up in the landing flare must increase noticeably (relatively speaking). When the main gear makes contact with the runway surface, the elevator is relatively far aft from its position at the beginning of the landing flare (Figure 19).

The amount of aft elevator travel shouldn't come as a surprise. You already experienced something similar during slow flight practice, when you noticed how much less responsive the airplane was to elevator control input. As a result, you had to pull the elevator control aft a considerable amount to sustain the desired slow flight attitude.

The aft elevator pull required to flare the airplane isn't linear. The slower you go (from position 1 to position 2), the more aft pull is required to flare the airplane. When the main gear makes contact with the runway, the elevator is often pulled aft a considerable amount from its starting position.

Additionally, the reduction in the wing's downwash on the tail as a result of ground effect causes the nose to pitch forward with decreasing airspeed. This requires even more aft elevator (yoke) deflection (and pressure) to maintain the desired attitude for the landing flare.

That's why, during the landing flare, you have to anticipate a relatively large aft movement of the elevator control to maintain flare attitude and control your rate of closure with the runway. Keep in mind that you've already gone through the motions of the landing flare even before you made your

Chapter 10: The Roundout and Flare

first landing. Where? During stall practice. As you prepared to perform your first power-off stall, the aft movement of the elevator essentially mimicked the movement you'll make in the landing flare, at least right up to the point where the airplane stalls. You do remember how much you had to pull aft on the elevator during a power-off stall, right?

Proper Trimming Helps You Land More Easily

In order to have more precise control of the airplane during the landing flare, make sure your airplane is properly trimmed for the correct approach speed. Without proper trimming on final, you're likely to spend more time trying to acquire the feel for landing. Why is that? Read on.

An improperly trimmed airplane on final approach presents you with a different elevator feel each time you begin the flare. Your landing flare will be like the haircut a drunken hairdresser gives you—each one will be different (and that's only good if you're in the witness protection program). That's why you should strive to ensure that the airplane is trimmed to maintain the same approach speed on every approach you make. At least that way when you begin the flare, the flight controls won't suddenly feel too heavy (or too light) because of improper trimming. This unexpected feel on the elevator control could easily cause you to over- or under-flare during landing.

Sampling the Response

Keep in mind that, during the roundout and flare, the *ideal* landing technique is one where you pull back consistently and smoothly on the elevator as the airplane approaches the ground at an ever decreasing descent rate until the main gear wheels gently squeak onto the runway (the squeak being made by the wheels and not the pilot's tiny biceps).

Creating You Own "Landing Time Machine"

For most students, the challenge of learning to flare an airplane is a time problem. I'm speaking of not having enough time as the airplane approaches the runway. A flight instructor can solve this problem if he or she can find a way to slow down the clock during the roundout and flare, which helps students gauge their height above the runway.

Believe it or not, your airplane has a built in time machine designed just for students having landing difficulties. That's right, you've got something on H. G. Wells. It's called a *throttle*. Instead of flaring with power completely off, the flight instructor should leave a little power applied during the student's roundout and subsequent flare (perhaps an increase of 200 to 300 RPM, but not much more than that) as shown in the figure below.

If you're a student using this technique, you'll immediately notice that the rate at which you approach the runway decreases, giving you more time to round out and flare your machine. Upon touchdown, immediately reduce power to idle. Keep in mind that flaring with power applied makes it easier to float or overcontrol during the flare. So only use this technique with your instructor on board. Don't use it on short runways, in gusty winds or when departure obstacles are present. You'll only need two or three landings using this technique to get a feel for the mechanics of the flare. After this, you'll want to ensure that your roundouts and flares are accomplished with power reduced to flight idle.

I've used this technique with great success over the years. Perhaps the biggest drawback to this time-distorting technique is that it has no delaying effect on the Hobbs meter. I'm working on that.

Just to be clear here, using power for landing is done as an *intermediate step* to help students learn how to flare. I'm not advocating power-on landings to touchdown.

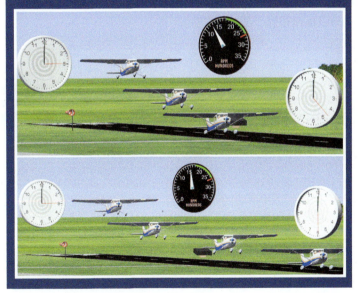

This ideal rate of aft elevator application is depicted by the yellow line in Figure 20. On the other hand, it's not uncommon for student pilots to move the elevator control in an exaggerated back and forth motion during the flare (represented by the red line in Figure 20). Hopefully this isn't followed by commentary such as: *Oops, too much; oops, not enough; oops, too much: no, no, not enough*, and *hoo chee mama!* What these students are doing is trying to compensate for over- or under-controlling pressures on the elevator during the flare. This certainly isn't ideal, but the behavior will diminish once the student has more experience at landings.

This pull-and-push behavior on the elevator control by student pilots is understandable, given that as soon as the airplane enters ground effect, the downwash on the tail diminishes and the airplane pitches forward. Students typically overcorrect with an excessive aft pull on the elevator control. The amount of aft pull necessary to flare the airplane is compounded by the fact that the aft pressure required to keep the airplane in the desired flare attitude constantly changes with the reduction of airflow over the tail as the airspeed decreases. So it's perfectly understandable that a student pilot might have difficulty finding the correct amount of elevator back pressure to apply.

Landing a Taildragger

At first glance it might look like landing a taildragger is something very different from landing an airplane with tricycle landing gear. Well, it's not. Let me explain why.

The approach and landing of a taildragger is done in almost the exact same way that it's done in an airplane with tricycle landing gear. The only difference is that your objective in a taildragger is to touchdown on all three wheels at the same time for a normal landing. This is known as a three-point landing because all three wheels should touch the runway at the same time.

To accomplish this type of landing, you perform the roundout and flare at the same altitude that you'd use in a tricycle geared airplane. In a taildragger, however, your objective is to keep the airplane from touching down until it's just a little above its stall speed. You accomplish this by holding the airplane off the runway while continuously reducing airspeed until you feel the wings are just about ready to stall. At that point, you let all three wheels to make contact with the runway at the same time. The wings are essentially stalled and the airplane has ceased flying.

The tricycle geared airplane lands at nearly the same nose-up attitude as the taildragger but it's not necessary for the wings to be stalled at the moment of touchdown. Why? Because the moment the main gear touches down, the nose is gently lowered to the runway surface. This essentially reduces the wings' angle of attack rendering the wings unable to generate the necessary lift for flight.

When you make a side-by-side comparison of a taildragger and a tricycle geared airplane landing, the only read difference between the two is that the tricycle geared airplane lowers its nose after the main gear contact the ground. The taildragger's nose always remains pointed slightly above the horizon after touchdown.

Of course, after a taildragger touches down, you must apply your considerable rudder skill to keep the airplane aligned with the runway. Why? Unlike the tricycle geared airplane, the center of gravity on a taildragger is located behind the main gear. If the taildragger is allowed to swerve sufficiently at higher speeds, it's possible for the nose and tail to attempt to switch places (the *groundloop*).

Chapter 10: The Roundout and Flare

There is, however, a very interesting technique that experienced pilots use to help them maintain the precise amount of elevator back pressure necessary to produce a smooth landing. Know as *sampling the response*, this technique allows them to precisely control the airplane's rate of closure with the runway, thereby minimizing the chance of over- and under-flaring the airplane. Here's how it's done.

During the flare, apply continuous elevator back pressure but do so in small pull-and-release motions as represented by the green line in Figure 20. Think about pulling just far enough aft so that the nose would begin to rise beyond the desired pitch attitude if you pulled even a tiny bit more. As you hold the elevator at this position, you've technically arrived at a point that I call the *threshold of control*—a point at which pulling further would raise the nose. But, as we've just discussed, this threshold is always moving elevator-aft as you slow down, so you have to keep sampling the elevator response to maintain that threshold of control. It's the constant recalibration of an aft moving elevator resulting from this pull-release motion that allows you to make the airplane's nose stay right where you want it to stay, and lets you retain immediate control of the airplane's attitude. This means that the airplane's nose shouldn't unsuspectingly pitch downward during the landing flare. (See *Postflight Briefing #10-1* on *Fanning* for a little history and detail about this technique.)

Now, you'd think the plane would be jumping up and down like one of those mechanical bulls in a Texas bar. The pull-release motions, however, are small enough (if they're done correctly) that no one in the cockpit will feel any vertical pitch acceleration. Nor will anyone inside or outside the cockpit see the nose pitching up or down. On the other hand, you will see the elevator control being

Say "No Thank You" to the Landing Stall

One of the techniques pilots occasionally use (and, remarkably, instructors occasionally teach) in tricycle geared airplanes is to touch down at the precise moment the airplane stalls. Sometimes referred to as a *full stall landing*, the intent of this maneuver is to minimize the landing roll by reducing the airplane's touchdown speed. The landing distance is affected by several things, such as wind, weight and speed; double the airplane's weight and you double the energy that must be dissipated to bring the airplane to a stop. Double the speed, however, and you quadruple the energy to be dissipated during landing. So slower is better when it comes to getting the airplane stopped. But everything comes at a price, doesn't it?

Trying to hold the airplane a few inches off the runway until it's just about to stall means that at the moment of touchdown the wings are near their critical angle of attack. You now have exactly zero margin to protect you from anything and everything.

In this condition, any wind gust or excessive pull on the elevator control can result in the airplane rising a few feet above the runway and dissipating the last of its energy. That's when fall comes early. The result is a hard landing, perhaps better characterized as an abrupt arrival. At this very slow speed, the flight controls are relatively ineffective. If a wind gust raises one wing instead of the entire airplane, you could lack the control authority needed to return the airplane to a normal landing attitude. This makes it easy to bend your landing gear or lose control of the airplane on the runway or both.

A full stall landing also requires an increase in any crosswind correction you're applying as you approach stall speed (more on crosswinds in the next chapter). Unless your timing is just right, it's possible to run out of crosswind control response before the airplane has actually touched down. Oops. You're landing north/south but the airplane is also moving east/west. The landing gear is not going to like this.

Yes, pilots essentially do full stall landings in a taildragger, but taildraggers touch down on three wheels at the moment of stall instead of two wheels for the tricycle geared machine). A three-wheeled base is more stable about the pitch axis than a two-wheeled base. Of course, taildraggers have their own special issues when landing, but the point stands, nevertheless.

In a tricycle-geared airplane, it's best to touch down a few knots above the airplane's stall speed, before the wings have stalled. Those few knots are your safety net, defending against gusts, ghosts, twitches, and other things that might or might not be of your doing.

Upon touchdown, you will of course gently lower the nose wheel to the runway surface to reduce the angle of attack, thus eliminating any chance of those wings allowing the airplane to lift off again.

Do not tell your instructor that hotrod Rod said you should speed down the runway to land. I'm advocating touching down at a speed at least a few knots above the airplane's current stall speed, before the wings have actually stalled. Since airplane stall horns typically activate at three to four knots above stall speed, it's possible you will actually hear the beginning of the stall horn on touchdown. That doesn't mean the airplane is stalled. It does mean that you have control of the airplane all the way through the flare and touchdown.

moved aft with small pull and release motions during its travel. These motions are more visible on larger single-engine airplanes where the airplane's mass requires a larger displacement of the elevator to change pitch slightly. The proper application of this technique requires proportionally smaller forward and aft yoke movements to remain in the threshold of immediate control when flying airplanes in the weight class of a Cessna 150 or J-3 Cub.

It's worth trying this technique on a few landings to see if it gives you a better idea of how to flare your airplane. It's certainly ideal to apply one continuous increasing pull on the elevator during landing, and you should always strive for the ideal. On the other hand, some folks have a difficult time flaring that way. So be it. While they may never be the Mohammad Ali of landings, at least they won't float like a butterfly and land like a bee.

An exaggerated form of the *sampling the response* (pull-and-release) technique is frequently used by pilots operating deep in the region of reversed command while making short-field landings on extremely short fields. Slightly larger forward and aft movement on the elevator lets them know how much (if any) aft elevator travel is still available to them, as well as how effective the elevator response is. I'll discuss this in greater detail in the chapter on short-field landing techniques.

As a final note on this technique, some pilots refer to this as *fishing for the runway*. OK, I'll take the bait on that. This is a *fishnomer* (OK, misnomer). Fishing for the runway is supposedly something pilots do when they have no clue as to where the hard surface is below them. They push and pull on the elevator slightly, waiting for those wheels to make contact with the ground. This is more myth than reality. It's actually quite rare to see a pilot fishing for a runway, though I've seen a few who hunted for one.

The Two Handed Flare

It's not uncommon for many student pilots to try placing two hands on the yoke during the landing flare. This isn't a wise idea for inexperienced pilots. So if you're a student pilot, I want you to keep one hand on the throttle and the other hand on the elevator control during the roundout and flare. Why? Because it allows you to have immediate access to engine power in the event you over-flared the airplane or the airspeed suddenly decreases. Student pilots, with few hours in their logbooks, haven't developed the necessary muscle memory to help them locate the throttle by feel. In other words, they aren't yet skilled at moving their right hand from the right side of the yoke directly down to the throttle.

Now, there are circumstances where I have let students use two hands on the yoke when they are having trouble learning to flare the airplane. Two hands give them greater fidelity on the elevator control. However, I typically do this for two or three landings, at most. I occasionally allow this because it can help students stop extreme over-controlling movements of the elevator. It only takes a few landings with two hands on the yoke for most students to get an approximate sense of how much elevator input is needed during the landing flare.

Chapter 10: The Roundout and Flare

Arms Control—The Case for the Two-Handed Flare

Why would anyone even think about flaring an airplane with two hands on a typical *wheel type* yoke instead of keeping one hand on the throttle and one on the yoke? There are several reasons why doing so is a reasonable idea.

One is when a pilot finds it difficult to manipulate an airplane's heavy elevator control forces, and the other is when an instructor needs a temporary technique to assist his or her student in the landing flare (as explained above). So let's explore the former here.

Biomechanically, it's simply easier to apply precise changes in elevator control pressure when you dedicate additional strength and more nerve endings to manipulating the control yoke. Two hands also provide better leverage. This is why some pilots opt to place both hands on the yoke during steep turns. Using two hands can also help overcome any binds or crimps in the yoke's gearing mechanism, a common issue in older airplanes (and older pilots, too).

It turns out that some pilots flying larger single-engine airplanes occasionally use two hands to flare their airplanes. These are typically airplanes such as the Cessna 182 and 210, the Cherokee Six and Saratoga. The handy use of two hands for the flare helps pilots to obtain greater precision in pitch control when the yoke is either aerodynamically heavy (i.e., in slow flight), mechanically sticky or because the pilot's physiology and seating position provides insufficient leverage on the yoke.

I am *not* talking about placing two hands on the elevator when the airplane turns final a mile out. I'm talking about using two hands on the yoke only in the latter portion of the flare when the plane is very close to the runway and the throttle is set at flight idle.

Some instructors ask, "What would happen during the flare if you encountered a gust, or heaven forbid, wingtip vortices, and had to apply power immediately? What about the critical time delay in finding that throttle? It could cost you your life."

A bit of experimentation on my part several years ago revealed that the time it takes a rated pilot (someone with a private pilot certificate or better) to apply power from a two handed yoke grip is just a fraction of a second and could be even faster with a pre-application of adrenaline. This is in comparison to the standard one-hand-on-the-yoke and one-hand-on-the-throttle technique. It is difficult to see how one's life hangs in the balance when an experienced pilot flares with two hands (under the previously stated conditions).

It's possible, I suppose, that the rotational forces encountered in a wingtip vortex might result in an inability to properly project your hand toward the throttle, thus delaying the application of power. My standard response to this suggestion is that wingtip vortices are things you avoid, not things you handle. If you encounter an actual wingtip vortex that close to the ground, time-to-throttle is highly likely to be the least likely of your problems. That's why we avoid wingtip vortices. That said don't use two hands when you suspect vortices are likely.

I'll reiterate that student pilots should always keep one hand on the yoke and the other on the throttle during the landing flare. This is simply good practice, given that students may not have enough practical experience to locate the throttle by feel or spatial memory.

Can a two-handed flare be done safely by rated pilots? The FAA thinks so, because it willingly certificates pilots having only one arm as described in Sherry Coin Marshal's book, *One Can do It* (shown to the left). This includes one-armed pilots who aren't required to use a prosthesis during flight. In fact, not only will the FAA certify one-armed individuals as private pilots, it has certified them as commercial pilots, flight instructors and multi-engine ATPs. We even have one-armed commuter airline pilots. Clearly, if a pilot only has one arm, that arm is on the elevator control when flaring the airplane, right? That means there are no hands left to place on the throttle. But it also means that the pilot can easily move his or her hand from one to the other and apply throttle quickly if that becomes necessary.

Ultimately, the ideal of having a hand on the elevator and a hand on the throttle is one we should honor. On the other hand (no pun intended here, honest!), it's also reasonable for an experienced pilot to use a two handed flare when flying an airplane with a heavy elevator control or when an instructor wants to apply a temporary training antidote to his student's excessive control inputs. Either way, this should be done only when the airplane is within a foot of the ground and with power at flight idle.

Over-control of the elevator during landing often stems from airplanes having poor elevator control leverage, sticky or worn elevator control gearing, or students with tiny little biceps that squeak when you pinch them. Most of the time this problem can be remedied with a bit of grease (no, not on those tiny biceps, either) or by proper use of the trim wheel prior to the roundout and flare. There is, however, a case to be made for use of the two handed flare if you're a private pilot or higher. Read about it in the sidebar titled, A*rms Control—The Case for the Two Handed Flare*.

Stabilized Approach

Here's an idea that may help you better approach and land an airplane. The more time you have to observe the runway on final approach without the airplane pitching up, down, right and left, the easier it is for your brain to compute the rate of closure with the runway as well as your height above the runway. If you can better estimate these two things, landings will be a snap instead of something that causes the landing gear to snap.

When you're having trouble learning to land, the objective for you and your instructor should be to arrive on final approach at least a half-mile from the threshold, at an altitude that allows a descent with minimal power changes (if power is being used). From this position, your objective is to establish the proper nose down pitch and power conditions for the target airspeed and descent rate, trim the airplane for this attitude, and use aileron and rudder control to keep the wings level and the nose pointed straight ahead (a no-wind condition is assumed here). This is what is known as a *stabilized approach*, and it offers you the best chance of making consistently good landings (Figure 21).

Once the airplane is stabilized on final approach, let it do as much of the flying as possible. After all, it already knows how to fly. *Your sole objective is to keep the ever-expanding runway picture steady in the windscreen during your approach to it.* Why? So your brain can do what it already does best, which is making estimates about your height and rate of closure with the landing surface.

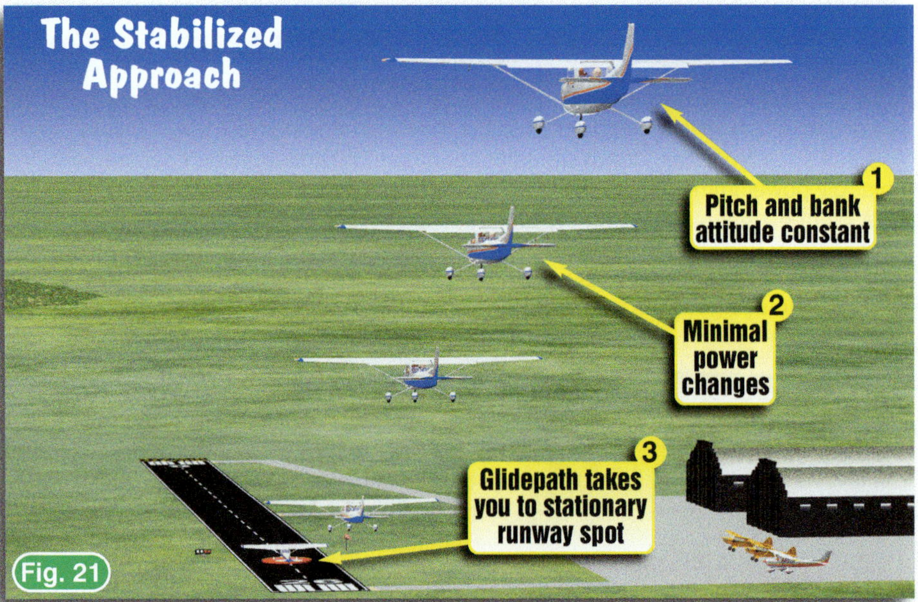

Jumble the picture by wandering all over final approach and your brain can't make these calculations as accurately. In fact, the *stationary spot method* for evaluating the landing location and the *trapezoidal shape method* of evaluating the glidepath angle are both based on your ability to keep the airplane stabilized on approach. Without stabilization, you simply can't make out how the runway and its environment change during the approach. This would be similar to having a child in the back seat who puts his hands over your eyes and holds them there until you're 10-15 feet above the ground. At this point the youngster removes those hands and says, "OK daddy, guess how high you are?" How can anyone make a reasonable estimate of roundout height in so little time?

Sometimes I have to remind students what they know as well as how to use what they know. An approach and landing is nothing but a wings-level, constant heading descent followed by a nose-up pitch at the appropriate time. This is why I often spend more time with new pilots initially practicing wings-level, constant heading descents. It's also why I make a very big deal about properly trimming an airplane on final approach (or at any time, for that matter). When they can keep those wings perfectly level, the airplane pitched downward to a precise degree below the horizon to maintain the desired airspeed, and not let their machine wander away, they'll be landing on their own in a short time. Of course, there's much more to learn about landings and it takes several additional hours to cover all the essentials.

Fig. 21 — The Stabilized Approach
1. Pitch and bank attitude constant
2. Minimal power changes
3. Glidepath takes you to stationary runway spot

A stabilized approach results when a pilot maintains a constant angled glidepath to a stationary spot on the runway. The approach is flown with minimum variation in pitch and bank and minimal changes in power.

Chapter 10: The Roundout and Flare

The Touchy Touchdown

Right after a proper landing flare, the airplane will touch down on its main gear first, followed by a gentle lowering of the nose gear. This portion of the landing is known as (drum roll please), the *touchdown*. Who would have guessed? (Probably you.) The transition between the wheels touching down and the airplane decelerating on the runway is known as the *touchdown roll* (Figure 22). We'll explore both here.

It's important to understand that airplanes should not be forced onto the runway during the touchdown phase. Think "gentle art of persuasion," not cage wrestling. You will rarely win a fight with an airplane.

You shouldn't need to shove the elevator control forward to make the wheels contact the runway surface. The objective here is to have the main gear touch down before the nose gear while the airplane is under complete control. How smoothly this transition occurs is a matter of practice and experience on your part.

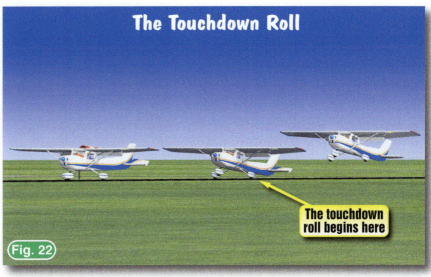

The touchdown roll begins the moment the airplane's main gear make contact with the runway surface and ends the moment the airplane comes to a complete stop after it taxis clear of the runway.

At the moment of touchdown, you must ensure that the longitudinal axis of the airplane is aligned with the runway (Figure 23). You have walking sticks (legs and feet). Make sure you use them just as the main gear is about to make runway contact. Push those rudder pedals as necessary to keep the airplane's longitudinal axis aligned (parallel) with the runway centerline stripe. Now is not the time to become Twinkletoes.

Keep in mind that the rudder is still quite effective during the landing flare. So, if the airplane's longitudinal axis is at some angle to the runway before touchdown, straighten it out by pushing on a rudder pedal. Push it as hard as necessary in order to point the airplane's nose straight down the runway, and use those ailerons to keep the wings level.

I'm assuming a no-crosswind condition here. We'll cover crosswind landings in the next chapter. Be assured that any normal or crosswind touchdown is accomplished with the airplane perfectly aligned with the runway's centerline. To land at some angle to this centerline

Just before the airplane touches down on the runway, you must make sure that the airplane's longitudinal axis (thus the airplane's main gear) is aligned with the runway centerline. Push on those rudder pedals to ensure that the airplane touches down in the direction it's moving.

means that side loads are imposed on the landing gear. Under extreme conditions this could lead to tire or landing gear damage. It can also lead to a *ground loop*.

A ground loop is essentially a loss of control after touchdown. The name probably originates with the behavior of a taildragger, which tends to pivot about its main gear after touchdown because the pilot lost control of his or her machine (Figure 24). It does this because unlike a tricycle geared airplane, the taildragger's center of gravity is located behind the main gear. This results in the front and back of the airplane wanting to swap ends if the airplane is allowed to swerve excessively during the touchdown roll. Swaping ends is not an advantageous position in which to place an airplane as it's touching down.

A groundloop occurs when the pilot loses control of the airplane during the touchdown roll. Taildraggers are especially sensitive to groundlooping given that the center of gravity is located behind the main gear. Groundloops can result in a damaged ego and a damaged airplane.

In an airplane with tricycle gear, the machine can also pivot about its main gear, but because of the way mechanical forces are distributed, instead of the front and back ends swapping places the more likely outcome is a wing and/or prop strike or, in extreme cases, the airplane actually flipping over on its back and playing dead. That's not a happy way to end a flight, is it? Your chance of ground looping increases when the airplane's longitudinal axis is misaligned with the runway centerline during landing. So the straight skinny here is to keep the airplane straight.

Houston, The Eagle Has Landed

Once those main wheels are on the ground, your job is to make sure they stay there. You have arrived, but you haven't fully landed. Do not stop flying the airplane until you are at the tiedown spot and the engine is shut down. A little complacency goes a long way in the wrong way post-landing.

Since your main gear will (should) touch down first, the wings will still be at some positive angle of attack. A strong gust of wind can produce sufficient lift to raise the airplane off the ground, or lift one wing off the ground in the case of a sudden crosswind gust. It can also cause the airplane to float or skip sideways across the runway, thereby exposing the airplane to a ground loop and/or tire and gear damage. We've already discussed how discomforting this can be. That's why you want to lower the nose gear smoothly and gently to the runway surface promptly after touchdown (Figure 25).

Notice that I said, "Promptly"? There is a far-too-prevalent view

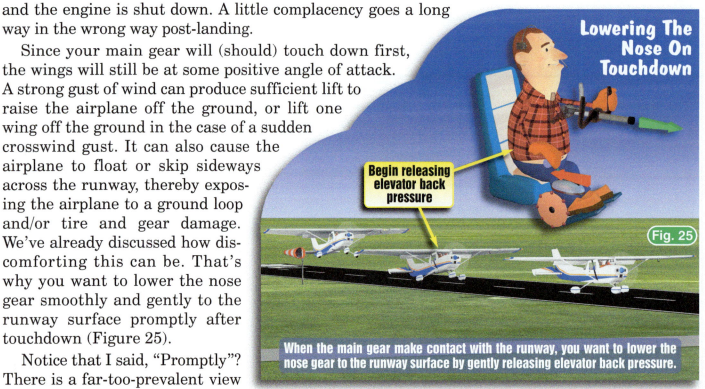

When the main gear make contact with the runway, you want to lower the nose gear to the runway surface by gently releasing elevator back pressure.

Chapter 10: The Roundout and Flare

Nose Strut Needs Compressing

Nose strut needs to compress for ground steering on some airplanes

When the nose wheel settles to the runway, the nose strut compresses.

Fig. 26

Over Compressed Nose Strut

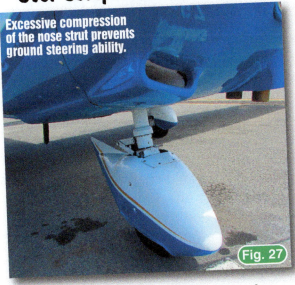

Excessive compression of the nose strut prevents ground steering ability.

Fig. 27

Normal Nose Strut Compression

As brakes are applied during the touchdown roll, apply elevator back pressure to reduce nose strut compression and maintain your steering potential.

Typical nose strut compression during landing with aft elevator applied

Fig. 28

that it is ideal to hold the nose wheel off the ground as long as possible, making it look as though you're doing a wheelie. I've been at airports where I thought all the landing airplanes were trying to "high-one" each other. I don't know where this wheel deal idea started, but I know where it should end—on the ground. Holding the airplane's wings at a high angle of attack after landing does create aerodynamic braking. But the idea that that's how you stop a general aviation airplane is very peculiar and you should get away from it. You aren't flying the space shuttle, and you haven't re-entered the atmosphere from orbit where aerodynamic braking is necessary to help dissipate your re-entry energy.

You, lucky pilot that you are, have an airplane equipped with wheel brakes! So use them, but use them in the right way.

Some pilots suggest that aerodynamic braking saves brake pads. Well, that may be true, but the cost of brake pads pales in comparison to the risks of ground looping your airplane because you insisted or performing an Evel Knievel wheelie on landing.

Another reason we don't use aerodynamic breaking is because it limits the ability to see what's ahead of you on the runway. Aerodynamic braking is reasonable when landing on a long, soft field, as we'll discuss in Chapter 12. Other than that, its risks far outweigh its rewards.

As you gently lower the nose wheel to the ground, the wings are at a very low angle of attack, producing little if any lift. As you apply the brakes gently, the airplane will tend to pitch forward about the main gear and compress the nose wheel strut mechanism (Figure 26).

Up to a point, that's fine, but excessive compression of that strut can diminish the ability to steer the via the airplane's nose gear steering mechanism (Figure 27). I don't want to milk a dead cow, but no steer is no good. That's especially true since the rudder is becoming less useful as a steering device as the plane slows. You need to be able to steer with *something*. That's why you'll want to reduce the compression of the nose strut by applying elevator back pressure during the deceleration (Figure 28). Apply just enough back pressure to prevent the nose strut from being excessively compressed but don't lift the nose wheel off the ground again. As the airplane decelerates, you'll have move the elevator control continually aft to reduce the nose strut pressure as the elevator control loses its aerodynamic effectiveness.

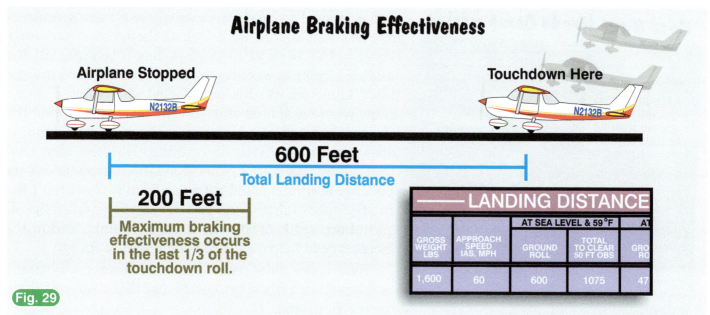

Fig. 29

Stopping an airplane just after landing means transferring the weight from the wings to the wheels as quickly as possible. This provides for more effective braking and deceleration. On the other hand, immediately after touchdown even with the nose wheel contacting the surface, it's possible that the wings are still developing a small amount of lift, which ultimately reduces braking effectiveness. An excessive application of brake pressure might result in skidding the tires. If you're someone who likes to make a dramatic airport arrival, this isn't the optimal way to do it.

If you sense that your tires are beginning to skid (it's possible that you'll hear or feel the skid), release the brakes and apply just enough brake pressure to keep the wheels from skidding. This is one reason why the maximum amount of braking effectiveness occurs in the last one-third of your total ground roll (Figure 29). In other words, if your performance charts suggest it would take you 600 feet to stop (the approximate distance between three sets of runway side lights along the length of the runway), then you can count on your braking action being most effective in the last 200 feet of the 600 foot ground roll (or, a single set of runway side lights). So don't apply heavy braking immediately after touchdown. Instead, apply brakes slowly at first then progressively increase the pressure on the brakes as the airplane decelerates.

Another thing you want to avoid doing is trying to turn a tricycle geared airplane too sharply while braking. The typical scenario for this is trying to make an early (or the first) turnoff to exit

Fig. 30

Chapter 10: The Roundout and Flare

Flap and Gear Handle Shapes

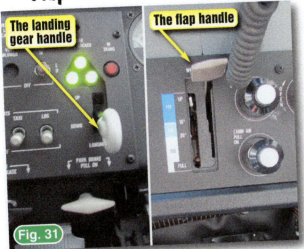
Fig. 31

the runway when you're still moving along briskly. It's easy to have the airplane's momentum lift it to the right or left front quarter of its tricycle base, resulting in it toppling over like a child on a tricycle who makes a sharp turn (Figure 30). Then you're doing a wing-y thingy. The potential for this happening is even greater if a quartering tailwind is involved. So decelerate straight ahead, then turn once the airplane is at or below normal taxi speed. Some airports have "high speed" taxiways, where the exit angle is more gradual and permitting a safe exit as a somewhat higher speed. That doesn't however mean that you have to exit at a higher speed if you don't feel it's safe to do so.

Of course, the proper use of the ailerons to keep a wing from rising due to a crosswind is also a very important part of touching down safely. We'll discuss proper use of the ailerons in a crosswind in the next chapter.

There's a lot going on during the touchdown. That's why you don't want to be messing with things like flap retraction immediately after landing. Despite flaps handles being shaped like *flat* flaps and gear handles shaped like *round* tires, pilots can easily mistake one for the other during the landing roll (Figure 31). It's that sort of thing that makes you—or your airplane—a sitting duck. Wait until the airplane has come to a complete stop off the runway before retracting the flaps. Doing otherwise means you might retract the gear (if it has retractable gear) and that means you'll need a lot more power to taxi. That's how you know you've landed gear up. (OK, just kidding on that one).

Using Flaps for Landing

What's the flap about flaps? There isn't much of a flap, actually. When an airplane extends its flaps (or sprouts aluminum), the size and shape of its wings are effectively altered (Figure 32). Now the wings are able to produce the required amount of lift at a slower airspeed. This can be easily seen in Figure 33.

Flap Extension

Flaps come in different shapes and sizes. Their primary purpose is to provide for the required lift at a slower airspeed. With increasing lift, you obtain increasing drag, which allows the airplane to make steeper descents.

Fig. 32

Flap Effectiveness

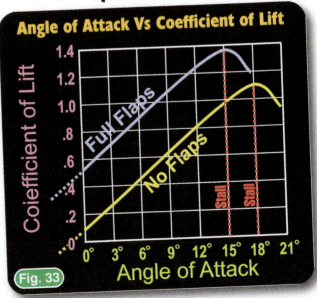
Fig. 33

Flaps provide a higher coefficient of lift for a given angle of attack. If you remember the lift equation in Chapter Five, the coefficient of lift is one of the direct multipliers in the lift equation. It's very uplifting, sort of the bench-press of coefficients. Double the coefficient of lift and you double the lift produced by the wings. With an increase in lift, however, there's also an increase in drag. What a drag, except when it allows the airplane to descend at a much steeper angle without an increase in airspeed. Let's see how this works in action.

First, by applying some flaps on takeoff it's possible for the airplane to become airborne at a slower speed and climb at a steeper angle. This is why some POH's recommend the use of 10-25 degrees of flap extension for short-field takeoffs (more on short-field takeoffs and landings in the Chapter 12). Since flaps also reduce the airplane's stalling speed, landing with flaps extended substantially reduces the airplane's landing roll, too. This is why short-field landings (especially when an obstacle is involved) are flown with full flaps. This allows a steeper descent over the obstacle at a slower speed, resulting in a shorter ground roll after touchdown (Figure 34).

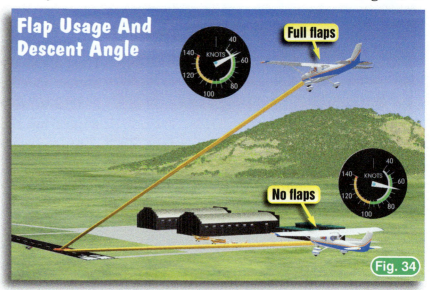

The application of flaps also increases drag which allows a pilot to make a much steeper descent without a commensurate increase in airspeed.

Depending on the specific type of flaps involved, flap extension might cause the airplane's nose to pitch upward or downward or upward with partial flaps and downward with full flaps as they are extended. It's important to counter this pitching tendency by using the appropriate elevator pressure. This action helps prevent large swings in airspeed. Once applied, the airplane should be retrimmed to maintain the desired attitude and to remove excessive elevator control pressure.

If you find yourself high on final approach, it's certainly appropriate to apply full flaps and simultaneously lower the nose to maintain the desired approach speed. In doing so, your descent rate and descent angle will increase.

If, however, you have flaps applied and you find that you are going to undershoot the runway, you don't want to remove the flaps unless you are beginning a go around and only then after adding full power (go arounds coming up next). Instead, you want to apply power—probably a lot of power—to change your glidepath. Removing flaps at the lower power settings associated with descents might

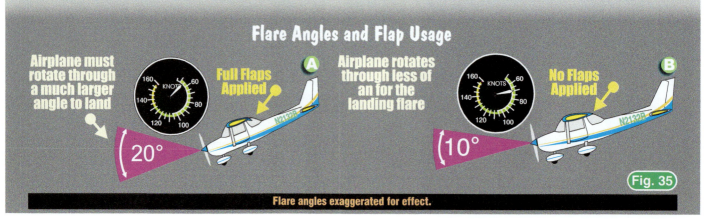

Chapter 10: The Roundout and Flare

cause the airplane to stall or to move into the region of reversed command, making a climbing recovery difficult, if not impossible.

When using full flaps for landing, there are two important items to consider. First, the nose is generally placed at a lower attitude when making a full flap approach (Figure 35, position A). More drag means that you must point the nose down more to allow gravity to sustain your descent speed. That means the roundout and landing flare require a rotation through a larger arc compared to rotating in a no flap condition (Figure 35, position B). Combine this with a slightly higher descent rate and it's clear that you must apply elevator back pressure for the landing flare at a slightly faster rate than you would in a no flap condition.

You also won't have as much time to make small corrections in pitch during the landing flare. Why? Because the lower approach speed along with the drag associated with the use of full flaps results in the airspeed decreasing to stall speed quickly (relative to a no-flap landing) . Ultimately, this means that if you begin the roundout too high above the runway or overflare during a full flap landing, you might be too high and/or at too slow an airspeed to recover by lowering the nose and attempting acceleration for another landing flare. So, when landing with flaps, you want to be ready to use engine power to help compensate for any overflare or bounce upon landing. Of course, the degree to which any of the above happens with full flaps depends on the type of flaps on your airplane. Some flaps (think *plain* flaps) just aren't as effective other types of flaps (think *Fowler* flaps).

The Go Around

You're about to learn why sometimes the most important landing maneuver is not landing.

Sometimes, no matter how much you want to land, the universe seems to do everything possible to prevent a smooth return to earth. You might be on final approach when someone decides to use the runway for takeoff (Figure 36) or a pickup basketball game. At other times some official representative of nature such as a deer or coyote might run out onto the runway. Shouting, "Oh, deer" is usually useless, especially if it's a coyote. And sometimes your approach is just not as stable or doesn't

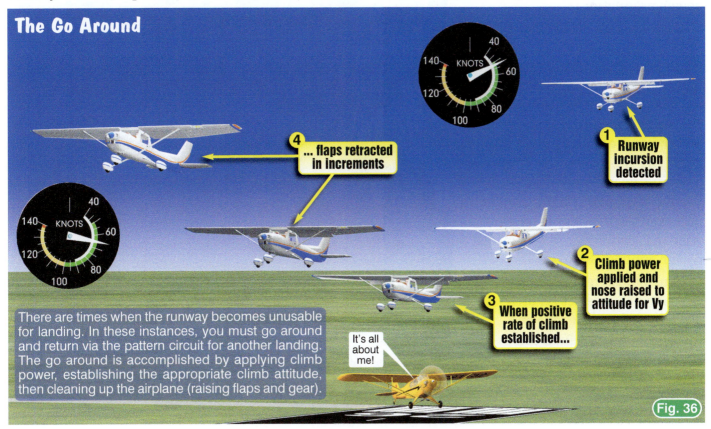

The Go Around

1. Runway incursion detected
2. Climb power applied and nose raised to attitude for Vy
3. When positive rate of climb established...
4. ... flaps retracted in increments

It's all about me!

There are times when the runway becomes unusable for landing. In these instances, you must go around and return via the pattern circuit for another landing. The go around is accomplished by applying climb power, establishing the appropriate climb attitude, then cleaning up the airplane (raising flaps and gear).

Fig. 36

feel as safe as you'd like it to be. These are the times when you must quickly reconfigure your mind *and* your airplane; both were set up to land, and now must be briskly transitioned into the right attitude for a *go around*.

The go around is just what the name says—you go around and try again. The go around is a maneuver that can be started at any altitude. You must be mentally and physically prepared to initiate a go around at any moment until the airplane is on the ground and safely off the runway (Figure 37).

Whether at 500 feet or in the flare, all go arounds begin the same way—with the application of climb power (Figure 38). Smoothly move the throttle handle forward. Don't jab it into and through the instrument panel. If carburetor heat had been applied, it should be turned off in order to maximize power production.

Because you've probably had the airplane trimmed for landing, when you apply climb power with flaps extended the airplane will tend to pitch nose-up quite dramatically. You might need to apply a great deal of forward elevator pressure to keep the nose attitude from increasing excessively. You'll also need a lot of right rudder to compensate for the airplane's left turning tendency with climb power applied (Figure 39).

Your objective after power is applied is to select an attitude that allows the airplane to accelerate to climb airspeed. In most instances, the airplane is already close to its climb airspeed so climb attitude can be immediately selected.

Executing a Go Around

You never quite know what might prevent you from landing on a runway. It can be a wandering animal, someone in a dragster (yep, that's happened) or a tower controller's command to execute a go around.

The first step is to add climb power, simultaneously raise the nose to climb attitude and remove any carb heat applied. You'll need to add right rudder, too. Next you'll need to remove the flaps in increments and add nose down trim.

Chapter 10: The Roundout and Flare

When You're Told to "Go Around," Then "Go Around"

This accident happened in the early 1980s at John Wayne Airport in Southern California. The pilot of this Boeing 737 was instructed to go around while on a short final due to another commercial airline delaying its takeoff. The 737 pilot, however, wasn't excited about going around and told his copilot to ask the tower if he could just slow down a bit, instead. After being told to go around a total of three times, the pilot reluctantly complied. Unfortunately, he had slowed down enough that he was now operating behind the power curve. He applied power and raised the gear but the airplane was just too slow. It stalled and hit the ground resulting in the crash you see here. Fortunately no one was injured. And several passengers crawled out through the broken fuselage with their briefcases, walked across the airport and went home. So how was your flight today, honey?

The moral to this story is to never let your airplane get so slow that you can't accelerate sufficiently to make a successful go around. Additionally, when the tower instructs you to go around, then go around. This isn't a good time to argue with the controller.

On the other hand, as you add power and raise the nose to begin a climb, you don't want to raise that nose too fast. Depending on the power available to you, the size of your machine, the type of flaps and the amount they're extended, the airplane simply might not accelerate quickly. Allowing the airplane to pitch up too early in this situation could easily increase the induced drag associated with slower speeds, nudging you into the region of reversed command and dangerously close to a stall.

So be prepared to keep the nose a bit lower than the desired climb attitude to accelerate properly. Only when the airplane is accelerating should you raise the nose and begin your climb. Be sure to use whatever nose-down trim is needed to help you maintain the desired attitude.

Time to kick back and open a cooling air vent? I don't think so. You still have work to do. You'll want to clean up the airplane once it begins accelerating. This doesn't mean picking up empty juice boxes and cookie wrappers. Now is when you put the airplane into an aerodynamically cleaner configuration by retracting the flaps and landing gear (assuming it is retractable, of course).

If you're flying a retractable-geared airplane, you only need to clean up the flaps during the climb. Start by reducing your flap setting to partial flaps first. This means ridding yourself of the major drag causing portion of the flaps. When you've established a positive rate of climb (meaning that the needle on your VSI is deflected upward), raise the gear if you're in a retractable. As the airplane continues to accelerate, remove the rest of the flaps in 10-15 degree increments. In airplanes having three notches of flaps (or three *nachos* of flaps if the airplane is from south of the border), flaps retraction typically means removing the last notch of flaps, followed by the other two notches with brief time intervals between each retraction. Of course, it's your POH that is the final arbiter about how flaps should be retracted in this condition.

Doing things in this order is the most reasonable means of transitioning from a dirty, high-drag airplane to a clean, low-drag one. Then get the kids to pick up the empty juice boxes and cookie wrappers.

Did you notice that I said to reduce flaps to their partial setting, but not to raise the gear until you've established a positive rate of climb? Think of this as an insurance policy. The plane is at or near the ground and headed downward. Even though you've applied power, there is a slight lag until the plane accelerates and removing flaps could cause the plane to settle slightly before it starts moving upward. If that happens, would you rather have the gear or the belly touch down?

That said, touching down during the go around is more likely if you happen to be flying a larger airplane having a lot of inertia. The point here is to have the gear out there to keep the airplane from contacting the runway.

If flaps are such a drag, why don't we just retract them completely as we begin a go-around? Because removing flaps at the lower power settings associated with descents might cause the airplane to stall or move into the region of reversed command, making a climbing recovery difficult, if not impossible. So, first dump the last 10-20 degrees or so of flaps (based on your POH's recommendation, of course).

Balked Landing Recovery Secrets

Simon & Garfunkel said there are 50 ways to leave your lover. There are at least four common ways to depart from a picture-perfect landing. A *balked landing* (which is just another way of saying that a pilot messed up the landing) often results from a *porpoise*, *float*, *balloon* or *bounce*. If you want to try making this an Olympic event, combine two or more of these options. Believe me when I say that all pilots who've landed more than four times have done all four. That's a fact. Good pilots, however, know how to correct for these events and turn a balked landing into a good landing. Let's examine each one individually.

Porpoising

Porpoising (the kind that actually resembles a porpoise popping in and out of the water) can occur if you attempt to force the airplane onto the runway at a higher-than-normal speed. This forces the nose gear to contact the runway slightly before the main gear does (Figure 40). It can also occur if you land hard on the main gear, resulting in the airplane pitching forward onto the nose gear. Either way, the airplane responds by pitching up and becoming airborne. Many pilots react to this by applying too much forward elevator pressure, resulting in the nose gear once again making hard contact with the runway. Boing, boing, boing. The cycle repeats itself, often with more devastating oscillations each cycle, until finally the nose gear collapses and the flight ends with a phone call to the insurance adjuster.

Here's how to handle the porpoise. The moment the airplane's nose gear contacts the runway and the airplane pitches up, you want to avoid *shoving* the nose down again. Instead, you'll lower the nose to maintain your airspeed but you won't shove the elevator forward to do so. You'll simply release the elevator back pressure you're most likely applying and gently let the

Porpoising and Why It's Not a Good Thing

1. The porpoise begins with a bounce followed by pushing forward on the elevator, causing another bounce
2. The porpoise continues as the pilot pushes the elevator forward and the airplane pitches upward

Fig. 40

Porpoising typically begins with the nose wheel striking the ground first, resulting in a nose-up pitch, followed by the pilot's reaction of pushing the elevator forward. The cycle then repeats itself as the pilot continues to push forward on the elevator as the airplane pitches upward. The end result is usually a collapsed nose gear assembly and sudden stoppage of the propeller.

Chapter 10: The Roundout and Flare

airplane return to the runway where you'll commence flaring at the appropriate height (Figure 41). Of course, you've probably lost a lot of airspeed in the process of pitching upward. Therefore, you should be ready to add whatever power is necessary to retain (or regain) your airspeed as you move closer to the runway. As you release that elevator back pressure, don't be afraid to move that throttle to its full forward position to increase your airspeed if you manage to get too slow during the bounce. As a general rule, the higher the bounce after the first porpoise, the slower your airspeed becomes and the more power you need to regain that speed. When you are once again at flare height, reduce your power to idle and flare.

Inexperienced pilots can learn to handle this problem by having an instructor simulate porpoising on landing, then practicing the appropriate defense. At a slightly higher-than-normal approach speed, the instructor can simulate the initial bounce of a porpoise by letting *the main-gear* wheels touch the runway (not the nose gear wheel!), then pulling back on the yoke *gently* and just enough to raise the airplane about two feet into the air.

At this point, after having followed the instructor through on the controls, the student takes the controls and practices the recovery. Release a little of the aft pressure applied, letting the airplane settle toward the runway and then *continue to flare* the airplane. What you don't want to do when you take over is shove the yoke forward. That's what gets you in trouble to start with. So the tip here is to release a little of the elevator pressure if the airplane porpoises. Free Willy!!

If you fail to release elevator back pressure soon enough, the airplane keeps rising and the speed keeps falling. You see where *that* winds up, right? Most likely in a stall several feet above the ground and a *very* hard landing. Using your slow flight and stall experience, you should know when the airplane is getting too slow to go. The feel of the controls, the high pitch attitude and the stall horn are good indications of this condition. High pitched sounds from the flight instructor can also be a sign of an impending stall.

And *always* keep the go-around option in mind. Always. Sometimes, too much is going too wrong too fast. It happens. Don't force the situation, especially when you are inexperienced. If you can't get solid control quickly, don't hesitate to go around. Consider it part of your education. A go around is a lot better than a wraparound prop.

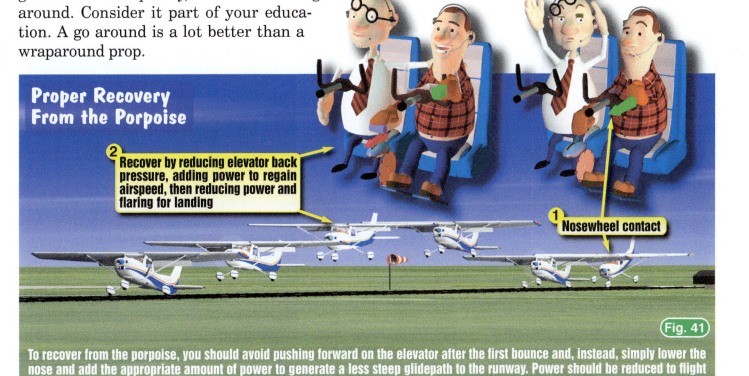

Proper Recovery From the Porpoise

2. Recover by reducing elevator back pressure, adding power to regain airspeed, then reducing power and flaring for landing

1. Nosewheel contact

Fig. 41

To recover from the porpoise, you should avoid pushing forward on the elevator after the first bounce and, instead, simply lower the nose and add the appropriate amount of power to generate a less steep glidepath to the runway. Power should be reduced to flight idle at flare height followed by a normal landing flare.

Floating

Floating during the landing flare is the result of an approach airspeed that is too high.

Landing is an exercise in energy management. Ideally, you arrive at the touchdown point with just enough energy; not too much, and not too little.

To float means that your airplane has too much energy—too much forward speed—to descend when you get to the spot where you'd like it to descend. The excess energy has to be dissipated before you can be repatriated with the runway.

You can't hold an energy yard sale, so the only option is to keep the airplane close to the runway while slowly pulling aft on the elevator to reduce the airspeed and increase induced drag. Depending on how fast you are going, it might be necessary to just fly level above the runway for a while before you can even start pulling the elevator control back. Pull back too soon and you balloon (see next section). But try and force the airplane onto the ground and you will porpoise for no purpose.

The problem with floating is that you can either run out of runway on which to land (Figure 42) or be blown off the runway by a crosswind for which you don't adequately compensate. Neither of these is much fun. Here's how to handle this problem.

If you find yourself floating during landing and aren't sure whether or not you have enough runway on which to land then go around. If there is any doubt in your mind about whether there's enough runway left, go around before that option isn't an option. One of the interesting things about runways is how much shorter they look when you're running out of them. And there are few things more useless than the sky above you and the runway behind you.

If you're convinced that you have sufficient runway, make sure power is reduced to idle and allow the airplane to remain at flare height, but don't shove the elevator control forward to get there. Let the airplane decelerate while it settles slowly to the runway. Do, however, keep the airplane in either a crab or sideslip condition to prevent drift (crosswind correction, to be discussed next chapter). Preventing drift is of course the big challenge associated with floating. So if you find yourself floating, you'll have to work hard at keeping the airplane positioned over the runway centerline.

As the airplane slows down to a normal roundout speed, you'll have to increase the crosswind correction to compensate for wind drift. This means you'll have to turn more into the wind to increase

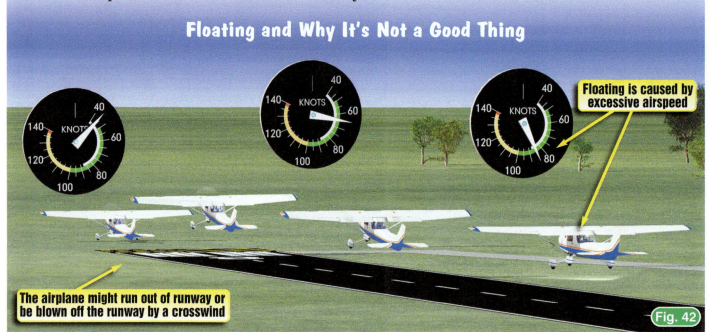

Floating and Why It's Not a Good Thing

Floating is caused by excessive airspeed

The airplane might run out of runway or be blown off the runway by a crosswind

Fig. 42

It's easy to float if you carry too much airspeed into the roundout or the flare. You have to dissipate the airspeed somewhat and, if there is insufficient runway on which to land, the best option is often to execute a go around and return for landing.

Chapter 10: The Roundout and Flare

the crab angle. If you're using a sideslip, you'll need to increase your sideslip angle while keeping the longitudinal axis parallel with the runway. Increase the crosswind correction as necessary to keep the airplane tracking down the centerline of the runway until a touchdown can be made. We'll discuss crosswind landings in detail in the next chapter.

Ballooning

One of the more common experiences that even high time pilots have is an increase in airplane altitude as they flare (Figure 43). This is called *ballooning* because the airplane moves upward during the landing flare instead of settling toward the runway.

Ballooning is different than porpoising. The porpoise usually results from bouncing off the runway, while ballooning results from excessive speed during landing, coupled with aggressive elevator technique in the flare where the wheels never actually touch the ground. It can also be caused by wind gusts or convective (rising hot air) currents in the runway environment.

As mentioned above, you are in an energy manager. Arrive hot at the landing spot, pull back abruptly (or sometimes even slightly) on the yoke, and the landing goes up instead of down.

In most cases, you can arrest ballooning behavior (no badge required, either) by simply releasing some back pressure on the elevator, followed by a normal increase in back pressure to continue the landing flare.

Releasing elevator back pressure might not be the right answer if the airplane's speed is too slow and its altitude too high. In that case, you'll want to release back pressure *and* apply generous amounts of power (perhaps even full power) to accelerate to a safer speed while returning to flare height and flare speed. At flare height, reduce power and commence a normal landing flare.

Once again, if it doesn't feel good, don't do it. A go around is your friend if you don't feel you can get the airplane under control and down on the runway that remains.

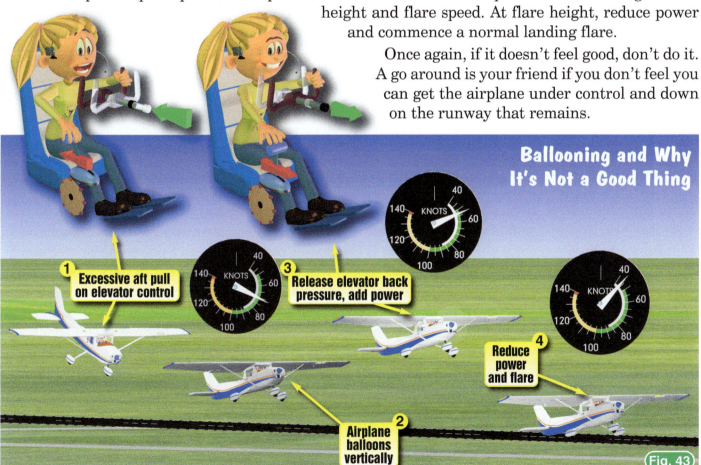

If you manage to balloon during landing because you pulled aft too aggressively on the elevator, then release that elevator pressure and be prepared to add a lot of power (perhaps full power) to regain the necessary airspeed to flare for landing.

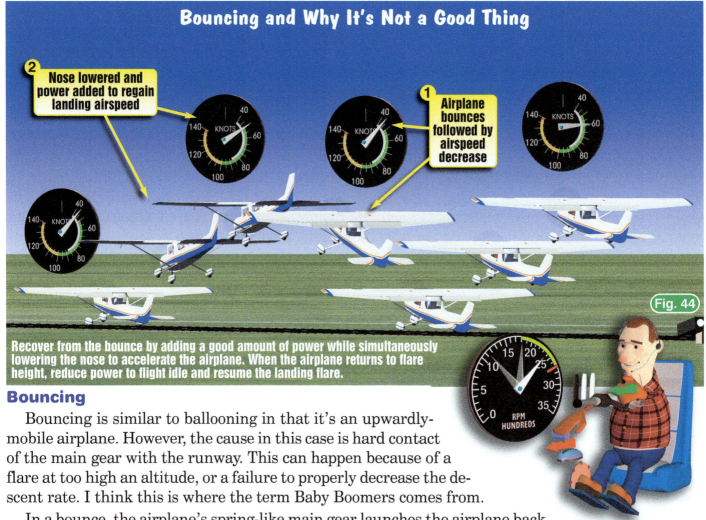

Recover from the bounce by adding a good amount of power while simultaneously lowering the nose to accelerate the airplane. When the airplane returns to flare height, reduce power to flight idle and resume the landing flare.

Fig. 44

Bouncing

Bouncing is similar to ballooning in that it's an upwardly-mobile airplane. However, the cause in this case is hard contact of the main gear with the runway. This can happen because of a flare at too high an altitude, or a failure to properly decrease the descent rate. I think this is where the term Baby Boomers comes from.

In a bounce, the airplane's spring-like main gear launches the airplane back into the air at a relatively slow speed (Figure 44). Because things happen faster during a bounce (as compared to ballooning), you need to respond faster. This usually means adding climb power and pointing the nose slightly below the horizon to accelerate the airplane as it returns to flare height. If you don't get some power under you, the plane will bounce again. And again. And again. And somewhere along the way the porpoise might come to play.

So don't be afraid to push that throttle forward. Push it! Don't wimp out on me here. Machiavelli is all for your power grab in this circumstance. Grab that power lever and power up as necessary. Here is where you have a need for power and speed. When the airplane is within flare height of the runway, reduce power and commence a normal landing flare.

These suboptimal landings can be challenging to explain to passengers. You can try saying you needed to get the dust off the plane, or that you're doing routine, required testing of the shock absorbers. You can also try telling your passengers that you experienced a microburst as a reason for landing hard, though they may suspect a microbrew was more likely at fault.

Believe me when I say that everyone, and I do mean everyone, lands hard on occasion.

More Advanced Landing Skills

Now that you have a basic idea of how to round out and flare the airplane for landing, it's time to talk about how to land when the wind blows from some place other than directly down the runway centerline. Crosswind landing skill is a must if you hope to fly relaxed, to say nothing about staying on the runway. So let's see how to handle crosswind landings so as to not get crossed by the wind.

Chapter 10: The Roundout and Flare

Postflight Briefing #10-1 Fanning

Fanning? No, this is not something you do after landing hot.

Fanning the elevator is similar to the technique we covered on Page 10-15 called *sampling the response*. There is, however, a distinct difference between the two techniques. Sampling the response requires small forward and aft movements on the elevator control during the flare to maintain precise control of the landing attitude. Fanning, however, involves similar movements performed in a slightly *quicker* and *exaggerated* manner. While all pilots might sample the response when landing an airplane, student pilots are sometimes taught to fan the elevator to learn how to land an airplane. Said another way, flight instructors often introduce their students to fanning for a short period of time to help them develop the proper landing behaviors.

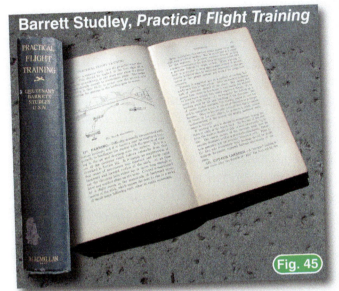

Barrett Studley, *Practical Flight Training*

Fig. 45

I first encountered the technique of fanning when I began flight instructing in the early 1970s. There were still quite a few WWll flight instructors around that were active in flight training. These instructors were very familiar with the concept of fanning.

Fanning, however, is a technique that even precedes WWll. I first read about it in Barrett Studley's 1928 flight training book titled, *Practical Flight Training* (Figure 45). Studley was a Navy flight instructor, teaching in an NY-1 Navy taildragger. Here's how Studley describes the technique of Fanning:

Fanning—Difficulty is usually encountered with normal landings, and if so, fanning may be employed temporarily to familiarize the student with the process of stalling in the air and dropping onto the surface.

Of course, taildraggers are often landed in a stalled condition, but there's essentially no dropping onto the surface except from just a few inches. Studley's point, however, is that fanning is a practical method of helping students learn to land.

When a student fans the elevator as he begins the roundout and continues through the flare, he is essentially pulling the elevator farther and farther aft, but doing so in a series of quick aft stick movements. Studley expresses the idea this way:

The plane is leveled off...by a series of quick backward movements of the stick. These movements are continued in order to raise the nose until the airplane stalls. After each one [aft stick movement] the stick must be allowed to go forward again, as if it is held back even momentarily the plane is likely to climb. (See Figure 46.)

Yes, it's true that at this early stage of landing, the nose is indeed moving up in small increments. No, it's not oscillating up and down as might be surmised from the small aft (and release) stick movements. Instead, the nose is being raised in small but distinctly visible increments, somewhat similar to applying aft pressure on a lever via a pulley system to raise a heavy weight. These increments should not be jarring or necessarily jerky if the technique is performed properly.

Studley expresses the point this way:

Control is maintained by a slight excess in the magnitude of backward movements of the stick, which causes the nose to rise in a series of small steps following each other in rapid succession.

The idea of fanning is based on the student having an opportunity to make, recognize and correct for the mistakes he or she is likely to make with the elevator during the first few hours of training.

That's right. Fanning is ultimately a mistake-making technique. It's the chance to see tiny little mistakes (raising the nose in small increments) then correct those mistakes—lots of them—that allows an acceleration in learning. Here's how Studley states it:

...tendency to keep the stick in more or less constant and regular forward and backward motion. The net result of this will be a marked decrease of the fluctuations in the plane's height. This tendency is normal at this time, as the student can progress only by making, recognizing and correcting mistakes. Free use of the elevators is one of the first things that must be learned.

The idea of fanning might appear to be more complex than just teaching someone to make a continuous aft pull on the elevator for landing. This, however, wouldn't comport with reality. Fanning is actually much easier on the beginner than learning to use a continuous, precise aft pull on the elevator for rounding out and flaring. Studley explains it this way:

While learning to land, it is simpler to keep approximate control of motion already initiated than to commence movement of the elevators at the proper instant and control its magnitude precisely.

Keep in mind that the objective of fanning is not to use it as the final skill one will use when landing. Instead, it's simply a step toward making a smooth continuous pull on the elevator for landing. Speaking early in the last century, Barrett Studley's words on this matter still ring true. Studley says:

Fanning is suggested, not as a method of landing, but solely as a step in instruction. After ten hours it indicates lack of adequate control of the plane. But during the period from three to five hours it may enable the student to learn more quickly two vitally important things: (1) to move his stick freely; (2) to recognize the feeling of a landing made by his own handling of the elevators. He of course makes mistakes, but quickly learns to feel for and to recognize a stall in the air preliminary to a proper landing. Once he has actually accomplished this a number of times by his own efforts, he acquires a much clearer understanding of the process and greatly increased confidence in himself.

If fanning is used it should be commenced during the third or early in the fourth hour. By the end of the fifth hour the student should be able to land consistently by its use. The excess motion of the elevators must then be steadily decreased until it is practically eliminated. Otherwise precision will be seriously interfered with. Prior to the first solo consistently good landings should be made without frequently repeated forward movements of the stick.

Keep in mind that fanning is not the same as sampling the response. Fanning is an exaggerated but similar technique that's used to help students *learn* how flare their airplanes for landing. Sampling the response is a technique typically *used* by rated pilots to flare their airplane. So add this to your bag of flight instructor techniques. You might find it useful. Your author certainly has.

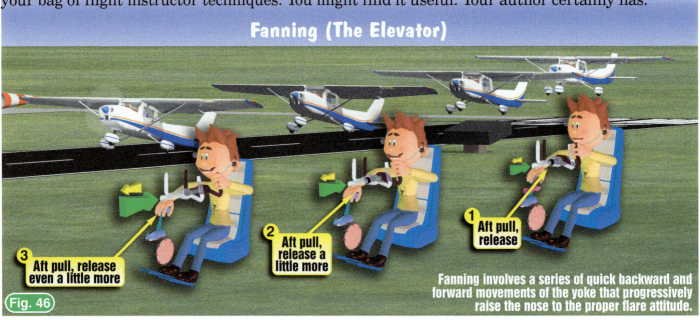

Fig. 46

Fanning (The Elevator)

③ Aft pull, release even a little more
② Aft pull, release a little more
① Aft pull, release

Fanning involves a series of quick backward and forward movements of the yoke that progressively raise the nose to the proper flare attitude.

Chapter 11
Crosswinds and Slips
Flying Sideways is Fun

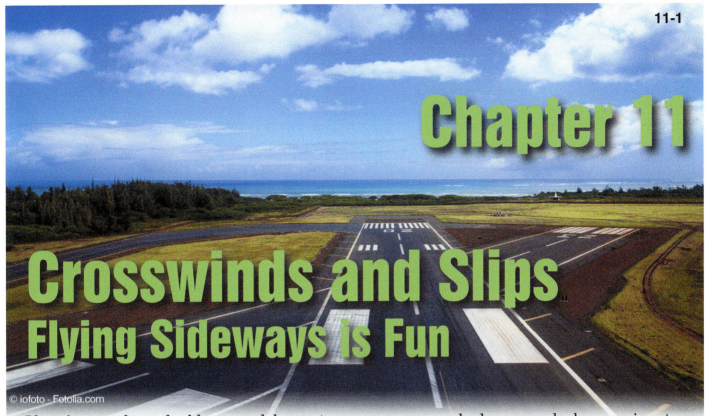

Prior to a crosswind touchdown, the longitudinal axis should be aligned with the runway. Fig. 1

If you've ever been double crossed, been at cross purposes, or had someone look crosswise at you, then you know that when two things cross it usually doesn't work out well for the home team. The same principle applies when there's a wind crossing a runway, but you have the ability to deal with this low blow.

If the wind *always* blows exactly down the runway everywhere you fly, you can skip this chapter. Still there, aren't you? You *know* that the fickle finger of the windsock points at you from many directions that are *not* perfectly aligned with the runway. Since runway builders haven't figured out how to perch a runway on a swivel so it always points into the wind, all pilots—including student pilots—need to acquire the skills that let them successfully and gracefully land in crosswinds great and small. Let's give you what you need.

Crossed by Crosswinds

In an earlier chapter we discussed how to correct for wind drift when flying a rectangular course. The same skills required for that maneuver—the *crab*—are all that's necessary to keep yourself aligned with the runway centerline on final approach, at least until you're ready to begin the roundout and the flare.

There's something you need to get straight—the airplane. There comes a point where you need to know how to transition between a crabbing condition and being perfectly aligned with the runway centerline. Except for some older airplanes no longer in production (See Sidebar: *Landing in a Crabbed Condition* on next page), the longitudinal axis of the airplane should always be aligned with the runway centerline just prior to touchdown (Figure 1). This prevents excessive side loads from being applied to the landing gear assembly, as well as minimizing the chance of a ground loop induced by these sideways forces.

Landing in a Crabbed Condition

Believe it or not, there are airplanes designed for landing in a crabbed condition. That's right. You land them at some angle (crabbed) to the runway centerline. These aren't, however, modern airplanes.

For instance, some Cessna 195 models have something known as a Goodyear *crosswind gear*. This refers to a specific brand of main gear wheels that swivel (think pivot or castor) and actually allow landing in a crab angle of up to 15 degrees. That means you'd hold the airplane at an angle to the runway, land, then align the fuselage with the runway centerline by applying rudder pressure after touchdown.

The Ercoupe was another airplane that was designed to land in a crabbed condition. Remarkably, it did *not* have swiveling (castoring) main gear. Since the airplane was designed without rudder pedals, you held the airplane in a crab all the way to touchdown. Its strong, hinged, L-shaped landing gear had sufficient flex, allowing the airplane to align itself in the direction of travel upon touchdown.

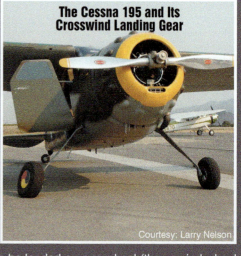
The Cessna 195 and Its Crosswind Landing Gear
Courtesy: Larry Nelson

The Ercoupe and Its Flexible Landing Gear

The fact is that all airplanes can be landed on one wheel (the upwind wheel as you'll learn shortly) in a sideslip condition. The implication here is that the average airplane's main landing gear is relatively strong, which it is. Usually, even poor technique that results in a pilot touching down with the wings level in a slightly crabbed condition won't damage the airplane's gear. Usually. But it's unwise to count on this margin to save your airplane skin. Larger side loads *can* damage the landing gear and even increase the likelihood of ground looping, and repeated stress of this kind is bad for the airplane and your instructor.

You have two choices for this transition (I feel like a waiter telling you the daily specials). One of them is a real kick. You can transition from a crab directly to the touchdown with a last-second *kick out*, or you can transition from the crab to the wing-low method for touchdown (otherwise known as the *sideslip*). Either one works, but I have a daily special to recommend for your aviating pleasure.

Let's first return to the position of having just turned onto final approach and discuss the crab method of crosswind landing.

As you turn onto final approach and align the airplane's longitudinal axis (the fuselage) with the runway, you will most likely notice the airplane beginning to drift to one side of the extended runway centerline (Figure 2, position A). The most effective method for determining the direction of drift is to use your eyes and see which way the airplane is moving in relation to the extended runway centerline. This will *always* give you the correct answer.

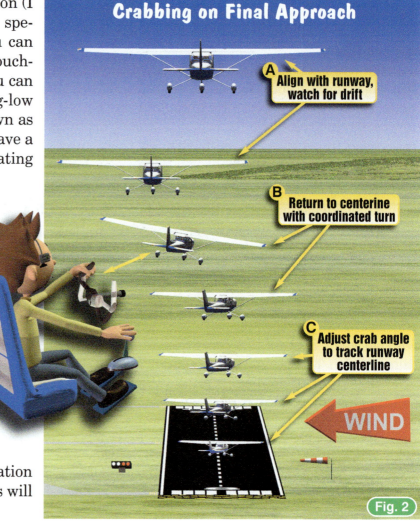
Crabbing on Final Approach
A – Align with runway, watch for drift
B – Return to centerline with coordinated turn
C – Adjust crab angle to track runway centerline
WIND
Fig. 2

Chapter 11: Crosswinds and Slips

Sock it to me. I can hear some of you asking why you can't just look at the windsock. You can, and it will tell you exactly what the wind is doing—on the ground right next to the wind sock. But you aren't yet on the ground, are you? What the wind does at several hundred feet in the air and half a mile from the runway might be something entirely different. Wind direction can shift (a little or a lot) several times as you descend through the final few hundred feet.

The least effective way to get the drift on how you'll drift on final approach is from wind reports from the tower, unicom broadcasts, or even the automated weather broadcasts. These reports are based on wind detection devices that are likely to be based at the location of the automated station or even the top of the tower cab. Since you aren't intentionally landing on the top of the tower cab, these wind reports do you little good. Stick with what you see. You literally don't need a weatherman to know which way the wind blows.

The Crab Method—It's Not Nebulous

It's time to get crabby, and that's not a matter of attitude. Once you've determined the direction of airplane drift, apply a crabbing angle into the wind to compensate for this drift. This requires that you make a *coordinated* turn into the wind and roll out into wings-level flight with the nose (longitudinal axis) pointed at some angle into the wind to compensate for the drift (Figure 2, position B). This angle is your *wind correction angle* or WCA.

As a general rule, the wind tends to shift to the left slightly as you approach the surface, because of the effects of the coriolis force and ground friction. Yep, that's right (no, I mean left). Faster moving winds are curved to the right more than slower moving winds. If the wind speed tends to decrease toward the surface because of surface friction, then those winds will shift slightly to the left. While this shift in direction might not be much, it's still something that could affect your airplane.

Since wind velocity tends to decrease as you approach the surface, you'll most likely need to reduce your WCA slightly during the descent (Figure 2, positions C). Of course, if your airspeed varies, then you'll have to adjust the crab angle for that, as well (but you'll keep your approach speed constant, won't you?). On final approach your airspeed should be stabilized at 1.3 Vs. Please remember that you modify the WCA by making small coordinated turns using rudder and aileron inputs, and not by use of rudder input alone, except in one instance. What's that one instance, you ask? Read on Big Foot.

Tower Winds? Not Always the Best Reference

It's not at all uncommon for pilots to call the tower as they enter the traffic pattern and ask for the wind direction and velocity. What is unusual is when they ask for the same information when they're on final approach. Here's why.

When you're on final approach, the only winds that you should be concerned about are the ones that are affecting you right now in your present position. By looking over the cowling and assessing wind drift (or drift correction) you can see what the wind is doing to your airplane. Sure, ask for the wind direction and velocity if it pleases you, but keep one very important thing in mind. The wind issued by the tower is often taken from a source different that in the first third of the landing runway (where you typically plan on touching down). More often, the windsock sitting right next to the runway is a far better wind reference than any tower provided winds.

The crabbing method of crosswind correction requires that you hold the crab angle throughout the landing roundout and flare, then *kick out* or eliminate the crab just prior to touching down, aligning the longitudinal axis of the airplane with the runway centerline (Figure 3). This is a crab kick, which is not to be confused with a crabcake. One is to eat, one is with your feet.

Your sole objective with this maneuver is to avoid placing excessive side loads on the main landing gear. You do this by pressing on the rudder and not by making a coordinated turn. You are too close to the runway to be making a turn. Besides, the airplane is just about to touch down. Attempting to turn and align yourself with the runway centerline might allow the crosswind to displace your airplane from the center of the runway. Instead, just as you're ready to touchdown at the end of the landing flare, apply sufficient rudder to align the nose with the runway and use opposite aileron to keep the wings level (applying rudder usually induces a turn unless this is corrected by input of opposite aileron) (Figure 3).

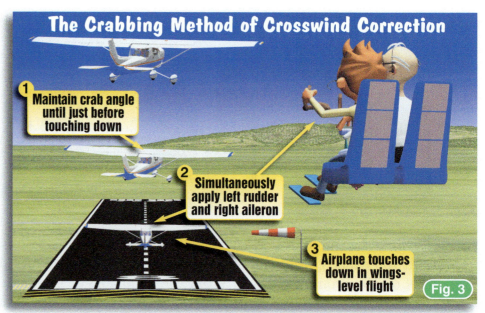

When using the crab method to keep aligned with the runway centerline, you must use rudder to align the airplane's longitudinal axis with the centerilne just prior to touching down. You must also apply a little opposite aileron to keep the upwind wing from rising. After touching down, you'll want to keep applying right aileron to force the right wing down and prevent it from rising.

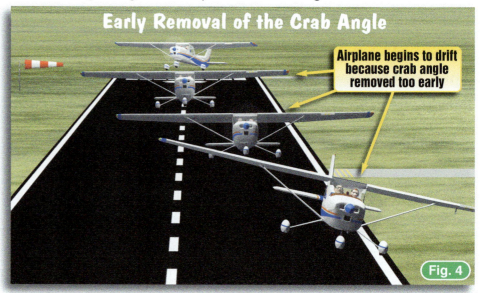

If you remove the crab angle and manage to balloon, overflare or hold the airplane off the runway to bleed off excess speed, you might begin to drift, resulting in the possibility of leaving the runway or in a groundloop or both.

Correct execution of the crabbing method of crosswind landings requires good timing on your part. It's not as easy to do as the *wing low* method, which is coming up next. Consider that during the landing roundout and flare the airplane's airspeed is decreasing. Since the airplane is crabbed into the wind at some angle, there's a sideways component of the airplane's speed that is neutralizing the wind's crosswind component. As the airplane slows down during the flare, that sideways component of movement decreases as the airspeed decreases, but the wind's crosswind component essentially remains the same. (Please read the sidebar titled: *Why Must Increase the Side Slip or Crab Angle During the Flare?*) If you don't touchdown immediately after removing the crab angle, you'll begin to drift (Figure 4). If that happens, you'll add a sideways component of force to the landing gear upon touchdown, which for reasons I already stated is something you want to avoid.

Chapter 11: Crosswinds and Slips

Increasing the Crab Angle During an Extended Landing Flare

As the airspeed decreases during an extended landing flare, the crab angle required to track the runway centerline must simultaneously increase. This does takes some skill to accomplish and isn't something that student pilots typically have the skill to accomplish

Fig. 5

Why You Must Increase the Side Slip Or Crab Angle During the Flare?

Let's assume you're on final approach at 65 knots crabbing to the right into a 10 knot crosswind. In order for you to maintain a ground track parallel to the extended runway centerline, your crab angle must be approximately 8.8 degrees to the right (Insert #1). Said another way, at 65 knots, by angling your nose 8.8 degrees to the right, a slight amount of the airplane's 65 knot speed acts perpendicular (to the right) of your flight path down the runway centerline. How much speed is this? It's exactly the same speed (10 knots) of the direct crosswind component, which allows you to track parallel to the centerline of the runway.

Now let's mentally do the roundout and flare where the airplane slows down to 50 knots before it touches down. Let's assume that the wind's direct crosswind component remains at 10 knots during your flare. At 50 knots, holding 8.8 degrees of crab will only produce 7.6 knots of sideways component by the airplane. Therefore, the airplane drifts to the left of the runway at 2.4 knots (10-7.6=2.4) if the crab angle isn't increased. As it turns out, for the airplane to maintain 10 knots of drift correction to match the 10 knots of crosswind, the crab angle must increase to 11.5 degrees during the flare (Insert #2). And that's why it's necessary to increase the crab angle during the flare when using the crab method of crosswind landing if you delay the touchdown. Of course, if you're using the wing low (a sideslip) method for crosswind correction, then the sideslip angle must also increase during the flare, too.

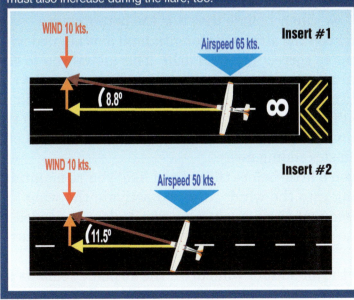

Technically speaking, if you stretch out the landing flare either because your approach speed is too high or because you are attempting a soft-field landing (discussed in the next chapter), you'll also have to increase the crab angle during the landing flare (Figure 5). It's true that an experienced pilot can turn slightly into the wind to increase the crab angle while he or she is actually in the landing flare. But this does take considerable practice to accomplish. Let me explain.

The way to induce a slight turn into the wind during the roundout or flare is by applying rudder pressure in the direction of crab. This accelerates the outside (downwind) wing, increasing its speed, thereby causing it to rise slightly and turn the airplane. In this instance, you don't want to hold the wings level with the ailerons. You want the wing to rise slightly and turn, but you don't want it to rise too much—perhaps five degrees or less. So you'll use your ailerons to keep the bank extremely shallow. Of course, when you use your rudders and ailerons in this combination you're making a skidding turn. Fortunately, you're only a few inches off the ground when you do this so there's no safety issue here in terms of spinning.

Just before the airplane is ready to touch down, apply rudder pressure to align it with the runway centerline and apply ailerons to keep the wings level. For instance, if you're in a right crab angle just before touchdown, apply left rudder (and a lot of it, too, since the airplane is very slow) and add sufficient right aileron to keep those wings level.

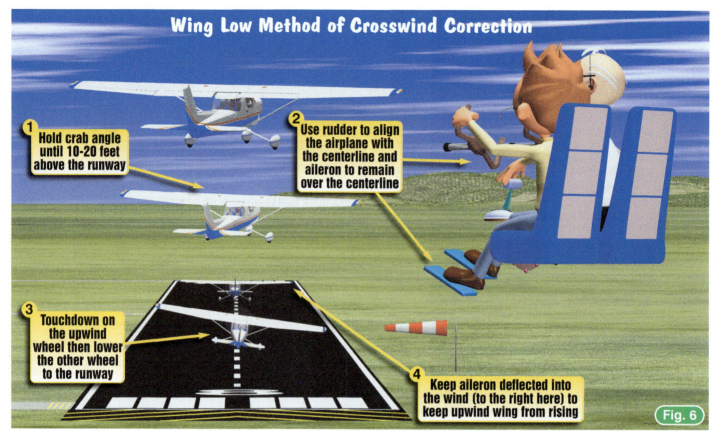

Fig. 6

Does this sound challenging? Well, it is. It can even be challenging for experienced pilots, but it's a perfectly acceptable way to handle a crosswind. While I certainly introduce the crab method to my students, I actually prefer that they use what's called the *wing low* method of crosswind correction. So what's the low down on the wing low method? Let's find out.

The Wing Low Method

Rumors that the *wing low* method of landing was created on the back of a napkin at a dingy Chinese restaurant are mostly not true. The restaurant was not dingy. The same maneuver was diagrammed at a Mexican-Chinese fusion place and dubbed the *Juan wing low*. Call it whatever you like, but we're calling it the wing low method of crosswind correction. This method of crosswind correction is a far easier method of preventing crosswind drift just prior to touchdown than the crab method, and from our rule that "easier is better," we can conclude that it is the better choice.

With this method, you use the rudder pedals to keep the airplane's longitudinal axis aligned with the runway centerline while deflecting the ailerons to correct for wind drift. This allows you to slip sideways into the wind while not exposing the main landing gear to excessive sideways stress at the moment of touchdown (it is also called the *sideslip* crosswind technique, too). Yes, you'll touch down on one wheel (the upwind wheel) after which you'll gently lower the other main gear wheel to the ground (followed by the nosegear last) while maintaining directional control of the airplane. Let's take a closer look at this maneuver, which has you slip sliding away.

Up to a point before the roundout begins (or even a little before that, if you like) you're maintaining the required crosswind correction by crabbing into the wind. Now you activate the wing low method. As you begin the roundout and the subsequent flare, apply whatever rudder is needed to align the airplane's longitudinal axis (the airplane's nose) with the runway centerline, and control for drift by using the ailerons (Figure 6).

If the drift resulting from the sideslip matches the amount of wind drift, the airplane remains directly over and tracks the runway centerline. So deflect the yoke into the wind until the airplane

Chapter 11: Crosswinds and Slips

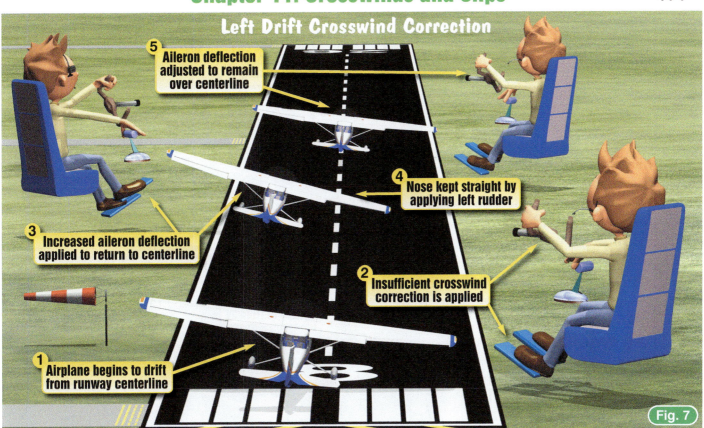

Fig. 7

stops drifting, while keeping the nose aligned with the runway centerline by use of the rudder pedals. It's as simple as that. Just as with the crab during the flare, you may have to increase the angle of sideslip (the bank angle) into the wind slightly as the airplane's speed decreases (Figures 7 and 8). This, however, is a lot easier to do than trying to increase the crab angle during the flare.

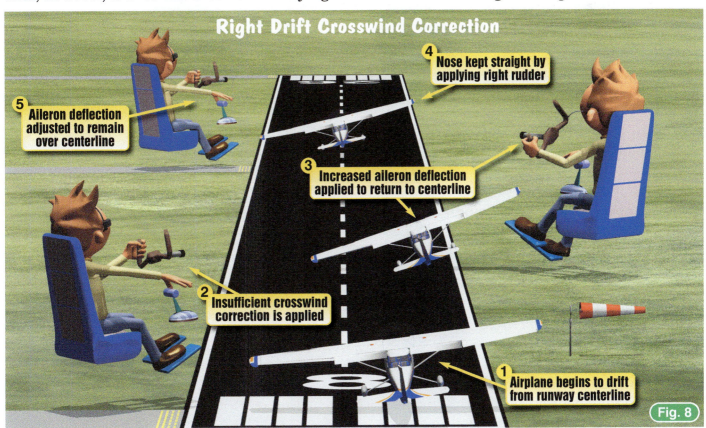

Fig. 8

It should be clear that a sideslip will result in the airplane touching down on one wheel (the upwind wheel), which is perfectly fine (Figure 9, position A). As soon as the upwind wheel touches down, the downwind wheel will tend to lower itself to the runway as the airplane loses momentum. Use your aileron control to keep the downwind wheel from slamming onto the ground (Figure 9, position B). After the upwind wheel makes contact with the runway and the downwind wheel begins to settle toward the runway, be prepared to deflect the aileron a bit more into the wind—in the same direction you're already applying it—to ensure a gentle lowering of the downwind wheel onto the runway (Figure 9, position B). During this entire process, you're continuing the flare while keeping the nose pointed straight down the runway with the rudder pedals (Figure 9, position C).

As soon as both tires are on the ground, continue deflecting the aileron control into the wind to keep that upwind wing from rising. If you used right (or left) aileron deflection during the sideslip, then you'll use right (or left) aileron deflection to keep the upwind wing from rising during the touchdown and subsequent ground roll. Think about it for a second and you will realize that his is exactly the maneuver you learned to use while taxiing the airplane in a crosswind. You've come full circle.

Since the airplane has slowed and is continuing to decelerate, feel free to fully deflect the control wheel into wind to keep the

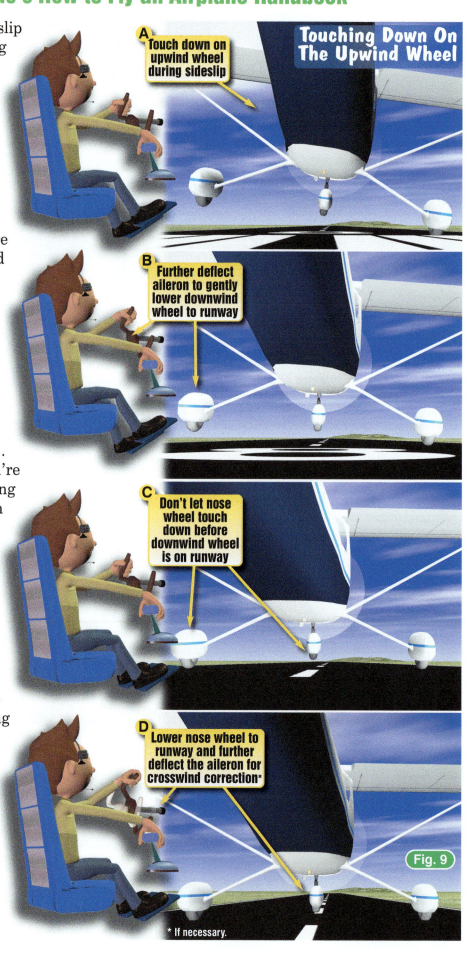

Chapter 11: Crosswinds and Slips

upwind wing from lifting if necessary (Figure 9, position D). There's no way you're going to roll the airplane back up on one wheel and strike the runway with a wing tip. At least not as long as you continue to decelerate. Remember, the slower you go the less effective those ailerons become on the ground. Thus, during the ground roll it typically takes a fully deflected control yoke to reduce the risk of that upwind wing lifting and sending the airplane running off the runway and taking you on a short trip to Embarrassment City.

Getting Nosey on the Touchdown

After touching down on one wheel, avoid letting the nose gear contact the runway before the other main gear contacts the surface (Figure 9, position C). In other words, you don't want to be on one wheel when you suddenly release whatever elevator back pressure you're applying. On many airplanes, when the nose gear extends (when it's no longer compressed by being in contact with the runway) it locks into place pointing straight ahead. Since you might still be applying pressure to the rudder pedal to keep yourself aligned with the runway, the moment that nose wheel contacts the ground, it will deflect in the direction of rudder travel, causing the airplane to swerve unexpectedly. Of course, this isn't a problem with castoring-type nose wheels (Figure 10). Nevertheless, you'll always want to lower the other main gear to the runway, followed by neutralizing rudder pressure before lowering the nose at the end of the landing flare.

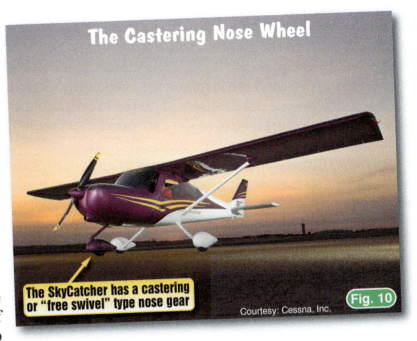

The Castering Nose Wheel

The SkyCatcher has a castering or "free swivel" type nose gear

Courtesy: Cessna, Inc.

Fig. 10

Flaring in the Sideslip

Throughout the entire wing low crosswind landing, the flare and touchdown are done the same way you would do them if there were no crosswind. The only difference here is that you're touching down on one of the main gear.

Now you're ready for the neatest little secret about the wing low method of crosswind landing.

How Do You Know How Much Crosswind You Can Handle?

One question that's often difficult to answer regards how we might learn the limits of our skill and abilities if we've never really put them to the test. There are a few ways to determine this.

You might simply guess at your capability to perform confidently. Yes, it's possible to guess correctly, within reason. For instance, if I know I've handled a direct 10 knot crosswind, it's not much of a stretch to assume that I might successfully handle one at 12 knots, especially if I've had a chance to practice in 10 knot crosswinds for some period of time. With a little common sense, it's possible to guess well.

You can also consult others you've flown with and ask them to make an assessment of your piloting ability. If you've recently flown with an instructor or another experienced pilot, then either of these individuals might be able to offer some insights into the practical limits of your skills.

Finally, there's simply no better way to know your limits than to do an experiment to discover them. Sometimes you just have to put yourself to the test to see what you've got under the hood. This often means testing your skills under the supervision of a capable flight instructor. It's why I would have encouraged my student to fly if he or she were reluctant-to-unsure of his or her ability to handle gusty crosswinds on flight review day. Even if he discovered he couldn't handle a 20 knot crosswind, at least he's learned an equally valuable lesson about the limits of his skill. Ultimately, if you don't actually do it, then you really don't know it and have no right to claim confidence about it.

Transitioning to the Sideslip from the Crab

As you approach the roundout altitude while in a crab, all you need to do to transition to the wing low method is to roll the yoke into the wind and watch the nose automatically align itself with the runway centerline. What? Get out. No way!

Yes, way!

For instance, let's say you're on final approach and crabbing into a right crosswind (Figure 11, position A). You decide to transition into the wing low method just a bit before you begin the roundout. By deflecting the yoke to the right and not applying any pressure on the rudder pedals, the airplane will bank to the right and adverse yaw will pull the nose in the opposite direction (to the left, in this instance), as shown in Figure 11, positions B and C. The nose is now nearly aligned with the runway centerline and the airplane is banked. At this point, all you need to do is apply sufficient left rudder pedal pressure to precisely align the longitudinal axis with the runway and modify the aileron input to keep the airplane over the runway centerline (Figure 11, position D). How easy is that? Relatively easy, as a matter of fact.

Perhaps you're wondering, "If this is so easy, why hold a crab angle at all on final approach? Why not begin using the wing low (sideslip) method when you're a half mile out on final approach?" There are two reasons. First, any passengers you might have won't feel comfortable being on "tilt" status for that long. Side slipping to counter crosswind drift is an uncoordinated maneuver. It forces you and your passengers to the low-wing side of the airplane. Doing this for a few seconds during the roundout and flare is one thing, but doing it on a long final approach will make your passengers crabby, perhaps even flattening one side of their hairdo. Since they already have *headset hair*, they won't appreciate the additional indentations. Besides, side slipping is a high drag maneuver that reduces your glide performance.

The second reason is that the POH may prohibit a prolonged slip. Why would it do that? Because of the potential for unporting a fuel tank. A tank low on fuel could suck air into the lines if you

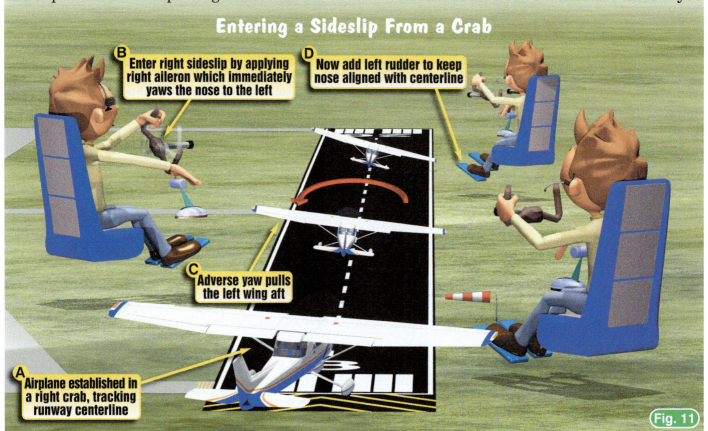

Chapter 11: Crosswinds and Slips

decided to lower one wing for, let's say, more than 30 seconds (check your POH for details). This is why the wing low method is best used at or just prior to beginning the roundout.

Of course, some pilots elect to enter the wing low method a little farther out on final when the crosswinds are strong. This allows them to see if it's actually possible to correct for crosswind drift by using only the wing low method. If not, they might have to bring in the big guns to handle the crosswind. How big are those guns? Dim some and read on.

The Really Big Guns

When the crosswinds are exceptionally strong, it's sometimes difficult to track the runway centerline when using the sideslip technique. The reason being that the sideslip depends on rudder effectiveness to keep the airplane aligned with the centerine. As the airplane's airspeed decreases, the rudder effectiveness also decreases, which might prevent you from maintaining the desired sideslip angle necessary to track the runway centerline (and flaps sometimes block airflow over the rudder which further reduces rudder effectiveness).

Therefore, when the crosswinds are very strong, you might want to use a combination of the wing low and crab methods throughout the flare and touchdown (Figure 12). This is a maneuver that requires some practice to perfect to perfection. Don't try this at home (except perhaps on a simulator), but do try it with a capable, competent instructor. It requires (and will sharpen) good stick and rudder skills.

How do you do it? Maintain the required crab angle needed to track the runway centerline. Just before beginning the roundout, deflect the yoke into the wind to begin the sideslip. Now, instead of letting the airplane automatically yaw in the direction of the runway centerline as it will do because of the adverse yaw on the raised wing, apply only enough opposite rudder to keep the nose crabbed at a slightly smaller angle while keeping the upwind wing banked into the wind. This technique allows you to apply both the crab and the sideslip to compensate for very strong crosswinds where any single method just wouldn't do the job.

Fig. 12. During exceptionally strong crosswinds, you might prefer to use a combination crab and sideslip technique for crosswind correction. While in the crab, lower the upwind wing with aileron and apply only as much opposite rudder as needed to maintain a slightly smaller crab angle. Now track the centerline with small aileron adjustments while maintaining a slight crab.

Since you'll touch down on one wheel, the fact that the nose is misaligned with the runway centerline isn't a factor here. What you must do, however, is promptly use rudder to align the nose (longitudinal axis) with the runway centerline when the upwind wheel makes contract with the runway surface.

You won't hurt the upwind main gear upon touchdown, but you will certainly cause your tire a bit more wear using this technique. Then again, it's not something you're likely to do very often. Besides, if your objective were to avoid tire wear, you'd fly a floatplane and wear down water molecules, instead. We have tires on airplanes so that we can use them. So have a good year—or 10 or 20—but don't be afraid to use your Goodyears. Just keep in mind that crosswinds requiring the combination slip-crab technique are those that should be avoided by inexperienced pilots, at least until they gain more experience with a qualified instructor on board.

Sideslip Angle Without and With Flaps

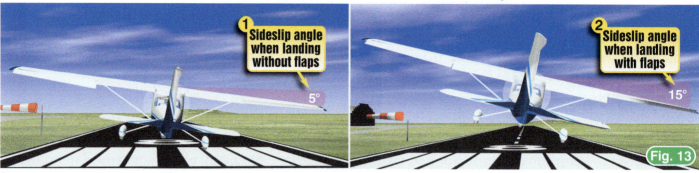

For a given crosswind, the sideslip angle necessary to handle a crosswind increases when flaps are deployed. The reason being that you approach and land at a slower airspeed when landing with flaps.

Full Flaps and the Crosswind Landing

If the crosswind component is particularly strong—10 knots or more of a direct crosswind component, for instance—you'll want to avoid using full flaps during landing. Full flaps require landing at a much slower airspeed (remember that the stall speed decreases with flap input). While your first thought might be that having things happen slower is better, think again in this situation. Slower means that you will need more of a crosswind crab angle or more bank in a sideslip to compensate for the crosswind during the roundout and flare (Figure 13). Larger crab angles and sideslip banks are more challenging for pilots with limited experience.

Landing at slower speeds means you'll typically need more aileron, rudder and elevator control deflection to maintain control of the airplane. Of course, if you're a good stick and rudder pilot, this shouldn't present a problem for you. If your skills aren't what they used to be (or there never was a *used to be*), then a full flap landing in a crosswind will certainly be more of a challenge for you. So keep the flap setting at a minimum, perhaps 10 to 15 degrees, when landing in stronger crosswinds.

Another issue with using full flaps during crosswind landings is that on some airplanes the flaps tend to blanket the rudder. It's like putting out a big force field deflector on the Enterprise. The result is that at the moment you most need rudder effectiveness during the sideslip, that effectiveness may be diminished (or absent entirely). For instance, on some Cessna airplanes having 40 degrees of flap travel, the POH recommend not side slipping with more than 30 degrees of flaps extended. On these machines, it's possible to experience unusual pitching motions and/or rotations with more than 30 degrees of flaps applied. This, however, seems to vary with center of gravity placement. So check your POH to see what (if any) flap restrictions are in effect during crosswind landings.

Flight Simulators for Crosswind Practice

Unfortunately, not everyone has the opportunity or the funds necessary to practice their crosswind landings day after day after day, despite their desire to do so (and assuming you could find a crosswind in which to practice when you're ready to do so). So what's a pilot to do? Well, I've got an answer, and it's one that many pilots use to enhance their skill level. It's called using your desktop PC aviation simulator.

I am a big, big fan of the "modern" PC aviation simulator. Of course, I'd be a big three-axis Boeing 777 simulator fan if I had a bigger garage and a profitable gold mine. Fortunately, most desktop PC simulation software can be purchased for $50-$100. With a reasonably fast computer, joystick and one nice size monitor (perhaps even two), you've got one heck of a crosswind training tool.

Here's how to make this work for you

Enter the software setup and place the airplane up on a 1/2 mile final approach on a reasonably long runway at approximately 300 feet AGL. Give yourself a starting airspeed appropriate for the airplane you typically fly. Then add a 10 knot crosswind that perpendicular to the runway. Don't start with anything fancy such as typhoon-like winds. Just try 10 knots to start, then increase the winds as you gain skill. Finally, make this the default flight, and begin your practice. Practice your crabbing, followed by the side slip for touchdown.

If you do this exercise in Microsoft flight simulator, for instance, you'll find that with an hour's practice, your crosswind skills will noticeably improve.

Chapter 11: Crosswinds and Slips

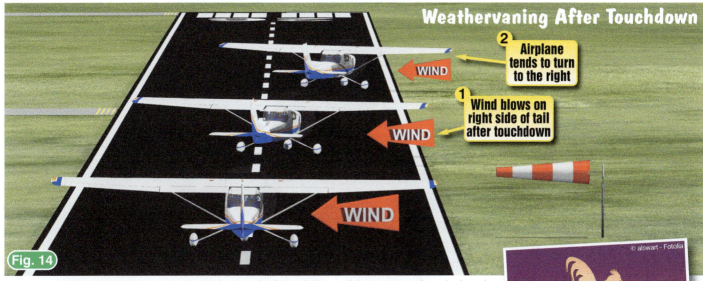

After the airplane lands in a crosswind, the wind that blows sideways on the airplane's tail attempts to rotate the tail about the main gear. This is known as "weathervaning" and can result in the airplane attempting to align itself into the wind.

Weathervaning

Weathervaning doesn't involve worrying about whether or not you look good as you read a weather report. It is the airplane's tendency to rotate about its ground pivot point (the main gear, for instance) when wind blows on the side of the airplane. Airplanes (especially those having large rudder surfaces) have a definite tendency to weathervane into the wind during the landing roll, despite all three wheels being firmly planted on the runway, as shown in Figure 14 (it's even more of a problem if you're flying a taildragger). Weathervaning primarily occurs because the wind pushes on the side of a long empennage and a sizeable vertical stabilizer. Pushing on these structures creates a turning moment about the gear, thus attempting to pivot the airplane into the wind. Fortunately, the nose gear that's planted on the ground helps resist this rotation to some degree. Nevertheless, this can still be a problem in tricycle geared airplanes, especially if you delay in lowering the nose gear to the runway surface after landing.

Counterintuitively, weathervaning also becomes more noticeable as the airplane slows down. Once those wheels are on the ground, the relative wind becomes more of a crosswind as the airplane's speed decreases. Huh? What? You brain hurts when you try to understand this point? OK, think of it this way. If the airplane is stopped and holding in position on the runway, then the relative wind blowing on it is, let's say, 30 degrees from the right. If the airplane had just touched down (it's wheels are on the surface and its tracking straight down the runway) and has a forward speed of 50 knots, then its relative wind is a combination of the 30 degree crosswind and wind generated by the airplane's forward movement. This means that the relative wind just after touchdown blows at less of an angle to the airplane's nose compared to when the airplane is moving slowly on the runway. The net result is that you might have to apply more rudder pressure to keep the nose straight as you slow down.

On very rare occasions in very strong winds after touchdown, it's possible that the nose wheel steering won't be able to compensate for this weathervaning tendency, and differential braking may be necessary to keep the airplane straight (especially in taildraggers). Fortunately, using differential braking is a lot easier than solving a differential equation after landing. The time you're most likely notice the airplane's weathervaning tendency is between the moment the main gear touches down and when the nose gear is lowered to the runway. Either way, always do whatever is necessary to keep control of the airplane. Sometimes that means using your brake pedals along with your rudder pedals to keep the airplane moving straight down that runway centerline or centered along a taxiway line.

Final Thoughts on Crosswinds

Are there crosswinds that are just too strong for a given airplane and pilot? Can you have a no-go due to blow? Yes, and either the airplane or the pilot can be the limiting factor, though it's more often the latter.

Some airplanes with smaller rudder surfaces and shorter fuselages are limited in the degree to which they can sideslip in correcting for a crosswind. Airplanes with larger rudder surfaces and longer fuselages (i.e., more leverage) make it much easier to sustain a large bank while keeping the nose aligned with the runway (Figures 15).

Most airplanes have something known as a maximum demonstrated crosswind component. That means pilots with average piloting skills should be able to handle a direct crosswind that's 20% of the airplane's power-off, gear down (of course), full flap stalling speed (your POH is the final source for this maximum demonstrated crosswind component). Keep in mind that this demonstrated crosswind component isn't a limitation or a restriction. I know of no POH for any common general aviation airplane that lists a maximum crosswind component limitation. The *real* maximum acceptable crosswind component is a personal limit that you should set based on your (ever-expanding) skills and your knowledge of the airplane's limitations.

Whether or not an airplane can be safely landed in a given crosswind is most often a function of the pilot's skill. Combining the sideslip and the crab methods often allows a landing in a mighty strong crosswind, but your stick and rudder skills must be up to the task.

A 20 knot wind blowing at a 30 degree angle to the runway is *not* a 20 knot crosswind (except when telling hangar stories). Some portion of the speed of any wind that is blowing at 90 degrees to the runway comprises the *crosswind component*. How do you determine what that portion is? By using the same crosswind component chart that you learned about in ground school, as shown in Figure 16. Every pilot

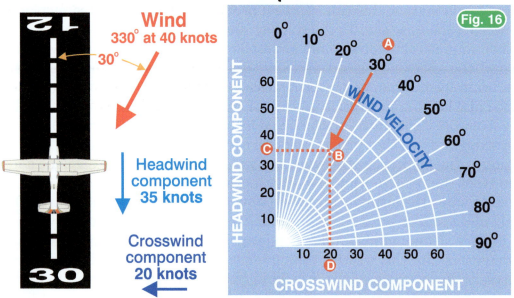

If the tower reports a wind from 330 degrees at 40 knots, you can find your headwind and crosswind components by finding the angle between the wind and the nose. That angle is 30 degrees. Find the 30 degree line (point A) and move downward to the 40 knot wind arc (point B). Move horizontally to point C to find the headwind component (35 kts). Drop straight down to point D to find the crosswind component (20 knots).

Chapter 11: Crosswinds and Slips

should have one of these handy in his or her flight bag. Fortunately your average cellular telephone can help you determine the crosswind component. How? By calling your flight instructor? No. By keeping a picture of the accompanying crosswind chart resident in your photo file, right next to uncle Wally or aunt Betty. Take a picture of Figure 16 right now and add it to your family album. If you have a small family, then adopt this picture.

Guts in the Gusts

It's one thing to land in a steady crosswind, and an entirely different thing to land in a *gusting* crosswind. A gusting crosswind is like landing in a lot of different crosswinds all at one time. Landing in gusting crosswind conditions puts your stick and rudder skills on display for all those at the airport to see. In some instances, you'll need to add, remove, add, then remove and add the sideslip configuration just to remain on or near the runway centerline. This *is not* a time when being smooth and gentle gets you anything except into a lot of trouble, as well as getting you blown away—away from the runway, that is.

Gusting crosswinds mean that you have to be aggressive on the flight controls. This is no place for the wimpy or weak of feet. You're going to have to make frequent, assertive control inputs to whatever extent is needed for complete control. This is something that many pilots are not used to doing. I can guarantee that if you have a steady crosswind at 15 knots with gusts to 25 knots, you're not going to have much fun landing unless you're willing to add and remove control inputs both quickly and firmly. While being a ballerina on the controls is great in smooth air, being an appropriate bully on them is an absolute necessity when landing in strong gusting crosswinds.

Best intent and effort notwithstanding, you will eventually find yourself at low altitude on a final approach somewhere when you suddenly realize that the wind is just too strong for you and your machine. What do you do in that instance? The best answer is to go around and find a runway with less of a crosswind. If that other runway doesn't exist at the airport you're at, you'll have to find another airport. If your preflight prep was thorough, you know what the alternatives are.

Getting Down by Slipping Down (Versus Up)

How do you get down in an airplane (no, not the disco-dance type getting down)? I'm now speaking about how to lose altitude when you're high on final approach. Sure, you can use flaps, but there is another method that's just as useful for losing altitude and it's called the *forward slip* (Figure 17).

Earlier, you learned to perform a sideslip to compensate for wind drift during a crosswind landing (Figure 18). The sideslip is a cross controlled maneuver that allows the airplane to move (slip) sideways relative to the runway centerline while the longitudinal axis remains parallel to that centerline. The forward slip is also a cross controlled maneuver; it differs from the sideslip in only one way:

The Forward Slip

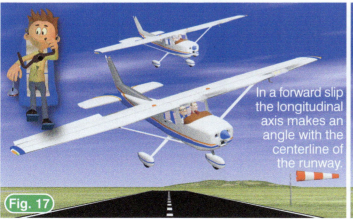

In a forward slip the longitudinal axis makes an angle with the centerline of the runway.

Fig. 17

The Sideslip

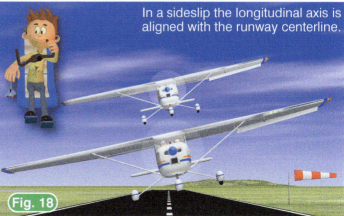

In a sideslip the longitudinal axis is aligned with the runway centerline.

Fig. 18

the longitudinal axis is kept at an angle to the runway while the airplane tracks directly along its centerline. This intentionally exposes one side of the airplane's fuselage to the relative wind for the purpose of increasing drag, which results in an increase in the rate of descent for a given airspeed.

The two slips are exactly the same maneuver as far as the airplane's flight controls are concerned because both involve using aileron and rudder in opposite (crossed) directions. The airplane can't tell the difference between the two slips.

The forward slip is an effective maneuver to use if you experience flap failure (or if your airplane doesn't have flaps) or if you're making an emergency landing and need to descend steeply over obstacles in a confined area but don't want to commit yourself to applying flaps (because it will reduce your glide potential), as shown in Figure 18. It's also an effective maneuver to use if you have to approach and land with your windscreen obscured. More than one pilot has made a landing approach with a windscreen made opaque by oil leaking from somewhere under the engine cowling (this isn't the origin of the term "greasing a landing," either), or from flight into a swarm of bugs or even from ice accretion aloft on the windscreen. The ability to see what's ahead of you out your side window in a forward slip sure comes in handy in these situations.

How to Slip Up to Go Down

To enter a forward slip during a descent, first apply aileron to lower the wing in the direction you want to slip (it's assumed that power is at flight idle, of course). In this example, enter a forward slip to the right by deflecting the yoke to the right, as shown in Figure 19, position A. Without using right rudder, the airplane's nose begins yawing in the opposite direction of bank (to the left in this instance) as shown in (Figure 19, position B). The adverse yaw resulting from the lowered aileron on the rising left wing pulls the nose to the left and this is precisely the movement you want to encourage in beginning the forward slip. As the right wing lowers and the nose yaws to the left, you'll want to continue that left yawing motion by pressing on the left rudder pedal (pressing the pedal opposite the direction of bank) while holding the aileron deflected as Figure 19 position C. All the while you're maintaining the attitude necessary to sustain your desired airspeed.

Of course, you will have to lower the nose slightly more than normal to maintain the desired airspeed, because the airplane is experiencing more drag and needs gravity to help sustain its forward momentum in the descent. During the forward slip, the descent rate (thus the bank angle of the slip) is controlled primarily by aileron input (Figure 19, position D), while the angle the longitudinal axis makes with the ground track is controlled by rudder deflection. The steepness of the slip (the descent rate) is ultimately

More Reason to Slip

There are additional reasons for slipping an airplane beyond just losing altitude in the traffic pattern.

It's entirely possible that an electrical fire and subsequent electrical shutdown might prevent you from extending flaps. Here is where a forward slip might come in handy.

Slips might become useful during an engine failure when the use of flaps alone can't not provide the required descent rate for landing. For most airplanes, slipping with flaps extended isn't an issue (you should check your POH to determine this for your airplane).

Forward slips can also be used for an emergency airspeed reduction. For instance, if you've shut down the engine due to an engine fire and are making a high speed descent to extinguish the fire, you'll definitely need to slow down prior to landing. A forward slip is one way to accomplish this.

A forward slip might also become useful to deflect smoke from the cockpit during an engine fire. If smoke pours from underneath the engine cowling directly toward the rear of the airplane, some of that smoke can enter windows or air vents. Slipping one way or another might minimize the amount of smoke you take into the cockpit. This is especially important if you need to open a side window (think of the Piper Warrior's small pilot side window) and need to deflect the smoke to the right side of the airplane when coping with this emergency.

You might also find the forward slip useful in helping close an open door on your airplane. A few airplanes use the forward slip as part of their door closing procedures. In particular, some airplanes have rear baggage doors that might bang and oscillate when open. A slip might apply sufficient pressure to the door to minimize its movement and subsequent damage.

Additionally, there are some airplanes whose design makes it very difficult to see what's ahead of you on the runway while on approach. The Cessna 195 is such an example. Performing a forward slip on final approach allows you to take a peek to ensure that no one is attempting to use the runway on which you want to land.

Chapter 11: Crosswinds and Slips

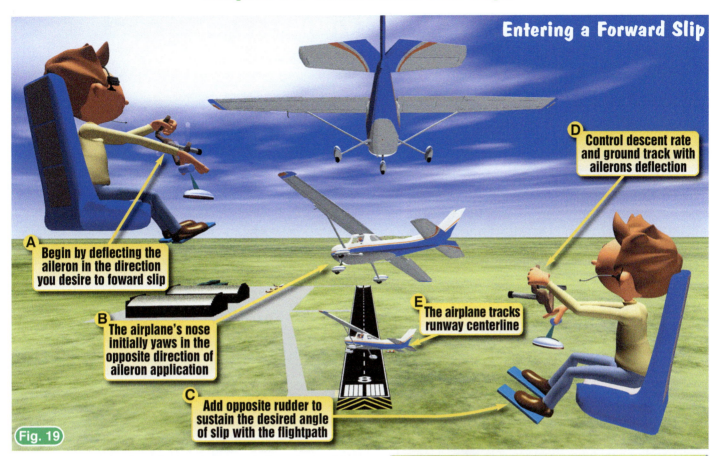

Entering a Forward Slip

A. Begin by deflecting the aileron in the direction you desire to foward slip

B. The airplane's nose initially yaws in the opposite direction of aileron application

C. Add opposite rudder to sustain the desired angle of slip with the flightpath

D. Control descent rate and ground track with ailerons deflection

E. The airplane tracks runway centerline

Fig. 19

limited by the efficiency of the airplane's rudder to maintain a heading at an angle to the flight path. This is known as the airplane's *practical slip limit*. For a dress, this is the length of hemline.

On airplanes with smaller rudder surfaces, it's difficult to induce more than a moderate amount of forward slipping. Fly an airplane with a large rudder surface and you'll be surprised at how steep the slip angle can be. Then again, even in airplanes that can make steep forward slips, it's not always necessary to slip steeply. You only need to deflect the rudder and aileron to the degree necessary to achieve the required descent rate (Figures 20 and 21). A little slip will do ya.

In a slip, one side of the fuselage is exposed to the relative wind, which produces an enormous increase in drag. This requires you to reduce the pitch attitude (decrease the wings' angle of attack) sufficiently to maintain the correct approach speed. In doing so you're actually moving slightly farther from the critical angle of attack. The exposure of the side of the airplane's fuselage to the relative wind is also providing some of the lift sustaining the airplane in a non-accelerated descent (meaning that the airspeed can remain constant while descending).

A Shallow Forward Slip

Less deflection of the controls

Fig. 20

A Steeper Forward Slip

More deflection of the controls

Fig. 21

When forward slipping, a large indicated airspeed error is possible. Deflection and/or redirection of airflow over the static port(s) and/or pitot tube might result in a small indicated airspeed error (perhaps 3 knots) or a large indicated airspeed error (perhaps 15 knots, or more). Either way, you'll use a slightly lower nose down attitude than you had prior to the forward slip to maintain the same or similar approach speed.

In this sense, the airplane's stall speed has decreased slightly and it's now a little less likely to stall in a slip (*less likely* does not mean *impossible,* so don't get careless; you can still stall it if you don't keep the angle of attack below its critical value). The net result of a forward slip is a rather large increase in descent rate, which is why you're performing the slip, right?

For some airplanes, there can be a noticeable change in indicated airspeed during a slip if there is only a single pitot tube and a single static port. When there is only one of each, whichever side they are on gets either more or less than the airflow in a non-slip condition, which leads to distorted airspeed readings. Airplanes with static ports on each side of the plane (dual static ports) typically experience less airspeed fluctuation than those with single static ports (Figure 22).

While the airspeed indication might provide a clue as to your actual airspeed in a slip, it's also very important to pay attention to other clues such as the airplane's attitude, control feel and sounds in assessing its actual speed through the air. It should be obvious that as you enter the slip you'll need to lower that nose a bit, no matter what the airspeed indicator says. On the other hand, you shouldn't try to maintain the precise approach speed you were using prior to slipping if it involves raising the nose upon entering the slip. That simply wouldn't make sense, would it? No, it wouldn't. No sense=nonsense. It's clear that the increase in drag resulting from any forward slip requires you to lower the airplane's nose to sustain the desired approach airspeed, not raising it.

How far should you descend in the slip during your approach to landing? You can forward slip all the way down to the beginning of the roundout, and if a crosswind is present, you can convert the forward slip into a sideslip and continue that maneuver through the flare to touchdown. On the other hand, most people use the forward slip only to reach a particular altitude or descent location. Then they roll out of the slip and make a normal descent.

Chapter 11: Crosswinds and Slips

11-19

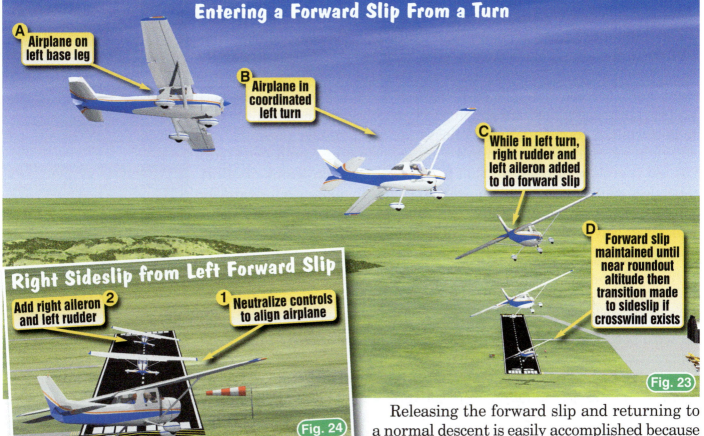

Releasing the forward slip and returning to a normal descent is easily accomplished because the airplane's positive static directional stability is always trying to align the fuselage with the relative wind. All you need to do is simultaneously neutralize the aileron deflection and the rudder pressure and the airplane will align itself with the relative wind. If you had the nose pitched down to a lower attitude in the slip, you'll want to raise it to the proper descent attitude to prevent an airspeed increase.

Which Way to Slip?

Another question to consider when making a forward slip concerns the direction of slip. When preparing to forward slip on final approach, you can do the slip in either direction, regardless of the wind (Figures 24 and 25).

Some pilots say that you should always slip into the wind, meaning that the lowered wing is on the upwind side of the airplane (Figure 25). For instance, if the wind is from the left, you add left aileron and right rudder and forward slip to the left. If you're making left traffic and are high on the turn to final approach from base leg (Figure 23, positions A and B), you might make the turn and, when within 10 to 15 degrees of alignment with the runway add right rudder while still in a left bank (Figure 23, position C). This allows the airplane's motion to track the runway centerline while forward slipping to lose altitude. Since the wind is from your left, when it comes time to flare, you can easily convert the left forward slip into a left sideslip (Figure 25) to compensate for the left crosswind. You'd do this by releasing a little of the right rudder pressure you've been holding and allow the longitudinal axis to align itself parallel with the runway centerline. This choice is simply a matter of convenience.

On the other hand, if you're making left traffic and have a right crosswind (or vice versa), you'll have the nose (longitudinal axis) already pointed into the wind a bit more than necessary to add a crabbing component to the slip. This is very similar to what you would already be doing if you were on final approach with a right crosswind (flying in a right crab), correct? You'd be crabbing to the right, but in this instance you're crabbing and forward slipping to lose altitude. When you're ready to perform the roundout, you'd release the right rudder pressure, and add right aileron to transition to a right side slipping condition (Figure 24). So there's really not all that much difference in terms of effort, much less control manipulation, when it comes to making a forward slip into or with the wind. Ultimately, you'll make a forward slip in whichever way is most convenient for you as you turn to final approach.

The Slipping Turn

There is one more variation of the slip that you should know about. It's called a *slipping turn*. This technique is not as prominent in the United States as it is in Canada, where it's regularly taught. As you'd be hard pressed not to conclude from the name, a slipping turn is one where the airplane slips as it turns.

Since the slipping turn is typically started from a coordinated turn, you'll simply apply rudder opposite the direction of bank and point the nose a little toward the outside of the turn. You'll use less rudder pressure than you would in a normal forward slip in order to keep the airplane turning (too much rudder could, of course, stop the turn). When would you use such a thing? One example would be if you turn from downwind to base leg and find yourself extremely high and needing to slip way before reaching final approach (Figure 26). As you approach the extended runway centerline, you would release a little of the rudder pressure you're using to sustain the slip, allowing the airplane to turn.

Slipping a 767

There are additional reasons for slipping an airplane beyond just trying to lose altitude in the traffic pattern.

For instance, in July, 1983, an Air Canada Boeing 767 was cruising at 41,000 feet and managed to run out of fuel at about the halfway point between Montreal and Edmonton (a miscalculated fuel load meant less fuel than expected was on board). The captain managed to glide the airplane to a safe emergency landing at Gimli Industrial Park Airport in Gimli, Manitoba.

It happened that Captain Pearson was an experienced glider pilot. He possessed a particular set of skills that most airline pilots don't have. These skills involved assessing an airplane's glide potential and modifying that glide to accomplish a successful landing. That's just what Captain Pearson did when he found himself too high on the approach to Gimli. Instead of making a 360 degree turn to lose altitude, he placed the airplane in a forward slip and managed to land successfully with no serious harm to crew or passengers.

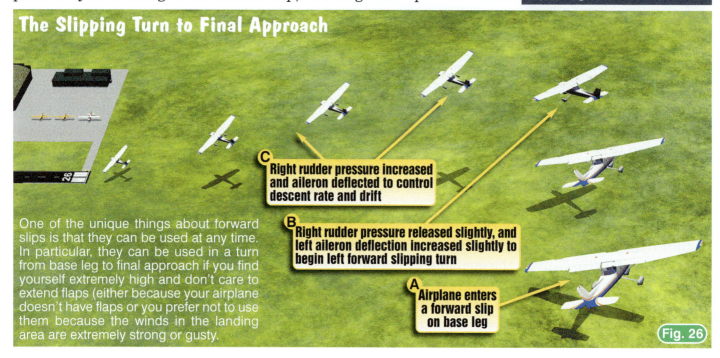

Fig. 26

Chapter 11: Crosswinds and Slips

Order Counts

As a final note on slips, keep in mind that a slip begins with a slip, *not* a skid. That's why it's always best to initiate a slip with aileron usage first, followed by rudder. Aileron application banks the airplane and yaws the nose in the opposite direction of turn, which fits the technical definition of a slip. As the nose yaws, the appropriate amount of opposite rudder pressure is added to either perform a forward or a sideslip. Some pilots start their slips by applying rudder first and induce a temporary skid before the slip. This is very poor technique, because it's dangerous if performed too close to the wing's critical angle of attack. After all, a skid at the moment of stall is how you enter a spin. So, apply aileron pressure then follow it with the appropriate application of rudder. This is how to keep the universe in balance.

More Advanced Landing Skills

Now you have a basic idea about how to land in a crosswind, as well as how to slip to lose altitude and correct for crosswind drift. I think you're ready to learn about some of the more advanced approach and landing skills you'll need as a pilot. These skills include power-on approaches to landings, landing on short and soft fields, accuracy landings and so on. So onward and earthward to the next chapter...and beyond.

Chapter 12

Advanced Landing Skills
Not All Runways Are Created Equal

It's hard to hide a bad landing. They don't fit under the bed or in a closet, and there are *always* those friends on board who will remind you about it on special occasions, such as every time they see you. So it pays to be proficient at getting an airplane down and stopped on a runway. This is, however, easier said than done in some circumstances.

It turns out that not all runways grow up to be long and wide; some become short and thin for their commissioning. Others never get the building materials they deserve and end up with sod or dirt surfaces. A few even rank as bona fide obstacle courses with trees, mountains, antennas, power lines, or chimneys located along the final approach path. Such runways can be perfectly acceptable places to land, but only if you have the skill to do so consistently. All you need is an angle, and this chapter will give it to you.

Short-Field Approaches and Landings—The Big Picture

Some runways are just plain short and they appear even shorter than they actually are the first time you try landing on them. Even when a runway looks long, it can have a prominent obstacle near the approach end that renders a significant portion unavailable for use during landing (Figure 1). That's why it's important for you to learn how to approach and land on a runway in the shortest possible distance, or the shortest possible distance after clearing an obstacle. This technique is known as a *short-field approach and landing*.

Before attempting a short-field landing at an unfamiliar airport, it's wise to perform a preliminary low altitude fly-by for a closer look at the landing environment. You don't want to be surprised by wires hanging from obstacles in the final approach path or difficult-to-see items such as potholes, stones, buffalo or other critters on the runway that are likely to make a short landing

Obstacles in The Approach Path
Courtesy: Matt Abrams
Fig. 1

thrilling while adding something to the airport restaurant's menu. You'll also want to evaluate any turbulence on final approach at altitudes closer to the obstacle. Given the slow airspeed associated with this type of approach, mechanical turbulence might suggest flying the approach at higher than normal airspeed for better airplane control (more on this later). If the runway is exceptionally short or other conditions make it not conducive to a safe landing, then go to Plan B. You do have a Plan B, right? The first thing you should do in considering a landing at Airport A is to formulate Plan B.

During the fly-by, you'll want to identify a spot on the runway where, based on your estimated landing speed, the airplane must touch down. This is important if you want to avoid running off the end of the runway, especially if there's a restaurant beyond the airport boundary (this is not what the restaurant means when it advertises the presence of a *drive through*, and dragging the buffalo along on top of the plane is not what they mean by *buffalo wings*). If there are no obstacles present along the final approach path, you'll want to choose a landing spot as close to the approach end of the runway as possible. Obstacles, however, require you to fly a steeper than normal approach while minimizing the touchdown roll so you can stop on the remaining runway.

Assessment of the airplane's stopping distance begins with the runway's length, its surface, and local obstacles. Information about all of these items can be found in the *Chart Supplement* (Figure 2). The question is, "How short is short? What makes a field a short field for purposes of landing?" The answer is, "It depends." It's obvious that if you need 1,000 feet of runway on which to land, then anything less than 1,000 feet is not only short, but unacceptably short. Don't go there. If the runway is exactly 1,000 feet in length, you could *theoretically* just make it—in theory. In practice, you should start preparing your explanation for the NTSB hearing at which you will testify (assuming you can even show up at your own NTSB hearing). Personally, I prefer to have at least 50% more runway than I actually need to get my airplane stopped. Now the question becomes, *How do you know how much runway you need to get your airplane down and stopped when approaching over an obstacle*? Here is where a visit to the POH can help.

The Chart Supplement and Runway Length

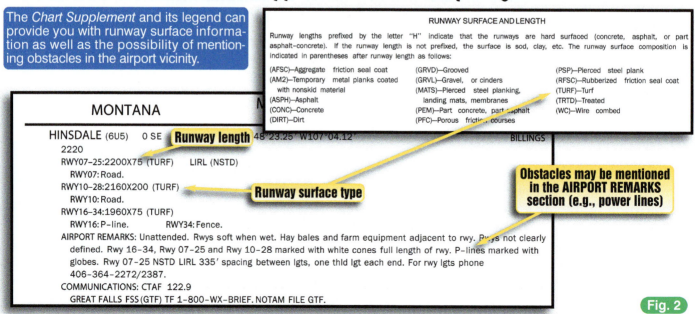

Fig. 2

Chapter 12 - Advanced Landing Skills

LANDING DISTANCE
FLAPS LOWERED TO 40 DEGREES - POWER OFF
HARD SURFACE RUNWAY - ZERO WIND

GROSS WEIGHT LBS	APPROACH SPEED IAS, MPH	AT SEA LEVEL & 59°F		AT 2500 & 50°F		AT 5000 & 41°F		AT 7500 & 32°F	
		GROUND ROLL	TOTAL TO CLEAR 50 FT OBS	GROUND ROLL	TOTAL TO CLEAR 50 FT OBS	GROUND ROLL	TOTAL TO CLEAR 50 FT OBS	GROUND ROLL	TOTAL TO CLEAR 50 FT OBS
1,600	60	445	1075	470	1135	495	1195	520	1255

NOTES: 1. Decrease the distances shown by 10% for each 4 knots of headwind.
2. Increase the distance by 10% for each 60 degrees F temperature increase above standard.
3. For operations on a dry, grass runway, increase distances (both "ground roll" and "total to clear 50ft obstacle") by 20% of the "total to clear 50 ft obstacle" figure.

Fig.3

The typical landing distance chart allows you to determine your airplane's ground roll (the time it takes to stop once the wheels make contact with the runway surface) and the total distance to clear a 50 foot obstacle (this distance includes the ground roll). These performance charts typically allow you to calculate landing distances for various types of environmental conditions such as temperature differences from standard and the specific type of landing surface (i.e., grass, dirt, etc.).

The POH for the airplane you are flying contains landing performance charts that provide the landing distances you can expect both in terms of *ground roll* and the *distance to clear an obstacle* (Figure 3). It is important to understand that the distance given as the distance to clear a 50-foot obstacle (the standard) *includes* the ground roll. If you subtract the ground roll from the 50-foot obstacle distance, you get the *minimum* distance down the runway where the plane could touch down after safely clearing a 50-foot obstacle at the threshold. Unless your plane is a helicopter, it is incapable of clearing a 50-foot obstacle and dropping straight down on the threshold.

These are provided as separate numbers because in the case where you are *not* landing over an obstacle, you can theoretically touch down right at the threshold and you then need to know only what the ground roll distance is to decide if the runway is long enough for a safe landing.

If you're landing on Runway 7-25 at Hinsdale field in Montana, the *Chart Supplement* indicates that the runway is 2,200 feet long. According to the performance chart, under standard conditions with no headwind, at a pressure altitude of 2,500 feet you'll need at least 1,135 feet of horizontal distance to clear a 50 foot obstacle, touch down and come to a complete stop on the runway. Since this runway is dry turf (dry grass), you'll need to increase the 50-foot obstacle distance by 20%. You will need a minimum of 1,362 feet to clear a 50-foot obstacle and come to a stop on this runway.

If there were *no* obstacle and you touched down right at the threshold, you would expect a ground roll of 697 feet. This comes from following the chart's instruction to increase the ground roll figure by 20% of the 50-foot obstacle distance. If such an obstacle existed for this approach, you could anticipate being on the ground and stopped just a bit beyond the midpoint of the runway. By subtracting the ground roll of 697 feet from the total landing distance of 1,362 feet, you can expect to have your wheels make runway contact at a little less than one-third of the runway's length beyond the landing threshold (or 665 feet from the threshold).

One of the more peculiar myths in aviation is that you must have a new airplane as well as test pilot flying skills to obtain the performance found in airplane performance charts. Well, that's not completely accurate. Yes, the part about having a new airplane is accurate in the sense that older airplanes don't necessarily perform as well as newer ones do. This statement, however, is more accurate for takeoff than it is for landings, because takeoff performance is clearly dependent on engine performance.

During landing, as long as you can control your airspeed properly and know how to properly decelerate the airplane after touchdown, you'll obtain something very close to the landing performance shown in your charts. So give those charts the credit they are due, but remain out of doo-doo by rejecting any thought of landing on a runway that's only as long as your calculated landing distance. Believe me when I say that you'll eventually come up short, and you'll take it in the shorts when you do. Wise pilots (which includes you) will always consider chart figures to be bare minimums, and add in their own safety factor.

Where the Short-Field Approach Really Begins

An important point to keep in mind is that the actual act of making the short-field landing begins on the downwind leg, not on final approach. That's because there's a bit of planning involved when flying this procedure.

Your objective when setting up the landing approach is to give yourself enough room and thus enough time to work your plan. That often means flying a slightly wider pattern for ease in configuring the airplane for landing. While your landing might be short, that doesn't mean your time in the pattern has to be short, too.

On the downwind leg you'll want to have your gear extended (if retractable) and at least partial flaps extended when abeam the threshold of the landing runway (Figure 4). The flight path objective is to turn base at a point where your descent rate allows you to begin a final approach for landing at least 500 feet above ground level. Why 500 feet? As you begin your descent to a specific spot on the runway and possibly over an obstacle, you'll need a little time to properly evaluate your glidepath, and modify it if necessary.

Arriving on final approach at 500 feet AGL makes it a lot easier to estimate the glidepath

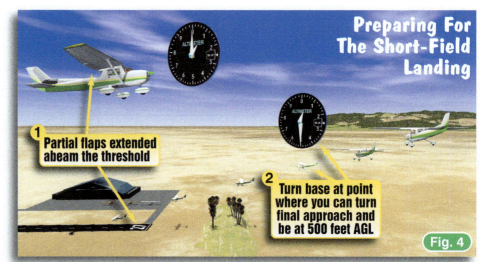

Your objective in preparing for the short-field landing is to turn base and begin a descent in such a way that you'll end up turning onto final approach at least 500 feet above ground level.

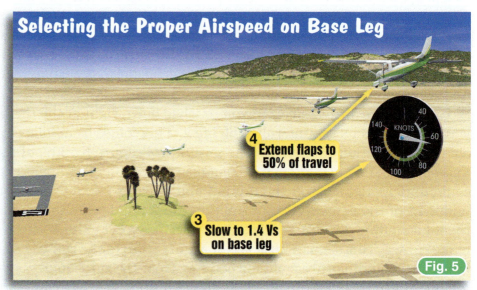

On base leg you'll want to extend flaps half way and slow to a speed that's 40% above the airplane's stall speed (1.4 Vs).

Chapter 12 - Advanced Landing Skills

needed to clear any obstacle, compared to starting the same procedure at a higher altitude (such as 1,000 feet AGL).

Think of this as aiming a gun at a target. The closer you get to the target, the easier it is to hit that target (assuming your target doesn't run off into the woods because it knows it's deer hunting season). In a similar way, being a little lower on approach makes it easier to establish the proper glidepath needed to clear an obstacle and land on a specific runway spot.

Proper approach planning

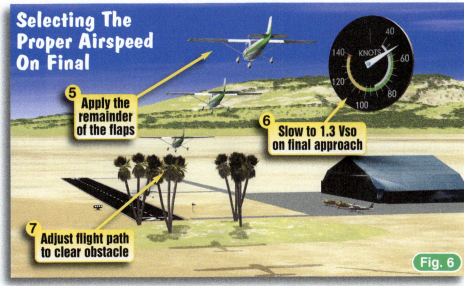

Selecting The Proper Airspeed On Final
5. Apply the remainder of the flaps
6. Slow to 1.3 Vso on final approach
7. Adjust flight path to clear obstacle

Fig. 6

As you turn onto final approach, you'll apply the remaining flaps and slow to a speed that's 30% above the airplane's full flap stall speed (1.3 Vso).

means slowing down to 1.4 Vs on base leg and having at least 50% of the flaps extended (Figure 5). As you turn final approach, your objective is to apply full flaps and decrease your airspeed to that recommended by the manufacturer for short-field approaches (Figure 6). Most of the time this will be approximately 30% above the airplane's full flap stalling speed, or 1.3 Vso (see sidebar: *Estimating Stall Speed With Variable Flaps Conditions*). If your POH doesn't recommend such a speed, then 1.3 Vso is a perfectly reasonable value to use. It's important to remember that this slower speed places the airplane near the bottom of the total drag curve (the "full flap" total drag curve in this case). That means the induced drag will increase as the angle of attack increases during the landing flare, resulting in an airplane that's less likely to float during the roundout and flare.

Now that you have a basic idea about how to accomplish the short-field approach, let's look more closely at the details. Specifically, we'll examine short-field approaches and landings with and without obstacles along the final approach path and the techniques used to fly each safely.

Estimating Stall Speed With Variable Flap Conditions

Keep the following in mind when operating older airplanes (typically pre-1980 *certificated* airplanes) having airspeed indicator color codes that read as *calibrated airspeeds*, CAS (color codes on post-1980 certificated airplanes might read as *indicated airspeed* values and not reflect significant pitot/static airspeed errors at speeds above V_{S1}). A value of 1.4 Vs is 40% above the airplane's stall speed for a given configuration (half flaps extended on base leg, for instance). Here's where you'll look at the difference between the beginning of the white arc (full flap stalling speed) and the green arc (no flap stalling speed) and multiply the middle value by 1.4 (Picture-1). In other words, if the full flap stalling speed (Vso) is 40 knots and the no-flap stalling speed is 50 knots, then 45 knots is a good estimate for a stall speed at half flaps. Take 40% of 45 knots (10% is 4.5, so 4 times 4.5 equals 18) and add that onto 45 to obtain 63 knots as your approach speed on base leg.

Remember that 63 knots is a calibrated airspeed on the airplane referenced here. Therefore, you'll want to use your airspeed calibration chart to determine the indicated airspeed (IAS) you must fly on the airspeed indicator to achieve a CAS of 63 knots (Picture-2). In this example, you'll need to fly approximately 59 knots on the airspeed indicator (IAS) to achieve a CAS of 63 knots. We'll also assume that your airplane is at or near its maximum gross weight here. If this were not so, then you'd have to make a correction for a reduction in stall speed based on a reduction in weight. As a general rule, your stall speed will decrease by 1% for every 2% decrease in weight. In smaller airplanes, however, this isn't often much of a concern, mainly because smaller airplanes aren't flown at a significant percentage of weight below their maximum gross weight. In many smaller and lighter airplanes your landing speed is based on a specific gross weight as shown in Picture #3. Other charts, however, offer you an approach speed based on variable weights as described in *Postflight Briefing #12-2*.

AIRSPEED CALIBRATION CH. Picture-2

FLAPS UP					
KIAS	50	60	70	80	90
KCAS	50	63	72	81	89
FLAPS 40°					
KIAS	40	50	60	70	80
KCAS	40	54	64	71	80

KIAS = Knots Indicated Airspeed

LANDING DISTANCE

Picture-3		AT SEA LEVEL & 59°F	
GROSS WEIGHT LBS	APPROACH SPEED IAS, MPH	GROUND ROLL	TOTAL TO CLEAR 50 FT OBS
1,600	60	445	1075

Short-Field Landing Without an Obstacle Present

There are fundamentally two types of short-field landings. Those where there is *no* obstacle, and those where there is an obstacle close to the threshold. In both cases, it's all about learning to wrangle the angle. Let's start with the no-obstacle case.

Without an obstacle on final approach, your objective is to land as close to the landing threshold as is safely possible (Figure 7). The angle of the glidepath isn't restricted and doesn't necessarily have to be steep. It need only be accurate enough to place you on the spot where the threshold begins (OK, a few inches or a few feet beyond that spot). It's entirely reasonable to fly this approach at a normal glidepath angle, power-on or power-off.

Short-Field Landing Without an Obstacle

1. Stabilized approach at 1.3 Vso
2. Glidepath need not be steep since no obstacle present
3. Touchdown on beginning of available landing surface

Fig. 7

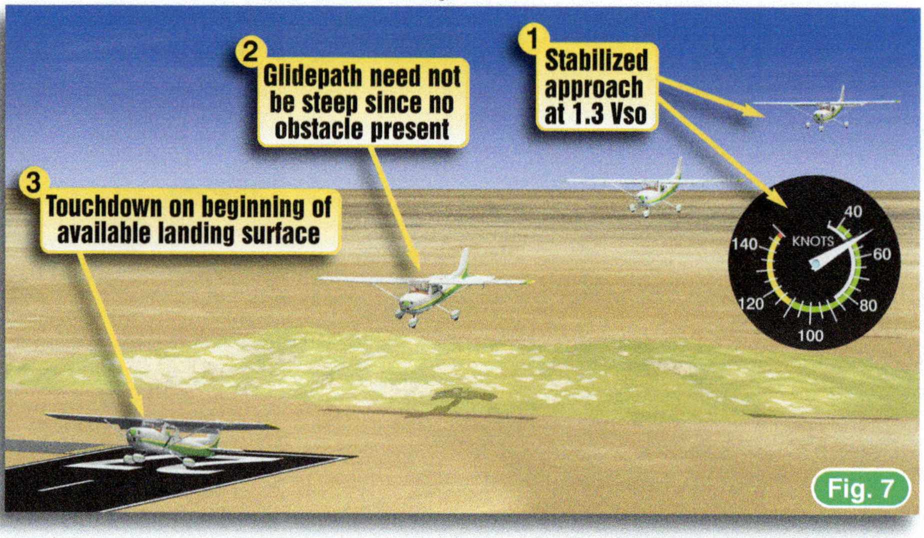

When no obstacle is present, the objective of the short-field approach and landing is to land at the slowest but safest speed possible on or near the beginning of the available landing surface.

After turning final, you'll add full flaps, trim the airplane for the desired speed and use a combination of pitch and power to establish a *stabilized approach*, which is an approach where the airspeed and descent rate remain constant. What you want is an approach with a descent rate that takes you directly to the selected landing spot at your minimum approach airspeed. You're not concerned about making the steepest descent here since there is no obstacle present. If you prefer, you can carry a little bit of power to correct for slight variations in glidepath (which is valuable if you find yourself high on approach. See sidebar: *A Practical Pitch-Power Technique for Short-Field Landings*).

Since the runway threshold (we'll use the runway numbers here) is the ideal landing spot, you'll use the *stationary spot method* to identify the touchdown location and the *trapezoidal method* for glidepath evaluation, as discussed in Chapter Nine. When landing on many really short fields, you typically won't find a VASI to assist you in evaluating the glidepath. That's because these runways tend to be so short and/or have sufficiently tall nearby obstacles that they can't be flown using the typical 3 to 3.5

A Practical Pitch-Power Technique for Short-Field Landings

In Chapter Three on Page 3-23, we discussed three different methods of controlling your airspeed and glidepath during an approach. The short-field landing lends itself very well to using the *elevator-airspeed* technique for three good reasons. First, even though you won't be flying on the back side of the power curve at 1.3 Vso, you're not that far from it. Therefore, it's wise to use the technique that favors using engine power to control your descent rate. If you accidentally slip into the region of reversed command, you're less likely to try stretching a glide by pulling aft on the elevator.

The second reason is that a short-field approach without an obstacle is often best flown with just a small amount of power (150-200 RPM) applied. Yes, the descent rate isn't maximized here, but there's no obstacle to clear, either. Since you can always add power to reduce the descent rate, now you have power to reduce if you find you're going to be a bit too high (the assumption is that you're already using max flaps and forward slips aren't practical).

The third reason the elevator-airspeed technique is favored for short-field landings is that some airplanes with high performance wings need a burst of engine power during the landing flare as they slip into the region of reversed command. In these types of airplanes, if you started to sink at 10 feet above the ground and pulled aft on the elevator control, you'd most likely slam onto the runway. High, slow flares make it easy to damage the airplane (and your neck). Your elevator is essentially ineffective in these airplanes when operating deep in the region of reversed command.

The Elevator-Airspeed Control Use Technique

Chapter 12 - Advanced Landing Skills

degree glidepath. VASIs also have glidepaths that intersect the landing surface several hundred feet beyond the runway threshold (a distance you can't afford to waste if you hope to stop on the runway). So using your eyeballs to determine the proper glidepath really comes in handy in these situations.

Because of your slower speed, it's not unreasonable for the stall horn to activate during the landing flare. That's a good thing. It shows that you're not carrying any excessive speed into the landing flare. For instance, when flying a short-field approach in your south-of-the-border, homebuilt airplane—the Tamale—you might see a stall warning horn/light activate during the landing flare. If you didn't, then you probably landed hot, meaning you landed a hot Tamale, which isn't advantageous on a short field.

Your flare and subsequent touchdown should be made close to stall attitude with the throttle closed. Upon touchdown, gently lower the nose to the runway and apply sufficiently strong braking to slow the airplane down without skidding the tires. You'll also apply sufficient elevator back pressure during deceleration to keep from over-compressing the nose gear. Whatever you do, don't even think about using aerodynamic braking during landing. No matter how much you wish it to be, you are not a space shuttle and you aren't landing at the Bonneville Salt Flats, either. You're in a small airplane that has real brakes. Use them.

There's one more very important thing to consider. Some pilots like to raise the flaps immediately after touchdown on a short-field landing. This helps transfer the weight from the wings to the wheels more quickly, which aids in braking effectiveness. Unfortunately, it also aids in increasing your gear-up landing potential, too (which makes a short-field landing *really* short).

When landing complex airplanes (those having retractable landing gear), it's very easy to mistake the landing gear handle for the flap handle. This becomes even more likely during short-field approaches when you are already a bit distracted by how short the runway actually is. It's true that flap and gear handles have different shapes, but so do snowflakes and you can't always tell them apart quickly, can you? My advice is to leave the flaps alone when and where possible and concentrate on stopping the airplane on the runway.

I'm not a fanatic about this advice. If you absolutely need to raise those flaps to stop the airplane on the runway, then raise them, regardless of whether you're in a fixed or retractable gear airplane. Just remember that while we benefit from our good habits, we must bear the burden of our bad ones. Take some time to consider just why you decided to land at this airport instead of landing somewhere with a slightly longer (and safer) runway.

Once the main gear are in contact with the runway, pull that throttle full aft, lower the nose wheel to the ground and apply moderate braking. Hold the elevator far enough aft to take the pressure off the nose strut as you apply those brakes (but don't let the nose gear rise from the runway since you'll need it for steering). Whatever you do, don't skid the tires, especially if you're landing on a grass strip. This would make it very easy to lose control of your airplane and turn it into a very expensive lawnmower. That would be a very sod story.

Now we're ready to examine the details of landing on a short field having an obstacle along its approach path. This is the most challenging—and in my opinion, the most fun—type of short-field landing to perform. It will give you a whole new angle on the short-field challenge.

The Lighter Side Of Aviation

Performing short-field landings in light sport airplanes, can offer you a big surprise when reducing power during the roundout and flare. Many of these airplanes will decelerate quickly, reaching the region of reversed command much sooner than you would normally expect when flaring.

These are typically light sport machines having high performance airfoils that are great for developing lift right up until the time they aren't. As the critical angle of attack is approached, the airflow over the wings quickly separates, resulting in an immediate and significant loss of lift. Flare too high and get too slow, and you'll find that you quickly run out of aft stick performance.

Landing airplanes that decelerate and/or stall crisply requires you to be quick on the draw with the throttle during the flare. A quick burst of power can arrest those sudden and unanticipated descents. Said another way, in some airplanes your throttle becomes a flight control that's just as important as the elevator during the landing flare.

To remain an aviation citizen in good standing with your insurance company, the moment you sense you're running out of aft stick response during the flare, move that throttle forward to arrest the descent (or the anticipated descent). Consider this a citizen's arrest.

Short-Field Landing Over an Obstacle

A short-field landing over an obstacle is the granddaddy of short-field landings. I don't say this because after doing one you feel old, worn out and in need of a nap. I say it because there's something solid in your flight path that you must avoid, while still getting the airplane safely stopped on the runway.

An obstacle? Really? Why would someone place an obstacle along the final approach path to a runway? Well, what makes you think someone did? It's more likely that someone put a runway in front of an obstacle that has been around for years, or even since the dawn of time. More than one flying farmer has awakened one morning with the inspiration to build a grass strip on an unused portion of his plantation—the unused portion that lies just beyond a grove of giant trees or towering asparagus spears.

If you made a standard approach over such an obstacle without using short-field techniques, you might leave a great deal of very valuable landing surface behind you (Figure 8). Given a short enough runway, you might not be able to safely stop on the remaining landing surface. Applying short-field approach and landing techniques allows you to clear the obstacle and land on a spot much closer to the beginning of the runway.

For the purposes of flight training and your private or commercial pilot examination, your instructor will play *make believe*

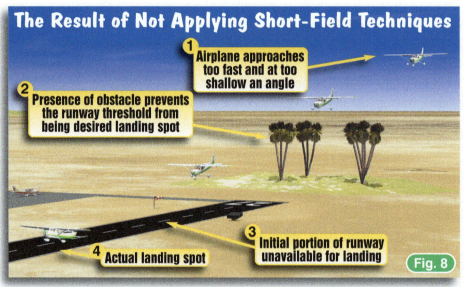

The presence of an obstacle along the final approach path can turn a runway of acceptable length into a shorter one. Using normal (non-short-field) approach techniques renders the initial portion of the runway unavailable for landing.

with you by having you imagine that a 50-foot obstacle exists on final approach somewhere close to the landing threshold. When he or she does, just play along as if you believe it's really there. Don't say, "That's unbelievable" or "Why would they do that?" or worse yet, "I don't see anything." Your objective is to land as close to the runway threshold as possible, meaning that you'll have to descend steeply over the no-see-um obstacle in a stabilized approach to a selected spot on the runway. This spot must be at or before the place where the remaining runway is more than the chart-given ground roll. Think of it as the no-crash-um spot.

The short-field landing over an obstacle (we'll assume an obstacle is involved from now on) involves a full flap, power-off approach on final, since that yields the steepest descent possible. This, however, implies that you were able to turn onto final approach at a minimum of 500 feet AGL at the precise distance where power can be reduced to flight idle, full flaps added, and a perfect stabilized descent established that clears the obstacle. Pulling this off might require more experience than you've acquired up to this point and more luck than you've ever had. Since we live in the practical and not the ideal world, let's look for a much more realistic way of performing a short-field landing.

The Practical Short-Field Landing Approach

Let's get real by making sure that your turn onto final approach positions you at least 500 feet AGL and between a half and three-quarters of a mile from the runway threshold. You can easily manage your power on base leg to place you at this altitude on final approach.

Chapter 12 - Advanced Landing Skills

When you turn final, your objective is to fly a steeper glidepath over the obstacle to a spot on the runway located as close to the landing threshold as possible. You'll use the same *trapezoidal* and *stationary spot* technique described in Chapter Nine to help evaluate your glidepath. If you've turned onto final approach at a distance of a half to three-quarters of a mile from the landing threshold, then your glidepath should be relatively steep, mainly because you won't need much, if any power and you'll be using full flaps (Figure 9, position A).

If you turn onto final approach farther from the runway threshold, then your glidepath is likely to be much shallower, which will require the use of power. The likely result of a shallower glidepath is a touchdown at a point farther from the runway threshold (Figure 9, position B). This is why I mentioned that the planning for flying the short-field approach begins on the downwind leg.

If you turn final approach too close to the runway threshold, you will certainly clear the obstacle or obstacles with a power-off, full flap descent. The problem here is that you'll clear the 50-foot asparagus spears by way too much altitude, resulting in a touchdown that is farther down the runway than desired. This defeats the purpose of a short-field approach, doesn't it? In such a case it's often wiser to go-around and make another approach.

On the other hand, what do you do if your turn onto final approach places you at an excessive distance from the runway threshold? Well, performing a go-around and coming back for another approach is,

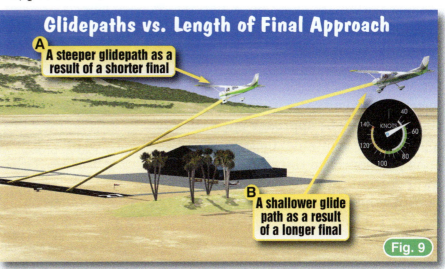

Turning onto final approach at a distance of 1/2 to 3/4 of a mile sets you up to make a relatively steep descent over the obstacle(s) in your flight path.

Turning onto final approach at less than 500 feet AGL or at an excessive distance from the threshold results in a glidepath that intersects the obstacle(s).

once again, a perfectly reasonable option. Then again, I try to be a practical pilot as long as it allows me to be a safe pilot, too. In this instance, it's perfectly reasonable to make a temporary modification to your glidepath that better positions you to clear the obstacle and land on the desired spot.

Let's say your turn-for-home plan didn't quite work out and you've turned onto final approach at an excessive distance from the threshold. If you immediately apply full flaps and continue the descent, there is a risk you will turn the 50-foot obstacle into a 40-foot obstacle. Your glidepath would be much too shallow to let you clear the obstacle (Figure 10). The most practical thing to do here is apply sufficient power and reduce the glidepath angle until you're where you should be. Then you'd apply the remaining flaps and reduce power which results in a stabilized approach to just the right spot.

Figure 11 shows how this problem might look from the cockpit as you turn onto final approach. It's clear that a full flap descent to the intended landing spot would not be prudent, even if you were in the tree trimming business.

The best way to handle these situations is to reduce your descent rate by adding power and raising the nose to maintain your present approach speed. Delay applying any additional flaps (Figure 12).

As you approach the runway at a shallower descent rate, you'll eventually reach a point where you can apply full flaps, slow to 1.3 Vso, progressively reduce power to clear the obstacle and trim for the final descent (Figure 13).

How do you know where that point is? Experience, that's how. By this time in your training you should have sufficient experience to make this assessment. Nevertheless, it's your eyes that provide the clue (Figure 13).

Now, I want to be very clear here that the technique of *temporarily* shallowing out the glidepath isn't a recommendation to routinely turn onto final approach at a *low altitude*, level out just above obstacle height using power, and then pull the power to idle and dump the nose for landing when you've passed the obstacle (Figure 14). That is very poor technique and it's potentially unsafe.

First, there's nothing stabilized about this type of approach. The immediate reduction of power at such a slow speed makes it hard to quickly estimate how far to lower the nose to maintain that airspeed. It's much too easy to mismanage your

Cockpit Clue - You're Too Low on Final

If you turn onto final approach too far from the threshold during the short-field approach, you might see the desired landing spot very close to or even below the top of the obstacle to be cleared.

Temporarily Reducing Descent Rate

By applying power and raising the nose slightly to reduce your descent rate, you'll eventually place yourself in a better position from which to commenced the descent to the desired landing spot.

Cockpit Clue - In Position to Clear Obstacle

When an obstacle-free approach to the desired landing spot becomes possible, resume steeper short-field approach descent.

Chapter 12 - Advanced Landing Skills

airspeed control in this condition. You might easily end up with an increased rate of descent at too slow an airspeed with insufficient elevator authority to arrest the descent prior to contacting the runway. This becomes even more likely if you enter the region of reversed command, which I'll explain shortly.

Second, wind currents near the ground and over an obstacle can produce an unpredictable effect on your airplane's performance. If the obstacle you're trying to clear consist of buildings or thick treelines or ridges (something relatively dense, which deflects, chops or churns the air flowing over it), it's possible for the mechanical turbulence generated from the obstacle to make the airplane difficult to control during a sudden reduction of power.

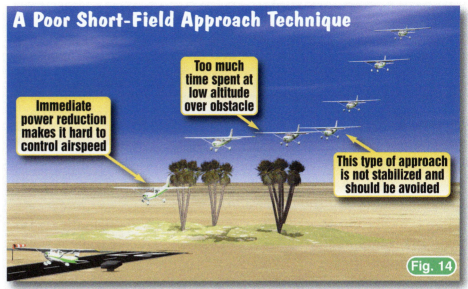

One of the things you want to avoid when making a short-field approach is to level off just above the obstacle, fly over the obstacle, then pull power, dump the nose and land. This is very poor technique and should be avoided.

Finally, an immediate power reduction over the obstacle does not give you time to evaluate the resulting glidepath. Sure, you're over the obstacle at a low altitude, but that doesn't mean you won't misjudge and descend dangerously close to it or even into it.

This is why it's always better to begin the final portion of the short-field approach in a stabilized condition starting at approximately 500 feet AGL. At this altitude, you are in a good position to evaluate your proximity to the obstacle during the descent.

Keep in mind that a short-field approach *without* an obstacle is typically flown with some power applied. In that case your main objective is to control the glidepath to reach the beginning of the runway. You can fly a glidepath of any safe, reasonable angle since there's nothing in your way. Approaches having an obstacle are *ideally* flown with power reduced to idle after passing the obstacle. This gives you the steepest descent possible over the obstacle, which ultimately provides you with the most runway on which to land and stop the airplane.

On the other hand, larger, heavier single-engine airplanes often require some power usage on a short-field approach regardless of whether or not an obstacle is present. This helps prevent exceeding the maximum allowed descent rate. For example, the POH of one popular six-seat, single-engine airplane recommends that power be used to prevent exceeding a descent rate of 900 FPM on final during a short-field approach. The reason for this limitation is that airplanes in this weight range have more mass to redirect during the roundout and flare. The slower airspeed associated with a short-field landing might not provide the elevator authority necessary to round out and flare these airplanes if the descent rate is excessive.

The Truth About True Airspeed and High Altitude Airports

Making a short-field landing at a high altitude airport is a little different than making one to a low altitude airport. The reason being that your true airspeed increases approximately 2% for every 1,000 foot of altitude increase. For example, when making a short-field landing to a sea level airport in a calm wind at 50 knots indicated airspeed, your groundspeed will be approximately 50 knots. Performing a short-field landing to an airport at 10,000 feet in a calm wind, you'd use the same indicated approach speed, but your groundspeed will be greater than 50 knots. In fact, it will be (2% x 10) 20% greater, or 60 knots. It's clear that your landing distance will be greater and this will be reflected in the longer ground roll and distance to clear an obstacle as shown in your performance charts. What you might not be familiar with is the perception of moving faster over the ground. Pilots often react to this by attempting to prematurely slow the airplane down as they approach the runway and sometimes end up stalling several feet above the landing surface. Some pilots might be over aggressive on the brakes and either damage their tires or lose control of their airplane. Let the flyer beware.

Either way, make a smooth, progressive reduction in power as you begin your descent on final. This provides a less dramatic transition to a nose-down attitude and allows you to better manage your airspeed during the transition.

In a typical (non-short-field) approach, you will normally fly final at 30% above stall speed (unless your POH recommends otherwise, of course). During a short-field approach, you will very specifically fly at precisely this speed. Every knot is of note when you're shooting for maximum performance in order to deal with minimum runway. You'll also use full flaps on every short-field approach. This means that any mismanagement of airplane attitude can result in the airplane losing airspeed quickly, perhaps bringing it to or very near its stall speed.

Given that you are flying slow with the potential for slowing down quickly during short-field approaches, you definitely want to know a little more about the *region of reversed command*. While it's true that a 30% margin above stall speed keeps you out of the region of reversed command in the typical small general aviation airplane, it doesn't keep you out by much. And once you are *in* the region of reversed command, things get a little weird, though it's not all bad news. So let's examine this region in more detail. In particular, we'll look at a few oddities that you might find useful when landing on a short field.

The Region of Reversed Command and Short-Field Landings

The essential feature of the region of reversed command is that a decrease in airspeed requires an increase in power to maintain altitude or your present descent rate. Figure 15 reveals how this appears on a traditional power curve for a small training airplane. The power curve (green line) represents the power-airspeed combination necessary for the airplane to hold altitude. For instance, at positions Y and Z, the airplane can hold altitude at two different airspeeds (54 and 76 knots, respectively) as long as the engine and propeller are producing 65% thrust horsepower. Now let's see what happens if you keep your power setting constant and vary the airspeed by raising or lowering the nose only.

Let's assume that you are at 57 knots (position A) with the power constant. In this instance, you are able to easily maintain your altitude. If you slowly pull back on the eleva-

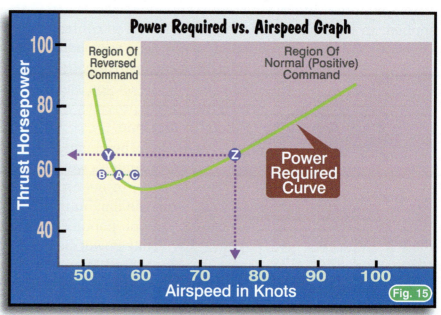

In the region of positive command, an aft pull on the elevator results in climb (at least temporarily). In the region of reversed command, however, an aft pull on the elevator results in a descent unless power is added immediately. The region of reversed command (the yellow "left" portion of this graphic) often begins at 75% to 85% of the airplane's best glide speed.

Chapter 12 - Advanced Landing Skills

tor control and let the airspeed decrease (position B) without adding additional power, your airplane is now operating behind the power curve (to the left and below it). It will start descending unless you immediately add power. Pulling further aft on the elevator won't result in a climb. If, however, you slowly lower the nose and increase your airspeed from position A to position C, the airplane will begin climbing. Yes, that's a strange

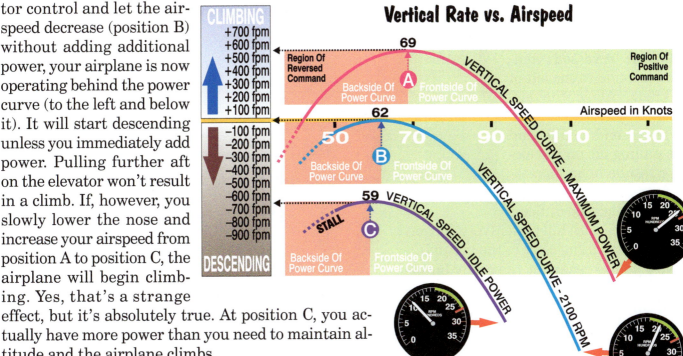

Fig. 16

effect, but it's absolutely true. At position C, you actually have more power than you need to maintain altitude and the airplane climbs.

Keep in mind that pulling back or pushing forward on the elevator control *quickly* might actually produce a temporary climb or descent respectively, because you're trading on the airplane's momentum to move up or down. You will, however, eventually see the airplane behave in the reversed manner, as described.

It's important to understand that your airplane has many power curves—one for each power setting to be exact. Since idle power is considered a power setting, this means that the region of reversed command still exists when the airplane is in a power-off descent. Let's see how this works with a slightly different version of the traditional power curve.

Instead of using a *power required* curve, let's examine three *vertical speed curves* based on three different power settings (Figure 16). These curves are not typically found in your POH, but you can easily calculate them for your particular airplane. Climb to a safe altitude, establish the desired power value, and adjust the attitude to obtain some higher speed (say 100 knots). Note the rate on your VSI. Then slow the airplane down in 10 knot increments and note the new climb or descent rate. These curves will shift slightly with altitude, but the difference isn't significant for our purposes.

Figure 16 shows three vertical speed curves for a typical small general aviation airplane. There's a curve for 2,500 RPM (climb power), for 2,100 RPM (low cruise power) and for 1,100 RPM (idle power). As I mentioned in Chapter Four, each vertical speed curve has a hump or peak that's associated with a specific airspeed and rate of climb or descent. At maximum power, the airplane's *best rate of climb* (Vy) occurs at 69 knots (Figure 16, position A) and produces a 550 fpm climb rate. At 2,100 RPM, the airspeed required to hold altitude is 62 knots, as shown in Figure 16, position B (the power required to maintain altitude varies slightly with altitude). When power is set to flight idle, the minimum sink rate occurs at 59 knots and is found at Figure 16, position C.

Each vertical speed curve also has regions of *reversed* and *positive* command. In the region of reversed command, an aft pull on the yoke and subsequent slowing of the airplane results in either a decreased rate of climb (the 2,500 RPM curve) or an increasing descent rate (the 2,100 and 1,100 RPM curves). With respect to flying the final portion of a short-field approach, you're interested in the 1,100 RPM vertical speed curve since this represents the airplane with its throttle set to idle thrust (the condition you're most likely to use on short final during this approach).

The takeaway point here is that when the power is reduced to flight idle, the region of reversed command is found to the left of 59 knots. Allow the airplane to slow to less than 59 knots and you'll find that pulling aft on the elevator results in an increasing descent rate—a descent rate that might be difficult to arrest even with full power (very dangerous when operating close to the ground).

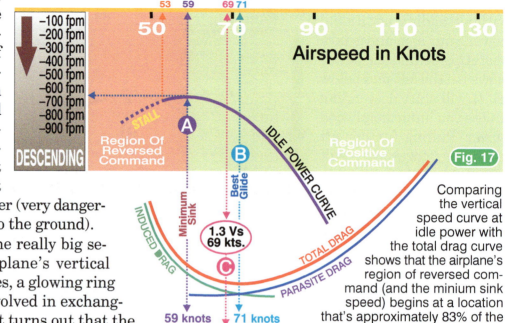

Comparing the vertical speed curve at idle power with the total drag curve shows that the airplane's region of reversed command (and the minium sink speed) begins at a location that's approximately 83% of the airplane's best glide speed.

Now you're ready for the really big secret revealed by your airplane's vertical speed curve (normally robes, a glowing ring and a wooden staff are involved in exchanging secrets on this level). It turns out that the region of reversed command for many smaller airplanes in a power-off descent typically begins at approximately 10-15% above the airplane's stall speed (Figure 17, position A). The airplane in this example stalls at 53 knots, with 59 knots representing an 11% increase above stall speed. (I'm using the clean configuration in this example for clarity, but the principle applies to full flaps with the curves shifting to the left slightly and the accompanying airspeeds obviously being a bit less.)

The purple-colored *vertical speed-idle power* curve in Figure 17 locates the airplane's stall speed at 53 knots and the minimum sink speed (Figure 17, position A) at 59 knots. To the left of the minimum sink speed is the region of reversed command. Moving to the bottom part of this graphic, you'll see the total drag curve (in red) for this airplane with the lowest point of the total drag curve located at position B. This is also known as the airplane's best glide speed, or L/D max.

At an approach speed of 1.3 Vs (Figure 17, position C) or 69 knots, you are below *this* airplane's best glide speed but above its minimum sink speed. This is the case with many smaller airplanes when approaching at 30% above stall speed (this can, however, vary between airplanes).

During the power-off descent at 69 knots, pulling aft on the elevator results in a *decreasing* descent rate. Why? The airplane is in the region of positive command. As your airspeed decreases, you'll reach the minimum power-off descent rate at a speed of 59 knots (Figure 17, position A). Once you reach 59 knots and continue to slow down, you're in the region of reversed command. Pulling further aft on the yoke now results in an *increase* in the airplane's rate of descent. Ooohhh. Magic.

The takeaway point here is that at 1.3 Vs you are *not* in the region of reversed command when flying your typical general aviation airplane. But you're lurking not far from its edge, and if you go over the edge more will suddenly be less, up will suddenly be down, and life will be different. This is why most POHs recommend short-field approach speeds no lower than 1.3 Vso (or 1.2 Vso in some cases).

Suppose you became distracted or got a bit sloppy with the flight controls when approaching at 1.3 Vs and let the airspeed decrease below your minimum sink speed. Now the airplane has strayed into the region of reversed command. Raising the nose without adding power increases your descent rate. Straying into the region of reversed command becomes even more likely when making short-field approaches in airplanes with high-drag flaps, such as the Cessna 150 or an older 172. The induced drag associated with slow speeds in these airplanes makes it very easy to decelerate quickly.

Chapter 12 - Advanced Landing Skills

Enter the region of reversed command and you'll need to be *Johnny on the spot* at adding power and/or lowering the nose (if you're not already too close to the ground) to reduce your descent rate. Delay adding power and you might end up as *Johnny is a spot* on the runway.

As a final note, notice that the minimum sink for the airplane in Figure 17 is 12 knots below the airplane's best glide speed of 71 knots but only 10 knots below our typical approach speed of 1.3 Vs (yes, clean configuration here, but the principle applies to any flap configuration). So how do you find your airplane's minimum sink speed? Well, you won't find it in your POH, since the regulations don't require that it be listed. The typical minimum sink speed for smaller airplanes is approximately 75% to 85% of the airplane's best glide speed. The very best way to find this speed is to fly the airplane at various slow speeds with power off and observe the VSI readings. The speed offering the lowest VSI indication wins. There's nothing like an experiment to make this assessment and you don't have to be a member of the Society of Experimental Test Pilots to do one, either.

The Roundout and Flare on Short-Field Approaches

During the final portion of the short-field landing, you won't have much of an airspeed margin above stall. This is why you'll want to be especially familiar with how the region of reversed command affects your ability to round out and flare the airplane for landing.

As you begin the roundout, your airspeed should be no higher at 1.3 Vso (full flaps assumed here) as shown in Figure 18, position A. This means that you are beginning the roundout in the region of positive command. That's positive. As you pull aft on the elevator control, the airspeed will decrease and the descent rate will also decrease. This is precisely what's supposed to happen in the region of positive command. It's what allows you to properly round out and flare the airplane for landing.

As the airspeed continues to decrease in the flare, you'll enter the region of reversed command (Figure 18, position B). This isn't a concern to you as long as your wheels are only a few inches above the runway, which is where they should be when flaring, right? Right.

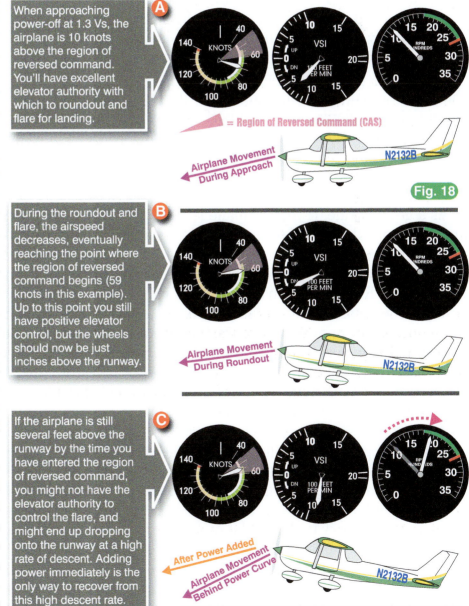

Elevator Control Authority and the Region of Reversed Command

A: When approaching power-off at 1.3 Vs, the airplane is 10 knots above the region of reversed command. You'll have excellent elevator authority with which to roundout and flare for landing.

= Region of Reversed Command (CAS)

B: During the roundout and flare, the airspeed decreases, eventually reaching the point where the region of reversed command begins (59 knots in this example). Up to this point you still have positive elevator control, but the wheels should now be just inches above the runway.

C: If the airplane is still several feet above the runway by the time you have entered the region of reversed command, you might not have the elevator authority to control the flare, and might end up dropping onto the runway at a high rate of descent. Adding power immediately is the only way to recover from this high descent rate.

Fig. 18

Despite being on the back side of the power curve, the airplane most likely has just enough forward energy to allow you to pull aft on the elevator and squeak those wheels gently onto the runway (if you don't hear the squeak, then feel free to make the squeak yourself. Passengers can't tell the difference).

On the other hand, if you began the roundout or flare too high above the runway (Figure 18, position C), it's entirely possible that you could blast right through the airplane's minimum sink speed and into the region of reversed command. For instance, if you're 10 feet above the runway in the region of reversed command and pulling aft on the yoke, it's very likely that you'll experience an increase in descent rate. This is precisely what you'd expect to happen in the region of reversed command. Unfortunately, this results in the bottom falling out of your airplane. Now that's just a figure of speech. The bottom of the fuselage doesn't actually fall away from the airplane, but you will certainly feel as if you're falling as you and the airplane drop to the runway. Here is where you'll immediately add sufficient power (if not before) to arrest the sudden descent rate. This, however, assumes you added power quickly enough and have enough of it available to stop or at least reduce the descent rate. Not all small airplanes have sufficiently powerful engines to make this happen quickly.

During any short-field approach, you need to be ready with the throttle to arrest any descent rate that might occur from rounding out or flaring at too high an altitude. This is especially important when flying airplanes with high performance wings, where there's a rapid decrease in lift when the wings reach their critical angle of attack. Several light sport airplanes fit into this category. In airplanes with these types of wings, it's not unusual to be in the landing flare a few feet off the ground and suddenly find yourself plopping onto the runway, sometimes damaging the airplane (and your ego) in the process. Ego repairs are expensive, and to be avoided.

As a general rule, if your airplane is a little too high above the runway during the landing flare and you sense that the elevator control is near its aft limits or you feel yourself descending as you pull aft on the elevator, you should add power *immediately*. How much power? Let's just say that it's always better to add too much than not enough. You can always reduce the power if you feel the airplane will float or balloon as a result of moving the throttle forward.

This is one reason that pilots flying extreme short-field approaches can occasionally be seen moving their joystick or yoke aft quickly then returning it to its previous position when they're on final approach. They do this to test how much aft elevator travel they have available to them as a result of their slower approach speeds. If there is no aft elevator travel left (because the yoke is nearly at its aft stop limits), then they know the only way they'll be able to flare is by applying power—perhaps a lot of power.

This *aft stick movement* technique isn't one you'll normally use, since you won't be flying your short-field approaches at these slower speeds. I'm speaking of speeds that are only 10-15% above stall speed and deep within the region of reversed command. Speeds in this range are typically used by professionals landing STOL (short takeoff and landing) airplanes on very short runways. When you see videos of pilots doing these things, you're also likely to see sherpas, llamas and mountain goats in the picture. It takes a lot of skill to feel comfortable making short-field landings at these speeds, and with llamas yakking.

If you understand these concepts and have a good understanding of the region of reversed command lodged in your noggin, then you're really going to enjoy making short-field approaches. When a friend says, "Let's go to Landlong airport for lunch," you'll most likely reply, "Why go to Landlong when we will have more fun going to Nolength Field?"

Stick and Move

During extreme short-field approaches at very slow speeds, pilots occasionally move their joysticks back and forth to assess how much aft elevator pull (for flaring) is available to them.

Chapter 12 - Advanced Landing Skills

Soft-Field Approach and Landing

When I previously mentioned that not all runways are created equal, I really meant it. Some runways are more unequal than you might imagine. It turns out that some are also pretty soft for a number of reasons. A few are made out of grass, some are covered with mud, while still others might be covered with snow (Figure 19). There are even a few that are full of rough spots such as pot holes and stones. The good news is that there is a way to land safely on many of those runways. Welcome to the wonderful world of *soft-field approaches and landings*.

The objective of any soft-field landing is to touch down as softly, as smoothly, and as slowly as possible, letting the wings bear the burden of lift as long as possible before the tires start doing the lion's share of the work. This reduces the chance that those wheels will sink into the soft field, possibly trapping or damaging the airplane in the process.

A soft-field approach is similar to a normal approach except that the landing is performed with full flaps to allow a touchdown at the slowest possible speed. There's no need to land near the threshold or on the numbers. Good thing, since grass doesn't have numbers. Nor is there a need to use a steep approach angle unless there is an obstacle associated with the soft field. You want to use the same approach speed as the short-field landing (or 1.3 Vso) unless your POH specifically recommends another speed. This speed minimizes the chance that you'll have to eliminate any excessive airspeed during the roundout.

A Typical Soft Landing Field

Fig. 19 — Courtesy Andrew Shacker

Soft-field landing techniques come in handy when landing on grass, wet grass, dirt strips, stone or rubble strewn fields, bush-covered surfaces and so on. A grass runway is shown here.

While the roundout and flare on a normal landing are done with the throttle set at flight idle, you'll actually want to carry a little power into the landing flare when landing on a soft field (Figure 20). It's the addition of power during the flare that makes this landing distinctly different from a normal landing or a short-field landing.

You'll begin by holding the airplane off the landing surface to help dissipate any excess speed (just in case you managed to get a bit too fast

Fig. 20

The soft-field landing is accomplished by landing at the slowest speed possible, meaning that you'll land with full flaps extended. The touchdown is made even slower by the addition of a slight amount of power during the landing flare.

on final). Then you'll add a little power during the latter part of the roundout and into the flare to help slow the airplane down even more prior to touching down.

Power adds to the vertical component of lift, meaning that the airplane can fly at a slightly slower speed and still develop the necessary lift for flight (Figure 21). This results in touching down at a slightly slower speed than normal. How much power should you add? Certainly not enough to flare at an angle that allows the tail or its tiedown ring to contact the runway surface when landing. Do that and the airplane owner will certainly rub your nose in it, meaning that you might end up with a nose ring. Add just enough power to land at a slightly slower airspeed and at a slightly higher attitude than you would during a short-field landing. You should be familiar with this attitude, since it's similar to the attitude used during a soft-field takeoff. Approximately 300 RPM above idle should do it. Your instructor will know for sure, since he or she is familiar with your airplane's performance characteristics.

What you don't want to do is slow down, stall and drop onto the runway, striking the tail of the airplane in the process. Your natural reaction when the airplane starts sinking is to pull aft on the yoke, which increases the likelihood of a tail strike. It's entirely too easy to destroy the rear end of an airplane with just a slight strike of the tail on the runway. To prevent this from happening, keep the airplane as close to the ground as is reasonable during the roundout (tall grass, shrubbery or even stones might be a good reason to be a little higher during the roundout before letting the airplane settle for the landing flare). Add sufficient power to slow the airplane down in the flare, but not so slow that the nose-high attitude increases the likelihood of a tail strike.

During the flare you should hear the stall horn blaring and experience all the appropriate sensory cues and clues that the airplane is approaching a stall. Keep in mind that the only thing that changes when adding engine power during the flare is the stall speed and attitude. The wings still stall at the same critical angle of attack. Despite the higher attitude, the stall horn sound and the pre-stall

How Engine Power Affects Touchdown Speed

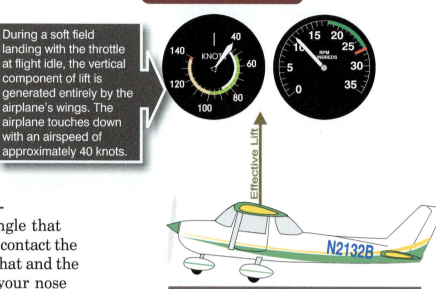

Landing Without Power

During a soft field landing with the throttle at flight idle, the vertical component of lift is generated entirely by the airplane's wings. The airplane touches down with an airspeed of approximately 40 knots.

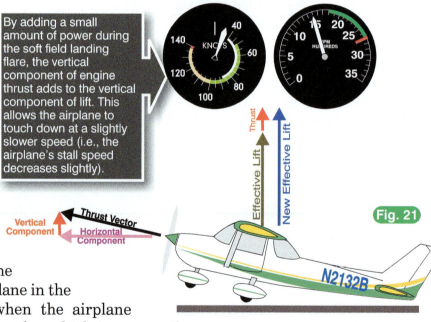

Landing With a Little Power

By adding a small amount of power during the soft field landing flare, the vertical component of engine thrust adds to the vertical component of lift. This allows the airplane to touch down at a slightly slower speed (i.e., the airplane's stall speed decreases slightly).

Fig. 21

Chapter 12 - Advanced Landing Skills

buffet feel of the controls are very similar to what they were during full flap stall practice. The senses you experience during a soft-field landing should be nothing new to you.

The moment the airplane touches down, reduce power to flight idle if you feel the airplane isn't likely to sink into the landing surface. There are times, however, where you might want to maintain a little engine power while the nose is still elevated, in order to more slowly transfer the airplane's weight from its wings to the main landing gear. You might not know how soft the field is on which you're landing. A friend of mine was landing on what he thought was dried mud. Turned out to be *partially* dried mud. He could feel his wheels sinking into the muck during the touchdown. Since he was carrying sufficient engine power into the flare, he was able to power up and take off, thus keeping his name from being Mudd.

With the airplane's main wheels contacting the surface as gently as possible, you'll also want to hold the nose wheel off the runway as long as possible (Figure 22). Why hold the nose wheel off the runway? Because lowering it onto a soft surface can cause it to abruptly dig into that surface, perhaps flipping, cartwheeling or even ground looping the airplane. Unless you're flying for Cirque de Avion, you'll definitely want to avoid these things.

When the nose gear starts to come down, try lowering it onto the runway surface as gently as possible. If the surface is especially soft, then feel free to use a little engine power to aid in this process. Increasing engine power slightly increases the elevator's effectiveness, allowing you more control in lowering the nose wheel to the landing surface. All the while, you're holding the elevator back to keep as much weight from pressing on the nose gear as possible. On some surfaces that are really soft, you may even need to keep that small addition of power applied, and perhaps even apply a bit more power to sustain your forward motion. Stopping or stopping too soon might mean that you get bogged down on the runway and become the new obstacle that students practice flying over.

This is why you want to avoid using brakes for as long as possible when landing on a soft field. It's time to break the brake habit. Use brakes on a soft field and the wheels can sink into the landing surface. If the field is wet, you might begin to slide. Airplanes are good for many things but sliding isn't one of them.

The Soft-Field Landing - Step-by-Step

1. Begin roundout and landing flare
2. Add a little power to touch down at slowest speed
3. Power off at wheel contact, hold yoke aft
4. Hold yoke aft, minimize brake application

Fig. 22

Rod Machado's How to Fly an Airplane Handbook

As with the short-field landing, consider doing an initial flight over any field on which you anticipate making a soft-field landing. A low pass allows you to see potential divots, grooves, boulders and other objects that could possibly damage you and your landing gear (and airplane) during landing. You might also get some idea about how wet or soggy the field is, too. Ducks paddling around are a sign that you should quack open the list of alternative airports.

If, during an emergency or precautionary landing you had to land on a field that looked rough and studded with stones or foreign debris, the soft-field landing technique would be the technique of choice. So choose it. It reduces the chance that you'll damage the landing gear, and minimizes the possibility of a flip-over, cartwheel or ground loop.

It turns out that the soft-field landing is one of the most challenging landings to do well. It requires a considerable amount of skill, timing and coordination to pull off a good softie. This is why, during flight reviews, I often ask pilots to demonstrate this maneuver as a means of assessing their piloting proficiency.

180 Degree Power-off Approach

When is a normal approach and landing *not* a normal approach and landing? If you said, "When it's not normal," you are correct. There are several non-traditional (non-normal, if you will) ways you can make an approach and landing that challenge your pattern skills as well as help you develop new landing skills. One of these is best known for helping you develop your ability to estimate the airplane's glide performance. It's known as the *180 degree power-off approach*. Let's see how this is done.

This 180 degree power-off approach to landing begins with reducing power to flight idle at a position abeam the chosen landing spot when downwind at an altitude 1,000 feet or less AGL (Figure 23). The chosen spot can be any spot on the runway and not necessarily the runway threshold. For our purposes, we'll elect to land on the end of the runway numbers, since they are easy to detect for this example (but please don't mistake these numbers for the numbers on top of a passing police car. You'll end up with a bad landing and a rap sheet).

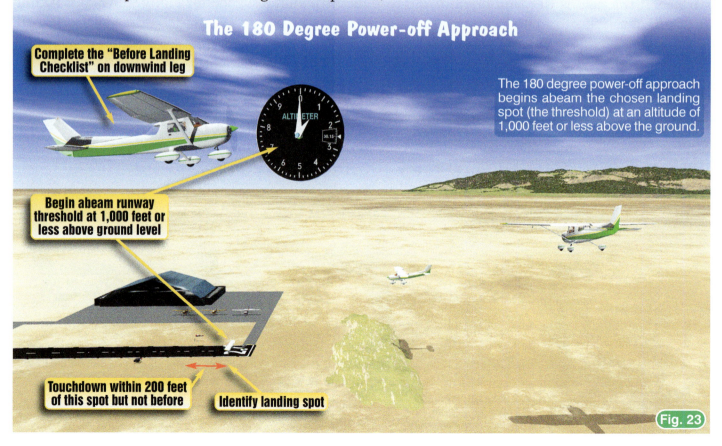
Fig. 23

Chapter 12 - Advanced Landing Skills

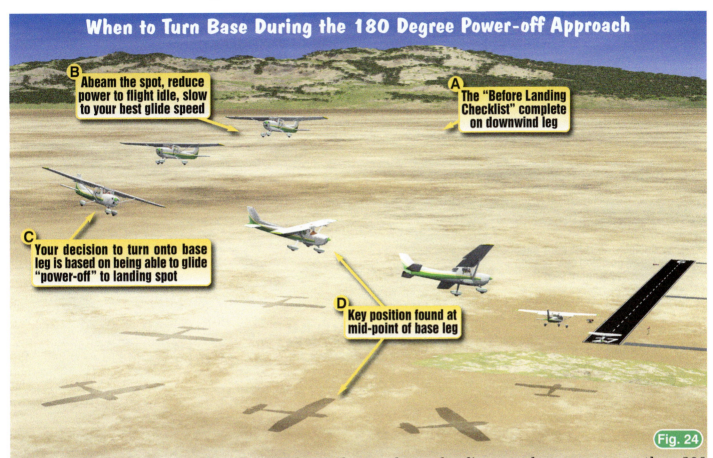

Fig. 24

Your objective is to touch down on or beyond your chosen landing spot but never more than 200 feet beyond it (that's the distance between the individual white edge-lights on the runway). And yes, you have to designate the spot before you begin the approach. You can't give it a shout out during the flare. Your instructor shouldn't be hearing, "I designate the spot to be there. No, wait, I mean over there. Wait, no, no. I mean there."

What makes this maneuver challenging is that the moment power is reduced, you can't power up again for the approach and landing. Of course, if you have to use power to avoid landing short of the runway, do so. No one expects you to land short of the runway, much less do any airplane dirt-biking. But the goal is to hit the spot without touching the throttle after your downwind power reduction to idle.

Why would you want to know how to perform such a maneuver? Well, you've probably guessed the reason already. Emergency landings. Master the 180 degree power-off approach to landing and you'll have no reason to doubt your ability to land safely if your engine quits over a suitable landing site. It's a tremendous confidence builder.

Let's get back to actually performing this maneuver.

On the downwind leg, make sure you complete the *before landing checklist* (see sidebar: *The Before Landing Checklist* on page 12-24) prior to reaching a position abeam of the landing spot (Figure 24, position A). If your airplane has retractable landing gear, the gear should be down by the midfield point. When downwind abeam the selected spot, reduce power to flight idle, raise the nose slowly (while maintaining your altitude) and slow the airplane to its best glide speed (Figure 24, position B). If that speed is not known, then use 1.4 Vs1 in the clean (no flap) configuration. Trim as necessary to keep the airplane in this attitude as you begin descending.

When should you turn onto base leg? Here is where good judgment is needed (if you don't have this judgment yet, don't worry. The purpose of this maneuver is to help you acquire it). If the winds

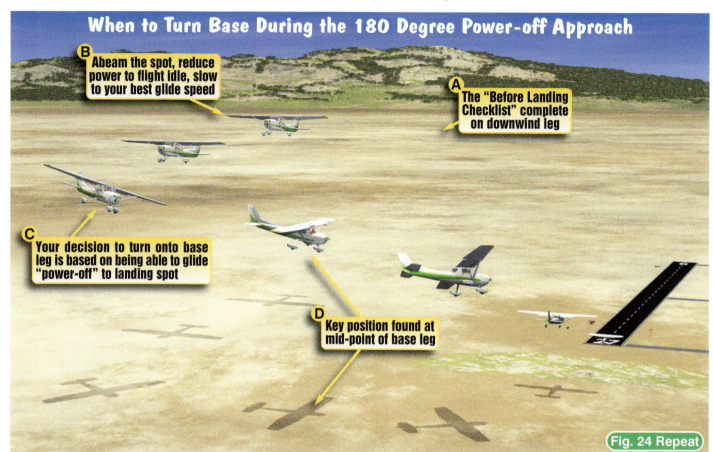

Fig. 24 Repeat

are strong, consider turning base leg closer to the landing spot. Delaying the base leg turn with a strong tailwind on the downwind leg means you might move beyond the gliding distance to the landing threshold (remember, a strong tailwind on downwind means a strong headwind on final approach, too). On the other hand, in a no wind or light wind condition, turning base leg too soon can cause you to end up high on final approach. So you make the call here (and not on your cellphone to me for advice, either). If you sense you've made an error in judgment, I'll show you how to correct for it shortly.

Use a medium or slightly steeper bank to turn onto base leg so that you'll be high enough and close enough to glide to the landing spot (Figure 24, position C). Why? Because it's easier to lose altitude if you're too high than it is to gain a better glide advantage if you're too low. Throughout the downwind and base leg, you're maintaining the airplane's best glide speed (or 1.4 Vs1 if the best glide speed isn't known). At this point, you're looking for something known as the *key position* located at the mid-point on base leg (Figure 24, position D).

You'll be at the key position when the landing spot is approximately 45 degrees to the left of the airplane's present ground track (or right of the nose if you're flying a right pattern). The key position is found to the left of the nose if the wind isn't too strong (i.e., no crosswind correction applied). If you haven't already done so, then move the propeller control to its full forward position in preparation for landing (assuming your airplane has a controllable pitch propeller).

At the key position on base leg you can make an estimate of how strong the wind is by examining the present wind correction angle needed to fly a ground track that's perpendicular to the runway centerline. As a general rule, it's a little more difficult to estimate your potential to glide to the runway on base leg compared to final approach, but that doesn't mean you can't do it.

Sometimes it becomes immediately clear that you are going to be too low. If so, this is where you'll want to cut corners—and I mean cutting them in a good way, by heading directly toward the runway threshold, resulting in an angled final approach (Figure 25).

Chapter 12 - Advanced Landing Skills

If You're Going To Be Too Low

At the *key position*, if you feel you are going to be too low, then make a turn toward the desired landing spot, rounding the corner of the turn from base leg to final approach.

Key position

Turn early toward the desired landing spot

Fig. 25

Sure, you're flying at an angle to the runway centerline but so what? You're also traveling less distance to get there, meaning that you have a better chance of reaching your landing spot. With little or no wind, you might want to make a square turn onto final or, if necessary, overshoot final a bit (if it's safe to do so) and then turn back for runway alignment. This gives you more distance to travel and helps you dissipate altitude as a result. Of course, you also have the choice of using a forward slip to lose altitude or applying flaps at any time while on base leg or final approach.

Ideally, you want to land on the desired spot with little or no floating. Using flaps will help bleed off the approach speed quickly and minimize the potential for floating. Then again, once those flaps are deployed, there's no retracting them in flight. This would be very bad form and would likely result in a dramatically shortened glide distance, as well.

As you turn onto final (or at some angle toward it), you can check the desired landing spot for upward or downward movement (the stationary spot method) to evaluate your glide potential. If you feel you're going to be low, then by all means maintain your best glide speed and keeps those flaps retracted. This gives you the best potential for reaching the desired landing spot.

If you feel you're going to be high, slow the airplane down to 1.3 Vs, which will be your stall speed based on whatever condition you'll use on final approach. Slowing to 30% above your present stall speed helps minimize your potential to float during the landing flare.

On base leg and final approach, if you feel you're too high, make S-turns, add flaps, slip the airplane, or do all three if necessary (Figure 26). Keep in mind that with some airplanes, slipping with full flaps can produce a vibration on the elevator surface since the flaps can disrupt the airflow over the airplane's tail feathers. This isn't dangerous, but it does tend to unnerve the pilot and cause the hair to stand up on the necks of any passengers. Slipping with full flaps can sometimes diminish the effectiveness of the rudder control. That means you might not be able to hold the airplane at the slip

If You're Going To Be Too High

At the *key position*, if you feel you are going to be too high, then overshoot final approach, followed by S-turns (if necessary) to lengthen the distance flown to the desired landing spot.

Overshoot turn and/or use S-turns if necessary

Fig. 26

The Before Landing Checklist

Before every landing it's always wise to use some form of checklist to ensure that the airplane is properly configured for landing. I recommend that you use a memory-type check list in the form of an acronym or mnemonic that you repeat to yourself. Or, if you must, an actual physical checklist in the form of paper or something on an electronic screen. To be practical about this, it's often more reasonable to use some type of mnemonic checklist because the last thing you want to do is start reading while operating in the traffic pattern. Here is where your eyes should be focused on what's outside the cockpit given that most mid-air collisions occur within five miles of an airport at less than 3,000 feet AGL.

I prefer to use the mnemonic *GUMP* before every landing. It stands for:

Gas - If you're far enough from the airport and at least 2,000 feet above ground, then you'll want to make sure that you're landing on the fuel tank with the most fuel (unless your POH requires that you land with the fuel selector set to "both," thus feeding from both tanks at once). If you're operating in the pattern, however, you're at too low an altitude to be switching fuel tanks. If there was some hiccough in the fuel system because you switched tanks, then you might not have enough altitude to restart the engine if it suddenly stopped. Of course, if you feel you are about to run out of fuel on one tank, then the safer of two poor choices might be to switch to the fullest tank even at lower altitudes. This checklist item is also a reminder to turn on the electric fuel pump if your airplane requires its operation when landing.

Undercarriage - If you're flying a retractable gear airplane, then you'll want to ensure that your gear is down and locked into the landing position. Under normal sea level conditions the gear should be put down by the midfield point on the downwind leg. My personal recommendation is to check that the gear is down at least four times in the traffic pattern. Here is where it's good to be a little paranoid. I check the gear on downwind, base, final and when crossing the threshold. That means I run through the GUMP checklist at least four times in the pattern.

Mixture - Your mixture should be at the appropriate setting when operating in the pattern. Under normal conditions that means it should be in the full forward position. It's entirely possible that you may have descended from your cross country flight altitude and forgot to enrich the mixture. Here's where this checklist item comes in handy. On the other hand, if you're landing at a high altitude airport in a non-turbocharged airplane, you'll want to try placing the mixture control in the position that allows you to develop maximum power in the event full throttle is applied during a go around.

Prop - In airplanes with constant speed propellers, you'll want to configure the propeller to allow the development of maximum engine power in the event you have to go around during landing. This means you'll want to move the propeller control full forward just prior to crossing the runway threshold. Moving the prop control full forward at this point is perfectly safe since you most likely aren't using very much engine power at the time. That means the propeller won't overspeed with the forward movement of the prop lever. If you've ever heard the engine of a complex airplane suddenly rev up and whine on the downwind leg, it's because the pilot moved the prop control full forward while the engine was developing substantial power. There's no way to hide this mistake, except to fly away and land at another airport (hopefully the pilots at the first airport won't alert the pilots at nearby airports to be on the lookout for Prop-sound Man (your new nickname).

---

angle desired. I know of no POH that *prohibits* slipping with full flaps but a few suggest that you should use *caution* when slipping with full flaps deployed. Check your POH to be sure, and follow the manufacturer's recommendations.

Suppose you just turned onto final approach and are now a little low. You do *not* want to try stretching the glide by pulling back on the elevator control, much less retracting the flaps (if you've extended them). But all is not necessarily lost. You have two little items left in your bag of tricks, and they're not rabbits.

Delay raising the nose and slowing to 1.3 Vs. Just remain at the best glide speed and don't further extend the flaps if they're already partially extended. This will provide the best shot at reaching the landing spot.

Another thing you can do is to make use of *ground effect*. When you're about 50 feet above the ground you can lower the nose slightly to quickly (but safely) move to within a wingspan's length above the ground, thus taking advantage of ground effect sooner. Level the airplane out as close to the ground as possible without touching down (assuming it's safe to be that low, of course). Hold the airplane off the surface but very close to it as you move toward your touchdown spot. Hopefully, you'll have enough energy to cover that distance and land on or within 200 feet of that spot. If not, then do what you need to do to land safely. Of course, this latter recommendation is meant more for the competition aspect of flying rather than its practical value for use in an actual emergency or everyday flying. After all, the tower controller isn't going to say, "Land on that spot because it pleases me, otherwise no more touch and goes for you today."

One very important thing to consider when making the 180 degree power-off landing is that you're not referencing landmarks to tell you where to begin and end your turns. In other words, you don't think, "OK, the 90 degree reference is over Bob's Biscuit Hut and I should always turn before reaching Bert's Burgers and Beans. This is known as the *biscuit and bean* approach technique because, if you have to use it to land after a real engine failure, you're probably going to get your buns kicked while being remembered as a has bean.

Chapter 12 - Advanced Landing Skills

How do you get good at maneuvers like this? Do them. Practice, practice and more practice. There is no substitute for practice. These maneuvers are easy to practice when there isn't much traffic in the pattern. If it's a busy pattern, then it's unlikely that you'll be reducing power to flight idle on the downwind leg. That's why it's often best to practice these landings when the pattern isn't crowded, or at a lightly-used airport.

Approaching and Landing When the Air is Bumpy

If there is a heaven for pilots, it must have airplanes with very slow-running Hobbs meters and airport weather that doesn't involve crosswinds, much less wind gusts that cause you to blow it when landing. Lo, that there is no such heaven on earth. That's why you should know something about approaching and landing in turbulent air.

It's entirely possible that strong gusts (i.e., wind shear), both vertical and horizontal, might cause a temporary change in indicated airspeed (Figure 27) and a significant change in angle of attack. Relatively speaking, this isn't so bad if you experience an increase in airspeed (a gust toward you, from in front of you), but it's certainly not good if you experience a loss of airspeed (a gust in your direction of motion from behind you), which always implies a temporary increase in angle of attack (perhaps at or beyond the critical angle of attack). That's why you need to know how to properly control the airplane if and when gusts are present on final approach.

How do you get better control in this condition? You increase your approach speed slightly, that's how. Flying slightly faster in gusty conditions means that a temporary variation in airspeed or angle of attack is less critical, because you've increased your speed and thus your angle of attack margin above stall. Sure, it's entirely possible that a wind gust could increase your indicated airspeed instead of decreasing it. Comparatively speaking, that's fine. You can easily live with a temporary increase in airspeed but you can't always say the same thing about a loss of airspeed resulting in a stall on final approach, right? You literally might not be able to live with that. So the question is, how much should you increase your indicated approach speed?

Fig. 27

I recommend initially adding half the reported gust velocity to your approach speed. If, for instance, the wind is gusting to 20 knots and you're approaching at 70 knots, then add 10 knots to 70 knots for a new approach speed of 80 knots indicated airspeed. Add a bit more if it's necessary to control your airplane.

What does this add-on give you? You get more effective control response to counter gust-induced pitches and banks. You also have the added safety factor of being less likely to stall if a gust subtracts from your indicated airspeed.

Of course, you aren't getting something for nothing, right? If there's one thing that aerodynamics teaches, it's that there is always a price to be paid. So what's the downside here? I'm glad you asked.

With the added gust correction, you're now making your approach 10 knots faster. That means you're likely to land longer. OK, fine. Just plan for a longer landing. As a consequence, you might plan on landing a little closer to the landing threshold on your initial approach to prevent running off the end of a short runway.

In turbulent or gusty conditions you actually want to carry a little extra speed into the roundout and flare, too. That means you'll land a bit flatter, while still selecting an attitude that allows the main gear to contact the runway before the nose gear. You aren't waiting for the airplane to stall before the main gear touchdown under these conditions.

You don't, however, want to force an airplane onto the ground and run the risk of landing on the nose gear first (Figure 28). That could cause the airplane to *wheelbarrow*, meaning that an unusual and unsafe amount of the airplane's weight is placed on the nose gear, much as it is in an actual wheelbarrow.

Wheelbarrowing increases the likelihood of a ground loop and loss of ground control (perhaps requiring the NTSB to call in one of its gardeners to help investigate the incident). So get the airplane on the ground and avoid unnecessary forward elevator pressure during the touchdown. Do, however, apply your normal aft elevator pressure to maintain the nose gear's steering ability during the landing roll. Apply heavy braking only when most of the airplane's weight is transferred from the wings to the wheels.

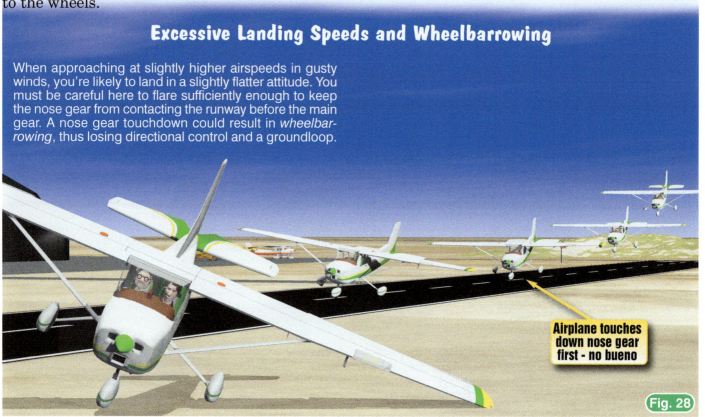

Excessive Landing Speeds and Wheelbarrowing

When approaching at slightly higher airspeeds in gusty winds, you're likely to land in a slightly flatter attitude. You must be careful here to flare sufficiently enough to keep the nose gear from contacting the runway before the main gear. A nose gear touchdown could result in *wheelbarrowing*, thus losing directional control and a groundloop.

Airplane touches down nose gear first - no bueno

Fig. 28

Chapter 12 - Advanced Landing Skills

Finally, when it comes to landing an airplane in gusty or turbulent winds, fly like a pilot who's not afraid to keep the airplane's attitude precisely where it should be. Muscle up! Landing in turbulence isn't a time to be a ballerina. It's a time to start horsing around and be a bronco rider. Be as assertive on those controls as needed to correct for turbulence-induced pitching, and keep the airplane's heading constant and its attitude precisely where you want it to be while on final approach. Yes, there is a time to be ballerina-like on the controls, and that's when the air is smooth. When it's rough, increase your control assertiveness as needed to keep the airplane under control.

How do you know how assertive to be on the flight controls? You look out the windscreen ahead of you and keep the airplane's nose from moving right and left or up and down. The runway is your calibration guide. If wind lifts the right wing and yaws the nose, then roll the airplane level while pushing the rudder to keep the nose from moving. Better yet, catch the rising wing and don't let it move in the first place. There's simply nothing more disconcerting (and revealing) than watching a pilot with poor stick and rudder skills ramble all over the final approach course in windy conditions.

In gusty wind conditions it's also best to keep flap use to a minimum. The greater the flap extension, the slower the landing speed and the less responsive the flight controls become during the roundout and flare. There's also a great deal of aerodynamic drag associated with the use of full flaps. A good gust from behind can slow the airplane considerably. Extra drag induced by the flaps can make airspeed recovery a bit more difficult. It's usually best to use 50% or less of the no-gust recommended flap extension when landing in gusty winds. Personally, if I'm flying an airplane with very effective flaps (think Cessna 150/172), I seldom use more than 10 degrees deflection in gusty winds. I have far more control of the airplane in this way. Landing with Fowler-type flaps extended to 40 degrees often means I have much less rudder effectiveness to help counter any gust-induced attitude changes.

You now know more than enough to help you land an airplane under more-than-normally demanding conditions. So where do we go from here? Onward and upward? To infinity and beyond? Well, hold on Buzz Lightsmear. First, we should make an attempt to learn certain advanced performance maneuvers. Not all of these maneuvers are required to become a private pilot. In fact, most are only *required* of those who seek to become commercial pilots. That doesn't mean, however, that you shouldn't practice these maneuvers simply to become a *better* pilot. I hope you'll go for it by reading Chapter 13, *Advanced Flying Maneuvers*.

Postflight Briefing #12-1 Landing at High Altitude Airports

More on Short-Field Landings at High Altitude Airports

There are several other factors to consider when performing short-field landings at high altitude (or high density altitude) airports. The first is runway slope.

If you have the option, it's better to land upslope on a short field. Every one degree of runway upslope gives you approximately a 10% decrease in landing distance. Additionally, a 10 knot increase in headwind gives you a 20% reduction in landing distance. So it's always wise to land upslope and into the wind whenever possible, especially if the runway is short.

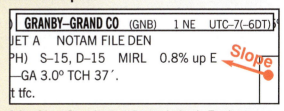

You can determine if there is a slope to the runway by making a quick check of the *Chart Supplement* (insert below). For instance, Granby airport shows that the east landing runway has a .8% upward slope. (Keep in mind that "slope" isn't an "angle." Instead, the runway's slope is the difference between each end of the runway divided by the runway's length and presented as *up* or *down*.)

Another thing to consider when making short-field approaches at high altitude airports is the use of power during approach. Because you approach at the same indicated airspeed that you would at lower altitude airports, your higher true airspeed means you descend through the air a bit faster than normal. Therefore your descent rate is higher for a given indicated airspeed. That's why it's often reasonable to use a little power to give you the same (i.e., slightly lower) descent rate you're used to at a lower altitude airport.

Inexperienced pilots attempting to make a power-off approach at a high altitude airport might find it much more challenging to identify when to begin their flare for landing. Using a little power provides a more moderate descent rate at high altitude airports.

Finally, there's a natural tendency for most pilots to make their approach and landing at higher than recommended airspeeds. The fact is that many pilots don't feel comfortable flying an airplane at 30% above its stall speed. Unfortunately, approaching at higher than normal speeds increases the odds of running of the end of an already short field. For instance, a 10% increase in your approach speed can increase your landing distance by 20%. So it pays to be comfortable at slower approach speeds.

Postflight Briefing #12-2 Estimating Approach Airspeed

Estimating Approach Airspeed With Variable Weight Conditions

Some landing performance charts are quite user friendly. A few landing distance performance charts automatically make the CAS-IAS conversion for the short-field landing by listing an IAS at which you'll fly the approach (Picture #1, position A). With these charts, there's no need to visit the airspeed calibration chart to find the speed at which to fly the short-field approach and landing.

These charts will also provide you with the appropriate speed at which to fly the approach based on the airplane's present weight (Picture #1, position B).

For instance, the landing distance chart in Picture-1 shows that the short-field landing should be flown at an IAS of 70 knots if the airplane weighs 2,950 pounds. At 2,200 pounds, you'll want to fly this approach at 60 knots to achieve the performance calculated when using this chart.

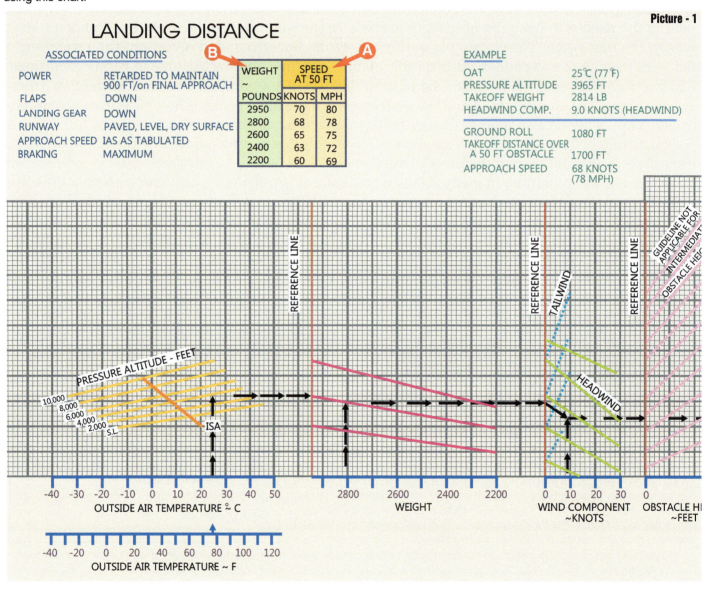

Picture - 1

Chapter 13
Advanced Maneuvers
Tools to Help You Become Proficient

Welcome to advanced flying class.

One of the great misconceptions about aviation skill development is that pilots don't benefit from acquiring a level of skill beyond that needed for everyday flying. Well, if you believe this, then you must also believe that the Bible Belt is something Baptists wrestle for. Not quite true. Let me explain.

If you ask any wise and highly experienced martial artist if he has ever used his martial arts training, he'll likely respond by saying, "I use it every day." No, he doesn't mean that he clocks a bully every day. Instead, he means that the higher-order martial skills of awareness, concentration and discipline are applied to everything he does.

In much the same way, if you learn to perform the higher order flight maneuvers contained within this chapter, you might never actually need to use them in flight. After all, very few pilots ever hear a controller say, "Quick, 2132 Bravo, give me an emergency lazy-eight, now!" Nevertheless, you will most likely apply the coordination and energy-management skills that these maneuvers teach every time your wheels leave the ground.

It's true that the maneuvers in this chapter are typically taught to those working on a commercial pilot certificate. Private pilots, however, can and will benefit by practicing them. Just as martial arts training can improve someone's character, these maneuvers, practiced to proficiency, will make you a much better pilot.

The Envelope Please

Airplanes have an operational envelope defined by airspeed and g-loading limitations. Most of the time you operate that airplane close to the center of that envelope, far from its limiting borders. This is a good thing. You seldom experience higher positive or negative g-loading or the extremes of higher and lower (stall regime) airspeed. That doesn't, however, mean you shouldn't know how the airplane behaves near the perimeter of its performance

Until you start learning to level out more smoothly, I'm going to need you to keep your seatbelt on a little tighter.

envelope. This knowledge prevents you from becoming rattled and helps you sustain a more rational frame of mind if and when you're subject to higher g-loading or find yourself closer to stall speed or design dive speed. It's also knowledge that helps you understand that the airplane's performance envelope is actually a bit bigger than you might suspect. Your airplane is a relatively strong machine that can withstand many more G's than you might think. It can also operate safely at a rather large range of speeds from stall to the never exceed speed. So let's begin our discussion with one of the most challenging maneuvers in our queue—the *steep turn*.

Steep Turns

As a flight instructor, I've taken a fancy to steep turns for one very important reason. It offers a lot of educational bang for the bank (Figure 1). From an airmanship perspective, practicing steep turns is like receiving a pregnant cat for your birthday. It's a gift that keeps on giving.

The *educational objective* of the steep turn it so help improve your coordination, control smoothness, division of attention, control of an airplane operating near its performance limits and spatial orientation (even if you're not from space or the Orient). All true, *and* there are additional benefits beyond these. One of these benefits is the message the airplane sends your way in the form of an immediate increase in apparent weight, as if it suddenly qualified for a weight loss scholarship. So what does this message mean?

It means the wings are not only producing the lift necessary to keep you aloft, but they're also producing an extra amount to pull you sideways, too. Your airplane and its contents (yes, you are contents) always resist any change in motion and protest it loudly with an increase in load factor. This is why you feel heavier in the turn, as if your machine and fanny have suddenly become too fat to fly. Consider this message the aviation version of a Western Union stall-o-gram: *You've just experienced an increase in load factor. Stop. This tells you something. Stop. Your wings have moved closer to their critical angle of attack. Stop. Your stall speed has increased. Stop.* This is just one of the many lessons steep turns teach. Please stay seated with your seatbelts fastened, because class isn't over.

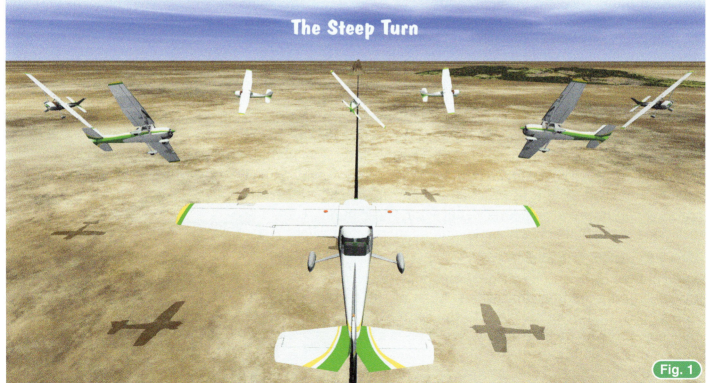

The steep turn is practiced at a maximum bank of 45 degree for private pilot certification and 50 degrees for commercial pilot certification. The objective is to roll into a steep turn to the right (or left) for 360 degrees then reverse course for a similar 360 degree steep turn in the opposite direction. (The pilot examiner specifies the initial direction of turn here.)

Chapter 13: Advanced Maneuvers

Turbulence and Load Factor

Steep turns expose you to g-forces that you wouldn't ordinarily experience unless you encounter some reasonably strong turbulence. If you experience turbulence-induced g-loading on a cross country flight before experiencing it during training, you'll most likely be concerned about whether or not the airplane is capable of handling these forces.

Years ago I sent a student on a cross country flight to Palm Springs, California. This airport is located right next to some very large mountains that can produce a great deal of mechanical turbulence. When the student returned from his flight, he told a story about how turbulence almost knocked him out of the sky.

It happened that he was flying a Cessna 150 Aerobat with a G meter. The G meter records the largest G-force it experiences with a needle deflection until it's reset. We looked at his G meter and it read 1.7 Gs. Would that have hurt his airplane? Hardly. Read on.

A steep turn at 60 degrees of bank (you don't normally do them that steep) can expose you to a load factor of 2 (or 2 Gs). This makes you feel as if you weigh twice as much as you ordinarily weigh. When you feel this much G-loading for the first time in turbulence you'll be convinced that the wings are coming off the airplane. Well, they aren't. Those wings aren't going anywhere.

A normal category airplane can take nearly twice as much positive g-loading as this before exceeding its limit load factor (which is 3.8 +Gs). That means the wings can hold 3.8 times its maximum gross weight without permanent deformation.

Airplanes are very strong machines and the steep turn is one maneuver that gives you confidence in your machine's integrity.

A Typical G Meter

In a 60 degree bank (we only use 45 or 50 degrees for the private or commercial certificate, respectively), the wings are supporting the weight of two airplanes. As you pull aft on the yoke to extract more lift from those wings, the increase in angle of attack *induces* them to throw a portion of their lift rearward, the same direction in which drag acts. Lift induced to act like drag becomes drag. You should recognize this as the *induced drag* that we discussed in Chapter Three (see sidebar: *Induced Drag and Angle of Attack* on page 13-4). This is the primary reason your airplane decelerates when turning steeply.

Of all the mischievous things you can do with a pair of wings, who would have thought you could make them work in opposition to engine thrust when flying at relatively low cruise airspeeds? Now you know why nothing happens quickly when you move the throttle forward in a steep turn. There's simply more induced drag to overcome. If your machine had barrel-sized pistons under the hood, you could accelerate in a steep turn, remaining far above the increased stall speed and below the critical angle of attack. Smaller airplanes, however, can't accelerate as well because of their *power-to-wait* ratio, meaning that there's always a long *wait* for anything to happen when power is applied, if anything happens at all. This is another valuable lesson that steep turns teach.

If you didn't consume too many Pop Rocks in the early 80s, you can still visualize what happens to the airspeed as you enter a steep turn using limited power or without using power at all. Imagine making a power-off turn to final approach from base leg with a combination crosswind-tailwind. The unanticipated higher ground speed results in overshooting the extended runway centerline. You steepen the turn and pull aft on the yoke only to find that the previous airspeed margin above stall has disappeared. Unless you immediately release elevator back pressure and unload those wings, you will receive another stall-o-gram, an *accelerated* stall-o-gram.

Steep turn practice should teach you at least four important lessons. The maneuver helps you understand how an increase in bank angle is associated with increasing angle of attack. It demonstrates how quickly any airspeed margin above stall speed can disappear as the bank angle steepens, especially during power-off approaches. In airplane engines equipped with little pistons (OK, small horsepower engines), steep turns teach that you can't necessarily trust the thrust to keep you well above an increased stall speed. Finally, the steep turn teaches you that the only good thing that comes from an increase in load factor is a recognition of the bad things that come with it. To make all these bad things go away you need only unload those wings by releasing elevator back pressure and/or by reducing your bank angle.

If you understand these fundamentals, then you've learned the essence of what steep turns actually teach. Now for the details.

Rod Machado's How to Fly an Airplane Handbook

Induced Drag and Angle of Attack

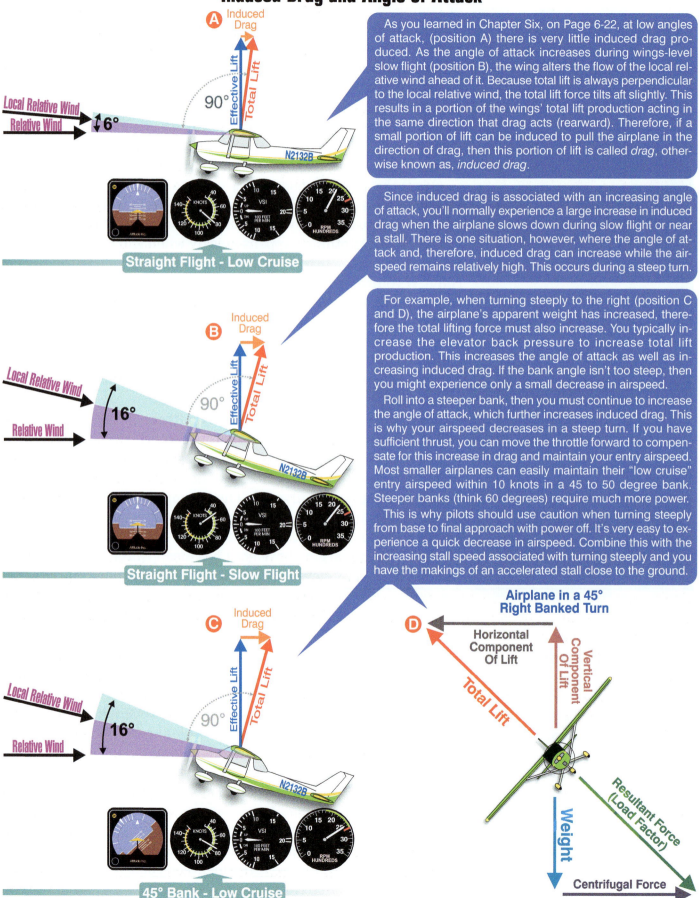

As you learned in Chapter Six, on Page 6-22, at low angles of attack, (position A) there is very little induced drag produced. As the angle of attack increases during wings-level slow flight (position B), the wing alters the flow of the local relative wind ahead of it. Because total lift is always perpendicular to the local relative wind, the total lift force tilts aft slightly. This results in a portion of the wings' total lift production acting in the same direction that drag acts (rearward). Therefore, if a small portion of lift can be induced to pull the airplane in the direction of drag, then this portion of lift is called *drag*, otherwise known as, *induced drag*.

Since induced drag is associated with an increasing angle of attack, you'll normally experience a large increase in induced drag when the airplane slows down during slow flight or near a stall. There is one situation, however, where the angle of attack and, therefore, induced drag can increase while the airspeed remains relatively high. This occurs during a steep turn.

For example, when turning steeply to the right (position C and D), the airplane's apparent weight has increased, therefore the total lifting force must also increase. You typically increase the elevator back pressure to increase total lift production. This increases the angle of attack as well as increasing induced drag. If the bank angle isn't too steep, then you might experience only a small decrease in airspeed.

Roll into a steeper bank, then you must continue to increase the angle of attack, which further increases induced drag. This is why your airspeed decreases in a steep turn. If you have sufficient thrust, you can move the throttle forward to compensate for this increase in drag and maintain your entry airspeed. Most smaller airplanes can easily maintain their "low cruise" entry airspeed within 10 knots in a 45 to 50 degree bank. Steeper banks (think 60 degrees) require much more power.

This is why pilots should use caution when turning steeply from base to final approach with power off. It's very easy to experience a quick decrease in airspeed. Combine this with the increasing stall speed associated with turning steeply and you have the makings of an accelerated stall close to the ground.

Elementary Components of Steep Turns My Dear Watson

As I mentioned earlier, steep turns are performed at the private pilot level with a 45 degree bank angle. On the commercial level, steep turns are performed with at least a 50 degree bank angle (Figure 2). During any steep turn, you don't want to exceed 60 degrees of bank. The reason is that everyone in your airplane (assuming you're not alone) must be wearing parachutes when exceeding 60 degrees of bank. At all times, you should keep your bank angle within +/− 5 degrees of either 45 or 50 degrees, depending on whether you're training for the private or commercial certificate, respectively.

Fig. 2

The private and commercial *Airman Certification Standards* require you to perform steep turns at 45 degrees or 50 degrees of bank, respectively. You're allowed a range of +/− 5 degrees of bank during the maneuver.

The *physical objective* of this maneuver is to complete 360 degrees of turn (for the private pilot examination) or 720 degrees of turn (a 360 degree turn in both directions) for the commercial certificate examination. You'll start on a specific heading or some outside reference such as a mountain peak (no, don't use a small cloud, either. It might dissipate, much like your dreams of passing your checkride would if you did this).

Before you actually try your first steep turn, here are a few *big picture* items I want you to consider.

When bank angles exceed 30 degrees, you'll notice that some airplanes have a tendency to overbank. Therefore, at 50 and 60 degrees of bank you should anticipate this overbanking tendency and correct for it. That means establishing the steep turn bank angle then applying aileron in the opposite direction of the turn to hold the bank constant (and use whatever rudder is necessary to maintain coordinated flight).

Using aileron to keep the bank constant is complicated by the fact that, as you enter the turn, your vertical component of lift decreases. The total lift component now tilts to one side, pulling the airplane in the direction of the turn. With less of the original component of lift acting vertically, you must increase your angle of attack to sustain the lift required for flight and to avoid accelerating in a downward direction.

You'll do this by applying sufficient elevator back pressure to increase the angle of attack and hold altitude. Here is where you must be careful not to let the bank increase as you apply back pressure on the yoke. This is a very natural tendency that all students have when they first attempt steep turns. Don't let this happen to you because you'll end up with a case of dropsy (OK, not the medical type of dropsy. I'm speaking of the aviation type where the nose pitches forward and the airplane loses altitude). Controlling your altitude during a steep turn is a very important sign of proficiency in this maneuver.

Increasing your angle of attack means that drag also increases resulting in your airspeed decreasing (unless you do something to maintain your airspeed). Wise pilot that you are, you've already learned that to maintain your airspeed in level flight you must increase your power to compensate for this increase in drag. Therefore, add power as necessary to maintain your entry airspeed.

So there you have the ingredients that make up this maneuver. Now it's time to put all these goodies in the oven and cook up a steep turn. Let's do some *baking*.

Rod Machado's How to Fly an Airplane Handbook

Enough Talk, Now Let's Do

You'll begin the steep turn at a speed below the airplane's present maneuvering speed (that's either Va if the airplane is at its maximum weight or Vo—*operational maneuvering speed*—which is maneuvering speed corrected for a weight decrease). Personally, I like doing these at a low to normal cruising speed, which is often a bit below maneuvering speed. If they're done at too high a speed, you may not have the extra power needed to sustain your entry speed as the bank increases (and the *PTS* expects you to maintain your speed within +/− 5 knots of your entry speed). You'll start the maneuver as you would start any in-flight maneuver by clearing the area in all four quadrants as well as above and below you. I know I emphasize this a lot but you simply don't want to take any chance of bumping into someone. When the clearing turns are completed you'll start the maneuver on a specific heading or with the nose pointed to some outside reference.

Oh, did I mention that you'll want to make a note of where the horizon line ahead of your seated position rests on your windscreen? Steep turns can be done almost exclusively by looking outside if you have a decent horizon (Figure 3). With the horizon line in mind, you'll want to either pick a spot on your windscreen that rests on the horizon directly ahead of you or, if there are no bugs on your windscreen (because you've developed the skill to avoid them in flight), you can simply make your own spot with a grease-based marker or the torn sticky edge of a Post-it. You make the call (perhaps to Staples for a pad of Post-its).

So let's begin with a right turn first. Here's the big picture of what you're trying to accomplish. You want to roll into a 45 or 50 degree bank and simultaneously increase the angle of attack to hold altitude while increasing power to sustain your entry airspeed, all while keeping the flight controls coordinated in the process. To do this you'll use a combination of outside references and a few

Preparing to Turn Steeply

The standard horizon reference dot you used when learning your basic flight training maneuvers is the same dot used when practicing steep turns.

Entering the Steep Turn

As you roll into the steep turn, you'll learn how high you must raise the reference dot above the horizon to establish the correct attitude for the steep turn (position A). It's also possible to use a pitch reference resulting from the intersection of the horizon and a portion of the engine cowling or instrument panel (position B).

Chapter 13: Advanced Maneuvers

instrument references. That means you must divert your attention outside then inside the cockpit, with most of your attention going *outside*. Now for the details.

To establish the correct pitch attitude for the steep turn, you'll want to look directly ahead of your seated position. This means that your vision is focused on the horizon reference dot located directly above the attitude indicator or control column (Figure 4). As you begin your roll toward the desired bank, you'll want to increase the angle of attack (by applying elevator back pressure) ultimately ending up at the desired bank with the reference spot typically located at a point approximately one to two inches above the horizon line (after you do a few steep turns you'll know exactly how much to raise your reference spot). What you're doing here is increasing the angle of attack to compensate for the decreased vertical component of lift in the turn. (See sidebar below: *Dot Is on the Level in Steep Turns*.) Keep in mind that the quicker you roll into the bank the quicker you'll need to increase the angle of attack. My preference, however, is for a medium rate roll into the turn, mainly because this gives you a chance to properly adjust your pitch as well as achieve the desired bank angle and maintain the entry airspeed.

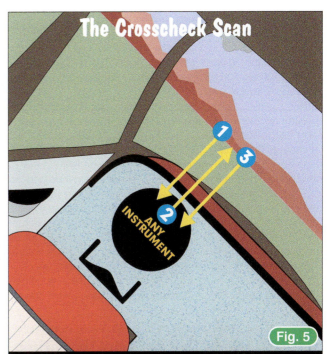

Step 1: Starting from the horizon line (or reference dot), look at an instrument (i.e., the attitude indicator and/or VSI) and determine what type of correction (if any) is necessary.
Step 2: Then look at the horizon and make the attitude change necessary to return the instrument to the desired reading.
Step 3: Return to the instrument to see if the desired change has taken place. If not, repeat step 2.

As you're rolling into the turn, increase your engine power to help maintain the desired airspeed. If you don't know how much to increase it, then add a few hundred RPM or a few inches of manifold pressure. Experience with a few steep turns will tell you how much to increase power during subsequent maneuvers. Modify that power to keep the airspeed with +/− 5 knots of the desired airspeed. Don't be dainty on that throttle, either. Move it quickly if necessary. Just maintain that airspeed.

The Steep Turn Crosscheck Scan

Your success at doing steep turns is based on how well you scan your inside and outside references. The crosscheck scan (the one we learned in Chapter Four) is based on a center point, much like the center spoke-hub on a bicycle, with items to be viewed at the end of each spoke radiating from the hub (Figure 5). With respect to steep turns, your hub is the horizon line or the reference dot.

Dot Is on the Level in Steep Turns

In Chapter Two I mentioned that the larger the bank angle, the greater the amount of back pressure that must be applied on the yoke to maintain level flight. Therefore, the higher that dot will have to be above its previous position on the horizon line due to the increasing angle of attack necessary to maintain altitude in the turn.  This, however, applies to shallow and medium banks only. As you increase the bank angle beyond 45 degrees, the increase in back pressure on the elevator control actually moves the dot a little more horizontally than it does vertically. In other words, as you bank beyond 45 degrees, the horizon reference won't need to be moved the same amount above the horizon that it moved when banking from zero to 45 degrees. It's true that at very steep bank angles your angle of attack is still increasing as you attempt to compensate for the loss of vertical lift component. This increase in angle of attack, however, is expressed more in a horizontal direction than a vertical direction as shown in the graphic above.

Then again, you're not likely to use banks beyond 60 degrees (mainly because you don't own a G-suit, much less a parachute), therefore you probably won't even notice this phenomena.

Setting Power With Airplanes Having Constant Speed Propellers

If you're performing a steep turn in an airplane having a constant speed propeller, you don't want to find yourself adding power while maintaining an unreasonably low RPM. This could result in excessive cylinder combustion pressures, which is never good for an engine (or the pilot).

This is why it's often best to increase your RPM value to some higher setting before beginning the steep turn. This allows you to move your throttle forward to increase engine power without worrying about exceeding the manufacturer's manifold pressure/RPM limits.

I recommend that you increase your engine RPM to the value used for climbing before beginning the steep turn. This allows you to increase the manifold pressure all the way up to the climb power value anytime during the maneuver to help you maintain the entry airspeed. While it's doubtful that you'll actually need to actually use climb power during the steep turn, it's nice to have it available to use just in case you lost several hundred feet of altitude and now need to climb back to your entry altitude (hopefully before your instructor or the examiner notices. OK, he or she will notice anyway).

(Note: This recommendation also applies to our upcoming discussion on the Chandelle since this maneuver always uses climb power. Therefore, before you begin the chandelle, you should set the RPM to the value used for climbing. Of course, this recommendation also applies to any maneuver that uses climb power, too.)

The first few times you begin a steep turn, you should roll into the turn using aileron and rudder and begin raising that dot above the horizon line while simultaneously moving the throttle forward slightly, about half an inch (just do it by feel, not by RPM/MP reference). Don't worry about a precise bank angle here. Just roll into a bank that places the top of your panel at an approximate 45 degree angle with the horizon and raise the dot a little above where it originally rested on the horizon line (Figure 6). If you can do that, you'll have a good first-time approximation for the proper pitch and bank needed for the steep turn. When you've established the approximate bank angle, you'll probably need to hold aileron opposite the direction of turn (to the left in Figure 6) to prevent overbanking. (I'll discuss how to use rudder to enter the turn and keep the controls coordinated shortly.) You'll modify this method of turn entry as you gain some skill at this maneuver. Now let's refine the entry.

Glance down at the vertical speed indicator and the 100-foot hand of your altimeter and note if they're showing a gain or loss of altitude. Immediately look at your horizon reference dot and adjust the pitch slightly so as to stop the needle movement. You shouldn't be far off your altitude by using the entry procedure mentioned above.

Now glance down again at your artificial horizon to see if you are indeed at 45 degrees of bank. Immediately look up and make any adjustment necessary to achieve 45 degrees of bank.

Repeat the same scan to further adjust your pitch and bank attitude until your altitude is constant and the bank angle is a steady 45 degrees.

Once these values are established, you should spend approximately 90% of your time looking outside the cockpit. Ten percent of your time is spent scanning the

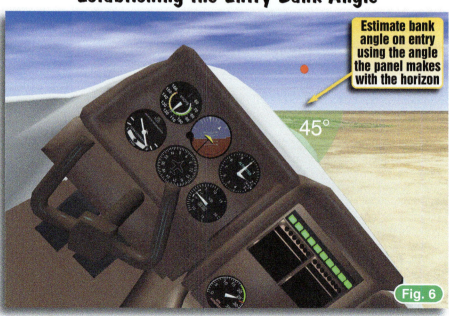

Establishing the Entry Bank Angle

Estimate bank angle on entry using the angle the panel makes with the horizon

45°

Fig. 6

The *initial* bank angle can be approximated by making a 45° angle between the panel and the horizon. You'll find that to maintain the desired bank angle, (to prevent overbanking) you'll likely need to hold aileron opposite the turn.

Chapter 13: Advanced Maneuvers

vertical speed needle, the altimeter's 100-foot hand, and occasionally checking the airspeed indicator and turn coordinator (if necessary). Any deviation of your panel instruments from their desired indications should be corrected by looking outside, not by looking at the panel instruments.

If you detect an airspeed deviation, then correct for it by a slight forward or aft movement of the throttle. You don't need to look at the RPM gauge to make a power change. Move the throttle forward or aft a tiny bit and crosscheck the airspeed indicator to ensure that it now reads the appropriate value. This is how you crosscheck scan your panel instruments during a steep turn.

Avoiding the Panel Illusion Trap During the Steep Turn Entry

One of the very big mistakes pilots make when rolling into a steep turn is looking to the left or the right side of their horizon reference dot, which is located directly ahead of their seated position (Figure 7). This is known as the *panel illusion* because your instinct is to take visual clues from the side of the cowling or panel on the opposite side of your seated position. For instance, in a steep turn to the left, the right side of the cowling or panel appears to rise above the horizon. You might try compensating for this by lowering the nose and losing altitude in a left steep turn. In a right steep turn, the right side of the cowling or panel appears to move below the horizon. You might try compensating for this by raising the nose and gaining altitude in a steep turn to the right.

If you look to the right of your red horizon reference dot to assess pitch attitude, you'll perceive the pitch attitude to be too high and correct for it by lowering the nose. If you look to the left of the dot, you'll perceive the pitch attitude to be too low and correct it by raising the nose.

The solution to this perceptual problem is to focus on your horizon reference dot (or where you imagine the dot should be on the horizon) that's located directly ahead of your seated position. So, don't look to the right or left of your seated position. Look directly ahead and you won't experience an issue with panel illusions.

Rudder Use During a Steep Turn

In a steep turn to the right, you'll find that you often need a great deal of right rudder to keep the airplane flying coordinated, despite the fact that you might be using left aileron to sustain the bank angle (Figure 8). Keep in mind that the increased angle of attack has increased p-factor. This, along with the propeller slipstream, is attempting to yaw the nose to the left. For most training airplanes, this means you'll need to apply a great deal of right rudder pressure as you *enter* the turn to the right, as well as sustaining the right rudder pressure *during* the turn.

A right steep turn requires left aileron deflection to prevent overbanking and a lot of right rudder to compensate for the airplane's power-induced left turning tendencies.

This is a cross controlled condition with left aileron applied to keep the bank from increasing and a generous amount of right rudder applied to compensate for the airplane's power-induced left turning tendency (Figure 8). Despite the cross controlled condition, the airplane is neither slipping nor skidding. The inclinometer's ball is perfectly centered because the airplane's nose is pointed in the direction the airplane moves around the turn arc.

During a steep turn to the left, you probably won't experience as much of a cross controlled condition. The airplane's power-induced left turning tendency will diminish your need to apply as much left rudder pressure during the turn *entry* as well as *during* the turn. Generally speaking, you might find yourself holding right aileron to sustain the steep bank angle and possibly a little left rudder to keep the controls coordinated (Figure 9). Then again, in some airplanes with powerful engines, you might find yourself holding right aileron and right rudder pressure to keep the controls coordinated in a left steep turn.

Reversing Course During A Steep Turn

When it's time to reverse course when half-way through a 720 degree steep turn, here are a few things to consider. First, you'll want to lead your course reversal by 10 to 15 degrees of the original entry heading. This, of course, assumes that you plan on making a relatively quick reversal. If you like slow reversals, then you should use a 20 degree heading lead. I'm assuming here that you used the heading indicator to determine your entry location, which is a bit more challenging than using a gigantic landmark for an entry reference. There's nothing like a mega-billion ton mountain moving across your panel to cue your turn reversal. Landmarks, in general, are easier to see than the tiny little numbers on your heading indicator. As you approach the reference (landmark or heading value) and begin your course reversal, you'll find that you can easily speed up or slow down the change in bank angle so as reverse course precisely on the same heading you used to enter the turn.

The benefit of using a landmark for course reversal is that it allows you to keep your horizon dot reference in sight and use it to roll into a turn in the opposite direction (see sidebar: *Course Reversal Tips*). This means you can keep the airplane's longitudinal axis nearly stationary during the reversal, keeping the controls perfectly coordinated during the most

Once established in a left steep turn, you'll need right aileron to prevent overbanking and, generally speaking, very little left rudder pressure to remain coordinated. Why? Because the airplane's power-induced left turning tendency tends to yaw the airplane to the left.

Course Reversal Tips

If your turn is coordinated, then the turn reversal results in the airplane *appearing* to pivot about its longitudinal axis (you'll see the airplane pivoting about the dot on the windscreen). If the nose yaws one way or the other during the reversal, then you've either underused or overused the rudder.

You're already familiar with this maneuver since you know how to do coordinated roll outs (See Chapter Two, Page 2-21.) It's the same maneuver except that you use it to reverse a turn instead of continually rolling right and left into and out of turns. So when you are within 10-15 degrees of the turn entry reference, roll in the opposite direction while being sure to use your rudder pedals to prevent the nose from yawing opposite the direction of the turn. This provides you with a nearly perfect coordinated reversal. Of course, there might be a very tiny bit of horizontal movement of the nose as the turn is being reversed because of the airplane's inertia, but the movement is hardly noticeable.

What makes this technique so helpful is that during the course reversal, you're also keeping the windscreen reference at the same height above the horizon line. Wait! Don't you have to lower the nose as you reverse direction since you'll roll through level flight? Well, no. Not if you do it quickly enough. If it takes you an entire lunch hour to roll from one turn to the next, then yes, you'll have to lower the nose to level pitch attitude as you roll through level flight followed by raising it again as the bank is established. But that's not what you want to do during a steep turn. Besides, you should be able to roll from one turn to the next within 10 degrees of heading change. So just keep your windscreen dot in its raised position as you roll quickly from one turn to the other.

Chapter 13: Advanced Maneuvers

challenging part of this maneuver. That's right. Suppose you're using your heading indicator to determine your turn reference. When you reach the desired heading lead for the reversal, you must change your focus from the panel to your horizon reference dot to make the reversal. That's a bit of extra work in my book. Using a distinct landmark for turn entries and reversals means you can change headings and control attitude without having to change where you were looking at a critical moment in this maneuver. This method easily prevents you from exceeding your entry heading during the reversal or during a rollout by 10 degrees (as required by the *PTS*).

After rolling into a steep turn in the opposite direction, you'll want to quickly crosscheck scan the attitude indicator to ensure that you're at the proper bank angle and the altimeter to see if your horizon reference dot needs a slight vertical adjustment. Of course, during the turn you'll periodically crosscheck scan the attitude indicator, altimeter, vertical speed indicator, airspeed indicator and inclinometer to ensure that you have the proper bank, altitude, airspeed and coordination. As a practical matter, once you're established in the steep turn, you only need to crosscheck scan the attitude indicator for bank angle and the VSI for altitude deviations. Airspeed and coordination shouldn't change much in an *established* steep turn once you've got the feel for the maneuver.

Correcting for Altitude Deviations During a Steep Turn

So what do you do if you find yourself gaining or losing altitude in a steep turn as shown in Figures 10 and 11? Some pilots like to reduce the bank a little if they're losing altitude and steepen it if they're gaining altitude so as to return to the assigned altitude. This alters the vertical component of lift slightly while the angle of attack remains the same.

For instance, if the airplane is losing altitude, rolling out of the bank tilts the vertical component of lift upward slightly and the airplane climbs (Figure 10). This, however, is not a good technique to use for altitude control during a steep turn, despite the FAA permitting pilots to vary the bank by one to three degrees to correct for small altitude deviations.

Why not? Well, this recommendation involves a small variation in bank that doesn't really do all that much to change the vertical component of lift. Besides, it's hard to tell the difference between one and three degrees of bank. Pilots ultimately end up changing their bank angle by 10 degrees or more in these instances and that's beyond the +/− 5 degrees allowed by the *PTS*. If you are going to change the bank angle to correct for an altitude change, then it's best to use up to but no more than five degrees, which is allowed by the PTS.

On the other hand, when doing anything other than a steep turn for the purpose of *passing a pilot checkride*, this technique is not only

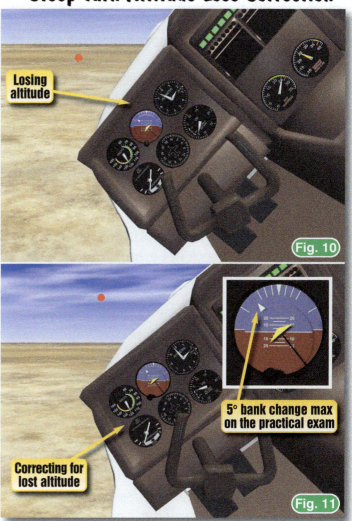

Steep Turn Altitude Loss Correction

You can correct for altitude loss during a steep turn by changing the bank slightly to alter the vertical lift component. You're allowed to vary the bank angle by +/− 5 degrees during the private or commercial checkride.

perfectly reasonable, it's absolutely essential. After all, if a steep bank is causing you to lose altitude, then roll out of the bank, especially if you're close to the ground. For instance, if you're making a turn from base to final and find yourself in a steep bank while losing altitude, then roll out of that turn to reduce the load factor. This also prevents an increase in stall speed.

When taking a private, commercial or flight instructor practical flight test, you shouldn't have to modify your bank angle to hold altitude in a steep turn. Instead, you should use your basic airmanship skills to control your altitude. So how do you do that? Let's see.

If you find yourself descending in a steep turn, apply back pressure while using enough opposite aileron along with the appropriate rudder pressure to prevent the bank from increasing (Figure 12). Raise the nose slightly above the attitude necessary for level flight so as to allow you to return to the desired altitude, perhaps at one- or two-hundred feet per minute. Unless you've had a wild swing in attitude, your airspeed shouldn't vary by more than 10 knots. Then again, if you've lost a lot of altitude (say, more than 200 feet), you may need to increase your power a bit as you return to your desired altitude. So do what you have to do to control your airplane and keep it within the parameters specified in the PTS.

If, however, you find yourself climbing in a steep turn, then apply slight forward pressure and maintain the bank at the desired angle with aileron and rudder (Figure 13). If you're making a large altitude correction, perhaps more than 200 feet, then you might need to make a small reduction in power to remain at the desired airspeed. Of course, it's entirely possible that you

Altitude Correction - The Proper Way

The proper way to correct for an altitude deviation is to pitch up or down slightly while using rudder and aileron in coordination to prevent over- or under-banking as you maintain the desired bank angle.

began climbing or descending because you failed to maintain the required bank angle to begin with. So return to the proper bank angle with the appropriate use of aileron and rudder.

Trim Use During a Steep Turn

One of the common questions pilots ask about steep turns is whether or not they can use trim to help control the airplane. Since trim was put on an airplane to make it easier on the pilot, you should use it as you see fit (Figure 14). Sure, the steep turn is a temporary condition, unlike a long climb or long descent. But some students have a difficult time maintaining the elevator back pressure necessary to keep the airplane in level flight. This is especially true with airplanes that have naturally higher stick forces such as the Cessna 182, 206 and 210. So feel free to use the trim as necessary to help you fly your airplane. That's what it's there for, but there is a price to pay. You can expect your workload to increase when using trim in a steep turn. Now you're not only working the flight controls and the throttle, you're working the trim. That's five items you must manipulate during a steep turn. If this were a job, you'd be getting bonus pay for your extra work. On the other hand, there's nothing

Chapter 13: Advanced Maneuvers

If you feel comfortable doing so, then it's perfectly reasonable to trim away elevators forces during a steep turn.

Sometimes using two hands on the yoke prevents having to trim during a steep turn.

at all wrong with using two hands on the yoke in a steep turn if you feel the need (Figure 15). This reduces the need for trim, which ultimately reduces your work load during this maneuver. Just don't make the machine gun "rat-tat-tat" sound while using two hands (unless you really want to).

When rolling out of the steep turn, you'll want to glance at your windscreen dot reference as you approach your entry heading or the entry reference point. Roll out so as to keep the airplane's longitudinal axis (use your dot reference here) aligned with the outside reference point. Simultaneously, lower the nose so that the windscreen dot reference is moved downward to the actual horizon line (to the point that held altitude in straight and level flight). At this point your power should be immediately reduced to that needed to maintain your entry speed for the maneuver. Hopefully you noticed and remembered the power setting used upon entry and can quickly return to that setting.

On the commercial checkride, your objective should be to make a 360 degree turn in both directions while keeping the bank angle within +/– 5 degrees of a 50 degree bank angle. Your altitude should remain within +/– 100 feet of the starting altitude and your airspeed should remain within +/– 10 knots of the entry speed. On the commercial checkride you'll be expected to rollout within +/– 10 degrees of the entry heading and reverse course within +/– 10 degrees of the entry heading.

Steep Spirals

While steep turns have great educational value, they actually have very little practical utility in flight. You seldom need to do one because you're not a fighter pilot nor should you suddenly find yourself close to buildings, mountains, trees or antennas and thus in need of evasive action. Steep spirals, however, are an entirely different matter. This is a maneuver that you might have to use someday and you want to make sure you're proficient at doing it.

The *physical objective* of a steep spiral is to make a power off, circling descent about a ground reference while maintaining a specific radius of turn around that reference without exceeding 60 degrees of bank (Figure 16).

The Steep Spiral

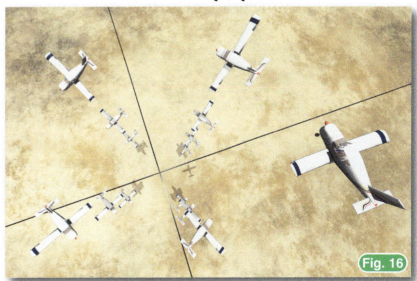

The steep spiral is a practical maneuver that involves descending about a specific reference on the ground. You might use this maneuver when descending over an emergency landing site.

The *educational objective* of this maneuver is to increase your skill at controlling airspeed, orientation, wind drift correction and dividing your attention.

When do you think you might use this maneuver? The commercial checkride? Yes, but where else? Correct. You'd use it to make an emergency landing resulting from an engine failure. If your engine quits and you're lucky enough to be over or near a desirable landing spot, you certainly don't want to fly away from that spot, right? Descending from directly overhead for a dead stick landing is probably your wisest choice here. More than one pilot

Steep Spiral Entry and Exit Altitudes

If possible, try entering the steep spiral downwind at least 3,000 feet AGL, make three turns at a constant radius and exit at approximately 1,500 feet AGL.

has selected an emergency landing spot only to turn away from it to lose altitude and returned for landing only to find him- or herself at too low an altitude (which really puts him on the spot).

An additional aspect of the *physical objective* is to make three, 360 degree spiraling turns during the descent from a starting altitude of approximately 3,000 feet AGL and an ending altitude no lower than 1,500 feet AGL (Figure 17). Of course, if the examiner asks you to continue the descent below 1,500 feet AGL for the purposes of simulating an emergency landing, please avoid descending less than 1,000 feet above the highest obstacle within 2,000 feet of your aircraft. If you're over a barren stretch of land, then a continued descent isn't an FAR issue. Remember, I said *barren* stretch of land, not a stretch of land with a Red Barron hotel on it, either. (Note. A few years ago the FAA used 1,000 feet AGL as the lower limit for steep spirals. Concerns about steep banks close to the ground initiated this change. So use caution during steeper banks when operating less than 1,500 feet AGL.)

Steep Spiral Radius of Turn

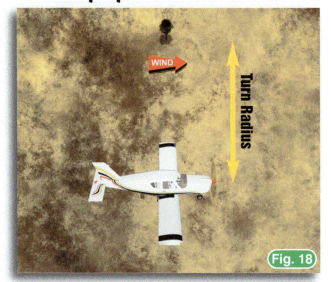

You'll want to choose a turn radius such that, upon entry, your bank angle doesn't exceed 60 degrees.

Since this maneuver is meant to be practical, you don't need to start it by flying downwind (although it makes it easier on you if you can enter downwind). In fact, in an actual emergency, you might not know the direction of the wind. This is, however, something you can discover by performing the maneuver and observing how wind affects your airplane.

What horizontal offset should you use during this maneuver (Figure 18)? Ultimately, this is determined by the bank limits established for the maneuver. You don't want to exceed 60 degrees of bank (parachutes, remember?) at the steepest part of the turn, which occurs on the downwind leg. So you'll just have to take a guess at first, then adjust your offset based on your assessment of wind speed.

Of course, this is one reasons why you have an instructor on board when you learn this maneuver.

Chapter 13: Advanced Maneuvers

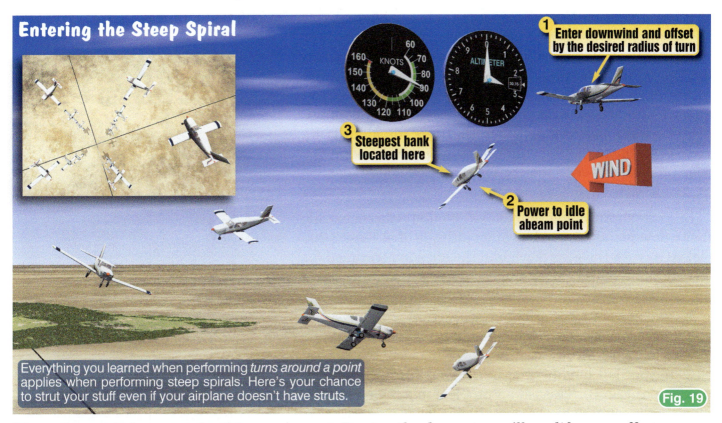

Fig. 19

He or she can help you make this assessment. During the descent, you'll modify your offset as necessary to prevent exceeding the 60 degree bank limit. At the slower speeds that general aviation airplanes fly, you should aim for angles of bank between 45 and 50 degrees at the maximum bank point (i.e., downwind).

One very unusual feature about starting the maneuver at 3,000 feet AGL is that your starting radius should look very small while not being small at all. That's right. While above your ground reference point, the radius at which you begin the maneuver appears to increase as you descend. No, it doesn't (or shouldn't) actually increase. This is simply a matter of perspective as you *close in* vertically on the ground reference. After one or two practice sessions with this maneuver you'll get a feel for what the approximate starting radius should look like at 3,000 feet AGL.

Keep in mind that your objective is to remain at a constant radius from the ground reference as you descend. Therefore, all that you've learned from doing turns about a point comes into play here. The steepest portion of the turn will be at the downwind point and the shallowest at the upwind point (Figure 19). The airplane will be crabbed into the wind on the upwind and downwind arcs to maintain the desired radius of turn just as it was when performing turns around a point.

What speed should you use during the descent? Well, that's up to you, as long as it doesn't exceed the airplane's present maneuvering speed and as long as it isn't too close to stall speed for the bank angle being used. It doesn't make sense to use cruise speed because you'll come down way too fast. And why would you want to come down that quickly during an emergency landing resulting from an engine failure? Typically you wouldn't, unless your airplane is on fire. Either way, it's best to use a speed that keeps you safely above stall for the steepest bank used in the maneuver, assuming you have no other speed that's preferable or no other reason to get down quickly.

What about doing this maneuver with the gear down if you're flying a retractable gear airplane? This is a good idea for a number of reasons. If this were a real emergency landing, you might forget to lower the gear as you get closer to the ground (assuming you'd land with the gear down which isn't always the best idea if you're landing in a swamp). Second, having the gear down increases the airplane's drag profile and reduces the chance of accelerating beyond the airspeed limit that you've designated for this maneuver. So I do recommend putting the gear down (or having it down already) when you commence the spiraling descent. If, however, you don't want to descend quickly perhaps because you're having difficulty communicating your position to the authorities (or identifying your position so as to communicate it), then leaving the gear up until closer to the ground might be a wise idea.

Enough Talk, Let's Do

Start by approaching your chosen ground reference while flying downwind (if possible) at an altitude of at least 3,000 feet AGL with the gear down and the airplane trimmed for level flight at your best glide speed (or any speed you desire below Va) as shown in Figure 20, position A.

As you approach the ground reference off your left wing, you'll notice that it appears to be almost inside the middle of your left wing if you're flying a low wing airplane, or very close to your left landing gear in a high wing airplane (Figure 20, position B). This isn't a problem in a high wing airplane but it can be a bit disconcerting in a low wing airplane because you often can't see the reference until you begin banking. So try using your mind's eye to help you estimate the position of the ground reference. Whatever you do, don't yell out, "I'm losing it! I'm losing it!" when losing sight of the reference. One of my students did this and I thought he was going bonkers and experiencing some temporary form of insanity. Yikes! You'll have a better chance of seeing the ground reference as soon as you begin your turn (Figure 20, position C).

Furthermore, when you descend through approximately 2,000 feet during the spiral, you'll find that you really weren't that close to the reference after all. In other words, your chosen radius of turn at 3,000 feet AGL looks a lot larger as you approach 1,500 feet AGL. It's like walking toward a friendly looking Chihuahua from a distance only to find that it's really a hungry Great Dane close up. Welcome to the world of perspective!

As you reach a position abeam the ground reference, apply carburetor heat (if necessary), reduce power to flight idle, and roll into a relatively steep bank, perhaps 45 degrees for starters (the appropriate bank for a downwind entry) as shown in Figure 20, position D. Even if you didn't enter downwind, you can make an immediate adjustment in bank angle to maintain the desired turning radius.

Make sure you simultaneously lower the nose as you reduce power and roll into the bank. Lower it to an attitude

Entering the Steep Spiral Turn

A Enter downwind with gear down at best glide speed

B In a low wing aircraft, your wing covers the reference

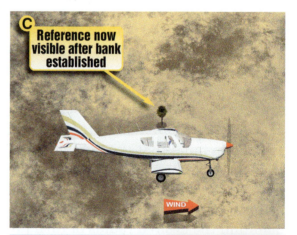
C Reference now visible after bank established

D Abeam reference, pull power, lower nose, start glide

Fig. 20

Chapter 13: Advanced Maneuvers

The Steep Spiral Turn

A. Steepest bank here where groundspeed highest

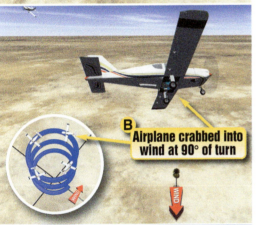

B. Airplane crabbed into wind at 90° of turn

C. Shallowest bank at 180° where groundspeed is the lowest

D. Airplane crabbed into wind at 270° of turn

Fig. 21

below the horizon sufficient to allow you to maintain best glide speed. This means that your horizon reference dot (it's still on the windscreen from the last maneuver, right?) is placed a little below the horizon line (Figure 20, position D).

At this time you should give the airplane a good twist of nose up trim. Since you're going to be making three full turns, it only makes sense to minimize the back elevator pressure you must hold during the descent. You don't, however, want to try trimming away the varying elevator forces you'll experience throughout the maneuver. These forces will change as your bank angle changes and you'll end up working yourself into a frenzy moving that trim wheel. So trim to remove the bulk of the elevator force you're holding then leave that trim wheel alone.

At 90 degrees of turn, you'll actually have to adjust your turn rate to crab into the wind slightly and maintain a circular ground track having a constant radius. You'll do this just like you did when making turns around a point (Figure 21, position B). Crabbing means continuing your turn toward the inside of the turn arc sufficiently enough to compensate for wind drift.

At 180 degrees of turn (Figure 21, position C), you're heading into the wind and your ground speed will be the slowest during this maneuver. Therefore, you will have the shallowest bank at this position, too.

At the 270 degree turn point (Figure 21, position D), you should be crabbed into the wind (now from your right) to maintain the desired turning radius. That means delaying the turn just enough so that the nose points outside the turn arc enough to compensate for wind drift. Throughout this entire maneuver you should adjust your bank angle with the coordinated use of aileron and rudder to maintain your starting radius of turn.

During the descent you'll want to cross-check scan your flight instruments the same way you did during the steep turn (Figure 22). The main difference here is that you aren't trying to hold a specific bank, much less hold an altitude. You're simply adjusting the bank angle to maintain the desired radius about the ground reference as you descend, all the while making sure you never exceed 60 degrees of bank. Therefore, the important instruments to scan are the airspeed and attitude indicator (for bank angle), but you do have to occasionally scan your altimeter and heading indicator (for entry heading), too. Keep in mind that 90% of your time should be spent looking outside the cockpit at the horizon and the reference point.

As you adjust the bank angle during the descent, you'll also need to adjust your pitch attitude slightly so as to maintain your desired descent airspeed, or best glide speed in this example. You can easily see how paying attention to your horizon reference dot is important during this maneuver. You simply don't want to let that pitch attitude vary too much, otherwise your indicated airspeed will vary wildly (you want to keep it within +/− 10 knots of the entry speed). Since no power is used during the descent, you'll find that there is a lot less difference between right and left rudder pressure when increasing or decreasing the bank angle. This is important because the steep spiral is the only maneuver where you spend a lot of time actually maneuvering with the power reduced to flight idle.

Now that you have an understanding of how the steep spiral is accomplished, let's examine a few of the typical issues you'll face when performing this maneuver.

You've Got "Spiral" Issues

Suppose, for instance, that you don't know what the wind direction is or aren't able to estimate it. If so, then pick a radius of turn from your previous experience with the maneuver (or use the radius used when performing turns about a point) and let the games begin. Enter the maneuver and use your eyeballs and those two enormous brain lobes to observe how the airplane drifts (Figure 22). With a little practice, it shouldn't take much more than 180 degrees of turn to estimate the direction from which the wind blows. In Figure 22, it's clear that by 180 degrees of turn the radius is decreasing. At position C you'll need to shallow the

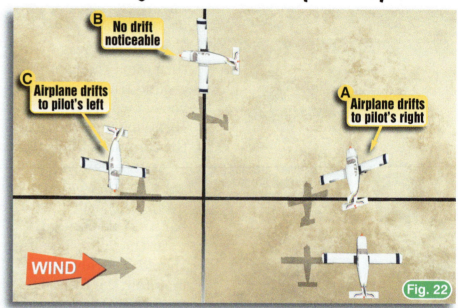

If you don't know the direction of the wind, then enter the spiral from any direction. Just assume you are entering downwind then use and hold a steep bank upon entry. Now observe how the airplane drifts to identify wind direction.

bank considerably if you want to maintain the entry turn radius. Assessing the wind during your descent is what you'll need to do if you were actually spiraling to land in an emergency, right? You definitely want to land into the wind, not with it. A 10 knot wind can mean a 20 knot difference in ground speed during landing, and that's significant, especially if the landing field is rough.

During the descent you'll want to occasionally clear the engine. No, this doesn't mean you yell, "Clear...the engine" out the side window during the descent. That's a great way to remain well *clear* of your commercial pilot checkride because your instructor will think you've *metally* lost it. You'll simply move the throttle to a higher power setting then bring it back to flight idle to remove any carbon and/or lead build up in the cylinders as well as to ensure your engine is still running. You don't have to add full power here. Simply move the throttle forward one-half to two-thirds of its forward travel then return it to the flight idle position. That should be fine. Clearing the engine at least once every thousand feet during the maneuver is a good thing to do, too. Be careful, however, not to let your airspeed exceed 10 knots of your entry speed during the clearing process. Years ago I demonstrated an emergency landing simulation to a new flight instructor who had never heard about clearing the engine. I cleared the engine twice during the descent and he commented, "Hey, that's cheating. You're trying to make the field with bursts of power."

Chapter 13: Advanced Maneuvers

I replied, "No, it's not cheating. It's only cheating if I have to clear the engine 150 times during the descent." I fully expected him to respond by saying, "No. The way you clear the engine is by opening the window and yelling, 'Clear the engine. Clear the engine'."

During the descent, you should expect the wind speed and velocity to change slightly, as it typically does when approaching the ground. Winds tend to shift to the left when they encounter surface friction (Figure 23). If the winds are stronger at altitude than they are closer to the surface (and they often are), then expect the wind correction angle you're using to decrease slightly during the descent.

One of the big challenges with steep spirals is dividing your time between flying the airplane, looking for traffic and paying attention to the ground reference. It's really a brain *time share* problem that requires practice to master. Perhaps the best bit of advice I can give you is to make sure that you pay close attention to your attitude during the maneuver. Using your horizon dot reference as the means by which you control and adjust your attitude is extremely important. You'll be in a nose down attitude all the time during this maneuver so be prepared to adjust your horizon dot reference as necessary to maintain the desired airspeed.

Changing Wind Speed and Direction With Altitude

Fig. 23

While descending during the steep spiral, be prepared for the wind's direction and velocity to change and to modify your drift correction, accordingly.

When you've completed three, 360 degree turns, you'll roll out, preferably on the downwind leg of a simulated traffic pattern. This does, after all, comport with how you'd ideally fly an emergency traffic pattern for a dead stick landing. So please remember that you've got to count the turns. So count them out loud during the descent if it pleases you. Saying something out loud makes it easier to remember. Trust me when I say that the first time you do this maneuver, you are just as likely to count, "one...three," and entirely skip two.

At this point, the maneuver is complete and you may either fly straight and level or begin a climb, depending on what the examiner has requested that you do. If you're taking your commercial checkride, then don't descend below 1,500 feet AGL unless the examiner wants you to simulate an emergency landing. At this point, acknowledge that 1,500 feet AGL is the lower limit of this maneuver then ask the examiner how he or she would like you to terminate it at the end of three turns. Be prepared for him or her to do a little comedy by saying, "I'd like you to terminate it successfully." So be prepared to giggle a lot and fake a false laugh. This can only help you. If you happen to mention that you haven't laughed that hard since your flight instructor slipped on a banana peel, you might find your performance score increasing slightly.

I've always like the descending spiral because it's one of the most practical maneuvers you'll learn. And, believe it or not, you can actually use it under instrument conditions, too. If you had an engine failure in the clouds, it's possible to use your moving map display to descend directly over an airport using a relatively small radius of turn (one-half mile or less). Hopefully, you'd exit the clouds at some reasonable altitude above the airport (hopefully above 500 feet AGL) and be able to land on some part of the airport surface. So this maneuver is a good one at which to become proficient.

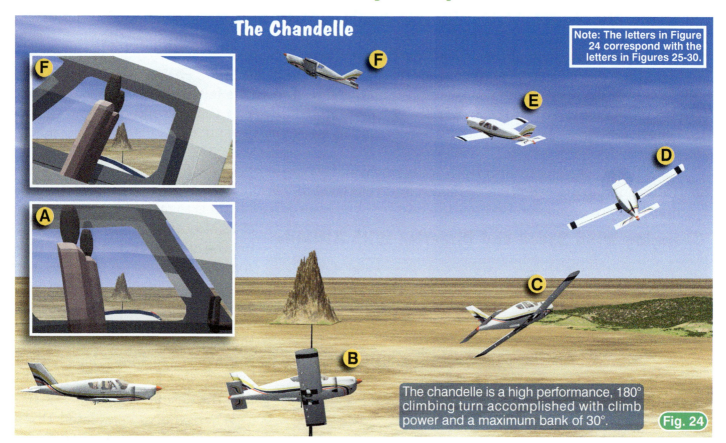

Fig. 24 — The chandelle is a high performance, 180° climbing turn accomplished with climb power and a maximum bank of 30°.

Note: The letters in Figure 24 correspond with the letters in Figures 25-30.

The Chandelle

No matter how you say the word *chandelle*, you just can't make it sound bad. Ouch, that chandelle just stung me! Hey, you just backed your car over my chandelle. I'll punch you in the chandelle if you look at my wife again. It just sounds nice for some reason, doesn't it? Well, it is a nice sound and it's a nice flight maneuver to become proficient at, too.

The *practical objective* involves a high performance, 180 degree climbing turn with a 30 degree bank limit. It starts approximately from straight and level flight, and ends with the wings level and the airplane at or near its minimum controllable airspeed in a nose high attitude (Figure 24). The *educational objective* of the maneuver is to develop your coordination, planning, orientation and flight control skills.

You might deduce that this means climb power is involved along with a bank angle allowing a reasonable rate of turn without extracting an excessively large penalty from a diminished vertical component of lift. Is there some hidden value to this maneuver that makes it worthwhile to practice for reasons other than proficiency or passing a checkride? As a practical matter, the answer is no. Some pilots say this maneuver can be used to help extract yourself from entry into a blind canyon. I'm pretty sure than entering a blind canyon is a rather poor time to be practicing your commercial maneuvers. As it is, the chandelle isn't the best maneuver for this a blind canyon extraction. A much better maneuver for this situation is to slow fly the airplane on the downwind side of the canyon, followed by a 180 degree turn into the wind, which gives you the shortest radius of turn.

On the other hand, the chandelle is one of the best maneuvers for helping you understand how to keep an airplane coordinated as you grapple with its power-induced left turning tendency. It's also a fantastic maneuver for teaching you to anticipate how the airplane performs through various attitudes and airspeeds. Finally, if you can do a chandelle well, then you've learned how to keep yourself oriented to some outside reference during flight. So enough talk young Skyflopper. Let's learn how to do this maneuver.

Chapter 13: Advanced Maneuvers

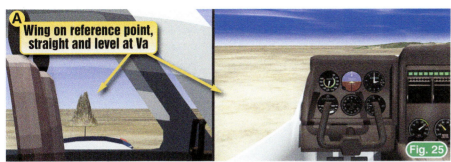

A — Wing on reference point, straight and level at Va

You'll begin by pointing your wing (it's actually the airplane's lateral axis but we'll use *wing* here) to some clearly identifiable reference point (Figure 24). This could be a mountain, a distant tree (a really big one) or anything that you can easily see out the left or right side of your airplane. If you're living in flat land, then you can even use a sufficiently long road or, if absolutely necessary, a specific heading on your heading indicator if outside references won't work for you.

The maneuver is entered in cruise flight, at or below maneuvering speed, with flaps and gear up. My preference is to enter this maneuver at maneuvering speed. If, however, the airplane manufacturer posts a recommended entry speed for the chandelle, then use that speed. This might mean beginning a slight dive to reach the desired airspeed, raising the nose to a level flight attitude, then beginning the maneuver.

Let's begin by making our first chandelle to the left from straight and level flight (Figure 25). Start by rolling into a 30 degree bank turn toward your distant reference (Figure 26). Thirty degrees of bank produces very little load factor (about 1.1Gs) but does produce a reasonable rate of turn. My preference is to enter this turn crisply, instead of slowly or lazily (if it's lazy you want, I've got just the thing for you coming up next).

B — 30° bank, then pitch up (Fig. 26)
C — Climb power added (Fig. 27)
D — 90° of turn - highest pitch (Fig. 28)
E — Begin rollout, maintain pitch (Fig. 29)

F — At 180°, wings level, at MCA

After you establish the bank angle, you'll begin climbing by applying elevator back pressure, while simultaneously applying climb power (Figure 27). This is the point where the planning begins. You're objective is to maintain 30 degrees of bank and reach the highest pitch used for this maneuver at the 90 degree of turn point (Figure 28). At 90 degrees of turn and beyond, you'll hold your pitch attitude steady (don't increase it or decrease it) and slowly begin your rollout (Figure 29). Your objective is for your opposite wing to end up on the starting reference point in a wings level (no bank) attitude after completing 180 degrees of turn (Figure 30). If you planned properly, the airplane will be at its minimum controllable airspeed at the completion of 180 degrees of turn.

It's clear that the first part of this maneuver—the first 90 degrees of turn—is relatively simple. I'd say it's almost a no brainer except for the fact that you need at least one of your lobes to be engaged during its performance. The last 90 degrees of turn is a definitely a double-lober. Here's why.

At the 90 degree of turn point (if you've planned properly), your airplane has achieved a pitch attitude that allows it to continue to decelerate through the last 90 degrees of turn (Figure 28). That's right. The slowest speed isn't achieved at 90 degrees of turn, only the highest

Fig. 30

pitch attitude is achieved at this point. This relationship is made clear by the graph in Figure 31 which shows the relationship between attitude, airspeed and bank angle during the chandelle. The airplane's airspeed continues to decrease throughout the last 90 degrees of turn. If your pitch attitude is too high at the 90 degree point, then you'll stall before completing 180 degrees of turn. How do you know how much pitch you need at the 90 degree point? Experience will tell you. Simply stated, you must perform the maneuver to learn how to perform the maneuver.

At the 90 degree of turn point, with the pitch attitude held constant, you want to begin rolling out of the turn. Now I don't gamble—despite the fact that I do eat at the buffet in Las Vegas—but I'll bet that you will roll out too fast on your first attempt at this maneuver (Figure 32). Let me explain.

As your speed decreases through the first 90 degrees of turn, your *rate of turn* is actually increasing. In other words, holding a constant bank while slowing down means your airplane is changing headings faster and faster. That means you'll get to the 90 degree turn point faster than you would if you had just made a level (constant airspeed) 90 degree turn to your left.

As you mentally plan your bank reduction from the 90 to 180 degree turn point, you're basing your rollout rate on your perception of how fast your heading changed during the first part of the maneuver. Since your airplane's nose appears to be moving through those headings rather quickly up

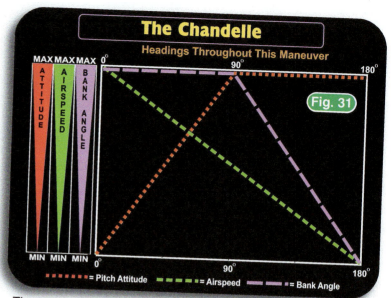

The graph above shows how the airspeed decreases throughout 180° of turn. The pitch attitude peaks at 90° then remains constant from 90° to 180°. Bank angle decreases to zero past 90° of turn.

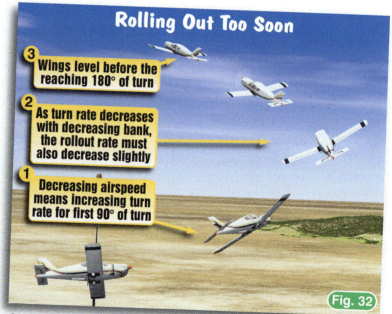

Students typically rollout too quickly when passing the 90° turn point. The reason for this is that the rate of turn is decreasing during the last 90 degrees of turn, thus requiring a slower rollout rate.

to the 90 degree point, your natural response is to roll out much too quickly. That's why you'll have to purposely resist the temptation to do this as you pass the 90 degree of turn point. Resistance is not futile here, either (unless you're a member of the Borg Collective).

Of course, the moment you start rolling out at the 90 degree turn point, your turn rate is no longer *increasing* as quickly, right? That's right. Despite your airspeed continuing to decrease which increases your turn rate, your bank reduction simultaneously *decreases* your turn rate. The two now counter or oppose one another. That means as you shed those 30 degrees of bank during the last 90 degrees of turn, your turning rate is relatively constant (or at least a whole lot less than it was). Ultimately, things don't happen as quickly as you think they will during the last 90 degrees of turn. This is why the last half of the chandelle is where you develop your ability to plan, or where a deficiency in

Chapter 13: Advanced Maneuvers

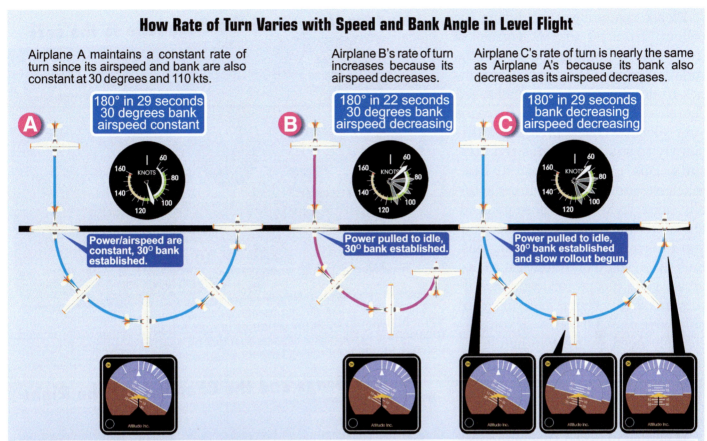

How Rate of Turn Varies with Speed and Bank Angle in Level Flight

Airplane A maintains a constant rate of turn since its airspeed and bank are also constant at 30 degrees and 110 kts.

Airplane B's rate of turn increases because its airspeed decreases.

Airplane C's rate of turn is nearly the same as Airplane A's because its bank also decreases as its airspeed decreases.

A — 180° in 29 seconds, 30 degrees bank, airspeed constant. Power/airspeed are constant, 30° bank established.

B — 180° in 22 seconds, 30 degrees bank, airspeed decreasing. Power pulled to idle, 30° bank established.

C — 180° in 29 seconds, bank decreasing, airspeed decreasing. Power pulled to idle, 30° bank established and slow rollout begun.

The airplane in position A banks at 30 degrees at a constant bank and airspeed. Its turn rate is constant. If a 30 degree bank is started and the power is pulled (resulting in the airspeed decreasing), the turn rate increases (position B). In other words, the airplane doesn't have to travel as far to complete a 180 degree turn as its airspeed decreases, so it completes the turn faster. This means its rate of turn has *increased*.

Now let's simulate something a bit closer to the actual turn rate in a chandelle. Enter a 30 degree bank and simultaneously reduce power to idle (position C). Then immediately begin a slow reduction in bank. If the bank is reduced as the airspeed decreases, the turn rate is similar (or approximately so) to that experienced by the airplane in position A. The takeaway point here is that your rate of heading change during the first half of the chandelle is increasing but it becomes relatively constant during the last half of the chandelle. If you base your rollout rate on what you experience in the first half of the chandelle, then you'll rollout too quickly during the last half of this maneuver.

The Mechanical Method of Rollout

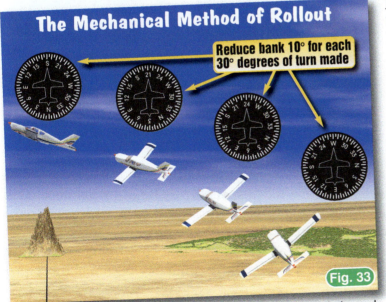

Reduce bank 10° for each 30° degrees of turn made

Fig. 33

A mechanical approach to eliminating 30 degrees of bank through the last 90 degrees of turn is to decrease the bank 10 degrees for every 30 degrees of turn.

planning reveals itself. See the sidebar above to help you better understand the relationship between turn rate, airspeed and bank angle.

If you want to reach 180 degrees of turn in a wings level attitude, you have to time the rollout properly. The easiest way to do this is to do it mechanically at first. Since you have 30 degrees of bank to shed through 90 degrees of turn, think about decreasing the bank by 15 degrees for every 45 degrees of turn or, if your lobes can handle the calculation, 10 degrees of bank for every 30 degrees of turn. Using this type of mechanical approach to the rollout should prevent you from rolling out of 30 degrees of bank at the very last minute (Figure 33). Once you get a little practice with this maneuver, you'll have a feel for how fast to rollout. This does, however, take a little practice.

Please remember that during the rollout (from 90 to 180 degrees of turn) you're holding the pitch attitude constant as the airplane continues to decelerate. As your airspeed decreases, you'll have to increase your elevator back pressure sufficiently to sustain the desired attitude. Don't be surprised at how much elevator back pressure it actually takes to keep the nose pointed above the horizon, either. Since you don't normally use trim during this maneuver, you'll definitely get to exercise your biceps (or *monoceps* if they are so tiny that it looks like you only have one). Of course, if you absolutely need to use two hands to hold the nose up, then do so. If you absolutely need to use trim, then do so. Do whatever you have to do to fly your airplane properly.

If you've planned this maneuver properly, you'll rollout with the wings level at the 180 degree point at minimum controllable airspeed. The stall horn or stall light should definitely be active since you are (or should be) very close to the wings' critical angle of attack. So hold the airplane at MCA just momentarily to show that you know what you're doing (but don't yell out, "I know what I'm doing") then reduce the pitch attitude and return to straight and level flight.

If you think the rollout isn't a two-lobe maneuver, then it's prob-

The chandelle to the left begins with a little left rudder to enter the turn (position A) followed by larger amounts of right rudder to remain coordinated (positions B to C). A little left aileron might be needed at position D to compensate for the right rolling tendency caused by right rudder application.

The chandelle to the right begins with a great deal of right rudder pressure (position A) to remain coordinated. More and more right rudder is needed as you approach the 180 degree turn point (position B). Left aileron will most likely be needed to keep the controls coordinated during the rollout (position C).

ably because I haven't discussed the effects of torque, slipstream and P-factor on the airplane. In a chandelle to the left, the airplane naturally wants to turn left, especially as its airspeed decreases. Relatively speaking, when you begin the maneuver to the left, your initial roll to 30 degrees of bank won't require too much left rudder pressure (Figure 34, position A). As the airplane slows down, especially past the 90 degree of turn point, you will need to feed in right rudder to remain coordinated (Figure 34, positions B and C). Remember, the airplane's left turning tendency becomes more pronounced at slower speeds.

As a general rule, you'll need to use relatively little right aileron when rolling out of a left chandelle (Figure 34, position D). This occurs because you are feeding in a large amount of right rudder during the last half of the chandelle. Right rudder tends to induce its own *right rolling* tendency. This could

Easy Chandelle Learning Strategy

Here's an easy way to develop your skill at the individual elements of the chandelle. Practice each element separately, then practice them together, and you'll be a master of the maneuver in a relatively short time.

The first element of the chandelle you'll practice is the *bank entry*, followed by the *bank rollout* (Picture - 1). Start by placing your left wing on a distant reference point in level flight at the airspeed used for a typical chandelle entry. Now roll into a 30 degree bank but leave the power alone. As you pass 90 degrees of turn, reduce the power to flight idle and apply sufficient elevator back pressure to hold altitude while gradually decelerating and progressively reducing the bank so as to arrive at the 180 degree turn point in wings level attitude near stall speed.

Picture -1

Practicing these elements of the maneuver allows you to practice rolling out as your rate of turn wants to increases due to your decreasing airspeed. It also allows you to get a feel for how much rearward elevator pressure is necessary to control the airplane's attitude. It's an excellent exercise in helping you divide your attention between the reference point and the bank angle.

The next element involves establishing a large pitch attitude in straight flight then holding that attitude constant as you allow your airspeed to decrease (Picture - 2). Begin by placing your left wing on the reference point in level flight with the airspeed used for a typical chandelle entry. Start raising the nose to a 20 degree nose up attitude (or the attitude used in your typical chandelle at the 90 degree point). As you raise the nose, add climb power. Your objective is to keep the wing's level, the controls coordinated and, when reaching the desired nose up attitude, maintaining that attitude until just above stall speed. Once you reach this point, you'll recover back to straight and level cruise flight. This is an excellent way to experience what it means to sustain a specific attitude as you watch the airspeed decrease. It's also a practical way to understand how necessary it is to add right rudder and (possibly) aileron to keep the wings level and the airplane coordinated.

Picture - 2

result in a *cross controlled* flight condition (left aileron with right rudder) despite the airplane flying perfectly coordinated, and that's perfectly OK, too. As you've already learned, crossed controls don't necessarily imply uncoordinated flight. As you complete the rollout in a left chandelle, you'll need to hold right rudder pressure in to maintain your heading. Then, as you lower the nose to accelerate to straight and level flight, you'll need to gradually release the right rudder pressure.

A chandelle to the right produces a slightly different control response at the beginning of the maneuver. Entering the right chandelle typically requires more right rudder pressure than a left entry thanks to the airplane's power-induced left turning tendency (Figure 35, position A). Past the 90 degree turn point, as you begin your rollout to the left, you'll find that you'll also need right rudder to remain coordinated along with a little left aileron to assist in the rollout.

Once again, you might end up at 180 degrees of turn with left aileron and right rudder applied in a cross controlled condition despite the flight controls being perfectly coordinated. In airplanes having large power plants, however, it's entirely possible that you'll need a lot of right rudder and even right aileron (Figure 35, positions B and C) to keep the airplane from banking to the left at the completion of a right chandelle.

Ultimately, any deficiencies in your understanding of rudder and aileron coordination are revealed in the performance of a chandelle. It's like one big SAT score demonstrating your coordination skill (or lack of it). So learn this maneuver well, and you'll make a big impression on those for whom you demonstrate your skill.

OK, enough work. Let's get lazy.

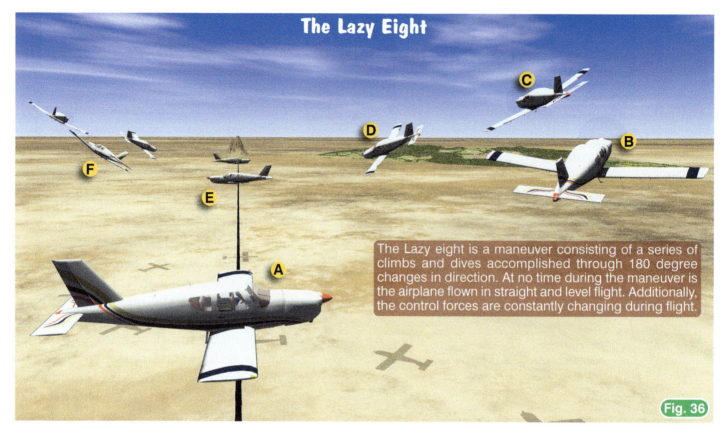

The Lazy eight is a maneuver consisting of a series of climbs and dives accomplished through 180 degree changes in direction. At no time during the maneuver is the airplane flown in straight and level flight. Additionally, the control forces are constantly changing during flight.

The Lazy Eight

Since you've been working so hard at these advanced maneuvers, you're probably looking forward to something a little less strenuous, a little less rushed, a little lazy, right? Well, good luck finding that in this maneuver. Despite its name, the lazy eight requires anything but a lazy approach to performing it. In fact, out of all the commercial maneuvers, the lazy eight is the one requiring the highest degree of skill to perform properly (Figure 36).

The lazy eight's *practical objective* involves a series of 180 degree turns requiring climbs and dives in alternating directions with airspeeds ranging from cruise to those found in slow flight. Two very distinguishing features of this maneuver are that the control forces are constantly changing and at no time is the airplane flown in straight and level flight except in transitioning from one turn to another.

The lazy eight's *educational objective* involves helping you develop your coordination skills through a large range of airspeeds and flight attitudes. To do it well, you must have good planning skills, the ability to keep yourself oriented to outside references, a good sense of speed as well as a subconscious feel for flying your airplane. If you don't have these skills at this point, then you will if you practice and perfect this maneuver.

How the Lazy Eight Got Its Name

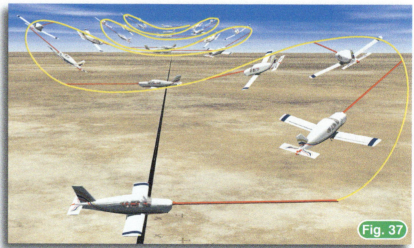

The lazy eight gets its name because an extended longitudinal axis appears to inscribe a lazy *eight* on the distant horizon. Unlike the chandelle, it's a maneuver performed slowly and smoothly.

Chapter 13: Advanced Maneuvers

The fact is that the lazy eight is lazy in name only. It's called a lazy eight for two reasons. First, the maneuver involves a relatively slower manipulation of the flight controls giving it a lazy feel. Second, if you were to imagine the airplane's longitudinal axis as a large pointer, then the maneuver would inscribe what can look like a droopy eight on a very distant horizon (Figure 37). You do, however, need a good imagination to see this. Pop Rocks fans need not apply.

The Big Picture

Here's the big picture. This maneuver starts with the airplane's wing (it's actually the airplane's lateral axis but we'll use *wing* here) pointed to an outside reference point and consists of two, 180 degree climbing and descending turns in the opposite direction, with each turn having symmetrical climbing and descending loops. No, the loops aren't perfect half circles either. In fact, the loop that's made above the horizon line

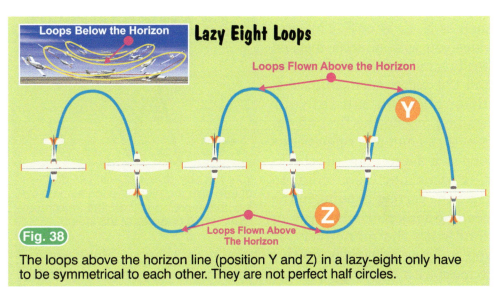

The loops above the horizon line (position Y and Z) in a lazy-eight only have to be symmetrical to each other. They are not perfect half circles.

is often slightly tapered (Figure 38, positions Y and Z). That's why these loops (or curving paths) as observed above and below the horizon line only have to be symmetrical with each other. At no time is the airplane flown straight and level nor is the airspeed constant during this maneuver. In fact, the airplane is rolled from one bank to another with its wings being level only at the moment the turn is reversed. Sounds like you're watching a moth fly, doesn't it? Well, let's head for the light and get enlightened, but not light headed.

The lazy eight is performed with gear and flaps up, at maneuvering speed or cruise speed, whichever is less (or the manufacturer's recommended entry speed, if provided). That's right. Unlike the chandelle, you don't need to accelerate to maneuvering speed before beginning this maneuver.

You'll set yourself up for the maneuver by pointing your wing (lateral axis) to a distant reference point (pick any wing...you only have two choices here) as shown in Figure 39, position A. Since you'll need to identify the 45 and 135 degree turn points, it's also beneficial if you can initially pick (or roughly guess at) outside reference points at these locations, too. If there are no outside references to be seen (because your practicing this maneuver over the No-Bikini Atoll atomic bomb explosion site), don't worry. You can

Begin the lazy eight with gear and flaps up and at cruise or maneuvering speed, whichever is less.

use 45 and 135 degree turn values on your heading indicator for these references. In fact, once you have your wing on the reference, you might rotate the heading *knob* and change the heading to a cardinal number, such as N, E, W or S. This provides you with quarter-marked heading indices to use for the 45 and 135 degree turn points. Additionally, you can set your heading *bug* to the first 45 degree turn point as a reference as long as it doesn't bug the checkride examiner (remember to reset the correct heading in the heading indicator when you're done with the maneuver). If you're flying an airplane with a slaved gyro, then you don't want to mess with unslaving it and rotating the heading indication. Instead, since most airplanes with slaved gyros are situated in an HSI (horizontal situation indicator) you should rotate the course selector to your entry heading and the heading bug to a 45 degree turn reference. Hopefully no one has freed your slaved gyro or fumigated the cockpit and killed your heading bug. Now you're set to "get set and go."

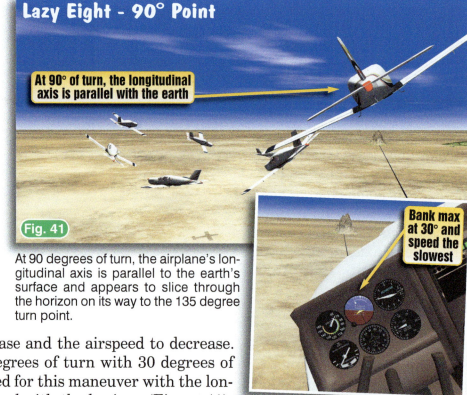

Fig. 40 — Your first objective is to reach 45 degrees of turn with the highest pitch attitude for the maneuver and half the maximum bank (or 15 degrees at this point).

Fig. 41 — At 90 degrees of turn, the airplane's longitudinal axis is parallel to the earth's surface and appears to slice through the horizon on its way to the 135 degree turn point.

Enrough Talk, Let's Do

You'll begin the maneuver by making a relatively slow climbing turn toward the distant reference point. Unlike the chandelle, you don't apply power as a standard practice in this maneuver (as you'll see later, you might need to adjust your power as you enter the maneuver). You're aiming to reach 45 degrees of turn at the highest pitch attitude used throughout the maneuver at 15 degrees of bank (which is ½ of the maximum 30 degrees of bank used for this maneuver) as shown in Figure 40.

At the 45 degree turn point, the bank will continue to increase and the airspeed to decrease. Your objective is to reach 90 degrees of turn with 30 degrees of bank at the slowest airspeed used for this maneuver with the longitudinal axis of the airplane *level* with the horizon (Figure 41).

Chapter 13: Advanced Maneuvers

Lazy Eight - The Slice

Longitudinal axis appears to slice across horizon at the 90° turn point

Fig. 42

At 90 degrees of turn, the airplane's longitudinal axis is parallel to the earth's surface and *appears* to slice through the horizon on its way to the 135 degree turn point. The slicing motion is more of a personal perception based on the use of proper aileron and rudder coordination at slow airspeeds.

Lazy Eight - 135° Point

At the 135° turn point: the lowest attitude, bank 15°

Speed increasing, bank decreasing

Fig. 43

At the 135 degree turn point, the airplane should reach its lowest pitch attitude while the airspeed continues to increase. Bank should be approximately half the starting bank, or 15 degrees.

Lazy Eight - 180° Point

At the 180° turn point: bank 0°, airspeed same as entry speed

Same altitude and airspeed as upon entry

Fig. 44

The airplane should pass through the 180 degree turn point in a wings level attitude at the same altitude and speed used upon entry. Here you'll immediately continue with a lazy eight in the opposite direction.

Keep in mind that from 45 degrees up to 90 degrees of turn, the nose is always elevated (to some degree) above the horizon. Therefore your airspeed continues to decrease until reaching 90 degrees of turn (to approximately 5-10 knots above stall speed). At this point, the airplane's nose (it's actually the longitudinal axis, but we'll use *nose* here) appears to slice diagonally through the distant reference point (Figure 42) as it descends below the horizon and heads toward the 135 degree of turn point.

Past 90 degrees of turn, the attitude continues to decrease while the airspeed increases and the bank decreases. Your objective is to reach the lowest pitch attitude for this maneuver at 135 degrees of turn at approximately 15 degrees of bank and airspeed increasing in value toward your entry speed as shown in Figure 43.

From 135 degrees to 180 degrees of turn, the pitch attitude increases, the airspeed increases and the bank continues to decrease (Figure 44). At 180 degrees of turn, you should be in wing's level flight (albeit for only a fraction of a second) at the same altitude and airspeed at which you entered the maneuver. At this point you'll immediately, without hesitation, repeat the maneuver in the opposite direction. The maneuver continues in right and left turns until the examiner says to stop or you're unable to hold the controls any longer because your arms went numb.

When performing the lazy eight to the left, you'll often find that you still need to apply a little right rudder pressure as the airplane climbs toward the 45 degree reference point (Figure 45). This should make sense since the airplane's power-induced left turning tendency increases as the airspeed decreases. You might also find that you really don't need that much left aileron to sustain an increasing bank angle given the airplane's tendency to roll to the left under higher power conditions and increasing angle of attack.

As you approach 90 degrees of turn, you'll typically need to apply a little left rudder and a generous amount of right aileron deflection (Figure 46). The right aileron deflection is necessary to keep the bank from increasing beyond 30 degrees at this point. A little left rudder is typically necessary here to keep the nose pointed in the direction of turn, despite the airplane's power induced left turning tendency.

The slice that typically occurs at the 90 degree turn point is one of the most beautiful aspects of this maneuver. Given the slow airspeed and steeper bank, the higher rate of turn at the 90 degree point results in your perceiving the airplane's longitudinal axis slicing diagonally through the distant reference point (Figure 47).

Just to be clear here, the actual amount of rudder and aileron you'll need during any lazy eight depends on the airplane you're flying. Airplanes with bigger more powerful engines produce a more noticeable left turning tendency. Therefore, there can be a distinct difference in control feel and control usage between airplanes.

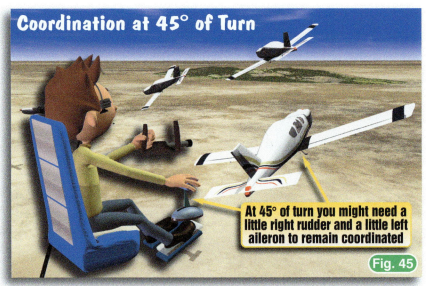

As you approach 45° of turn in the left lazy eight loop, you'll need a little right rudder to counter the airplane's left turning tendency. A little left aileron might also be necessary to maintain the increaseing bank angle.

At 90° of turn in the left lazy eight loop, you'll most likely need a little left rudder to remain coordinated as you slice through the reference point and a sufficient amount of right aileron to prevent over banking.

The perceived slicing motion through the reference point at 90° of turn results from the higher rate of turn that's associated with the slowest airspeed and the steepest bank found at this point in the maneuver.

Chapter 13: Advanced Maneuvers

Figure 48 shows a graphic representation of the maximum and minimum locations of attitudes, airspeeds and bank angles throughout the lazy eight. Now for the itty, bitty, gritty, details.

Lazy Details

Let's examine the finer details of the maneuver while continuing the lazy eight to the right, from 180 to 360 degrees of turn.

The one big challenge you'll find in doing this maneuver is to keep from doing everything too quickly and too abruptly. This is a maneuver that's best performed slowly and methodically, thus the reason it's called a *lazy* eight and not a "I never saw that coming" eight.

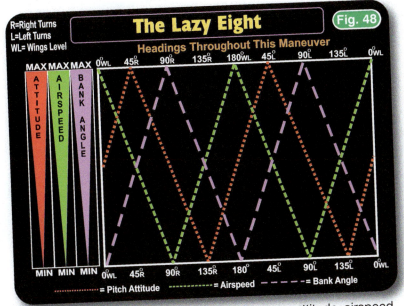

The graph above shows the relationship between attitude, airspeed, bank angle and heading in a lazy eight to the right then to the left.

As you begin the lazy eight to the right (or left), the natural tendency is to increase your bank too quickly. Why? Because most pilots roll into a turn using a moderate rate of roll to establish a specific angle of bank. They have very little practice rolling into a turn using a progressively increasing bank angle. They just deflect the yoke to the right (or left) to initiate the roll, then center (or neutralize) the yoke when they reach the desired bank angle.

As you begin the turn and pitch up toward the 45 degree reference point, the rate of turn increases and continues to increase until reaching 90 degrees of turn. The reason the rate of turn increases results from the airspeed decreasing and the bank angle increasing through 90 degrees of turn. Therefore, you'll want to begin the lazy eight by banking slowly at first, then gradually increasing the rate at which you steepen the bank as you turn toward the 90 degree point. If you increase the bank too quickly, you'll reach the 45 degree turn point with more than 15 degrees of bank. Mechanically speaking (which has nothing to do with talking to a mechanic), you can *initially* strategize your way through the maneuver by planning to increase the bank angle approximately five degrees for each 15 degrees of turn. Of course, with practice you'll develop a feel for this and won't need to go all "Einstein" here by trying to match specific headings to bank angles.

As you pass through 90 degrees of turn your turn rate will be the highest for this maneuver. That means the longitudinal axis (or the nose) will be moving horizontally relatively fast. This is why the airplane's longitudinal axis appears to slice diagonally through the distant reference at this point. Of course, the beauty of this slicing action is dependent on the proper use of aileron and rudder to keep the controls coordinated. Let's examine how that's done in the right lazy eight loop.

Rod Machado's How to Fly an Airplane Handbook

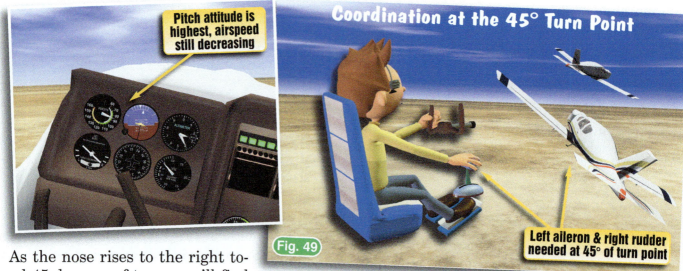

Fig. 49

As you approach the 45 degree turn point, you'll most likely need to increase your right rudder pressure to keep the nose pointed in the direction of turn and left aileron to keep the bank from increasing too quickly.

As the nose rises to the right toward 45 degrees of turn, you'll find that you need to begin adding right rudder to counter the power-induced left turning tendency. You'll also find that you might need to apply opposite aileron (left aileron in this instance) to keep the bank from increasing too quickly as it's likely to do when right rudder is applied (Figure 49). Yes, you're in a cross controlled condition but that's just fine since this is the control combination it takes to keep the flight controls perfectly coordinated.

Another challenge most pilots face at 45 degrees of turn is determining how high to raise the nose. Ultimately, you want to pass through the 90 degree turn point at 5-10 knots above stall. That means you'll want to pitch the airplane upward sufficiently so that by 90 degrees of turn, the airspeed has decreased substantially. This means that you have to keep the longitudinal axis pointed some degree above the horizon right up until reaching 90 degrees of turn, at which point the longitudinal axis should be parallel to the earth's surface. If the longitudinal axis points below the horizon at any time prior to reaching 90 degrees of turn, then your airspeed will have already begun increasing (or at least stopped decreasing) by this point. That's not what you want, right? Right.

Fig. 50

As you approach the 90 degree turn point, you'll need to add a great deal of right rudder pressure to remain coordinated and a large amount of elevator back pressure, as well as needing left aileron to keep the bank from increasing too quickly.

Chapter 13: Advanced Maneuvers

Perhaps the best way to approximate your attitude is to plan on losing half of the total expected airspeed loss for this maneuver by the 45 degree turn point. Yes, this is a suggestion to initially fly the lazy eight mechanically. There's nothing wrong with this method since it's how you learn to do most things, right? So fly it mechanically at first and soon, with practice, you'll find that you're able to perform the maneuver in a very smooth and pro manner.

To keep the flight controls coordinated from 45 to 90 degrees of turn (Figure 50) and to keep the bank from increasing too quickly, you'll have to keep increasing right rudder pressure and deflecting the yoke to the left. Your maximum cross control condition occurs at 90 degrees of turn when the airspeed is slowest and the airplane's power-induced left turning tendency is greatest. This is the position where you'll typically find yourself with a large left deflection of the yoke and a large (and I do mean LARGE) amount of right rudder pressure applied. If you're not applying a relatively large amount of right rudder pressure here, then you're most likely not performing the maneuver correctly.

From 45 to 90 degrees of turn, you'll also need to hold a relatively large amount of elevator back pressure as your airspeed decreases. This is necessary because the slowest airspeed is reached at 90 degrees of turn with the nose (longitudinal axis) parallel with the horizon. Your airspeed won't continue to decrease from 45 to 90 degrees of turn unless you keep that nose above the horizon at least until reaching 90 degrees of turn. If you release elevator back pressure too soon, then your airspeed stops decreasing or perhaps even increases prior to the 90 degree turn point.

When reaching the 90 degree turn point (Figure 50) with your airspeed about 5-10 knots above stall, the longitudinal axis should be level with the earth's surface. As the nose passes through the reference point at a high rate of turn, and because you should be using a great deal of right rudder at this point to keep the controls coordinated, it will appear to *slice* through the reference point diagonally from upper left to lower right.

As you turn pass the 90 degree reference, you want to be careful not to let the nose drop too quickly as it is inclined to do when the vertical component of lift is tilted in a banked condition. That's why you should apply sufficient back pressure to actually lower the nose at a slow controlled rate below the horizon from 90 to 135 degrees of turn (Figure 51). Your objective is to continue decreasing the pitch attitude while simultaneously beginning your rollout. You want to reach 135 degrees of turn (the 135 degree reference point) at the lowest pitch attitude used for this maneuver and with your airspeed approximately half way between the entry speed and the speed at the 90 degree turn point.

Fig. 51

As you accelerate toward the 135 degree turn point, you'll have to gradually release the right rudder pressure you had previously applied while simultaneously rolling out with left aileron.

Helpful Hints

Typically, most pilots roll out too slowly when passing 90 degrees of turn, which dramatically alters the symmetry of the loop. They tend to hold their bank at 30 degrees as they lower the nose and remove the majority of it when passing 135 degrees of turn. This is easy to do given the high rate of turn resulting from the slow airspeed and steep bank found at 90 degree turn point. So begin decreasing your bank slowly but progressively when you turn past 90 degrees while simultaneously allowing the

At the completion of the second lazy eight loop you should continue the maneuver in the opposite direction unless the examiner or the instructor suggests otherwise.

attitude to progressively decrease. Strive to reach 15 degrees of bank at 135 degree of turn (Figure 51) where you should have the lowest pitch attitude for this entire maneuver.

Keep in mind that the lowest pitch attitude found at 135 degrees of turn doesn't mean that the airspeed peaks at this point, either. Because the airplane is pointed below the horizon, it is still accelerating as you raise the nose during the last 45 degrees of turn (from 135 to 180 degrees), which is also where you'll remove the last 15 degrees of bank. The highest airspeed (which is your original entry speed) is reached at the 180 degree turn point as the airplane passes through a level flight attitude. As your airspeed increases when turning from 90 to 180 degrees, you'll need to progressively release the right rudder pressure you've previously applied. Done properly, you'll arrive at 180 degrees of turn at the same airspeed and altitude at which you entered the maneuver (Figure 52). At this point you don't stop the maneuver. Instead, you continue it in a turn to the left, repeating the process until the examiner is satisfied with your performance (or your arms have fallen off).

One of the other challenges with this maneuver is that pilots often find that they've gained or lost altitude after one or two 180 degree turns (typically, it's a gain of altitude). Consider that the lazy eight is entered from level flight at a speed that's often considerably higher than the airplane's best rate of climb speed. As the airplane slows down during the climb, its climb efficiency increases (as it always does when flying at Vy or approaching Vy). This makes it easier to gain a little excess altitude when the airplane slows down during the maneuver. Unfortunately, if you try to lose this excess altitude in the nose-down portions of the lazy eight, you'll end up at a speed higher than your entry speed.

The *Airman Certification Standards* wants you to be at the same altitude and airspeed during each 180 degree turn point. That's why you'll often have to start the maneuver then reduce your power slightly. How much of a power reduction should you make? That depends, but it's typically about one or two inches of manifold pressure or a few hundred RPM. Of course, you'll know exactly how much to reduce the power once you get a little practice with the maneuver. On some occasions, however, it's actually necessary to increase power slightly, depending on the airplane used. Sorry, but airplanes and their performance do vary and it's hard to predict just what will happen until you observe the results in flight.

So there you have it, the commercial maneuvers explained in detail with quite a few observations to help you perform them better. I hope I've shed some light on this subject for you, especially since I'm going to get pretty dark as we talk about night flying in the next chapter.

Chapter 14
Night Flying
Taming the Dark Side

History doesn't record who made the first night flight, but my guess is that he probably wished he had a real live echo-locating bat in his pocket to help with the navigation. The experience had to be a real eye opener, or a real pupil opener to be exact. In the same way you roll down a car's window to let more air into the vehicle, you widen the pupil to let more light into the eye. After all, it's dark at night. This makes everything harder to see. Now your ability to estimate practical things such as your speed and proximity to a reference in your environment is diminished. We simply don't see as well at night.

The problem for pilots is that we often don't know we can't see as well. Sure, we might know it intellectually, but we don't necessarily act on that knowledge, at least not until we have our first encounter with (or fall victim to) any one of the physical and/or psychological limitations that night operations impose on us. Either way, night flying can be quite safe as long as you know how to deal with the dark times—those times beginning after sunset and ending before sunrise. Since we often spend a great deal of time in the dark, let's shed the light on the night by examining what you need know to fly safely during these times.

It's true. There are approximately three times more aviation accidents at night than there are during the day. Why the difference? It's not necessarily because it's harder to see *lighted* objects at night. In fact, it's actually easier to see lights at night but that doesn't mean that night lighting conveys the same information to your brain as does the illumination of the object and its surroundings by direct sunlight.

Flying at night deprives you of the essential peripheral information used to assess runway closure rate, terrain closure rate, the distance between you and any

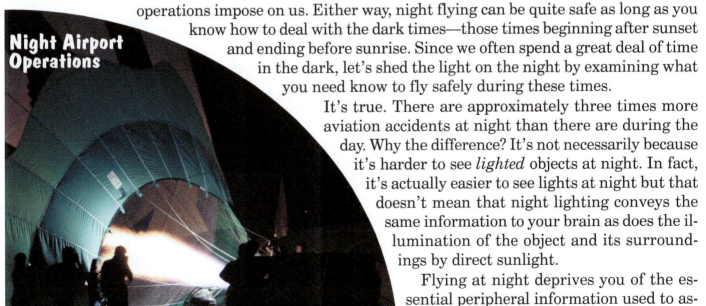

Night Airport Operations

object, and your airplane's attitude which means identifying the horizon line when it's not clearly definable at night. Under daylight conditions, however, we obtain (see) additional information from our environment which allows us to more accurately judge our speed, closure rate, distance, attitude and so one. When the sun isn't shining, we need to make adjustments in our mental and physical behavior to compensate for this loss of information.

The problem with night flying is that some pilots tend to fly at night the same way they fly during the day. In other words, they don't adjust their behavior to the diminished peripheral information available to them. This is one of the reasons automobile drivers have more accidents at night. They typically drive at the same speed as they do during the day while having less peripheral road and traffic information. Is it any wonder that drivers might round a curve too quickly when they can't use the surrounding terrain to properly assess their speed or approach other automobiles at excessive speeds when they see car lights but not the actual car? A lighted object provides relatively little information about that object's distance, much less your closure rate with that object while driving at night. The same applies to flying airplanes at night, too.

That's why night flying is an art unto itself, and thus the reason for a chapter entirely dedicated to the subject. It's also why the FAA requires three hours of night flight training to obtain an unrestricted private pilot certificate.

So let's start with those two marvelous optic orbs you own, each having its own socket, connecting cable and protective covering. I'm speaking about your eyes, of course.

Flight Vision: Your Eyes in the Sky

To understand just how magnificent a creation your eyes are, consider how well they actually allow you to see. In his book, *The Seven Mysteries of Life*, author Guy Murchie stated that it's possible for someone to see a match struck on a mountain top on a clear night from as far as 50 miles away. No, that's not one of Murchie's mysteries, either. In Chuck Yeager's autobiography, the General states that his vision was so good that he could detect enemy airplanes at a distance of 50 miles during the day. Of course this was during the latter stages of WWII and he was in combat. So he was motivated to see things, especially things that would point guns at him. Nevertheless, you are quite capable of seeing things at a great distance, especially at night, but only

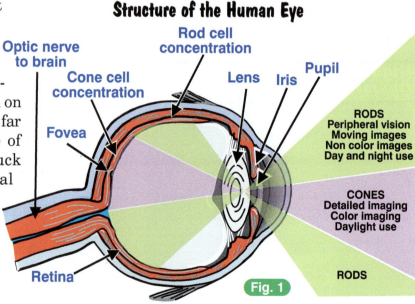

The human eye has separate structures for aiding both night vision and day vision. Cone cells, located within the fovea, are very effective during the day for detailed imagery and color imagery. Rod cells, located outside the fovea, are best used for detection of moving images and non-color images. They are effective during day and nighttime hours.

Chapter 14: Night Flying

if you know how to do it. And that means knowing a little something about how your eyes work.

Figure 1 shows a side view of the human eye. Light passes through the pupil and lens, then falls upon the retina at the very back of the eye. The light sensitive area of the retina is made up of individual cells known as *rods* and *cones*.

Cone cells are concentrated in a small section in the center of the retina known as the fovea. These cells decrease in number with distance from this center point. While the eye can observe an approximate 200 degree arc at a glance, only the light falling on the fovea has the ability to send the brain a *sharp, clearly-focused* image. All light falling outside the fovea will be of less detail (Figures 2 and 3). For example, an airplane at a distance of 7 miles which appears in sharp focus within the foveal center of vision would have to be as close as 7/10 of a mile in order to be recognized if it were outside the foveal field of vision.

Cone cells are responsible for allowing you to perceive color and detail during the day. By looking directly at an object, most of the image is focused on the fovea. Unfortunately, the cones don't work well when it's dark. This explains why it's difficult to perceive color at night compared to the daylight hours.

Rod cells (no, they aren't named after me) are concentrated on the outside of the fovea and are known as dim-light receptors (that's why I'm happy they aren't named after me). Since these rods are located outside the fovea, they are responsible for our peripheral vision, as shown in Figure 4. *Moving* images are more easily detected by rod cells than by cone cells. Catching an object out of the corner of your eye is an example of rod cells at work.

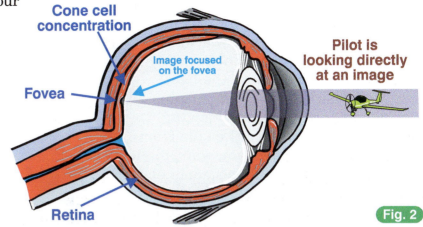

Fig. 2 — Looking directly at an object focuses the image on the fovea. The image falls on the cone cells that are effective at distinguishing color and image detail. Unfortunately, cone cells are less effective when it's dark. This is why it's difficult to distinguish color and detail at night.

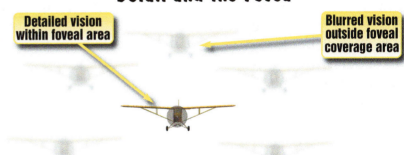

Fig. 3

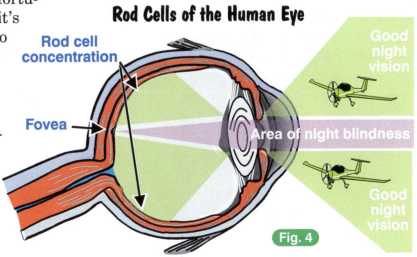

Fig. 4 — Looking directly at an object at night makes it difficult to see. At night it's best to look 5 to 10 degrees offset from center for better vision. This allows the light from dimly lit objects to fall on the rod cells (surrounding the foveal region) which are better for night vision.

Since cone cells don't work well in the dark, it's difficult to see an object at night even though you're looking directly at it (Figure 4). If you want the best view of a dimly lit object you need to expose the rods to the light. You can do this by using your peripheral vision for off-center viewing. Look 5 to 10 degrees to the side from the center of the object you want to view (Figure 5). Doing so allows some of the object's reflected light to fall on the rods. You can demonstrate this process at night by looking directly at an airplane's strobe light head on, then looking at the same light offset a few degrees. Big difference. A direct view dims the object while an indirect view increases its brightness.

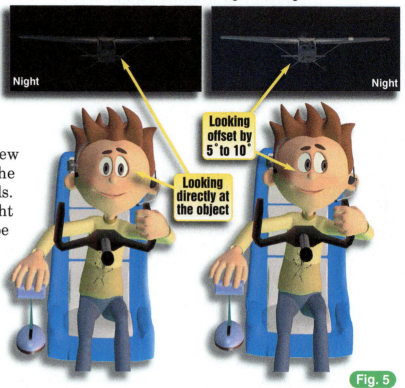

At night it's much easier to see an object if you direct your vision 5° to 10° degrees to the side of the object you're attempting to identify.

Night Vision

How well you see at night is determined by the amount of light passing through your pupils (Figure 6). As you know, pupils close to prevent the eyes from receiving too much light and open when light intensity diminishes. They also open (dilate) to let in more light when it's dark. In fact, those pupils increase in diameter by a factor of five, from 2 mm to 10 mm. This increases the light entering the eye by about 25 times. You would think that this enormous opening would assure you adequate vision at night. It might do that but only if you haven't bleached a very important chemical located in those rod cells, known as *rhodopsin*. No, I don't mean bleaching as in someone bleaching their hair. I'm speaking of exposing rhodopsin to sunlight in such a way that it prevents your eyes from seeing properly at night regardless of their gigantic dilated pupils.

Let's look at the eye's visual cycle (Figure 7) to see how bleaching of rhodopsin occurs. When light energy (photons) enter the eye, it stimulates the chemical rhodopsin (position A) located in the rod cells which are located in the retina. Rhodopsin is a light sensitive chemical that absorbs this photonic energy and converts it into both electrical and chemical energy (position B).

The molecule cis-retinal (known to you as Vitamin A) now begins to straighten and detach from the opsin protein. As it does, electrical energy is released and sent to the brain via the optic nerve (position B). This is the electrical energy responsible for forming an image in your brain. The straightening cis-retinal molecule is now fully straightened and is *transformed* into trans-retinal (position C).

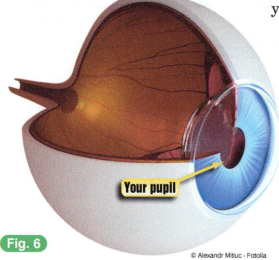

The pupil controls the light entering the eye. If your eyes have adjusted to daytime lighting, it might take 30 minutes or more for the eye to adapt to night conditions.

Chapter 14: Night Flying

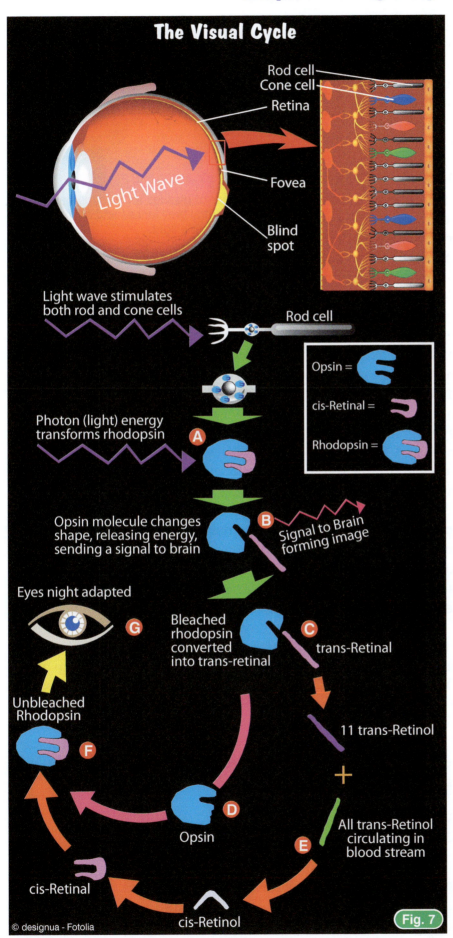

The Visual Cycle

Fig. 7

At this point the rhodopsin molecule has been completely bleached, meaning that it has been converted into trans-retinal and opsin (position D). This is what is known as (photobleaching). Neither opsin or trans-retinal are useful for vision until they recombine to form rhodopsin again.

The chemical recombination process occurs in several steps (position E) until the rod cells are re-supplied with rhodopsin (now unbleached) as shown in position F. At this point, your eyes are considered to be night adapted.

The problem is that if your eyes have adjusted to daytime lighting, then you have bleached a great deal of the rhodopsin molecule. If this occurs close to sunset, then it's possible you might find yourself flying with eyes that haven't had a chance to resupply themselves with rhodopsin. Believe me when I say that you will have a much more challenging time seeing things under these conditions.

As a general rule, it might take at least 30 minutes for your eyes to completely adapt to the dark. This is especially true if you've spent a lot of time in direct and intense sunlight.

You can, however, achieve a moderate degree of dark adaptation within 20 minutes under dim red cockpit lighting. This is one reason you want to avoid very bright lights for at least a half-hour before a night flight. If you suddenly find yourself in need of using a bright white light in the cockpit at night (such as a flashlight), try closing one eye while the light's in use. This keeps the closed eye night adapted. It also makes you look like a pirate, perhaps a private pirate.

Fortunately, rhodopsin isn't as affected by red light, so its use doesn't diminish your night vision. This is why most airplane cockpits offer you the choice of red overhead lighting to illuminate the cockpit and panel. Now you know why red lighting is often used in darkrooms. Photosensitive paper isn't so photosensitive to red wavelengths (when there were such things as darkrooms).

A good pair of glasses for aviation have either green or neutral gray lenses and absorb at least 85% of the visible light.

One time I spent an entire day shooting an aviation video outdoors. This was done on a bright clear day with several members of the production crew aiming light reflecting mirrors at my face to enhance the video quality. My body felt like a big ant being zapped by a magnifying glass. After eight hours of sun fun we wrapped up the shoot and I flew home in my Bonanza. Arriving 20 minutes later near sunset, my airplane turned onto base leg where the runway, 45 degrees to my left and resting just below the setting sun, was completely invisible to me. My eyes were night blind after absorbing nearly a full day's worth of sunlight. This was one time where a "pocket bat" would have helped me find my way around the traffic pattern. My initial approach ended up as a go-around, followed by circling for about 20 minutes until my eyes had adapted to the dark. It would have been better for me had sunglassess been worn for the entire video shoot (or an arc welding helmet).

Using sunglasses for protection from glare is most helpful in preventing night vision deterioration as well as preventing eye strain and eye damage (Figure 8). Find sunglasses that absorb at least 85% of the visible light (15% transmittance) and have minimal color distortion. Green or neutral gray are recommended colors. Do, however, avoid pink flamingo framed glasses. These won't help you pass your checkride. I make it a point to ensure all my sunglasses have a high degree of impact resistance, too. Why impact resistance? They are excellent eye protectors in the event that something—such as hail, a pink flamingo or any other bird—penetrates the windshield during flight.

You can enhance your night vision by using supplemental oxygen if it's available on board your airplane. No, you don't blow it on directly onto your eyes, either. You breathe it. It turns out that our eyes can experience the effects of diminished oxygen levels at cabin altitudes as low as 5,000 feet. You won't notice the loss of visual acuity during the day as much as you would at night. One of the neatest experiments you can do is to climb to 5,000 or more on a clear night, and before using supplemental oxygen, look up at the stars. You'll see a few, of course. Now breathe supplemental oxygen while keeping an eye on the stars. Suddenly your vision dramatically improves and the star field appears to become much brighter (unless they've brightened because you've just made the jump to warp speed). Your vision improves because your eyes now have more oxygen available to them.

Aging and Night Vision

We'd all like to think we're forever young, but there are undeniable effects of aging and one of the most noticeable is a decline in night visual acuity.

This happens for number of reasons. First and foremost, significantly less light hits the retina as we age, due mostly to a reduction in pupil size. By age 60, even

Chapter 14: Night Flying

in the daytime, the retina receives only one-third the amount of light it did at age 20. At night, the retina of an 80-year-old receives one-sixteenth the light that falls on the retina of a 20-year old.

As if this weren't bad enough news, other aspects of night vision are also adversely affected with age. The time it takes to achieve dark adaptation lengthens in our later years. Once rhodopsin has been photobleached, it takes longer for opsin and trans-retinal to recombine. This means that, on average, there isn't as much active rhodopsin around to absorb photons and thus detect light.

Turn down the lights and you initially have no un-split rhodopsin in the rods to detect photons. If you're young, the reunion of retinal and opsin happens quickly, so you can see well in the dark pretty quickly. If you're not so young, you have to wait longer for the reunion and thus for your night vision to return to a level that's considered normal for you (whatever level that might be).

Color vision and contrast sensitivity also decline with increasing age, making it more and more difficult to discern what lies beyond your cockpit windscreen. Some colors (primarily blues and blue-greens) are more affected and thus less detectable at night. No, you can't use this as a ready excuse if you accidentally fly through a Blue Angel's formation during a TFR'd airshow. You'll gain no points with the FAA by saying, "Ahh, Mr. Inspector, I'm 80 years old and those jets are blue. Do I need to connect the dots for you?"

Finally, as you age, the ability of the lens to bend (much like your back) and focus an image sharply on the retina starts to wane. This is why most people eventually end up wearing glasses by age 40 or so. The lens, supple in youth, becomes less flexible with age and can't be bent over as great a range to focus images from both near and far.

Visual Illusions

There are situations where you can encounter instrument-like conditions without being in a cloud during visual meteorological conditions (VMC). At night, a blending of the earth and sky is often responsible for creating an indiscernible horizon which can make you feel as if you're in actual instrument condition. This is most prevalent on moonless nights where stars take on the appearance of city lights and city lights appear to be stars (Figure 9).

Another common visual illusion occurs when you are flying in the direction of a lit shoreline. With a dark foreground underneath you (think: the unlit surface of water), it's easy for shoreline lights (the background) to be mistaken for stars (especially if you frequently skipped high school astronomy class to go surfing) as shown in Figure 10.

False Horizons

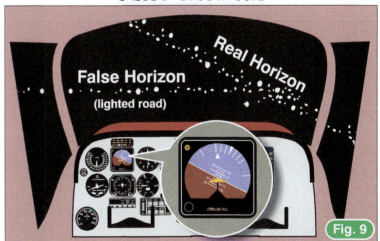

In this example a lighted road can be misinterpreted as the actual horizon at night. This can be very disconcerting to a pilot.

When the foreground is unlit and the background contains stars, it's possible for a pilot to think he or she has gone inverted.

The airplane's position lights are required to be on from sunset to sunrise. This simply makes it easier to identify aircraft in flight.

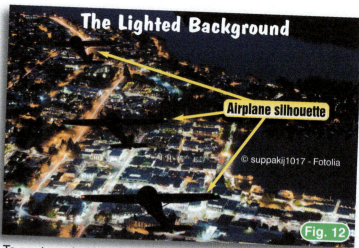

To spot an airplane below you at night against a lighted background requires you to look for the motion of its silhouette and position lights against the background.

Then there's the visual illusion known as *autokinesis*, which has nothing to do with your automobile. It's a visual illusion that occurs when you stare at a stationary light located in a dark background. The light appears to move because of small, frequent, involuntary movements of your eyeball. This is especially likely when there's nothing in the background on which your eyes can focus. As a result, there's a tendency to attribute motion to a stationary lighted object.

Believe me when I say that more than one pilot flying IFR on top of the clouds has yanked and banked in response to staring at the planet Venus. Of course, if you scream, "Look out! It's Venus," then everyone onboard will know that you actually passed your high school astronomy course but didn't do so well in pilot school. To prevent this type of astronomical embarrassment, don't stare directly at stationary light sources when it's dark. Besides, looking askew allows you to better see and identify lighted objects at night.

Night Scanning for Traffic

As a general rule, it's easier to spot an aircraft by its lights at night than it is to spot it during the day. This, however, doesn't mean it's easier to identify an aircraft's distance, size and direction of movement at night. That's why airplanes are required to have their position lights on from sunset to sunrise (anticollision lights are to be on at *all times* when the airplane is in operation)

The Parallax Effect

The "parallax effect" describes a type of visual illusion in which the position of an object in 3-dimensional space appears to change, due to a shift in the position of the observer. The parallax effect can make distant fixed objects, such as a planet or star, appear to be close and in motion. The twinkling planet Venus is a well-known example in aviation. Tower con-

trollers have often cleared Venus to land, while pilots have mistaken the planet for nearby aircraft lights.

The parallax effect is especially apt to occur during night operations when there may be few, or no, visible references to the horizon as an aircraft moves through space. Several ASRS reports illustrate this phenomena, beginning with a First Officer's account of a nighttime evasive maneuver that startled crew and passengers:

I observed what I believed to be an imminent traffic conflict. I manually overrode the autopilot and started an immediate left turn. The perceived conflict was a result of slight parallax of green and red wingtip lights of another aircraft. A bright white star also appeared as one of the running lights on the perceived conflict. The maneuver was a gut reaction on my part, as I perceived the aircraft to be within a few thousand feet from us. Passengers and flight attendants who were not seated with their belts fastened were upended in the cabin. One passenger received an abrasion to a knee and one complained of a neck injury after landing. No passengers required medical attention. The aircraft was inspected for overstress and no discrepancies were found.

A conservative approach, followed by the First Officer in this instance, is to avoid the perceived hazard first, and verify the nature of the hazard afterwards. Although this report didn't mention crew fatigue as a factor, fatigue is known to be associated with susceptibility to the parallax illusion. U.S. Air Force research has shown that a few minutes of breathing 100% oxygen will help to refocus pilots' thinking—and eyesight.

ASRS Report

Chapter 14: Night Flying

as shown in Figure 11 (more on position lights shortly). Spotting an aircraft at night, however, becomes much more difficult when it is imposed on a lighted background, such as city lighting (Figure 12). Therefore, when descending into a lit background at night, your ability to identify traffic requires that you look for the relative motion of position lights and a dark silhouette against the lit background.

Night Flying Skills and Techniques

If you're a private pilot you've probably had at least three hours of night flying experience. Therefore, you'll have at least minimal experience when you take off with passengers at night for the first time. But minimal isn't always comforting. That's why I'd like to give you the benefit of all the little things I've learned over the years about flying safely at night. So let's begin by shedding a little light on the subject by discussing flashlights.

Flashlights—You Can Never Have Enough of These

The very first thing you want to do when considering flying at night is to make a visit to the nearest hardware store and buy flashlights (Figure 13). One? Two? How many? Buy four or five. I'm not kidding. You can never have enough flashlights when flying at night. No, it's not that you'll likely need them. Instead, you have them in case you need them. Just imagine being above an overcast on a moonless night or above the deserts of the southwestern United States at night and having your electrical system fail. It could be dark enough that you wouldn't be able to see any distinct horizon, much less your panel.

Bring Along Flashlights!
And Even More Batteries!
Fig. 13
© Sandra van der Steen - Fotolia

Believe it or not, this might be a perfectly legal thing for a VFR pilot to do (I said, "legal," I didn't say, "wise"). Without the ability to obtain some basic instrument reference to help you control your airplane, you're no better off than a pilot in the clouds without the necessary instruments to control his or her flying machine.

Fortunately, there are a large variety of flashlights from which to choose. You can purchase the standard flashlight you hold in your hand, as well as the type that you connect to your body or headset. I've always been a fan of the miner's flashlight (no, that's not a flashlight limited to those under 18 years of age). This is the type that's connected to your headset or hangs from your neck by a small rope. There are even mega-powerful small book lights that help you read in the dark. One of these clipped to your shirt pocket can provide adequate panel lighting in an emergency as well as allow you to read uplifting aviation poetry just in case your wings aren't developing enough lift.

A Sign of Trouble

A Tower Controller submitted this report of a night taxi incident in which an aircraft, apparently with no lights on, encountered an unlit sign with an ironic message.

It was still dark out when I issued taxi instructions to a PA28 to [taxi to] the runway via Taxiway Foxtrot. After a minute or so had passed and I hadn't seen the aircraft begin his taxi, I asked him where he was. Radio problems are not uncommon in that area as there are spots that are obscured by a hangar. He told me he had just passed an intersection and was going to have to get out of the aircraft and assess some damage. I again asked him where he was and found him on a service road south of taxiway Foxtrot. He didn't have any aircraft lights turned on. He had run into a "This Is Not a Taxiway" sign.

ASRS Report

The Dark Preflight

Doesn't that sound like a preflight you do while wearing a black robe with a hood? Well, flying at night often requires preflighting in the dark, and here is where your flashlight comes in handy (Figure 14). Of course, there have been times when I've driven my car up to the airplane and shined its headlights on the fuselage to make the preflight a bit easier. So don't be stingy with your photons. Use whatever light source is available to you for preflighting.

Checking all the external lights before departure is a must if you want to remain legal as well as be safe at night. You need the navigation lights and anti-collision lights to help other people see you. They don't call it an *anti-collision* light for nothing, right?

One instructor I chatted with told me that he had to complete some night dual instruction since his student was taking a checkride the next day. It turned out that his rotating beacon stopped rotating during the last 10 minutes of the night touch and go landing session. The tower informed him of his beacon's rotational failure. So for the last 10 minutes he sat there turning the switch on and off to simulate beacon rotation. Right or wrong—OK, mostly wrong—you do have to give him credit for creativity.

It's important to get one very important point lodged in your noggin regarding night flying: if it's dark outside, it's most likely dark inside the cockpit. Sure, most airplanes have cockpit lighting, which varies in intensity from that produced by a flamed-out firefly to that of a Hollywood search light. Typically, you want to keep those bright white lights down in the cockpit which means organizing your charts, papers and pens so that they're easy to find. The last thing you want to do is deprive yourself of dark adapted vision because you had to illuminate the cockpit just to find a chart that's slipped under a seat. If, however, you do have to use that flashlight to hunt for charts, this is where it would be wise do close one eye to keep the other eye night adapted.

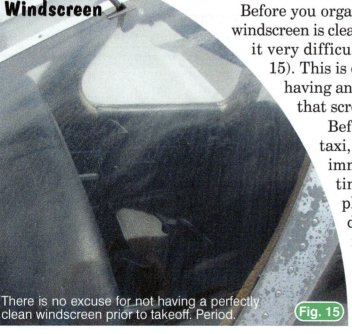

There is no excuse for not having a perfectly clean windscreen prior to takeoff. Period. Fig. 15

Before you organize your cockpit, I suggest you make sure your windscreen is cleaned. A dirty windscreen scatters light and makes it very difficult to see anything outside the airplane (Figure 15). This is especially true when taxing near bright lights or having another airplane's bright light shine on you. Clean that screen and give it a sheen.

Before you enter the airplane to begin your night taxi, please take a look around the airplane and the immediate taxi path. You'll be surprised how many times people park cars at night in obstructing places where they wouldn't dream of doing so during the day (maybe because they were dreaming while they parked their cars). Sometimes lock boxes are moved and forgotten, or objects are dropped from cars that can't be easily observed at night. One friend told me he saw a suitcase in the middle of a taxiway at a non-

Chapter 14: Night Flying

Smartphone, Smart Preflight

You paid good money for that Smartphone so it's time to get your money's worth. During your next night (or day) preflight, activate the phone's video camera with the light on (assuming your phone has a video camera and a light). Now stick that phone into those dark crevices that are often challenging to inspect during a preflight at night. That's right, poke that phone around the corners inside the cowling and get a photonic revelation about the well being of your airplane's pipes, tubes and wires. This is a handy tool for being able to look around where it's dark and where it's hard to inspect with a flashlight. Whatever you do, however, don't drop the phone inside the cowling. If you do, you'll need to use your passenger's phone to find yours. Whatever you do, don't drop that one. That wouldn't be smart.

An Embarrassing Lesson

Taxiing and flying an airplane will always involve some degree of multi-tasking, but this C172 pilot learned an embarrassing lesson when the "heads-down" usage of an electronic tablet conflicted with the "heads-up" requirements of safe taxiing.

We were cleared by Ground to taxi on the outer ramp area to Taxiway Bravo to Runway 22 and hold short. It's a "no-brainer" taxi route and there were no other aircraft taxiing out. I was with another pilot and was showing him the information I had available on my iPad with ForeFlight. I was showing how I had the enroute charts for our trip and then went to the checklists, also on the iPad. I was definitely multi-tasking as I taxied and demonstrated the software. I was aware of the runway area approaching but missed the hold short line until Ground said, "[Callsign], stop. Stop!"

I would never dream of texting on my phone while driving, but wasn't this sort of the same thing? There was no traffic for the runway, but it was still an embarrassing lesson learned.

ASRS Report

---

towered airport at night. Most likely a pilot placed it on top his car after returning from a night trip and forgot it as he drove away from his tiedown spot. Can you imagine hitting this suitcase with your prop, disintegrating the luggage only to have someone's shorts fly up and land on your windscreen? That would certainly cause a short in your visual system, wouldn't it? To prevent taking it in the shorts, give the ground a look around before you enter your flying machine.

Night Taxiing

Let's get it on…get your taxi or landing lights on, that is. After engine start, when you're ready to make your move on the airport surface, you'll want to ensure you can see where you're going. For airplanes with both taxi and landing lights, you'll want to operate your taxi light (Figure 16). The taxi light allows you to see what's ahead, but it gives you little or no information about what's next to your airplane's wings. This is why it's important to taxi slow enough so that you can evaluate your wing's distance from nearby objects. Believe me when I say that it can be very difficult to estimate your distance from an airport fence, pole or building at night. Is this a good enough reason for you to stay perfectly centered on the yellow taxiway centerline? You bet it is.

Make sure you use your taxi light at night. The taxi light normally (not always) shines downward at a larger angle than the landing light. Nevertheless, be prepared to turn your landing and taxi lights off if either point directly at another aircraft for any length of time.

Another reason to carry at least one powerful flashlight is that it can be used to illuminate a nearby obstruction in the proximity of your wing during night taxi. Then again, if your taxi space is that tight, it's sometimes better to stop the engine, exit the airplane and use the towbar to pull the airplane through the critical area. If you have passengers on board, you can shut the engine down and have them do the pulling, while you direct them with your "point and yell" management skills.

Courtesy is another aspect of good airmanship during night operations (no, not curtsey, which you'd only use when taxiing past a King or Queen Air). If you're taxiing toward someone while operating a taxi or landing light, it's often best to turn it off to prevent that pilot's pupils from clamping shut so tight that WD-40 won't open them. This also applies to the strobe light that you might be using, too. During ground operations, strobe lights from your airplane don't typically affect you as much as they do other pilots in your vicinity. If you're in the runup area close to another airplane, it's often best to turn the strobes off until you resume your taxi. And please, if someone in the cockpit asks if your strobes are on, don't say, "Yes, no, yes, no, yes…." You'll be picked up by the humor police and taken to a no-bail jail.

Zapped by Little Green Men

I had been playing "Space Invaders" for about two straight hours when I and an inexperienced co-pilot were launched to find a man believed to be injured who was lost in dense underbrush. After we got to the search pattern [and are] only 100 to 200 feet above the ridgeline we were searching, I started "seeing" (imagining) the Space Invaders descending down the windscreen. I gave the helicopter to my co-pilot, who continued the search at a higher, safer altitude. It took me about two minutes to de-program the Space Invaders out of my vision. Why did this happen? Two hours of self-induced strong visual programming plus mental exhaustion from a normal day and intense game "arcade fever" combined to catch me off guard in a quiet moment in the cockpit....The knowledge that I was dangerously close to "granitus" and a well-developed ability to concentrate on the instruments and facts pulled us out of that situation. Needless to say, I don't spend that... [much] time... in the arcade anymore!

NASA Report

Ready, Set, Go

If you're like most pilots, you get a little nervous when a tower controller has you taxi into position and wait on a runway at night. Since it's difficult to crank your neck around to see what's behind you, how do you know that there's not someone on final with the potential to land on you? Well, aside from all the normal things you'll do, such as listening carefully to what other airplanes in the pattern or on approach are saying, consider this bit of advice. When lining up and waiting on the runway at night, you might want to position yourself slightly offset (perhaps two or three feet) from the runway centerline and ensure that your taxi or landing light is on (Figure 17). This makes it slightly easier for an airplane on final approach to identify you. Of course, when cleared for takeoff, you'll want to return to the centerline before adding full power. Am I recommending this strategy because I don't trust the tower controller to keep another airplane from landing on me? Yes, absolutely! That's not an affront to the tower controller, either. Instead, it's a statement of my concern about being flattened by another airplane. This recommendation harms no one, but it does reduce the risks of holding in position for takeoff.

Night takeoffs are unique for a few reasons. First, you have less and less chance of avoiding some-

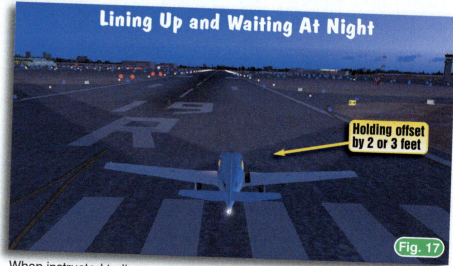

When instructed to line up and wait on the runway at night, it's often best to move a little to the side of the centerline with your landing/taxi light on to make it easier for an aircraft on final approach to identify you.

Chapter 14: Night Flying

Fig. 18

At airports in rural areas at night, it's possible that you might rotate the airplane and suddenly find that there is no visible horizon for attitude control. You might have to temporarily rely on your instruments.

Lights Out!

A corporate pilot almost found himself left in the dark when his aircraft experienced a total electrical failure.

I activated the pilot-controlled runway lighting and proceeded with my run-up and pre-flight checks. [After takeoff], I turned off my aircraft landing light, after which I lost all electricals. I turned back to the field... I did not feel I could spend much time in the pattern because the pilot-controlled lighting might go out and I would have no way to reactivate the runway lights. I decided to land in the reverse direction...

Posting of "on times" (5 minutes, 10 minutes, etc.) for lighting on charts, airport guides, etc. would allow pilots to determine how much time is left before shutoff of runway lights in emergency electrical failures.

Some additional pre-flight reading might have saved our reporter a lot of worry. The Chart Supplement indicates that this airport has pilot-controlled Medium Intensity Runway Lighting (MIRL), an FAA-approved system. The AIM explains that FAA-approved lighting systems illuminate the lights for a period of 15 minutes from the time of the most recent activation. The AIM suggests that, even when runway lights are on, pilots should key their mikes seven times, to ensure that the full 15-minute lighting duration is available.

ASRS Report

thing ahead of you as you accelerate during the takeoff roll. The faster you go the harder it is to stop, right? So you'll have to do your best to ensure that there's no one or nothing else on the runway that you're using for takeoff. Here is where turning on the landing light can help for takeoff. Sometimes your landing light shines farther down the runway (I say sometimes because sometimes it's the taxi light that shines farther down the runway. It all depends on the manufacturer. Go figure). So activate the light that shines the farthest down the runway when taking off. This just makes it easier to see and be seen on the takeoff roll.

Of course, I'm assuming that the runway edge lighting is active during your night takeoff, too. There's no practical reason for taking off with these lights off. If the lights are pilot controlled, it pays to remember that *pilot controlled lighting* should remains on for 15 minutes before shutting off. You don't want to begin your takeoff roll 10 seconds before these lights shut off, otherwise you'll experience something known as the, "What the hay?" phenomena. This is where something strange happens and your entire emergency procedure consists of saying, "What the hay?" So, unless you want a good case of "What the hay?" fever, it's best to key the mic seven times before taking the active runway at night at an uncontrolled field. This recues the lights to remain on for another 15 minutes.

Lifting off at night can be interesting, especially if there is no discernable horizon. You may rotate only to find that you have no visible reference by which to calibrate your pitch attitude. If this happens, then it's entirely reasonable to use your attitude indicator and airspeed indicator to establish your climb attitude. Remember, this is night flying and it's unlikely you'll be able to see as well as you can during the day.

This type of scenario is most likely when departing from a desert airport on a moonless night (Figure 18). Without the moon's presence in this figure, you might have a very difficult time identifying the horizon line after liftoff. It's interesting to note that the *Aeronautical Information Manual* (AIM) provides information on moon phases for helicopter operations since helicopter pilots tend to operate close to the surface for long periods of time. But don't airplane pilots sometimes operate close to the surface at critical times such as departing at night? You bet they do. So, take a peek at the AIM for any relevant moonshine information. At least you'll have a little more info about a potential horizon-identification problem when departing a desert airport at night.

While the landing light may be a useful reference during the night takeoff roll, it's not really helpful during the climb. If you're departing in haze or low visibility conditions, it's entirely possible that the landing light beam might become distracting. After all, it's a beam of light that's reflecting off the particulate matter in the air and it's really doing nothing for you, unless you're a Star Wars fan—then it looks like your airplane is equipped with a light saber, and you might become distracted imagining all the neat things you could do with it. So, with all due respect to Obi Wan, don't "be one" of the distracted in hazy conditions. Turn your landing light off after liftoff if it distracts you.

Personally, at night, when no haze is present, I prefer to keep the landing light on when I'm near an airport or in a busy terminal area (and not because I like to yell out, "Darth Vader, who's your daddy?" when landing, either). It just makes it easier for other airplanes to see and avoid me. During the enroute phase of flight where you'll find far fewer airplanes, then turn the light off.

Night Enroute Conditions

Once again, let me remind you that it's dark at night. What does that mean in terms of seeing other airplanes? Well, you can certainly spot an airplane easier at night than during the day. But that really is the only benefit you have (unless your complexion looks a bit spotty in direct sunlight). As far as identifying the direction and speed of the airplane, well, that's not so easy.

It's far more challenging to identify whether or not an airplane is moving toward or away from you at night than during the day. Why? Because the only reference by which you can compare closure is the relative distance between the airplane's position lights (Figure 19A and 19B). Typically, you will see two of these lights at any one time. This might consist of the white tail light and one wing light, or two wing lights when the airplane is coming directly at you, or a white tail light and two wing lights when the airplane is heading away from you. These lighting angles vary between airplane manufacturers.

For instance, an airplane can be flying a path from right to left across your flight path and you can see the tail lights and the left wing (red) light (Figure 20). You might close in on this airplane without being able to detect the increasing distance between the lights as you would the increasing size of the actual airplane during the day. So what's a pilot to do?

At night you simply have to be more cautious of the aircraft you see (or the lights on the aircraft you see) while airborne. You really have no choice

The relationship between the right and left wing position lights helps identify if the airplane is coming or going.

The relationship between the right and left wing position lights helps identify if the airplane is moving to the right or left.

but to fly defensively, going out of your way to maneuver around suspect aircraft. Consider that any lights seen above the horizon are a potential threat, assuming that these aren't celestial objects. These lights might belong to an airplane or a mountain peak (assuming there's a light on that peak and you're operating at an altitude below it) or a tower (again, assuming there's a light on the tower and you're operating below it). Lights below the horizon can be a potential threat, too. An airplane ahead and below you that's climbing toward you often blends in with any terrestrial lighting below the horizon. This is one reason why the movement of lights relative to the background (the sky or the ground) becomes an important means of assessing potential targets.

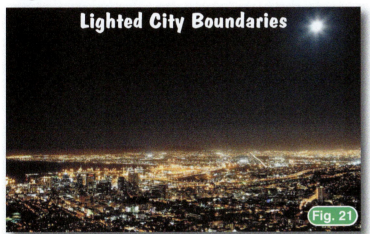

The boundaries of cities are easily identified by lights at night. This makes night cross country navigation by pilotage a little bit easier, but not as easy as it is during the day.

Navigating at night is when pilots learn the real challenge of night operations. Pilotage is still possible, but let's face it, unless a river is filled with electric eels or phosphorescent algae, it's harder to identify ground objects at night. Then again, roads and city outlines are relatively easier to identify (Figure 21). So that's a plus for you in the pilotage box. In general, it's much easier to get lost at night for one simple reason: you most likely acquired all your cross country navigation skills during the day. Whether you realize it or not, you've come to rely on landmarks to help you find your way around your local area. I've taken students on *dual* cross country flights at night then, upon returning home, they became location challenged (lost) a few miles from the airport. They couldn't orient themselves without knowing where Saddleback peak or the Hilton Hotel were located (despite a big fat lighted runway filling their windshield).

You can expect to rely more on other types of navigation at night, such as GPS or VOR navigation (Figure 22). Of course, if you were worried about a GPS equipment failure during a day cross country, you might want to double that worry when flying at night. I've heard rumors about pilots becoming quite disoriented at night when the depleted batteries in their handheld GPS revolted by giving up their volts. The problem here is that these pilots were lost the moment they took off but didn't know it.

Once the GPS failed, their "lostness" became quite apparent. Isn't that interesting? You can know precisely where you are on a moving map but still be lost. That's because not being lost implies knowing how to get where you want to go. If your moving map fails and you know precisely where you are, that means nothing unless you know how to use that info to get where you want to go. More than a few pilots knew their location when their moving map failed but then lost track of their position as the airplane continued to move while they attempted to plot a course

With GPS, night navigation becomes much easier. It's also much easier to become lost at night if you lose your GPS capability.

Circling Descent to Mountain Airport

A safe way to approach an airport surrounded by mountains at night is to descend from overhead on the side of the airport where the traffic pattern is flown (within the normal boundaries of that traffic pattern). This allows you to descend to pattern altitude and enter the downwind leg safely.

to their desired destination. One pilot with a failed moving map was spared embarrassment at night when he spotted a big fat road and followed it to the nearest city (where there's likely to be an airport nearby).

One of the other problems pilots face at night involves the mountains. Believe it or not, pilots can have trouble knowing where the mountains are at night. This is why you must know your exact location and altitude in relation to mountainous terrain. At night, I always plan to cross any mountain range at an altitude that's at least 2,000 feet above the highest peak within several miles of my planned route.

For many pilots, however, the tricky part of crossing mountainous terrain involves knowing when to descend to clear those peaks or hills. Perhaps the safest way to descend into an airport *surrounded* by mountains, or where mountains concern you, is to descend to traffic pattern altitude from directly over the airport. You'll do this on the side of the runway where the traffic pattern is normally flown. This is made especially easy if you happen to have a moving map display in your airplane (Figure 23). Keeping your airspeed at the same speed at which you fly the pattern, then descending on the pattern side of the runway, allows you to descend to pattern altitude with a high degree of safety.

Mystery of the Disappearing Lights

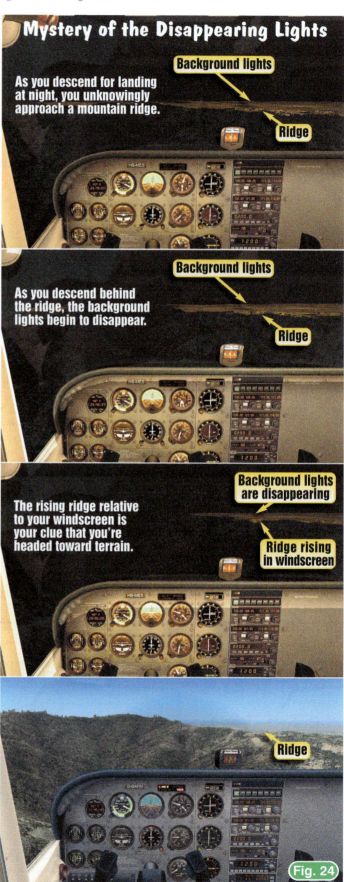

As you descend below the ridge, it rises relative to your windscreen, blocking out background lighting. You must immediately climb and/or turn to avoid higher terrain ahead of you.

Chapter 14: Night Flying

While descending from an enroute altitude for landing where mountains or hills exist, keep an eye out for disappearing lights. Huh? A black hole? UFOs? No, I mean lights in the vicinity of the airport that disappear because you're descending behind a mountain range (Figure 24). In this instance, any background lighting will disappear as a mountain comes between you and the light source. If you see this happening, then immediately reduce your descent rate or, even better, climb (this will help save your "background").

Keep in mind that even though you might not have an instrument rating, you might feel like you need one when flying across the desert, large bodies of water or, for that matter, across many parts of this great country at night. As we've already discussed, it's entirely possible to have no discernable horizon through the windscreen at night.

The Value of Lunar Light

Fig. 25 Moonshine (the *light* kind), often provides excellent illumination of clouds. Without lunar or city lights, however, it's often extremely difficult to detect clouds at night.

Not only can you not identify your pitch attitude with an outside reference, you also can't tell if you're banking. This can be quite disconcerting to the uninitiated. What do you do? Well, you have no choice but to rely more on your instruments than you're used to under daylight conditions. That's why it's often best to get that instrument rating (or instrument training), even if you don't ever intend to fly under instrument meteorological conditions (IMC). You might end up flying hard "night" VMC and need instrument skills.

Speaking of that instrument rating, how easy is it to see and avoid clouds at night? Well, it's a lot easier under a moon's reflection (Figure 25) or above the reflection of city lights. It's not that easy when there's no ambient light available. That's why special VFR isn't allowed at night unless you have an instrument rating. After all, how can you remain clear of clouds that you can't see?

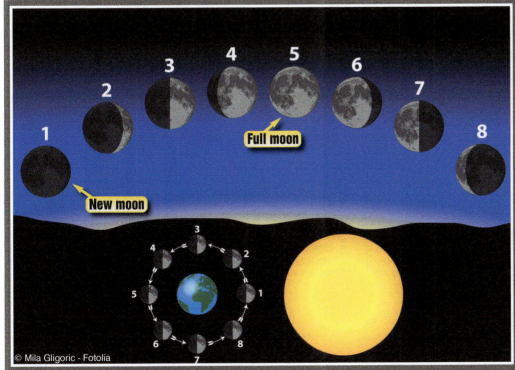

Why Does the Moon Appear In Different Phases?

We see the moon in different phases from the *new moon* to a *full moon* because the moon orbits the earth.

A *new moon* occurs when the moon is positioned between the earth and the sun. None of the moon's illuminated surface is visible from earth (position 1). As the moon circles the earth to position 3, half of it is seen as illuminated. In position 5, the moon is fully illuminated, thus the name *full moon*. The lunar phase cycle from new moon to full moon takes 29.5 days.

Some pilots pay close attention to moon cycles to know the amount of celestial illumination they can expect on night cross country flights. Check out the U.S. Naval Observatory on the web for moon cycles.

If you do manage to accidently fly into a cloud at night, your instrument rating is your extraction ticket. What do you do if you fly into a cloud? Sure, make a 180 degree turn, but don't forget to look at the bottom of the heading indicator and say the number you see *out loud*. That's right. You might be a little discombobulated (even if your name isn't Bobulated) and begin the turn without remembering the heading to which you're turning. Saying something out loud reinforces it your short term memory. It's also is tremendously entertaining to your passengers if they don't know what's going on. You might suddenly yell out, "Three three zero," and a passenger might reply with, "Three three one," thinking this is some sort of aviation counting game.

At night, don't discount major highways with their mobile runway lights (we call these *cars*) as a reasonable option on which to make an emergency landing. Of course, this assumes that there aren't too many cars using the highway at the time so as to make an emergency landing an even bigger emergency.

Now for the big question. Would you feel comfortable flying cross country at night over mountains? If not, I certainly would understand this. However, can this be done in such a way that you can minimize the risks of engine failure? The answer is, yes. Here's how.

Since most of the places you want to go are probably connected by big roads, then follow the roads at night (or follow them closely enough to see them as well as to be able to glide to them). Major highway, freeways and interstates are acceptable emergency landing spots at night (Figure 26). If your engine quits you simply turn your airplane into a car. That sure beats turning it into a night dirt bike. You'll benefit by something known as the *FLS* or *Ford Lighting System*, which you should think of as mobile runway lights. The neat thing about major freeways and highways is that they (relatively speaking) tend to have few powerlines crossing them. So, if you're planning on flying to Las Vegas at night, then keep an eye on Interstate 15, which takes you from Los Angeles directly to Las Vegas. Do this and you'll reduce the gamble as you travel to gamble at night.

Approaches and Landings at Night

You'd think that finding an airport at night would be a bit easier because the FAA requires all public lighted land airports to be identified by a rotating *green and white* light beacon (Figure 27). The problem is that you still have to find the beacon, which isn't necessarily easy when the airport is surrounded by city lights. So here's a little secret that can help you. When you suspect you are within 10 miles of the airport, blur your vision slightly, and look for something that flashes white and green. It's the contrast

Public (non-military) airports having runway edge lighting (position B) are identified by a rotating green and white lighted beacon.

Chapter 14: Night Flying

of flashing over a steadily lit background that helps find the airport in these conditions. Please unblur those eyes for the approach and landing. Based on this technique, you'd think that anyone over 50 would have no problem finding airports at night. So for slightly more mature pilots, you can accomplish the same objective by avoiding the squint and *temporarily* looking over the top of your glasses.

With the airport in sight, you'll do exactly the same thing you do during the day in terms of entering and flying the pattern. The one thing you always want to keep in mind at night is never to let the airport out of your sight at night. It's amazingly easy to lose the location of the landing runway when your airplane or your eyes turn away from the field. If you're going to turn away from the airport, then take note of where it is now, then turn, followed by immediately looking back in the previous direction while the sight picture impression is still fresh in short term memory. You can also take a peek at your heading indicator and identify the number value around the heading disc that points to the airport (Figure 28). You can even rotate your heading bug to it. When you turn back toward the airport, you only need to fly that same number value.

Turning Away From the Runway at Night

When turning away from a runway at night, find the number on the heading indicator that most nearly points to the runway and set your heading bug to it. This is the heading you'll use if you lose sight of the runway while maneuvering.

As a general rule, you shouldn't do anything different in terms of flying downwind, base and final approach at night, with one exception. Since you might not have the visual clues to help you identify your glidepath (i.e., no VASI), you might have to apply a little higher math (math done higher in the air) to enhance your safety.

Night Landing Approach Strategy

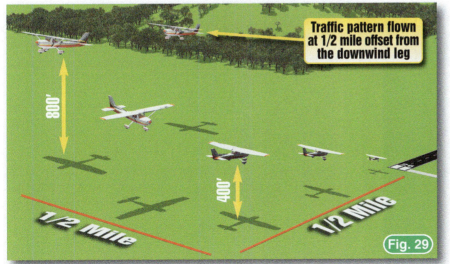

Night landing approaches are made safer by remaining relatively close to the runway (1/2 mile offset on downwind) and planning your base-to-final turn at one-half of the traffic pattern altitude.

Let's suppose that your downwind is flown at one-half statute mile horizontally from the runway centerline at 800 feet AGL. You'll turn base when the runway threshold is 45 degrees behind your wing. (You can often make the one-half distance offset from the runway by comparing your downwind offset to the length of the runway. A 5,000 foot runway means your offset should be approximately one-half the runway's length. In this sense, your runway becomes a pattern calibration tool.) Ideally, this would have you turning final (no wind assumed) at approximately one-half mile from the threshold (Figure 29).

That means that you should be no less than 400 foot AGL on the turn to final. This leaves you with approximately 400 feet to eliminate at a distance of one-half mile from the threshold.

At an approach speed of 75 mph or 65 knots (no wind assumed here), you're covering 1.25 miles per minute. You must lose 400 feet in 24 seconds, which requires that you descend at a rate of 1,000 feet per minute to touch down on the runway threshold. In a calm wind, the resultant glidepath would have you landing on the threshold or the numbers. But that's not necessarily something you want to do at night. Instead, it's better to land somewhere in the middle of the first third of the runway, which gives you a little more protection behind and below you on the approach, especially when the runway doesn't have a VASI. Therefore, descend at a rate a bit slower than the maximum necessary to get you down on the beginning of the runway (perhaps 800 feet per minute or less).

What you want to avoid doing is flying a long final approach (i.e., a *straight in approach*) when landing at an airport without a VASI and where the background is lighted and the foreground is dark. This type of runway environment is conducive to something known as the *black hole illusion* (see sidebar: *The Black Hole Illusion,* next page). Flying a rectangular pattern that's one-half mile from the runway centerline and one-half mile from the threshold on base and final keeps you closer to the landing surface. It gives you a better chance of establishing a safer glidepath when a VASI isn't present. It also helps you avoid the dangerous black hole illusion.

Fortunately, there are quite a few airports that have VASIs, which takes all the painful calculations and estimations out of night approaches. Well, it does, but only if you know how to use the VASI.

One of the first things you should learn about VASIs for night approaches is that they are limited in terms of the distance at which you can use them as well as the angle you can use them when turning onto final approach. As a general rule, your typical two- or three-bar VASI is visible up to 20 miles or more at night. Yes, these VASI units can be seen at a relatively great distance at night, but that doesn't mean they provide safe glidepath information for 20 miles. In fact, these VASI types typically provide safe obstruction clearance up to 4 nautical miles from the runway threshold within +/− 10 degrees of the runway centerline (Figure 30).

The PAPI (precision approach path indicator) also uses high intensity lighting that allows it to be seen up to 20 miles at night (Figure 31). Safe obstruction clearance is also typically provided up to 4 statute miles from the runway threshold within +/− 10 degrees of the runway centerline. So don't assume that because you're inbound on the PAPI's glidepath 15 miles out that you're flying an obstruction free path. There could be wires, spires and other things you just can't see until it's too late.

The two-bar *visual approach slop indicator* can be seen at great distances but it only provides obstruction clearance for four statute miles from the threshold.

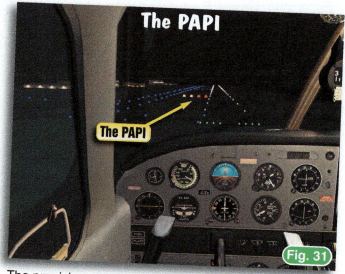

The *precision approach path indicator* can be seen at distances up to 20 miles at night. It also only provides obstruction clearance for four statute miles from the threshold.

Chapter 14: Night Flying

Night Magic – The Black Hole Illusion

Do you know what magic is? It's really pretty simple. It's the exact opposite of what a (good) teacher does. The teacher provides perceptual information that leads to insights and ultimately ends with you understanding something.

The magician, however, prevents you from understanding anything. The magician does this by using misdirection to keep you from seeing what he's actually doing. If you can't *see* what's happening, it's hard to *understand* what's happened. This is why I still check behind my ear when I need a quarter. Let's call this the *magic effect*, because it can lead us to believe what we see, when seeing shouldn't lead to belief.

I'll bet the last rabbit in my hat that anyone who's ever driven a car at night has experienced the magic effect to some degree. At night, we can see lighted objects at great distances in much the same way we see normally illuminated objects during the day. We can't, however, easily see non-lighted objects such as the road, curves, or foreign objects along the periphery of the road. When it's dark, we're deprived of vital visual information that keeps us from understanding our speed in relation to the road.

It's magic, right? Without this information to stimulate our brake gland, we tend to drive faster than is safe. This is one very big reason that 40% of the fatal car accidents occur at night despite there being 60% less traffic during that time. Said another way, we're bringing daytime driving strategies to the road at night, and we're paying a hefty price for it. It's as if we're at a magic show being fooled, and we don't even know it.

For those of us who fly at night, the magic effect is also in full force, especially when the approach environment offers a dark or featureless foreground next to a lighted background. Approaching an isolated desert airport at night or an airport from over the water at night is a good example (Picture 1). The dark environment below prevents us from having sufficient visual clues with which to assess our height above the ground. Our natural response is to use what lights we do have to make this assessment. This means using the distant runway edge lighting as well as the far off environmental lighting around the airport to make this assessment. This is where the magic begins.

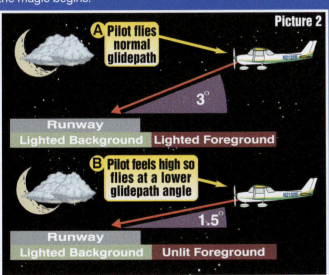

More than one study has confirmed that using only background lighting clues when approaching from over a dark foreground tricks the mind into thinking the airplane is higher than it actually is (Picture 2, position A). Sometimes, twice as high. If we act on that effect, our response is to descend prematurely or increase our descent rate. The end result is often a landing when there's no airport beneath the airplane, otherwise known as CFIT, or *controlled flight into terrain*. The lack of perceptual information from beneath our airplane lures us downward, as if our machine is being drawn into a black hole. And now you know the reason for calling this the *black hole illusion*.

Avoiding the black hole illusion means avoiding the use of daytime flying strategies when operating an airplane at night. So let's begin with a very common daytime landing strategy that we surely want to avoid at night—the *straight-in approach*.

Long straight-in approaches at night to runways having no visual or electronic glidepath information provide the perfect setup for the magic effect. A good nighttime strategy for landing is to overfly the airport and enter a normal traffic pattern for landing. You might even gain a tactical advantage by keeping the pattern a bit tighter and using short-field (over an obstacle) landing procedures even when no obstacle actually exists in the landing environment. Why? Because remaining closer to the runway environment means having more perceptual lighting clues with which to assess your height above ground. This is why the research shows that the black hole illusion tends to become less effective (less illusory) as you move closer to the runway.

What happens if you're making an approach to a runway having a VASI or a WAAS-based advisory glidepath? The answer is simple—use it. But use it based on its stated limitations. For example, most VASIs offer obstacle clearance only when the airplane is within 10 degrees of either side of the runway centerline. Keep in mind that some VASIs are offset from that centerline, to provide a descent path away from local obstacles (read about those things in the *Chart Supplement*).

Let the buyer beware. Even with VASI (or electronic glidepath) information, the black hole illusion still tempts some pilots to leave the glidepath prematurely, resulting in red and white lights turning green as the light filters through the grass (OK, not really). This is one instance where you don't want to feel either the magic or the grass beneath your feet.

In his book *Illusions*, Richard Bach wrote that when you know what the magician knows, it's not magic anymore. The magic works only as long as the magician can limit what we see. Unfortunately, a dark environment often accomplishes the same thing for pilots, leading us to a big misunderstanding of our airplane's proximity to the ground.

That's why it's important to understand how the black hole illusion works. It's one instance where seeing the lights does not mean that we've "seen the light."

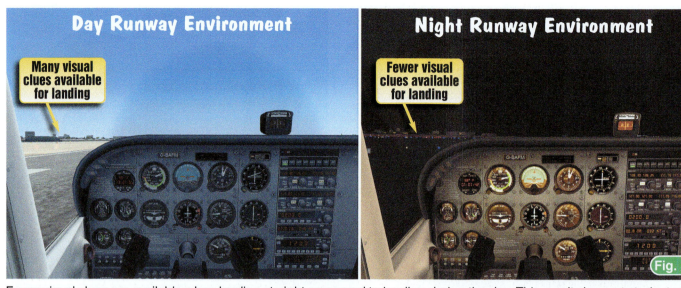

Fewer visual clues are available when landing at night compared to landing during the day. This results in most student pilots becoming ground shy at night. As a result, they initially tend to flare a little too high during their first few night landings.

Beginning the Roundout and Flare, Mon Frere

Many years ago I remember asking a student why he was having trouble landing at night. He said, "Because dark air has less lift in it that light air does." Silly student. Silly me for not anticipating that answer. Once I pointed out a few basic principles of night landings, he was no longer in the dark on the subject and neither will you be.

One of the things that makes a night landing a challenge is that you simply don't have the runway visual clues you typically use during the day. I'm speaking of seeing the runway surface, the foliage along the side of the runway along with peripheral structures such as the windsock, control towers, airport buildings and a rabbit or two (most likely, two) as shown in Figure 32. Without these peripheral visual clues available to you during a night landing, you're likely to perform the roundout and flare at too high an altitude during your first couple of night landings. Why would you tend to flare too high? Because you'll have a less-than-certain idea about how high you are above the ground. Therefore, you're likely to be ground shy, and have every reason to be, too. So how do you gauge your height above the ground at night?

Believe it or not, you already have sufficient experience with one of the most important visual clues you'll need to land at night. I'm speaking of the runway's edge lighting. During the day, you can't help but notice where the edges of the runway are when landing because they're often darker in color than the

At night, the runway edge lighting provides the visual clues to help identify the roundout and flare.

Chapter 14: Night Flying

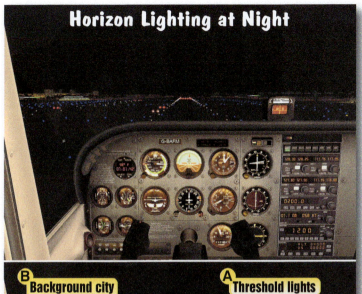

At night you might be able to see the distant (lighted) horizon for pitch clues. Even with your landing/taxi light on, the runway lights might be your only significant source of height information.

terrain surrounding the landing surface. Therefore, the contrast between the runway and its borders has always provided you with a geometric (shape) reference to help gauge your round-out and flare height for landing during the day.

The runway's edge lighting provides you with the same geometric (or shape) information that you have during daytime landings (Figure 33). Since it's easier to identify lighted objects out of the corner of your eye at night, you'll find that edge lighting actually makes it easier to identify the runway's borders in the dark. In fact, the *runway expansion effect* that you learned about in Chapter 10 on Page 10-6 now becomes even more noticeable to you. The sudden expansion of runway geometry now becomes your primary method for deciding when to begin the roundout for landing at night.

What's Missing at Night

On the other hand, there are two important sources of height information that are diminished at night. I'm speaking of sighting the distant horizon and the actual runway surface (i.e., the *sweet spot* discussed in Chapter 10 that you use to gauge your height above the landing surface).

The distant horizon might not be visible at night, especially if you're landing at an airport located somewhere away from a major city or town. Nevertheless, you might still have a satisfactory source of pitch information if you can see the red (runway end) threshold lights on the far end of the runway (Figure 34, position A). During a normal night landing in some airplanes (certainly not all), it's sometimes possible to see the distant red runway end threshold lights to the left of the raised nose/cowling. They're colored red as a means of identifying where the runway ends. You're more likely, however to see a distant horizon defined by environmental/city lights (Figure 34, position B)

During night landings, you'd identify the landing sweet spot (assuming you can see it in the dark) in the triangular (pizza shaped) area made up of the left window border, the engine cowling on the right and the distant horizon on top as shown in Figure 34, position C (also see Chapter 10, Page 10-10). Ultimately, anything you can do to make it easier to see over the airplane's nose during the landing flare makes it easier to identify the end of the runway, thus providing you with a source of pitch information. That's why seating height becomes very important during your first

Using a more flaps when landing at night typically allows you to land in a slightly lower nose attitude. This provides you with a better view over the nose with which to keep the distant threshold lights in sight.

few night landings. Generally speaking, the higher you sit the more likely you are to have a better source of pitch information during the roundout and flare at night.

There are two additional ways to help you identify the end of the runway during night landings. The first is the use of flaps. Flaps allow you to land in a slightly flatter attitude (achieving the necessary angle of attack at a lower nose attitude) as shown in Figure 35. That means during the roundout and flare, it will be easier for you to see the distant runway end threshold lighting to help you determine your pitch attitude. Using partial if not full flaps for a night landing generally works to your benefit (it also makes the approach and landing a little slower, which gives you a little more time to assess the necessary visual clues for landing). Additionally, making sure the runway edge lighting is on a brighter setting (medium or high intensity) can also make it easier to identify the distant threshold lighting. But not everyone shines in bright lights. Some people experience a reduction in visual acuity in the presence of bright lighting. In other words, their eyes see bright lights as scattered or blurred light. So be sure to choose the runway edge lighting intensity level that's optimal for your vision at night.

The other source of runway information that's limited at night is runway surface information. I'm speaking of seeing the *sweet spot* on the runway 50 to 80 feet ahead and to the left of the engine cowling that you've previously used to judge your height above the landing surface. It's very difficult and often impossible to identify this spot at night unless there's peripheral lighting available (moonlight, ambient electrical light, etc.). Sure, the

Depending on the airplane, it's possible that use of the taxi light along with the landing light could offer greater illumination of the landing surface (especially the sweet spot).

Chapter 14: Night Flying

landing light shines on a patch of the runway during the descent, but this lighted spot is often directly ahead of you and you'll typically lose that surface lighting once you've begun the flare (Figure 36, position A). A lot of good that does you, right? Most landing lights on small airplanes just don't have a sufficient photon spread or candle power to keep the sweet spot lit as the nose rises during the flare. Then again, this might be a reason to also have the taxi light on during a night landing. Taxi lights tend to shine downward at an angle closer to the airplane and, depending on the desires of the airplane manufacturer, the beams can have a greater horizontal light spread (Figure 36, position B). This could help you see the runway a bit sooner and a bit longer as you approach the runway.

Of course, as the nose comes up during the flare, your taxi and landing light are likely to shine more into space than on the sweet spot. Since there is no runway in space, this doesn't do you much good. So use both of these lights on when you're *learning* to land at night if it helps. Yes, I know some flight schools are reluctant to have you operate both lights when landing because they're concerned about costs. This is understandable. Fortunately, once you learn to land at night, you won't need to have the taxi light on for night landings. You'll have acquired a feel for landing at night and will tend to rely more on the runway edge lighting to help you make your roundout and flare decisions.

As a general rule of thumb when learning to land at night, it's often best to acquire this skill mechanically at first. Using the runway expansion effect allows you to rely less on identifying the sweet spot and focus more on keeping the top left hand side of the cowling on the distant horizon (as best as that can be seen or estimated) during the landing flare. If your instructor doesn't think you have an identifiable horizon and/or sufficient lighting to actually see the runway surface, then this technique will most likely be used during your initial introduction to night landings.

The Shallow Descent Technique

There's a particular method that some pilots use to help them land on an unlit surface at night and it has some merit. When landing a seaplane during the day on still or glassy water, it's very hard to identify your height above the mirrored surface (Figure 37). Slowing the descent rate down to a descent rate of approximately 150 feet per minute on final approach at a speed and flap configuration that provides a slightly nose up pitch attitude allows the seaplane to descend safely onto still or glassy water.

To do this, you'll need to make a power-on approach without using an excessive amount of flaps. You'll also need to make your approach at no more than 30% above stall speed. Ultimately the speed and flaps condition chosen for this technique results in the nose gear being positioned above the main gear during the landing. Generally speaking, a speed of 1.3 Vs1 will work, but you might have to experiment to find out for sure. You'll typically commence the power-on, 100 to 150 foot per minute descent rate when you are above the runway and at an altitude at which you typically begin the flare for landing (Figure 38).

Keep in mind that using power to sustain a descent rate of 100 to 150 feet per minute will consume a great deal of landing real estate in the process, despite being initially close to the runway. So let the buyer-flyer beware. Don't try this on a short runway. Period.

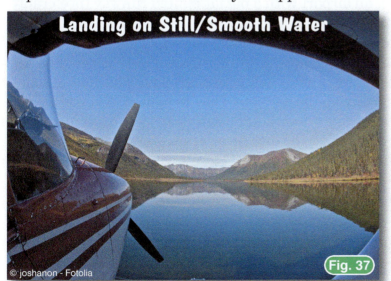

The *shallow descent* landing technique is used by seaplane pilots when landing on smooth water where it's hard to identify your height above the landing surface.

When would you use this technique? There are two occasions when this might come in handy. One is when landing without the use of a taxi or landing light and the other is when landing on a runway that doesn't have runway edge lighting.

One of the bigger challenges you'll face is landing at night without a landing or taxi light (or when these lights are inoperative). I purposely avoided saying that this was the *biggest* challenge you're likely to experience at night because your runway might still have runway edge lighting. While runway edge lighting can and does provide the necessary clues to help you determine your roundout and flare height at night, you have an entirely different issue on your hands if that lighting isn't working or doesn't exist. To land at night without these lights is a very big challenge (if not a risky proposition), indeed.

If you have a long enough runway, you can fly a shallow glidepath after crossing the threshold so as to minimize your closure rate with the runway. This is the same method used by seaplane pilots when landing on still water where it's very difficult to assess height above the landing surface.

In many instances, it might not be possible to land on a runway without active runway edge lighting. On a moonless night you might not be able to identify the runway's location, much less see its surface during landing. On the other hand, strong moon beams often allow you to identify the runway's location and shape, making it possible to land safely at night (assuming you can make a safe approach and descent into the airport environment). Here's where the shallow descent technique over the runway that I previously mentioned might be useful in helping you make a controlled touchdown. Then again, it doesn't take much brain power to realize that the darker the runway is and the less you're able to light it up, the less safe the landing. Period. Sometimes it's better to mimic the moth and head for the light, meaning that you should find yourself an airport with a big fat lighted runway (preferably with an FBO having a closet full of tasty clothes so you can have a pocket sandwich to eat).

Of course, the landing isn't over until it's over. That means keeping your airplane under control until it has slowed to taxi speed and has taxied off the runway. While this is relatively easy to do, some pilots have difficulty estimating distances to the runway exit points at night. This makes sense since we can't see these points as easily as we can during the day since they're lighted. As I mentioned earlier in this chapter, it's the peripheral clues that are missing, and that means you can't judge distance and runway closure rates as well as you can during the day. As a result, you might approach a runway exit and suddenly realize that you are going to overshoot it. Here's where some pilots get a bit too aggressive with brake pressure in an attempt to make the turn. In some cases, a ground loop results from this loopy behavior. So don't let your mind fool you.

Night Flight

So there you have the essentials of night flying. Sure, you have to be a little more cautious, but I can assure you it's worth it. There's nothing quite like a flight at night. It's often peaceful, beautiful and sometimes it seems as if you're the only person in the air (OK, you and your pocket bat, if you're fortunate enough to have one). Once you're hooked on night flying, there's no going back. Welcome to the bright but dark side of flying.

Appendix 1 - Desired Skills to Achieve

15-1

Graphic Representation of Flight Skills

The following are graphic representations of the desired skills for selected maneuvers from this book. The standards shown here might change over time in slight ways. Nevertheless, these graphics do represent the basic elements of airmanship. To obtain the precise requirement for any maneuver on a practical airman checkride, please visit the FAA's site and download the appropriate copy of the *Airman Certification Standards*.

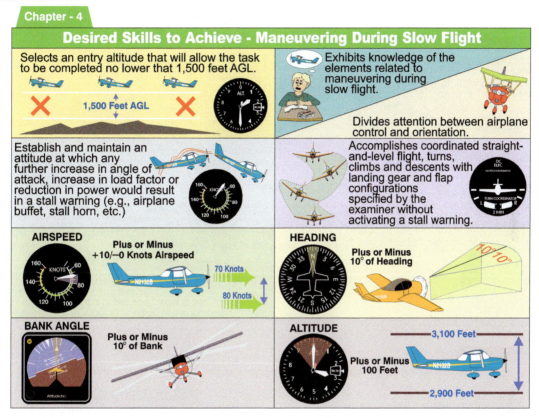

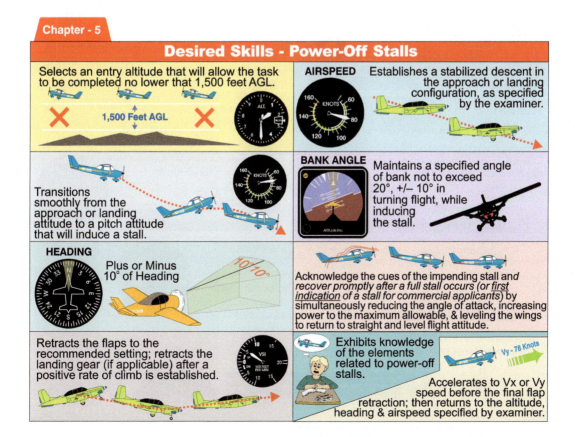

Appendix 1 - Desired Skills to Achieve

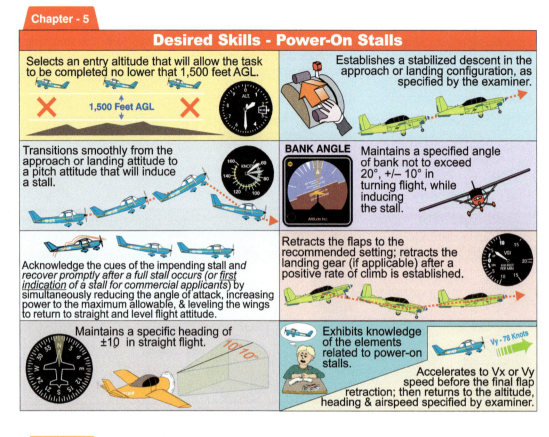

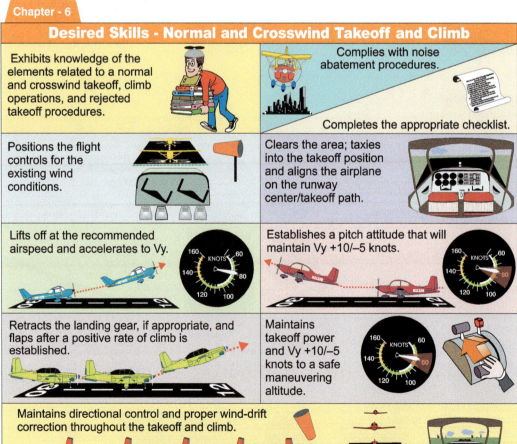

Appendix 1 - Desired Skills to Achieve

Chapter - 6

Desired Skills - Soft-Field Takeoff and Climb

Positions the flight controls for existing wind conditions and to maximize lift as quickly as possible.	Exhibits knowledge of the elements related to a soft-field takeoff and climb. Completes the appropriate checklist.
Clears the area; taxies onto the takeoff surface at a speed consistent with safety without stopping while advancing the throttle smoothly to takeoff power.	Establishes and maintains a pitch attitude that will transfer the weight of the airplane from the wheels to the wings as rapidly as possible.
Lifts off at the lowest possible airspeed and remains in ground effect while accelerating to Vx or Vy, as appropriate.	Establishes a pitch attitude for Vx or Vy, as appropriate, and maintains selected airspeed +10/–5 knots, during the climb.
Retracts the landing gear, if appropriate, and flaps after clear of any obstacles or as recommended by the manufacturer.	
Maintains takeoff power and Vx or Vy +10/–5 knots to a safe maneuvering altitude.	Maintains directional control and proper wind-drift correction throughout the takeoff and climb.

Appendix 1 - Desired Skills to Achieve

Chapter - 6

Desired Skills - Short-Field Takeoff and Maximum Performance Climb

Exhibits knowledge of the elements related to a short-field takeoff and maximum performance climb.	Positions the flight controls for the existing wind conditions; sets the flaps as recommended.
Clears the area; taxies into takeoff position utilizing maximum available takeoff area and aligns the airplane on the runway center/takeoff path.	Applies brakes (if appropriate), while advancing the throttle smoothly to takeoff power. 
Lifts off at the recommended airspeed, and accelerates to the recommended obstacle clearance airspeed or Vx. 	Retracts the landing gear, if appropriate, and flaps after clear of any obstacles or as recommended by manufacturer. 
Establishes a pitch attitude that will maintain the recommended obstacle clearance airspeed, or Vx, +10/–5 knots, until the obstacle is cleared, or until the airplane is 50 feet above the surface.  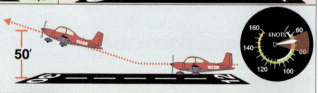	
After clearing the obstacle, establishes the pitch attitude for Vy, accelerates to Vy, and maintains Vy, +10/–5 knots, during the climb. 	
Maintains takeoff power and Vy +10/–5 to a safe maneuvering altitude. 	Maintains directional control and proper wind-drift correction throughout the takeoff and climb.

Appendix 1 - Desired Skills to Achieve

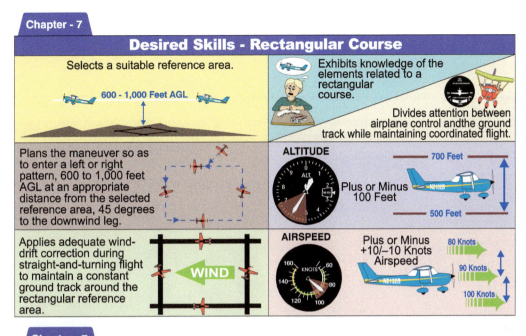

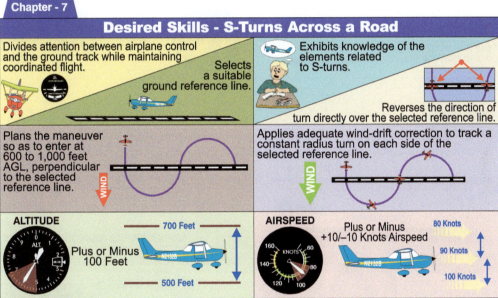

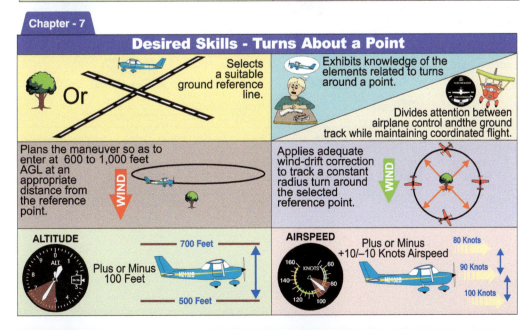

Appendix 1 - Desired Skills to Achieve

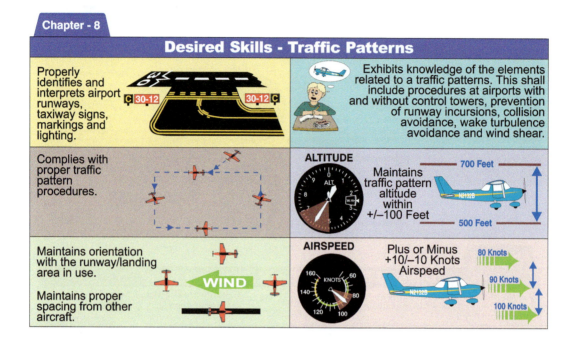

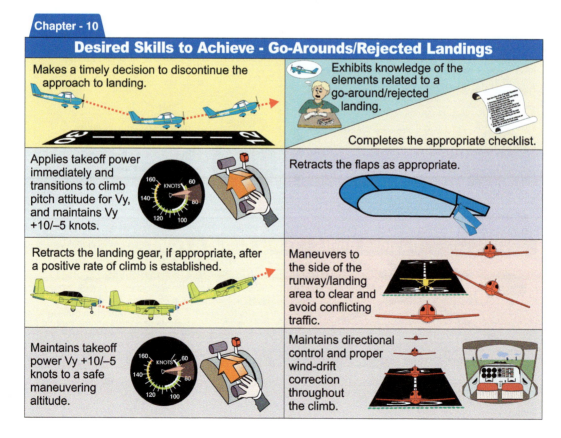

Appendix 1 - Desired Skills to Achieve

Chapter -11

Desired Skills - Normal and Crosswind Approach and Landing

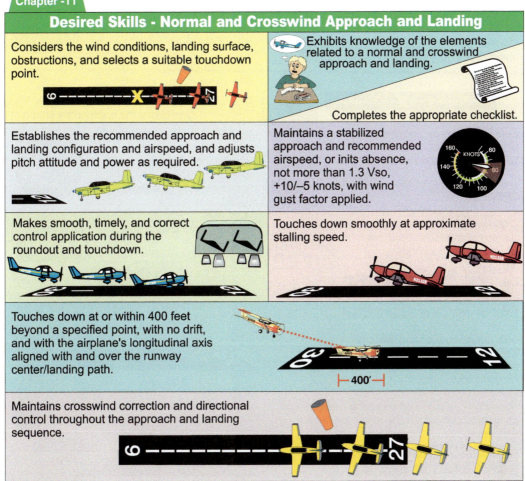

- Considers the wind conditions, landing surface, obstructions, and selects a suitable touchdown point.
- Exhibits knowledge of the elements related to a normal and crosswind approach and landing.
- Completes the appropriate checklist.
- Establishes the recommended approach and landing configuration and airspeed, and adjusts pitch attitude and power as required.
- Maintains a stabilized approach and recommended airspeed, or inits absence, not more than 1.3 Vso, +10/–5 knots, with wind gust factor applied.
- Makes smooth, timely, and correct control application during the roundout and touchdown.
- Touches down smoothly at approximate stalling speed.
- Touches down at or within 400 feet beyond a specified point, with no drift, and with the airplane's longitudinal axis aligned with and over the runway center/landing path.
- Maintains crosswind correction and directional control throughout the approach and landing sequence.

Chapter - 11

Desired Skills to Achieve - Forward Slip to a Landing

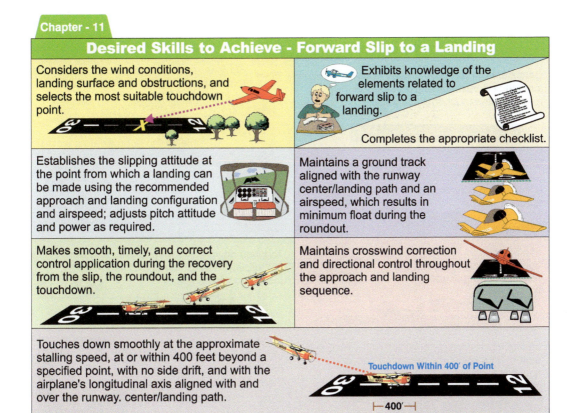

- Considers the wind conditions, landing surface and obstructions, and selects the most suitable touchdown point.
- Exhibits knowledge of the elements related to forward slip to a landing.
- Completes the appropriate checklist.
- Establishes the slipping attitude at the point from which a landing can be made using the recommended approach and landing configuration and airspeed; adjusts pitch attitude and power as required.
- Maintains a ground track aligned with the runway center/landing path and an airspeed, which results in minimum float during the roundout.
- Makes smooth, timely, and correct control application during the recovery from the slip, the roundout, and the touchdown.
- Maintains crosswind correction and directional control throughout the approach and landing sequence.
- Touches down smoothly at the approximate stalling speed, at or within 400 feet beyond a specified point, with no side drift, and with the airplane's longitudinal axis aligned with and over the runway. center/landing path.
- Touchdown Within 400' of Point

Appendix 1 - Desired Skills to Achieve

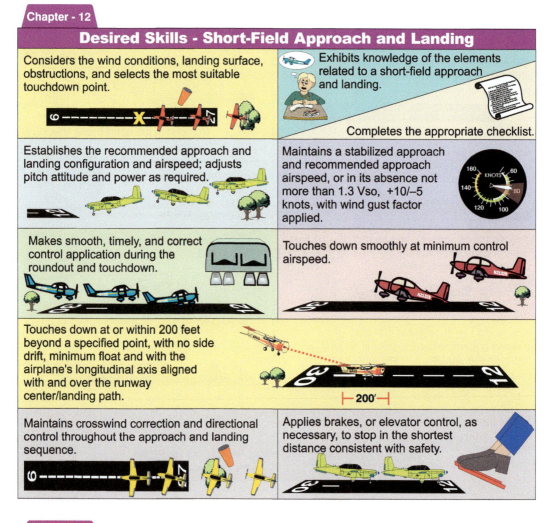

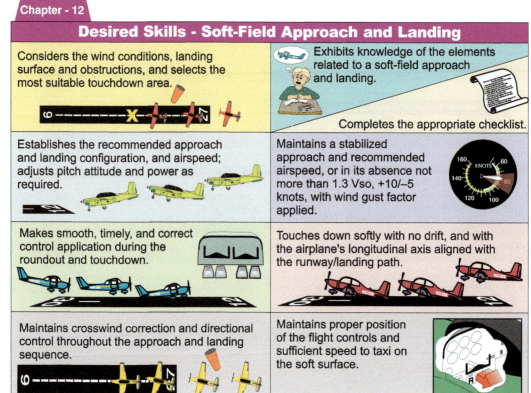

Appendix 1 - Desired Skills to Achieve

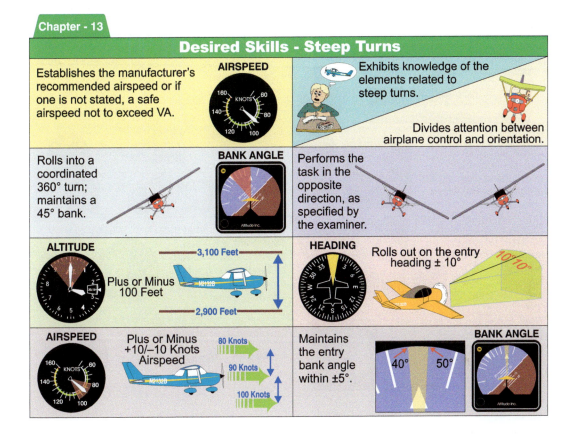

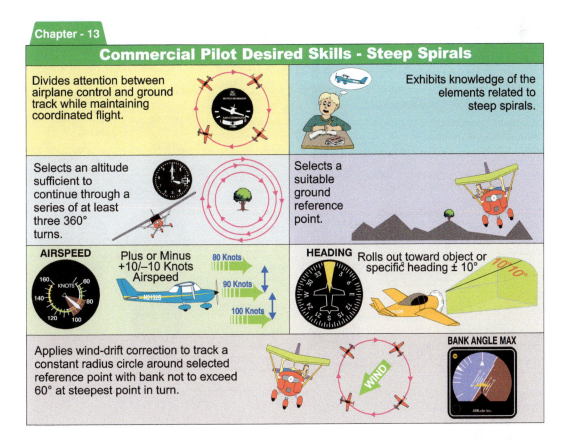

Appendix 1 - Desired Skills to Achieve

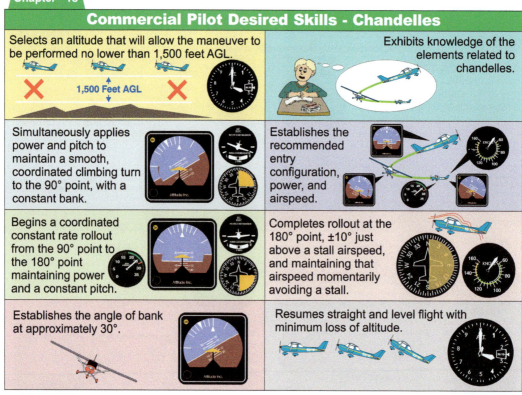

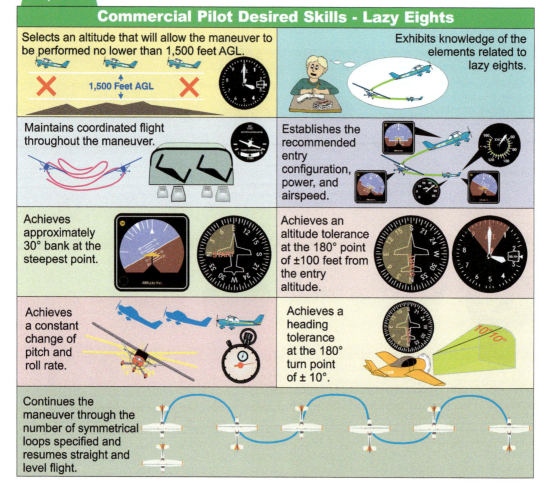

Appendix 1 - Desired Skills to Achieve

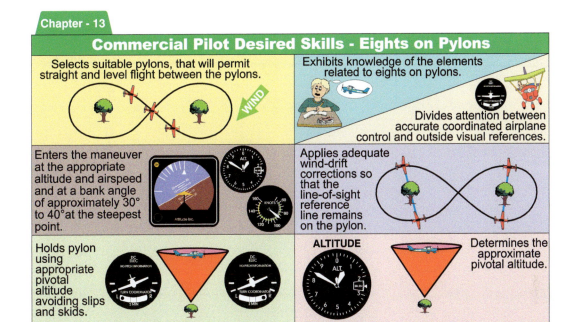

Back of the Book Information

The Senior Editor - Chapters 1-12

The Senior Editor: Mr. Brian Weiss

Brian Weiss is the owner of WORD'SWORTH, a marketing communications and design company. WORD'SWORTH provides services for all forms and formats of communications materials. Capabilities include the creation of brochures, books, newsletters, direct response letters, advertising, catalog sheets, slide shows and videos.

WORD'SWORTH clients have included Bank of America, Xerox Corporation, the National Childhood Cancer Foundation, Childrens Hospital (Los Angeles), the University of California (Irvine and Los Angeles campuses), Health Valley Foods, McGraw-Hill/CRM Films, Saint Joseph Hospital, *American Health* magazine, *Psychology Today* magazine, *Equity Quarterly*, Saint John's Hospital, *Aviation Safety* magazine, Long Beach and Santa Monica airports, and many others in a wide variety of fields.

In addition to general business expertise, WORD'SWORTH provides specialized background and knowledge in the areas of medicine and health care, science and technology, aviation and fundraising.

WORD'SWORTH also offers consulting on marketing strategies, direct mail campaigns, and fundraising proposals.

A little about Brian Weiss:

Founder (1977) and owner, WORD'SWORTH
Former editor, *Baja Explorer* magazine
Former associate editor, *Psychology Today* magazine
Served on the faculties of UCLA and the University of Michigan teaching introductory courses and advanced seminars in departments of human behavior, geography, and journalism.
Author for six years of a nationally syndicated consumer newspaper column (*FREEBIES*), and creator of a national magazine of the same name
Former medical/science editor, *Aviation Safety* magazine
Member (and former Board of Directors member), of Angel Flight, a not-for-profit community service organization.
Brian has been a pilot since 1980. He packs a private pilot certificate with an instrument rating and is the proud owner of a Cessna 172. He's one of the organizers of Flight Log, a group which provides information for pilots flying in Baja and throughout Mexico.

WORD'SWORTH
626-510-9180
bweiss@aol.com

Brian Weiss

"Brian is one of the most talented, energetic and intelligent people with whom I've had the pleasure of working. His advice and dedication to this project were simply invaluable!"

Rod Machado

The Gal With Talent and a Lot of Patience

The Aviation Speakers Bureau
Providing Quality Aviation Speakers Since 1986

The Aviation Speakers Bureau features speakers for your banquet, educational seminar, safety standdown, convention, conference, forum, trade show, keynote, corporate training, airshow, safety program or association meeting. We guarantee a perfect match for your needs and objectives, and recommend only the very best in speakers. Our professionals shine and make YOU look good every time!

"We will help you find the perfect speaker for your budget and there is **never** a charge for our service."

Presentation and Topics

Safety, Weather, Instrument Flying, Inspirational, Cockpit Resource Management, Aviation Humor, Understanding Airspace, Test Pilots, Teamwork, Stress, Fighter Pilots and Aces, Weather Radar, In-flight Emergencies, Multi-engine Procedures, Celebrities and Heroes, Vietnam Pilots, Aviation Management, Interpreting Instrument Charts, Comedy, Air Racers, Policies and Politics of Aviation, Motivational, Industry Specific Training, Maneuvers, Success, Patriotic, Aviation Firsts, Stunt Flying, Air Combat, Aviation Psychology, Survival, Aviation Careers, Jeppesen Charts, Aerobatic Pilots, Wright Brothers, Accident Investigations, Survival and much more.

For information on our speakers call
800-247-1215
For all other calls 949-498-2498

P.O. Box 6030
San Clemente, CA 92674-6030

Read speaker biographies and view video clips:
www.aviationspeakers.com

Charter Member

Diane Titterington

Learning to fly in 1973, Diane holds a commercial certificate with an instrument rating. Her logbook is a Heinz 57 mixture of different makes and models. Flights include ferrying aircraft from the factory, flying fire patrol and a number of air races. Until 1981, she worked as a radar qualified air traffic controller on the high/low sectors at Houston Center. Diane has been a passenger on a carrier landing and takeoff, flown a T-38, rode dozens of airline jumpseats and logged a few blimp flights.

Her father, who worked at WPAFB, told tales of test pilots Bob Hoover, Scott Crossfield and Chuck Yeager when she was young. Diane never dreamed that she would later work with such aviation greats. As the President of The Aviation Speakers Bureau, Diane supplies speakers for hundreds of safety seminars, banquets and conventions. She places aviation speakers, celebrities and specialists at events across the United States, Canada and other countries.

The Ongoing Editor: Diane Titterington

"It is a pure pleasure to work with dozens of brilliant and gifted individuals such as Jim Tucker, Bob Hoover, Col. Joe Kittinger, Brian Udell, Al Haynes, Dave Gwinn, Dr. Jerry Cockrell and Ralph Hood. With their unusual experiences, unique delivery styles, and vast knowledge of aviation, our speakers are the most sought after in the business. By providing inspiring speakers for aviation events, we help motivate and educate. And we help to keep the skies safe too." Visit our web site: www.aviationspeakers.com

Diane has been the ongoing editor of *Rod Machado's Private Pilot Handbook* and *Rod Machado's Instrument Pilot's Survival Manual*. She is the designer, compiler, managing editor and producer of *Speaking of Flying*, a book of stories from 44 aviation speakers.

Rod Machado's Private Pilot Handbook

15-15

See website for eBook version!

"As if your instructor is explaining everything in *PLANE* English."

"...switched to Rod's book because of something as small as Zulu Time – no one else covers it – Now, I AM HOOKED. For CFIs that attach as much importance to ground school as I do, YOU SIMPLY CANNOT GET ALONG WITHOUT THIS TEXT."
  Jim Trusty, 1997 National Flight Instructor Of The Year

"EXTREMELY VALUABLE TO STUDENTS... great book for CFIs to use in teaching... those needing a BFR."
  Dave Sclair, Editor "General Aviation News & Flyer"

"At last, the book we've all been waiting for... ONE YOU JUST CAN'T AFFORD TO BE WITHOUT."   *"Angel Flight News"*

"MY STUDENTS ARE LOSING SLEEP BECAUSE THEY CAN'T PUT IT DOWN! Marvelous book so beautifully explains information needed."
  Ed Shaffer, 30,375 TT, Active CFII, Retired Airline Check Captain

"BRILLIANTLY WRITTEN AND ORGANIZED... elevates a thorough education to a fun experience."
  Dave Gwinn, CFII, Airline Captain, Aviation Writer

"...FULL PREPARATION FOR THE NEW PILOT, rather than a quick memorization of test questions...great way to refresh your knowledge for a flight review...pleasant way to brush up on new information."   *"AOPA Pilot Magazine"*

"...LOTS OF PICTURES, BIG, EASY-TO-UNDERSTAND ILLUSTRATIONS AND HUMOR – a combination you won't find in any other pilot handbook."
  Rafael Blanco, "Private Pilot Magazine"

"THE REAL TREASURE IS THE TEXT. This is the way to write a teaching manual."   *Henry G. Smith, FAA Designated Examiner*

"FINALLY, a reference book that puts the basic knowledge factors required by all pilots in an EASY TO GRASP, ENJOYABLE FORMAT."   *Ralph Butcher, CFII, Airline Captain, Aviation Author*

"simplifies complex subjects.... INVALUABLE REFERENCE BOOK... You'll be a better pilot for it."
  Bill Cox, Senior Editor Plane & Pilot Magazine

Rod Machado's Private Pilot Handbook is a serious text written in a fun and witty style. With more than 1,100 color illustrations and photos, this 656 page manual makes preparation for the FAA private pilot oral and knowledge exams (flight reviews too) a pleasant and enjoyable experience. Here's some of what's inside:

- Easy to understand analogies and examples for technical subjects such as engines, aerodynamics, flight instruments and the airplane's electrical system.
- New weather codes: METAR, TAF, GFAs,
- Alphabet airspace made E-Z with 3-D color illustrations
- Step-by-step procedures for planning a cross country
- Clear, down-to-earth explanations of pertinent FARs –Part 61, Part 91, NTSB Part 830
- Easy to apply navigation methods for VOR & GPS
- ICAO Flight Plans, Graphical Forecasts for Aviation
- Practical tips and techniques for ensuring safe and enjoyable flight

$74.95

Rod Machado's Private Pilot Handbook 656 pages 8-3/8 x 10-7/8, softbound

Visit our web site at: **www.rodmachado.com**

Rod Machado's Private Pilot Audiobook

Rod Machado's Private Pilot Audiobook - MP3 Files (30 Hours+)

Retention can increase by 70% with auditory learning!
SHOULDN'T YOU BE REVIEWING?

Welcome to your instructor in an audiobook. Rod's entire Handbook is presented in a warm, conversational manner. His tried-and-true method of instruction can be enjoyed during your commute, relaxing at home, or almost anywhere. It allows you to learn in a new, novel and often more efficient manner. Turn wasted freeway time into learning time. As one pilot said, "I felt like I had a flight instructor right there in the car with me."

Perfect if you don't have the time or inclination to read, or for "tired" eyes at the end of the day. It's a pleasure to be read to, especially from a lively text spiced with humor. You can listen to the first eight chapters without referring to the book's graphics. For some chapters, you'll want to review pictures, picture text, graphs and charts in the Handbook.

This valuable one-stop audiobook will help you:

Fly as a knowledgeable and competent pilot
Prepare for the Private Pilot FAA Knowledge Exam
Prepare for the Private Pilot practical oral exam
Refresh for required currency training
Remain an up-to-date confident pilot

Download MP3 Version $74.95

See website for download version!

Narrator: Capt. Philip E. Hewitt Ph.D., CFII, ATP, Pilot Examiner, pro narrator
Guest Narrator: Alec Cody, CFII, comedic impressionist

LISTEN and LEARN while:
- DRIVING
- RELAXING
- GARDENING
- EXERCISING
- EATING LUNCH
- BUILDING A KITPLANE

**Rod Machado's Private Pilot Handbook
30 Hours of MP3 Audio Files
Only Available as a Download**

Price: $74.95

Pilots Say...

If it wasn't for Rod Machado's Private Pilot Handbook on CDs, I wouldn't be a pilot. I'd finished the flying requirement. But hadn't taken the written or prepared for the oral portion of the checkride. It was difficult to find time to read. I'm a long-haul trucker. With these (MP3 files) I was able to study while driving. Only because of Rod's CDs was I able to get my pilot's license.
Long-haul trucker and new pilot

The longer I listened the more I realized how much I had forgotten or just haven't thought about for years.... These (MP3 files) are great fun to listen to.
David Lau, Watertown, WI

I have never met anyone who was a more informative speaker or better teacher than Rod Machado.
Kurt, C-177 pilot

Hey, I don't want to sound like a groupie, I just want to say thanks. I really enjoy Rod's books, etc., as well as his "technique" for getting his point across. I ENJOY learning from Rod! He is the best at what he does (come to think of it, no one else does what he does!) and I hope he keeps at it.
T.S.

Rod has wonderful and innovative ideas about learning to fly! I am an active flight instructor and find myself quoting him on almost a daily basis. When a student asks a question about a complicated subject, I usually answer with something like, "Well, Rod Machado explains it like this..." Rod is a true professional and has an innate ability to simplify and put into 'layman's' terms the difficult subjects encountered when learning to fly.
T.J. CFI

Rod Machado's Private Pilot Workbook/Speaking of Flying

Rod Machado's Private Pilot Workbook

The new *Rod Machado's Private Pilot Workbook* is now available. As a programmed learning guide, this book will help prepare you for the FAA Private Pilot Knowledge Exam. The questions are organized to follow the presentation of material, section for section, as found in the *Handbook*. Not only will this book prepare you for the Private Pilot Knowledge Exam, it will help you understand and absorb the knowledge necessary for you to fly safely. You can test your knowledge and comprehension in each subject area with numerous weight and balance, performance, and flight planning problems.

This valuable one-stop workbook contains:

- An excellent, thorough and complete self-study system when used with *Rod Machado's Private Pilot Handbook*.
- 1,811 FAA Private Pilot Knowledge Exam and general aviation knowledge questions.
- Questions organized to follow the layout of *Rod Machado's Private Pilot Handbook* so you can test your knowledge and comprehension in each subject area.
- Color navigation charts & numerous weight-and-balance, performance, and flight planning problems.
- An FAA approved, Part 141 ground training syllabus for use in an FAA approved Part 141 ground school.

Only available as an ebook! $19.95

Speaking of Flying

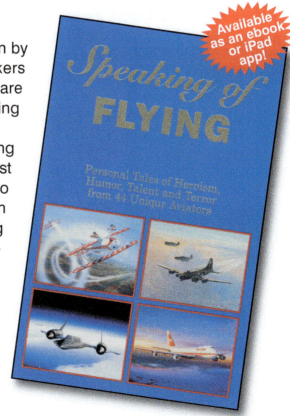

This wonderful 438 page hardbound book was written by 44 pilots who are speakers with The Aviation Speakers Bureau. These funny, dramatic, and inspiring stories are some of aviation's finest tales. You would expect nothing less from aviation's celebrities, experts and specialists.

Our flight plan sees us barnstorming in the U.S., flying aerial combat missions in World War II and Vietnam, test piloting new aircraft, performing air rescue, winging to exotic places, and flying to historically important aviation places from Kitty Hawk to the moon. You will go along as history is being made and hear the pilot's perspective on some of these aviation firsts. You will find ACES and true heroes within these pages. *Speaking of Flying* is your ticket to adventure. Step aboard, and be prepared to laugh, cry, and feel the excitement.

$29.95

Available as an ebook!

Rod Machado's Video DVDs/Downloads

Rod Machado's eLearning Courses

Would you like to try a fun, new and exciting way to learn? Then purchase one of Rod Machado's *Interactive eLearning Courses*.

Each course is narrated and accompanied by interesting graphics, animations, videos and educational interactions. In addition, each section within a course is accompanied by questions to help test your knowledge and reinforce important concepts. Of course, if questions aren't your thing, then simply skip them and continue with the course. While this course can be viewed on an iPhone or Android phone, the graphics would be difficult to see (unless you are an ant). These courses were designed to be used on an iPad, Android tablet device, laptop or desktop computer. Check them out at: rodmachdo.com.

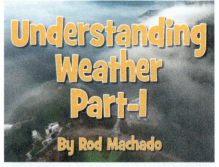

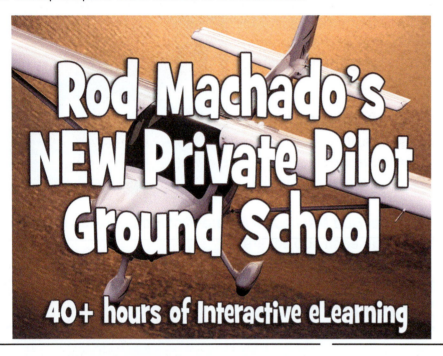
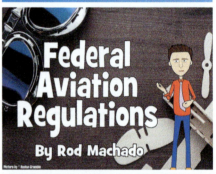

Rod Machado's Instrument Pilot's Survival Manual

Fourth Edition - eBook Only

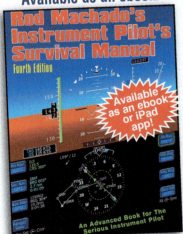

Rod Machado's *Instrument Pilot's Survival Manual* is written to answer the instrument pilot's most important and frequently unanswered questions. For the price of one hour's worth of dual you will learn the following:

1. How GPS approaches are constructed and how to fly them
2. How to differentiate between benign cumulus clouds and those that can damage an airplane
3. How to measure flight visibility at DA & MDA
4. A unique three-step method of scanning your instruments
5. Secrets of using Jeppesen and TPP charts
6. Using Center radar, ASR-9 radar, NEXRAD and Stormscope (sferics) to avoid thunderstorm and icing conditions
7. New ways of thinking about the IFR system and managing cockpit resources and much more!

(Available as an ebook only, 531 colored pages) $29.95

Aviation Humor Video/DVD

Laugh along with over 2,000 pilots as Rod delights and entertains his audience with some of the best of his aviation stories. As a professional humorist, Rod has always been known for his ability to move people off the edge of their seats and onto the floor with his fast paced, humorous presentations. As Scott Spangler, Editor of *Flight Training* magazine says, ".. Get a copy of Aviation Humor. It's Rod Machado at his best. His humor is effective and funny because it strikes at the truth pilots seldom admit, such as the pride a new pilot feels when he uses his certificate as identification when cashing a check and the clerk asks, 'What is that?' If you're in need of a good laugh, get this video. You won't regret it. "After so many requests for a video version of his very popular audio tapes, this video of Rod's is sure to be a popular addition to your library. Funny, Funny stuff!

Aviation Humor - $19.95   Approximate Length 1:00

Rod Machado's Plane Talk
The Mental Art of Flying an Airplane
You'll Learn, You'll Laugh, You'll Remember!

Welcome to a collection of Rod Machado's most popular aviation articles and stories from the last 15 years. *Rod Machado's Plane Talk* contains nearly 100 flights of fun and knowledge that will stimulate your aviation brain and tickle your funny bone. In addition to the educational topics listed below, you'll read about higher learning, the value of aviation history, aviation literature, aviation art and how an artist's perspective can help you better understand weather. You'll also find more than a few articles written just to make you laugh.

In this book you'll discover...

Available as an ebook!

How to Assess and Manage Aviation Risks
Learn how safe pilots think, how to apply the safety strategy used by General Jimmy Doolittle (known as the master of the calculated risk), how famed gunfighter Wyatt Earp can help you cope with aviation's risks, how misleading aviation statistics can be and why flying isn't as dangerous as some folks say it is.

Several Techniques for Making Better Cockpit Decisions
Discover how to use your inner copilot in the cockpit and the value of one good question asked upside down.

New Ways to Help You Cope With Temptation
Fly safer by developing an aviation code of ethics, understand how human nature can trick you into flying beyond your limits, why good pilots are prejudiced and how a concept like honor will protect you while aloft.

How to Use Your Brain for a Change
You can learn faster by understanding how the learning curve—the brain's performance chart—is affected by the little lies we tell ourselves, the mistakes we need to make, our need to please our instructors, and simulator and memory training.

The Truth About Flying, Anxiety and Fear
Learn why it's often the safest of pilots that make excuses instead of flights, why anxiety should be treated as a normal part of flying, and a three-step process to avoiding panic in the cockpit.

How to Handle First Time Flyers and Anxious Passengers
Discover how to behave around new passengers, how to avoid most common mistakes that scare passengers in airplanes and how to reduce the cockpit stress between pilot and spouse.

Favorite Skills Used By Good Pilots
Learn why good pilots scan behind an airplane as well as ahead of it, are sometimes rough and bully-like on the flight controls, occasionally fly without using any of the airplane's electronic navigation equipment, don't worry about turbulence breaking their airplanes, master airspeed control as a means of making better landings and much more.

$24.95

Rod Machado's IFR Audiobook and Best of Machado Live Audio

Download MP3 files - Price: $74.95

Rod Machado's Instrument Pilot Audiobook in MP3 Format

Now you can enjoy Rod's popular *Instrument Pilot's Handbook* during your daily commute or at home in the comfort of your own chair. This audiobook is a 30 hour narration of the *Instrument Pilot Handbook* by Rod Machado.

While you can listen to the first ten chapters of the book without referring to the text, you'll still want to use the actual *Instrument Pilot's Handbook* as a reference for reviewing pictures, graphs and many of the incidental ASRS stories scattered throughout the text. This exciting audiobook is the key to learning quickly and efficiently while maximizing use of your scarce time.

Download MP3 Version $74.95

See www.rodmachado.com for download version!

Download MP3 files - Price: $24.95

The Best of Rod Machado's Live in MP3 Format

Rod combined 10 of his best "live audience" recordings from the original "Laugh and Learn" tape series and added four additional live recordings to produce this exciting 14 program set. Included are Rod's popular *Handling In-flight Emergencies* seminar and his latest programs on defensive flying, the art of flying, the non-pilot's guide to landing an airplane, and three additional live programs containing some of Rod's funniest standup aviation humor. You can laugh and learn while driving, gardening, or building your own plane.

Download MP3 Version $24.95

See www.rodmachado.com for download version!

How to Order

Order Form

Credit card ordering 24 hours - 7 days a week
Call: **(800) 437-7080** for ordering only

For more information and secure internet ordering visit *www.rodmachado.com*
Questions: Email us from web site.
FAX: (888) MACHADO (622-4236)

Title	Quantity	X	=	Total
Aviation Humor Video - MP3 Download		$19.95		
eLearning Couses - please visit website to order				
Rod Machado Live on 14 Lectures		$24.95		
Instrument Pilot's Survival Manual (ebook only)		$29.95		
Rod Machado's Instrument Pilot's Handbook		$74.95		
Rod Machado's Private Pilot Handbook		$74.95		
Rod Machado's Private Pilot Workbook (ebook only)		$19.95		
Rod Machado's Private Pilot Audiobook-Mp3		$74.95		
Rod Machado's IFR Handbook Audiobook-Mp3		$74.95		
Rod Machado's How to Fly an Airplane Book		$59.95		
Rod Machado's How to Fly an Airplane Audiobook		$59.95		
Rod Machado's Plane Talk		$24.95		
Speaking of Flying		$29.95		
		Product Subtotal		
Sales Tax - CA Residents only		Product Subtotal x .0775		
Product shipping & handling				
		Total		

Name _____

Address _____

City _____ State ____

Zip _____

Phone (___) _____

Check # _____ or:

We accept checks, money orders, MasterCard, VISA, American Express and Discover.

Credit Card # _____

Expiration Date: _____

Authorized Signature _____

Index

1.3 Vs 9-4, 9-5, 9-8, 9-9, 9-11, 9-16, 9-19, 9-23, 9-28, 10-13, 11-3
1.3 Vso 12-4, 12-5, 12-6, 12-10, 12-15, 12-17
1.4 Vs 9-4, 9-6, 9-8
100LL 1-14
180 degree power-off approach 12-20
45 degree angle 8-24
45 degree bank limit 7-9
45 degree entry 7-8

A

a left turn at MCA 4-15
A+P=P 2-12, 3-2, 3-4, 3-5
abeam the landing threshold 8-13
absence of slipstream/p-factor 3-15
accelerated stalls 5-44
accelerator pump 1-30
adding right rudder - slow flight 4-5
adjust pitch for airspeed 3-12
adjusting climb attitude 3-3
advanced landing skills 10-34
advanced maneuvers 13-1
adverse yaw 2-5, 2-6, 2-19, 2-21, 2-22, 2-23, 2-24, 2-28
Aeronautical Information Manual 8-23, 14-13
AFM 1-11
aft elevator pull 10-14
aging and night vision 14-6
aileron 2-2
aileron and rudder coordination 2-26
aileron application and angle of attack 5-21
aileron hinge 1-17
ailerons 1-37, 2-4
ailerons and rudder in stall recovery 5-17
airplane axes 2-3
airplane flight manuals 1-11
airplane tilting 1-3
airplane's drag curve 3-20
airplane's left turning tendencies 2-24
airport recycling center 1-16
airport remarks 12-2
airport surrounded by mountains at night 14-16
airport traffic pattern 4-2
airport traffic pattern 8-1
airworthiness certificate 1-14
aligning the airplane before touchdown 10-21
altitude loss during stall recovery 5-15
ammeter 1-33
angle of attack 2-12, 4-2, 4-3, 4-4, 4-11, 4-13, 4-14, 4-15, 4-18, 5-2, 13-3
angle of attack and airspeed 4-2
angle of attack and coefficient of lift 10-25
angle of attack and the relative wind 5-6
angle of attack changes with wing rotation 5-22
angle of attack in a loop 5-5
angle of attack, estimating your 5-14
angle of attack, how power affects AOA 5-13
angle of incidence 4-3, 6-9
anti-collision light 14-8
AOI 4-3
apparent weight 5-28
apparent weight increase in a turn 5-29
applying a wind correction angle 8-21
applying flaps in a turn 5-57
applying power in a stall recovery 5-11
approach speed, recommended 9-4
approach to landing stalls 5-30
approaching at 30% above stall speed 1.3 Vs 9-4, 9-5, 9-8, 9-9, 9-11, 9-16, 9-19, 9-23, 9-28, 10-13, 11-3
approaching to land 9-1
approach-to-landing stalls 5-31
attitude 2-12
attitude plus power equals performance 2-12
Australian Transportation Safety Board study 10-5
auxiliary fuel pump 1-31
auxiliary tip tanks 1-5
average relative wind 6-21
AVGAS 1-14
aviation sunglasses 14-6
avionics master 1-8
avionics master switch 1-8

B

back side of the power curve, entering the 4-12
balked landing recovery 10-30
ballooning 10-33
bank angle and climbs 3-7
banking 2-4
base leg 7-6
base leg 8-15
base leg, when to turn to 8-15
before engine start 1-28
before landing checklist 12-20, 12-21, 12-22, 12-24
before lifting off 6-8
before takeoff checklist 6-5
before-landing checklist 12-21
beginning the level off 3-5
bendable rudder tab 3-16
best "L over D" 3-20
best angle (Vx) and best rate (Vy) 6-31
best angle of climb speed (Vx) 6-14, 6-30, 6-31, 6-37, 6-38
best glide speed 3-19, 3-20
best L/D speed 3-20, 9-4
best rate of climb 3-3, 6-37, 6-10
black hole illusion 14-21
bladder tanks 1-15
blind spots, airplane 8-14
bouncing 10-34
brake - hand lever 2-11
brake fluid 1-12
brake lines 1-12
brake pedals 2-5
brakes, riding the 1-35
braking effectiveness 10-24
burning insulation 1-6

C

calculating when to descend 3-16
carburetor's accelerator pump 1-30
carburetor's butterfly valve 1-30
castering nose gear 1-25
center of lift 5-10, 5-26
center of the first third of the runway 9-3
centrifugal force in a turn 5-29
Cessna 150 1-4
Cessna 152 1-8
Cessna 172 1-20
Cessna 182 1-8
Cessna 210 1-4
chandelle - control usage 13-24
chandelle 13-20

chandelle bank limit 13-20
chandelle learning strategy 13-25
chandelle performance graph 13-22
charge/discharge ammeter 1-33
Chart Supplement 12-2
check fuel indication 1-9
check the brakes 1-34
circling descent to mountain airport 14-16
Cl 5-4
Cl vs. angle of attack 5-5
Clark-type airfoils 12-7
climb attitude 3-2
climb attitude, establishing 3-2
climb attitudes vs density altitude 6-12
climb prematurely out of ground effect 6-11
climb rate decreases with bank angle 3-8
climb, entering the 3-4
climb, initial 6-2
climbing - complex airplane 3-6
climbing at the best rate of climb speed (vy) 6-10
climbing in slow flight 4-16
climbing or descending in slow flight 4-15
climbing turns 3-7
climbing with full power 3-4
climbs 2-3
climbs 3-2
climbs and descents 3-1
cockpit management 1-28
coefficient of lift 5-4
coefficient of lift vs angle of attack 5-5
collapsing runway trapezoid 9-27
combination crab and sideslip 11-11
common traffic advisory frequency 8-9
complacency 1-2
compressed nose strut 10-23
cone cells 14-3, 14-4
configuring for landing on downwind 8-13
congested area 7-5
constant speed propellers - setting power levels 13-8
Continental engines 1-31
control cable tension 1-17
control placement during taxi 1-36
control response in slow flight 4-7
controllable propeller 1-23
coordinated 2-22
coordination in slow flight 4-10
coordination rolls 2-28
correcting for a takeoff crosswind 6-18
counterweights 1-17
cowling 1-23
cowling plugs 1-12
crab method 11-3
crabbing angle 7-16
crabbing in the pattern 8-20
crabbing into the wind after takeoff 6-20
crabbing on final approach 11-2
crabbing on the downwind leg 8-20
crankcase breather tube 1-19
critical angle of attack 5-2, 5-3, 5-5, 5-6, 5-7, 5-8, 5-10, 5-13, 5-14, 5-15, 5-16, 5-19, 5-20, 5-22, 5-23, 5-24, 5-27, 5-29, 5-32, 5-35, 5-36, 5-38, 5-40, 5-44, 5-51, 5-56
cross checking a flight instrument 4-7
cross controlled 13-10, 13-25, 13-32
crosscheck scan 13-7
crosscheck VSI and altimeter in slow flight 4-6
cross-controlled slipping stall 5-48
cross-controlled stall 5-49

crossed controls 2-30, 2-32, 13-9, 13-25
crosswind component chart 11-14
crosswind correction after liftoff 6-18
crosswind landing gear 11-2
crosswind leg 7-6, 8-6
crosswind limit 6-20
crosswind turn illusion 8-7
crosswind, how much can you can handle? 11-9
crosswinds 11-1
crosswinds on takeoff 6-17
cruise descent 3-18
cushions in the airplane 10-9

D

danger of premature flap retraction 5-33
dark adaptation 14-5, 14-7
defining a normal glidepath 9-19
delaying the base leg 8-16
density altitude 2-12, 6-35
density altitude chart 6-36
departure (power-on) stalls 5-38
departure leg 8-5
departure stall 5-15
departure stall attitude 5-40
departure stall, how to enter the 5-41
departure stall, performing the 5-39
departure stall, recovering from the 5-40
departure stall, rudder use in the 5-41
departure stall, setting up the 5-39
departure stalls in complex airplanes 5-42
descending in slow flight 4-16
descending turns 3-14
descent for landing 9-5
descents 2-3
descents at cruise speed 3-18
desired landing spot 9-13
desired landing spot moves 9-14
determining pitch in a turn 2-33
dihedral 2-37
dipstick 1-25
dirty windows 1-26
disappearing lights at night 14-16
distance to clear a 50 foot obstacle 12-3, 12-12
distractions and stalls 5-17
divide your attention between airplane and ground 7-17
dividing your attention 7-13
downwash and the average relative wind 6-22
downwind leg 7-6, 8-8
drag profile, airplane 9-4
drain holes 1-19
draining fuel sump 1-25
dress a propeller 1-22
drift angle 7-4
driving and landing 10-10
dynamic air pressure 5-4

E

effective lift 6-21
eights along a road 7-25
eights along a road, essentials of 7-27
eights around pylons 7-28
eights around pylons, essentials of 7-29
eights on pylons, essentials of 7-38
eights-on-pylons 7-30
electric gyro-based instruments 1-9

Index

electric stall horn 1-16
electric trim switch 2-10
electrical insulation 1-7
elevator 1-20, 1-37, 2-2
elevator counterweights 1-21
elevator instinct 9-16
elevator pressure 1-37
elevator trim stall 5-34
elevator-airspeed method 4-5
elevator-airspeed pilots 3-23
elevator-airspeed technique 3-22
elevator-altitude technique 3-24
elevator-attitude relationship 10-16
elevator-glidepath pilots 3-25
empennage 1-18
engine cowling 1-23
engine fires 1-30
engine power configurations 6-15
engine start 1-29
engine start checklist 1-29
engineered shape of the wing 5-2
enter at a 45 degree angle 8-24
Ercoupe 11-2
eye - structure 14-2
eye's pupil 14-4
eye's dilate 14-4
eye's visual cycle 14-5

F

fabric covered airplane 1-7
false horizons at night 14-7
FAR 91.113(f) 8-11
FAR 91.117 8-13
FAR 91.119(b) 7-5
FAR 91.119(c) 7-5
final approach - long and low 12-9
final approach 8-17
final approach speed (1.3 Vs) 9-4, 9-5, 9-8, 9-9, 9-11, 9-16, 9-19, 9-23, 9-28, 10-13, 11-3
final approach, essentials on 9-10
finger-decoder method of pattern entry 8-10
fire extinguisher 1-31
fishing for the runway 10-18
fixed power condition 3-22
flap effectiveness 10-25
flap extension 10-25
flaps 1-18
flaps and descent angle 10-26
flaps moving symmetrically 1-18
flaps, extend 1-9
flaps, using for landing 9-24, 10-25
flare 10-3
flare 9-2
flare angle and flap usage 10-26
flare height, low level passes to learn 10-13
flare, how fast do you flare? 10-12
flaring in the sideslip 11-9
flashlight 1-10, 14-9
flight control use on takeoff 6-13
flight simulators for crosswind practice 11-12
flight vision 14-2
floating during landing 10-32
flooded engine start procedure 1-32
flooding the engine 1-31
foot position with heel brakes 6-8

forward slip 11-15
forward slip from a turn 11-19
forward slip, entering a 11-17
forward slip, shallow 11-17
four basic flight maneuvers 2-3
fovea 14-3
fuel dipstick 1-10
fuel injected engine 1-30
fuel lines 1-24
fuel recirculation line 1-31
fuel sampling 1-13
fuel sumps 1-24
fuel vapor 1-31
fuel volatility 1-7
full flap stall 5-31
full flap stall, recovering from the 5-32
full flaps and the crosswind landing 11-12
full moon 14-17
full power 3-2
full stall 5-16
fuselage 1-18

G

gas truck 1-15
gear doors 1-13
gear handle position 1-6
gear handles 1-8
glide ratio 3-19
glidepath angles and power usage 9-29
glidepaths vs length of final approach 12-9
gliders 3-19
g-loading 13-1, 13-2, 13-3
g-loading limitations 13-1
G-meter 13-3
go-around 10-27
going around 10-27
Google Earth 7-13
green and white airport beacon 14-18
ground effect 6-10, 6-11, 6-21, 12-24
ground effect and induced drag 6-21
ground effect and pitching motion 6-23
ground effect and takeoffs 6-23
ground loop 10-21, 10-22
ground reference maneuvers 7-1
ground roll 6-2, 12-3, 12-8, 12-12
ground track 7-4
GUMP 12-24
GUMP memory aid 8-15
gust locks 1-8
gusts 11-15, 12-25
Guy Murchie 14-2

H

hand propping 1-38
headwinds for takeoff 6-6
heel brakes 2-11
high boost pump 1-31
high density altitude takeoff 6-11
High Flight poem 3-1
high on final approach 9-18
higher stick forces 5-27
horizon reference 13-6
hot exhaust manifold 1-24
how cg affects stall speed 5-26
how cg position affects stick forces 5-27

how engine power affects stall speed 5-28
how the runway disappears 10-8
how to grip yoke 2-7
how to increase lift in a turn 2-35
how your glidepath changes 9-15, 9-17

I

IAS and CAS chart 9-11
identifying bank angle 2-32
imminent stall recovery procedure 5-16
imminent stalls 5-15
incipient stage of the spin 5-54
inclinometer 2-25
inclinometer and coordinated turns 2-26
indicated airspeed lag 3-13
indicated airspeed variation in a slip 11-18
induced drag 6-21, 13-3, 13-4
induced drag and angle of attack 13-4
inertia 2-22
inside cowling 1-24
insufficient runway 6-11

J

jammed rudder pedals 6-3
jet fuel 1-14
joystick 2-7

K

key position 12-21, 12-22, 12-23
kick out method 11-2
kinesthesia 5-14
kneeboards 1-29

L

laminar flow wings 12-7
landing distance chart 12-3
landing flare, learning the 10-13
landing in a crabbed condition 11-2
landing in bumpy air 12-25
landing location on runway 9-9
landing long on the runway 9-17
landing short of the runway 9-15
landing stall 10-17
landing time machine 10-15
landing with power 12-18
landing, looking only at the horizon during 10-12
lapboard 1-29
lateral axis 2-2
lateral reference 7-30
lateral stability 2-28
lazy eight - the slice 13-29
lazy eight 13-26
lazy eight description 13-27
lazy eight entry configuration 13-27
lazy eight performance graph 13-31
leaning while taxiing 1-40
left climbing turn, entering a 3-9
left drift crosswind correction 11-7
left quartering headwind 1-36
left quartering tailwind 1-36
left turn, entering a 2-4
left wing aileron 1-17
left wing position light 1-17
level flight 2-17, 2-20
leveling off - complex airplane 3-8
leveling off 3-5

leveling off from a climb 3-5
leveling off from a descent 3-14
lift 6-21
lift equation 5-4
liftoff 6-3
liftoff point 6-2
lighted background at night 14-8
lighted city boundaries 14-15
lighter stick forces 5-27
limited battery energy 1-8
lining up and waiting at night 14-12
lining up with the runway centerline 6-7
load factor/stall speed chart 5-30
load on the propeller 3-4
loadmeter 1-33
local relative wind 6-21
long coupled airplanes 6-26
longitudinal axis 2-2
longitudinal dynamic stability 2-19
low wing airplane 1-12
lunar light 14-17
lunar phases 14-17

M

maintaining altitude during slow flight turns 4-10
maintaining pattern spacing 8-11
maneuvering altitude 6-15
maneuvering speed, 13-21, 13-27
manifold pressure 3-6
manual flap extension 4-19
master switch 1-6
MCA 4-2
medium bank 2-28
medium bank, definition 2-28
merging in heavy pattern traffic 8-24
minimum controllable airspeed 4-2
minimum sink speed 3-21
modifying your glidepath 9-15
moon 14-17
moving with the wind 7-3
multiple layers of traffic in the pattern 8-8

N

Navy pilots 3-26
negative dynamic stability 2-19
new moon 14-17
night - approaches and landings 14-18
night - GPS navigation 14-15
night emergency landing sites 14-18
night enroute conditions 14-14
night flight training 14-2
night flying 14-1
night flying skills 14-9
night horizon vanishing 14-13
night landing approach strategy 14-19
night roundout and flare 14-22
night runway expansion effect 14-22
night scanning for traffic 14-8
night shallow descent technique 14-24
night sweet spot identification 14-23
night taxiing 14-11
night vision 14-4
night vision adaption 14-5
non-towered airports 8-3
normal engine start procedure 1-31

Index

normal power-off glidepath 9-3, 9-20
nose down attitude - descent 3-10
nose gear 1-25
nose strut inflation 1-26
nose-up trim - slow flight 4-5
not releasing elevator pressure after stalling 5-10
no-wind condition 7-2

O

obstacle along final approach 12-1
off center viewing at night 14-4
oil 1-33
oil pressure 1-33
operational maneuvering speed (Vo) 13-6
opsin 14-5
over the top stall 5-47, 5-49
overflowing fuel 1-7
overpriming 1-29
overshoot final approach 12-23
overshooting final to lose altitude 8-18
overtaking another airplane 8-11

P

panel illusion 13-9
panel illusion trap 13-9
PAPI 14-20
parallax effect 14-8
parallax error 2-35
parasite and induced drag 3-19
pendulum effect 2-31
p-factor 3-4, 2-25, 2-38
PFD 2-26
photobleaching 14-5
pilot controlled lighting 14-13
pilot in command 2-6
Pilot Operating Handbook 1-11
pilotage 14-15
Piper Cherokee 1-37
Piper Warrior 1-4
pitch and power techniques 3-22
pitch reference dot 2-34
pitot cover 1-12
pitot tube 1-12
pivotal altitude 7-32
plastic window cleaner 1-27
pneumatic stall horn 1-16
POH 1-11
porpoise, recovery from the 10-31
porpoising 10-30
position lights 14-8
post stall attitude 5-32
power and aircraft motion 5-12
power induced left turning forces 6-8
power required curve 12-13
power required curve 4-5
power required to maintain altitude 4-11
power required vs. climb/descent rates 4-17
power-off approach - 180 degree 12-20
power-off descents 3-10
power-off landings 9-9
power-off stall in a complex airplane 5-35
power-off stall, recovering from in a complex airplane 5-36
power-on approach 3-17
power-on descents 3-16
Practical Test Standards 5-10, 5-15, 13-5, 13-6, 13-11, 13-12, 13-34

precision approach path indicator 14-20
preflight 1-3
preflight at night 14-10
preflight audio recording 1-12
preflight begins 1-5
premature flap retraction 5-33
premature turn onto base leg 8-15
pressure altitude 6-35
prevent propeller overspeed 3-4
preventing entry into a spin 5-52
primary flight display (PFD) 2-26
prime, pump the throttle to 1-29
priming 1-29
propeller 1-22
propeller control 3-6
propeller face 1-22
propeller loads 1-22
propeller slipstream 2-25, 3-4
propeller tips 1-18
propeller, back side of the 1-22
proper trimming helps you land 10-15
public (non-military) airport lighting 14-18
push down on tail 1-14
pylon separation 7-31

R

raise the landing gear, when to 6-16
rate of turn 13-20, 13-21, 13-22, 13-25, 13-30, 13-31, 13-33, 13-34
recognizing the stall 5-13
recovery phase of the spin 5-55
rectangular course 7-6
rectangular course, essentials of the 7-12
reducing speed on downwind 9-3
reducing speed on final 9-8
region of reversed command - elevator authority 12-15
region of reversed command 4-10, 4-26, 12-12
rejected takeoff - fixed gear airplane 6-34
rejected takeoff - retractable gear airplane 6-34
rejected takeoffs 6-33
relationship between angle of attack and airspeed 5-2
relative wind 5-6
releasing elevator back pressure after stalling 5-11
retractable gear 1-26
retracting the flaps and gear 5-37
returning to a normal glidepath 9-22
rhodopsin 14-4, 14-5, 14-6, 14-7
right climbing turn, entering a 3-9
right drift crosswind correction 11-7
right quartering headwind 1-36
right quartering tailwind 1-36
right wing position light 1-17
rod cells 14-3, 14-4, 14-5
rotate 6-2
rotating beacon 1-9
rotating beacon for airports 14-18
Rotax engines 1-38
roundout 9-2, 10-2
roundout and flare 10-1
roundout and the flare 9-2
roundout, flare and touchdown 10-2
roundout, when do you begin the? 10-4
roundout, where to look for the 10-5
roundout/flare, focus your vision 10-10
rudder 1-21, 2-2
rudder pedals 1-34, 2-5

rudder surface 2-5
rudder-how to check 1-22
runup 6-3
runup area 1-22
runup checklist 6-3
runway alignment 9-7
runway centerline 6-7
runway expansion effect 10-6
runway hold lines 1-35
runway hold lines 6-4
runway length 12-2
runway surface type 12-2
runway trapezoid, expanding 9-27
runway with an obstacle 6-29
runway's trapezoidal shape 9-20

S

sampling the response 10-15, 10-17, 10-18
seat of the pants flying 2-28
seat of the pants for coordinated flying 2-28
seat of the pants in slow flight 4-10
seating height 2-8
see with your ears 8-17
sensory-rich runway environments 10-5
serpentining 1-34
shallow bank 2-30
shallow bank, definition 2-30
short coupled airplanes 6-27
short-field approach 3-18
short-field takeoffs - retractable gear 6-32
short-field takeoffs 6-29
short-field approach - where it begins 12-4
short-field approach 3-18
short-field approaches - roundout and flare 12-15
short-field approaches and landings 12-1
short-field landing over an obstacle 12-8
short-field landing without obstacle 12-5
short-field landings - high altitude airports 12-29
Short-field landings in lighter airplanes 12-7
short-field landings, pitch-power technique for 12-6
side slip 11-15
side slip or crab angle increase during the flare 11-5
side slips 11-1
side stick 2-2
sideslip 11-2
sideslip after takeoff 6-19
sideslip angle without and with flaps 11-12
sitting height 10-8
sitting just right 10-9
skidding left turn to final approach 5-47
skidding turn to final approach 5-47
slipping 9-25
slipping turn 11-20
slipping turn to final approach 11-20
slipping with full flaps 12-23
slips to landing 5-49
slip-skid indicator (trapezoid type PFD) 2-26
slow flight - complex airplane 4-23
slow flight 4-1
slow flight at MCA 4-13
slow flight in complex airplanes 4-25
slow flight maneuvering with flaps 4-21
slow flight rudder usage 4-16
slow flight turns 4-8
slow flight with flaps 4-18

slow flight with flaps extended 4-18
slow flight with half-flaps 4-19
slow flight with partial flaps 4-18
slow flight without flaps 4-18
slow flight, entering 4-4
slow flight, exiting - complex airplane 4-24
slow flight, exiting "full flap" 4-22
slow flight, exiting 4-6
slow flight, how to enter 4-4
slow flight, how to exit 4-6
small ladder 1-10
Smartphone 14-11
Smartphones for preflights 1-24
smell during preflight 1-24
smell smoke 1-30
smoke 1-30
soft-field takeoff - after liftoff 6-27
soft-field takeoff - retractable gear 6-28
soft-field takeoff 6-25
soft-field takeoff, performing the 6-26
soft-field takeoffs - short coupled airplanes 6-27
soft landing field 12-17
soft-field approach and landing 12-17
soft-field landing approach 12-17
speed, rate and radius 7-10
spin to the left 5-51
spin to the right 5-51
spin, entry stage of the 5-53
spin, fully developed 5-50
spin, fully developed stage of the 5-54
spinner plate 1-23
spins 5-50
spirals 5-54
stabilator 1-20
stabilized approach 9-13, 9-20, 10-6, 10-20, 12-5, 12-6, 12-8, 12-10,
stabilized glidepath 9-21
stabilizer's drain holes 1-21
stall - definition 5-2
stall characteristics 5-26
stall horn 1-16, 4-14
stall pattern progression 5-18
stall sensations, recognizing 5-13
stall speed with variable flap conditions 12-5, 12-27
stall warning light 4-14
stall warning systems 1-16
stall, gear-flap retraction sequence 5-37
stall, what is a...? 5-2
stall, your first 5-8
stall/spin proof airplanes 5-19
stalling in a nose-high attitude 5-24
stalling in any attitude and at any airspeed 5-7
stalling in coordinated flight 5-18
stalling while turning 5-22
stalling with flaps extended 5-30
stalling with gear and flaps extended 5-35
stalling with the nose pointed 5-24
stalls and cross-controlled flight 5-46
stalls and spins 5-1
stalls one wing before the other, why? 5-20
stalls, spins and the conditioned reflex 5-38
standard conditions 6-35
static port 1-19
static pressure reduction in ground effect 6-24
static wicks 1-21

Index

stationary spot 9-13
stationary spot method 9-13, 9-20, 9-23, 9-25, 10-20
stationary spot method, short-field landings 12-6
steep bank, definition 2-30
steep spiral and wind direction 13-18
steep spiral entry 13-15
steep spiral, bank limit 13-13
steep spiral, entry configuration 13-16
steep spiral, turn radius 13-14
steep spirals 13-13
steep turn, altitude deviations 13-11
steep turn, bank limit 13-3
steep turn, components 13-5
steep turn, cross controls 13-9
steep turn, crosscheck scan 13-7
steep turn, reversing course 13-10
steep turn, rudder use 13-9
steep turn, trim use 13-12
steep turns 13-2
steeper forward slip 11-17
still-engaged starter 1-33
straight and level 2-1
straight and level flight 2-3, 2-12
straight in approach at night 14-20
s-turn across a road 7-20
s-turns 12-23
s-turns across a road, essentials of 7-24
s-turns on final approach 8-18
sumping the tank 1-13
sunglasses 14-6
Super EZ glidepath evaluation clue 9-28
sweet spot 10-11
sweet spot moves closer during the flare 10-11

T

T tail 1-18
tail light 1-17
taildragger 1-37
taildragger, landing a 10-16
takeoff expectations 6-33
takeoff memory aid 6-5
takeoff picture 6-1
takeoff power 6-15
takeoff roll 6-2
takeoffs and climbs 6-1
tandem seating 2-6
TAS 6-37
tasting fuel 1-14
taxi light 14-11
taxi speed 1-34
taxiing 1-34
taxiing in strong winds 1-36
taxiing too fast 1-35
taxiway 1-34
taxiway centerline 1-35
thigh method of runway alignment 9-7
three types of turns 2-30
threshold as the stationary spot 9-28
threshold of control 10-17
tiedown ring 1-18
tires 1-26
Tomahawk 1-18
too high on final approach 9-24
too low on final 9-23
torque 2-25

total drag curve 3-19
total drag curve 4-5
touch-and-wiggle procedure 1-24
touchdown 10-21
touchdown roll 10-21
touchdown speed and engine power 12-18
touchdown spot 9-28
touching down on the upwind wheel 11-8
tow bar 1-20
tower controlled airports 1-35, 8-3
track 7-2
traffic on downwind 8-8
traffic pattern components 8-5
traffic pattern entry altitude 8-25
traffic pattern entry, recommended 8-23
traffic pattern speed 8-13
traffic pattern, entering the 8-22
transitioning to the sideslip from the crab 11-10
trans-retinal 14-4
trapezoidal method - short-field landings 12-6
trapezoidal runway shape, when it varies 9-27
trapezoidal shape 9-20
trapezoidal shape 9-22
trapezoidal shape method 10-20
tricycle gear 1-37
tricycle gear instability 10-24
tricycle geared airplane 1-37
trim wheel 2-8, 2-9, 2-14, 2-15, 2-16, 2-17
trimmed airspeed 3-11
trimming for level flight 2-14
true airspeed 6-37
true airspeed and high altitude airports 12-12
turbulence and load factor 13-3
turbulence or gusty winds 12-25
turn arc 2-26
turn onto base leg 9-5
turn, rolling into a 2-22
turn, rolling out of a 2-21
turn, rudder use to enter a 2-22
turning crosswind 8-6
turning downwind 8-8
turning onto final approach 9-7
turns 2-3
turns around a point - graphically explained 7-18
turns around a point 7-14
turns around a point, essentials of 7-20
two handed flare 10-18

U

U.S. Air Force pilots 3-26
uncompressed nose strut 10-23
uncongested area 7-5
uncontrolled airports 8-3
under the bottom stall 5-47
unexpected maneuvers in the traffic pattern 8-11
upwind leg 7-6

V

variable glidepath angles 9-19
variable length runways 6-29
variable power condition 3-22
variable runway shapes 9-26
variable winds in the pattern 8-22
VASI 3-23, 9-12
VASI distance limitations 14-20

vertical component of engine thrust 3-10
vertical speed curves 4-17, 12-13
VFR transponder code (1200) 6-5
visual approach slope indicator 3-23, 9-12
visual illusions 14-7
visual meteorological conditions 14-7
visual method for coordinated turns 2-27
VMC 14-7, 14-17
Vo—operational maneuvering speed 13-6
Vx 6-14,
vx and vy change with altitude, why? 6-37
Vx, rotating to and climbing at 6-30
Vy 12-13
Vy 3-3
Vy vs Vx 6-14

W

water contamination 1-13
WCA 7-4
weathervaning 11-13
wheelbarrowing 12-26
when a spin isn't a spin 5-54
when a spin isn't a spin, it's a spiral 5-56
whiff of AVGAS 1-6
why things appear to move faster closer to the ground 7-29
why you feel heavy in a bank 5-29
wind correction angle 7-4, 11-3
wind correction angle in the pattern 8-21
wind indicators 7-8
wind speed/direction change with altitude 13-19
window polishing 1-27
window ring formations 1-27
window scratches 1-27
windscreen - keep it clean 14-10
windscreen 1-26
wing overstressing 1-17
wing rotation and unequal angle of attack 5-50
wing speed differential 2-24, 2-30
wing sump drain 1-13
wing tip 1-17
wing tips 1-16
wing-low method 11-4
wing-low method of crosswind correction 11-6
wingtip height 1-4

Y

yelling "clear" 1-29
yoke 2-1
yoke and pedal 2-3